MW01675339

INTERNATIONAL BUSINESS 93/94

Second Edition

Annual Editions

A Library of Information from the Public Press

Editor

Dr. Fred Maidment
Kean College of New Jersey

Dr. Fred Maidment is associate professor of management at Kean College of New Jersey. He received his bachelor's degree from New York University in 1970 and his master's degree from Bernard M. Baruch College of the City University of New York. In 1983 he received his doctorate from the University of South Carolina. His research concerns training and development in industry. He resides in Lebanon, Pennsylvania, with his wife and four children.

Cover illustration by Mike Eagle

The Dushkin Publishing Group, Inc.
Sluice Dock, Guilford, Connecticut 06437

The Annual Editions Series

Annual Editions is a series of over 55 volumes designed to provide the reader with convenient, low-cost access to a wide range of current, carefully selected articles from some of the most important magazines, newspapers, and journals published today. Annual Editions are updated on an annual basis through a continuous monitoring of over 300 periodical sources. All Annual Editions have a number of features designed to make them particularly useful, including topic guides, annotated tables of contents, unit overviews, and indexes. For the teacher using Annual Editions in the classroom, an Instructor's Resource Guide with test questions is available for each volume.

VOLUMES AVAILABLE

Africa
Aging
American Government
American History, Pre-Civil War
American History, Post-Civil War
Anthropology
Biology
Business Ethics
Canadian Politics
China
Commonwealth of Independent States
Comparative Politics
Computers in Education
Computers in Business
Computers in Society
Criminal Justice
Drugs, Society, and Behavior
Dying, Death, and Bereavement
Early Childhood Education
Economics
Educating Exceptional Children
Education
Educational Psychology
Environment
Geography
Global Issues
Health
Human Development
Human Resources
Human Sexuality
India and South Asia
International Business
Japan and the Pacific Rim
Latin America
Life Management
Macroeconomics
Management
Marketing
Marriage and Family
Microeconomics
Middle East and the Islamic World
Money and Banking
Nutrition
Personal Growth and Behavior
Physical Anthropology
Psychology
Public Administration
Race and Ethnic Relations
Social Problems
Sociology
State and Local Government
Third World
Urban Society
Violence and Terrorism
Western Civilization, Pre-Reformation
Western Civilization, Post-Reformation
Western Europe
World History, Pre-Modern
World History, Modern
World Politics

Library of Congress Cataloging in Publication Data
Main entry under title: Annual Editions: International Business. 1993/94.
1. International business enterprises—Periodicals. 2. Business—Periodicals. I. Maidment, Fred, *comp.* II. Title: International business.
ISBN 1-56134-206-8 338.88′05

© 1993 by The Dushkin Publishing Group, Inc., Guilford, CT 06437

Copyright law prohibits the reproduction, storage, or transmission in any form by any means of any portion of this publication without the expressed written permission of The Dushkin Publishing Group, Inc., and of the copyright holder (if different) of the part of the publication to be reproduced. The Guidelines for Classroom Copying endorsed by Congress explicitly state that unauthorized copying may not be used to create, to replace, or to substitute for anthologies, compilations, or collective works.

Annual Editions® is a Registered Trademark of The Dushkin Publishing Group, Inc.

Second Edition

Manufactured by The Banta Company, Harrisonburg, Virginia 22801

Printed on Recycled Paper

Editors/ Advisory Board

Members of the Advisory Board are instrumental in the final selection of articles for each edition of Annual Editions. Their review of articles for content, level, currentness, and appropriateness provides critical direction to the editor and staff. We think you'll find their careful consideration well reflected in this volume.

EDITOR

Fred Maidment
Kean College of New Jersey

ADVISORY BOARD

Riad A. Ajami
Ohio State University

Jeffrey Arpan
University of South Carolina
Columbia

Robert T. Aubey
University of Wisconsin
Madison

Martin S. Bressler
Thomas College

Charles R. Chittle
Bowling Green State University

Kerry Cooper
Texas A & M University

John D. Daniels
Indiana University

Frank L. DuBois
American University

Donald G. Howard
University of Akron

Basil Janavaras
Mankato State University

Paul E. Jursa
College of Charleston

Nana Amu Korsha
Nova University

Michael Kuryla
Broome Community College

Frank P. Land
University of North Carolina
Greensboro

Joseph LeMay
Ramapo College of New Jersey

Wendell H. McCulloch, Jr.
California State University
Long Beach

Taylor W. Meloan
University of Southern
California

Richard W. Moxon
University of Washington

Lucie Pfaff
College of Mt. St. Vincent

Betty Jane Punnett
University of Windsor

William E. Renforth
Florida International University

John E. Richardson
Pepperdine University

Douglas Ross
Towson State University

Belay Seyoum
Nova University

Claus Sinai
University of Portland

Arienne Turner
Fullerton College

STAFF

Ian A. Nielsen, Publisher
Brenda S. Filley, Production Manager
Roberta Monaco, Editor
Addie Raucci, Administrative Editor
Cheryl Greenleaf, Permissions Editor
Diane Barker, Editorial Assistant
Lisa Holmes-Doebrick, Administrative Coordinator
Charles Vitelli, Designer
Shawn Callahan, Graphics
Meredith Scheld, Graphics
Steve Shumaker, Graphics
Lara M. Johnson, Graphics
Libra A. Cusack, Typesetting Supervisor
Juliana Arbo, Typesetter

To the Reader

In publishing ANNUAL EDITIONS we recognize the enormous role played by the magazines, newspapers, and journals of the *public press* in providing current, first-rate educational information in a broad spectrum of interest areas. Within the articles, the best scientists, practitioners, researchers, and commentators draw issues into new perspective as accepted theories and viewpoints are called into account by new events, recent discoveries change old facts, and fresh debate breaks out over important controversies.

Many of the articles resulting from this enormous editorial effort are appropriate for students, researchers, and professionals seeking accurate, current material to help bridge the gap between principles and theories and the real world. These articles, however, become more useful for study when those of lasting value are carefully *collected, organized, indexed,* and *reproduced* in a *low-cost format*, which provides easy and permanent access when the material is needed. That is the role played by *Annual Editions*.

Under the direction of each volume's *Editor*, who is an expert in the subject area, and with the guidance of an *Advisory Board*, we seek each year to provide in each *ANNUAL EDITION* a current, well-balanced, carefully selected collection of the best of the public press for your study and enjoyment. We think you'll find this volume useful, and we hope you'll take a moment to let us know what you think.

International business is where the economy of the world is heading. Virtually all countries and all organizations will be engaged in doing business with other organizations outside their home country. Students of business administration, indeed, all people involved in business, need to be aware of the new international environment; they need to be aware of the opportunities and the problems associated with doing business outside their home markets; and they need to understand that the same type of opportunities await all who engage in business.

Business must respond to this change in the environment by keeping an open mind about the opportunities available to it on a global basis. The 46 articles that have been chosen for *Annual Editions: International Business 93/94* comprise a cross section of the current literature on the subject. The collection addresses the various aspects of international business with emphasis on Japan, the European Economic Community, and Eastern Europe. Articles have been selected from a variety of sources including *The Wall Street Journal*, *The Economist*, *Industry Week*, and *Forbes*.

This publication contains a number of features designed to make it useful for people interested in international business. These include a topic guide for locating articles on specific subjects, and a table of contents with abstracts that summarize each article with key words in bold italics. The volume is organized into seven units dealing with specific interrelated topics in international business. Each section begins with an overview that provides the necessary background information to allow the reader to place selections in the context of the book. Important topics are emphasized, and challenge questions address major themes.

This edition of *Annual Editions: International Business* will provide the reader with the most complete and current selection of readings available on the subject of international business. We would like to know what you think. Please take a few minutes to complete the article rating form at the back of the volume. Anything can be improved, and we need your help to improve *Annual Editions: International Business*.

Fred Maidment

Editor

Contents

Unit 1

Overview of International Business

Five articles discuss how today's business community has become global.

The concepts in bold italics are developed in the article. For further expansion please refer to the Topic Guide and the Index.

Unit 2

The Multinational Corporation

Five selections examine the necessity of international alliances and joint ventures in order to be able to effectively compete in world markets.

Unit 3

International Management

Seven articles discuss different approaches to management around the world.

The concepts in bold italics are developed in the article. For further expansion please refer to the Topic Guide and the Index.

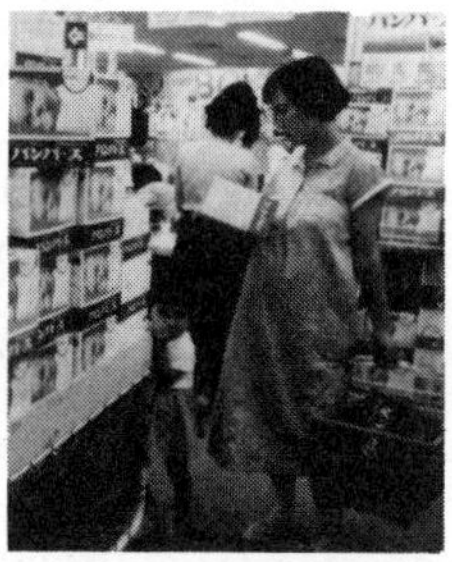

Unit 4

International Marketing

Five articles examine various methods used by corporations to effectively enter different world markets.

Unit 5

International Finance

Five selections discuss some of the challenges faced by corporations when they finance international businesses.

Unit 6

International Production

Four articles examine the different approaches to production in various parts of the world.

Unit 7

International Issues of the Twenty-First Century

Fifteen articles examine areas of the world that will compete for future markets. Areas considered are Japan, Eastern Europe and the Commonwealth of Independent States, the Western European Community, North America, and the Third World.

The concepts in bold italics are developed in the article. For further expansion please refer to the Topic Guide and the Index.

The concepts in bold italics are developed in the article. For further expansion please refer to the Topic Guide and the Index.

Topic Guide

This topic guide suggests how the selections in this book relate to topics of traditional concern to students and professionals involved with international business. It can be very useful in locating articles that relate to each other for reading and research. The guide is arranged alphabetically according to topic. Articles may, of course, treat topics that do not appear in the topic guide. In turn, entries in the topic guide do not necessarily constitute a comprehensive listing of all the contents of each selection.

TOPIC AREA	TREATED IN:
Automobiles	1. Are We Building New Berlin Walls? 5. World's Trade Topography 10. Stepping Up to Global Competition 31. Myth of 'Made in the U.S.A.' 36. Does Japan Play Fair? 39. Locking Up Tomorrow's Profits
Communications	4. International Communication 5. World's Trade Topography 9. Corporate Globalization 12. Sources of Information 13. What Executives Should Know 14. Companies in Europe 17. Foreign Director 21. It's in the Mail! 28. Manufacturing's New Economies of Scale 29. Search for a Truly Pan-European Manufacturing System 33. RJR Nabisco 34. Companies Use Cross-Cultural Training
Developing Countries	2. Global Frontiers of Business 7. U.S. Companies Come Back Home 13. What Executives Should Know 15. Super Manager 26. Foreign Direct Investment 27. Report on the Debt Crisis 31. Myth of 'Made in the U.S.A.' 32. Adapting Ethical Decisions 33. RJR Nabisco 37. "Mountains Are High, the Emperor Is Far Away" 38. Doing Business With the Soviet Republics 41. Megamarket 43. Do We Want Free Trade With Mexico? 44. North-South Split 45. Don't Forget Latin America 46. But What About Africa?
Education	3. Global Economy 4. International Communication 10. Stepping Up to Global Competition 11. Who Is Them? 12. Sources of Information 14. Companies in Europe 30. Global Innovation 34. Companies Use Cross-Cultural Training
Environment	3. Global Economy 9. Corporate Globalization 10. Stepping Up to Global Competition 12. Sources of Information 13. What Executives Should Know 17. Foreign Director 20. Exporter's Guide to Selecting Foreign Sales Agents and Distributors 28. Manufacturing's New Economies of Scale 32. Adapting Ethical Decisions 33. RJR Nabisco 35. How Japan Sees Itself 40. Now the New New Europe 42. Quebec 43. Do We Want Free Trade With Mexico?
European Economic Community	1. Are We Building New Berlin Walls? 2. Global Frontiers of Business 5. World's Trade Topography 6. Global Corporate Competition II 10. Stepping Up to Global Competition 14. Companies in Europe 21. It's in the Mail! 26. Foreign Direct Investment 28. Manufacturing's New Economies of Scale 29. Search for a Truly Pan-European Manufacturing System 39. Locking Up Tomorrow's Profits 40. Now the New New Europe
Human Rights	11. Who Is Them? 13. What Executives Should Know 15. Super Manager 32. Adapting Ethical Decisions 33. RJR Nabisco 37. "Mountains Are High, the Emperor Is Far Away" 38. Doing Business With the Soviet Republics 43. Do We Want Free Trade With Mexico? 45. Don't Forget Latin America 46. But What About Africa?
IMF/World Bank	24. Competitiveness and the Global Capital Shortage 27. Report on the Debt Crisis 44. North-South Split 45. Don't Forget Latin America 46. But What About Africa?
Manufacturing	2. Global Frontiers of Business 3. Global Economy 7. U.S. Companies Come Back Home 9. Corporate Globalization 10. Stepping Up to Global Competition 11. Who Is Them? 15. Super Manager 16. Challenging Global Myths 24. Competitiveness and the "Global Capital Shortage" 26. Foreign Direct Investment 28. Manufacturing's New Economies of Scale 29. Search for a Truly Pan-European Manufacturing System 30. Global Innovation 31. Myth of 'Made in the U.S.A.' 36. Does Japan Play Fair? 37. "Mountains Are High, the Emperor Is Far Away" 41. Megamarket 43. Do We Want Free Trade With Mexico?
Marketing	1. Are We Building New Berlin Walls? 4. International Communication 5. World's Trade Topography 6. Global Corporate Competition II 9. Corporate Globalization 10. Stepping Up to Global Competition 12. Sources of Information

Overview of International Business

The world has changed. The global business environment is much smaller than it was 50, 30, or even a few years ago. After World War II the United States was the only major industrialized nation that had been spared the ravages of the conflict. Europe, with the exception of Sweden and Switzerland, was flattened, and even victorious Britain had been bled white. Germany had been conquered and divided, and the countries to the East were under Russian control. The Soviet Union, itself, had suffered horribly during the war, in addition to Stalin's repression and the gulags.

Japan had experienced two atomic bombings and numerous firebombings of its cities and industrial base. Its army was scattered and its navy sunk. The Japanese population faced almost immediate starvation, as did many of the people around the world, especially those who had been in the war zones. They had avoided the quick death of the war, only to be met with the specter of slow death by starvation.

As the only industrialized nation with its factories, infrastructure, agriculture, government, and society intact, the United States had very little alternative other than to assume world political and economic leadership. Basically, the United States had not suffered economically or physically in World War II, with the exception of Pearl Harbor in Hawaii and part of Alaska, both of which were not yet states. True, various American possessions had been lost to and retaken from the Japanese in the Pacific, but the nation itself had not been touched. American casualities, which numbered in the hundreds of thousands, were almost exclusively connected to the regular armed forces. While certainly not to be discounted, compared to the Soviet Union or China, where the only certainty concerning casualities is that they numbered in the tens of millions, U.S. losses were relatively light.

Shortly after the end of the war, the United States and the Soviet Union broke their alliance and the Soviets established what Winston Churchill called the "Iron Curtain." The United States tried to bring Europe back from starvation and economic disaster. First the U.S. government fed the people of Europe and Japan, turning the once mighty convoys carrying arms to Europe and the Pacific into vessels carrying food and other products. Then the United States initiated economic recovery in both Europe and Japan with such programs as the Marshall Plan, perhaps the most successful foreign policy program in the history of the United States.

These programs helped to bolster Japan and Western Europe against the threat of Soviet aggression that became known as the "cold war." Not that it was always cold—Korea, the Berlin airlift, the Berlin Wall, Afghanistan, Cuba, and Vietnam were all examples of how the cold war could get hot. The cold war became a contest between the Soviet system of socialism/communism and the U.S. system of capitalism. The struggle went on for over 40 years, and finally the Americans won.

The Americans won on a number of fronts—they essentially outspent the Soviets militarily in hardware and technological innovation, they outproduced the Soviets in goods and services, and they assisted and allowed formerly poor, backward, and often war-devastated nations to develop themselves and their economies so as to experience a prosperity previously unknown in their history.

North and South Korea probably provide the best example. The peninsula was devastated after the Korean War, which occurred after a long history of exploitation by both the Japanese and the Chinese. After the war, the Communist North and the capitalist South started about as even as could be expected. They were the same people with the same culture, language, and traditions, but they were using different economic systems. Today, South Korea is one of the economic "tigers" of the Pacific Rim, and North Korea is an economic "basket case," an experience that did not go unnoticed in the rest of the world.

The world has changed. The United States has won the cold war and the economies of Japan and Germany are challenging the American dominance in many fields. For the first 20 or 30 years after World War II, U.S. firms really did not have to worry about foreign competition, but that has changed. In the early 1970s General Motors was concerned about antitrust problems, as it controlled roughly half of the U.S. automobile market, and it was worried that the federal government might break it up. Today, GM has about one-third of the market, Toyota is on the verge of passing Chrysler in the United States, and nobody is worried about antitrust litigation at General Motors.

Unit 1

Firms must think globally. If they do not, then they are doomed to failure. Markets are global in nature when applied to raw materials, manufacturing, labor, and customers. For a U.S. firm to ignore the European Economic Community is to ignore a market larger than the United States and Canada combined, and European firms are certainly not ignoring North America.

It is a new world. The Soviet empire has broken up and new opportunities await in the old Communist bloc. Change in China will be delayed only as long as the old gerontocracy remains in power, and that change is already on the way. Japan, if for no other reason than to avoid a massive world-wide backlash, will be forced to open its markets and career opportunities to non-Japanese. It will be a slow process, but it is inevitable. The United States is now faced with a different challenge than it faced during the cold war. It must make the change from a military and ideological struggle to an economic and industrial struggle. While there will still be conflicts and minor brush wars, such as the Persian Gulf War, the main challenge will be economic; the struggle will be to compete on a global basis, not just with GM, or Ford, or Chrysler, but with Toyota, Volkswagen, Nissan, Honda, and Fiat.

Looking Ahead: Challenge Questions

After World War II, the United States and the Soviet Union had a falling-out as allies. How did the U.S. government respond to the Soviet challenge? What were some of the policies initiated? How were they successful?

American firms are more involved in world markets than at any time in the history of the country. Why do you think this is? What are some of the consequences?

The automobile industry in the United States is in decline while the Japanese automakers prosper. Why do you think this happened? What can U.S. firms do about it?

Are we building new Berlin walls?

Is the world rushing toward new trade wars? The circumstantial evidence suggests it is, but there are deeper trends at work.

Susan Lee

WORLDWIDE FREE TRADE. That notion used to stir the hearts of politicians and economists; it was the imprimatur of the enlightened view on world affairs. Global free trade meant good-paying jobs for workers in Peoria making tractors for export. It meant these well-paid workers could buy the best goods the world had to offer at the lowest prices. Ditto for American farmers who could sell the food they efficiently produced to the less efficient Europeans and Japanese and could take, in return, gleaming Japanese electronics and stylish Italian clothing. Indeed, as recently as four years ago, phrases like "regional trade blocs" and "bilateral agreement" would have been dismissed as drivel coming from the left wing of the Democratic Party.

Well, for those of you who think that trade blocs and bilateral trade deals are something from the bad old days, listen up. Enthusiasm for regionalism has so firmly replaced multilateralism that, when the Uruguay round of the General Agreement on Tariffs & Trade wheezed its last recently, there wasn't enough interest to reschedule talks.

The media is full of speculation about trade wars and the rebuilding of tariff barriers. The President of the U.S. zips down to Mexico and South America to chat about making regional trade deals. Even warrior free-traders like Columbia University Professor Jagdish Bhagwati seem resigned to a world system that will fall short of multilateral free trade: "One wishes to do without regionalism, but it's not that dangerous. I wouldn't lose any sleep over it," he says.

Not so fast. The current trade trends are inherently dangerous.

The idea of regionalism is deceptively neat. The world will consolidate into three free trade blocs: By 1992 the 12 nations of the European Community will—they hope—have knit themselves into a sort of United States with free flow of goods and services, harmonious tax and regulatory policies. With a need to protect its inefficient but politically noisy farmers and its weak computer and electronics industries, the EC will be tempted to throw up new tariff or quota walls and otherwise give preferences to locally produced products.

Meanwhile, the U.S., building on last year's free trade treaty with Canada, will make similar agreements with Mexico, Chile, Colombia, Ecuador and Bolivia and, quite possibly, Brazil and Argentina—thereby creating an American bloc. It, too, will begin, perhaps slowly at first, giving preferences to goods produced within the bloc at the expense of stuff from Europe or the Far East.

The third bloc will encompass the Pacific—Japan, Hong Kong, Singapore, Taiwan, South Korea and, for what it's worth, North Korea.

Those taking a calm view of the developing trade blocs deny regions might Smoot-Hawley each other to death. They argue the internationalization of trade and direct foreign investment by multinational corporations make such an event unlikely.

Don't worry, says Robert Lawrence of the Brookings Institution: "These deals will enhance multilateralism; once the commitment to market forces has been made at the regional level, then it will be easier to move on to bigger levels." Bloc dealing with bloc, he thinks, could be easier than nation dealing with nation: Just 3 seats at the table instead of the 100 chairs required for a GATT powwow.

But Lawrence may be paying insufficient attention to the Eurocrats in Brussels who, while working furiously to meet the EC 1992 deadline, are not laboring to dismantle its barriers to external competition—the various quotas on agriculture, cars, textiles, footwear and electronics. As barriers to full integration become more serious, we can expect the Eurocrats to offer protection for local industry as a sop to nationalistic feelings: You, France, put up with an influx of Portuguese workers and we'll keep your farmers happy. You, Italy, give German cars a better chance to compete against your Fiats and Germany will absorb more workers from depressed southern Italy.

Nor is the U.S. pure on protectionism. It is politically easy for President Bush to stump around South America talking about a trade region from Alaska to Argentina. It is more difficult to do battle with the protectionists in Congress who in 1989 extended quotas on steel and last year tried to push through another multifiber agreement to restrict textile imports.

Regionalism could, in other words, degenerate into a severe spate of protectionism. And that's not an academic issue for the U.S., where exports accounted for 75% of manufacturing growth and 12% of GNP in 1989. Indeed, it's a critical issue in an economy slipping into recession. Without open world markets, U.S. exporters won't be able to take complete advantage of the cheap dollar, and

Reprinted by permission of *Forbes*, January 7, 1991, pp. 86-89. Copyright © 1991, Forbes, Inc.

their rising exports won't moderate the recession.

Keep this in mind: Trade is equal to almost one-fifth of gross world product. If the current recession turns out to be severe, pressures will mount within the various trading blocs to protect local jobs against imports. Sylvia Ostry, a former GATT negotiator who is now teaching at the University of Toronto, says: "What if we're facing a giant global recession? If you get a crazy quilt of bilateral agreements, it will make the world more complicated and impair growth because it is bound to create uncertainty."

Does it matter if international trade is crimped slightly? It does indeed. Trade allows countries to consume more than they could if left to themselves; whatever the temporary dislocations, the bottom line is that international trade raises everybody's standard of living. By permitting countries to specialize in producing whatever they are most efficient at and exchanging those products with countries that are also producing efficiently, trade boosts real incomes and standards of living. My country's sale abroad of its laptop computers lets me buy more of your country's kumquats (which my country doesn't produce very efficiently), just as your sale of kumquats lets you buy more of my laptops (which your country doesn't produce efficiently).

Look at little Chile: After suffering for decades under a policy of economic self-sufficiency, this Latin American nation has performed a minor economic miracle by reorienting its tiny economy toward free trade. Chile simply decided: We'll produce wine and grapes and salmon for your tables more efficiently than you can produce them yourselves; you pay us in computers and shoes and other things that you can produce more efficiently than we can. The net result was a big gain for the Chilean economy and a better standard of living for the nation's depressed rural poor.

Trade insures efficiency, too, through the brutal system of competition. Ask the many firms sheltered from global competition in the 1950s and 1960s. They grew lazy and unable to compete in the world of the 1970s and 1980s: Britain's auto industry, the U.S.' steel industry, Japan's aluminum industry.

The classic problem of trading blocs is that they divert trade from efficient nonmembers to less efficient members. During the formation of the European Community, for example, the customs union allowed special free entry to products from former African colonies. Thus relatively cheaper Latin American bananas faced a tariff, making them more expensive, while relatively expensive African bananas slipped in duty free. So Europeans pay more for bananas and poor Latin American countries tighten their belts—and turn to the U.S. in hope of getting preference from us to offset Europe's discrimination. Of course, African countries benefit. That may make political sense, but it makes no economic sense.

Trade diversion could be enormous. Each of the envisioned regional trade blocs has an enormous stake in trade outside its area. Outside-the-region trade for North America is 12% of GNP, 13% for Western Europe and Asia; these are big numbers, and it is in everybody's interest to see those numbers grow bigger.

Regionalism spawns trade frictions. You discriminate against my cars and I'll block your cognac; ban our chickens and we'll tariff your wine; put a quota on my textiles and I'll buy my computers elsewhere. The potentials for retaliation and counter-retaliation are endless.

Assuming that regional trade walls are inevitable, many big corporations have decided to jump the walls even before they are built. They are building plants and acquiring companies within each of the blocs. Gary Becker at the University of Chicago points out, "There will be various inefficiencies because companies outside of the blocs will have to set up plants and invest capital in each bloc to gain access to the market." How would this work? Badly. To gain access, say, to the Latin American market a European auto company might have to build a plant there, where low volume would make it a high-cost producer.

These are not idle possibilities. Intel, the U.S. maker of semiconductors, has announced plans to build in Europe in part because it was concerned that the European Community will apply tariffs and quotas to protect local chipmakers. Roger Stone put his Stone Container Corp. deeply in debt to buy Canada's Consolidated Bathurst, a major paper producer with large holdings in Western Europe. He explained that he did so to protect Stone's European markets, which might turn hostile against imports from the U.S.

Michael Aho at the Council on Foreign Relations says: "Bilateral trade agreements could eventually fragment the world trading system and produce the same disastrous effects as an overt policy of protectionism."

Why is the world suddenly abandoning the difficult but fruitful trend toward freer trade?

Part of the reason has to do with the changed position of the U.S. in the world. After World War II the U.S., with the only nondevastated industrial economy, was eager to export. Free trade was in the U.S.' national interest. So U.S. commitment to the General Agreement on Tariffs & Trade served us—and the world—very well. Thanks to GATT, world trade expanded faster than global output after 1945. Under GATT, tariffs have been cut from an average of 40% in 1947 to less than 5% today, and consumers have reaped rich rewards in the form of lower prices and better goods.

Now, of course, we aren't the only ones with stuff to sell—Germany and Japan have become formidable export machines. Competition is fierce—and not always fair, since many countries, Japan in particular but the U.S., too, cheat sometimes on free trade. It is no longer as clear as it once was that free trade is in the national interest. Ask any autoworker.

The obvious result of the U.S. loss of hegemony in trade is the appearance of new sorts of trade protection, like Voluntary Export Restraints, antidumping regulations and countervailing duties. During the 1980s the share of total imports into the U.S. subject to quotas or restraints went from 9% to 15%. And the Omnibus Trade & Competitiveness Act of 1988 strengthens the 301 provision allowing the U.S. to mount trade retaliation on a unilateral basis rather than under the multilateral approach mandated by GATT. While griping at the Japanese and the Europeans for throwing barriers to free trade, we've thrown a few of our own.

The U.S.' large and persistent trade deficit with Japan also sparked a fright—especially after the gap could no longer be blamed on an overvalued dollar. So, certainly, did protectionist tendencies in Europe, many of whose countries have openly discriminated against Japanese exports. If Japan, why not Canada and the U.S.?

The trade deficit caused strong protectionist mutterings in Congress and even produced a protectionist presidential candidate in Representative Richard Gephardt (D-Mo.). "It was," says Carla Hills, the chief U.S. trade cop, talking about the trade deficit, "a bad backdrop for good trade policy. It drove Congress in directions that may not be the best way to deal with the deficit."

Obviously, everyone has grown impatient over the cumbersome process of GATT—joke: GATT stands for the

General Agreement to Talk and Talk. Talk and talk, stall and stall. In April 1988 the U.S. brought suit at the GATT Secretariat in Geneva against the European Community over the EC's payment of internal subsidies to producers of oil seeds. GATT agreed with the U.S. in a 1989 decision, but so far the EC has not complied with its ruling.

As the failure of the Uruguay round of GATT talks so vividly demonstrates, agreements are difficult to negotiate. John Taylor of the Council of Economic Advisers says, "Multilateral trade is the preferred solution, but it's so slow to come."

Must we then batten down the hatches and get ready for a trade war?

Maybe not. Powerful counterforces are at work.

Remember this: Regionalism received its main impetus from political considerations. The driving force behind EC '92 in the early 1980s was European fear of Soviet military might and U.S. economic prowess. U.S. anxiety over EC '92, in turn, set off talk about an Americas bloc.

But the political impetus behind the EC has been dissipating in recent years. The Soviet Union is a basket case, and the U.S. is a diminished giant. Meanwhile, European nationalism is not dead; this is a continent, after all, still divided by language and culture and centuries of history—a continent where Flemish mobs will still beat on Walloon mobs, where Germans still possess a kind of national superiority complex. The EC has a long way to go before it is a U.S. "We could see a revival of the pre-1919 world with Europe as a collection of nation states," says Robert Mundell, economics professor at Columbia University.

If Mundell is right, Washington should go slow on regional trade and exercise a certain amount of forbearance when confronted by European provocations on agriculture.

A slowing of European integration may not be a bad thing for the world and for Europe itself if it ends the pressure to rush toward the creation of trade blocs and puts world trade back on the path that has served it so well since World War II: a totally free interchange of goods among nations on a basis of economic advantage rather than political expediency. Mundell's talk of a revival of nationalism in Europe may be good news rather than bad for the world.

Global Frontiers of Business

Business leaders looking to position their companies for the next century will take advantage of innovative technologies, new management techniques, and new trade opportunities in the Pacific Rim and Europe to develop winning strategies. So say the experts quoted by the Monitor for this special section on the 'Global Frontiers of Business.'

Advice to Execs: 'Think Globally'

David R. Francis
Staff writer of The Christian Science Monitor

BOSTON

FOR business, the frontier is the globe.

Business executives and business-school professors often talk about "globalization." Peter Drucker, professor of management and social science at Claremont Graduate School, has told corporate officials, "If you don't think globally, you deserve to be unemployed, and you will be."

"The global marketplace surely has arrived when villagers in the Middle East follow the Gulf war on CNN [Cable News Network], via Soviet government satellite, and through a private subsidiary of a local government enterprise," notes Murray Weidenbaum, an economist at Washington University in St. Louis. "Both public and private business are involved and they are located in three different continents."

More than half the products manufactured in the United States have one or more foreign components. Half of all imports and exports—foreign trade—are transacted between domestic companies and their foreign affiliates or foreign parents. Foreign operations of US-owned companies account for more than $1 trillion in annual sales worldwide, four times the total export of US-made goods.

Robert Reich, an economist at Harvard University, maintains that globalization has gone so far that the managers of supranational corporations feel little allegiance to the nation of their headquarters.

"In the global enterprise, the bonds between company and country . . . are rapidly eroding," he writes in the latest issue of the Harvard Business Review. "Instead, we are witnessing the creation of a purer form of capitalism, practiced globally by managers who are more distant, more economically driven—in essence more coldly rational in their decisions, having shed the old affiliations with people and place.

"Today corporate decisions about production and location are driven by the dictates of global competition, not by national allegiance."

In his new book, "The Work of Nations" (Knopf), Professor Reich goes further: "We are living through a transformation that will rearrange the politics and economics of the coming century. There will be no *national* products or technologies, no national corporations, no national industries. There will no longer be national economies, at least as we have come to understand the concept. All that will remain rooted within national borders are the people who comprise a nation. Each nation's primary assets will be its citizens' skills and insights."

Some say Reich has exaggerated, that the nationality of a corporation still matters. Another Harvard professor, Michael Porter, writes in his massive tome, "The Competitive Advantage of Nations" (Free Press): "As globalization of competition has intensified, some have begun to argue a diminished role for nations. Instead, internationalization and the removal of protection and other distortions to competition arguably make nations, if anything, more important. National differences in character and culture, far from being threatened by global competition, prove integral to success in it.

"The home base is where strategy is set, core product and process development takes place, and the essential and proprietary skills reside. The home base is the platform for a global strategy in the industry in which advantages drawn from the home nation are supplemented by those from an integrated, worldwide position."

Certainly business, using modern technology, is bringing together the world's peoples, whether they like it or not. It was business that turned the US from a conglomeration of states and regions into a nation. It is business that today is unifying

Reprinted by permission from *The Christian Science Monitor*, April 11, 1991, pp. 9-11. Copyright © 1991 The Christian Science Publishing Society. All rights reserved.

Europe into the European Community.

Further, it is business that is turning English into the main international language. When the directors of Asea Brown Boveri (ABB) meet, they speak English, despite the fact that the $25 billion company is the result of a merger of Swedish and Swiss companies and its headquarters is in Zurich. Though it has 240,000 employees in dozens of nations, the official company language is English.

"Technology and economics are outpacing our traditional way of thinking about international politics," Mr. Weidenbaum says. "The standard geopolitical map is out of sync with the emerging business and economic map."

Reich says governments are still struggling to catch up to global business managers. He advocates the creation of an "Office of the United States Investment Representative," or USIR, paralleling the US Trade Representative. Instead of negotiating international trade deals, this new office would negotiate international investment issues.

At present, Reich says, states and cities bid keenly for investments in plant and equipment, granting various tax breaks and subsidies. They become "easy pickings" for global managers. Partly as a result, corporations contributed only 16 percent of local government revenues in 1989, compared with 45 percent in 1957. The concessions to companies make it more difficult for states and cities to finance education and infrastructure, he says.

Reich's USIR would preempt by federal law the separate state and local laws that authorize their officials to offer investment incentives. It would bargain for only those global investments that would likely provide maximum benefits to the US and guide the investments to locations that would do the most good. "It would put America on an equal footing with other large nations and emerging trading blocs that are already bidding effectively for global investment," he writes.

Reich also suggests a GATT (General Agreement on Tariffs and Trade) for direct investment in plant and equipment. GATT establishes rules for global trade. The new institution would establish rules by which nations bid for global investment and processes for settling disputes over such bids. Without such rules, Reich says, wealthy nations can always outbid poorer ones.

Mr. Porter cautions: "One nation's firms need not succeed only at the expense of another." Such competition is not a zero-sum game, where what one wins the other loses, he says. "World economic prosperity depends on rapid innovation by advanced nations, which creates new products and cedes relatively less-productive activities to developing nations." That means what blesses one nation economically can also bless other nations. Prosperity there promotes prosperity here.

"Technology has liberated us from the zero-sum game of traditional economics," writes Paul Zane Pilzer in "Unlimited Wealth: The Theory and Practice of Economic Alchemy" (Crown). "We live today in a world of effectively *unlimited* resources, a world of *unlimited* wealth."

Small Firms Wary of One-Market Europe

By Howard LaFranchi

Staff writer of The Christian Science Monitor

PARIS

FOR Luc Doublet, the key to succeeding in Europe's single market will be treating everybody the same, while knowing what makes people different.

His philosophy may sound contradictory. Yet the Lille, France, manufacturer of flags, banners, and traffic-control products says that two-tier approach will be the answer for small and medium-size companies that want to succeed in a 12-nation borderless Europe after 1992.

"It's a variation of the absolutely essential advice to 'think globally, but act locally,' " says the employer of 350 people from France to Belgium, Spain, and California, who works out of a pyramid-shaped headquarters and quotes futurist Alvin Toffler.

To make his point, Mr. Doublet notes that his company is about to publish a European-sales catalog in which all prices will be listed in the European Community's ECU—European Currency Unit. "That way, the price will be the same for everyone, each customer will feel he's being treated like the next," he says.

Doublet also says that companies branching out from a local market will be wise to understand what makes their various customers different.

Here he gives another example: "We had to be ready for the effect the Gulf war would have on us," he says. Flag sales in the United States, "a country I understood would need to identify itself as a nation," jumped 30 percent. In France, on the other hand, "an old and hardly gregarious nation," sales plummeted 45 percent.

Doublet is a Euro-enthusiast. For many of Europe's small and medium-size companies, however, the prospect of a market of 350 million consumers, with no barriers to the free movement of goods, capital, and persons, is daunting.

Economists say the single market, which has sometimes been criticized as a boon primarily to large corporations, holds traps and opportunities for smaller companies.

In many cases they will have to expand to survive; in other cases, their specific talents will be sought out by larger companies looking to boost their own products' attractiveness.

"Many small companies are going to die in the single market, but I am not pessimistic about their future in Europe," says Arnoud De Meyer, a specialist in European manufacturing at the European Institute of Business Administration, or INSEAD, one of Europe's top business schools, in Fontainebleau, France. "Those that learn to become part of emerging networks will do very well."

Europe will emerge as a "laboratory" for 21st-century manufacturing, where companies will learn to produce efficiently nearly customized products, Mr. De Meyer says. He says companies that give up the idea of "protecting a piece of a local market" but instead learn to capitalize on their specific talent, selling it on a regional basis or subcontracting to a

'Ninety percent of the small and medium-size companies do not have a strategy.'

– Bruno Calzia, consultant

large corporation, will succeed in a culturally diverse Europe.

Still, problems of information, financing, language, and culture, remain high hurdles for many companies.

"The big corporations are already multinational, so they generally know what they are doing. But 90 percent of the small and medium-size companies do not have a strategy," says Bruno Calzia, an Italian attorney and consultant specializing in helping small companies survive in the European market.

To ease the transition for businesses, the EC set up a netowrk of 195 "Euro Info Centers" in its 12 member countries (the centers are linked to Brussels by computer) to disseminate information on new laws and opportunities concerning the single market. The Community has also set up a network to help companies find potential joint-venture partners in other EC countries.

Despite these programs, "The Community really hasn't developed an environment for small companies," De Meyer says. "There is definitely a communications gap."

Three principal changes will affect the way Europe's successful smaller companies operate, De Meyer says: a "regionalization" of markets across national lines; the growing need for large companies to have diversified supply networks; and a greater customization in the manufacture of products.

"Rather than thinking about making the best product, companies are going to have to think about making the best components to use in the most versatile ways," says De Meyer. "The advantage for small companies is that they are very good at components."

This trend in production toward extreme specialization favors European small businesses, says De Meyer, because they are accustomed to Europe's cultural diversity.

'Mega-Markets' Shine on Pacific Rim

Daniel B. Wood

Staff writer of The Christian Science Monitor

LOS ANGELES

WAKE up and smell the green tea, America. Go East, young Europeans. Don't dillydally, Gorby: In the next century, a growing chorus of Pacific Basin ballyhooers say, the world economy will be controlled by Asians – and there's still time to get in on the ground floor.

The opening of Eastern Europe, German reunification, and the expanding Common Market is a blip on the screen compared to the "mega-markets" emerging in Asia, these observers say.

Five years ago, United States trade with Pacific countries surpassed trade with Atlantic countries by 50 percent. In five more years, Pacific Rim-US trade is projected to be twice that with Western Europe.

Already, 40 percent of world trade is done by Asian nations – and the number jumps by ever greater increments each year.

"The whole Atlantic is excited about a new market of 17 million East Germans, when they should be thinking about the 170 million Indonesians," says Jeffrey Rosensweig, an economist at Emory University in Atlanta.

Caught up in "Europhoria," Professor Rosenweig and others warn, the US and Europe are neglecting to take advantage of the Asian countries that are both investing and opening themselves to investment. These include Thailand, Malaysia, and Indonesia, which are following the earlier patterns of South Korea, Taiwan, and Hong Kong.

"We are still a Eurocentric country; the Old Country is still easier and more obvious," says Frank Gibney, director of the Pacific Basin Institute in Santa Barbara, Calif. Outside the West Coast, the awareness of Asia has not been communicated to the country, he says.

Meanwhile, intra-Asian trade is the growth story of the past two years and the foreseeable future:

- Small countries such as Hong Kong and South Korea are out-investing the US in countries such as Thailand, China, and Indonesia.
- Regional trade is expected to exceed US-Asia trade by the year 2000. (In 1989, intra-Asian trade amounted to $200 billion, compared with $271 billion for transpacific trade.)
- The so-called "four tigers" – Taiwan, Hong Kong, Singapore, and South Korea – are receiving unprecedented investment from other Asian countries. Despite unofficial barriers to investment in Japan, Asian investment there has more than doubled since 1986.

"The idea of the Pacific Rim is past its 'gee whiz' stage, where everyone said, 'Isn't this great we can get together?' to a stage where everyone is standing back to assess the problems of so much trade," says Ernest Preeg, a professor of international business at the Center for Strategic and International Studies.

Two years ago, foreign ministers from 12 countries set up the region's first intergovernmental body: the Asian-Pacific Economic Cooperation (APEC) consists of the US, Canada, Japan, South Korea, Australia, New Zealand, Indonesia, Malaysia, the Philippines, Singapore, and Thailand.

"They are moving beyond the stage of just exchanging views across a table to scratching out serious solutions to region-wide problems," Mr. Gibney says. This bodes for a switch in bilateral (US-Japan) dominance of the Pacific Rim to a multilateral focus that will transcend national boundaries.

'The whole Atlantic is excited about 17 million East Germans, when they should be thinking about 170 million Indonesians.'
– Economist Jeffrey Rosenweig

"In the next few years, you will see a recognition that it is very hard to make regional economics follow single-country policy or domination," says Larry Krause, professor of international economics at the University of California, San Diego.

Rosenweig predicts "huge conglomerations of nations in trading zones" in the next 10 years in Asia.

Without a formal policy to deal with Pacific Rim trade, US strategists are dividing into two schools of thought:

Although most see a bipolar trading world, with Europe and Asia at the two poles, a tri-polar world is seen by Dr. Preeg and C. Fred Bergsten, director of the Institute for International Economics. That would divide the Asian Pacific into an East Asian and North American camps (US, Canada, and Mexico). Europe would be the third pole.

Krause says the US must make a dramatic shift toward a focus on Asia. "The US is a Pacific country, not an Atlantic one," he says. "The fact that we don't recognize this in our policy is sheer accident... our capital and New York City face the wrong way."

Both sides see the Pacific Rim countries as opportunities ripe for aggressive business dealings of a cooperative nature – where the US, European, and even Soviet businesses must take initiative and be ready to stay in for the long haul.

Anticipating an easing of protectionism on both sides of the Pacific, Gibney sees a "leveling of the playing field" in coming years – one that could be accelerated if US policymakers would address the issue head-on.

TWO KEY MARKETS

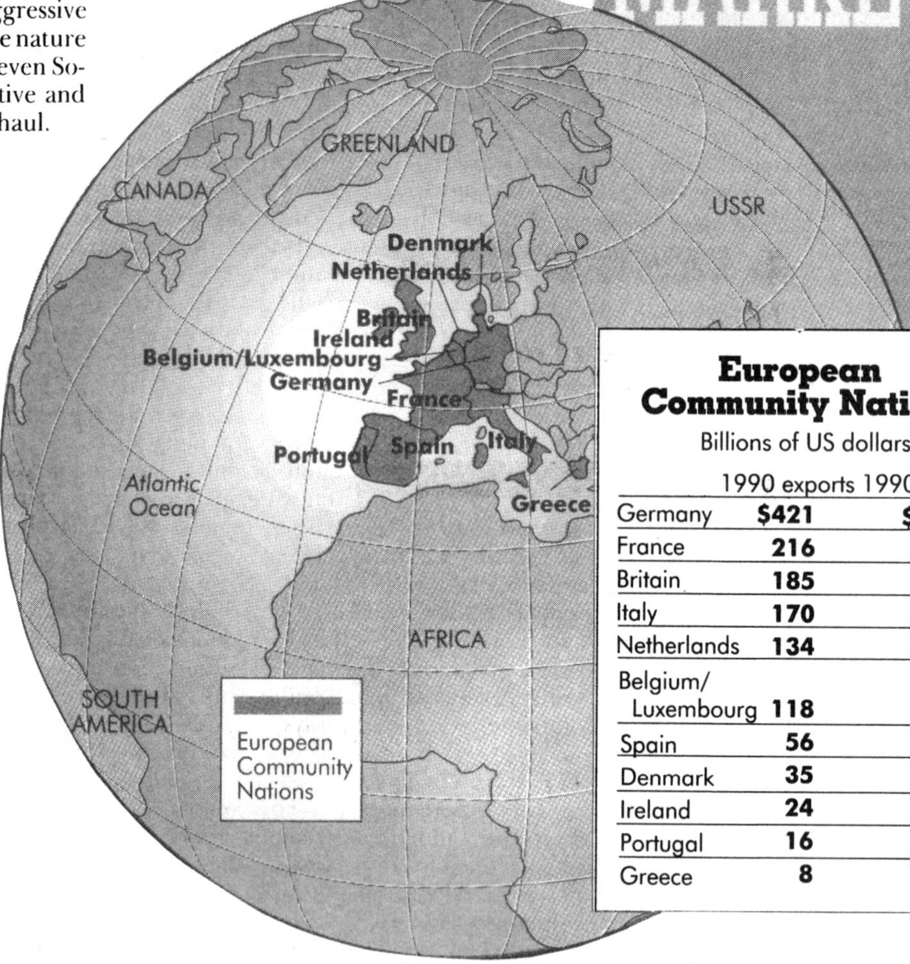

European Community Nations

Billions of US dollars

	1990 exports	1990 imports
Germany	**$421**	**$356**
France	**216**	**234**
Britain	**185**	**224**
Italy	**170**	**182**
Netherlands	**134**	**127**
Belgium/ Luxembourg	**118**	**120**
Spain	**56**	**88**
Denmark	**35**	**32**
Ireland	**24**	**21**
Portugal	**16**	**24**
Greece	**8**	**21**

Brazilian Businesses Shackled by Low-Tech

By Julia Michaels

Special to The Christian Science Monitor

SÃO PAULO, BRAZIL

IN the back room of an old house hidden away in an industrial neighbor hood, a muscular young man pulls on a hand loom for eight hours every day. With each movement, a row of knitting emerges, slowly becoming part of an elegant sweater that will be handstitched together, hand-finished, hand-washed and ironed, and hand-carried into the front room, where store owners buy them.

The Bruar knitwear factory's 10 workers painstakingly produce 100 pieces a day. "Modern machines are very expensive, and loans are hard to come by," says factory manager Claudia Guedes. "We work more using goodwill than with technology."

Bruar's problems are only the tip of an iceberg that affects just about every sector of Brazilian business. Here, as in many developing nations, modern technology is sorely lacking. United States auto companies operating in Brazil see some car models that are 20 years behind Detroit.

"Our technology varies from state of the

From *The Christian Science Monitor*, April 11, 1991, p. 11. Copyright © 1991 Julia Michaels. Reprinted by permission of the author.

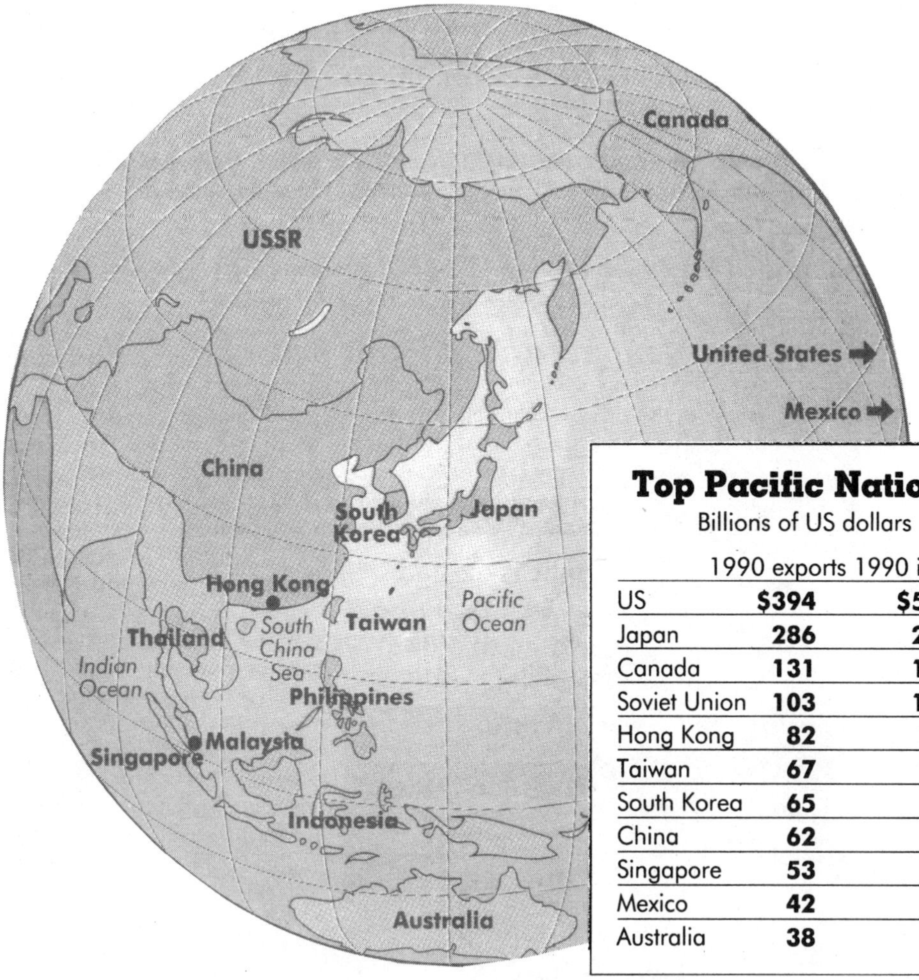

Top Pacific Nations

Billions of US dollars

	1990 exports	1990 imports
US	**$394**	**$515**
Japan	**286**	**234**
Canada	**131**	**119**
Soviet Union	**103**	**121**
Hong Kong	**82**	**82**
Taiwan	**67**	**55**
South Korea	**65**	**70**
China	**62**	**54**
Singapore	**53**	**61**
Mexico	**42**	**41**
Australia	**38**	**42**

art . . . to out of the ark," says James Donaldson, director-superintendent of Autolatina, a Brazil-Argentina joint venture between Ford Motor Company and Volkswagen AG. "Some of our equipment dates from just after World War II." Mr. Donaldson blames Brazil's high taxes and import duties, plus a generally unstable business environment.

Latin America's largest economy, with a territory the size of the continental US and a gross national product of about $350 billion, has come a long way. Before World War II, Brazil imported almost all its manufactured goods. Today, it produces its own steel, automobiles, soft drinks, electronic cash machines, tableware, and telephones. It makes airplanes and tanks.

However, according to a study by the University of Campinas, the technology available in Brazil lags behind that of industrialized nations by about 10 to 15 years.

The problem, analysts say, has been a widespread belief that Brazil could develop technology the same way it replaced imports with local industrial output just after World War II.

"The last 20 years were a period of technological breakthroughs," says a long-time American consultant to Brazilian industry. "During the same period of time, Brazil was trying to start from scratch and get up to state-of-the-art, and that equation just doesn't work," he adds. The government, he says, could not invest enough in education to provide training in high-tech research and development on a par with the US and Asia.

The start-from-scratch policy protects local computermakers, for example, but keeps out many state-of-the-art products and increases costs. "I recently bought a new [computer system] from a smuggler," says a São Paul computer user. "It cost me $4,000, $800 over the US price. If I wanted to buy the same equipment in Brazil, I couldn't find it, and the closest thing to it would cost $7,000, without the monitor."

The technology gap is evident even in the simple act of making a phone call. Callers must wait for dial tones, and put up with busy circuitry and frequent disconnections. That is because Brazil's 8.8 million telephone lines run on the old rotary system, an immediate need for 6 million new lines. The cost of this would be $24 billion, says telecommunications consultant Luiz Carlos Morals Rêgo. He notes that the cost needs to be funded by phone-rate hikes and foreign investment. But the hikes cause inflation, and Brazil's unstable economy isn't attractive to investors.

THE government of Brazilian President Fernando Collor de Mello is trying to remedy this. Mr. Collor has begun changing the policy that long instead of a modern digital one, and there is kept out foreign computer technology, and recently announced a program to help business use more modern technology.

But so far, Collor has met with formidable obstacles.

"Brazilian legislation is very complicated, so the political decision to open up the computer market, for example, depends on congressional approval," says José Goldemberg, the national science and technology secretary. "Also, there is [the opposition of] a technocracy that has been forming for the past 30 to 40 years and is firmly entrenched."

To open up the country to modern processes, the government also faces resistance from businesses. "Some companies are doing fine in the market, they're not really keen on changing," says George Hegedus, a business professor at the Getulio Vargas Foundation. For if everyone can get technology, "where does that leave the big fish?"

THE GLOBAL ECONOMY: WHO GETS HURT

FREE TRADE IS A NET PLUS—BUT NOT FOR EVERYONE

You'll have to excuse the McAmis family of Greeneville, Tenn., if they cringe at talk of free trade. After 12 years of assembling Magnavox TVs at a North American Philips Corp. plant, Allen McAmis was laid off in February and his $13-an-hour job moved to Juarez, Mexico, where it pays $2 an hour. He was recalled in June to fill in for workers on sick leave. But Allen and his wife, Sherry, who also works at the plant, fear that Philips will move more jobs south. The couple have cut out birthday gifts and allowances for their children, Christina and Brian, and survey the future with dread. If Allen loses his job again and "I get laid off, too, we'll be a welfare family," Sherry says.

Ever since the British economist David Ricardo advanced the theory of comparative advantage in 1817, conventional economic wisdom has held that the benefits of dropping trade barriers—lower prices and higher growth—outweigh the loss of jobs and pay that some workers suffer in the process. Most analysts have held to this view as global competition soared in the 1980s and the U. S. negotiated a free-trade pact with Canada and contemplated one with Mexico. But now, a flurry of studies by disparate economists—everyone from middle-of-the-road academics to ardent defenders of Reaganomics—are finding that the tradeoff isn't nearly that simple.

SERVICE SURPLUS. These analyses still call growing trade a net plus. But they also pinpoint more precisely than ever who gets hurt, and the scope of their findings is sobering. In the 1980s, the first and worst hit by global trade were factory workers whose companies competed with foreign rivals. As these people were laid off or suffered wage cuts, they created a glut of job candidates that helped hold down pay among the 64 million workers, across a wide spectrum of industries, who never went beyond high school. Only the college-educated did well. These 54 million Americans, blessed with high skills and fortified by the fact that new technologies boosted

HOW TRADE AFFECTS WAGES...

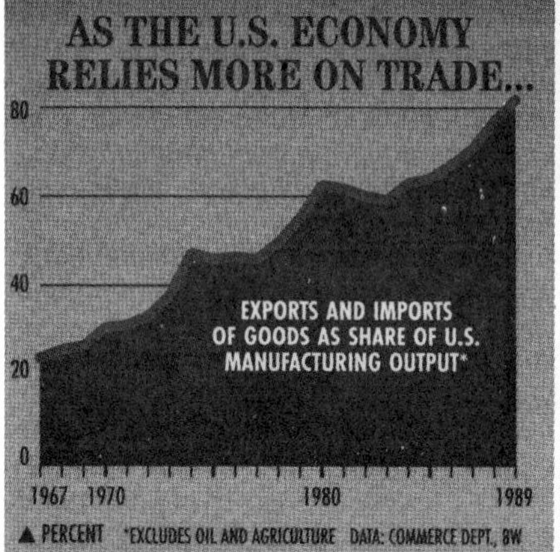

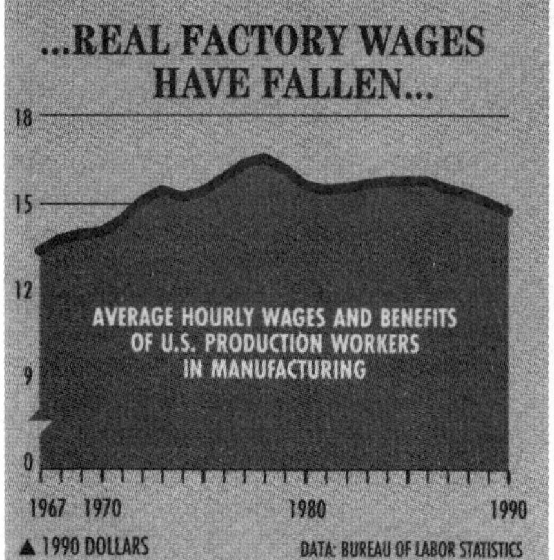

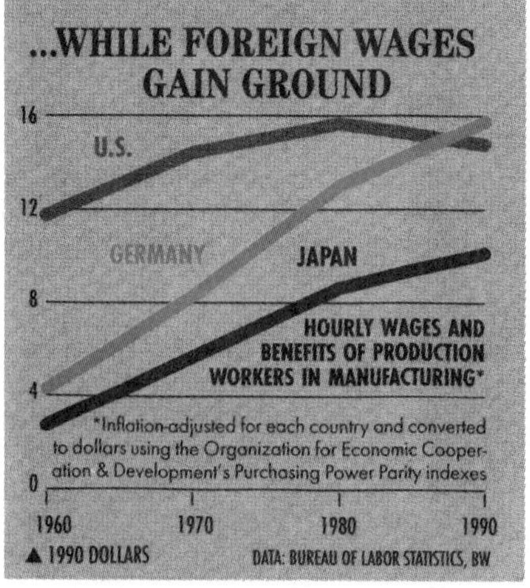

...AND FUELS INCOME INEQUALITY

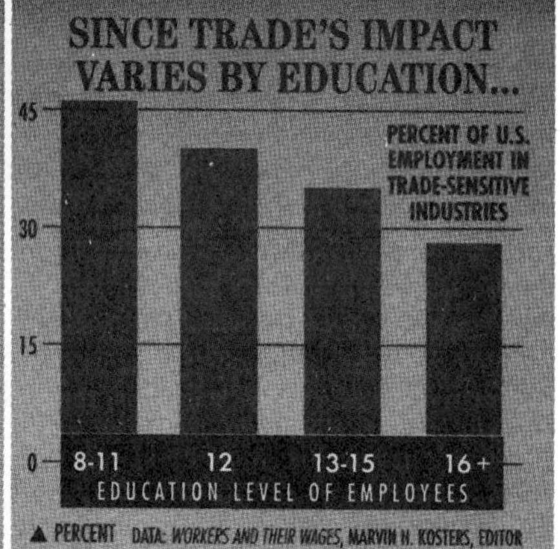

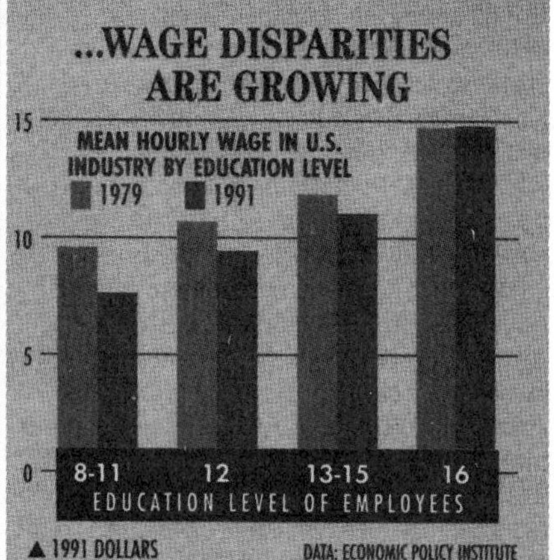

Charts by Erick Hoffmann

FIRST AND WORST HIT

The North American Free Trade Agreement will mean more U.S. exports to Mexico, but that could include low-skill jobs.

Reprinted from the August 10, 1992, issue of *Business Week*, pp. 43-53, by special permission. Copyright © 1992 by McGraw-Hill, Inc.

demand for the work they do, were insulated both from foreign competition and the struggles of the less educated.

These trends sound familiar, but their broadest implication is news: The increase in trade bears much of the blame for an unprecedented surge in income inequality between the most- and least-educated halves of the U. S. work force. To cite the extremes, the real wages of high school dropouts have fallen by up to 20% since 1979, while real incomes of employees with more than four years of college have grown by 8%, according to the Economic Policy Institute, a liberal think tank in Washington, D. C. Marvin H. Kosters, an ardent free-trade advocate and director of economic policy studies at the conservative American Enterprise Institute, has just edited a book called *Workers and Their Wages,* which tries to explain the new inequality. It results, he says, from the potent combination of "trade and technology."

What makes this conclusion especially unsettling is that trade is bound to pick up. U. S. and Mexican negotiators are close to reaching a North American Free Trade Agreement that will phase out many trade barriers between the two. This will no doubt create U. S. jobs as exports to Mexico increase—but will also send more lower-skilled ones south. Meanwhile, the seven major industrial countries are trying to expand the 108-nation General Agreement on Tariffs & Trade (GATT), which will leave labor-intensive industries such as textiles more vulnerable to foreign rivals. And countries such as Malaysia and China are rapidly boosting exports. All this "will have a dramatic impact on lower-skilled workers in the U. S.," predicts Edward E. Leamer, a trade economist at the University of California at Los Angeles.

CLASS WARFARE? The impact will reach much further than that. Declining pay for the bottom half may not slow U. S. growth, since average incomes should rise as the top half does better. But widening inequality poses other problems. The poverty rate could stay up. The tab for welfare and unemployment could mount, inflating taxes. Ultimately, resentment of the wealthy could reach a boiling point, leading to ferocious attacks on executive pay and even to more riots like last May's in Los Angeles. "One possibility is for us to become a class society like those in Latin America," which have unequal distributions of wealth and chronically unstable governments, says Richard B. Freeman, an economist at Harvard University. "That's the direction we're headed."

This will be a potent issue in the Presidential campaign, where Democratic candidate Bill Clinton is attacking the

▲ LEVI STRAUSS

Teams of workers are doing higher-skilled tasks, such as eliminating bottlenecks and setting up the line

Reagan-Bush legacy of wage stagnation for all but the most well off. In accepting his nomination, Clinton vowed that "American companies must act like American companies again—exporting products, not jobs." On July 27, meanwhile, House Majority Leader Richard A. Gephardt (D-Mo.) called for a tax on companies that move to Mexico to fund training for workers who are left behind. At the Republican convention on Aug. 17, President Bush is likely to blame the Democratic Congress for failing to enact his plan for growth—cuts in spending and taxes.

Neither candidate embraces protectionism, and other strategies would work. For one, Corporate America could compete globally by adopting a high-skills strategy. Rather than push pay to the lowest common denominator, companies such as Deere, Ford, and Motorola are training workers to improve their skills, boost productivity—and keep jobs at home. If most companies did likewise, the ranks of the less skilled would shrink, easing the glut of them. To hasten this trend, Washington could spend more on education and training, for example, or curtail immigration of low-skilled workers.

For the moment, however, Washington seems unwilling to act. And for every Motorola or Ford, a trendsetter such as AT&T is turning high-paying jobs into

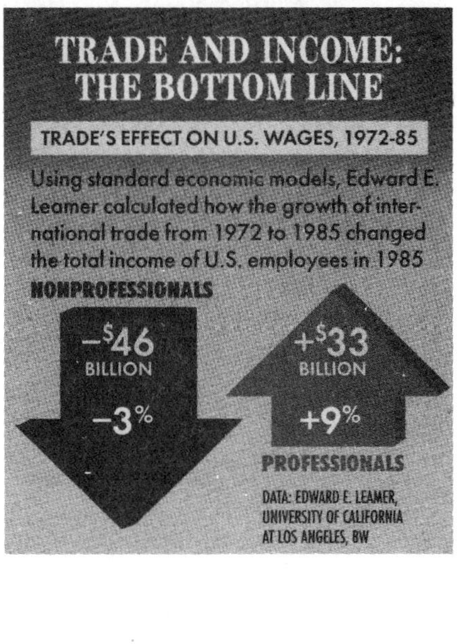

low-wage ones. Even those that upgrade worker skills, such as Ford Motor Co. and General Electric Co. (page 17), still shift work to cheap-labor countries—thus pursuing both approaches.

Meanwhile, the bottom half faces another ominous trend. Service industries —banks, insurers, and retailers, among others, which employ 75% of the work force—are automating jobs and displacing lower-skilled workers. Since 1990, Sears has dumped 21,000 positions this way. "If service productivity rises in the '90s, the question is how neutral this will be between educated and less educated workers," says University of Chicago economist Kevin M. Murphy. "If the gains come mostly in low-skilled jobs, the story will be the same as [for manufacturing] in the '80s."

The specter of inequality hasn't changed most economists' conviction that globalization is good. Economic theory has held for decades that as foreign countries sell more to the U.S., they use the revenue to buy U.S. exports. They also set up shop and create jobs in the U.S., as the Japanese and Germans are doing. The latest example: a $400 million BMW plant that will bring 2,000 jobs to Spartanburg, S.C. There are other benefits, too, such as a freer exchange of technology and managerial ideas. Historically, the net benefit of all this in terms of jobs and growth has been difficult to quantify. Still, economists project that a new GATT deal would add 0.5% a year to world GDP growth, and that free trade with Mexico would lift output in both countries and create tens of thousands of new U.S. jobs.

TECHNO TRADE. There's at least equal proof, however, of the link between trade and inequality. Wolfgang F. Stolper and Paul A. Samuelson, the father of neoclassical economics, first expressed the concept in 1941, with elegant equations that built on Ricardo's comparative advantage theory. If goods trade freely, the idea goes, prices will equalize, and so will production costs. To compete, countries must specialize where they have a relative edge. Low-wage countries will make labor-intensive goods, while those with capital will do better in technology-intensive products. Thus, U.S. low-skilled work should flow overseas, or wages of low-skilled workers must fall.

This didn't happen for much of this century, largely because trade—the sum of exports and imports—was less than 10% of U. S. gross domestic product. In the past 20 years, as that figure grew to 25%, imports began to displace low-skilled workers or depress their wages in industries such as textiles, auto parts, and electronics. But the U. S. wage gap didn't widen: The baby boomers, plus an influx of working women, produced a

▲ PHILIPS
So far, Philips has shifted 900 jobs to Juarez. The threat of moving more enabled it to win union concessions

surplus of college-educated employees, which kept their incomes from rising faster than those of the less educated.

These forces reversed in the 1980s. The rush of college graduates eased, reflecting the baby bust and the slowdown of women entering the work force. New technology investment, spurred in part by foreign competition, swelled demand for college grads such as engineers and technicians, so their pay rose. Meanwhile, 350,000 less skilled immigrants entered the U. S. each year, and soaring imports eliminated factory jobs. Soon, "workers displaced by trade were competing in service industries," says Harvard economist Lawrence F. Katz.

American Telephone & Telegraph Co. illustrates how all this happens. Since 1984, it has eliminated 21,000 blue-collar manufacturing jobs in the U. S., leaving 32,000. It also has created 12,000 mostly lower-paying factory jobs elsewhere. Meanwhile, its U. S. white-collar work force has grown by 8,000, to 118,000. "We're losing low-skilled jobs overseas or to technology," says William J. Warwick, president of microelectronics manufacturing at AT&T. "I need more engineers, designers, and high-skilled technicians, but fewer people who make circuit boards."

Jacqueline A. Gregory proves his point. A 29-year-old electrical engineer at AT&T's Allentown (Pa.) microelectronics facility, she was hired last September to help develop software that AT&T customers use to design semiconductor chips. AT&T created Gregory's group of six engineers shortly before she signed on, then added four positions. "We're now trying to hire three more people," she says. And Gregory is back in college part-time, aiming for a masters degree.

BORDER CROSSING. Dreama B. Fields, 33, has had the opposite luck. She worked for nine years as an assembler and packer at an AT&T plant that made transformers and other devices in Radford, Va. Then, in 1990, after moving work to Matamoros, Mexico, for five years, AT&T shut the plant. By then, 800 of Radford's 2,100 blue-collar jobs had migrated south. Labor comprised about 50% of production costs at Radford, says Warwick. He won't give the figure in Mexico. But workers there earn an average $2.35 an hour in wages and benefits, vs. the $13 Fields earned.

Fields has suffered less than many of her peers because her husband, James, has a job as a state park ranger. But they have cut back so she can attend community college. They buy second-hand clothes for Audrey, 4, and often don't spend the $10 a month for Candi, 13, to enter bowling contests. Fields hopes accounting classes will help her get work as a payroll clerk—a $5-an-hour job in Radford. "It will be years before I get back to where I was," she says.

Even workers who still have jobs feel the fallout. From 1979 to 1989, as the sum of exported and imported goods rose from 55% of U.S. manufacturing output to 82%, the average pay and benefits of U.S. factory workers fell 6% after inflation. Meanwhile, plant productivity rose 42%. In fact, factory pay in Europe and Japan, where companies and governments train workers, gained on the U.S. average after inflation and exchange-rate adjustments. German factory compensation has passed U.S. levels for the first time in modern history.

This trend probably won't turn around soon. UCLA's Leamer recently tried to project how much free trade would cost less skilled workers in the future. To do so, he looked at how trade changed prices for goods from 1972 to 1985 in 38 labor- and capital-intensive manufacturing industries, then figured the pay effect on professional and blue-collar employees across the economy.

He found that trade raised demand for higher-skilled work, as Stolper and Samuelson predicted. So the average annual pay of 17 million professionals was 9%, or $1,900, higher than it would have been without trade growth. But annual pay of more than 90 million other workers was $465, or 3%, lower than it would have been otherwise. Leamer predicts that lower-skilled workers will suffer similar declines in the 1990s—and that professionals will reap similar gains—if manufacturing trade grows the 60% it did in the period he studied. "Gains from the expansion of trade will continue to be very unequally distributed," he adds.

This may be true even if trade growth slows, as the mere threat of exporting jobs keeps pay down. In June, Philips wrung concessions from the McAmises and 1,600 colleagues who have so far survived the transfer of 900 jobs to Juarez. The International Union of Electronic Workers accepted $1.50 an hour less for new hires than current workers get—and no benefits. These conditions will apply to 600 or more laid-off workers who may be recalled. The union consented, officials say, because Phillips

▲ BELL LABS
AT&T has cut 21,000 low-skill jobs since 1984 but expanded white-collar hires, such as Jacqueline Gregory, by 8,000

threatened to shift all TV production to Mexico and leave 300 distribution jobs in the U.S. Says F. Joseph Brang, the Greeneville plant manager: "There is great pressure to move work to Mexico because of the low labor costs there."

Free-trade advocates such as Massachusetts Institute of Technology economist Rudiger Dornbusch argue that the loss of lower-skilled jobs is not only inevitable in a world awash with cheap labor—but may be a blessing in disguise. If trade growth indeed spurs exports of value-added products, where the U. S. has an edge, then higher-paying jobs should spring up to replace lower-paying ones that are lost, he says.

POSITIVE STATIC. But for this to occur, most companies must try the approach taken by those such as Motorola. Today, only 44% of its 100,000 employees work in the U. S., vs. nearly 100% in 1960. Part of the shift overseas reflected a desire to manufacture in its best markets. But nearly half of the change stemmed from a search for low wages, says A. William Wiggenhorn, Motorola's vice-president for training and education. Then, in the early 1980s, Motorola reexamined itself in light of moves it was making to just-in-time inventory control, total quality management, and teamwork systems. More than cheap labor, "today, we want high quality and a short time to market," says Wiggenhorn. "So we don't move employment to low-cost countries anymore."

Take Motorola's cellular phone business. When the company started making the phones in 1983, it eliminated larger parts by putting their functions on computer chips. This required less assembly, cutting labor costs to 10% to 15% of production costs, vs. 25%-plus in previous products. The company also switched to a labor relations strategy that encourages its 3,000 cellular phone employees in Arlington Heights, Ill., to boost quality and productivity.

Last year, for instance, Lemel Lewis, who makes circuit boards for phones, joined a plantwide team formed to reduce static in the air, which causes defects as boards are produced. The team tested various antistatic packages used to move the boards along the assembly line and "discovered that a clamshell-shaped package is the best," says Lewis. The change has helped boost quality and keep Motorola ahead of its rivals abroad.

A few companies are even trying the higher-skills approach in apparel, one of the most labor-intensive industries. In traditional piecework, each worker at a machine sews the right pocket, say, onto 30 garments that arrive in a bundle. Then the bundle moves to the next machine for the left pocket. Recently, companies such as Russell, Levi Strauss, and Sarah Lee Corp.'s Hanes have begun to create teams of 30 to 50 workers that make an entire garment. Operators within each team move between machines to eliminate bottlenecks. And they, not supervisors or engineers, decide how to set up the line.

Levi Strauss & Co. just began converting its 27 U. S. plants last fall, so it doesn't yet know if teams boost productivity. But other benefits are clear. Each plant now can make a bundle of 30 jeans in seven hours from start to finish instead of the six days it often took as bundles got stuck at different stages of the old system. So a factory can rapidly switch styles and sizes to respond to consumer demand.

MORE GRADS? At Levi's 432-employee Blue Ridge (Ga.) plant, which last spring became the first to convert entirely to teams, defects fell to 1.9% of production in April, from 2.6% during the same month in 1991. "Our factories couldn't compete with overseas ones on a pure cost basis," says Peter Jacobi, Levi's president of global sourcing. "If the team system succeeds, there are a lot of products, like shirts and Dockers jeans, we could produce here" at current wage rates.

Foreign factories may not be far behind, however. One of General Motors Corp.'s highest-quality plants is in Ramos Arizpe, Mexico. And AT&T's Warwick uses teamwork in Juarez. "The average education level in Mexico is about the ninth grade, but it doesn't take more than that to use new manufacturing techniques," he says.

If U. S. companies' efforts to boost skills don't reverse wage inequality, it's unclear what will. Until recently, Kosters, among others, thought labor market forces might narrow the gap. He notes that college enrollment rates jumped from 33% of 14- to 24-year-olds in 1984 to 39% in 1990. If the lure of higher pay hastens this trend, then in theory the supply of college grads should eventually match the demand for them. And a resulting shortage of lesser-skilled workers could ease the downward pressure on pay for these people.

The problem is, this scenario requires a lot more college grads. John H. Bishop, an economist at Cornell University,

GE'S HARD LESSON: PAY CUTS CAN BACKFIRE

When international competition hit the U. S. full force in the early 1980s, most manufacturers slashed labor costs by extracting concessions or shipping jobs overseas. Some now wonder if this was wise. If getting ahead turns as much on quality and productivity as on cost, they reason, maybe there's a better way. That's the thinking behind one change in plans at General Electric Co.

Back in 1987, GE's electric motors division was in trouble. A chief domestic rival, nonunion Emerson Electric Co. in St. Louis, paid its workers $7.20 an hour, vs. GE's $11, GE says. Both companies had opened motor plants in Singapore and Mexico, where wages were 80¢ to $1.50 an hour, and GE remained No. 1 in motors that go into everything from refrigerators to computer disk drives. But the division's revenues had fallen by 7% since 1984, to $710 million. Return on sales was less than 2%, vs. an average 6% at other GE units—even though the division had in the course of a decade shed 5,300 jobs, 42% of its total.

BLUNDER. CEO John F. Welch Jr. had threatened to jettison any GE business not No. 1 or No. 2 in its market, so the division decided to act. It demanded that its hourly workers accept an 11% cut in pay and forgo scheduled raises of $1.30 an hour. They did. Then, after closing 2 of its 12 motor plants, GE guaranteed the remaining 5,400 workers their jobs for three years and sank $200 million into new equipment and product development. "At the time, investing at [existing] wage levels didn't seem sane," says Frank P. Doyle, GE's senior vice-president for external and industrial relations.

What looked like a sweet deal then, GE now sees as a blunder. True, the pay cuts saved $25 million a year. And the plant closings eliminated 1,000 jobs. But both company and union officials say worker morale sank like a stone. "Productivity went to hell," says Doyle, although he won't give figures.

So, the division is remaking itself again. This time, the strategy centers around modern techniques: just-in-time inventory systems, quality control, design-for-manufacture, and Japanese-style teams of seven to eight workers who rotate tasks and make daily decisions about how work should be done. GE hopes these approaches will offset its wage disadvantage—it still pays $10 an hour—by boosting efficiency. Indeed, in the past year the division's productivity gains have been "above moderate," says a GE official, even though the new strategies are just being implemented. Welch has given the unit until 1994 to boost returns. By then, GE wants it to match the efficiency gains—generally, 4% to 8% a year—in its other units that have tried teamwork. "The biggest change in our thinking since 1988," says Doyle, "is that we now see that the productivity available is really extraordinary."

NEW CRITERIA. It's too early to tell if the new tactic will work. GE still may farm out some labor-intensive work on motor parts such as switches or washers. And the bad feelings from the wage cut persist. In early May, 1,000 workers in Fort Wayne, Ind., voted down contract changes their union negotiated to make teamwork blossom, in part because some people would have lost up to $5 an hour in incentive pay. But Fort Wayne has set up some teams, and union leaders want them to work. "If we're going to stay in the motor business, we have to make it profitable," says Dewey D. Minton, who heads the GE contingent of the International Union of Electronic Workers.

If the latest effort works, does it mean GE erred in giving up on such businesses as TV's and housewares, which seemed doomed against low-wage rivals? GE officials say they haven't done such hypothetical calculations. But, adds Doyle, "the decision criteria would be different today."

Aaron Bernstein in New York

puts the figure at 1.2 million a year, vs. 1 million now. Both President Bush and Democratic candidate Clinton support tuition-loan programs that would help more students finish college. But boosting the graduation total will be hard to do, given that there are only 25 million 18- to 24-year-olds today, vs. 30 million in 1979. In fact, says Bishop, based on these demographics, "I project a slowdown in the growth of college-educated workers and a continuing escalation of wage premiums for college graduates."

Companies and government could help even things out by training more existing workers. Washington now spends about $4 billion a year on training. Employers spend $30 billion more, mostly to upgrade the skills of professionals. To match Japan and Germany, U. S. industry should be investing $15 billion more a year, says the American Society for Training & Development. "Even if you need $60 billion a year in training and education, we should spend it," argues MIT's Dornbusch. "What else can you do, given that we're now seeing the results of not doing so, like the L. A. riots?"

Economists once thought that the inequality of the past decade occurred mainly because sluggish productivity gains slowed growth—and because lower-wage workers suffer most when growth stagnates. They assumed that as productivity rose, wage inequality would recede. But global competition may now prevent this. "You can't expect an automatic link anymore between the overall economy and less educated workers," says Harvard economist Katz.

This isn't an argument for protectionism, with all its negative effects. Instead, it should prompt debate on ways to ensure that the benefits of free trade don't go just to America's top half. "If there really is a net gain from trade, we ought to compensate the losers" with subsidized training or lighter tax burdens, argues Andrew M. Sum, an economist at Northeastern University in Boston. Otherwise, there will be no lifeboats for Allen McAmis, Dreama Fields, and millions more whose ship is sinking.

By Aaron Bernstein in New York, with Walecia Konrad in Blue Ridge, Ga., and Lois Therrien in Arlington Heights, Ill.

International Communication: An Executive Primer

Ronald E. Dulek, John S. Fielden, and John S. Hill

One must recognize the type of culture when engaging in international business, and then apply the correct principles in dealing with foreign nationals.

Euphoria frequently turns to paranoia when domestic executives face their first overseas assignment. Disturbing memories come pressing to the fore:

- A college anthropology professor gleefully pointing out that thousands of languages (and even more thousands of dialects) exist in the world;
- A semester or two of a foreign language that was hated, never mastered, and is now well forgotten;
- A once-hilarious book documenting the communications blunders American businesspeople apparently make every time they set foot on foreign soil (Ricks 1983).

These and a variety of other doleful thoughts cause now-wary executives to wonder how they—or anyone—could even begin to cope with thousands of different cultures and languages involved in international business. And there is ample evidence that coping with those cultures and languages is necessary:

Fact 1: By the year 2000, experts have predicted that multinational corporations will control approximately half the world's assets. So even if you are not now working for one of these companies, the odds are high that you will be—or that you will be interacting and communicating with other people who work for "foreign" companies.

Fact 2: Today English dominates the international business scene. But it is blind provincialism to believe that English will continue to be used everywhere for all occasions. Even today an ever-increasing number of foreign countries are demanding that contracts be drawn and negotiations be conducted only in the language of that area.

Fact 3: Sad but true, U.S. businesspeople have the lowest foreign language proficiency of any major trading nation. Despite accreditation association pressure, U.S. business schools do not emphasize foreign languages, and students traditionally avoid them.

Fortunately, some generalizations will help U.S. businesspeople communicate more effectively internationally. These generalizations derive from a seemingly simple division of cultures into two polar types, which Edward T. Hall (1976) named high- and low-context societies.

Cultures (see the **Figure**) were divided by Hall into those in which:

1. The social context surrounding a negotiation counts as nothing; all that counts are the actual written agreements. These cultures he called low-context; and
2. The social context that surrounds a formal, written document is far more important than the written, legal documentation. These he called high-context cultures.

Low-Context Cultures

In low-context cultures (from the German to the North American) what counts is primarily what has been written in contractual form and sanctified by lawyers on both sides. The social context in which the agreement has been forged has no legal standing and hence, does not count.

High-Context Cultures

Just the reverse is true about very high-context cultures (from the Chinese to the Arab). These cultures are historically oral cultures; what a per-

Reprinted from *Business Horizons*, January-February 1991, pp. 20-25. Copyright © 1991 by the Foundation for the School of Business at Indiana University. Used with permission.

son says in writing is held to be much less important than who that person is, his or her status (or rank) in society, and his or her general reputation. The social context in which an agreement has been made counts for at least as much as, and usually far more than, the written agreement. Therefore, in high-context cultures the process of forging a business relationship is as important as, if not more important than, the written details of the actual deal.

Figure
Arrangement of High- and Low-Context Cultures

High Context	↑	Chinese
		Korean
		Japanese
		Vietnamese
		Arab
		Greek
		Spanish
		Italian
		English
		North American
		Scandinavian
		Swiss
Low Context	↓	German

Source: Edward T. Hall, Beyond Culture *(Garden City, NY: Anchor Press/Doubleday, 1976), and "How Cultures Collide,"* Psychology Today, *July 1976, pp. 67-74.*

APPLYING CONTEXT TO INTERNATIONAL COMMUNICATIONS

Knowledge of where a particular culture falls in the high- and low-context spectrum gives business people valuable clues about how to communicate with people from different cultures. In this article, these clues have been put in the form of three sets of specific "dos" and "don'ts" for businesspeople to remember when they engage in international communication:

1. Conversational Principles—those that should be remembered in all aspects of communication, ranging from informal luncheon chats to boardroom meetings.
2. Presentation Principles—those applicable when making oral presentations to a foreign group.
3. Written Principles—those to remember when exchanging written information internationally.

Conversational Principle #1: Recognize that many high-context cultures need to know as much as possible about you and the company you represent. Always remember when you are in Latin America, Asia, and parts of Western Europe that even the most seemingly casual, insignificant conversations have a level of significance far beyond that dictated by the content being discussed. **Conversations about your family, your company, or current events are used to "warm up relationships," just as one might warm a car engine on a cold day. You should also give your hosts insights into you as a person and recognize their need to find out what makes you "tick." Americans are not used to talking openly about personal or family intimacies; yet overseas, once the trust "bond" has been established, there are in many cases few things foreigners will not talk about.**

The best approach to high-context negotiation, then, is to acknowledge that you and your company are under close scrutiny. You should take pains to provide your prospective Japanese or Arab client with as much information as possible about you and the company you represent. It is often best to provide information before you visit or entertain visitors from high-context cultures. Americans, it is said, like "to meet and get to know you." Persons from high-context societies often prefer "to get to know about you first and then meet you." Copies of your resume as well as those of other people who hold important positions in your organization, documents, pamphlets, or annual reports that provide details about your company's history, other pieces of information detailing you and your colleagues' personal interests—all can be forwarded to associates in high-context cultures before your visit begins.

Conversational Principle #2: Speak slowly, clearly, and simply. Avoid jargon, slang, cliches, and idiomatic usage. When foreigners learn English, they learn a "correct" version of formal English. When they listen to Americans (or Britons, or Australians) lapsing into slang or idiom, they become confused. We must realize that even an everyday expression such as "Let's get rolling" or "I'm all ears" can be perplexing if the foreigner tries to translate it literally. Imagine foreigners having to translate a simple English idiom such as "So long" into their language. Also, sayings such as "first among equals" and "last but not least" are often untranslatable because, even when translated correctly, they appear illogical and contradictory.

Conversational Principle #3: Sprinkle your conversation with at least some words and phrases in the language of your listeners. It is regarded as "good manners" to make at least an attempt to learn a few phrases in your host's language. This shows that you have made a good faith effort to learn something about the other person's language—and, by implication, his or her culture and background.

All of us have seen how statesmen regularly make use of their partial knowledge of another country's language when they visit that country. If the President of the United States visits Mexico and says in Spanish, "*¡Hola! ¡Me gusta estar aquí!*" the audience cheers wildly. We have all seen the care Popes have taken to deliver at least part of their sermons in the native language of the country visited.

Conversational Principle #4: Be careful about what your body language and your tone of voice communicate. When listeners cannot follow what is being said, they will pay far greater attention to body language. And if they do understand English, they will look for contradictions between what is said and how it is said. If the words carry a message that is not reinforced by concomitant bodily expressions, either confusion results, or the listener may conclude that the speaker is not being sincere. When people say to foreigners, "I'm very pleased to meet you," but say so in a bland monotone and an expressionless face, this contradiction between words and action may convince the listeners that the speakers are not at all pleased to meet them. They may immediately wonder how much of what else is said will be truly sincere.

"If the words carry a message that is not reinforced by concomitant bodily expressions, either confusion results, or the listener may conclude that the speaker is not being sincere."

Many of our hackneyed expressions can actually undermine our credibility. In the U.S., someone asks us, "How are you doing?" Regardless of how we actually are doing, we usually answer something on the order of, "Fine, fine." However, when a question like this is asked abroad, Americans should fully expect to receive a sincere answer that may include detailed reasons as to why the respondent is feeling either great or terrible. If after inviting this response we register impatience, foreigners have every right to believe that they have been deliberately made to look foolish, although they may not really understand what was foolish about it.

Tone of voice also plays an important role when communicating internationally. There are vast cultural differences at play here: notice, for example, how softly people from most Asian cultures speak. Americans often seem loud and aggressive in negotiations and vigorous in arguments. And negotiations in Latin American, Greek, Italian, and Central European countries are far louder, often including heated, arm-waving exchanges of opinion that rarely mean anything personal.

Loud oral communications in Asia or the Middle East, however, are socially unacceptable. There is a Japanese saying that "The nail that sticks out will always be beaten." Disruptive elements such as loud or argumentative voices, waving of arms, and exaggerated hand gestures are all frowned upon.

Presentation Principle #1: Respect many foreign audiences' desire for greater formality of presentation. Different cultures have varying ideas about what constitutes an effective oral presentation. Americans generally like presentations that seem natural and spontaneous, not "canned" or overly rehearsed. Most other countries, both high- and low-context cultures, expect more formality. "Natural" presentations, it is thought, give the impression that the speaker has not respected the audience sufficiently. Speakers who write on blackboards or on transparencies inadvertently give the impression that the presentation is not important enough for them to have prepared proper sets of visual aids prior to the actual presentation.

Also, efforts to customize what you present, as opposed to giving an off-the-shelf generalized presentation, will be appreciated.

Presentation Principle #2: Allow for differences in behavior of foreign audiences. U.S. presenters must not be "thrown off" by seemingly odd behavior of an overseas audience. Japanese audiences, for example, usually sit and nod their heads (which means they understand, not that they agree) and say nothing. However, on some occasions, they may start frenzied talking among themselves. Or, in open discussions, they may suddenly become evasive. What this usually means is that something that has been said is disturbing to them. At this point, presenters should take heed; get off that topic and go on to something else until they can find out, either directly from the audience or through a go-between, what the problem is.

To Americans, "looking people in the eye" is a sign that mutual respect has been established. U.S. businesspeople traveling overseas are often disappointed by their inability to establish eye contact. This is true especially in superior/subordinate relationships, but is also true in presentation to members of cultures where staring is considered "brash and insolent." Hence, in such countries, audiences will not seem attentive because they will spend most of the time staring down at the floor. It is hard for Americans to realize that this usually means the audience is showing respect, not inattention.

Presentation Principle #3: Have patience; design your presentation's length, completeness, and "interruptability" with the audience's culture in mind. Americans are impatient and are used to fast-paced, efficient presentations. Most foreigners, with the probable exceptions of Germans and the Swiss, prefer slower, more deliberate efforts. In situations where interpreters are used, the pace is automatically slowed. When the presentation is in English and there is no interpreter, a speaker must go very slowly. Be patient also in allowing those who raise questions to have time to search for the precise English word they need. Signs of impatience will be unfavorably received, and the presenter will be downgraded for not showing proper respect and courtesy.

Audiences in high-context cultures, such as Japanese, Latin American, and Arabic audiences, expect a presentation to be in short, separate segments that allow time for questions and digestion of what has been presented. This is wise because many high-context people communicate in what is referred to as "loops"; they will mix circuitous, irrelevant (by American standards) conversations with short dashes of information that go directly to the point. Because they are not as time- or efficiency-oriented, Arabs, for example, prefer presentations that allow frequent deviations from the major business topic. This allows them to relax for a while, after which they will be ready to loop back and listen intently to further discussions. These interruptions can prove wearing even to those who are experienced in international dealings. Yet companies whose presenters are the most patient, tolerant and, in their audience's eyes, "mature" will get the contracts. Impatience in these circumstances is interpreted as childish; the prevailing attitude is, "Who wants to do business with children when there are adults around?"

Presentation Principle #4: Match rank and age of presenter to rank and age of important members of foreign audiences. In many American companies, meritocracy is dominant and fairly young executives rise rapidly to powerful positions early in their career. In high-context cultures, however, age (or seniority) is a major indicator of status. Therefore, sending young executives, regardless of their rank, to negotiate important contracts with businesspeople in high-context cultures can be a disaster. In those cultures, wisdom is associated with age, a throwback to the days when wisdom was assured through years of experience, when knowledge was passed on by elders, not by books or data sets. Hence a young presenter is unlikely to command the same respect as would an older, more seasoned executive. Sending a young hotshot may even invite interpretation that the American company does not take the foreign venture seriously enough to send in its "first team."

Writing Principle #1: Only in low-context cultures where communication efficiency is highly prized should you organize your communication so that its central point is directly and immediately stated. The higher the context a culture is, the more we should question whether we should write terse, concise, "bottom-line" communications to persons in that culture. In cultures where language is used not so much to document as to reveal the personal qualities of the individuals and their companies, written communications may need at times to be longer, more elaborate, more personally revealing, and less focused on getting the job at hand completed with dispatch.

"Audiences in high-context cultures, such as Japanese, Latin American, and Arabic audiences, expect a presentation to be in short, separate segments that allow time for questions and digestion of what has been presented."

But, oddly enough, just the reverse is frequently true. People from high-context cultures may settle for written business agreements that are extremely short and bottom-lined, in some cases merely stating the bare bones of the agreement. The reason for such brevity is that the parties to the agreement have already spent a great amount of time circuitously finding out about each other's integrity. Thus, when both parties are assured of each other's trustworthiness, a brief written statement for the record may be all that is required for this transaction and perhaps those that follow.

U.S. executives should also realize that if a formal, American-style contract is drawn up, the high-context partners will not read it in detail. They will assume that no one would be so crass as to conceal anything in the fine print. While this knowledge might tempt unscrupulous companies to slip in provisions favorable to themselves, one can be sure that succumbing to such a temptation will guarantee that their company will never again do business, not only with the company that was cheated, but probably not even with any other companies in that country.

There is another factor influencing whether communications should be bottom-lined. In international writing, hierarchical power differences between readers and writers affect the organization of messages even more than they do in the U.S. In Malaysia, for example, government bureaucrats bottom-line almost everything they write "down" to the citizenry (analogous to the imperial or bureaucratic "command"). But a businessperson writing "up," asking governmental permission for some action, is expected to be circuitous to the greatest possible extent. The longer the letter, the more "respect" it shows. Moreover, the businessperson is expected to include many long paragraphs praising the bureaucrat (or more subtly, the bureaucrat's administration) in the most lavish terms. This "respect" is necessary because high-context cultures usually have definite social divisions, and there are appropriate sets of verbal behavior depending upon whether one is speaking to another who is higher or lower in the social order.

But remember, not all cultures are high-context. Low-context cultures such as German, North American, Swiss, and Scandinavian prefer business messages to be very direct, even to the point of being terse.

Writing Principle #2: Adapt your style of writing to the preferences of the culture to which your readers belong. The culture in which a piece of writing takes place clearly affects the style in which messages are expected to be written. In high-context cultures, there is a marked emphasis on politeness and decorum. Even communications going down in an organization will be phrased in polite and respectful ways and will appear to have less force attached to them. There will be differences in how instructions are given. Where there are close business relations between sender and receiver, great care is taken to observe social writing etiquette that to Americans seems vague and obscure. Underlings are asked to "consider" doing certain things and completion of a task may be "requested, if at all possible." These give the appearance that the recipient of the request has at least the option of refusing to do what is asked (although in reality, there is no such option). As result, what is to be avoided are forceful imperatives such as "Do this!" or "Do that!" A much greater reliance should be placed on a more passive, subtle style.

There are cultural differences and expectations about how formally one should write. In high-context countries much informal written communications takes place. Information is often exchanged through informal personal notes written at the bottom of documents. In high-context cultures there is far less need for subordinates to file CYA memos for the record (a person who does so will be thought of as insecure and as calling unnecessary attention to his or her activities). In such cultures writers do not have to document everything formally because they will not be held personally responsible if something goes wrong. Responsibility will be taken by the top of the organization. The subordinate need not fear being the "fall guy" for a mishap. If mistakes are made in the Middle East, Asia, or some parts of Europe, the person at the top will resign, regardless of whether he or she had anything personally to do with the blunder. In the U.S., responsibility flows all too often to the lowest organizational levels.

Not all cultures prize our flat, objective, "Business English" style of writing. Some cultures exhibit styles of writing that are quite colorful compared with English. Arabic, for example, is a poetic language filled with exaggerations, colorful adjectives, and metaphors. Arabs do not react, as English readers might, with shock or surprise at such colorful writing. Such language is just their normal way of expressing ideas. Compared with English, the Latin languages also delight in colorful verbal turns of phrase. Hence, when Americans write in English to members of these cultures, they need not be so hidebound in their expression as they are in standard English.

But many low-context cultures prefer just the reverse. Germans, for example, avoid colorful exaggeration and hyperbole in their writing, believing that people from other cultures (even Americans) exaggerate, abuse superlatives such as "most," "best," and "newest," and demonstrate egocentrism by overusing the personal pronouns "I" and "my." A passive, impersonal style is therefore best in communications with low-context cultures.

Writing Principle #3: Don't count on non-native readers being able to understand English in all its subtleties and technicalities. Therefore, whenever possible enclose a translation in the recipient's language. If writers are unsure about a foreign reader's ability to understand English, even when it is written as simply and unidiomatically as possible, then they should include a translation. Doing so will often better guarantee a response. Readers with limited command of English may simply not respond because (a) they do not know whether the unreadable communication is worth the cost of hiring a translator or (b) they may not want to admit publicly that they really don't understand English. Enclosing a translation into the reader's language will not be taken as an insult; instead it will be regarded as helpful and a diplomatic courtesy.

This primer will not make Armand Hammers out of ordinary domestic-variety executives. What it can do, however, is increase U.S. managerial effectiveness, especially in the high-context cultures of Latin America, the Middle East, and Asia. By avoiding cultural *faux pas* and by being sensitive to the needs of other cultures, participants in international business meetings and negotiations can better focus on the real issues in a more relaxed atmosphere. This should enhance the probabilities of successful outcomes, and plant the seeds from which international business relationships can be successful both at the corporate and the all-important personal level.

References

Culturegram Series, Brigham Young University, David M. Kennedy Center for International Studies.

Ronald E. Dulek and John S. Fielden, *Principles of Business Communication* (New York: Macmillan, 1990).

John S. Fielden and Ronald E. Dulek, "How to Use Bottom-Line Writing in Corporate Communications," *Business Horizons*, July-August 1984, pp. 24-30.

Edward T. Hall, *Beyond Culture* (Garden City, N.Y.: Anchor Press/Doubleday, 1976).

Edward T. Hall, "How Cultures Collide," *Psychology Today*, July 1976, pp. 67-74.

David A. Ricks, *Big Business Blunders: Mistakes in Multinational Marketing* (Homewood, Ill.: Dow-Jones-Irwin, 1983).

Ronald E. Dulek is a professor and chair of management and marketing, **John S. Fielden** is university professor of management communications, and **John S. Hill** is an associate professor of international business, all at the College of Commerce and Business Administration, The University of Alabama, Tuscaloosa.

THE WORLD'S TRADE TOPOGRAPHY:

HOW LEVEL IS IT?

Perceptions abound that the playing field between countries is indeed uneven—to the advantage of Japan and the disadvantage of the U.S., with European nations somewhere in the middle. That's the perception. What is the truth? IW editors have tracked four products as they move around the world—airplanes (because aerospace is an extremely competitive, risky, winner-take-all business); automobiles (surely the most visible and publicized product facing competitive international pressures); bluejeans (because they can teach us how a truly American product travels the trade lanes); and cellular phones (because they are high-tech and comparatively new products). What does a U.S.-made export face when it reaches Japan? What barriers do Japanese products face on American shores? How do European countries greet Japanese as well as American products? Whose policies are the fairest? Whose are the least fair? Is any trade truly free? The following four profiles are a step in mapping the trade topography of the world. They show that, although automobiles get most of the attention, the story does not end there.

AUTOS

'TILT' IN THE SECTOR

BRIAN S. MOSKAL

How can a Made-In-The-USA Chrysler Jeep Cherokee sell for roughly $44,000 in the Japanese market while Toyota's luxury Lexus LS400 sells for $44,300 in the U.S. market?

The two vehicles have little in common. According to J.D. Power & Associates, the 1991 Lexus LS400 had the highest quality levels of any car sold in the U.S., and it competes easily with the best American and European luxury cars sold in North America; it is the very best that Toyota offers the U.S. market. The fully optioned Jeep Cherokee, on the other hand, is a sports util ity vehicle that simply doesn't compete in that stratosphere.

It seems unlikely that these dissimilar vehicles could sell for roughly the same dollar amount when they are imported in the U.S. and Japan respectively. In the U.S., a fully optioned Cherokee Limited version sells for about $27,000.

There are other examples of Big-Three-made products that carry a much stiffer price tag in Japan than they do in the U.S.:

A Chrysler LeBaron retails for $18,176 in the U.S. and carries a retail price in Japan of $33,077, an 82% difference.

A Buick Park Avenue lists for $27,420 in the U.S., yet retails for $43,617 when a Japanese consumer looks at the sticker, a 59% markup. These statistics come from the Economic Strategy Institute in Washington.

Yet a Honda Accord that retails for $17,645 in the U.S. sells for $20,272, or only 15% more, in Japan. Ford's Taurus model sells for $31,845 in Japan, or 67% more than the U.S. list price of $19,024.

How can this be?

In short, there are impediments—both direct and subtle—that face U.S. carmakers in getting their products into the Japanese market that are not faced by the Japanese when it comes to penetrating the U.S. These impediments can jack up the cost of U.S.-made autos sold in Japan, and they put U.S. manufacturers at a distinct price disadvantage. In addition, the very scarcity of U.S. automotive products in the Japanese market also serves to drive up their cost.

In order to be approved for sale in

Reprinted with permission from *Industry Week,* May 18, 1992, pp. 24-36. Copyright © 1992 by Penton Publishing, Inc., Cleveland, Ohio.

Japan, cars not made there must go through a tangled web of regulations, equipment modifications, certifications, and inspections that add thousands of dollars to an imported vehicle sold in Japan.

For example, side mirrors must snap off easily if they come into contact with a pedestrian. Headlights must be refocused because cars drive on the left side of the road. Also, import manufacturers must install a warning light on the dashboard to signal failure of the catalytic converter.

In addition, the inspection process can take months before imported cars reach Japanese consumers. In contrast, in the U.S., foreign-made cars can be in dealer showrooms about two weeks after they arrive at U.S. ports.

The average tariff on imported goods in the U.S. is 5%, and sedans like the Lexus face a 10% luxury tax on the portion of the transaction that exceeds $30,000.

Japanese car buyers are subject to a tax of up to $2,500 at the point of purchase if the engine size exceeds 2 liters and an additional tax of $1,500 each year to own such vehicles. This creates a natural bias against foreign-made autos sold in Japan because 80% of Japanese automotive products sold at home have an engine size of less than 2 liters.

Specifically, in the case of the Jeep Cherokee, Chrysler attributes the $17,000 price differential between U.S. and Japanese versions to four costs: government requirements and certifications, about $3,000 per unit; overseas freight and customs clearance, $1,000; sales tax, $1,500; and distribution and dealer margins, $11,500.

For an imported-car manufacturer that sells 1,000 or fewer units of a particular model annually, the Japanese Transportation Ministry requires that each car be individually tested for gas mileage, emission standards, and crash-worthiness. The Japanese, unlike their U.S. counterparts, won't accept U.S. manufacturers' test data for low-volume nameplates of imports, even though California's emission standards and in most cases federal regulations are more strict than Japan's in every category. When made-in-Japan cars enter U.S. ports, on the other hand, U.S. officials accept Japanese test data for safety, mileage, and emissions standards.

(High-volume imports to the Japanese market are not inspected individually, but they do require rigorous documentation.)

"It's very expensive to distribute fewer than 1,000 cars in a market like Japan," says Sean McAlinden, an automotive and manufacturing economist with the Office for the Study of Automotive Transportation at the University of Michigan, Ann Arbor. "But if you sell 2 million units in a car market—like the Japanese do in the U.S.—you can spread your market entry costs over a much larger base."

One of the largest barriers to the Japanese market is the cost of distribution, starting with a customs-clearance expediter and four middlemen. Distribution and dealer margins can add roughly $12,000 to the cost of an automotive product before it reaches the Japanese consumer.

In addition, while U.S. car dealers can own more than one franchise to sell different makes of cars under one roof, Ford, General Motors, and Chrysler were blocked from reaching franchise agreements with Japanese dealerships and gaining easy access to the Japanese consumer market until a Japanese law changed two years ago.

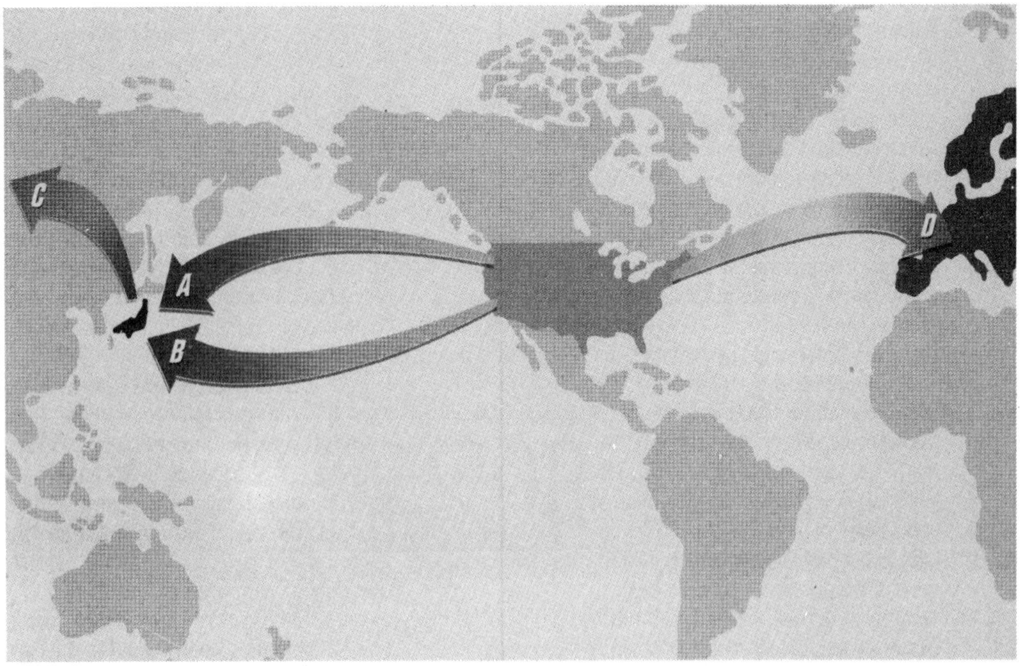

Auto Trade Market

A. *After traveling a tangled web of Japanese-imposed inspections, regulations, and equipment modifications,, a U.S.-made Jeep Cherokee sells for $17,000 more in Japan than in the U.S.*

B. *In contrast, a Japanese Made-In-USA Honda Accord sells for just $2,700 more in Japan than in the U.S.*

C. *Europe has frozen Japanese import cars to their 1990 level until 1999.*

D. *No major tariffs; most U.S. cars sold in Europe are made in Europe.*

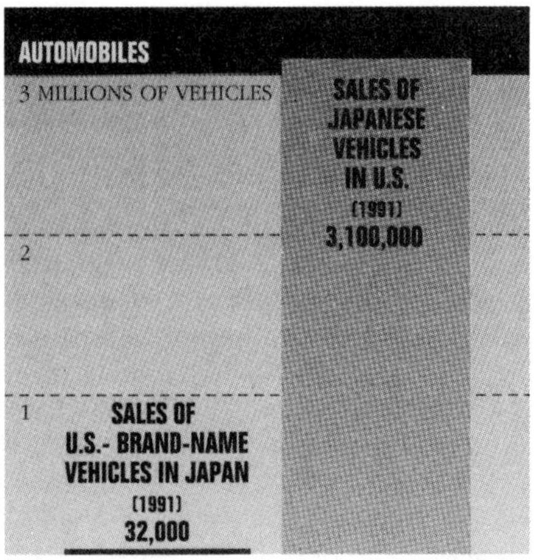

Source: IW

Even so, foreign-made vehicles are sold at only 7% of Japanese dealers, while every Big Three dealer in the U.S. is free to sell Japanese or other imported products. Big Three vehicles are sold in 19,000 dealerships in the U.S., while foreign vehicles, including Japanese and European products, are sold in 23,000 dealerships. The Japanese, in effect, didn't have to build a single dealership in the U.S., through some products such as the Lexus models are sold at standalone dealerships.

"The land under the Imperial Palace in Tokyo is worth more than the real estate value of the state of California," observes Mr. McAlinden. "So the cost of building a GM stand-alone dealership in Tokyo is about $100 million—just so GM can sell 10,000 units a year. And that amounts to a barrier." (Ten times that amount, $1 billion, will build a car-making plant in the U.S. that will pump out 25 times more vehicles—250,000 units or more a year.)

Without a direct highway to Japanese consumers, sales of American-brand-name cars and light trucks in Japan (like the Jeep Cherokee) built in North America totaled only 32,230 units in 1991. Total foreign penetration of the Japanese market totaled 199,922 vehicles, or 2.66% of the 7.5 million cars and trucks sold last year, led by prestigious German makes that sold 119,573 units.

Meanwhile, 3.1 million Japanese vehicles were sold in the U.S. in 1991—including 1.8 million imported vehicles and another 1.25 million made at Japanese-owned assembly plants in North America. Total passenger-car and light-vehicle sales reached 12.3 million units last year in the U.S. market.

American cars account for only 0.4% of the market in Japan, compared with the 30% share of the U.S. vehicle market captured by Japanese manufacturers. Last year, automotive vehicles and parts accounted for about 65% of Japan's $43 billion trade surplus with the U.S.

In Europe, the 12-nation European Community (EC) and Japan's Ministry of International Trade & Industry agreed to a plan last year that will allow Japanese penetration to rise to 2.5 million units by 1999, or 16% of a projected 15.5-million-car market, from the current 12% share. Under the plan, imports from Japan are frozen at the 1990 level of 1.2 million units until 1999. In the interim, Japanese production of cars in the EC countries will be allowed to account for the balance.

U.S. car companies exported only 350,000 cars to the rest of the world last year, with the bulk going to Europe. U.S.-badged cars sold in Europe are almost universally made in Europe, so U.S. car products don't face the maze of tariff and nontariff barriers when their products are sold there.

The Big Three moved into Europe with their assembly plants in the early 1900s to avoid unfair import taxes and unfavorable political pressure. The Japanese may find setting up transplant assembly operations more difficult because of Europe's history of managed trade and the nationalistic natures of the French, Italians, and Germans. (But cars made in the U.S. by Japanese-owned firms so far aren't counted against the voluntary Japan-Europe trade agreement, and thus some analysts think the Japanese share of the European market could reach 20% by the end of the decade.)

Also tilting the international automotive playing field in favor of the Japanese is a $550-to-$600-per-car health-care cost advantage over U.S. carmakers.

The Japanese have a capital-cost advantage of $300 per unit, and U.S. automakers pay five times the pension costs of the typical Japanese automaker, according to University of Michigan research.

"High Japanese penetration in the U.S. [where the car market peaked in 1986] means that one company or one country wins as another company or country loses," says David J. Andrea, senior research associate for the Office of Automotive Transportation at the University of Michigan.

And getting back to the Lexus, "there's a heck of a lot of cost in that product," says Mr. Andrea. "I don't know how much Toyota is making on the Lexus. It might truly be a $50,000 car [selling for $44,300]."

BLUEJEANS

A RED-HOT AMERICAN PRODUCT

WILLIAM H. MILLER

Travel anywhere in the world—the Amazon jungles of Brazil, the chic boulevards of Paris, the mountain valleys of Nepal, or the crowded subways of Tokyo—and you'll see a bit of America: people wearing bluejeans. Lots of people.

First sold by Levi Strauss & Co. to California gold miners in 1850, bluejeans are products that practically scream "America." American-branded bluejeans are the world's standard. They're so much in demand that Levi Strauss, the world's "name" jeans producer, is combatting an increasingly alarming wave of counterfeiting.

In an environment in which overall textile and apparel imports into the U.S. have reached record levels—intensifying cries for protection for what already is one of the nation's most-protected industries—bluejeans are an exception. Although quotas and other restraints on American-made bluejeans are common in many countries that wish to protect their home jeans industries, that's not the case in Japan or the European Community (EC). Neither has a particularly large jeans industry that needs to be protected, so they don't strive to keep American jeans out. Similarly, because neither Japan nor European countries are significant exporters of bluejeans, the U.S. has no need to limit such imports from them.

In bluejeans, trade among the U.S., Japan, and the EC "is very reciprocal, very straightforward," describes Steven Kott, director of member services at the American Assn. of Exporters & Importers, New York.

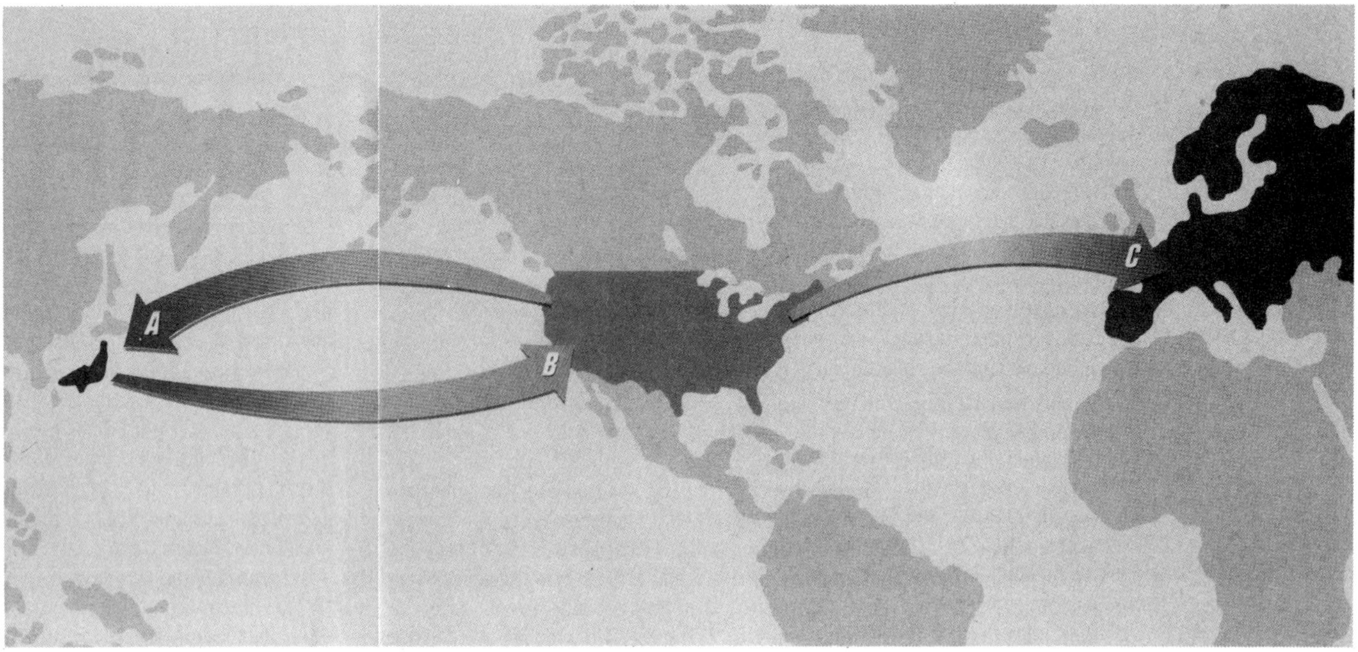

Bluejeans Trade Market

A. Duty payment of 11.2% plus 3% consumption tax.

B. Duty payment of 17.7%.

C. Duty of 13% plus value-added taxes ranging from 12% to 25%.

Thus, paperwork required for bluejeans imports from one another is minimal and routine. Customs duties are basically harmonized. Although duties for bluejeans imports are somewhat higher in the U.S., EC nations impose a value-added tax and Japan a consumption tax, whereas America doesn't.

Specifically, in exporting to Japan, American and European jeans manufacturers, after finding a buyer, need to do only the following:

1. Complete a shipper's declaration form for U.S. Customs describing the contents of the shipment and listing the appropriate international commodity classification number.

2. Complete a Japanese customs clearance form—again declaring contents of the shipment and verifying that it has been inspected.

3. If using a freight forwarder (as most exporters do), include a commercial invoice, a packing list, and a bill of lading.

4. Pay a duty of 11.2%—the tariff set for the category of "cotton trousers"—plus a 3% consumption tax.

Meanwhile, in shipping to EC countries, American and Japanese jeans producers need to:

1. Prepare a commercial invoice.

2. Complete a shipper's export-declaration form.

3. Submit a certificate of origin, usually obtainable in the U.S. from a company's local chamber of commerce, showing where the product was manufactured.

4. Pay a 13% duty plus a value-added tax (similar to the Japanese consumption tax) that ranges from 12% in Spain to 25% in Denmark.

Requirements are equally straightforward for Japanese and European jeans makers exporting to America:

1. A commercial invoice, packing list, and bill of lading.

2. A "textile declaration" stating where the fabric and accessories originated, and where the jeans were cut and sewn.

3. For Japanese shippers, a visa from Japan.

4. A duty payment of 17.7%.

This ease of entry into the U.S. hasn't always been the case, at least for Japanese jeans manufacturers. Until this year, they were affected by U.S. quotas on Japanese textiles and apparel.

The quotas were first introduced in the 1950s when Japan, aggressively reindustrializing after World War II, pursued a strategy of emphasizing textile and apparel exports. Over the years, as the Japanese shifted toward more sophisticated, capital-intensive industries, the quotas gradually dwindled. They were lifted entirely at the end of 1991.

The last agreement, covering 1990 and 1991, limited Japanese exports to the U.S. of cotton, wool, and manmade fiber apparel—a broad category into which bluejeans fall—to 85 million square meters a year. Actual Japanese exports to the U.S., however, fell far below that ceiling; they reached only 18.9 million square yards—22% of what was permitted—in 1990 and, although final figures aren't in, were running at a similarly low level last year. "There simply was no need to continue the quotas on Japan," says Anne Novak, international trade specialist in the Commerce Dept.'s Offices of Textiles & Apparel.

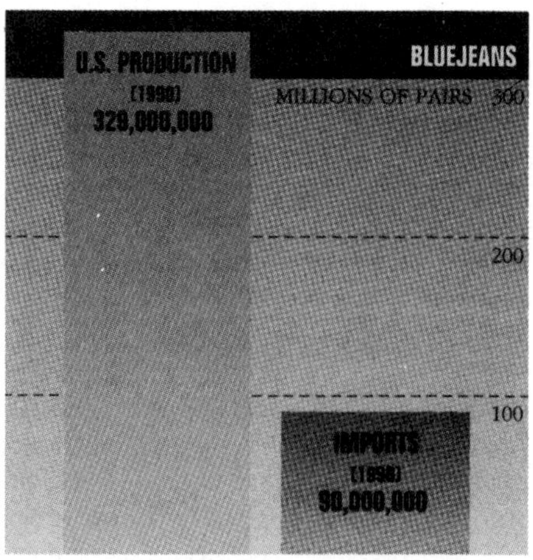

Source: AAMA

Even though bluejeans specifically have never been much of a factor in Japan's overall apparel exports, a study of import data at the Commerce Dept. suggests how dramatically Japanese bluejeans shipments to the U.S. have plunged in recent years. As recently as 1984, Japan was the second highest volume exporter of men's and boys' cotton trousers to the U.S. (behind Hong Kong), accounting for 13.6% of the total; in shipments to this country of women's and girls' cotton trousers, Japan ranked 12th, with only 2% of the total.

Contrast that with 1991. Japan did not even make the list of the top 48 major shippers of apparel to the U.S. in the men's and boys' cotton trousers category. And it was 44th in the women's and girls' category.

Where, then, are U.S. bluejeans imports coming from? In 1991, the Dominican Republic, with 14% of the total, led the men's and boys' cotton trousers category, trailed by Hong Kong, Mexico, and Costa Rica. In the women's and girls' category, pacesetters in order were Hong Kong (19%), Mexico, the Dominican Republic, Guatemala, and Taiwan.

In truth, though, there *aren't* significant imports of bluejeans into the U.S. In the home market, American bluejeans manufacturers are the undisputed kings. Levi Strauss and VF Corp., a Wyomissing, Pa., firm that makes the popular Lee, Wrangler, and Rustler brands, lead the market, but smaller firms such as Gitano Group Inc. (maker of the Gloria Vanderbilt line) are also players.

Altogether, reports the American Apparel Manufacturers Assn. (AAMA), domestic production of bluejeans and jeans-like dungarees in 1990 totaled 329 million pairs, valued at $4.09 billion. In contrast, imports were only 90 million pairs, valued at $960 million. And much of that represents U.S. companies that source part of their domestically sold product abroad.

A main reason why U.S. bluejeans are relatively immune to serious foreign competition in the domestic market is their sheer popularity. Unlike other apparel products, "bluejeans can be made with a high degree of automation," observes Carl Priestland, chief economist at AAMA. "When you have more than 300 million units of one type, you can engineer the heck out of their production."

He points out that Americans per capita buy 1.5 pairs of bluejeans a year—fully 10% of U.S. spending on apparel. Worldwide, the market penetration of American-made bluejeans isn't as high. But American producers—and particularly Levi Strauss—do well, acknowledges John Pachtner, the company's manager of corporate communications. Although he won't divulge exact numbers, he says that "in each of the countries in which we operate, we either have the dominant share or hold a very large chunk of the market."

Despite its strong market presence abroad, Levi Strauss *does* face competition. Mostly, says Mr. Pachtner, it comes from a proliferation of local jeans makers who manufacture for their local markets, exporting little.

Indeed, adds Dennis Klainberg, vice president of sales and corporate counsel for Berklay Air Services Inc., a freight-forwarding firm based at New York's John F. Kennedy Airport, "there are lots of jeans makers out there. However," he emphasizes, "no one really gives a damn about them. American jeans have tremendous name-brand strength. They're the most demanded product on earth."

That may be overstating the case. But there is no denying that their popularity has led to one instance in which free trade is alive and well.

CELLULAR PHONES

HELLO! HELLO?

BY JOHN S. MCCLENAHEN

By yearend 1991, says the U.S. Commerce Dept., 15 million subscribers in 83 nations were enjoying cellular-phone service. And the U.S., by more than a factor of six, was the world's largest cellular-phone market. With 7.6 million subscribers on the line, the U.S. was well ahead of the United Kingdom (1.2 million), Japan (1.2 million), Canada (0.7 million in mid-1991), Sweden (0.6 million), Italy (0.6 million), and Germany (0.5 million).

Global growth in cellular-phone use has been spectacular. For instance, the number of subscribers around the world rose 50% between 1990 and 1991 alone.

But at least among the U.S., Europe, and Japan, cellular phones don't cross national borders simply at the push of a few buttons.

For example:

- American-made phones being shipped to Europe and Japan require a "general" export license from the U.S. Commerce Dept.
- In addition to filing U.S. Customs Service forms listing the units and dollar values of European- and Japanese-manufactured cellular phones, American importers must certify on a Form 740 to the Federal Communications Commission that each shipment of phones meets U.S. standards limiting radio-frequency emissions.
- The U.S. imposes a 6% tariff on cellular phones imported from Europe and Japan, as well as from Hong Kong and South Korea, the two other major offshore suppliers to the U.S. market. In 1991, the U.S. imported 1 million cellular phones valued at $300 million, the Commerce Dept. calculates. Japan accounted for 36% of the units and 40% of the dollar volume.
- U.S. cellular phones exported to any of the dozen countries that constitute the European Community (EC) face a 6.5% duty.
- Although Japan assesses no import duties on U.S.- or European-made cellular telephones, it does require that they be type-certified by its government radio-equipment approval authority.
- Europe also imposes type-certification requirements on American and other foreign-made phones.

In Europe the certification process is being complicated in at least two major ways. First, Europe is in the midst of switching from analog phones and their associated gear to more sophisticated digital equipment. Second, looking ahead to its coming "single" market, Europe is simultaneously

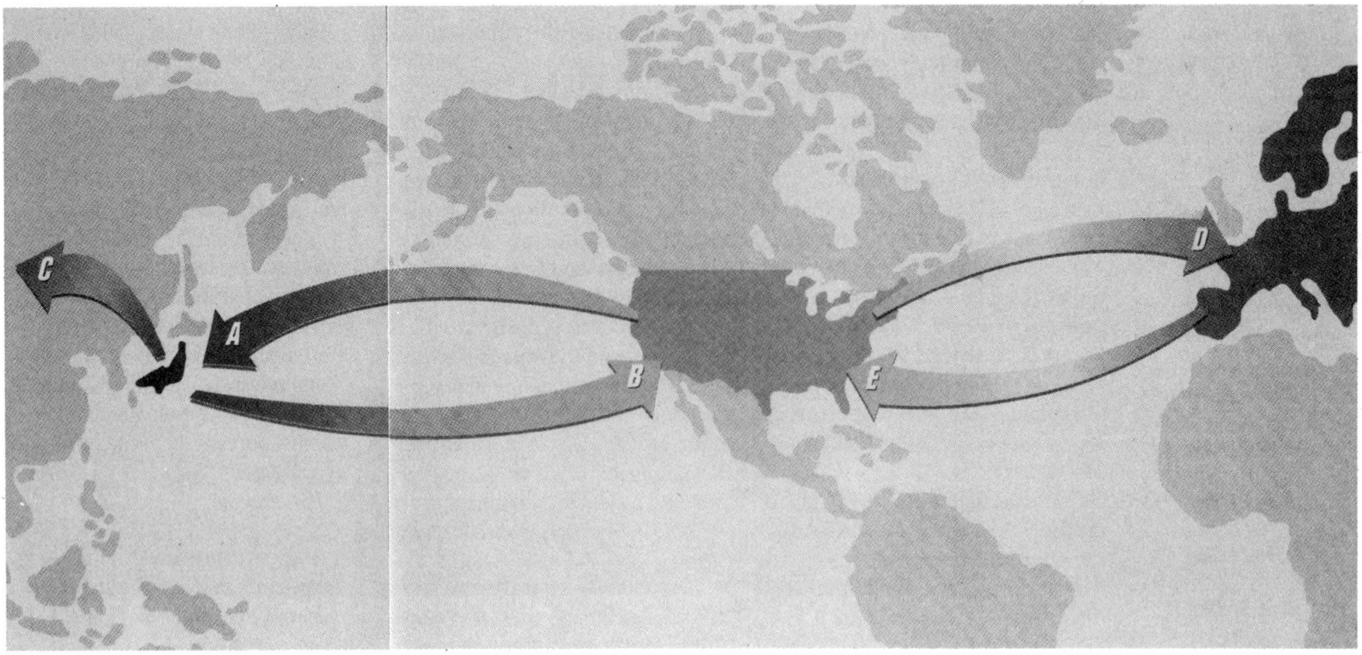

putting in place new, and rather detailed, equipment-approval procedures.

How difficult is the situation?

Well, "full" type-certification for digital phones is not now possible because laboratory test equipment needed to evaluate equipment samples isn't yet ready. What's more, as of two months ago, the software for running tests for "interim" type-certification on digital cellular phones was still being debugged.

So about the best a U.S. or other foreign phonemaker can expect at the moment is something called "interim-interim" type-certification, a process that involves 160 tests of phone samples in one of six designated European laboratories.

And, because one-stop EC-wide certification won't be possible until 1993, foreign phonemakers must get lab results to officials in each of the European countries in which they want to be type-certified.

Europe isn't the only significant example of just how involved selling cellular phones around the globe can get. Consider some of Motorola Inc.'s efforts in Japan.

There are no tariffs to keep Motorola's cellular phones from connecting with hundreds of thousands of people in Japan. Yet, for much of the last seven years, the Schaumburg, Ill.-based firm has not heard as loud a ring of success as it would have liked. Japanese regulations and delays are to blame.

"While we have been very successful in getting good penetration in the Kansai area [in western Japan], we [have been] much less successful in the [business-intense] Tokyo-Nagoya area," says Arnold S. Brenner, executive vice president and general manager of Motorola's Japan Group. "You can say we got into Japan, but we got into only half the country. We are trying to make it into the other half."

Motorola makes its Micro TAC series of portable cellular phones in Arlington Heights, Ill., just outside of Chicago, and exports them to Japan. But getting them to consumers on the other side of the Pacific "is not like exporting stuff [from the U.S. for the Japanese] retail market or even [like selling] automobiles," stresses Mr. Brenner. "It's more complicated."

Indeed, it is.

Relevant elements of Japan's highly regulated telecommunications environment include:

- The 1985 partial privatization of Nippon Telegraph & Telephone Corp. (NTT), which until recently had not come close to Motorola's technology.
- Japan's alleged failure to remove geographical and technical restrictions as envisioned in a 1986 trade agreement with the U.S.
- Japan's cost-increasing, innovation-discouraging, and, thus, sales-depressing requirement that cellular phones be leased through NTT and other common carriers rather than customer-owned.

The net effect for Motorola has been a notably uneven business playing field—even in the wake of a 1989 boost from the Bush Administration. Acting on a Motorola complaint that Japan had not lived up to the terms of the 1986 market-opening telecommunications accord, on Apr. 28, 1989, U.S. Trade Representative Carla Hills

Cellular Phones Trade Market

***A.** No import duties, but require type-certification and radio-equipment approval.*

***B.** Tariff of 6%.*

***C.** Type-certification requirements.*

***D.** 6.5% duty plus type-certification requirements.*

***E.** 6% tariff.*

World Share of Cellular Phone Sales

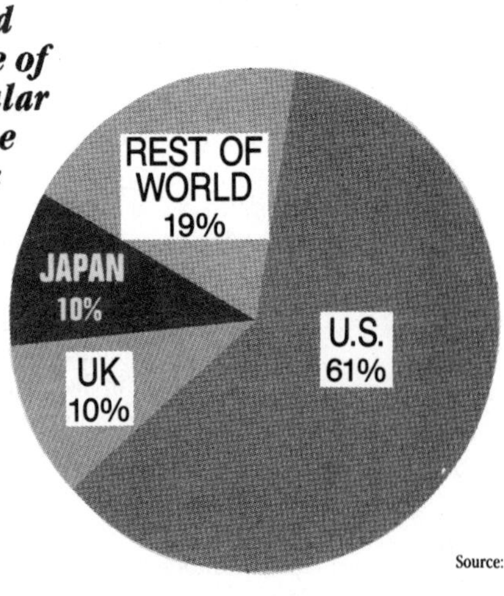

Source: Commerce Dept.

set in motion a series of steps that could have resulted in special duties, fees, and other trade restrictions being slapped on selected Japanese exports to the U.S.

Retaliation never occurred, because at the 11th hour Japan agreed to make space on Tokyo's busy airwaves available for Motorola's cellular phones and to allow the interconnect that would make nationwide "roaming" possible.

However, for many months the pace of implementation in Tokyo was disappointing, says Mr. Brenner. For example, it took about two years to secure sufficient antenna sites for the initial system. Expansion of Tokyo coverage seemed to be on hold, even though the necessary equipment had been ordered. In Tokyo, total sales of Motorola's cellular phones were fewer than 2,000 units.

What's more, Motorola didn't yet have Nagoya or the all-important business corridor between Nagoya and Tokyo covered, asks Mr. Brenner.

Not surprisingly, by early this year, Motorola was knocking on official doors in Washington and Tokyo and asking: "Are we ever going to speed things up or have [the Japanese] been delaying this . . . until digital systems are ready?" indicates Mr. Brenner.

The fact is that within two years of the signing of the 1989 telecom pact with Japan, NTT had developed a compact, lightweight portable cellular phone similar to Motorola's.The bottom line: Delay blunted Motorola's competitive edge in Japan's most populous region.

However—and this is significant for Motorola—it now looks as if there will be a happy ending to the saga, relates Mr. Brenner.

"As a result of the efforts of Washington and Tokyo, Motorola has received notification that the Tokyo-Nagoya system will be fully implemented per the 1989 agreement," he says. The expansion is expected to be completed in about two years, the time it'll take to select cell sites and manufacture equipment, he says.

"Quality and customer satisfaction are very important in Japan," emphasizes Mr. Brenner. "Perseverance also is."

AIRPLANES

'TOP GUN' HITS TURBULENCE

David Altany

More than half of the vapor trails seen streaking across the globe's skies are, in a sense, made in America. U.S. companies dominate the world's aerospace market. They generate the largest trade surplus of any U.S. industry. In 1991 that surplus hit $30 billion on a record $43 billion in exports Overall, the U.S. commands a 60% share of the worldwide market for aerospace products. Europe, by contrast, has 33% of the market, and Asian producers trail with a meager 7% share.

The aerospace industry is extremely competitive—and risky. Building a new jet consumes $2 billion to $4 billion in fixed development, tooling, and certification costs. A study of the aerospace industry conducted by Gellman Research Associates indicates that even a successfully launched aircraft program can generate a five-year cumulative deficit of $5 billion—far beyond the means of most companies.

The cost of producing military aircraft often surpasses that of civilian aircraft. The European Tornado fighter aircraft cost more than $8.5 billion to develop—double the annual military R&D budget for any single European Community nation.

In this hostile atmosphere, competitors need some type of edge to survive. That edge doesn't come in the form of direct trade barriers or tariffs, however, as these were reduced beyond significance by the Trade in Civil Aircraft agreement signed by the major industrial countries in 1980.

Instead, for U.S. companies, the edge has been their size and experience. After World War II, the U.S. immediately emerged as the dominant power in aerospace, while German and Japanese companies largely dismantled their operations.

Even today, U.S. aerospace companies' link to the U.S. government—the world's largest consumer of military aircraft—provides a strong source of support. In 1988, the U.S. military budget totaled $308 billion. By comparison, the combined military budgets of France, Germany, and the United Kingdom totaled only $101 billion.

"The expertise and technologies that U.S. companies develop while doing defense work is a great boost to their civilian side of the business, too," says a spokesperson at Europe's Airbus Industrie.

Though not unfair when viewed by the terms of existing trade agreements, this alliance, coupled with U.S. companies' high-quality aircraft, provides a U.S. edge that foreign firms have had difficulty competing against.

This is especially true in the case of Japan. Despite its product-development prowess in other areas, Japan lags far behind the U.S. in its aerospace capabilities. Japan has primarily exported helicopters and small commuter and business aircraft—market niches that U.S. companies have abandoned to avoid exposure to prohibitive U.S. product-liability laws.

Rather than launching into high-risk large-aircraft development, Japan has chosen to settle for the role of subcontractor for the major players in the U.S. and Europe. Japan's strategy is to build expertise in a growing number of aerospace product areas while facing a minimum of risk. According to the Aerospace Industries Assn. of America, Japan currently provides spoilers, ailerons, flaps, tailcones, rudders, and other parts used in Boeing and McDonnell Douglas jets.

There are no obvious trade barriers with Japan in the aerospace area. As with most other countries, though, Japan often pushes to have a growing portion of military aircraft it purchases from the U.S. manufactured or assembled in Japan. This supports employment and expands Japan's expertise in aerospace.

In time, Japan will acquire enough experience to become a full-fledged aircraft manufacturer. Already, it excels in several specializations, most notably aircraft materials and casting

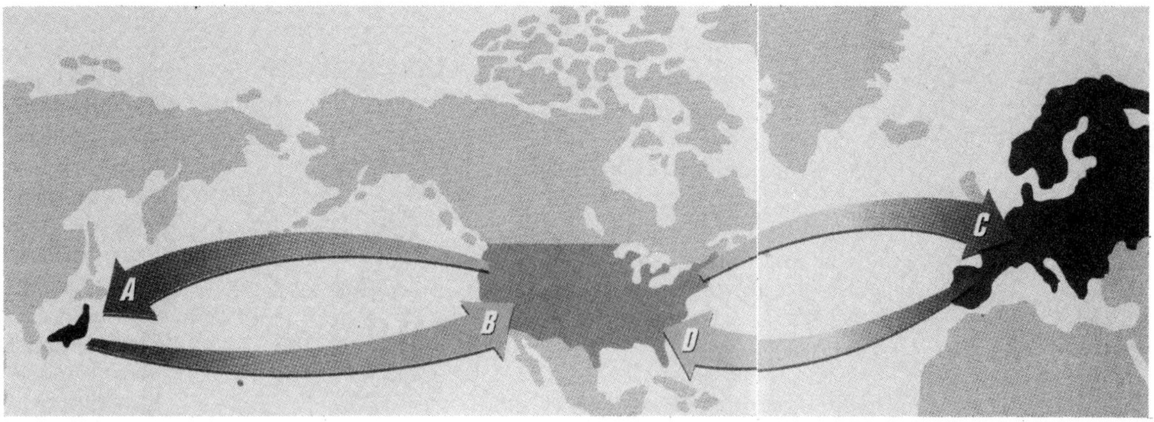

Trade barriers were reduced beyond significance by 1980's Trade in Civil Aircraft Agreement. Competitive edge remains in size and experience. Export volume is most telling:

A. $4.1 billion.

B. $0.5 billion.

C. $15.7 billion.

D. $6.9 billion.

processes. Japan produces roughly half of the world's supply of carbon fiber for composite materials.

Overall, though, Japan's importance in the aerospace industry is as a purchaser, rather than a producer. Japan is the second largest single-country export market for U.S. producers, exceeded only by the United Kingdom. Japan's aerospace trade balance has been consistently negative. The Aerospace Industries Assn. of America indicates that since 1982, the ratio of aerospace imports to exports in Japan **has been 10:1. The U.S. has been the biggest exporter of aerospace products to Japan, accounting for 87% of its imports in 1988. Japan's foreign direct investment in the aerospace industry has been small. The U.S. Commerce Dept. lists only one Japanese investment in the U.S. aerospace sector. Industry analysts suggest that American political sensitivity toward Japanese investments in U.S. high-tech industries is the underlying reason. The 1987 attempt by the Japanese firm Fujitsu to purchase 80% of Fairchild Semiconductor—which had previously been purchased by the French in 1976—generated so much anxiety in the U.S. that the sale fell through.**

In contrast to Japan, the competitive dynamics between Europe and the U.S. are far more intense. As is the case with Japan, direct trade barriers and tariffs are not significant. But several indirect factors work to the advantage of the Europeans.

Two of these, ironically, are aspects of the U.S. system itself that work against domestic producers:

- Product-liability laws, which expose American firms to hugely expensive lawsuits and penalties, while allowing foreign firms to escape their scope.
- The U.S. government's tough transfer-of-technology restrictions, which pertain mostly to military-aircraft sales. The U.S. government has been more active than competitors' governments in curtailing sales of high-tech aircraft and electronic components to Middle Eastern countries and nonmembers of the NATO alliance. This policy is supported by most Americans, but it nevertheless has a negative impact on U.S. aerospace companies.

Of much greater significance to U.S. aircraft manufacturers, however, are the European government subsidies provided to members of the Airbus Industrie consortium.

Airbus was established in 1969 by the four largest European aerospace companies and their respective governments to help Europe establish a strong presence in the aerospace industry. Because of the high development costs associated with the industry and the countries' relatively small defense budgets, finding private sources of capital for such a venture was not possible.

As a result, during the last two decades the governments have provided funds in the form of direct grants and non-interest-bearing loans for research and development. To date, these funds have totaled $13 billion. If the interest Airbus avoided is included, the benefit of the subsidies jumps to $26 billion. Very little of the loans has been repaid yet, and some analysts suggest little ever will be.

The subsidies have been crucial to Airbus' survival. During Airbus' early years, the subsidies covered up to 90% of the consortium's aircraft-development costs and have averaged more than 75% during the life of the consortium. These subsidies, along with Airbus' pricing policies, have allowed the consortium to capture one-third of the world aerospace market.

The subsidy situation now appears to be in a state of change. When Airbus was first established, its member companies were nationalized firms. Market share—not profitability—was the consortium's emphasis. After 20 successive years of operating in the red, however, "member governments have become less tolerant of funding the [now privatized] consortium's consis-

World Share of Aerospace Sales

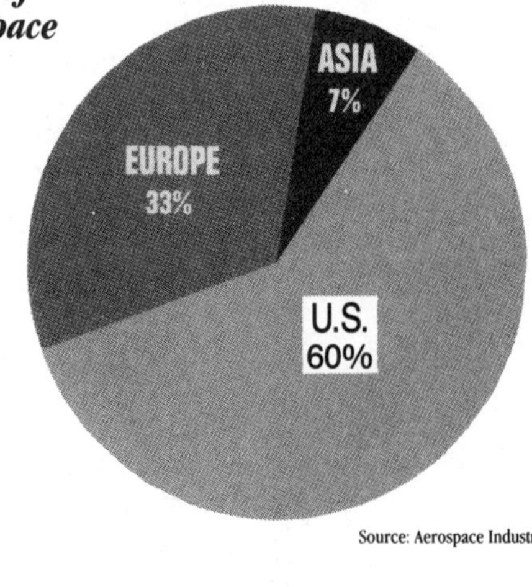

Source: Aerospace Industries Assn.

What's Behind The Acronyms

An Abbreviated Guide To Trade Terms

The **EC**, primarily an economic alliance, presently embraces 12 nations—Belgium, Denmark, France, Germany, Greece, Ireland, Italy, Luxembourg, the Netherlands, Portugal, Spain, and the United Kingdom. The European Community, the association's formal name, has spent the last seven years trying to establish the so-called single European market that will debut Jan. 1, 1993. In fact, next New Year's Day will dawn with matters of market access, technical standards, and taxes not fully resolved—and the future composition of the EC less than certain. (It's unclear how many of the seven European Free Trade Assn. countries and the nations of the former Communist Eastern Europe will secure membership.) Key elements of the EC are the Commission of the European Community, the Council of Ministers, the Court of Justice, and the European Parliament.

Created in 1947, **GATT** is both a set of international trade rules, formally known as the General Agreement on Tariffs & Trade, and the collective noun for the bureaucrats in Geneva, Switzerland, who administer the trade pact. GATT's current round of world trade talks, the so-called Uruguay Round, is the seventh in a series of multilateral negotiations aimed at reducing tariffs and such nontariff trade barriers as quotas, subsidies, and "buy national" procurement rules. Two of GATT's shortcomings are the absence of effective enforcement and the lack of rules covering global trade in banking, insurance, and other business-related services. Including the U.S., the 12-nation European Community, and Japan, GATT's membership totals 103 countries. These nations account for roughly 90% of total world trade in automobiles, computers, machine tools, steel, and other merchandise.

Like references to the tax-initiating U.S. House Ways & Means Committee, descriptions of Japan's **MITI** usually begin with the adjective *powerful*. But there the similarities end. The U.S. doesn't have a government institution comparable to Tokyo's Ministry of International Trade & Industry, mainly because most American business and government officials remain uncomfortable with the Japanese kind of closeness between the economy's private and public sectors. (MITI is most famous, or perhaps infamous, for the strategic counsel—so-called administrative guidance—it provides to Japanese industry.) Since the late 1970s, presumably to boost U.S. competitiveness in global markets, proposals have been put forth for a U.S. MITI. The basic notion has been to consolidate the U.S. Commerce Dept. and as many as a dozen other trade-related agencies in a more influential Dept. of International Trade & Industry (DITI). The idea has not progressed very far at the White House or on Capitol Hill, partly out of the fear that a DITI would start picking industrial winners and losers. Too, there's the realization that Presidential understanding and leadership in global economics are probably more essential to U.S. trade success than just a bureaucracy that's organizationally neat.

MFN, most-favored-nation trade status, suggests special trade treatment by the U.S.—or any other trading nation. In fact, it's the basic GATT principle of nondiscrimination that extends to all of a country's trading partners—except those specifically denied the customs and tariff terms accorded to the country's most-favored partners. At last count, the U.S. treated 168 other countries as most-favored nations. This spring, Congress unsuccessfully tried to condition a one-year continuation of MFN for China contingent on Beijing's clear protection of human rights.

NAFTA, the pending North American Free Trade Agreement, envisions a powerful Canadian, U.S., and Mexican trading zone extending from the Arctic to the Yucatan. Though NAFTA is still being drafted and may not be submitted to Congress until after the Nov. 3 U.S. Presidential election, the White House isn't exactly discouraging talk of eventually extending free trade in goods and services beyond Mexico to Central and South America.

—John S. McClenahen

tent losses," says economist David Vadas of the Aerospace Industries Assn. of America.

Recently, negotiators from the European Community agreed to reduce subsidy levels by more than half, placing them in the 30% to 33% range. The agreement falls short of the 0% subsidy American negotiators ultimately desired, as well as the 25% level they were bargaining for. Still, the agreement appears to be a step in the right direction.

The agreement comes just in time, as tensions were beginning to escalate, especially on the American side. "None of Airbus' aircraft have been profitable, and we find this situation quite troubling because the subsidies have allowed Airbus to stay in the market and offer products at below-fair market prices," says Mr. Vadas. "If this had continued, they soon would have knocked McDonnell Douglas right out of the market."

Indeed, that danger still lurks, as McDonnell Douglas recently made it known that it has insufficient funds for the development of a wide-body jet to compete with Boeing's 747-class jet. Having failed to find a domestic source of development capital, the company now says it may sell 40% of its business to a Taiwanese firm—29% owned by that country's government—to raise $2 billion.

A longer-term threat to U.S. manufacturers looms as the nonmarket and pseudomarket economies of China, the former Soviet Union, and Eastern Europe begin competing for a slice of the world's aerospace market. It is unlikely the U.S. will be able to maintain market share against these players with their heavy government support.

Debate over the subsidy issue is complex because it pits two valid but incompatible rights against each other.

On the one hand, each country has the right to stake at least an initial claim in the economically important aerospace industry, which, because of enormous start-up costs, requires some form of initial government aid.

On the other hand, companies in countries with already-established aircraft industries have the right to compete within a fair and open-market environment free from the distortions of government subsidies.

The Multinational Corporation

Multinational corporations, for the most part, did not start out to become multinational corporations. Indeed, the word was not even invented when most companies started business as small firms years ago. Multinationals evolved over a period of years. They did not happen overnight, but gradually grew as their markets and industries expanded.

The energy business (oil) is a case in point. When John D. Rockefeller was first operating Standard Oil in Cleveland, Ohio, he had no idea that the organization he was starting would be the direct ancestor of such corporate giants as Exxon, Chevron, or Mobil. Rockefeller was too busy trying to meet the daily demands of his new company to worry about yet-to-be-discovered oil fields in Kuwait—oil fields for which the United States would go to war in the following century. As the oil business grew, so did Rockefeller's little company, and it grew fast. Rockefeller shrewdly developed business practices that helped to drive the competition out of business. He dominated his industry to such a degree that he was able to demand and

Unit 2

get kickbacks from the railroads for goods that the competition was shipping. Of course, there was a reaction in the form of antitrust laws that made many of Rockefeller's practices illegal. But Standard Oil, and the companies into which it was divided as a result of antitrust action, were major organizations and often the model for the multinational corporation.

Multinational corporations are business organizations with all levels and degrees of business interests all over the world. They export, manufacture, import, and sell a variety of goods and services worldwide. While they may have started out in their industry as being from a particular country, they have often lost that nationalistic identity and are frequently considered to be "domestic" firms in host countries. Often, they can be one of the largest business organizations in a particular country that is not the country of origin. Ford, while it is the number two automaker in the United States, is often the number one automaker in a variety of markets; Shell Oil is simply the American division of Angelo-Dutch Petroleum; and IBM is a member of the European Economic Community's electronics and data processing consortium.

Multinational corporations know no political boundaries. They do business on a worldwide basis and on a worldwide scale. While, perhaps, a relatively small operation in a particular country, on the global level they can be organizations with sales in the hundreds of millions and tens of billions of dollars.

Many of the multinational corporations tend to be American in origin, but that is not always the case. Indeed, the world's five largest industrial firms, according to *Forbes* magazine, are Japanese and include Sumitomo, C. Itoh & Co., Mitsui, Marubein, and Mitsubishi. Others include such household names as the already mentioned Shell Oil, Seagrams (Canadian), and Phillips (Dutch).

Multinationals often will get together with a local firm to form a joint venture. This is a favorite tactic to enter a market because it often allows the multinational access to markets that it would not normally have. These joint ventures can be very beneficial to both parties involved, but they are not without problems. Often the joint venture becomes a race to learn—to learn from each other, to learn the product, and to learn the market.

Multinational corporations are not without difficulties and critics. Many countries have severe and harsh restrictions on what multinational corporations can do in their countries. This is particularly true in the lesser and least developed countries that have had a history of colonial exploitation. After over a generation of political independence, these countries are still wary of foreign organizations. They do not want to trade political colonization for economic colonization. Often, one of the first acts of a newly politically independent state was to nationalize the various holdings of foreign corporations as a symbol of, and end to, foreign economic exploitation. Many of the former colonies still do not trust their former masters or the multinational corporations. It would seem to them that there would be little difference between a past of colonial/political exploitation and a future of colonial/economic exploitation.

Multinational corporations view the world as one market. They are no longer American, British, Canadian, or French firms. To be truly multinational means to lose national identity, to view all markets on an equal basis, to manufacture without regard to such national concerns as the balance of payments or national defense, and to offer equal opportunity to all employees to make it to the top of the organization. Perhaps the most American of all products, Coca Cola, is a case in point. The three top executives at Coca Cola in the 1980s were a Cuban refugee, an Englishman with an Argentine passport, and an American, and it was the Cuban refugee who headed the firm.

Multinational corporations represent the future of industry as the world gets smaller and experiences greater economic and political interdependence. They will continue to grow and expand, and their numbers will continue to climb as more corporations take on a truly multinational character. Even the Japanese will eventually be forced to give up their very Japanese orientation and to join the rest of the world in developing true multinational organizations because they will not be able to ignore or leave unrewarded the world's pool of talent in their organizational structure.

Looking Ahead: Challenge Questions

Multinational corporations did not just grow up overnight. What are some of the ways they have evolved? How are they different?

One of the favorite ways for a multinational to enter a market is through a joint venture. What are some of the problems associated with joint ventures? When would they be useful?

What makes a successful multinational corporation? What are some of the factors for success?

Global Corporate Competition II: Is the Large American Firm an Endangered Species?

Lawrence G. Franko

> *U.S. firms have declined in relation to foreign competitors in almost every industry.*

This article provides a 30-year overview of global corporate competition. In large measure, it is an update through 1990 of findings presented in the article, "Global Corporate Competition: Who's Winning, Who's Losing, and the R&D Factor as One Reason Why," published in the *Strategic Management Journal* (Franko 1989a). Like this past summer's film, *Naked Gun 2 1/2*, the results turn out to be "more than a sequel." Alas, those results—at least from the perspective of U.S.-headquartered big business firms—are vastly less amusing than the aforementioned film.

The 1960-80 erosion of the global position of large U.S. industrial and banking enterprises documented two years ago not only continues, it appears to have accelerated during the late 1980s. Indeed, the erosion of the U.S. corporate position—or, if one prefers, the rise of non-U.S. enterprise—has begun to be noticeable in high-tech and resource-based sectors, such as computers and office equipment, aerospace, pharmaceuticals, and paper and forest products—areas seemingly immune from declines in U.S. dominance even during the mid-1980s.

Propelled by computer downsizing, small copiers, and a monopoly on fax machines, the Japanese onslaught on computers and office equipment appears stronger than ever. Airbus continues to do more than irritate Boeing and McDonnell-Douglas in aerospace. Heavy electrical and telecommunications equipment are more and more dominated by European firms, as Japan and, more recently, South Korea consolidate the non-U.S. hold on consumer electronics. BMW joins the "top 12" for the first time in autos and trucks, and European firms also seize the high road to 1992 in paper and non-ferrous metals. U.S. dominance of the world banking industry is but a dim memory, with no U.S. bank on the list of the top 12 by assets and only one—Citibank, at number 18—among the leading 25.

Table 1 summarizes the numbers of firms headquartered in different countries in the top 12 by sales revenues in each industry, and their collective world market share, defined as their percentage of sales revenues of the world's 12 largest firms in each sector, for 1960, 1970, 1980, 1986, 1988, and 1990. **Table 2** lists the firms in each industry group and their individual world market shares for 1980 and 1990. The primary data source for these tables has been the *Fortune* U.S. 500 and non-U.S. 500 lists, which have been merged over the years by industry. *Fortune* lists have been supplemented by company annual reports. Industrial classifications are essentially those of *Fortune* (see the July 29, 1991 issue, whose "Global 500" format greatly facilitated the rapid updating of Table 1) as modified in the interests either of historical consistency or accuracy. For example, Table 1 divides *Fortune*'s metals and metal products sectors into iron and steel and non-ferrous metals categories. Table 1 also classifies Swedish/Swiss Asea Brown Boveri as an electrical equipment company; Xerox is included in computers and office equipment; AKZO and Montedison are classified as chemicals firms.

Although firm-based data are surely better indicators of the global competitive position of U.S., European, or Japanese-based enterprises

Reprinted from *Business Horizons*, Vol. 34, No. 6, November/December 1991, pp. 14-22. Copyright © 1991 by the Foundation for the School of Business at Indiana University. Used with permission.

Table 1
Changes in "World Market Share" in Major Industries, 1960-1990
Numbers of firms and percentages of consolidated worldwide sales accounted for by the 12* largest companies in each industry, by home country.

	Numbers of Firms					*% of Sales*				
	'60	'70	'80	'88	'90	'60	'70	'80	'88	'90
AEROSPACE										
USA	**9**	**9**	**9**	**9**	**9**	**85**	**88**	**81**	**84**	**79**
France	0	1	2	1	1	3	6	5	5	4
UK	3	2	1	2	2	15	9	6	11	17
AUTOS AND TRUCKS										
USA	**6**	**4**	**3**	**3**	**3**	**83**	**66**	**42**	**44**[a]	**38**[a]
Japan	0	3	3	3	3	0	12	17	21	23
Germany	2	2	2	2	3	7	11	14	15	21
France	2	1	2	2	2	4	4	15	10	10
Italy	1	1	1	1	1	3	4	10	7	8
UK	1	1	1	1	0	3	4	3	0	0
Sweden	0	0	0	0	0	0	0	0	3	0
BANKING (% of Total Assets)										
Japan	0	0	2	8	7	0	0	15	71	66
France	0	2	4	2	3	0	12	37	14	21
Germany	0	0	1	1	1	0	0	8	7	7
UK	3	2	1	0	1	22	15	15	0	6
USA	**6**	**6**	**3**	**1**	**0**	**61**	**67**	**26**	**8**	**0**
Italy	0	1	0	0	0	0	6	0	0	0
Canada	3	0	0	0	0	17	0	0	0	0
CHEMICALS										
Germany	3	3	3	3	3	18	27	36	39	39
USA	**8**	**5**	**4**	**4**	**3**	**68**	**40**	**31**	**29**[b]	**23**[b]
UK	1	1	1	1	1	14	11	10	10	11
Italy	0	1	1	1	1	0	9	7	6	6
France	0	1	1	1	1	0	6	5	6	7
Norway	0	0	0	1	1	0	0	0	5	5
Japan	0	0	1	0	1	0	0	5	0	4
Netherlands	0	1	1	1	1	0	7	0	5	5
COMPUTERS/OFFICE EQUIPMENT										
USA	**7**	**9**	**8**	**6**	**6**	**95**	**90**	**86**	**74**	**70**
Japan	0	1	2	3	4	0	3	7	18	23
Italy	1	1	1	1	1	3	5	4	4	4
UK	1	1	1	1	0	2	2	3	3	0
France	0	0	0	1	1	0	0	0	3	3
ELECTRICAL EQUIPMENT/ELECTRONICS										
Japan	2	3	3	5	6	8	17	21	42	47
South Korea	0	0	0	2	1	0	0	0	13	11
USA	**6**	**5**	**5**	**1**	**1**	**71**	**59**	**44**	**12**[a]	**11**[a]
Germany	2	2	1	1	1	10	12	11	11	10
Netherlands	1	1	1	1	1	8	9	11	9	8
France	0	0	2	1	1	0	0	12	7	7
UK	1	1	0	0	0	4	5	0	0	0
Sweden/Switz.	0	0	0	1	1	0	0	0	6	7
FOOD & BEVERAGE PRODUCTS										
USA	**9**	**10**	**8**	**7**	**7**	**62**	**67**	**50**	**51**	**52**
UK	1	1	3	3	2	24	25	36	28	23
Switzerland	1	1	1	1	1	10	8	14	17	15
Italy	0	0	0	0	1	0	0	0	0	6
France	0	0	0	0	1	0	0	0	0	3
Canada	1	0	0	0	0	4	0	0	0	0
Japan	0	0	0	1	0	0	0	0	5	0
IRON & STEEL										
Japan	1	4	4	5	5	5	30	31	43	44
Germany	2	3	2	2	3	11	21	24	20	26
France	0	0	1	1	1	0	0	5	12	12
Australia	0	1	0	1	1	0	7	0	6	8
UK	1	1	1	1	1	5	12	7	6	6
South Korea	0	0	0	0	1	0	0	0	0	5
USA	**7**	**3**	**3**	**2**	**0**	**74**	**31**	**26**	**12**	**0**
Netherlands	0	0	1	0	0	0	0	7	0	0
Luxembourg	1	0	0	0	0	5	0	0	0	0
NON-FERROUS METALS										
Germany	1	1	2	4	4	8	10	18	34	44
USA	**8**	**5**	**3**	**2**	**2**	**63**	**39**	**21**	**16**	**16**
France	1	2	1	1	1	7	19	16	11	13
Canada	2	2	2	2	2	22	18	14	20	12
(Non-Ferrous Metals cont'd.)										
UK	0	2	1	1	1	0	14	11	7	7[c]
Japan	0	0	1	2	1	0	0	7	10	5
Switzerland	0	0	1	0	1	0	0	7	0	4
Belgium	0	0	1	0	0	0	0	6	0	0
NON-ELECTRICAL MACHINERY (INDUS. & FARM EQUIP.)										
USA	**5**	**6**	**5**	**3**	**3**	**37**	**51**	**41**	**28**	**26**
Germany	4	3	2	3	3	42	28	23	26	25
Japan	0	1	1	3	3	0	7	6	21	23
South Korea	0	0	1	1	1	0	0	9	15	17
UK	0	1	1	1	1	0	7	5	5	5
France	1	0	1	1	1	7	0	12	6	5
Canada	1	1	1	0	0	8	6	5	0	0
Sweden	1	0	0	0	0	6	0	0	0	0
PAPER & PAPER PRODUCTS										
USA	**10**	**9**	**8**	**8**	**7**	**86**	**81**	**66**	**73**	**62**
Sweden	0	0	1	1	2	0	0	7	8	18
Canada	1	1	0	0	1	6	5	0	0	8[d]
New Zealand	0	0	0	1	1	0	0	0	7	7
Finland	0	0	0	0	1	0	0	0	0	6
Germany	0	0	1	1	0	0	0	10	6	0
UK	1	2	2	0	0	8	14	17	0	0
Japan	0	0	0	1	0	0	0	0	6	0
PETROLEUM PRODUCTS										
USA	**10**	**10**	**7**	**7**	**5**	**77**	**78**	**61**	**59**	**47**
Netherlands	1	1	1	1	1	17	16	15	18	18
UK	1	1	1	1	1	6	6	9	11	10
Italy	0	0	1	1	1	0	0	5	6	7
France	0	0	1	1	2	0	0	5	5	10
Brazil	0	0	0	1	1	0	0	0	4	4
Venezuela	0	0	1	0	1	0	0	4	0	4
PHARMACEUTICALS										
USA	**10**	**9**	**7**	**7**	**6**	**87**	**70**	**55**	**52**	**49**
Switzerland	2	3	3	3	3	13	30	32	35	30
Germany[e]	0	0	2	1	1	0	0	13	6	6
UK	0	0	0	0	1	0	0	0	0	9
Japan	0	0	0	1	0	0	0	0	7	0
Sweden	0	0	0	0	1	0	0	0	0	6
TEXTILES										
Japan	1	5	3	5	5	7	32	21	42	42
USA	**7**	**5**	**5**	**3**	**3**	**58**	**44**	**41**	**18**	**21**
UK	2	2	2	2	2	19	23	22	18	16
South Korea	0	0	1	1	1	0	0	8	10	11
Turkey	0	0	1	1	1	0	0	8	11	10
Netherlands	1	0	0	0	0	10	0	0	0	0
Italy	1	0	0	0	0	6	0	0	0	0
TIRES										
Japan	0	1	2	3	3	0	3	10	33	32
France	1	1	1	1	1	6	8	18	19	19
USA	**6**	**5**	**7**	**2**	**1**	**76**	**69**	**50**	**23**	**19**
Italy[f]	1	1		1	1	7	9		15	14
UK[f]	1	1	1[f]	0	0	11	9	18[f]	0	0
Germany	0	1	1	1	1	0	3	4	10	9
Australia	0	0	0	0	1	0	0	0	0	7

*(*Certain industry columns don't add up to 12.)*
[a]Excludes revenues of financial subsidiaries consolidated under new accounting rules for the first time in 1988.
[b]Includes only the chemical and diversified product sales of Du Pont; excludes the petroleum and coal sales of acquired Conoco.
[c]RTZ added to Fortune industry group.
[d]Forest products division only of Noranda.
[e]Pharmaceuticals divisions only of Bayer and Hoechst.
[f]Dunlop/UK and Pirelli/Italy sales were consolidated in 1975 and 1980.
(NOTE: Totals may not equal exactly 100% due to rounding.)

Table 2
Largest 12 Companies Worldwide in 15 Industries:
Sales in $Billion and "World Market Share" of "Total Industry Sales," 1980 and 1990

	1980	*%*		*1990*	*%*
INDUSTRIAL & FARM EQUIPMENT			**INDUSTRIAL & FARM EQUIPMENT**		
Caterpillar	8.60	0.14	Mitsubishi Heavy Industries	16.40	0.12
Schneider	7.60	0.12	Mannesmann	15.09	0.11
Mannesmann	7.22	0.12	Daewoo	22.26	0.17
Gutehoffnungshutte	6.91	0.11	Tenneco	14.89	0.11
Hyundai	5.54	0.09	Caterpillar	11.54	0.09
Deere	5.47	0.09	MAN	10.83	0.08
Dresser Industries	4.02	0.07	Deere	7.88	0.06
Ishikawajima-Harima Heavy Industries	3.60	0.06	Komatsu	6.43	0.05
FMC	3.48	0.06	Schneider	6.80	0.05
Combustion Eng.	3.15	0.05	Hoesch	7.83	0.06
Massey Ferguson	3.13	0.05	BICC	6.38	0.05
BICC	2.98	0.05	Kawasaki Heavy Industries	6.53	0.05
TOTAL	61.70	1.00	TOTAL	132.86	1.00
NON-FERROUS METALS			**NON-FERROUS METALS**		
Pechiney	9.03	0.16	Preussag	14.99	0.14
Rio Tinto Zinc	6.50	0.11	Pechiney	14.12	0.13
Alcan Aluminum	5.22	0.09	Viag	12.17	0.11
Alcoa	5.15	0.09	Metallgesellschaft	11.97	0.11
Metallgesellschaft	5.08	0.09	Alcoa	10.87	0.10
Degussa	4.85	0.08	Alcan	8.85	0.08
Alusuisse	4.12	0.07	Degussa	8.26	0.08
Nippon Mining	3.94	0.07	RTZ	7.20	0.07
Reynolds	3.65	0.06	Reynolds	6.08	0.06
Metallurgie H.O.	3.36	0.06	Mitsubishi Metal	5.58	0.05
Kaiser	3.22	0.06	Noranda (ex. forest)	4.68	0.04
Inco	3.02	0.05	Alusuisse	4.56	0.04
TOTAL	57.14	1.00	TOTAL	109.32	1.00
CHEMICALS			**CHEMICALS**		
Hoechst	16.48	0.13	BASF	29.18	0.14
Bayer	15.88	0.12	Hoechst	27.75	0.13
BASF	15.28	0.12	Bayer	26.06	0.12
Du Pont	13.65	0.10	Imperial Chemical Industries	23.35	0.11
Imperial Chemical Industries	13.29	0.10	Du Pont (ex. Conaco)	22.06	0.10
Dow Chemical	10.60	0.08	Dow Chemical	20.01	0.09
Union Carbide	9.99	0.08	Rhône-Poulenc	14.47	0.07
Montedison	9.10	0.07	Montedison	13.03	0.06
DSM	7.51	0.06	Norsk Hydro	9.87	0.05
Rhône-Polenc	7.16	0.05	AKZO Group	9.51	0.04
Monsanto	6.57	0.05	Monsanto	9.05	0.04
AKZO Group	6.27	0.05	Mitsubishi Kasei	8.22	0.04
TOTAL	131.78	1.00	TOTAL	212.56	1.00
IRON & STEEL			**IRON & STEEL**		
Thyssen	15.24	0.16	Thyssen	21.49	0.15
Nippon Steel	13.10	0.14	Nippon Steel	21.16	0.15
U.S. Steel	12.49	0.13	Usinor-Sacilor	17.64	0.12
Krupp-Konzern	7.67	0.08	Krupp	9.70	0.07
Estel	7.05	0.07	Sumitomo Metal	12.78	0.09
British Steel	6.77	0.07	Broken Hill Proprietary	10.83	0.07
Bethlehem Steel	6.70	0.07	NKK	10.25	0.07
NKK	5.93	0.06	Kobe Steel	9.44	0.07
Armco	5.68	0.06	Kawasaki Steel	8.65	0.06
Sumitomo Metal	5.56	0.06	British Steel	8.45	0.06
Usinor-Sacilor	5.15	0.05	Pohang Iron & Steel	7.00	0.05
Kawasaki Steel	5.02	0.05	Hoesch	7.83	0.05
TOTAL	96.36	1.00	TOTAL	145.23	1.00
AEROSPACE			**AEROSPACE**		
United Technologies	12.30	0.20	Boeing	27.60	0.18
Boeing	9.40	0.15	United Technologies	21.78	0.14
Rockwell	6.90	0.11	British Aerospace	19.33	0.13
McDonnell Douglas	6.06	0.10	McDonnell Douglas	16.35	0.11
Lockheed	5.40	0.09	Allied-Signal	12.40	0.08
General Dynamics	4.74	0.08	General Dynamics	10.18	0.07
Textron	3.64	0.06	Lockheed	9.98	0.07
British Aerospace	3.31	0.05	Textron	7.92	0.05
Aérospatiale	3.12	0.05	Rolls Royce	6.62	0.04
Rolls Royce	2.93	0.05	Aérospatiale	6.47	0.04
Martin Marietta	2.62	0.04	Martin Marietta	6.14	0.04

Table 2 (cont'd.)

	1980	*%*		*1990*	*%*
Dassault Aviation	2.55	0.04	Northrop	5.49	0.04
TOTAL	62.97	1.00	TOTAL	150.26	1.00
BANKING			**BANKING**		
Citicorp	114.92	0.10	Sumitomo	407.91	0.10
Bank America	111.62	0.10	Dai-Ichi	426.86	0.10
Banque Nationale de Paris	107.28	0.10	Mitsubishi	412.78	0.10
Crédit Agricole	105.91	0.09	Mitsui	407.50	0.10
Crédit Lyonnais	98.15	0.09	Sanwa	401.47	0.10
Societé Generale	90.16	0.08	Fuji	398.32	0.10
Barclay's	88.62	0.08	Crédit Agricole	302.98	0.07
Dai-Ichi	88.52	0.08	Banque Nationale de Paris	289.75	0.07
Deutsche Bank	88.47	0.08	Industrial Bank of Japan	289.18	0.07
National Westminster	82.59	0.07	Crédit Lyonnais	285.24	0.07
Mitsubishi	76.43	0.07	Deutsche Bank	267.70	0.06
Chase Manhattan	76.20	0.07	Barclay's	260.05	0.06
TOTAL	1,128.87	1.00	TOTAL	4,149.74	1.00
COMPUTER & OFFICE EQUIPMENT			**COMPUTER & OFFICE EQUIPMENT**		
IBM	26.20	0.42	IBM	69.02	0.36
Xerox	8.20	0.13	Xerox	18.38	0.10
Sperry	4.78	0.08	Fujitsu	17.97	0.09
NCR	3.32	0.05	Hewlett Packard	13.23	0.07
Hewlett Packard	3.10	0.05	Digital Equipment	13.09	0.07
Burroughs	2.86	0.05	Canon	12.21	0.06
CDC	2.75	0.04	Unisys	10.11	0.05
Fujitsu	2.62	0.04	Sharp	9.93	0.05
Olivetti	2.54	0.04	Olivetti	7.54	0.04
Digital Equipment	2.37	0.04	Bull	6.41	0.03
Canon	1.85	0.03	NCR	6.40	0.03
ICL	1.67	0.03	Ricoh	5.96	0.03
TOTAL	62.26	1.00	TOTAL	190.24	1.00
AUTOS & TRUCKS			**AUTOS & TRUCKS**		
GM	57.70	0.23	GM	110.80	0.19
Ford	37.10	0.15	Ford	81.84	0.14
Fiat	25.16	0.10	Toyota	64.52	0.11
Renault	18.98	0.08	Daimler-Benz	54.26	0.09
Volkswagen	18.34	0.07	Fiat	47.75	0.08
Daimler-Benz	17.11	0.07	Volkswagen	43.71	0.08
Peugeot	16.85	0.07	Nissan	40.22	0.07
Toyota	14.23	0.06	Chrysler	26.97	0.05
Nissan	13.85	0.06	Renault	30.05	0.05
Mitsubishi Heavy Industries	11.00	0.04	Peugeot	29.38	0.05
Chrysler	9.20	0.04	Honda	27.07	0.05
British Leyland	6.69	0.03	BMW	17.29	0.03
TOTAL	246.21	1.00	TOTAL	573.85	1.00
ELECTRICAL			**ELECTRICAL**		
GE	24.96	0.15	Hitachi	50.69	0.13
ITT	18.53	0.11	GE	44.88	0.11
Philips	18.40	0.11	Samsung	45.04	0.11
Siemens	17.60	0.11	Matsushita Electric Industrial	43.52	0.11
Matsushita Electric Industrial	13.60	0.08	Siemens	39.23	0.10
Hitachi	12.87	0.08	Philips	30.87	0.08
Western Electric	12.03	0.07	Toshiba	30.18	0.07
CGE	10.85	0.07	Asea Brown Boveri	27.71	0.07
Thomson-Brandt	8.66	0.05	Alcatel-CGE	26.46	0.07
Westinghouse	8.51	0.05	NEC	24.39	0.06
Toshiba	8.15	0.05	Mitsubishi Electric	21.23	0.05
RCA	8.01	0.05	Sony	20.93	0.05
TOTAL	162.17	1.00	TOTAL	405.13	1.00
FOOD & BEVERAGE			**FOOD & BEVERAGE**		
Unilever	26.43	0.26	Philip Morris	44.32	0.19
Nestlé	14.62	0.14	Unilever	39.97	0.17
Dart & Kraft	9.41	0.09	Nestlé	33.36	0.14
Beatrice	8.29	0.08	Pepsico	17.80	0.08
Pepsi Co.	5.98	0.06	Conagra	15.52	0.07
General Foods	5.96	0.06	Grand Metropolitan	14.77	0.06
Coca-Cola	5.90	0.06	Ferruzi	13.97	0.06
Consolidated Food	5.34	0.05	Sara Lee (Consolidated Foods)	11.65	0.05
Grand Metropolitan	5.10	0.05	Anheuser Busch	10.75	0.05
Associated British Food	5.00	0.05	Coca-Cola	10.41	0.05
Ralston Purina	4.88	0.05	BSN	9.72	0.04
Greyhound	4.76	0.05	Archer-Daniels-Midland	7.89	0.03
TOTAL	101.67	1.00	TOTAL	230.13	1.00

Table 2 (cont'd.)

	1980	*%*		*1990*	*%*
PAPER & FOREST PRODUCTS			**PAPER & FOREST PRODUCTS**		
International Paper	5.04	0.11	International Paper	12.96	0.14
Georgia-Pacific	5.02	0.11	Georgia-Pacific	12.67	0.13
Flick Group	4.64	0.10	Stora Kopparbergs Berg.	11.07	0.12
Weyerhaeuser	4.50	0.10	Weyerhaeuser	9.02	0.09
Bowater	4.09	0.09	Noranda	8.12	0.09
Champion International	3.75	0.08	Fletcher Challenge	7.13	0.07
Statsforetag Group	3.34	0.07	Kimberly-Clark	6.45	0.07
Reed International	3.31	0.07	Repola	6.04	0.06
Crown Zellerbach	3.07	0.07	Stone	5.77	0.06
Boise Cascade	3.02	0.07	James River	5.42	0.06
Mead	2.71	0.06	Scott	5.39	0.06
Regis	2.70	0.06	Svenska Cellulosa	5.33	0.06
TOTAL	45.19	1.00	TOTAL	95.38	1.00
PETROLEUM PRODUCTS			**PETROLEUM PRODUCTS**		
Exxon	103.10	0.20	Royal Dutch/Shell	107.20	0.18
Royal Dutch/Shell	77.10	0.15	Exxon	105.89	0.18
Mobil	59.50	0.11	British Petroleum	59.54	0.10
Texaco	51.20	0.10	Mobil	58.77	0.10
British Petroleum	48.00	0.09	ENI	41.76	0.07
Chevron	40.50	0.08	Texaco	41.24	0.07
ENI	27.20	0.05	Chevron	39.26	0.07
Gulf	26.50	0.05	Elf Aquitaine	32.94	0.06
Standard of Indiana	26.10	0.05	Amoco	29.28	0.05
CFP	23.90	0.05	Total-CFP	23.59	0.04
Atlantic Richfield	23.70	0.05	Petróleos de Venezuela	23.47	0.04
Petróleos de Venezuela	18.82	0.04	Petrobrás	20.47	0.04
TOTAL	525.62	1.00	TOTAL	583.41	1.00
PHARMACEUTICALS			**PHARMACEUTICALS**		
Ciba-Geigy	7.11	0.17	Ciba-Geigy	14.48	0.14
Johnson & Johnson	4.84	0.11	Johnson & Johnson	11.23	0.11
American Home Products	3.80	0.09	Bristol-Myers Squibb	10.51	0.10
Hoffmann-La Roche	3.50	0.08	Sandoz	8.90	0.09
Warner-Lambert	3.48	0.08	SmithKline Beecham	8.64	0.09
Bristol Meyers	3.16	0.07	Merck	7.82	0.08
Pfizer	3.03	0.07	Hoffmann-La Roche	6.96	0.07
Sandoz	2.93	0.07	American Home Products	6.92	0.07
Hoechst	2.80	0.07	Pfizer	6.60	0.07
Merck	2.79	0.07	Procordia	6.34	0.06
Bayer	2.70	0.06	Hoechst	6.22	0.06
Lilly (Eli)	2.56	0.06	Abbott	6.21	0.06
TOTAL	42.70	1.00	TOTAL	100.83	1.00
TIRES			**TIRES**		
Goodyear	8.44	0.20	Bridgestone	12.40	0.21
Michelin	7.73	0.18	Michelin	11.52	0.19
Dunlop	7.51	0.18	Goodyear	11.45	0.19
Firestone	4.85	0.11	Pirelli	8.46	0.14
Goodrich	3.08	0.07	Continental	5.30	0.09
Bridgestone	3.02	0.07	Pacific Dunlop	3.88	0.06
Uniroyal	2.30	0.05	Sumitomo Rubber	3.79	0.06
GenCorp	2.22	0.05	Yokahama Rubber	2.96	0.05
Continental	1.74	0.04	TOTAL	59.77	
Yokohama Rubber	1.12	0.03			
Armstrong	0.40	0.01			
Cooper	0.32	0.01			
TOTAL	42.73	1.00			
TEXTILES 1980			**TEXTILES**		
Courtaulds	3.97	0.16	Toray Industries	6.05	0.12
Burlington	2.90	0.12	Hyosung	5.26	0.11
Levi Strauss	2.84	0.11	Haci Ömer Sabanci	5.13	0.10
Kanebo	2.06	0.08	Kanebo	4.63	0.09
Haci Ömer Sabanci	1.98	0.08	Courtaulds	4.33	0.09
Hyosung	1.95	0.08	Levi Strauss	4.25	0.08
J P Stevens	1.92	0.08	Teijin	4.11	0.08
Toyobo	1.73	0.07	Toyobo	3.69	0.07
Coats Patons	1.60	0.06	Wickes	3.65	0.07
Unitika	1.57	0.06	Coats Viyella	3.29	0.07
Armstrong World	1.32	0.05	VF	2.62	0.05
West Point Pepperel	1.25	0.05	Unitika	2.96	0.06
TOTAL	25.07	1.00	TOTAL	49.97	1.00

than are macroeconomic or trade data, some cautions and caveats must be noted. Arguably, exchange-rate fluctuations could influence relative rankings. However, in the industries surveyed here, the vast majority of firms have either markets in many currencies or the potential of selling or producing in many currency areas through export or multinational production operations. The dollar is but a *numeraire* for firms selling primarily in globally spread markets. Moreover, should a "weak dollar" be asserted to distort rankings significantly in 1990, one must ask why rankings were not similarly distorted in 1980 and 1988, when the dollar was also "weak."

Extensive corporate diversification, especially of the "unrelated" or conglomerate variety, could also distort rankings absolutely and, if undertaken by acquisition, on a year-to-year basis. However, in general, unrelated diversification moves have been far more typical of U.S. (and British) firms than of European or Japanese. Therefore the U.S. position would—as in the case of Xerox's early 1980s insurance acquisitions, or GE's late 1980s moves into financial and broadcast services—be most likely exaggerated upwards. (In one case where the impact on company sales was especially dramatic, Du Pont's acquisition of Conoco, the sales figures and rankings for that firm in the chemicals sections of Tables 1 and 2 have been adjusted to include chemicals only.) Moreover, while unrelated diversifications and acquisitions may introduce short-term upward distortions in firm rankings, the longer-term performance of firms pursuing such strategies has been almost invariably such as to move them down or off the leadership lists. Indeed, there is ample reason to conclude that the pursuit of unrelated diversification has been a principal cause of U.S.-company defeats in global competition (Franko 1989b).

Acquisitions or mergers per se, even of the "related" variety, may of course alter rankings year by year; the sharp increase in the Swedish position in the world paper and forest products industry noticeable in the 1990 figures is largely due to Swedish acquisition and consolidation in the European paper industry on the road to 1992. But acquisitions sometimes indicate real strengths of the acquirer. If not, the truth will usually out over the two- to ten-year periods used to gauge strategic success or failure. U.S. firms, too, have sometimes raised their rankings in the top 12 and world market share by acquisition or merger. Burroughs probably avoided dropping off the top 12 list in computers by merging with Sperry as Unisys in the mid-1980s, yet without notable longer-term, strategic business success. (Unisys dropped from number five in 1988 in computers and office equipment to seventh in 1990 while losing more than $400 million.)

WINNERS AND LOSERS

While firm-based data on winners and losers in rankings and "world market share" constitute an imperfect scorecard, over time they do help keep score. In very broad outline, the story told by the numbers in Tables 1 and 2, industry by industry, is as follows.

Aerospace. American firms are still dominant, with a nearly 80 percent world market share in 1990. The rise of British Aerospace and Rolls Royce may be exaggerated by those firms' recent acquisitions outside of their main industry (Rover cars by British Aerospace, and Northern Engineering, a turbine firm, by Rolls Royce). Still, the decline in U.S. position since the mid-1980s is consistent with the end of the U.S. defense contract boom, with Rolls Royce's technology-led gains in the jet engine business, and with British Aerospace's participation in the European Airbus consortium—whose worldwide sales prowess, if not profit success, is now uncontested.

Autos and Trucks. The mid-1980s resurgence in the competitive position of the U.S. auto producers may well have been ephemeral. The world market share of Detroit's Big Three has fallen from 50 percent in 1986 to 38 percent in 1990—both figures a far cry from the two-thirds share enjoyed by U.S. firms in 1970 and the total dominance of the 1960s. The appearance of BMW on the list of the top 12 in 1990 seems symptomatic of a German, if not wider European, ability to have exploited the model and market opportunities of 1992 and beyond. And the American firms are faced with a continuous gnawing away of their domestic position by Japanese transplants at home.

Banking. Much of the blame for the decline in the world position of U.S. banks can be laid to macroeconomic factors, such as the (much) higher savings rates in Japan and Europe, as well as to the manifest absurdities of American banking law restraining interregional and financial services expansion by U.S. banks. Notwithstanding this, it is hard to escape the feeling that it took some special managerial genius for American banks to go from global dominance (67 percent of the assets of the world's top 12) in the 1970s to no presence at all by 1990. One clue may lie in the fact that the only U.S. bank still to be among the top 25 was also the only U.S. bank that seriously built a multinational presence within foreign markets when the opportunity was available. (Regarding the benefits to Citibank of being "global," see Lascelles 1991.)

Chemicals. Last year saw the disappearance from the top 12 of Union Carbide, and thence the first truly notable realignment of rankings since the mid-1970s, the time when each of the three German giants overtook Du Pont. The fruits of the Bhopal disaster, however, only accelerated a broader U.S. decline long signaled by a low level of R&D investment relative to industry peers and the distractions of unrelated diversifications.

Computers and Office Equipment. As already noted, the Japanese challenge to the U.S. is alive and well. Massive dominance by giant U.S. firms has been replaced by fragmentation among industry segments at home and a strong Asian incursion. But the large U.S. firms that have maintained their leadership position, especially Hewlett Packard and DEC, have notably maintained their R&D investments relative to sales revenues at levels in the industry reached only by Japan's Fujitsu among the big 12. All of the large firms, to be sure, also face attack on another front from smaller U.S. firms such as Apple, Compaq, and Sun Microsystems. Whether these smaller U.S. firms will in turn grow large enough to "pick up the slack" of U.S.-company world market share lost by the declines of IBM and Unysis, and the departures from the list of CDC and Honeywell, remains to be seen.

Electrical Equipment and Electronics. The Japanese have won in consumer electronics and are being joined by the South Koreans. Were it not for General Electric, U.S. firms would have exited the list of the world's top 12 by 1988. The Europeans, especially Asea Brown Boveri of Sweden and Switzerland and Siemens of Germany, appear to be relegating GE (and Westinghouse) to also-ran status in heavy electrical equipment. And the telecommunications equipment part of France's Alcatel alone is larger than the equipment division of AT&T. (The equipment part of AT&T itself is not large enough to make the top 12 list, although it used to be on it in the 1970s as Western Electric. That was before AT&T allowed itself, among other things, to be preempted in digital switching systems in its home market by Canada's Northern Telecom. On global competition in telecommunications, see Yoffie and Vietor 1991.) The diversifiers—or, as Peter Lynch of Magellan Fund fame used to put it, "deworsifiers"—ITT, RCA, and the UK's General Electric, are long gone from the majors.

All is not necessarily lost for the U.S. electronics industry. Motorola is among the top 25 in the world; Intel ranks 35th. But they do not (yet) rival the non-Americans in scale and scope.

Food and Beverage Products. In spite of the best efforts of the leveraged buy-out movement in the U.S.—which, as Alfred Chandler has noted (1990), especially affected and afflicted this sector of American industry—sales rankings show American firms (just) holding onto their historic majority of world sales in these businesses. The departing Beatrice and Dart and Kraft have been replaced by Conagra and a transformed Philip Morris. Indeed, the "new news" is the rise of Continental European groups such as France's BSN and Italy's Feruzzi. Renewed European market growth and future promise appear to have called forth renewed entrepreneurial dynamism.

Iron and Steel. Asia has won; big U.S. steel is no more. Indeed, U.S. firms, no longer large enough to be among the top 12, are largely exiting the business, selling out to the Japanese, or both. And "mini-mills" are just that relative to the impact this industry once had on U.S. economic activity, employment, and incomes.

Non-Ferrous Metals. The surprise here is of a resurgent Germany, with the world market share of Metallgesellschaft, Degussa, Preussag, and VIAG advancing rapidly during the 1980s to 44 percent by the end of 1990. The U.S. at 16 percent maintains its activity through Alcoa and Reynolds in aluminum, but the days of dominance of copper are no more.

Industrial and Farm Equipment. The battering taken by Caterpillar in the early 1980s appears to have stopped; Deere is even back to number seven in the world rankings, after starting out the decade in sixth place, then falling to 11th in 1986. The U.S.-firm share holds in the upper 20s, but the major successes during the 1980s were Japanese and Korean.

Paper and Forest Products. The stimulus of 1992 is visible again, with the Swedes leading the charge to consolidate their position in the EC through vertical and horizontal integration. In 1990, the "world market share" of Swedish firms reached 18 percent, while that of U.S. companies dropped to 62 percent. Some American firms, notably International Paper, have also been "going global" in Europe, but they appear to be following, not leading.

Petroleum Products. For the first time, U.S. companies accounted for less than half of the world market in 1990. The era of the "seven sisters" is no more; Royal Dutch Shell, not Exxon, is now the world's largest oil enterprise; third-world National Champions joined the list; and French company discoveries in the North Sea, dynamism, and acquisitions have altered the industry.

Pharmaceuticals. In pharmaceuticals, U.S. companies also slipped just below half of the "world market share" of the 12 largest companies in 1990 for the first time. Notable was the reappearance of a UK firm on the list, SmithKline-Beecham, albeit due to the UK's Beecham taking over U.S. SmithKline. Notwithstanding the influence of acquisition, this development does seem to reflect a broader surge of UK-firm activity in the world pharmaceutical industry; on recent growth form, it would not be a surprise to welcome Britain's Glaxo (number 16 by our count, which includes Ciba-Geigy and the Pharma divisions of Bayer and Hoechst, not included in *Fortune*'s ranking) to the top 12 in the near future. The appearance of Procordia of Sweden on the list also appears to realistically reflect a notable R&D dynamism in health care of firms based in that country.

Textiles. It was fashionable in the early

1980s to assert that the scale advantages of U.S. textile mill firms, plus the eternal appeal of Levi Strauss's blue jeans, would maintain the U.S. dominance of this industry. But something happened that halved the U.S. share of the "world industry" from 41 percent to 21 percent during the 1980s. Part of what happened was the rise of large Korean and Turkish producers; part was a lack of eternal appeal of Levis; and part may have been leveraged buy-outs of formerly leading U.S. textile mill producers and a subsequent lack of investment therein.

Tires. As noted in my 1989 *SMJ* article, the handwriting had been on the wall for the U.S. tire industry for several years, even though the world market share figures (at 50 percent in both 1980 and 1986) showed a deceptive stability in the U.S. firms' global position. Too little R&D, too little presence in non-U.S. markets of more rapid market growth and leading-edge technological development, and too much conglomeration by Uniroyal, Goodrich, General, Firestone, and even (so far) survivor Goodyear, caused the decline of the U.S. share of this industry to play out during the decade of the 1980s like a slow-motion Greek tragedy. The late 1980s LBOs of the terminally ill patients, and subsequent sales of the carcasses to France's Michelin, Japan's Bridgestone, and Germany's Continental, extracted the last bit of "shareholder value" from once-leading companies, but neither the LBOs nor the foreign acquisitions drove the underlying dynamic of the U.S. demise. Thus, the U.S. representation is down to one firm, itself a bit of a conglomerate struggling with a useless, unsaleable pipeline activity, doing less R&D than at least two of its rivals, and without great presence in many of the growth markets of the new Europe and the newly industrializing countries.

POSSIBLE CAUSES

There is a rich agenda of possible causes of the shifts in the global position of large firms based in different countries summarized in Table 1. Although statistical analyses along the lines of those undertaken for the 1970s are yet to be done, many of the hypotheses discussed therein retain their validity.

It seems no accident, for example, that in the computer and office equipment industry the survivors and gainers in rank through 1990 tended to have above average R&D intensity (R&D to sales ratios) during the 1980s, whereas those who dropped off the list were of low R&D intensity, unrelated diversifiers, or both. Likewise, firms that were above average in R&D intensity in the early 1980s maintained or improved their rankings in aerospace, electrical equipment, and pharmaceuticals, whereas firms neglecting R&D either slipped (American Home Products declined from 3 to 8 in pharmaceuticals), or dropped off (Westinghouse in electrical equipment, Warner-Lambert in pharmaceuticals).

The conglomerate, unrelated diversifiers of the 1970s, disproportionately of U.S. provenance and especially prevalent in electrical equipment and tires, also largely disappeared during the 1980s—both from the "world's largest" lists, and frequently altogether. Focus, on the other hand, was related to success.

A global spread into foreign growth markets and lower-cost production sites appeared to count too. The American firms surviving at or near the top of the computer, aerospace, chemical, auto, paper, pharmaceutical, and tire industries had foreign sales percentages—and therefore access to non-U.S. growth markets—well above the majority of those leaving the top rank. The late 1980s resurgence in European company dynamism so noticeable from Table 1, and so different from the Asian-dominated results through 1986 presented in the 1989 *SMJ* article, surely has much to do with the replacement of "Eurosclerosis" with "Europe 1992" and After-the-Berlin-Wall European market dynamism. Those American (and Japanese) firms that had already built a marketing and production network capable of accessing renewed European growth and dynamism could now grow with the new Europe; those U.S. firms and banks (several of whom withdrew from Europe just in time for the Euro-boom) that looked mainly to their domestic market could not.

Intriguingly, there is not much evidence here for blaming leveraged buy-outs or "the financial excesses of the 1980s" for declines in U.S.-company dominance. LBOs were not much of a feature in most of the industries, especially the higher-technology industries, surveyed here. They affected large U.S. companies principally in food products—therein "restructuring" or moving around parts of companies apparently without great effect on world rankings by country of headquarters (albeit France's BSN was able to expand its European activities by buying pieces of what once had been RJR-Nabisco)—and in tires. But in tires, the (strategic) deed was almost surely done. Perhaps the LBOs hastened the process through industrial euthanasia; perhaps the LBOs had a more ecological function, like wolf packs killing weak caribou—and recycling their meat into "shareholder value"—before death from natural causes occurred. To blame the LBO practitioners for not "saving" Uniroyal-Goodrich seems a little like blaming ordinary mortals for their inability to resurrect the dead.

Will the waning of the large American firm continue? Perhaps some respite is possible: the "deworsified" conglomerates of the 1970s are already LBO'd, restructured, or deceased. Still, some of the American firms appearing at or near the top of the electrical equipment, aerospace, and chemicals rankings do not seem to be giving the priority to R&D they once did. And there are still some domestically oriented U.S. firms that could become unviable as others' technologies, costs, or market locations provide competitive advantages—which is a longish way of saying that the fears of Chrysler's eventual demise often expressed in the business press are hardly irrational.

Does the waning of the large American headquartered firm matter? Pundits like Robert Reich (1991) would have one believe not, or not very much. After all, the newly dominant non-U.S. firms can and do contribute to U.S. productivity and economic growth by setting up efficient plants in the U.S., like Honda's and Nissan's transplants. Or, they can acquire U.S. firms or factories and (potentially) render U.S. capital and labor more productive (Bridgestone's acquisition of Firestone? Michelin's of Uniroyal-Goodrich? Beecham's takeover of SmithKline? Hoechst and Celanese? Bayer's extensive U.S. activities? Schneider and Square D? St. Gobain and Norton? Rhône-Poulenc and Rorer? Samsung's investment in Zenith Electronics?). With such a long and growing list, the U.S. had better hope so.

Yet even if all those good productivity effects happen, losses of U.S. headquarters do matter. The most highly skilled (and highly paid) jobs are nearly universally located at headquarters. It is not for nothing that headquarters cities are more culturally dynamic than "branch plant towns." (Boston-area pundits and professors will begin to notice this as Wang, never having quite made it to the world's top 12 in computers, quietly disappears into the bureaucracy of IBM.) Headquarters also is where tax allocation decisions among countries are made. Perhaps even more important, R&D activities and jobs are concentrated at headquarters: the "transnational" corporation with R&D and decision-making jobs broadly dispersed among countries is, in the real world, a mythological beast, far more discussed than observed.

Others may argue—or hope—that small firms will ride to the rescue of U.S. industry and employment. But the success of the Japanese, Europeans, and Koreans argues that the relationship of scale and scope to cost and risk reduction, and ultimately to global competitiveness, has yet to be repealed. Small firms matter in the aggregate not when they are small, but when through technological, capital, and human investment they become large, globally dominant enterprises and create large numbers of well-paying jobs. And during the past 30 years, European, Japanese and newly industrializing country firms have been performing this transformation more effectively than have their American counterparts.

References

A.P. Chandler, "Underinvestment in American Industry: Is There a Short-Term Investment Perspective?" Unpublished draft manuscript, Harvard Business School, 1990.

L.G. Franko, "Global Corporate Competition: Who's Winning, Who's Losing, and the R&D Factor as One Reason Why," *Strategic Management Journal, 10* (1989a): 449-474.

L.G. Franko, "Unrelated Diversification and Global Corporate Performance," in A.R. Negandhi and A. Savara (eds.), *International Strategic Management* (Lexington, Mass.: Heath-Lexington Books, 1989b).

D. Lascelles, "Global Strategy: Banking on Boulevards to Build the Business," *The Financial Times*, Management Page, July 24, 1991.

R. Reich, "Who Is Us?" *Harvard Business Review*, January-February 1990, pp. 53-64.

"Special Report/The Global 500," *Fortune*, July 29, 1991.

D. Yoffie and R. Vietor, "International Trade and Competition in Global Telecommuncations." Unpublished manuscript, Harvard Business School, 1991.

Lawrence G. Franko is a professor of finance and strategy in the College of Management, University of Massachusetts at Boston, and a senior investment associate with ValueQuest, Ltd., Marblehead, Massachusetts.

U.S. COMPANIES COME BACK HOME

Tired of hearing about corporations that are giving up on America as a place to make things? Some have returned, and here's why they're glad they did.

Edmund Faltermayer

SO YOU THINK that the day Americans take electronic manufacturing jobs from Asians will be the day men bite dogs? Well, watch out, Fido. In Charlottesville, Virginia, GE Fanuc Automation turns out a new programmable logic controller—a kind of black-box drill sergeant for factory machines—that's twice as powerful and cheaper to make than one formerly sourced in Japan. And oh, yes. While other factories are laying people off, this one, part of a fifty-fifty joint venture between General Electric and Japan's robot giant, recently hired 60 production workers to meet demand.

GE Fanuc is not alone. FORTUNE turned up a score of companies, from high-tech electronics to low-tech apparel, that in recent years have discovered a little secret already known by foreign corporations erecting transplant facilities: The U.S. can be a dandy place to make things. A report by the Manufacturing Studies Board of the National Research Council, due early next year, will strongly endorse the view that more American manufacturers should consider coming home or switching to domestic suppliers of key components. The report's tentative title is *Dispelling the Manufacturing Myth: America Can Compete in the Global Marketplace*.

Has the arsenal of democracy halted its slide down the post-industrial path to decline? Maybe, but this is no time to breathe easier. Much of the manufacturing that has returned occupies special niches. All the camcorders and many of the best cars still come from Japan, and the U.S. runs a sizable deficit in manufactured goods despite the deeply discounted dollar. And it's not just American R&D that's lagging. According to *American Machinist* magazine, the U.S. ranked 21st among industrial countries in the purchase of metalworking machine tools per capita last year—behind Romania.

What kind of manufacturing *does* make sense in the U.S. these days? Look at the reasons why some companies that skipped off have skipped back:

■ THE NEW MATH OF LABOR COSTS. U.S. workers are no longer the world's factory aristocrats. Adjusted for inflation, their wages have essentially stood still since the late Sixties, while pay has climbed elsewhere. The return of the once sky-high dollar to levels that prevailed in the late Seventies has further narrowed the gap—or eliminated it. According to the Bureau of Labor Statistics, Germany's wages have leaped from 74% of America's in 1985 to 144% in 1990, and Japan's have moved from 50% to 87%. Even in Hong Kong, says Bud Konheim, president of the Nicole Miller apparel firm in New York City, "they don't work for a bowl of rice." Konheim, who moved his garment making across the Pacific in the mid-Seventies, has brought it all back.

■ PRODUCTIVITY GAINS. Some manufacturing operations have become so efficient that wages are almost irrelevant. Credit automation, working smarter, and new product designs that shrink the number of parts and simplify assembly. Direct labor used to comprise up to 25% of the cost of producing a key electronic module at Modicon, a company in Andover, Massachusetts, whose factory controllers compete with GE Fanuc's. Production was handed off to a Hong Kong contractor in 1988. But two years later, after Modicon was bought by Daimler-Benz's AEG unit, back it came. The labor content of today's Massachusetts-made module: a mere 5%. As a rule, says CEO George Fisher of Motorola, "the days of chasing low-cost labor are over."

■ QUICK RESPONSE. It's the Nineties, when customers wait until the last minute to order. Says William Wheeler, a Coopers & Lybrand partner specializing in manufacturing strategy: "What many companies compete on today is service—the ability to produce with lead times of a day or two." Speed is everything for Harbor Seal, a small outfit in Southern California that has begun making products formerly brought in from Taiwan and South Korea. The company's seals for the shafts of industrial pumps come in thousands of varieties. If a leaky one has shut down an American customer's pump, Harbor Seal can sometimes custom-make a replacement for same-day delivery—an impossible feat from across the Pacific.

■ FAST PRODUCT DEVELOPMENT. "Having the engineering in Boston and the factory in Singapore doesn't play out that well anymore," says Todd Hixon, vice president of the Boston Consulting Group. It's better, he believes, for the design and manufacturing folks to be physically close so that they can "talk elbow to elbow, modifying continuously." That kind of interaction became easier when AT&T moved some of its electronic circuitboard manufacturing from Hong Kong to a 2,000-employee plant in Richmond several years ago. The board is the electronics industry's basic platform for holding wiring, semiconductors, and other bits and pieces. "It's the last thing you design in a product," says Richmond AT&T executive Robert Heinz, "but the first thing you need, and it gets changed a lot."

■ BAD LUCK ABROAD. "We had our heads handed to us in Mexico," says Randy Snyder, president of Invalco of Hutchinson, Kansas, which makes industrial flow meters and oil field valves. His Achilles' heel: border hassles for goods shuttling between U.S. and *maquiladora* operations. Today ten Americans in Kansas have taken over electronic assembly and light machining work formerly performed by 30 Mexicans south of the border. The Kansans' pay is four times as high, but their productivity—along with less need for rework and lower turnover—puts Invalco ahead. Snyder says he won't return to Mexico even if it joins a free-trade area with the U.S. and Canada.

REPORTER ASSOCIATE *James A. Anderson*

From *Fortune*, December 30, 1991, pp. 106-108, 110-112. Copyright © 1991 by The Time Inc. Magazine Company. Reprinted by permission.

PATRIOTISM. Don't ignore it. Since 1985, Wal-Mart Chairman Sam Walton has been prodding his retail chain to buy American to help close the trade deficit. Signs at headquarters in Bentonville, Arkansas, proclaim that Wal-Mart has created or brought back 131,000 manufacturing and related service jobs. About 45 of them are at a Texas Instruments factory in Lubbock, Texas, that two years ago resumed making hand-held calculators after they had been produced entirely in Asia during a nine-year interim. Paul Greenwood, the TI manufacturing executive who spearheaded the revival, says he took the offshore move as "a major-league defeat. We wanted to prove we can be competitive." This year Lubbock will build over two million calculators, prominently labeled MADE IN U.S.A. and sold for $10 or less by Wal-Mart and other retailers.

The homeward movement has surfaced most visibly in America's $265-billion-a-year electronics industry. Just-in-time delivery was the deciding factor for Applied Digital Data Systems (ADDS) of Hauppauge, New York. This subsidiary of NCR, in turn part of AT&T, furnishes its corporate parent and others with computer terminals, mainly of the nonintelligent type and worth about $600 each. Just what you'd expect to procure in Seoul or Taipei, right?

Not anymore. ADDS farmed out production to Asian sources in 1985, only to resume production on Long Island five years later. The terminals come in 4,000 different combinations of screen color, keyboard, power supply, and other specifications, and the company likes to promise delivery in 48 hours or less. Keeping that pledge required maintaining a four-month inventory of finished products when terminals were sourced in Hong Kong, Taiwan, and South Korea.

That burden, says David Laws, ADDS's Australian chief executive, forced the company to study "what it really would cost" to produce a redesigned terminal in America. At $10 an hour, counting benefits, the wages ADDS pays on Long Island are about 3½ times higher than they would be in Hong Kong. But when freight and other savings got figured into the calculations, Laws says, "it was pretty much a push"—Australian for wash. Since production came home, ADDS has actually come out ahead by cutting its inventory of finished terminals and raw materials to one-eighth the former level.

In terms of value added, the amount of American manufacturing recaptured at Hauppauge is modest. "Make," in this case, means little more than assemble and test. Essentially, ADDS bakes a cake whose ingredients—picture tube, keyboard, chips—come overwhelmingly from the great Asian electronics mart.

The American content is higher at GE Fanuc, whose decision to produce at home was inspired by the declining dollar. The joint venture, headquartered at the foot of Virginia's Blue Ridge Mountains, is the successful remnant of GE's failed effort to sell turnkey "factories of the future." The most sophisticated programmable logic controllers were always made in Charlottesville. Low-end PLC's came from Koyo, a Japanese company.

By 1986, GE Fanuc decided it had to develop a homemade version. Production of low-end controllers, which sell for $300 to $1,500, got under way last year. These black boxes are a hit at home and abroad, and Charlottesville is working Saturdays to fill orders. Robert Collins, CEO of GE Fanuc North America, says, "We've exploded the myth that you can't produce competitively in the U.S., and with better quality." GE Fanuc just won an award given annually by Automation Forum, an industry-supported group, to companies that bring production back or decide against moving offshore.

Even if the dollar doubled, Collins says, the company would go on making the controllers in the U.S. The labor content is down to 5%, he explains, and these days it's important to look not only at labor and material costs but also at the "total cost" of getting a product to a customer, including the time value of fast service. From Charlottesville, made-to-order PLCs, tailored to the types of machines they electronically boss around, can be delivered with two weeks.

MOTOROLA ships its pagers even faster. Manufacturing cycle time at its plant in Boynton Beach, Florida, including insertion of a customer's individual code, is less than three hours. Four years ago, says Len DeBarrows, manufacturing vice president in Motorola's paging division, the company decided to "support markets by manufacturing from within those markets." Thus, the new $200 Bravo Express pager is made in Singapore for Asians but in Florida for Americans.

The U.S. content of the domestic Bravo is higher than in past pagers, DeBarrows says. He puts the figure at "upwards of 70%," including plastic case, circuitboards, display crystals, labels, and "most of the silicon," which comes from Motorola plants in Arizona and Texas. Because of the company's continuous improvement policy, he says, the circuitboard design is tweaked "every goddamn day." In the past it would have taken an Asian circuitboard maker three or four weeks to make a change. Now a domestic supplier—like the one DeBarrows can see from his window—furnishes modified boards in less than a week.

Tandy Corp. never stopped expanding its American factories. They were essential to keeping new products flowing to its Radio Shack stores. But two years ago the fourth-largest U.S. maker of personal computers shifted production of a popular model from Korea to Fort Worth, and the trend has been to bring production for domestic customers back home. Robert McClure, president of the company's Tandy Electronics manufacturing arm, claims a major reason is the need to shorten the interval between design and production.

At highly automated U.S. facilities, Tandy also makes notebook computers for its own label as well as for Grid and Victor, which it owns. It even supplies a competitor, Panasonic, through a joint venture agreement with Matsushita. The company aims to be vertically integrated when it comes to components. Excluding disk drive and screen, about 75% of a new $1,300 desktop com-

TEN THAT BROUGHT WORK BACK

COMPANY	PRODUCT	PREVIOUS SOURCE	WHERE IT'S MADE NOW
ADDS (part of AT&T)	Computer terminal	Asia	Hauppauge, New York
American Tourister	Softside luggage	Asia	Jacksonville, Florida
Chicago Pneumatic Tool	Impact wrench	Joint venture in Japan	Utica, New York
Esprit	30% of women's apparel	Asia	California and the Southeast
GE Fanuc Automation	Programmable logic controller	Japan	Charlottesville, Virginia
Modicon (part of Daimler-Benz)	Module for programmable logic controller	Hong Kong	Andover, Massachusetts
Nicole Miller	Apparel	Hong Kong	New York City and eastern Pennsylvania
Tandy	Desktop computer	South Korea	Fort Worth, Texas
Texas Instruments	Hand-held calculator	Asia	Lubbock, Texas
Xerox	Replaceable cartridge for desktop copiers	Japan	Webster, New York

FORTUNE TABLE

puter is American, says McClure. Assembly labor in such machines costs a mere 2%. Tandy is even gearing up for Texas production of digital compact cassette players—a business most people would assume has migrated permanently from American shores. Cordless phones too could "eventually" come back, McClure figures, as production becomes "a matter of just snapping things together."

AGGRESSIVE U.S. suppliers have played a part in bringing electronics manufacturing home. Cardinal Technologies, a private four-year-old company in Lancaster, Pennsylvania, has displaced a Taiwan company as the maker of display terminals for Quotron, owned by Citicorp. Cardinal chirped again when Xerox, abandoning a Korean source, picked it to make an interactive video-screen for a new high-performance copier now exported to a number of countries, including Japan.

Xerox straddles the boundary between electronics and a different manufacturing realm, that of big machines with moving parts. In such operations the cost of direct labor is higher, often approaching 10%, and the case for bringing production back to the U.S. is sometimes less compelling. But Xerox, for one, has already raised the American content somewhat in copiers for the home market. A line of desktop copiers features a replaceable $300 "copy cartridge" containing the basic xerographic system, including the copier's equivalent of film. The cartridges formerly came from Japan; now they're made in Webster, New York. Says Ray Stark, Xerox's vice president for materials management: "We are on the cusp of a substantial shift to dealing with suppliers engaged in the markets in which we sell."

Chrysler pledges allegiance to a similar credo. Says Thomas Stallkamp, vice president for procurement: "We prefer suppliers who are close geographically and domestically owned." In recent years the North American content of Chrysler's cars has fallen a bit, to 91% on average. But that includes a lot of items that the automaker used to import, such as corrosion-resistant steel, antilock braking systems, aluminum wheels, and compressors for car air conditioners.

For years some of Chicago Pneumatic Tool's power equipment has come from a fifty-fifty joint venture in Japan. But with currency fluctuations, says Richard Besser, CEO of the Swedish-owned company, "one year I'm a big winner and the next year a big loser." In addition, commitments to take Japanese tools sometimes produce inventory backlogs that "you wouldn't believe." By the end of 1994, he hopes to have "repatriated a significant portion of that block of tools back to the U.S." To Utica, New York, to be precise. Chicago Pneumatic has already introduced a new impact wrench, which is lighter, faster, and cheaper to make than any imported model.

Repatriation, it would seem, is a much tougher proposition with another class of goods: those stitched together as clothing or accessories. But style is changing this picture too. If consumers suddenly want a different color or shape and the unwanted stuff is coming from abroad, goods rapidly pile up.

About 85% of the softside luggage sold in the U.S. is imported, mostly from the Pacific Rim. Early this year American Tourister, a division of Hillenbrand Industries, turned to Dallas's Thomas Group for advice on how to get a jump on the competition. The suggestion: Move faster. "Asia is a long-cycle-time culture," says Philip Thomas, chairman of Thomas and a leading advocate of what he calls total cycle time, which entails "cutting out non-value-added steps wherever they are."

American Tourister's wait from order to delivery was running seven months. It didn't help that suppliers in Taiwan and Korea, to counter their own rising wages, had begun to manufacture in Thailand, the Philippines, and China. "That makes the lead times even longer," says Tom Korbas, senior vice president for operations. To telescope response time to 60 days, the company had to look homeward.

Today 95% of the materials for a growing portion of American Tourister's line come from the U.S., and the company has just opened a fabric-cutting plant in Jacksonville, Florida. Sewing is done in the Dominican Republic. Under the so-called 807 law, the company pays a tariff only on the 20% of value added there. U.S. manufacturing doesn't get the whole pie back, Korbas says, but it gets most of it.

APPAREL MAKERS were among the first to flee the U.S. In the late Eighties the exodus slowed, and it may even have reversed this year. One cause is temporary: A recession is on, and some debt-ridden retailers can't qualify for bank letters of credit to finance imports that take months to arrive. A more lasting reason, says Konheim of Nicole Miller, is the need to be nimble in a business where merchandise often enjoys the shelf life of lettuce. "Domestic sourcing means we never have to commit big to an idea in advance," says Konheim, whose business has doubled in the past year. "Instead, we have the luxury of seeing if it sells."

A lot of repatriated production, like Konheim's clothing, is upscale. At Cherry Tree, a two-year-old maker of children's outerwear in Rhode Island, labor eats up 30% of revenues, but speed gives it an edge. Says President David King: "Saks came to us with a November order in mid-October. There's no way they could have sourced that delivery with such short notice offshore." Three years ago Esprit, the San Francisco maker and retailer of casual wear, had nearly everything made in Hong Kong, Taiwan, and Singapore. Today, says vice president Phillip Lighty, 30% of the women's line is made in the U.S.

What if trade barriers disappear between the U.S. and Mexico? Would some of the rag trade returnees rush south? Esprit would consider it, Lighty says, if a free-trade area didn't drive up costs below the Rio Grande. No way, says Konheim, whose factories are in Pennsylvania's slate-mining region and in Manhattan's garment district. Says he: "I'm set for a long time."

It would be folly to expect a surge in production jobs from manufacturing's homeward movement, even if the trend gathers force. Except where a product is unique, American manufacturing must win by being the world's most efficient, like American agriculture. But just as a few million farmers support a vast food industry, work in the plant makes possible far more: service jobs, industries that supply equipment and raw materials, the enhancement of a company's production skills, and the ability to convert intellectual property from the R&D labs into the plump profits that come from getting to market first.

The new religion of speed is not only bringing some companies back but also deterring others from leaving. Digital Equipment, says Charles Christ, the company's vice president for mass storage systems, has just turned its production strategy "upside down." Looking for a place to manufacture a next generation of high-capacity disk drives for Digital and others, Christ scoured the globe.

To compete in that $10 billion market, Christ says, "conventional wisdom says you've got to go to the Far East." That may still be true of low-end disk drives for personal computers, he believes, but not for more sophisticated, higher-priced devices. Production will begin in six months, not in Singapore but in Digital's own plant in Colorado Springs. Says Christ: "You've got to get the new product cycle down to 12 to 18 months to stay in the hunt. That requires close coupling between design and manufacturing."

THE STAY-PUT MOVEMENT, as well as the homeward trek, needs no subsidies from Washington. But the tax treatment of new investment in equipment, which worsened considerably in the Eighties, needs adjustment. A dose of the old American can-do attitude would also help. Consider the electronics business that moved to Asia. "There's not much that comes from there that can't come from here," says Harold Krall, the upbeat RCA alumnus who runs Cardinal Technologies. "After five cups of sake, the Japanese will tell you they can't believe that we've essentially abdicated the whole thing." It doesn't take an act of Congress to stamp out defeatism.

GLOBETROTTER

Ken Reynolds brings a New World order to Baldwin Technology.

SARAH GLAZER

Sarah Glazer is a freelance writer based in Cambridge, Massachusetts.

The road has narrowed to two tree-shaded lanes, and the cab driver is asking once again if I'm sure we're not lost. I'm beginning to wonder myself. The coastal Connecticut village of Rowayton seems an incongruous spot for the headquarters of Baldwin Technology Co. Inc., a multinational manufacturer of material handling, control, and accessory equipment for printing presses.

A jumble of sailboats and fishing vessels appears on the right, bobbing up and down in Five Mile River, which flows into Long Island Sound. Is that it? The low gray building nestled at the water's edge? There is no corporate logo on the weathered clapboards, but this does appear to be the Baldwin building.

Inside, in a snug office facing a panorama of water and well-appointed cottages, Kenneth W. Reynolds, CFO and vice president of finance and administration, explains that Baldwin's unlikely location is no accident. It is indicative of the company's efforts to fight becoming a stuffy, top-heavy organization, despite a recent acquisitions spree and revenue spurt that put it squarely in the ranks of middle-market companies.

During fiscal 1990, ended last June 30, Baldwin logged $183 million in sales, up 45 percent from the previous year. During fiscal 1989, sales had jumped 31 percent. Although the $108 million in sales reported for the first half of fiscal 1991 was less than anticipated, one analyst says 1991 total sales should top $239 million. Looking further out, chairman and chief executive officer Wendell Smith predicts that revenues will double over the next five years. For his part, Reynolds will assure that "tight financial controls" coexist peacefully with Baldwin's ambitious expansion plans.

A cornerstone of Baldwin's business strategy is to hire foreign nationals to run its overseas units—an approach Reynolds describes with pride. "There are people in every country who are built to be entrepreneurs; some of them just don't know it. Give them the right incentives and the freedom to run their own shows" and you have a winning formula, he asserts. But to keep everything running on an even keel, he quickly adds, "you must have good control mechanisms, a clear delegation of authority." Indeed, for the past two and a half years, Reynolds, 52, has been boarding planes at a furious pace, helping to "bring logic and organization" to Baldwin's burgeoning network of small businesses.

A "lean and mean" extreme

Today, Baldwin has 42 separate business units (20 are operating companies) with manufacturing and product development taking place around the world. Overseas, it has plants in Germany, France, Sweden, England, and Japan. Even in the United States, manufacturing sites are scattered from Connecticut to California. Despite the company's far-flung operations, it has just nine people at the Rowayton office. "We may have the smallest corporate headquarters staff of any company our size," says Reynolds.

Relying on a skeleton crew composed of an assistant treasurer, a chief accounting officer, an assistant corporate secretary, an accountant, and three clerical assistants, Reynolds develops financing strategies for acquisitions, coordinates global cash and tax management, oversees all financial reporting tasks, and handles investor relations. "We all have to be ready to roll up our sleeves and help each other. For example, when we're in the middle of an acquisition, I do a lot of the due diligence work myself," Reynolds says. At times, he can be found burning the midnight oil in Rowayton, helping his staff meet reporting deadlines. Or he may be globetrotting with Smith, meeting an acquisition candidate or evaluating the financial infrastructure of a new business unit.

Baldwin's products range from automatic cleaning systems and ink control equipment to machinery that guides paper through presses and cuts and folds finished pages. It has two primary markets: first, manufacturers of printing presses, which resell a variety of accessories and controls to printing companies along with their presses; and, second, the printing companies themselves. The printing industry, Reynolds explains, is a robust and dynamic business arena. Worldwide, the market for printing equipment appears to be especially ripe "as developing countries begin to

From *CFO*, July 1991, pp. 22-26. *CFO*, The Magazine for Senior Financial Executives. Copyright © 1991 by CFO Publishing Corp.

lean toward democracy" and sanction public debate in the print media.

Reynolds's responsibilities often take him far from the typical CFO's turf—sometimes frighteningly far—like the day, two years ago, when he found himself camped near Beijing, just as student demonstrators were starting to mass in Tiananmen Square. He and Smith made two trips to China to see about setting up a new subsidiary there. On their first visit, they ended up "in Red Army barracks north of Beijing, negotiating with a commune for utilities and cafeteria rights for the new subsidiary." By the time of the second visit, political tensions had mounted, and "it was kind of scary to be standing there watching 17-year-old country kids marching around with AK-47s," Reynolds recalls. "Now how many CFOs have the opportunity to do that?"

Bursting at the seams

When Reynolds joined Baldwin in early 1989, he was faced with a less hair-raising but far more critical challenge: A series of recent acquisitions had made the company's completely decentralized organization untenable. Prior to the spate of acquisitions, "Baldwin had 18 units, and Wendell [Smith] was pulling it all together himself.

All the unit presidents were reporting directly to him," says Reynolds. But "the company reached a point where it needed a structure that would let it grow in a more logically controlled manner and let it integrate units and finance in local currencies in a tax-advantaged way. When I arrived, Baldwin was bursting at the seams," recounts Reynolds. For example, "we needed a way to be sure that the controller of the Swedish operation wasn't borrowing locally [above a set amount] and inadvertently causing a violation of the parent company's loan covenants."

Reynolds hunkered down with Smith and came up with a total corporate reorganization, a project that has just recently been completed. "We're now what I call 'plug-compatible.' If I buy a Dutch company, for example, I can structure it for the best tax advantage because I know what holding company to put it under," says Reynolds. He also proposed a uniform set of "control documents that allow for the delegation of authority in a decentralized environment." Reynolds's rules govern issues ranging from internal reporting to handling bad debts.

The delegation of authority became the battleground for a series of spirited debates between Reynolds and Smith about corporate controls. "Wendell kept accusing me of taking away the entrepreneurial spirit. He once said if it was up to me, we would have a book of procedures this thick," recalls Reynolds wryly, holding his hands more than a foot apart. "We compromised."

Smith agrees that he and the CFO are philosophically poles apart on the issue of controls. "We openly argue this point, even in front of the troops sometimes," says Smith, lean and athletic looking at 55. "I'll say, 'Come on, get off their backs, Mr. Vice President and CFO. Let them alone. These guys know how to run their business.' Yet, I admit that we have to know how things are going financially on a timely basis."

> *"It was scary watching 17-year-olds marching with AK-47s. How many CFOs have a chance to do that?"*

A veteran's perspective

Thanks to his long tenure and broad background in printing industry finance, Reynolds was able to hit the ground running when he joined Baldwin. A Chicago native, he joined printing behemoth Moore Business Forms and Systems Inc. in 1963, after a stint in the Navy. Reynolds spent 12 years with Moore in Chicago and in Dover, New Hampshire, moving through finance and internal audit to become the controller of a printing equipment plant. Meanwhile, he attended night school, earning his BA from the University of Connecticut.

From Moore, Reynolds went to Harris Corp., in Melbourne, Florida, joining the Harris Graphics division, which manufactured printing presses. As a planner and later a controller, he worked his way through each of the division's business units. After Harris Graphics was sold by its parent and eventually broken up, Reynolds spent two years as vice president of finance at the Modicon division of Gould Inc. Test and Measurement Group, in Rolling Meadows, Illinois. In a simple twist of fate, one of his responsibilities turned out to be selling the Gould division. In 1988, Reynolds found himself once again looking for a job.

It was "pure coincidence" that Baldwin needed a new CFO "just when I was available," says Reynolds. He had done deals with Smith in the past and was eager to work for "someone with a hands-off style. It's very exciting for a CFO to work for a guy like Smith who will let you run," offers Reynolds. The two men quickly agreed they could form an effective corporate team.

Shaping up, going global

The new blueprint divides the company's 42 units into three geographical sectors: the Americas, Europe, and Asia-Pacific. Each sector has a holding company that provides financial functions and managerial support, and a trading company, which provides distribution capability the local units lacked on their own. Individual business units, however, remain autonomous in many respects. Each unit is responsible for manufacturing, engineering, marketing, and finance, yet benefits from the access to capital and coordination of tax and cash management activities provided by the sector finance staff. Each of the three sectors has a CFO who reports to a sector president, but "the CFOs report on a dotted line to me," explains Reynolds.

The beauty of this organization from a financial standpoint, says Reynolds, is that the local business unit has control of its day-to-day affairs, but the company as a whole enjoys financial harmony. For example, each unit manages its own working capital, but the sector CFO secures loans for expansion or large equipment purchases. "Each unit has access to better credit terms and options, thanks to the clout wielded by the sector CFO who represents, say, a five-company entity," notes Reynolds. If a unit has trouble getting working capital, "the sector can guarantee the credit," he adds.

Reynolds's control guidelines spell out who signs off on what. For example, "I review capital expenditures over $250,000, while the controls are tighter at the sector or unit level," Reynolds explains. More important, tax, cash, and investment management are now far more efficient. Since the reorganization, Baldwin's overall tax rate has dropped from 58 percent to 49 percent, says Reynolds. And rather than repatriating profits from abroad, he prefers to leave cash overseas and invest it locally. "We don't have to worry about currency fluctuations that way. The ups and downs tend to balance each other out," he says.

Strategic decisions, such as joint ventures, are made by the unit's board of directors under the watchful eyes of Reynolds and Smith. The idea is to provide guidance but give the unit manager a true sense of responsibility. "There's a good reason why we don't consolidate things like purchasing or data processing. We want the unit manager to behave like an entrepreneur and cut the best deals he can for the things he needs." As far as developing annual operating plans, "we let the unit head set his own revenue targets, but that also means he has to hit the bottom-line targets he sets," says Reynolds. "If they low-ball their sales forecasts, they must also establish a proper head count and cost structure to give an adequate operating margin. We manage on a ratio basis."

The "highly fragmented" nature of Baldwin's business makes this structure more sensible than it might at first appear, explains Reynolds. While the whole corporation manufactures some 120 products, no single unit makes more than a dozen at most. The sector-level trading companies can take on the job of marketing Baldwin's overall product line throughout the three regions, allowing the individual business units to stay tightly focused on promoting the products they make to their traditional customer bases. "For example, it was difficult for our company in Kansas to sell its products in Taiwan," says Reynolds. "But now, it will have someone with a regional presence who can do deals easily." Even better, says Reynolds, "the company as a whole is benefiting from cross-fertilization. We're learning how to sell products globally. For instance, our people in Japan can take a product made in America and customize it for the Japanese market. If we tried to go in as Americans with an American product, it would be like trying to drive a Cadillac down a tiny Japanese side street."

As long as the individual units can stay lean and nimble enough to compete effectively in their own markets, Baldwin's size will be a formidable advantage, notes Andrew Beja, vice president of research for Advest Inc., an investment firm in Hartford. "They're in an enviable position," he says. "They're globally diversified, and their product line is diversified. When one area is down, another will be up. That's why they're solidly profitable when their smaller competitors are full of red ink."

Today, Baldwin's revenues are generated almost equally by its three regional sectors. This balance helps protect the company from the effects of regional economic slumps, as does its market being split between press manufacturers and printers, which have unique business cycles.

With his predecessor now serving as CFO for the Americas sector, Reynolds has been busy hiring and training the two other sector CFOs, who will operate—in true Baldwin fashion—with the leanest of staffs. The first hired was Yungyi Huang, an accountant from Beijing, who will take over responsibility for coordination of the Asia-Pacific sector, headquartered in Hong Kong. The rationale: "We don't think that as Americans we necessarily know how to do business in Japan, China, or any other country," says Reynolds. "The Germans, for instance, like to manufacture everything themselves, while Americans have a bias toward subcontracting. To put an American manager in charge of a German business wouldn't work. You can't impose American logic and controls that [other] people don't understand."

Daring deals

Despite the global nature of Baldwin today, until fairly recently it was a small, family-owned concern. The company was founded in 1918 in Baldwin, New York, by William Gegenheimer, the inventor of two widely used printing press accessories. Under the founder's guidance, and later his son Harold's steady hand, Baldwin continued to develop new products and to prosper. During the 1960s, Baldwin decided to rev up its international sales, and in 1966, Harold Gegenheimer hired Wendell Smith to provide the spark.

The third week on the job, Smith flew to Tokyo. Unaware of how difficult it was for most U.S. companies to gain a toehold in Japan, he rushed in where more experienced executives feared to tread. "I didn't know you couldn't do business in Japan," says Smith. He found Japanese partners and established a joint venture, one of the first such American-Japanese deals. Baldwin Japan Ltd., which in 1989 became a wholly owned subsidiary, is managed completely by Japanese nationals. It does business like a typical Japanese company—upholding rigid rules of protocol among employees and, in Reynolds's words, "doing business president-to-president."

In the late 1960s, Baldwin began to focus on domestic growth through acquisition. And like their Japanese counterpart, the new U.S. subsidiaries enjoyed an unusual degree of independence. "The combination of wanting foreign nationals to run our foreign businesses and making U.S. acquisitions that we wanted the former owners to continue to run, which meant plants were not relocated, built us automatically into a decentralized business," Smith observes.

In 1985, Smith got backing "from a group of investors" and organized a management buyout to purchase the company from the Gegenheimer family. In 1987, the company went public to pay back its debt; the stock is traded on the American Stock Exchange.

Defying the credit crunch

Reynolds joined Baldwin just in time to arrange the financing for the

Baldwin Collars Its Interest Rate Risk

A standard feature of mergers and acquisitions in the 1990s is likely to be a strategy for minimizing risks associated with leverage. The story of how Baldwin Technology Co. Inc. hedged the interest rate risk associated with a recent acquisition is a case in point.

In July 1990, Kenneth W. Reynolds, CFO and vice president of finance and administration, borrowed $45 million from a syndicate of U.S. and European banks to finance Baldwin's purchase of Misomex AB and Misomex of North America. Because of the leverage this transaction created, the credit agreement included language requiring Baldwin to obtain interest rate protection on 60 percent of its acquisition-related debt. Specifically, Baldwin had to limit its interest exposure to a LIBOR base rate of 9.5 percent over three years. Reynolds sought a method that would minimize hedging costs and help him avoid paying an upfront premium.

Manufacturers Hanover Trust Co., one of the syndicate banks, proposed a hedging technique known as PIRA (Participating Interest Rate Agreement) for three years. A PIRA is essentially a structured interest rate collar in which the notional principal on the cap is less than the notional principal on the floor. Like a standard interest rate collar, a PIRA protects a company from a rise in interest rates, and in exchange the company surrenders a portion of the benefits derived from a drop in interest rates.

With the PIRA, Baldwin hedged 60 percent of its acquisition debt at a LIBOR rate of 9.5 percent. But, because Baldwin simultaneously sold Manufacturers Hanover an interest rate floor of 8.33 percent for *100 percent* of the debt, it was able to achieve a lower-than-normal floor level at no cost.

In all, Baldwin obtained a floor 46 basis points lower than a straight collar and avoided paying an upfront premium. Of course, anytime LIBOR falls below 8.33 percent, Baldwin is obligated to pay the bank the difference between that rate and the prevailing market rate. That was the bet Reynolds was willing to make.

most ambitious acquisitions program in company history. In January 1989, Baldwin acquired Kansa Corp., in Emporia, Kansas, for $7.4 million, consisting of stock and $4.5 million in cash. In July, it acquired Enkel Corp., in Rockford, Illinois, for $22.3 million, made up of stock and $10 million in cash. In September 1989, it acquired part of Stobb Inc., in Clinton, New Jersey, for $1.3 million in cash and the assumption of $2.4 million in liabilities. Then, in July 1990, the company acquired Misomex of North America Inc., in Rosemont, Illinois, and Misomex AB, in Stockholm, for a total of $44 million in cash.

Before taking on the large Misomex deal, Reynolds decided to shore up the company's financial structure. Baldwin had only about $22 million in debt, but the additional $44 million it needed for the Misomex acquisitions would have made the company too highly leveraged, says Reynolds. "We decided to do a public offering to pay down the debt," he says. The company raised $24.5 million in an October 1989 stock offering.

Then a fly hit the ointment. When it came time to finance the Misomex purchase, Reynolds found himself a victim of the credit crunch that began to blight the U.S. banking scene in spring 1990. Seemingly overnight, U.S. banks "got caught up in the HLT problem," recalls Reynolds, in reference to banks sudden reluctance to lend to any company that wasn't a veritable blue chip. The banks feared loans to lesser credits would draw fire from federal regulators concerned about the amount of so-called highly leveraged transactions on the books of large commercial lenders. So, despite a healthy balance sheet, Baldwin was left out in the cold.

"One bank that would have done 100 percent of the deal three months earlier couldn't even take 10 percent of the deal," recalls Reynolds in amazement. Annoyed but undaunted, Reynolds resolved to "maneuver around the HLT scare" by looking overseas for financing. It wasn't long before he had assembled a syndicate of banks in the United States, Germany, France, and Sweden, and borrowed $45 million. Although Baldwin's current debt-to-capital ratio of 47 percent is "higher than we are comfortable with, we have the means to bring the debt down," says Reynolds.

With a new corporate structure in place, the company is ready for future growth. "By bringing logic to the company early on," says Reynolds, "we hope to avoid the problems that so many companies experience when they grow past a certain size." While Baldwin strives to manage its growing cadre of global entrepreneurs, Reynolds, who travels as much as one week out of four, is enjoying "a job I've prepared my whole life for." Describing a new unit just launched in Hungary, Reynolds's words tumble out in a flurry. "We have the chance to give somebody there an opportunity they've never known before. That's what's really exciting."

Corporate globalization: a new trend

Koh Sera, Sumitomo Corporation, Tokyo, Japan

Mr. Koh Sera is General Manager of Sumitomo Corporation's Communications Development Group in Tokyo. He has wide experience in international business having worked for extensive periods in the U.S. and Europe. He is a graduate of the University of Tokyo earning a B.A. in American Studies. He has tri-lingual fluency in French, English and Japanese.

Executive Overview

The internationalization and globalization of world markets has forever changed the way that companies must conduct business. Until recently, manufacturers believed in the strength of goods created from self-complacent concepts. Today's wealthier and more selective consumer expects products that reflect status, provide comfort, and save time.

This viewpoint article explores the issues and ramifications to business and society that are associated with the corporate globalization trend. The author draws on his experience at Sumitomo Corporation located in Tokyo, Japan to illustrate his viewpoint.

In My View

As economic borders rapidly lose their strong demarcations, each corporation must rethink its challenge in dealing with the new global economic environment.

Internationalization and Globalization

It is necessary at the outset to define the terms internationalization and globalization. Globalization, in particular, has not even been printed in the dictionary until fairly recently, as it has been merely four or five years since business people started to use it. This word is profusely and easily used, because it exactly characterizes the reality occurring in the business world—"the big changes." Until recently the international interrelationship among businesses of various nations was defined as internationalization because the term globalization did not exist. These two words are not synonymous, and therefore should be used selectively in their respective meanings.

What then, is the difference in the meanings between these two words? In my opinion, internationalization connotes expanding interfaces between nations sometimes even implying political invasion or domination. Internationalization of business, therefore, is a concept of an action in which nationality is strongly in people's consciousness. It means the flow of business, goods or capital from one country into another. Globalization, by contrast, looks at the whole world as being nationless and borderless. Goods, capital, and people have to be moving freely. In the current corporate environment, where capital funds have to be used efficiently, borders between nations have less significance; people are least concerned about their nationality. Globalization is a reality that has emerged out of the needs of the contemporary world. It is not as nationality-conscious or intrusive as internationalization.

Invasion and Expansion

Having worked in Europe, the United States, and Asia for more than thirty years with Sumitomo Corporation, an integrated trading company, I have watched the

From *The Executive*, Vol. 6, No. 1, February 1992, pp. 89-96. Copyright © 1992 by The Academy of Management Executives, a quarterly journal for professionals in the management field.

company on its course of international expansion. Sumitomo has accomplished its expansion by adding overseas offices, increasing the numbers of rotating Japanese staff, and employing national staff in each locality.

The status of most overseas offices have changed in the meantime, from simple liaison or representative offices into branch offices as profit centers, and finally into companies incorporated by the laws of the nations where the offices are located. Internationalization has thus made its rapid progress. Past growth had been achieved for a variety of reasons: because the volume of trade had increased, because it was better to establish a national entity in that locality to deal with tax issues, or because changes in the political or social situation, had made it possible for the company to set up a new office there. Not all the offices are productive, but they are in place in expectation of prospective profit in the long term, or have a flagship office in a strategic market. These measures have been taken to comply, and catch up, with the changing circumstances outside the company. By nature, they were patchworks, produced out of passive and reactive posture. They might as well be called 'band-aid remedies' that were administered to cope with a new situation each time it arose.

Japanese corporations in the manufacturing sector have been no exception to the trend. Automobile manufacturers have sought new production units in the U.S., Europe, and Asia so they could secure these markets in which they used to sell Japanese-made cars. Some woodpulp manufacturers made investments in forest-rich countries enabling permanent access to a woodchip supply, the raw material for virgin pulp. A cement manufacturer, largely dependent on the U.S. market for its exports but plagued by repeated anti-dumping lawsuits, examined the feasibility of building and operating a bulk cement distribution center in the U.S. in partnership with its U.S. counterpart. By this, the Japanese cement manufacturer thought it could alleviate and better handle trade friction with U.S. cement manufacturers.

These are only a few examples of moves toward internationalization that occurred in the 1960s and '70s. Irrespective of the difference between business sectors the approach was the same: "Specific remedies for specific symptoms." It had been just like administering pain-killer Tylenol for pains; or prescribing Bufferin for high fever. In a nutshell, they were nothing more than tactical relief measures. Through such processes, considerably reactive as they were, people in the world witnessed more and more foreign goods coming into their own markets. Increasing numbers of people experienced foreign travel. They were less xenophobic and people cared less about national identity when purchasing goods. For example, consider a typical Japanese shrimp dish called "Tempura Udon." The major ingredients of noodles, deep-fried shrimp, soy sauce, and even chopsticks are imported. Leeks and water are the only ingredients obtained domestically.

Amazing 1980s

Internationalization, however, entered a new epoch in the early 1980s. People witnessed unprecedented changes in their lives and lifestyles.

First and foremost, they have become wealthier as reflected in the figures of per capita GNP (in 1988, US$19,813 in U.S.A.; US$23,382 in Japan—source: Bank of Japan, Comparative International Statistics 1989). This indicates that the citizens of developed countries are not living from hand to mouth, but are enjoying an upgraded quality in food, clothing, and housing.

For example a Japanese bride, by custom, is to bring several household appliances and some furniture into her new home as dowry for the marriage. In the early 1960s, a Japanese bride was to provide a washing machine, refrigerator, and TV set. In the 1970s, an air-conditioner, microwave oven, and stereo audio set was expected. Now, in addition to these items, more sophisticated products such as a home computer, satellite TV set, and a CD audio-visual set could be included on her dowry list. Young consumers have become wealthier, so they can afford to buy more expensive items.

The quality of Japanese life has also been greatly improved. Chairs used to be simply for sitting in, but now they have become aesthetic goods used for home decoration. The kitchen is no longer a place where cooking appliances are brought in at random to prepare foods. Now, thanks to the comfort that a well-designed system-kitchen provides, it is a place where a homemaker spends a pleasant time watching TV or reading magazines as well. Trains and buses do not simply provide mass transportation anymore; they are now temperature-controlled for warmth and coolness, so passengers can enjoy an optimum atmospheric amenity. For many people automobiles are already a part of their total living environment. Ownership of cars is no longer only for utilitarian purposes, but for luxury and pleasure as well. It is often the manifestation of social status.

People have become more particular and diversified in their lifestyles. They do not want to own a car that others are driving. They want to feel that the car they drive is different in some respects from all other cars. Hong Kong, Hawaii, and Guam are no longer on Japanese honeymooners list of destination spots. Instead, Bali, Seychelles, or Maldives are attracting honeymooners, mainly because they are unusual and somewhat new. The Japanese used to enjoy a variety of Japanese, Chinese, and Western style foods; now in addition to those, they are after so-called ethnic dishes that hold more exotic interest, such as Cajun, Moroccan, and Thai cuisines. Different things are more attractive, more appealing.

There is also increased interest in fashionable articles with exclusive brands. Expensive jewels, brand-name handbags, gorgeous watches, designer-clothing are the symbols of the contemporary lifestyle that satisfy more than minimum necessity. Often they are desired because they are prestigious and enhance the user's perception of their own identity. Purchasers are ready to pay more for the brand name, in addition to the product's practical utility. This is an amazing phenomenon for businesspeople who have long been used to negotiating on price. To illustrate, physical exercise is no longer practiced in a dark and bleak gym as a tough, muscle-twisting torture. Today it is enjoyed in a posh sport-plaza equipped with shiny machines with high-tech calorie-indicators. After perspiration, the participant, colorfully clad in body-hugging spandex can relax by chatting in a cozy coffee shop adjacent to the club.

Consumers are now more willing to pay more money for something invisible or intangible, things that cannot be kept for long-time appreciation. Instead of investing money only for precious art works or for expensive antiques, that can be kept for a long time and later resold for capital gains, contemporary people spend money for overseas trips, live concerts, theatrical play watching, and golf-matches—all activities that are experienced and appreciated only on the spot. They want to enrich, not merely their attics or sitting room walls, but also their own hearts with something that quenches their intellectual and artistic thirst. They want to have some unusual experience even at the sacrifice of some necessities.

People also want technology that saves them time and are easy to use. Most people wouldn't buy a camera if not equipped with an auto-focusing and automatic light-exposure adjustment system; people prefer to use a vacuum cleaner that can monitor various surface conditions of the floor, and set itself in the best cleaning conditions by means of a 'fuzzy' sensor system. Car-drivers give preference to a car that has an automatic cruising device.

The last, but not least, trend in modern buying behavior is that buyers, users, or consumers do not care much about the nationality of products. As long as the commodity meets their specific needs, its country of origin is not important. Honda cars made in the U.S., Coca-cola produced in Singapore, Burberry's raincoats tailored in Japan under license, and Kellogg's cereals made in Korea are only a few examples of popular items the Japanese buy. What is good is good anyway, wherever it is made. It's not producers' confidence in nationality or traders' hard-sell efforts that open potential users' wallets. On the contrary, it is because of the users' choice and appreciation that one sole item is selected out of many competing alternatives.

Borderless World

Europeans have been counting the days to witness the birth of the European Economic Community in 1992. The EC-92 is the epitome of the borderless economy, in its significance and magnitude. People in the European Community agreed that it would be wiser for them to remove their economic borders and unite into one market, despite the differences in national ego and interests.

I define August 21, 1989 as one of the most significant days since World War II ended. On that day about 660 East Germans who had gathered in Hungary near the Austrian border, allegedly to participate in a peace rally, suddenly rushed across the border into Austria. History showed later, that this was the very beginning of the subsequent collapse of the Eastern European order that had been dominant throughout the après-guerre era. In a mere 3 months of time thereafter, the Berlin Wall was destroyed. In less than a year after the Wall collapsed, two Germanies were unified into one; Indonesia opened diplomatic relations with China; and The Republic of Korea has entered into an official relationship with the USSR.[1]

Changes have occurred not only in the Western/Eastern relationship, but inside the Eastern world as well. *Perestroika* released the Soviet's satellite countries from the communist's tight rein and accelerated liberalization of each member country. In August 1991, the movement proved itself to be firmly rooted, when the attempted coup failed in only a few days. It didn't take much more time then, until the Soviet Union had to allow the member republics to become independent. Even in Albania, a maverick among the Eastern European communist circle, there are reports about the people's rise for more freedom.

What has caused such monumental and rapid change is a question everybody must be asking. I believe that it is because of communication facilitated and prompted by current technology. People have much easier access than ever before to international news.

The circumstances as such have already disabled the tyranny of oppressing poor people for long without receiving wide-spread criticism. They have also revealed that Eastern Europe's ostensible military strengths were built on fragile economic ground. Thus, politically and socially, the basis for globalization, or interlocked relations across borders, are coming into reality. Globalization, therefore, is the natural corollary of the richness and diversification of people's lives combined with increased communication—borderless by nature.

Corporate Globalization

Any company that fails to catch up with recent trends and fit into the new environment, will perish. How then are companies to survive and prosper?

First, customers' (or users') needs must be identified. Until recently, manufacturers believed in the strength of goods created from their self-complacent concepts. As long as those goods satisfied people's minimum living requirement which was at a level far lower than today, users would buy those goods with little complaint. A low price used to be the most attractive point in purchases.

In the business world today, it is imperative for a supplier to listen carefully to users' needs in usefulness, usability, function, effectiveness, aesthetics, and after-purchase services of the good. Now users dominate the market; the time of suppliers controlling the market is gone for good. Japanese consumers know that good quality semi-conductor chips can be obtained in Malaysia at cheaper prices. American consumers are interested in Japanese small-sized cars for quality, reliability, and economic advantage.

Sumitomo Corporation has a joint-venture with Otto Versand of Germany, the world's largest women's apparel sales company by direct-mail order system and is the parent company of Spiegel. The joint-venture's solid strategy is and will continue to be that it will only cater to the needs of female consumers. Hence, merchandising, or the identification of the market propensity for commodity, is of utmost importance to this company.

The Japanese government, as opposed to the private sector, has been gradually transforming in accordance with the changing environments. Each one of the governmental ministries had long positioned itself as regulatory office for suppliers, providers, and manufacturers for any industry. It has had little concern for consumers, users, weak citizens, handicapped persons, or senior citizens. (Ironically, contrary to what many foreigners claim, the Japanese government has not been recognized as the sweet and helpful patron even in the eyes of some industries, but rather as a giant that tended to interfere, regulate, and control the industries to a great extent.)

For many years, the Ministry of Finance (MOF) has been known for the stringent regulations it imposed on financial institutions in Japan. It appears so strict that in the eyes of foreign people, banks and securities companies seem to have little management autonomy. In actual fact, the government and the private sector apparently work together in harmony. Some may believe that the notorious "Japan Inc." case is typically applicable here, and that banks and securities companies have been enjoying MOF protection in the name of regulation.

Fortunately, some signs of improvement in the Japanese government dealings is occurring with the changing economic environment. Even the MOF has begun to loosen its rigid control over financial institutions. It is endeavoring to deregulate savings and loans interest rates. It is also reducing regulations previously set to define the roles of banks, securities companies, and insurance companies, each of which had been confined inside its own territory of activity. Recent outside pressure to deregulate and create a more open and free financial market in Japan has caused the MOF to decrease its bureaucratic interference.

Autonomy of local branches and de-nationalization are the essence of a successful corporation that wants to develop a business with a global outlook.

What must not be forgotten is the surge of environmental issues. Industrial negligence has long contributed to the destruction of the environment. Polluted industrial waste water, acid rain, greenhouse warming effect, nuclear waste radiation, devastation of tropical rainforests are all reasons why our planet is becoming unlivable. These culprits do not choose nationality. Pollution travels everywhere—over the borders—as in the disastrous Chernobyl nuclear power unit meltdown. To deal with the borderless environmental disasters, people also need to take global and borderless measures, both at governmental and corporate levels.

Another issue that needs to be examined is where companies make their business decisions. Most Japanese companies engaged in international business activities have corporate headquarters in Tokyo. Strategic decisions are, therefore, made in Tokyo, and are then conveyed to their overseas branches for execution. The reality, however, is that New Yorkers know more about New York than Tokyoites.

How can Tokyo headquarters be so presumptuous as to believe that they can make better decisions about good community relations in their overseas offices than the nationals? It makes more sense for the local people to deal with legal matters and the like than the executives in Japan. In our rapidly changing business environment, constantly asking headquarters for a decision and direction will surely cause the local branch office lost business opportunities. Instead, if a company is globally coordinated and two-way communications between the headquarters and their overseas offices are feasible, it is truly a global corporation, and on the path to survival.

A global corporation is an added-value inventor and provider. At Sumitomo Corporation, my team is currently performing a feasibility study of a public relations business. The main role of a P.R. agency is to create added-value in its client companies through consultation, on the basis of which they will use communication as a powerful means to establish their corporate objectives and strategy. Although Japan is still in its infancy in regard to the awareness of the importance of strategic communication, some Japanese companies are beginning to accept the idea that communication is a strong weapon for the corporation to fight and survive in this inexorably competitive world.

Each company should find a unique added-value. One camera maker has created a huge success by selling a 2,000 yen (or $16) throw-away camera with a twelve exposure film and flash mounted in it. A Japanese laundry dryer manufacturer has introduced a laundry washing machine with a dryer equipped on top of it. It was highly successful because of the extremely limited extra space in most Japanese homes. Refrigerators with automatic ice-cube makers and soft-chilling storage-tray combined with the main body; and elevators with auditory devices that call each floor's number for the handicapped, are only a few more examples. Adding value on ordinary and conventional goods and services creates a tremendous differentiation over competitors, and customers will buy your goods—even over the border.

Money Game

Cross-the-border capital flow is the most dramatic and ultra-modern phenomena of globalization. According to the 19th century textbook of international trade, monies that traveled over country borders were mainly the counter-value of goods that were traded to the opposite direction. As time went on, overseas investments became routine and more diversified. Investment in foreign countries used to be a way to support and strengthen existing trade transactions. Today, more investments are made purely for capital return.

In Japan there is a new business term "*Zaiteku*," an artificial word (that sounds like high-tech) derived by combining *zaisan*, which means assets or wealth, and technology. The word describes the reality of corporations making profits through pure capital maneuvering. In other words, manufacturers are less dependent on product sales for profit. While the value of total world imports and exports was about US $5 trillion in 1989, the magnitude of the capital flow in the same year was estimated at US $102 trillion. Thus, capital flow was twenty times the size of trade volume of goods.

Consequently, more companies are less interested in getting profit out of their manufactured goods. Instead, they are chasing higher interest rates across the border and nervous about the fluctuations of foreign-exchange rates. They are figuring out what country risks to take into consideration and they daydream about good returns of capital investment.

This trend has induced the so-called "hollowing" of solid industries throughout the world. In reflection of this trend, until the Black Monday shock and the subsequent appearance of a recessive stock market, college graduates who had studied technology or engineering had been less interested to work in manufacturing or technological sector, but rather sought jobs in securities companies. In Japan, a similar trend prevailed until the "Bubble Economy" began to collapse in early 1990, following a sharp drop in stock prices.

Money used to be a means to buy goods. People have long desired money (and gold) because of its convertibility into goods. Now that the total volume of capital flow in the international market is dozens of times greater than that of the world trade of goods, money has gradually lost its significance of convertibility with goods and services. Money has become the most important merchandise to deal with in business. This trend has enormously increased the degree of gain or loss accrued out of such money games. Some individual and corporate investors incur big losses. So big is the magnitude of the losses that it is beyond their control and compensation capabilities. The amount that an investor company spends for an M&A deal is sometimes greater than the company's paid-in capital value. Where these excessive money-games will take us is a big question. Is this really a sound and solid practice for an economy and business?

If the world's economy is not built on a substantive and solid basis, and if people become more interested in the short-lived and speculative money games, there will be little difference between business and gambling.

In Japan, for the last year and a half, we have witnessed certain deterioration of our economy which had been flourishing. The ever-soaring stock prices and astronomically high land values once created inflated collateral for money lenders. Fragile and transient as soap bubbles, such an economy was to dissipate, sooner or later. A misuse or abuse of borderless economic transaction will lead the corporate structure into decay.

Epilogue

A healthy and desirable investment is accomplished through a long-term perspective and by use of risk management. Capital should not be invested abroad only to bring profits back to the home country. It should contribute to the benefit of the host country or the community that receives the investment. Therefore, monies used and profit accrued through over-the-border investments should not be repatriated quickly. The off-shore investment that is really welcomed and appreciated is the one that is not homebound, but one whose capital gain should be reinvested outside home to produce more added-value. It is like the Pilgrim Fathers that came into the land of opportunity, never to go back to England. Capital has no nationality per se. At this point, the borders are rapidly phasing out in economic and financial terms. In light of this fact, corporate viability and prosperity largely depend on the company's comprehensive awareness of the current business environment, which is borderless.

It is apropos to consider a quote from a speech made by Richard von Weizsaecker, president of new Germany, on October 3, 1990, the day of the German unification. "Those who believe that one country alone can open a way into the future are merely living in the past."

Endnote

[1]This article was written prior to the breakup of the U.S.S.R. in 1991.

Stepping Up to Global Competition

Interview with Harold A. Poling chairman, CEO, Ford Motor Company

Harvey Kahalas, University of Massachusetts Lowell

Harvey Kahalas is dean of the College of Management, professor of Management, and executive director of the Center for Industrial Competitiveness at the University of Massachusetts Lowell. He recently served as executive director of the General Motors/New York State Project on Industrial Effectiveness and Economic Development. Professor Kahalas has held positions with Ford Motor Company and a major U.S. governmental agency as well as serving as the dean of the School of Business at the State University of New York at Albany, a fellow at the Rockefeller Institute of Government of the State University of New York, and on the faculties of Virginia Polytechnic Institute and State University, and Worcester Polytechnic Institute.

Kathleen Suchon, University of Massachusetts Lowell

Kathleen Suchon is assistant professor of Management in the College of Management and Director of the Center for Industrial Competitiveness at the University of Massachusetts Lowell. She has had a wide variety of research, consulting and training experiences in the public, private, and not-for-profit sectors. Professor Suchon received a BA degree from the University of California at Berkeley, and an MBA and PhD from the State University of New York at Albany.

In My View

"You not only have to meet the needs and expectations of customers, you have to exceed them . . ."

During the eighties we witnessed the apparent unraveling of what had once been the proudest of American industries. In the face of foreign competition, largely Japanese, the domestic auto industry appeared paralyzed. In fact, during this critical period, the big three domestic automakers were treated to a crash course in global competitiveness. The stakes were high, mistakes were costly, and strategies were eventually reconfigured to meet the new cost, quality, and marketing challenges.

Ford Motor Company has earned a reputation as the U.S. automotive company that has most effectively refocused its operations to meet global competition and CEO Harold (Red) Poling was instrumental in developing and implementing its strategy. In 1980, after leading Ford of Europe to record earnings as its president, he took over as executive vice president of Ford Motor Company in charge of North American Automotive Operations.

In that capacity, in the midst of huge domestic losses during the early eighties, Poling took part in the senior management decision to approve a $3 billion new car program that put Ford's future on the line. Said Poling, "We bet the company. It was a tremendous gamble, but it has paid off." The strategy was to win while losing—to move forward with the fundamental changes that would ultimately restore profitability. And indeed, in 1983, when Ford achieved the greatest turnaround from a loss position in U.S. corporate history, Poling was given much of the credit.

Poling also established the single-minded focus on quality that has become the

From *The Executive*, Vol. 6, No. 2, May 1992, pp. 71-82. Copyright © 1992 by The Academy of Management Executives, a quarterly journal for professionals in the management field.

hallmark of Ford's operating and marketing strategies. While heading North American Automotive Operations, he was instrumental in gaining the assistance of W. Edwards Deming, the quality guru so long respected by the Japanese and ignored by Americans. With the guidance of Dr. Deming, and Poling's demonstrated, bottom-line commitment to quality principles, Ford was the first domestic automaker to effectively implement a comprehensive quality program. That early success proved critical in re-establishing Ford's reputation with the American public.

Poling became COO of Ford Motor Company when he was named president in 1985. In 1987 he was appointed vice chairman, and he has been chairman of the board and CEO since 1990.

Poling was among the twenty-one business leaders that accompanied President Bush on his recent trip to Japan. He was invited because of the importance of the auto industry to the overall trade relationship with Japan—a relationship that is currently receiving close scrutiny. While in Japan, Poling reiterated his position that Japan must assume greater responsibility for balance within the world trading system.

As CEO of a multinational that has long relied on foreign as well as domestic markets, in an industry that continues to experience phenomenal levels of competition worldwide, Poling sees trade and productivity issues in a broad context. He does not seek protection for the domestic auto industry. Instead he advocates more open markets worldwide. He is convinced that U.S. companies can and must succeed by producing world-class products and services. This is the strategy he has pursued as CEO. Ford's response to the changing competitive environment in the global automotive industry has been a strong, and fundamentally successful, focus on restoring product quality while improving productivity.

In this interview, Poling reflects on the changes that have taken place at Ford. He assesses the current and future prospects for the auto industry—focusing on world markets, recurring issues of capacity, cost and quality, and workforce prospects. Also, as a veteran of many years of competition with the Japanese, he provides broad suggestions for American managers and policy makers in meeting the challenges they pose.

Question:
How would you describe global competition in the auto industry today?

HAROLD POLING:
Competition today is more intense than it's ever been. A major reason is that we have substantial world-wide excess capacity. We estimate that in a normal situation—without a U.S. recession—there's a world excess capacity of about 8.4 million units, and about 6 million are directed at the U.S. market. For example, a North American customer now has the opportunity to choose among 650 different car and truck models compared with about 530 ten years ago. As a result we have heavy competition for market share, and that's causing very costly marketing programs, and putting severe pressure on margins for everyone. That situation will intensify in Europe.

By 1993 the capacity of the Japanese manufacturers will reach about 800,000 units. Whether the market grows fast enough to absorb the additional capacity that's being created, largely by the Japanese who are initiating a very aggressive attack on automotive markets around the world, remains to be seen. The excess capacity level we have currently may actually increase in the years ahead.

A great deal of the excess capacity appears to be directed at the U.S. market.

It's the most open market, and the easiest one to access. There are three basic

automotive markets in the world: the U.S., European, and Asian. The most open is the U.S. market, the next is Europe, and the last is Asia.

What do you think of the prospects for the Asian market?

There are good growth prospects in Asia during the next ten to fifteen years. China will eventually represent a significant opportunity and our operations in Taiwan, which are very strong, could provide us a good entree into that market. It's very difficult to get into markets such as China because they want you to come in and export to generate hard currency. It will take some time before they're in a position to compete with the West in terms of quality and efficiency in automobile manufacture.

Interestingly enough, worldwide, I think that the main growth in the next ten to fifteen years will occur in markets where most major manufacturers have little or no presence today: Eastern Europe, Russia, India, China, and other Pacific Rim countries.

Do you think that at some time Japan could be a growth market for Ford?

I'd like to think so. We do currently export to Japan, but our penetration there isn't good. I think it's really questionable whether Japan will be a massive market for anybody unless approaches are changed.

My view of global markets and free trade is that the major economic powers have a responsibility to provide an example for their global trading partners. But the major economic powers must move in concert, and one country should not take the leadership role to the detriment of its economy. Any one of the major powers that maintains a high and chronic imbalance of trade with another is doing a disservice to global trade, and I think it's their responsibility to modify that. If they don't, then the other power should address the problem. It provides a poor example in terms of free trade, it severely impacts the economy of the country that's attacked, and I think there's no justification for it.

We have proven in our approach to free trade with Japan that the micro approach does not work. We pick out a little thing here and there and look at the trade balance—nothing really happens. The Japanese should be given five years to correct it. Get down to plus or minus five or ten billion dollars. It doesn't have to be zero—there will always be fluctuations. But there shouldn't be very high imbalances.

So you would prefer to see some form of managed trade between the U.S. and Japan.

Free trade was great when I took economics in college, but that isn't the real world. There are no free trading countries in this world. There are relative degrees of protectionism. The objective of achieving conditions as close as possible to free trade is something we should strive for, but all the major economic powers should work together. If we're going to help the developing countries of the world then we have to provide a market for their products so that they can generate hard currency and purchase products from the developed world. If a major economic power maintains a high imbalance of trade with other developed countries that relationship channels resources away from the developing countries around the world. I think that such a coordinated approach to trade would be beneficial to the global economy. Without such an approach the risk is high that the global economy will not mature properly.

So you're not talking about special protection for particular products or industries, but rather a macro-level management approach.

The major economic powers ought to work together on this. We do not have large problems with our other trading partners. And other countries would not

tolerate the imbalances we have with Japan. You know the European Community is not going to say to Japan, "Come on in the water's fine. We're going to treat you just like they do in the United States." They're not going to do it. They're coming over here to learn what we did wrong to prevent the same thing from happening in the Community.

What do you think of the Japanese transplants in the U.S.?

Japanese coming in and locating a plant in the United States certainly have some human resource cost advantages. They can pick up an advantage of $5 to $10 an hour by virtue of not having the pension or the medical benefit costs of the domestic manufacturers. That creates a significant disadvantage for the domestic manufacturers. Also, it's unfortunate that the Japanese don't attempt to utilize the domestic suppliers, but want to use Japanese, or Japanese transplant, suppliers. Most people say, 'look at the tremendous number of jobs the Japanese bring to this country.' Well, many are still imported products from domestic content standpoint. They have fifty percent or less domestic content, and to be considered domestic you have to have seventy-five percent domestic content. If you're substituting a transplant product for a domestic-made product, you're giving up jobs.

You're giving up the supplier chain as well.

Absolutely. And so it's really costing jobs in this country. Another unfortunate misperception is that domestic manufacturers used the voluntary import restraints as a basis for increasing prices. That is wrong. You go back to 1985—and I pick that time because that was the Plaza Accord—the Japanese increased their prices twenty percentage points more than domestic manufacturers, significantly more than the rate of inflation, and we increased our prices less than the rate of inflation. Those are the facts. Or you can go back to 1980, and a similar pattern is involved. In 1981 when we introduced the Escort, it was priced higher than comparable Japanese products; today it's priced about $800 lower.

What do you think of the competitiveness of Ford's product line compared to Japanese products?

I think we have done an extremely good job with the competitiveness of our products—from a product, quality, and cost standpoint. Ford hit a low point at 16.6% of the car market in 1981. We ended up 1989 with 22.3%. That's a pretty dramatic improvement, and compares very favorably with the total increase by all the Japanese in this country. I think that demonstrates that if you design, develop, and produce products that meet the requirements of the customer—that have good quality—you can succeed.

In the nineties, quality's got to be a given. We will be competing for customer satisfaction, and that includes the way customers are treated from the moment they walk into a dealership, when they take their purchase back for service, and until they complete the process by hopefully going back and buying another Ford or Lincoln-Mercury product. We have a very aggressive program working with our dealers to provide them the tools to meet our objective of providing the best customer satisfaction.

The Japanese have excelled at integrating their dealers with the rest of their operations. How is Ford doing?

We have customer satisfaction research data for each of our dealers, not based on our assessment but based on their own customers' assessment of how they believe the dealership treats them. The average for all our dealers was 8.3 last year on a scale of 10, and that has improved each year in the last seven since we started measuring it. Our most prestigious award for the dealers has been

awarded for seven years now. The first year we made the presentations to the dealers there were 89 winners, and as each one came up to accept the award they said, "we'll be back next year." Equally important, or maybe more so, were the number of letters I got from dealers that didn't win who said they'd win the next year. There's tremendous competition among the dealers to provide quality service, and the customer's the winner. To the customer, dealers are the face of Ford. As they are perceived, so are we. The good dealers see the benefit of it. It turns into the bottom line. Customers will change products, they'll change dealers if they can find a dealer that treats them the way they think they should be treated.

How do you see Ford positioned in the European market?

I think we're well positioned. Our strongest market is the UK, we're a significant player in Germany and Spain, and we've improved our position fairly substantially in France and Italy.

It's been said that Ford of Europe is a European car company.

That's the approach that U.S. domestic companies have used in competing with the rest of the world. We've become effective corporate citizens of the areas in which we sell our cars, as opposed to initiating an export program from our country. And we have totally integrated operations in Europe. The Japanese, in the last part of the decade, have just started to locate around the world, and only because of pressure. They would much rather export from Japan.

Let's focus specifically on Ford's goals, its operations, and the U.S. auto industry. What are Ford's strategic objectives in its automotive business?

Our objective is to maintain a strong position in our markets and then move into the growing markets around the world in a responsible fashion as those markets develop and our resources are available to capitalize on opportunities. I have personally been a little conservative on the approach to Eastern Europe. There have been a lot of very aggressive moves and some concern expressed by some of our people that we weren't moving fast enough into Eastern Europe. I believe that Eastern Europe has good potential. My assessment of the time frame in which that potential will be realized is a little longer than some others'. So far I feel vindicated in my position.

How did you arrive at your evaluation of the situation?

I actually went and met with some of my top officials in Europe and got their assessment, and then based on my knowledge and experience from living and working in Europe for six and a half years, I developed my conclusions.

My first assessment was that one of the problems is forty-five years of a culture that is completely alien to competing in a free economy. There are antiquated facilities, gross inefficiency, and heavy pollution. There is dramatic political change, and it appeared that would have to be followed very quickly with equally dramatic economic change to support the political change. There are three potential sources of support for this economic change. First, the private sector. But if demand doesn't create a need for additional capacity, then why would you build something in Eastern Europe, why make a substantial investment? Private sector investment will develop only in accordance with the growth in the countries' economy. A second potential source of support could be other countries. But in the United States we've got enough problems of our own, and no resources to pour in there. The German unification has been more costly than they anticipated. Then there's Japan, but they haven't moved aggressively into that area. So I concluded that other countries would only be a modest source of support. The third potential source is banks, but they've got problems

of their own. So I didn't see the source of economic resources to support what was necessary.

In particular, I felt that West Germany was overly optimistic in terms of the time frame of East Germany's turn around, the magnitude of the problem, and the financial resources that would be required.

And you've been right on all three.

Well, when I talked to the West German government they likened their support for eastern Germany to West Germany after the war. They said, "We got the Marshall Plan. We performed an economic miracle. We provide the financial resources now, and there will be another economic miracle." I submit there's one big difference between West Germany after the war and eastern Germany today. West Germans' expectations after the war weren't that high. Residents of eastern Germany want what residents of western Germany have, and they want it now.

Another reason for my caution in Eastern Europe is that I have some experience in moving into countries with significant growth potential. One of those was Spain. In 1973 we approved a program to make a substantial investment in Spain. I think at that time it was the largest investment ever undertaken by Ford Motor company—approximately a billion dollars. To get into Spain we had to have sixty percent local content, export two-thirds of the production, and we were limited to ten percent of the market. For others that came in later, those restrictions were mitigated substantially. So, for those who say you have to get in early, I say, well the Japanese have done pretty well in the United States, and they came in later.

Among domestic producers the American public believes that Ford's products are of highest quality. This perception was created partially by an extremely effective advertising campaign—Quality is Job 1—but also by the dramatic quality improvements made at Ford during the eighties. How did you achieve this quality turnaround?

First was the commitment, then the reality, and then the change in perception. We had a very strong commitment to quality that started in 1979. In the early eighties we began doing things that demonstrated that commitment. These actions changed the perceptions in our employees' minds about our emphasis on quality.

Could you give an example of such an action?

We have a program that our new products go through called Four P's—the production process proveout program. You're supposed to have all parts off production tooling. Well, when the Escort was to be introduced in 1981 it went through Four P's and we didn't have all the parts, and there were a fair number of problems identified. So the question arose, do we proceed with the launch or do we delay? And remember, at this time the worst thing you could do was to shut down a launch. I had that decision to make, and I must tell you there were split opinions in the company. Some said we should go ahead, iron out the problems, and we'd be okay when we got into production. Others said, if we do that it'll be the same thing we've done before. I elected to delay the launch, and that decision affected the organization like a lightning strike.

A delay for quality.

Yes. That was a major signal. And we reinforced it by everything we did. We concentrated on the quality of the product from the earliest design stages. When we had the engineers determine the feasibility of the product, they looked at whether it could it be done, and could it be done at high production with good quality. So the quality focus started with the design stage, and continued

throughout our operation—throughout everything. We emphasized that everyone has a customer, and we have to have a happy customer every step of the way. Everybody provides a service or a product to somebody in the company, and if everybody does their job to the best of their ability then the end product will be right. We made dramatic progress in our quality.

The launch of the Taurus was a pivotal point in terms of perceptions.

It was a very good symbol because it was an all new product with a dramatic style that hit the marketplace at a good time, when it was in an upward move, so I think it helped us convince the public that our commitment to quality was more than just words.

What was the role of the "Quality is Job 1" advertising campaign?

We had quite a discussion, by the way, with our advertising agency. They planned to use actors. They felt that employees could not do the job that actors could do. And I remember that Phil Benton [now Ford president and COO] and I said no. We've got to use the employees. To me it was a matter of integrity. So we pursued our position, and we did use the employees, and the record speaks for itself. They do an outstanding job. And not only, I think, does it come through on the TV clips, but it's important to the employees in the plant. They're proud of what they accomplish, to get the recognition, and to tell the public how committed they are. I think it's very important.

What about what you did with the employees at all levels at Ford to change the operating culture from one that said "let's launch anyhow" to . . .

Well, we had very aggressive programs in employee involvement and participative management. We tried to secure the ideas, expertise, commitment, and dedication of all our employees, hourly and salary, throughout the organization. For example, when we had the prototypes of the new products we took them to the plants and asked for suggestions to improve the quality or the efficiency with which those products could be built. We got a tremendous number of ideas, and the majority of those were included in the products.

What was the role of Dr. Deming?

He was very influential. He worked very closely with our top management, he talked with Don Petersen [former Ford CEO], who became a convert, and he worked closely with our top quality personnel at the staff level. Then he moved into the operating level of the company. I think that was a very strong signal to our employees that we were serious about quality. Dr. Deming was the thrust for statistical process control, and if you go through our plants today you'll see control charts all over the place.

Do you feel SPC has been successful at Ford?

Oh, yes. And if it's going to be meaningful, you better get the results. Otherwise it's just a piece of paper on a wall. You go through our plants and talk to the employees on a given operation, they talk with pride about their SPC charts. They pay attention to them. They understand what they mean. And they tell you what they do any time something starts to slip from the band.

How did the employees learn to use the control charts?

Very extensive training programs. If you don't have training it's worthless. So we've used outside facilitators, trained our own, and it's been very beneficial.

You seem to have achieved a quality focus within Ford. What about your suppliers? How have you managed to get the same quality level for your inputs?

We started a program in the early eighties working with our suppliers on

quality, when we initiated the Q1 award. And that had a very positive impact. I'm convinced that everyone wants to do a job to the best of their ability but they need to know what your expectations are. So conveying our expectations to our suppliers, and working with them on the approach to meeting those quality objectives, was very beneficial not only for us but for the suppliers. If you talk to the suppliers they'll tell you that. It helped them immeasurably. They recognize that they have to compete in the global economy, and the only way to do it is to produce good quality.

We have focused on Ford's automotive business. What is Ford's corporate level strategy, and how does the automotive business fit into that strategy?

Let me just talk about the strategic objective of the company in terms of the businesses that we are in. Our major business is the car and truck business around the world. It is a cyclical business. So we need something as a counterbalance to that—something that is less cyclical or countercyclical to the automobile business. We've decided on financial services, so we've invested a fairly significant sum of money to expand into it. Presently, that strategy has proven to be quite effective. Financial Services contributed $927 million in 1991. The objective is for financial services to represent thirty percent of the profitability of Ford Motor Company in a normal year when our auto business is doing well. Unfortunately since we're in a recession in the United States and a depressed market in the UK—our major market in Europe—it wasn't enough to offset the losses in the automotive division. But that is the objective, and why we're in financial services. We have pretty well completed moving out of the other businesses we were in at Ford Motor Company. So now our focus will be on those two businesses.

As CEO what do you feel Ford has to do, and do right, during the nineties to position itself for the twenty-first century?

The actions we have to take aren't headline grabbers, but they're fundamental to our success. They are the things that helped us during the eighties and I think they're applicable to any company.

First, product—the car, truck, components that we make. It has to be designed to meet customer needs and requirements. We have to focus on the consumer and try to find out exactly what those needs are and make sure that we're responsive to them. We've got all of the efforts in place to accomplish that.

Second, quality. Quality is our number one objective. Not only do the needs and expectations of the customers have to be met, they have to be exceeded. The customer must be surprised and delighted and Ford must distinguish itself from the competition.

Third, cost. I believe we should strive to be the low cost producer worldwide. It's a tough task, but it's difficult to compete unless you move in that direction. You need at least to be on a par with the best and I always like to do better than the competition. If you're the low cost producer, you're in control. Regardless of what the competition does, you're going to be in a better position.

Next, relations with suppliers and dealers. Suppliers represent approximately fifty percent of the content of our vehicles. We need their ideas, expertise, and commitment to be the best. We can't succeed unless they do. The dealers represent the company and interact directly with the consumer. We need to continue to work on and enhance that partnership. And, of course, the employees. Whatever we accomplish, all that we've accomplished in the eighties, and all we hope to accomplish in the future, will depend on the commitment, dedication, and ideas of our employees.

If we continue to focus on those things, and do them to the best of our ability, I'm confident that we'll succeed in the nineties, and beyond. We intend to find

ways to build on what we've done in each of those areas. And I think if we just continue to focus on that, not to provide any magic solution, we will be well positioned for the future. We've got a lot behind us in sharing our commitment to quality. Our people understand it, believe in it, and are supportive. We have excellent training programs. We've committed the resources necessary to ensure that we continue to proceed with the focus that we've been successful with in the eighties. We've proven that we can introduce new products that create the excitement necessary to attract new customers, not just with the Taurus and the Sable, but with products like the Town Car and the Explorer. We spent $28 billion on new product development from 1987-1991, including $5.8 billion in 1991, and we plan to spend more in the next five years.

Has the credit crunch caused some of those plans to be put on hold?

We have not cancelled any programs. We have moved timing on some of them, but much of it was to be responsive to workload as opposed to financial constraints. One of the reasons that we've increased our debt is so that we can keep our product programs going. And our commitment is to do that.

Finances aside, what about the design cycle time for your products?

That's one of the significant problems that we've had to focus on. We have a program in our operations to reduce significantly the time it takes to bring products to market. But you have to put the problem into perspective. When you talk new products you can talk anything from a minor change to a major facelift to an all new product. When you talk an all new product with all new powertrains and a new platform as well as skin, then my understanding is Lexus took five years to come to market. And that's what it took us to bring Taurus and Sable. The Town Car took us thirty-one months. We would like to take twenty-five percent out of the time it takes us to introduce a new product, from concept to customer, and currently we're implementing actions to accomplish that.

Moving to workforce issues, advancing technology and expanding line worker responsibility are increasing worker skill demands at the same time illiteracy and innumeracy problems are growing. What is the effect of this skills gap on Ford and other American manufacturers?

It poses a significant problem, an added burden that we shouldn't have. We have to supplement the basic education of students, which we shouldn't find it necessary to do, as opposed to providing specific training programs to provide special skills applicable to our business or the specific job that an individual is going to hold. The changes in technology and process in our business are very dramatic. And this is true of other industries as well. It's estimated an engineer's college education will have expended its useful life in five years. I think the same is true of all the other skills and professions. One of the things that students today have to recognize is that education and training are going to be a continuous process necessary if the country is to be successful in the years ahead. Companies will continue to develop training programs to enhance that process and to ensure that they have the quality of personnel necessary to compete on a global basis. But changes also have to take place in our educational system to ensure that the graduates that we turn out are competitive on a global basis. If not, how are companies expected to compete? I'm not sure that it requires additional resources. Effective use of the resources we have is the first goal, and then if additional resources are needed we have to determine why they're needed and how best to channel those resources to accomplish this country's objectives.

Is there some role that private firms can play in enhancing the process by which the educational system is improved?

Yes, in fact Ford is involved in virtually every educational program there is today. In addition we work with the Business Roundtable on their focus on education. We stay informed and are supportive of the President's federal programs. We work closely with state agencies.

One of my concerns is that there are so many people focusing with slightly different perspectives on educational problems and requesting huge sums of money to address these issues. I think some overall program that is responsive to this country's educational needs would be much better to more fully utilize resources.

Industry can work effectively with the educational system to provide inputs about their needs. The course structure can then be designed to enable students to respond to the needs of the jobs that will be available. We've started a program called Ford Academy of Manufacturing Sciences to give high school students an indication of what manufacturing is all about and to show them that it isn't a dull, uninteresting type of business. It's exciting, dynamic, and they should eagerly look forward to an opportunity to work in the business and get an understanding and appreciation of what is necessary to succeed. Others have done similar things. I think American Express has a program in financial services.

Another major workforce issue—unions. Their role and how you have worked with unions to get competitive.

We've had a very good program working with the unions at Ford in terms of better understanding the issues that we face as an industry and working together to address those issues to compete successfully. I'm very pleased with the relationship that we've had with the unions. It's been a very cooperative one. In fact, the UAW has said that Ford has the best union relations in the industry. And I'd like to continue to emphasize the importance of this critical area.

What do you think about the mushrooming cost of medical insurance?

Medical care is one of the biggest problems that the industry faces today—not only the automobile industry but all U.S. industry. It's a serious problem from several standpoints. There are about 33 million people that don't have access to medical care. The quality of medical care, and cost are major concerns. It represents a substantial and significantly greater portion of GNP in this country than any other. That says that we're noncompetitive, and something needs to be done. What is the solution? I'm not sure. We're working with all our constituents trying to find ways to address this problem, and I'm convinced that we will find a solution. The question is how soon, and what form will it take? Just saying that business should provide the benefits to all employees is too easy a solution. This directly affects competitiveness. We have to find a way to spread the cost across a broad section of the community, and find a way to reduce the rate of cost increase. Costs increase at two and a half to three times the rate of inflation, so if there isn't a cost containment as part of the new approach to health care, it will not be successful.

Would you support a joint business-government relationship to focus in on that issue and look at it?

Absolutely.

As you look at American manufacturing prospects, what are your overall assessments and how do you think it will fare in the twenty-first century?

I think that American prospects are good. We need to address some of the major

issues facing this country—education, drugs, health care—all critical issues of national importance. But I think that people can become too pessimistic about America. Americans are very resourceful. We still devote huge resources to research and development. It's easy to look at R&D as a percentage of GNP and not at the total dollars invested. If you look at the total dollars invested in research and development you'll see that this country still maintains a substantial lead. We have an excellent record in new technology, though we could do a better job in commercializing some of our technology. We need to focus a lot more attention on that. To assume that any country or any company is invulnerable would be a mistake, but this country has proven that we can come out of a very severe recession and be successful—as we did in the eighties. I think we can do it again.

We need a closer relationship in this country between business and government in the cause of our country's goals, and I think that it hasn't developed to the extent that it should. However, I'm encouraged by several things. The meetings of the three domestic manufacturers with members of the administration and ultimately the President was very beneficial. Also, the visit by representatives from Congress to the auto industry to see for themselves the actions that we have in place to address national issues of environmental concern and fuel efficiency was very positive. It gives a different perspective and a better understanding of what's going on. It's difficult to understand the impact some of the proposals have on the industry unless you can see it for yourself. Ongoing relationships of this type—and I'm not talking just about the automobile industry, I'm talking about business in general—would be desirable. Congressmen could get out and learn more about all industries, especially those affected by major pieces of legislation that are under consideration. Such activities take place in other countries, and they have proven successful. Certainly, we're going to do everything we can from our side. And if we get a greater focus on applying the total resources of business and government we'll see earlier resolution of some of the national issues, more efficiently and effectively, and we'll see a more competitive industrial base in this country.

International Management

Perhaps the rudest awakening ever experienced by American management came at the hands of the Japanese. American firms had been supremely confident during the 1950s, 1960s, and into the 1970s, but with the first gasoline crisis of the early 1970s, that started to change. Up until that point, the Japanese had been producing some very nice small cars, but their success in the American market had been limited. With the first gas crisis, the Japanese suddenly had the right product at the right time. Then, just as the American cars were starting to make a comeback, the second gas crisis occurred—a one-two punch that sent the U.S. automobile industry reeling. While the Japanese refined their products, making them better, American industry tried to ignore the change in the market and responded with the Dodge Aspen and the Plymouth Volare, perhaps the largest group of "lemons" in the history of the automobile industry. They were the wrong cars at the wrong time.

Japanese management ideas were not new. They were the result of the work of Edward Deming, a professor of management at New York University. Deming had tried to get U.S. firms to at least try his ideas, but there was no

Unit 3

interest. The Japanese, on the other hand, found Deming's work to be extremely useful and adopted much of it for their own use in what has come to be called "Japanese management." One of the more interesting coincidences in the development of management in the second half of the twentieth century is that the two leading management theorists of the time were in the same college of the same university at the same time, and yet each had very different experiences. Peter Drucker, whose ideas were readily accepted by American industry, and who now teaches in California, has for years been considered the number-one thinker on management in the United States. The other expert, Edward Deming, is considered the number-one thinker on management in Japan, and the Japanese have named their annual award for the best-managed company in Japan after him.

Management is by nature an eclectic discipline, drawing on many and all fields of knowledge that can be useful. In managing international firms, the need to draw on these areas of knowledge is even greater. Managers use what works and discard what does not. Whether a particular principle originated in the United States or Japan or Europe really is not important. The only important criteria is "Does it work and how well?"

There are some special considerations in international management that need to be taken into account. The first is to recognize that international management implies a recognition of different cultures, ideas, and values, and that trying to impose Japanese or American or British values outside of their normal context can lead to problems. Charges of "Ugly American" or "Ugly Japanese" are just symbols of this problem.

Second, it must be recognized that while two partners in joint ventures may have differences, these differences must be recognized and worked out if the joint venture is to be successful. This is especially true of American and Japanese firms. The natural conflict between the two countries and their corporate counterparts is far outweighed by the benefits of cooperation, and the same can be said for Euro-Japanese and Euro-American ventures.

Third, international management must recognize the importance of viewing each business location on an equal footing. Firms with origins in the United States, Europe, or Japan need to recognize this if they are going to be truly multinational organizations. The interests of one country cannot automatically be dismissed in favor of the interests of the "home" country. Indeed, a truly multinational firm with multinational managers cannot do this.

National societies and governments have been slow to recognize this change in the way multinational firms have to do business. Multinational corporations and their managers are now citizens of the world, not just citizens of a particular country. They view the world as their market, their source of raw materials, labor, and capital. The managerial expertise of the corporation can be applied anywhere, and if they do not have it for a particular market, then they can buy it. Americans do not necessarily lead "American" corporations, nor do Europeans necessarily lead "European" firms. While the Japanese still insist upon Japanese senior control, it will be a matter of time before even Japanese organizations will be headed by non-Japanese. Talent and the competitive forces of the marketplace will eventually force the issue. Today, it is possible for the chairman of the board of a Fortune 500 firm to be the son of an English missionary to China and a Chinese mother, married to a Japanese woman, with virtually no American domestic experience, as was the case with William Anderson, the recently retired chairman of the NCR Corp.

Managers make their decisions based upon what is good for the firm. As economist Robert Reich has pointed out, those same decisions are not necessarily based upon what is good for the country, and those countries lacking a comprehensive industrial policy or some other way to deal with it are going to be at a disadvantage. Nations and societies need to catch up with the development of multinational organizations or they are likely to find themselves with frequent and large scandals in the future. The recent B.C.C.I. (Bank of Credit & Commerce) scandal could never have occurred in a single developed country, but needed the lack of coordination and regulation between nations in the commercial sphere in order to happen.

Looking Ahead: Challenge Questions

"Japanese management" is one of the hot "buzz" words in the managerial dictionary. How did the Japanese ideas on management develop? Who was behind them?

Japan and the United States are the two largest economies in the world. Why do they need to cooperate? How can Japanese and U.S. firms do a better job of cooperation?

The development of the multinational corporation has led to a change in the way organizations do business. How has it changed? What is the role of government in those changes?

WHO IS THEM?

Robert B. Reich

Robert B. Reich teaches political economy and management at the John F. Kennedy School of Government, Harvard University. His article, "Who Is Us?" appeared in the January-February 1990 issue of HBR. His newest book is The Work of Nations: Preparing Ourselves for 21st-Century Capitalism, *published by Alfred A. Knopf.* [In 1993 Robert Reich was appointed Secretary of Labor in the Clinton administration. Ed.]

"We" are seated at a negotiating table. "They" are seated across from us. The outcome of these talks will shape America's future competitiveness and economic well-being. But "us" is not necessarily companies based in the United States. "Them" is not foreign nations. Rather, us is the people – most prominently, the work force – of the United States. And them is the growing cadre of global managers – supranational corporate players, whose allegiance is to enhanced worldwide corporate performance, not to any one nation's economic success.

> In the global enterprise, the bonds between "us" and "them" are rapidly eroding.

Unlike their preglobal predecessors, global managers feel little allegiance to us. In the global enterprise, the bonds between company and country – between them and us – are rapidly eroding. Instead, we are witnessing the creation of a purer form of capitalism, practiced globally by managers who are more distant, more economically driven – in essence more coldly rational in their decisions, having shed the old affiliations with people and place.

Today corporate decisions about production and location are driven by the dictates of global competition, not by national allegiance. Witness IBM's recent decision to transfer 120 executives and the headquarters of its $10 billion per year communications business to Europe, a move that is partly symbolic – a recognition that globalization must take companies beyond their old borders – and partly practical – an opportunity for IBM to capitalize on the expected growth in the European market.

As this and countless other examples show, business competition today is not between nations. Nor do trade flows between nations accurately keep score of which companies are gaining the lead. For the past two decades, U.S. businesses have maintained their shares of world markets even as *America* has lost its lead.

Nor does a nation's wealth turn on the profitability of corporations in which its citizens own a majority of shares. Cross-border ownership is booming: Americans are buying into global companies based in Europe and East Asia; Europeans and Asians are buying into companies based in the United States.

Reprinted by permission of *Harvard Business Review.* "Who Is Them?" by Robert B. Reich, March-April 1991, pp. 77-88.
Copyright © 1991 by the President and Fellows of Harvard College. All rights reserved.

And most corporate profits are plowed back into new investments spread around the world.

Ultimately, our wealth and well-being depend on the value that the world places on the work we do, on our skills and insights. Hence the importance of the negotiations between us and them about what jobs we are to perform in the new global economy.

In this regard, the logic of the global manager is clear: to undertake activities anywhere around the world that will maximize the performance of the company, enlarge its market share, and boost the price of its stock. Our logic is just as clear: to get global managers to site good jobs in the United States. Our best interests are served by making it easy, attractive, and productive for them to do so, regardless of the nationality of the company they represent. At the same time, we need to structure the talks between us and them over the kinds of jobs they put here in a way that represents and secures our interests.

The Logic of the Global Manager

The image out of the past is a compelling one. A strong and proud American company is centered in an American community and is run by American managers. The offices, the factories, the community all bear the unmistakable mark of connectedness. But it is an image that is fading, an ideal that is more in our memories than in reality. Gone is the company town, the huge local labor force, the monolithic factory, and the giant vertically integrated corporation that dominated the entire region. Gone is the tight connection between the company, its community, even its country. Vanishing too are the paternalistic corporate heads who used to feel a sense of responsibility for their local community. Emerging in their place is the new global manager, driven by the irrefutable logic of global capitalism to seek higher profits, enhanced market leadership, and improved stock price. The playing field is the world.

This is not to impugn the patriotism of those Americans (or Italians or Germans) who manage globally. In their private lives, global managers are no doubt one of "us": no less patriotic, no less concerned about their countries' futures, no less involved in civic causes or social issues. But it is in business that global managers become "them." Their outlook is cosmopolitan – corporate citizens of the world, wherever they conduct their business. As one top IBM manager told a reporter, "IBM has to be concerned with the competitiveness and well-being of any country or region that is a major source of IBM revenue."

When it comes to global managers, no group of citizens, no government, has a special claim. Edzard Reuter, chairman of Daimler-Benz and one of the most powerful men in German industry, insists that

> **When it comes to global managers, no group of citizens or government has a special claim.**

the company has no special duty to invest in the former East Germany. "We are not national or nationalistic pioneers, but entrepreneurs," he has said. "When [there are good returns] in East Germany, we will invest. But not to do some politician a favor."

Regardless of the manager's national background, the principles are the same. The emerging global manager invests in the most promising opportunities and abandons or sells off underperforming assets – no matter how long they have been part of the corporate family or where they may be located. "You can't be bound emotionally to any particular asset," Martin S. Davis, chairman and CEO of Paramount Communications, told a reporter. Charles (Mike) Harper, head of ConAgra, the giant food-processing and commodity-trading company, which is crucial to the economy of Omaha, Nebraska, recently threatened to move the company unless the state changed its tax code. The bonds of loyalty could slip over the weekend, Harper warned: "Some Friday night, we turn out the lights – click, click, click – back up the trucks, and be gone by Monday morning."

While the tone of such a statement may sound menacing, in fact Harper's logic is anything but sinister. The new global manager's job is to exploit the opportunities created by the high-powered technologies of worldwide communication and transportation and by the relaxation of national controls over cross-border flows of capital. The global manager efficiently deploys capital all around the world, seeking the highest returns for shareholders or partners. Competition is intense and growing. The global manager who fails to take advantage of global opportunities will lose profits and market share to global managers who do.

In deciding where around the world to do what, the global manager seeks to meet the needs of customers worldwide for the highest value at the least cost. Some production will be done under the company's direct supervision; much will be outsourced. Often design and marketing activities will be sited close to the markets to be served; research and complex engineering, where skilled scientists and engineers can be found; routine fabrication and assembly, where workers are available at lowest cost. But there are exceptions – depending on products, markets, and circumstances. When there is danger that a market might be closed to imports, production might be shifted there. When two or more locations are about the same, the decision will be based on where the global manager can secure the most profitable deal.

The global manager's task is to put it all together, worldwide. For example, Mazda's newest sportscar, the MX-5 Miata, was designed in California, financed from Tokyo and New York, its prototype was created in Worthing, England, and it was assembled in Michigan and Mexico using advanced electronic components invented in New Jersey and fabricated in Japan. Saatchi and Saatchi's recent television advertising campaign for Miller Lite Beer was conceived in Britain, shot on location in Canada, dubbed in Britain and the United States, and edited in New York. An Intel microprocessor was designed in California and financed in the United States and Germany, containing dynamic random-access memories fabricated in South Korea. Chevrolet's best-selling Geo Metro was designed in Japan and built in Canada at a factory managed by Japan's Suzuki. Boeing's next airliner will be designed in Washington state and Japan and assembled in Seattle, with tail cones from Canada, special tail sections from China and Italy, and engines from Great Britain.

The logic of the global manager is not confined to large, well-established global companies. In 1989, in the first six months of its cosmopolitan life, the tiny Momenta Corporation, headquartered in Mountain View, California with 28 employees, had raised almost $13 million from Taiwanese and American investors. A small band of U.S. engineers was designing Momenta's advanced computer; the components would be engineered and produced in Japan; the actual product would be assembled in Taiwan and Singapore. Kamran Elahian, Momenta's Iranian-born founder, said to a reporter that global financing was "one of the only ways we [could] be assured of the $40 million we needed," and global production was required to "make use of the best technology that is available to the company." Switzerland's Logitech, the world's leading supplier of the "point and click" mouse for personal computers, relies on just 20 Swiss and Italian engineers, 520 technicians and marketing specialists in California, and 350 production workers in Ireland and Taiwan. Weng Kok Siew, president of Singapore Technologies, another upstart, has described his worldwide strategy in words that could stand as the global manager's credo: "We plan to manufacture in any country in the world where there is an advantage – to make things in Thailand where the cost is low, in Germany because the market is big, to do R&D in Boston."

Headquarters for the new global web can be a suite of rooms in an office park.

As competition globalizes, so must the vision of the manager. The dictates of capitalism are clear: the global manager gains profits and captures markets by putting worldwide resources to their most efficient uses.

The Logic of the Global Web

If the company town, a relic of the 1950s, is vanishing, so too is the old multinational corporation disappearing, a reminder of the 1960s and 1970s. Like the company town, the multinational exuded a sense of hierarchy, place, and order. World headquarters was, very simply, both in the center and at the top of the worldwide corporate pyramid. The location of the headquarters was a reflection of company history (the founder had begun the company in this place) or of industry requirements (headquarters had to be where the biggest factory was located or where the research and engineering was done). Managers in worldwide headquarters made all the crucial decisions, of course. Foreign subsidiaries were just that – *subsidiary* to headquarters. Their work usually consisted of exporting materials and components back to the parent corporation for assembling and finishing or of selling the parent's finished products in a foreign market. The lines of power, of communication, of corporate decision making and corporate governance all led back to headquarters.

The Fading Significance of World Headquarters. The emerging global manager works within a global web, which operates according to a new and different logic. The location of headquarters is not a matter of great importance; it is not even necessarily in the country where most of the company's shareholders or employees are. Headquarters for the new global web can even be a suite of rooms in an office park near an international airport – a communications center where many of the web's threads intersect.

In 1988, for example, when RJR Nabisco moved its worldwide headquarters to Atlanta, Georgia from Winston-Salem, North Carolina – where, years before, it had built the city's largest skyscraper, created a community arts center, and been the chief patron of Wake Forest University – the citizens of Atlanta were expecting great things. But the new worldwide headquarters turned out to be leased space in a suburban mall, housing only 450 executives and staff (about a third of 1% of the company's worldwide work force). Ross Johnson, then RJR-Nabisco's president, cautioned Atlantans to expect no more from the business than they would from any tiny 450-person company in their midst.

In fact, the global web may have several worldwide headquarters, depending on where certain markets or technologies are. Britain's APV, a maker of food-processing equipment, has a different lead country for each of its worldwide businesses. Hewlett-Packard recently moved the headquarters of its personal computer business to Grenoble, France. Siemens A.G., Germany's electronics colossus, is relocating its medical electronics division headquarters from Germany to Chicago, Illinois. Honda is planning to move the worldwide headquarters for its power-products division to Atlanta, Georgia. ABB Asea Brown Boveri, the European electrical-engineering giant based in Zurich, Switzerland, groups its thousands of products and services into 50 or so business areas (BAs). Each BA is run by a leadership team with global responsibility for crafting business strategy, selecting product-development priorities, and allocating production among countries. None of the BA teams work out of the Zurich headquarters; they are distributed around the world. Leadership for power transformers is based in Germany, electric drives are in Finland, process automation is in the United States.

The global web's highest value-added activities – its most advanced R&D, most sophisticated engineering and design, most complex fabrication – need not be in the nation where most of the company's shareholders and executives are. Ford's state-of-the-art engine factory is in Chihuahua, Mexico, where skilled Mexican engineers and technicians produce more than 1,000 engines per day with quality equal to the best in the world. Texas Instruments is fabricating some of its most complex wafers in Japan at its Sendai facility and is building an R&D center in Japan's science city of Tsukuba. Other recently or soon-to-be opened research labs in Japan: Procter & Gamble's technical center on Rokko Island in Kōbe; Ciba-Geigy's facility in Takarazuka; and Carrier Corporation's engineering center in Shizuoka prefecture. By 1990, Hewlett-Packard's German researchers were making significant strides in fiber-optic technologies; its Australian researchers, in computer-aided engineering software; its Singaporean researchers, in laser printers.

> Whirlpool International's management committee is made up of six people from six different nations.

A recent study of where U.S.- and European-based global corporations site their high value-added activities confirms the trend. There was little evidence of any bias in favor of the headquarters nation, except in companies that had only recently become multinational and had not yet had an opportunity to site their high value-added activities abroad. Among more advanced companies working to spin their global webs, the tendency is to site high value-added activities all over the world.[1]

The Cosmopolitan Management Team. Increasingly, the managers who inhabit the global web come from many different nations. Take, for example, Whirlpool's approach to going global in the white-goods business. Headquartered in Benton Harbor, Michigan, Whirlpool recently formed a joint venture with the Major Appliance Division of Philips, headquartered in Eindhoven, Holland. The administrative headquarters of this U.S.-Dutch joint venture – Whirlpool International – is in Comerio, Italy, where it is managed by a Swede. On the six-person management committee sit managers from Sweden, Holland, Italy, the United States, and Belgium, with a German to be named later. Such cosmopolitanism is equally apparent at the top of the world's leading companies: IBM prides itself on having five different nationalities represented among its highest ranking officers, and three among its outside directors. Four nationalities are represented on Unilever's board; three on the board of Shell Oil. Sony has attempted to address the global team in a characteristically compact fashion: recently named as president and chief operating officer of Sony America was Ron Sommer, who was born in Israel, raised in Austria, and carries a German passport.

The threads of the new global web extend, as well, across the old boundaries of the company to include transactions between global managers in different companies. Investment decisions travel through far-reaching relationships between global companies headquartered on opposite sides of the world. Profit-sharing agreements, strategic alliances, joint ventures, licensing agreements, and supply arrangements tie together units and subunits. In the 1980s, for instance, Corning Glass abandoned its national pyramidlike organization in favor of a global web, giving it the capability to make optical cable through its European partner, Siemens A.G., and medical equipment with Ciba-Geigy. In 1990, these

1. John Cantwell, Technological Innovation and Multinational Corporations (Oxford: Basil Blackwell, 1989).

kinds of foreign alliances generated almost half of Corning's earnings. AT&T has also sought to transform itself from a self-sufficient bureaucratic monopoly into a multilateral global web: Japan's NEC helps AT&T supply and market memory chips; Dutch-owned Philips helps AT&T make and market telecommunications switching equipment and application-specific integrated circuits; Mitsui helps it with value-added networks.

No nation or continent is immune to the logic of the global web. In the 1950s and 1960s, for example, Europe sought to create and nurture "national champion" companies in key industries as a way to shelter domestic businesses from the onslaught of U.S. multinationals. Today these same champions are transforming into global webs with no particular connection to their own countries: France's Renault has teamed up with Sweden's Volvo to create Europe's fourth-largest industrial group; Daimler-Benz, Germany's largest industrial group, is discussing a wide assortment of links with Mitsubishi; Fujitsu, Japan's largest computer company, has acquired Britain's ICL; Pilkington, Britain's largest glassmaker, has joined with France's Saint-Gobain and Japan's Nippon Sheet Glass; Italy's Olivetti is distributing mainframe computers for Hitachi and developing laptops with Japan's YE Data.

The Japanese Exception? If there is one country that is criticized for not playing by these emerging global rules, it is Japan. But the logic of the global web is so powerful that the Japanese will either be forced to comply over time or else face a stiff penalty from the marketplace, the talent pool, and competitors and governments. For example, in the competition for global talent, corporations that are reluctant to consider foreign nationals for top managerial positions will lose out: the most talented people simply will not join an organization that holds out no promise of promotion. Japanese-owned companies that have been notoriously slow to open their top executive ranks to non-Japanese will operate at a competitive disadvantage.

> The Japanese will be forced to comply over time or pay a stiff penalty.

Similarly, Japanese companies that have traditionally done most of their highest value-added work in Japan now must reconsider the economic and political advisability of this strategy. Indeed, there is evidence suggesting that the leading Japanese companies – those that are already the most international – are beginning to change. Many of the companies that were the earliest to recognize the need to establish manufacturing facilities in Europe and the United States are now investing in R&D laboratories and complex fabrication facilities outside Japan. By 1990, more than 500 U.S. scientists and engineers worked for Honda in Torrance, California; another 200 worked in Ohio. At Mazda's new $23 million R&D center in Irvine, California, hundreds of U.S. designers and engineers are undertaking long-term automotive research. Nissan employs 400 U.S. engineers at its engineering center in Plymouth, Michigan; Toyota employs 140 at its technical research center in Ann Arbor. Fujitsu is now constructing an $80 million telecommunications plant and research center in Texas. NEC has opened a research laboratory in Princeton, New Jersey.

Japanese investment in Europe has also skyrocketed. According to the Bank of Japan, direct investment in the 12 European Community countries totaled $14 billion in 1989 and grew by a factor of eight between 1985 and 1989, even faster than in the United States. And much of this new investment is at the high value-added end. Fujitsu, for example, has established an R&D center in Britain for semiconductors used in communications equipment; Hitachi, a British R&D laboratory for telecommunications switching equipment.

As the Japanese experience shows, to be successful globally, the global manager cannot bias investment decisions in favor of the corporation's home base. Even the appearance of bias is likely to cause political problems for the company in less favored nations – making it more difficult for the global manager to utilize the people, capital, technology, and natural resources across the global web. Successful global competitors like IBM, GE, McDonald's, Ford, Shell, Philips, Sony, NCR, Unilever, The News Corporation, and Procter & Gamble have willingly shed their national identities and become loyal corporate citizens wherever they do business around the world – siting high value-added activities in many nations, hiring foreign nationals for senior positions, and giving local and regional managers substantial discretion. As a result, these companies are usually treated by governments around the world on an equal footing with locally based companies.

By contrast, the worldwide operations of multinational giants like NEC, Fujitsu, and Mitsubishi, and even some European-based companies like Siemens, are still considered to be *foreign* subsidiaries – subunits whose identities derive from the nation where their worldwide headquarters are. As a result, these companies sometimes have difficulty gaining equal treatment with locally based companies. In fact, even the most cosmopolitan Japanese companies are finding that the general reputation of Japanese business for putting Japan's interests first is creating a competitive disadvantage, making it increasingly difficult for these companies to export their products or undertake foreign investment around the world without encountering political opposition.

Furthermore, the well-known predilection of Japanese companies to do business with each other and in a way that uniquely benefits Japan has created a backlash among corporate competitors. In recent years, U.S. and European global managers have grown wary of depending too heavily on Japanese companies for critical high-tech components. Specifically, they worry that Japanese suppliers will allocate the parts they make to other Japanese companies first and withhold them from foreign partners or that Japanese companies will use the parts to gain a predatory foothold, gradually displacing their foreign partner as the relationship becomes more and more lopsided.

These concerns of Western managers about Japanese corporate practice are not necessarily yielding more investment in the United States; they are leading to more alliances across the Atlantic or with non-Japanese Pacific Rim partners. For example, IBM's recent efforts to ensure itself a supply of random-access memory semiconductor chips independent of Japanese companies has led it into a spate of investments and alliances across Europe – a joint venture with Siemens, membership in the European Community's semiconductor research consortium called JESSI. IBM's strategy, like that of other Western global corporations, is not pro-United States – it is pro-IBM and non-Japanese.

In fact, as corporations spin their global webs, other corporations, rather than governments, are likely to engage in strategic countermoves. The more companies decentralize their operations, the less authority and control any single government can assert over them. A company that is comfortable investing all over the world can negotiate with governments all over the world and, with enough leverage, dictate the specific terms and conditions of its investment.

The National Interest

They, as global managers, want to increase their world market shares, profits, and share prices. *We,* as citizens of a particular nation, want to secure national wealth and national economic well-being. They parcel activities around the world according to economic criteria, putting them wherever they can get the best return, intentionally playing no favorites to avoid setting off political alarms. But we do play favorites. We feel a special allegiance to our country and to our compatriots. Global corporations exist within world markets; we are members of a society.

Our interests diverge from theirs for two specific reasons: we are concerned about our nation's relative wealth and power, and we want to capture for our nation the public benefits that spill over from global investment.

Relative Wealth and Power. Consider the following two possible scenarios for economic growth between now and the year 2000 for the United States and Japan:

The United States economy grows 20%, but the Japanese economy grows 90%.

The United States economy grows only 8%, and the Japanese economy grows 8.2%.

When I have offered this choice in classes and corporate training seminars, a majority of the Americans in my audience usually select the second option. Many Americans are more concerned with our country's relative wealth and power compared with Japan's than with our country's absolute growth. We not only want global managers to favor the United States – locating their high value-added activities in America – more than they favor Japan, but many would also sacrifice some additional wealth in order to prevent the Japanese from enjoying even greater gains. Whether or not these sentiments should be commended as a principle of international economic behavior, they cannot be ignored. Despite the logic of the global manager and the global web, national wealth and power continue to drive us to think about our national interests not only in absolute terms but also relative to our perceived national competitors.

Spillovers from Corporate Investment. Even those of us who select the first option might still want global managers to favor the United States because of national benefits that do not typically appear on the global manager's balance sheets. Specifically, these spillovers might include the jobs that result from having sophisticated factories, laboratories, and equipment in the United States, whose high wages multiply throughout the economy, raising other incomes. Good jobs also generate higher tax receipts, which permit government to invest in public facilities such as improved schools and transportation and also to care for the elderly and the disadvantaged in society. Moreover, on-the-job training and the resulting technical know-how enable Americans to innovate and thus generate more wealth for the United States in the years to come. This know-how spreads beyond individual Americans to create entire regions of U.S. innovation – the San Francisco Bay area and greater Boston in science and engineering; Los Angeles in music and film; New York in law, advertising, and publishing; Minneapolis in medical devices and instruments; Irvine and Pasadena, California in industrial design, and so on.

The logic brings us to this central issue:

Their goal is to maximize profits by siting their production activities around the world for the highest return and investing wherever it is most efficient and strategically profitable.

Our goal is to attract into the United States the most high value-added global activities with the greatest positive spillovers – and to keep and grow them here.

We can pursue our goal by ensuring that we give America's children a first-class education – starting with preschool and extending through college or vocational training – and that our transportation and communications infrastructure is second to none. But even if we make the United States an attractive place for high value-added investments, that alone will not be enough to guarantee the kind of global investment we need. In a world in which every other nation is bidding for high value-added jobs, America must negotiate as well.

The Logic of Global Negotiations

When trade was the primary engine of global economic integration and corporations were rooted in particular countries, negotiations were government-to-government. Each nation's objective was to open foreign markets to the exports of its own companies or to protect its own companies from foreign competition at home. Countries measured their success by the extent to which they were able to sell their goods and services within foreign nations and how much world market share their own companies could command.

But the new global economy renders obsolete these old forms of negotiating and keeping score. Global investment is supplanting merchandise trade as the major engine of world economic integration – and the key to a nation's wealth and well-being. And negotiations between governments and global managers – between the new "us" and the new "them" – are displacing the old government-to-government talks.

The Growing Importance of Direct Investment. Between 1983 and 1988, world trade volumes grew at a compounded annual rate of 5%. Over the same period, global direct foreign investment increased by more than 20% annually in real terms. As a result, sales by foreign-owned affiliates within a nation now typically exceed foreign exports to that nation. In fact, when the foreign sales of U.S.-owned companies are calculated against the total purchases by Americans of the products of foreign-owned companies, America's trade deficit turns into a net surplus. The foreign operations of U.S.-owned corporations now account for more than $1 trillion in annual sales around the world, roughly four times the total export of goods made in the United States and about seven to eight times the value of America's recent trade deficits.

Today much of what is actually "traded" across borders are intangible services – research, engineering, design, financial, management, marketing, and sales – transferred within global corporations from one location to another. IBM exports relatively few machines from the United States to the rest of its global web; most of its U.S. "exports" are ideas and insights. Honda now imports relatively few automotive components into the United States from Japan; most of its Japanese "imports" are technological specifications and management know-how. The threads of the new global web are computers, facsimile machines, satellites, high-resolution monitors, and modems – linking up ideas and money from each of the company's worldwide locations with every other. In 1990, some 20,000 privately leased international telephone circuits carried video images, voices, and data instantaneously back and forth among managers, engineers, and marketers working together on different continents.

The New Negotiations. This change in the locus of economic activity – from trade to direct investment – implies a change in the nature of negotiations: while we focus our attention on the Office of the United States Trade Representative in Washington, D.C., looking for government-to-government talks to open up foreign markets to the products of "our" companies, that is no longer where the important action really is. Even when these old-fashioned trade talks succeed in opening a foreign market to a U.S. company, the effect on *us*, on our incomes and standard of living, is often tangential. For example, the recent agreement secured with Japan after intense government pressure to permit Toys "R" Us to open a large retail outlet in Tokyo will have almost no effect on the U.S. work force, apart from a few U.S. managers. Almost everything that Toys "R" Us sells in Japan will be conceived, designed, and manufactured outside the United States.

Another sort of negotiation is becoming far more important – one that occurs between a different set of parties. On one side of the bargaining table still sit the government representatives; but on the other side *they* sit – the global managers. The government negotiators represent the citizens of the nation, not the nation's corporations. Their job is to induce the global managers to site certain activities in the nation and thus provide the nation's citizens with good jobs. In return, the government negotiators offer a carrot – an assortment of tax breaks, financial inducements, and public investments. There is also a stick: government negotiators may threaten to close the national market to the company unless it makes the desired investments.

Third World nations have long bargained along these lines with multinationals headquartered in advanced nations. But the logic of the global web means that practically every nation now ends up sitting on that side of the table, including some of the most unlikely parties. Hoping to attract labor-intensive light industries like electronic-parts manufacturers, Vietnam has recently created an industrial zone on the outskirts of Ho Chi Minh City; the government is prepared to negotiate rock-bottom leases to global companies willing to invest in production facilities there. In these types of negotiations, moreover, governments make virtually no distinction between domestic and foreign-owned companies. "There is no flag on capital," says Argentina's President Carlos Menem. "I ask myself, what is national capital? Is it the $50 billion in flight capital that has left the country via Argentine business executives? Or resources used by multinationals to produce here?"

America's Negotiators. Like every other nation, the United States is taking an active part in these new sorts of negotiations. But unlike other countries, we are not represented by a high-ranking federal official like the United States Trade Representative. Instead, we are represented by 50 state governors and hundreds of mayors and city managers. Like the bargaining agents of other nations, these governors and mayors pay no attention to the nationality of the global managers on the other side of the table. In fact, 43 U.S. states maintain permanent offices and staffs in foreign capitals to conduct negotiations with foreign managers full-time. And these offices are not limited to the major commercial centers of the world: 10 states have recently opened offices in Taipei, and 4 more have announced plans to locate there. Just as often, the global managers sitting across the table are American, whose companies are headquartered in the United States – but they drive just as hard a bargain as the global managers from other countries.

> In the bidding for global investment, U.S. bargaining agents often compete against themselves.

The process works in a crude but effective fashion: the possibility of a new factory, laboratory, headquarters, or branch office within a state or a city sets off a furious auction; a casual threat to move an existing facility starts an equally impassioned round of negotiation. The governor or mayor who successfully lures or keeps the jobs is a hero; the one who loses the bidding may soon lose his or her own job.

The problem for us is that our U.S. bargaining agents often compete against themselves. A case in point: in the early 1980s, the Hyster Corporation, a manufacturer of forklift trucks, notified public officials in eight locations where Hyster had factories – five U.S. states, three foreign locations – that some of the facilities would be closed. Hyster invited each political jurisdiction to bid to keep its local jobs. The resulting auction was a great success for Hyster. By the time the bidding had closed, American states and cities had surrendered a total of $18 million to preserve about 2,000 Hyster jobs. The big "winner" was Danville, Illinois – a town with a population of only 39,000. In exchange for 850 blue-collar jobs, Danville and the state of Illinois agreed to provide Hyster with roughly $10,000 in subsidies.

Just as frequently, these kinds of auctions are global affairs. For example, when Diamond Star Motors, the Mitsubishi-Chrysler joint venture, announced in 1985 that it would begin assembling automobiles in the United States, four states competed for the factory. Illinois came out the winner with a bid of ten years of direct aid and incentives worth $276 million – roughly $25,000 for every new job the factory would create in the state. The city of Bloomington, Illinois threw in an additional $10 million of land and $20 million in local tax abatements.

Over time, the bidding has become more ferocious and the incentives more generous. In 1980, Tennessee paid the equivalent of $11,000 per job to entice Nissan to Smyrna. By 1986, Indiana had to spend $50,000 per job to induce Subaru-Isuzu to set up shop in Lafayette. When ConAgra threatened to leave Omaha, the state of Nebraska felt the heat of the bidding war directly. "It's like a poker game," said Donald Pursell, former director of Nebraska's Bureau of Business Research. "Nebraska makes a bid, Iowa ups it."

Bidding to attract new plants or keep existing ones requires that such state and local largess be routinely parceled out. Few global managers expect to pay the same rate of property tax in proportion to the assessed value of their land as local residents pay. Using the threat of the global web, it is relatively easy for global mangers to insist on a better deal simply by pointing out to state or local officials that, without more favorable tax treatment, the company will move to one of its other global locations. Partly as a result of this kind of leverage, corporations now contribute a much smaller percentage of local taxes in the United States than they did in the past. In

1957, corporations accounted for about 45% of local revenues; by 1989, corporate taxes comprised only 16%.

Paradoxically, such tax breaks and subsidies make it more difficult for states and communities to finance public education and infrastructure. For example, General Motors's successful effort to cut its annual taxes by $1 million in Tarrytown, New York, where the company has had a factory since 1914, has forced the town to lay off dozens of teachers and administrators and to cut back on school supplies and routine school maintenance. Ultimately, these kinds of "beggar thy neighbor" ploys by some global managers undermine our ability to attract global investments – since the quality of the work force, good transportation facilities, and a good quality of life are ultimately more important lures for attracting global managers' investments than tax concessions and subsidies.

The Advantages of Bargaining as a Whole. It is simple common sense that large nations that bargain as a whole with global managers – or groups of smaller nations that pool their bargaining strength behind a single agent – have much more clout than small nations or separate states and cities. By avoiding internal bidding contests, they end up paying far less to attract investment and have an easier time getting the jobs they want when and where they want them. For example, the European Commission reviews location incentives offered by member nations in order to minimize bidding by one against the other. As a result, when Honda decided in 1989 to locate its first European plant in Britain, it did not receive a shilling of inducement from Downing Street.

After 1992, a united Europe will be in an even stronger bargaining position in negotiations with global managers. Access to Europe's newly integrated market of 230 million people will itself be a powerful lure. Global managers are already scrambling to set up facilities there in anticipation that Europe's gates will shut. "You can't pick up a piece of paper that says why Intel has got to manufacture in Europe," one Intel executive told a reporter. "The rules don't exist." But when they do, Intel wants to be already well-established inside the gates.

> No one would seriously propose that each U.S. state conduct its own foreign trade policy.

Another illustration of the same principle: for years, before Japan caught up with the West technologically, Japan's Ministry of International Trade and Industry acted as a single bargaining agent for the country, acquiring foreign technology at cut-rate prices. By effectively barring auctions for licenses in Japan, MITI forced foreign licensors to sell at a fraction of the cost of developing the technology originally. According to estimates, between 1956 and 1978 Japan paid some $9 billion to acquire U.S. technologies that cost between $500 billion and $1 trillion to develop.

The Logic of a *United* States of America

Think back to any earlier time. Before the ratification of the U.S. Constitution, every state carried out its own trade policy, negotiating separate trade pacts with foreign nations. This approach allowed the other nations – Britain in particular – to play one state against another, gaining agreements that favored Britain at the expense of the states.

When John Adams, representing the Continental Congress, sought Britain's agreement to open its ports to U.S. shippers, British Foreign Secretary Charles James Fox contemptuously suggested that ambassadors from all 13 states would have to sign any such treaty. As a result, when the founding fathers met in Philadelphia to devise a new constitution, they agreed with little debate that Congress should have the power to "regulate commerce with foreign nations and among the several states." This unprepossessing clause in Article I became the charter of our national economy.

Today no one would seriously propose that each U.S. state conduct its own foreign trade policy. That responsibility is firmly lodged in the federal government. Trade negotiations are centralized in the Office of the United States Trade Representative, with its own expert staff. But today, with direct investment supplanting trade as the engine of world commerce, we lack any similar vehicle to negotiate on our behalf with global managers. As a consequence, we are relatively easy pickings for them.

What is needed is a shift of authority over global investment, from states and cities to the federal government. What little authority the federal government now exercises over global investment is negative. That is, under the Omnibus Trade Act of 1988, the federal government can block foreign investors from gaining a controlling interest in a U.S.-owned corporation if the purchase is likely to "impair national security." Under several other recent statutes, the federal government subsidizes private sector R&D only if it is undertaken by a U.S.-owned company. Even more recently, Congress has sought to impose special tax and disclosure burdens on non-U.S. companies operating in the United States.

Most of these investment disincentives make little sense. Global managers at U.S.-owned companies are no more "us" than are the global managers of non-U.S. companies. And it is in our interests to attract investment from global managers all over the world, rather than raising investment barriers on the faulty basis of national identity. Most important, while other nations are improving their bargaining power to attract global investment, the United States continues both to dissipate its bargaining power by permitting state and local bidding wars and to discourage foreign investment by creating federal barriers.

A United States Investment Representative. A response that would serve our interests and accede to the logic of the global manager and the global web is both the creation of an Office of the United States Investment Representative, paralleling the United States Trade Representative, and the preemption by federal law of separate state and local laws that authorize their officials to offer investment incentives. In other words, the federal government should effectively bar states and cities from bidding for global capital; just as the USTR negotiates national trade issues, the USIR would negotiate investment issues.

The USIR would determine what sorts of global investments we need in order to enhance our wealth

> Other nations are improving their bargaining power to attract global investment; America still creates federal barriers.

and create important spillovers, but which would not be made without special incentives. Do we want more of the public benefits associated with microelectronic fabrication and manufacturing? More microbiological research? More state-of-the-art auto assembly plants? Just as important, where do we want to see these investments located – in regions of high unemployment and relatively low skills? In regions where there already exist the beginnings of a critical mass of suppliers and relevant skills? The USIR would also monitor major factories, laboratories, and offices in the United States that global managers were planning to close and move abroad. Is it worth trying to keep them here? Why, and at what cost?

The tools available to the USIR in negotiating on our behalf already exist but are now scattered across the national landscape: tax abatements, tax credits, R&D incentives, loans and loan guarantees, use of public lands, public capital investment, and more. Moreover, working with the USTR, the USIR could offer trade concessions in exchange for the investments we seek – lowering tariffs on certain components to be used in the proposed U.S. manufacturing facility, providing relief from voluntary restraint agreements on other parts and components, granting immunity from certain antidumping levies. And if other nations threaten to close off their markets to global corporations unless they make certain investments there, America would be in the position to use similar threats as a means of ensuring its fair share of such investments.

The creation of a USIR would thus solve four problems at the same time. By pooling our now diffuse bargaining power, the USIR could bargain more effectively and at a lower cost on our behalf – thus preserving scarce resources for the important tasks of educating our work force and building a world-class infrastructure. It would bargain only for those global investments that promised large beneficial spillovers and that would not come to our shores automatically. It would seek to guide these investments to locations that would maximize the benefit to us. And it would put America on an equal footing with other large nations and emerging trading blocs that are already bidding effectively for global investment.

Without question, the activities of the USIR would be the subject of intense political interest. State and local governments would still compete against each other, but the competition would be contained among us, rather than channeled as payments to global corporations. And yes, the USIR would be selecting certain technologies and industries as more critical than others – which is exactly what Carla Hills, the United States Trade Representative, does now when she gives priority to certain industries during trade negotiations.

A GATT for Direct Investment. Just as we need a United States Investment Representative to parallel the efforts of the United States Trade Representative, so we need a GATT for Direct Investment to parallel the GATT that establishes rules for global trade – and for precisely the same reasons. So long as relative economic wealth and power figure prominently in national calculations, some framework for negotiations is necessary – lest nations fall prey to the same zero-sum investment bidding as America's states now engage in. Moreover, in the absence of such a new international forum, wealthy nations will always have the capacity to outbid poorer ones.

A GATT for Direct Investment would establish international rules by which nations bid for global investment and processes for settling disputes over such bids. For example, threats to close off a domestic market unless certain investments were made in it would be carefully circumscribed – for it is precisely threats such as these that rapidly unravel into zero-sum contests. The amount of permissible subsidies to attract investment might be proportional to the size of the nation's work force, but inversely proportional to its average skills – so that nations with large and relatively unskilled work forces would be allowed greater leeway in bidding for global investments than nations with smaller and more highly skilled work forces.

Other kinds of investment subsidies would be pooled and parceled out to where they could do the most good globally, as the European Community has begun to do regionally. For instance, nations would agree to fund jointly those basic research projects whose fruits are likely to travel across international borders almost immediately – projects such as the high-energy particle accelerator and the exploration of space. How such funds were apportioned and toward what ends would, of course, be subject to negotiation. The rules of the GATT for Direct Investment would also specify fair allocations of tax payments by companies operating across several borders and would reconcile various regulatory regimes.

Come back to the global negotiating table where we started. We are on one side; they are on the other. There is nothing sinister or hostile about this setting. It is, in fact, an inevitable, practically inexorable extension of the emerging global economy. It is not, however, absolutely true that our interests and theirs conflict. Both sides, for example, benefit from our having a well-educated, well-trained work force; a well-developed, well-maintained public infrastructure; a high-quality environment and a high overall standard of living.

Global managers are adapting with agility; U.S. government lags behind momentous events unfolding around the globe.

But there are differences as well, places where our interests naturally diverge. Many global managers, more sensitive to the requirements of the bottom line and thus more agile in adapting, have realized the implications of globalization. We and our governments are still struggling to catch up. They are changing the shape, size, location, and operating principles of global businesses. We are mired in the obsolete practices and attitudes of a previous era; our government lags behind the epoch-shaping events unfolding around the globe. Other nations – other groups of "us" – are reacting to these same events: EC '92, Japan's cautious emergence in world councils. Now we must move in the United States to create the new institutions and new attitudes that will permit us to negotiate effectively with them – that will allow us to negotiate as if our future depended on it.

Sources of Information (and Misinformation)

BENJAMIN WEINER

Benjamin Weiner is president of Probe, a Stamford, Conn.-based consulting firm that specializes in political analysis.

In this ever changing global environment, U.S. businesses find it increasingly difficult to know where to find a good location for a foreign project.

Where does one begin? There seem to be so many confusing issues and events before us that it is hard to establish priorities. There is the on-going fragmentation of nations, and one must consider which of the new entities are viable and which will turn into economic Bangledeshes or worse. The increasing ebb and flow of peoples is another contribution to instability. Will there be a Slavic flood into Western Europe, of people desperate for jobs or charity? Is Mexico a renewed opportunity or should it be viewed as a tenacious dictatorship scheduled for turmoil?

Considerable background information and opinion on a specific country or foreign situation can be accumulated without leaving the United States. Newspapers and news magazines are an obvious source of general information, but coverage is sometimes spotty and dependent on resources and the crisis of the moment. Most important, news coverage generally takes place *after* an event—a coup, a revolution, civil war, rioting, etc.—rather than in anticipation of it.

Specialized magazines and newsletters often provide greater depth and insight. For example, if you are considering an involvement in Singapore, go to a library that maintains the *Far Eastern Economic Review* or the *Asian Wall Street Journal* and start reading issues of the past six months. This simple exercise will provide you with the names of the players and the issues at hand, and also will tell you how effective the reporters were in evaluating events.

Be careful in approaching chambers of commerce for objective perspectives on the country they represent, since their job is to boost rather than criticize. However, some can be effective on an off-the-record basis. The Philippine-American Chamber, for example, frequently holds informal, small breakfast meetings that permit an interested executive to meet one-on-one with senior Philippine officials passing through the United States.

There also are specialized international and regional councils that provide forums on specific international issues or luncheon meetings for visiting dignitaries. Unfortunately, these gatherings sometimes are so large that a participant ends up listening to a canned speech with no opportunity to meet the guest of honor, no less hold a conversation with him or her.

Much more effective are the smaller, highly professional organizations such as the Carnegie Council or the Business Council for International Understanding, both located in New York City. The Carnegie Council holds small gatherings on specific international issues in an elegant Manhattan townhouse, which permits a participant to talk at some length with the speaker at hand. The American Management Association and other management organizations also sponsor seminars and conferences on opportunities and problems in foreign markets.

Also, do not lose sight of activist organizations that often criticize the overseas activities of the private sector. For example, the publications of the Interfaith Center for Corporate Responsibility can be quite revealing. This group, ensconced in the National Council of Churches building in New York, has taken it upon itself to function as a moral SEC. Many other church-related groups run similar operations.

WASHINGTON'S RESOURCES

Washington represents an intense concentration of current information and speculation on international developments, and a visit to the capitol is a key step in the serious evaluation of political developments in a particular country.

To many businesspeople, the U.S. Department of State is a murky repository of mismanagement and indecision, aptly described as Foggy Bottom, the informal name of the part of Washington in which it is located. And at first glance its dull, two-block-long facade reinforces the concept of bureaucratic anonymity—a monument to monotony designed by cost accountants rather than architects.

Yet if properly approached, officials within the Department can prove a valuable source of current information on political developments around the world. The core of the Department are the geographic bureaus, within which are country offices, formerly and often still referred to as "desks." The country director is usually a career Foreign Service officer and generally willing to meet informally with an American executive for an off-the-record discussion of the primary political and economic issues, as well as of the key personalities within his or her

From *Management Review,* January 1992, pp. 24-26. Copyright © 1992 by Benjamin Weiner. Reprinted by permission of the author.

country of responsibility. Moreover, the director often can provide the names of other officials in Washington who can provide additional perspectives.

This is important since numerous government agencies have international responsibilities, including Defense, Treasury, CIA, Agriculture, Commerce, the Special Trade Representative's Office, and on and on into the distant bureaucratic horizon. But don't stop there. A host of congressional committees conduct international research, and your congressperson would be pleased to provide you with copies of these studies. Also, the Washington offices of international organizations are sources.

Official Washington is a rather compact geographical entity and it is possible to conduct a dozen interviews in a two-day period.

GOING ABROAD

The wealth of information available in America, however, cannot match the immediacy and significance of an on-the-scene evaluation. By now the corporate executive should have an initial understanding of the range of political and political-economic problems within the country. It's time to go abroad.

A trip to the country in question, preferably for at least a week, offers direct insight into the political mechanisms and forces at play and allows for some immediate face-to-face evaluations. This could be conducted as an integral element of the feasibility and market evaluations normally carried out prior to approval of a joint venture or other operation.

A visit to the American Embassy should take place early on. Many executives put off going to the embassy, having heard it is of marginal value. When conducting a political evaluation, however, a meeting with one of the officers from the political section can be of great help. The names of the heads of the political section and other key embassy officers are available in a booklet, "Key Officers of Foreign Service Posts," published quarterly by the Department of State. Sometimes, the political officer will attempt to foist you off on the commercial section. However, insist that you are seeking a political and not a commercial evaluation.

As was the case with the country director in Washington, the ensuing discussion should generate a rundown of specific political and political-economic developments, regionally as well as nationally, and highlight potential areas of difficulty. And the political officer, if he or she has been in the country for a while, can provide names.

It is surprising how accessible these contacts are to an executive seeking to learn about the country. Time and language are the two constraining factors. Many foreigners speak some English, but I have found some more forthcoming if they speak in their native language, so you might want to arrange to have a competent interpreter. Here, obviously, knowledge of the native tongue would be invaluable.

Meetings with heads of government or cabinet ministers often are not worth the effort required to arrange them. It may satisfy an individual's ego to have been able to call on a president or minister of finance but it usually contributes little to the political evaluation itself. Far better to seek out the anonymous senior civil servants that run the pertinent government agencies year in and year out, regardless of who heads the ministry. Given the choice between meeting a minister of foreign affairs or the permanent secretary of that same agency, I invariably would choose the latter. The minister may or may not be around in six months and may not even understand the workings of his or her own portfolio. But you can be certain that the permanent secretary knows what is going on.

One of the difficulties companies must deal with is misleading information, from sources that have a stake or vested interest in a particular country or market. There is a remarkably tenacious cabal of U.S. government officials, bankers, attorneys, market researchers and consultants committed to selling their services to corporations considering international activities. The problem is that they eschew reality in favor of drum-beating. Perhaps they suspect they would not be able to develop a clientele were they not excessively positive on a particular country or situation. Accordingly, one never sees a brochure or attends an investment conference entitled "Limited Opportunities in Country X." It's always pitched within the hysteria of great opportunity.

Perhaps the best way to deal with the flow of exaggerated information is to develop a sense of professional skepticism.

The USSR is a case in point. Although political and economic realities a few years ago provided a clear signal of impending social and ethnic instability as well as economic malaise, the general atmosphere was one of unsullied opportunity. At conference after conference speakers from the government and the private sector stood up to urge American business to move forward in the USSR "before it was too late." Unfortunately, a number of American companies accepted this positive approach as gospel and were burned in the process.

Sadly, certain U.S. government agencies are regular contributors to this drum-beating approach to American business abroad, two of the culprits being the Department of Commerce and the Overseas Private Investment Corporation. Perhaps the best way to deal with the flow of exaggerated information is to exercise a sense of professional skepticism. A cynical international executive once commented half-seriously that if the U.S. Government was promoting a particular country that meant it was time for his company to move in the opposite direction.

What Executives Should Know About Political Risk

BENJAMIN WEINER

Benjamin Weiner is president of Probe, a Stamford, Conn.-based consulting firm that specializes in political analysis.

Life was simple. For decades the American business community had conducted its international activities within the cozy confines of U.S. foreign policy. Out there were the good guys, the bad guys and an amorphous and constantly changing middle group representing various gradations of risk.

The Cold War defined much of what the U.S. corporate executive could accomplish abroad; it qualified the countries in which a company could invest and those with which it could trade, as well as the goods that could be sold. If Washington's policy changed toward a traditionally hostile nation, then that country suddenly became an immediate opportunity for the business community. After President Nixon's visit in 1972, China was transformed from frog to shining prince to the ensuing regret of a number of firms that pursued this prospect without first conducting a realistic appraisal.

In this environment American businesspeople were satisfied with the simple political measure of "safe" and "unsafe" and were secure in selecting foreign projects against traditional commercial and financial benchmarks. Little or no effort was made to probe and analyze the political equation within a country or region in terms of how events might affect the success of the venture.

The astounding political changes of recent years, however, are forcing the U.S. business community to face up to new and confusing uncertainties. For example, the naive but happy presumption that the end of the Cold War meant the end of political conflict was quickly laid to rest by the Iraqi invasion of Kuwait and the eruption of intramural violence in Eastern Europe and the USSR.

FALLEN POWERS

These changes began well before the unleashing of perestroika and glasnost. The seemingly sudden demise of the powerful and friendly Shah of Iran at the hands of what was assumed by many to be a small minority of religious fanatics is a case in point. Iran had been an eager, cash-up-front customer of American goods and services, and the end of the Shah's regime adversely affected many American companies that had assumed that profits from Iran were an eternal phenomenon.

Remember, also, how the markets of Mexico, Nigeria and other OPEC members expanded geometrically under the beneficence of upwardly spiraling crude oil prices? That is, until mismanagement, corruption and the decline of oil prices destroyed their economies and caused irreparable harm to foreign creditors, foreign suppliers and foreign investors.

Fortunately, companies are beginning to recognize the impact of political issues upon international ventures, and that a sure-fire opportunity in a foreign country can deteriorate into a tremendous headache—affecting the safety of personnel as well as of profits—if political factors are not measured and provided for along with traditional market and investment perspectives.

Let's identify a variety of issues that fall within the political rubric, and then consider what a company can do on its own to identify and cope with these problems.

Political problems range from catastrophic events such as revolution or war, through a broad range of destabilizing issues including endemic corruption, labor unrest, crooked elections, religious violence, coups d'etat and incompetent economic management by government agencies, and then on to narrow but nevertheless dangerous matters such as the political leverage of your competition or ethnic conflict within a specific worksite. All of these phenomena spell trouble if not considered in advance.

Identifying these issues within a country and measuring their impact on political and economic stability requires an alertness to changing events and a healthy respect for reality. This becomes self-evident when we realize that more than one-third of the world's governments change hands each year, many by processes that would not qualify as democratic.

At the top of the scale is the potential for armed conflict with a neighbor or a civil war within a country's borders. In this category are perennial issues such as the India-Pakistani crisis and problems in the Middle East, and now the emerging ethnic-driven crises in Eastern Europe and the USSR that also signal potential bloodshed, terrorism and lingering instability.

These seeds of instability

From *Management Review,* January 1992, pp. 19-22. Copyright © 1992 by Benjamin Weiner. Reprinted by permission of the author.

LESSONS LEARNED

Specific, narrow political events—the kind that affect a particular venture rather than the nation as a whole—are difficult to categorize. However, a few examples get the message across rather quickly:

In the '60s, Mack Truck established an assembly plant in Pakistan but eventually left because of complications generated by its principal Pakistani competitor, whose managing director happened to be the son of the dictator. *Lesson*: Assay the political strength of your competition as well as of your own potential venture partner or agent. Mack Truck apparently failed to do this and paid the price.

Initially dazzled by the publicity surrounding EC 1992 (remember all those conferences?), an American manufacturer took the time to measure local political attitudes within the Common Market. It turned out that his product line would remain constrained by local customs and local regulations and that he was better off operating on a country-by-country basis despite the advent of a unified marketplace. *Lesson:* Don't always believe what the experts are proposing.

A West Coast manufacturer was invited by a group of Saudis to establish a joint venture in Saudi Arabia. They claimed impeccable credentials. The lead "Saudi" was named George, which piqued the curiosity of one of the company's executives, since it was a Christian name not normally used by a Saudi Arabian. After a discreet investigation it turned out that George was a Lebanese passing as a Saudi to foreigners. The manufacturer wisely terminated discussions. *Lesson:* Learn the ethnic equation early on.

B.W.

within a country thrive on any number of identifiable issues—historical, tribal, religious, linguistic, social, political or economic in nature. The questions are obvious:

□ Is conflict predictable and is it imminent?

□ Would it affect production and access to raw materials, and would it affect the marketplace?

□ What about your workforce? Does it comprise different ethnic groups and are they compatible?

□ Whose side are they on?

On a more specific note, it is incumbent upon the corporate executive to make certain that a prospective agent or joint venture partner fits into the political and ethnic equation in which he will be operating. This in turn requires an understanding of the ethnic and religious composition of the nation in question.

For example, an approach to the Nigerian potential could prove disastrous were an Ibo or Yoruba tribesman chosen to head an operation that was primarily concerned with the Hausa-Fulani region, or vice versa. In Pakistan one must understand the differences between Punjabi and Sindi. In Malaysia it is essential to recognize the special economic relationship between Chinese and Malay. In the Philippines it is important to understand the significant and sometimes lead financial role played by Filipino-Chinese.

POLITICAL ISSUES

If we were to select a "most important" political phenomenon, it would be ethnicity. It is the dominant engine behind current and potential instability throughout the world and will remain so for decades to come. Many of the conflicts attributed to struggles between political groupings are in fact the result of ethnic differences. And it is a vital issue for management to understand because it affects specific operations as well as general instability in a given country.

Ethnic violence is shaped by two factors, one historical and the other relatively recent. In some countries ethnic rivalries go back for hundreds of years and have managed to resist the influences of modern nationalism. (Perhaps the two most important components of ethnicity are religion and language, as we can see from events in Yugoslavia, Lebanon and the USSR.)

More recently, large numbers of foreigners with alien religions and customs have established themselves in wealthier nations, the result of the imbalance between labor-short Western industrial nations and labor-surplus Third World countries. Accordingly, France suddenly finds itself burdened with 3 million Muslims, Germany with nearly as many and England with between 1 million and 2 million. These new alien communities represent a source of political and social instability.

It is worth looking at the ethnic issue in terms of its impact upon a number of countries:

□ *Canada.* French-speaking, Roman Catholic Quebec has maintained its identity for some two centuries despite its being part of English-speaking, Protestant Canada. In recent decades the Quebecois have begun to assert their singular identity and position themselves as distinct from the remainder of Canada. It is possible that this trend will lead to partial or complete separation for the Province. (See *MR* December 1991, page 10.) In turn, this could lead to the further disintegration of Canada with the western provinces, for example, seeking economic and perhaps political union with the United States. The impact of this political dissolution upon U.S. interests depends on where the American company is located and the nature of its Canadian markets.

□ *Soviet Union.* The dissolution of the Soviet Union into autonomous or independent republics is generally along historical ethnic lines. This creates two problems. One is that although the new republics may possess all the political attributes of independence, some may not be able to function effectively as independent economic units, either because of the absence of raw materials or the inability to access foreign markets or markets within the other republics.

Second is the painful reality that there may be groups of differing ethnic background within many of the new republics, and they may resist integration. This is the case with the Abkhazian people within Georgia, who inhabit prime coastal territory in Georgia and seek autonomy.

A GUIDE TO POLITICAL EVALUATION

The following is an abridged version of Probe's Political Agenda Worksheet, which may serve as a guide for corporate executives initiating their own political evaluations.

EXTERNAL FACTORS AFFECTING SUBJECT COUNTRY

- □ prospects for foreign conflict
- □ relations with border countries
- □ regional instabilities
- □ alliances with major and regional powers
- □ sources of key raw materials
- □ major foreign markets
- □ policy toward United States
- □ U.S. policy toward country

INTERNAL GROUPINGS (POINTS OF POWER)

Government in Power

- □ key agencies and officials
- □ legislative entrenched bureaucracies
- □ policies—economic, financial, social, labor, etc.
- □ pending legislation
- □ attitude toward private sector
- □ power networks

Political Parties (in and out of power)

- □ policies
- □ leading and emerging personalities
- □ internal power struggles
- □ sector and area strengths
- □ future prospects for retaining or gaining power

Other Important Groups

- □ unions and labor movements
- □ military, special groups within military
- □ families
- □ business and financial communities
- □ intelligentsia
- □ students
- □ religious groups
- □ media
- □ regional and local governments
- □ social and environmental activists
- □ cultural, linguistic and ethnic groups
- □ separatist movements
- □ foreign communities
- □ potential competitors and customers

INTERNAL FACTORS

- □ power struggles amongst elites
- □ ethnic confrontations
- □ regional struggles
- □ economic factors affecting stability (consumer inflation, price and wage controls, unemployment, supply shortages, taxation, etc.)
- □ anti-establishment movements

FACTORS AFFECTING A SPECIFIC PROJECT
(Custom designed for each project)

Then there is the problem of the Shi'ite Meskhetians in Sunni Uzbekistan. Nor can we ignore the tensions between the Catholics and the Orthodox in the Ukraine. All of these issues represent potential friction, instability and bloodshed.

□ *South Africa.* The problem is no longer just black/white. It now is also black/black, with thousands of blacks killed in recent years as the result of struggles between two dominant tribes in that country, the Zulus and the Xhosa. For some reason the media hesitate to describe the bloodshed as tribal or ethnic in origin, but rather prefer to describe it in political terms as if the violence stemmed from profound ideological differences, for example the Inkatha Party versus the African National Congress (ANC). The reality, however, is that the Inkatha is almost exclusively Zulu, whereas the ANC is dominated by the Xhosa.

Tribalism in Africa is the paradigm of ethnicity. It not only encompasses the fundamentals of creed and language but also dictates for individuals the clothes they wear, the food they eat, how they dance, where they work, whom they marry and for whom they vote. In this context and until the tribal issue is resolved, American companies had best practice caution before renewing or establishing operations in South Africa.

Political analysis is rapidly becoming an integral element of the procedure by which companies evaluate foreign prospects. It's about time, given the chaotic political changes in play around the world.

But whether a company conducts its own research or contracts out for analyses, two important ground-rules must be observed: Focus on political issues before they become headlines; it's too late if you first learn about a problem on the evening news. And never, ever try to shape the outcome of political events in a given country. The consequences can be painful. The task of political evaluation is to protect a venture against the impact of political developments. Or to take advantage of them if they signal opportunity.

Companies in Europe Seeking Executives Who Can Cross Borders in a Single Bound

Bob Hagerty

Staff Reporter of The Wall Street Journal

When Vittorio Levi decided to leave the warmth of Italy for a job in Sweden, everyone told him he was crazy.

Scandinavians may dream of working in a Mediterranean climate, but Italians aren't supposed to be willing to go north. Nonetheless, Mr. Levi says he made the right choice when he joined **Oy Nokia**'s Stockholm-based computer division, where he became president early last year.

Expatriate executives are no novelty, of course, As more companies try to compete globally, more executives are crossing borders—not just as a brief detour but as a critical, and sometimes inevitable, stage in their careers. That trend is particularly pronounced in Europe, where plans for a unified market after 1992 are spurring companies to reorganize.

Responsibilities are rapidly shifting from national to regional or pan-European units. At the same time, companies want to stay in touch with local tastes. So they need managers who can think big while understanding local nuances.

Mastering that tricky mix often means hiring what some companies call Euromanagers; people skilled at dealing with a variety of cultures and at bringing a diverse team together. And that means hiring and promoting more foreigners.

"You need as much cultural mix and diversity and experience as possible . . . if you are running a global company," says Bob Poots, personnel director for the European division of London-based **Imperial Chemical Industries** PLC. ICI's executive ranks were predominantly British 20 years ago; now, only 74 of the company's top 150 executives world-wide are British.

That sort of change isn't easy to effect. The problem, headhunters and personnel managers say, is that Europe has a shortage of good senior executives who are willing to move. Tax and pension hassles, family ties and simple chauvinism keep many top managers in their own back yards.

"It's easy to say 'Euromanager,' " notes Brian F. Bergin, president of the European division of **Colgate-Palmolive** Co. "In fact, [hiring them] is an extremely difficult task. But it's happening."

To help realign its management, Colgate appointed a pan-European human-resources director, Peter Dessau, a Dane who moved to Brussels in 1989. His job is to encourage mobility among managers in the U.S company's European units.

Colgate quizzed all of its top European managers about what kind of executive works best in an international setting. Among the main attributes, Mr. Dessau says, is flexibility in managing. "You don't always go by the book," he says.

ICI's Mr. Poots says he looks for people who are good at getting along with colleagues at home. "That skill travels remarkably well," he says. Any problems an executive has in dealing with colleagues, he figures, will be magnified in a foreign setting, where much more effort is needed to build understanding and trust.

Unilever Group, the Anglo-Dutch food and soap giant, shies away from bossy executives. "We tend to look for people who can work in teams and understand the value of cooperation and consensus," says Floris Maljers, chairman of Unilever NV, the group's Dutch arm.

Some recruiters want candidates who have learned at least one foreign language besides English. Even if the foreign language won't be needed much in a particular job, having learned it "shows you are willing to dive into someone else's culture," says Marc Swaels, a Brussels-based partner for **Korn/Ferry International,** a U.S. executive-search firm.

Not surprisingly, many companies are above all looking for executives who have already succeeded in running at least one big operation outside their home countries.

Once the right kind of executive is found, companies wanting to move managers across borders must overcome differences in pay scales, pensions and tax systems. In time, the European Community is expected to bring greater harmony in these areas, but for now the costs of solving such problems make some companies hold transfers to a minimum.

Even if the red tape can be cut, many European executives—especially senior ones with families—are reluctant to live abroad. British managers are often willing to leave their children in distant boarding schools, but Continental Europeans tend to want the family close together.

Another barrier to the free flow of executives is prejudice. Especially among older executives, history weighs heavily. Asked why his company wasn't moving into the German market, the chief of a Dutch retailer replied without hesitation, "Because we [in the company] don't like Germans."

To overcome these obstacles, companies are trying to be more flexible in managing people. Nokia Data, for instance, made it possible for the Italian Mr. Levi to keep his main residence in Turin. The company provides him with a small apartment in Stockholm and flies him home to Italy for weekends about twice a month.

Reprinted by permission of *The Wall Street Journal,* January 25, 1991, pp. B1, B3. Copyright © 1991 by Dow Jones & Company, Inc. All rights reserved worldwide.

Mr. Levi says such benefits have helped him make a smooth transition. At age 52, he is older than most executives in their first senior position abroad. Though he doesn't expect to spend the rest of his career in Stockholm, he says his international job gives him a better understanding of Europe's political and economic transformation. "In a time of great change," he says, "you get a closer view if you are in a position like this than if you stay home in Italy with your friends."

Companies also try to identify potential Euromanagers at an early stage. ICI has long recruited heavily from British universities; now, it is trying harder to attract Continental students. A new program offered 20 university students two-month internships last summer at an ICI site outside their home country.

Rainer Goldammer, personnel chief for the European division of **Minnesota Mining & Manufacturing** Co., asks the company's local operating units for lists of young managers who might do well internationally. The company would like to send more young managers abroad for experience, but relocation and other expenses mean such managers cost about twice as much as local hires, Mr. Goldammer says.

An alternative is to give young managers international experience without moving them out of their home country. Both 3M and Colgate put managers on project teams with colleagues in other countries. "It's a way of seeing the light," says Colgate's Mr. Dessau. "You find out that you don't need to stay in the boundaries you're used to."

Honeywell Europe, a Brussels-based unit of **Honeywell** Inc., encourages managers to relocate by clearly showing them how such international experience could lead to promotions later on. Jean-Pierre Rosso, a Frenchman who heads Honeywell Europe, says the company persuaded a reluctant Frenchman to take a post in Hong Kong by telling him that the next step would be a top job back in France.

In general, it helps if foreign executives feel they have a chance to rise to the top. In Honeywell's European division, 12 of the top 13 jobs are held by non-Americans. Mr. Rosso, a Frenchman who in 1987 became the first non-American to head Honeywell Europe, says he hopes a European executive eventually will sit on the board of Honeywell in the U.S.

Unilever has six nationalities on its board, but most companies' executive directors come almost exclusively from the home country. A boss's natural inclination, says Korn/Ferry's Mr. Swaels, is to surround himself with people from a similar background, speaking the same language. But Mr. Swaels and others say it will be vital for global companies to build up "an international culture" at the very top.

Partly because true Euromanagers are in short supply, some European companies turn to Americans or other non-Europeans who have worked for U.S.-based multinationals. U.S. companies sometimes have an edge in Europe because—whether through naivete or foresight—they have always tended to view Europe more as one big market than as a series of small nations. Colgate's top executive in Europe, Mr. Bergin, is Australian. The top finance man is Argentine.

At 3M, more Americans are filling top jobs in Europe these days. But Mr. Goldammer, a German who moved to Brussels a year ago, says the next generation of European managers will be more internationally minded and mobile. That would let 3M send more Americans back home.

SUPER MANAGER!

Xerox is beating the Japanese throughout Asia. Pat Martin is leading the fight.

Marlene C. Piturro

In his well-worn corduroy jacket, blue shirt, and half-moon spectacles, the ruddy-faced, fiftyish Patrick J. Martin resembles a college professor. He's not.

Martin, a mathematician and electrical engineer with a stint at Harvard's executive training program, is now a top global manager at Stamford, Connecticut-based, Xerox Corporation. Xerox grew its business from a 1949 quirky invention, a machine that replaced carbon paper, to a giant with annual revenues above $13 billion.

Martin, father of five, wasn't always a globetrotter. Before joining Xerox in 1977, he worked at the Department of Agriculture on school lunch and food stamp programs. Through years of hard work, he has blossomed into a top executive.

Martin joined a cadre of Xerox senior managers who are homegrown—managers who understand each other, the copier business and the international market. They're high-energy, entrepreneurial types operating within a huge company. To succeed, they learn their assigned parts of the international business. That means long stretches of time overseas, immersed in a foreign business that's also part of Xerox.

The global route is the way to go at Xerox. Paul Allaire, Xerox chairman and CEO since May 1991, did it. An electrical engineer with an MS in industrial administration, much of Allaire's career has been spent overseas. Allaire's ascendancy must be inspiring to Martin and other major executives still hacking their way through the thicket of international postings.

Like Allaire, David Kearns (former CEO), Wayland Hicks, David Myerscough, Yotaro ("Tony") Kobayashi, and other Xerox executives, Martin spends lots of time outside the U.S. Since January 1991, Martin has been president and general manager of the Americas operation, a promotion that added Latin America and Canada to his Pacific Rim responsibilities. He reports to Hicks, executive vice president of marketing and customer operations of the Xerox empire.

Martin radiates energy. The three times we spoke, twice in Hong Kong, he was at his desk by 7 a.m. His secretary manages to be there before him, so as to not lose face. Six-day workweeks are the norm, but if he and his staff need to work on Sundays, they do. "We set the pace for everyone," he says of his staff, "especially the ex-pats. I gear my reward systems for people who know how to work hard."

He seems thoroughly at home in Hong Kong. It's easy to forget that it's his first foreign posting. And for a novice, the assignment—to lead the Xerox Shanghai joint venture—was a humdinger.

Before Martin's arrival, Xerox was preoccupied with the same dreams that mislead most companies in China—"If we just get all of the 1.1 billion Chinese to buy one of our widgets, we'll be rich." The Chinese, of course, did nothing of the sort. So Martin developed a strategy to crack this market. He chose to work the bureaucracy.

In contrast to the entrepreneurial types in Hong Kong, Martin found a whole other world in Shanghai. Shanghai was attractive because of its proximity to Hong Kong, its progressive mayor, Zhu Rhongji, and its long exposure to Western culture. But Shanghai was also a part—a victim, you might say—of China's bloated bureaucracy, uncompetitive industries, and workers who had no reason to produce quality goods on time. Martin gritted his teeth and plunged ahead.

He set a goal of sourcing 70% of supplies locally. Strategically, this would upgrade the suppliers' technical skills and tie them closely to the success of the joint venture. Under the ever watchful eyes of bureaucrats heavily invested in the government's central economic planning, Martin moved cautiously.

Getting to know the locals, Xerox people worked one-on-one and in small groups. They trained the suppliers, gave or sold them tools, and brainstormed technical problems. Xerox engineers, foremen, and procurement officers showed them how to meet Xerox standards. Martin felt that even if a supplier wanted to produce to Xerox standards, he'd be taking a risk with the local authorities, who might accuse him of politi-

From *World Trade*, April 1992, pp. 80, 82. *World Trade*, 500 Newport Center Drive, Suite 450, Newport Beach, CA 92660. Reprinted by permission.

cally incorrect behavior. Martin bided his time.

Eventually, someone came through. One supplier, Changzhou Electric Motor Company, got very excited about the quality control program and produced excellent electro-mechanical parts. Xerox spread the word and Changzhou became both a role model and a potential exporter to companies other than Xerox.

But the Changzhou managers, trained by politics and culture to be risk-averse, faced a big hurdle. Should they invest in upgrading the plant with a chance for more lucrative contracts in the future?

After some hand-holding from Xerox, Changzhou Electric's managers went ahead with the upgrading. It paid off: They landed a multi-million dollar expert contract with an Italian buyer.

Even with the Changzhou example to guide them, other Xerox vendors remained fearful about forging straight away into capitalism. Martin needed to do more. He convinced the Shanghai Economic Commission (SEC) to pour millions of dollars into local companies that upgraded their machines, thereby lessening the vendors' risk of investing in capital. It also relaxed currency controls so that companies had the hard currency to buy parts and equipment.

Shanghai was becoming more economically independent and resourceful every day. Things were running smoothly. Until June 4, 1989, a day that changed everything. On that day, the People's Liberation Army gunned down pro-democracy demonstrators in Beijing, triggering shock waves around the world. Pat Martin and all other Americans got a painful lesson about how quickly and awfully things can change in China.

Martin's hands-on style served him well during the dark days after Tiananmen Square. Would the violence spread from Beijing, nearly 1,000 miles away? Worried about his 560 Chinese employees, ex-pat managers and their families, he moved everyone to safety and shut the plant. After waiting several days and seeing that things in Shanghai were stable, he sent people back to work. Martin might have simply flown back to safety in the U.S. Instead, he went to marches in the street, trying to gauge the people's mood. He had what he calls "very long conversations with local officials," particularly Zhu Rhongji, then mayor of Shanghai and now vice premier of China. Martin urged them to keep

REVOLUTIONS

Teaching the Giant to Dance

Xerox went through dark days during the late '70s. After years of ignoring Japanese competitors, the Stamford, Connecticut-based giant watched its own market share plunge from 82% to less than 35%. The Japanese were selling small copiers for what it cost Xerox to make theirs. They were building them in Japan, shipping and selling them here—and making money.

Xerox blamed no one but itself for the decline. It didn't look to the government for a bailout—Xerox does not support government subsidies, trade barriers or import quotas. David Kearns, then CEO, decided to shake things up. He turned to McKinsey & Co., management consultants, for an analysis of what was wrong and how to fix it.

The McKinsey staff hit hard with these findings: Xerox had no global strategy. It had missed the Japanese strategy of going in at the market's low end and working up the product line. Turf wars and career advancement meant more than productivity. Managers worked at cross-purposes; one faction wanted to cut prices, others wanted to hold market share, others wanted profits.

Kearns bit the bullet. He cut staff by 20%, brought in new blood at the top and insisted that all top people have international experience. He broke the company into small businesses, urging all managers to be entrepreneurs. Xerox adopted competitive benchmarking; each plant had to turn out products as good or better than the Japanese.

Everyone had to work faster, smarter, in smaller groups—and overseas when appropriate. Other "radical" changes: Automation, just-in-time manufacturing, sophisticated market research, and rallying around a new product line.

The strategy worked. From 1980, its low point, through 1986, Xerox regained a substantial portion of the market share it had lost to the Japanese, thanks to the hard work of its top managers.

Although all senior managers worked hard during the turnaround, Wayland Hicks at Rank Xerox (Europe), Pat Martin's boss, stands out. Hicks is a legendary high-energy workaholic, noted for his 14-hour days and 6- or 7-day weeks. In the late '70s and early '80s, while other Xerox top executives worried about competition from IBM and Kodak, Hicks had this on his mind: "Our real enemy is Japan. Canon is waging total war on us. . . . I'm not going to let those bastards beat us. . . . The next story I see about the Japanese competing with us I'm going to put on the wall . . . until I can paint black over them."

Hicks was one of Xerox's first international managers to carry out McKinsey's strategy. Hicks' straightforward approach was a blueprint for other managers, including Pat Martin.

the peace by keeping out the troops. In the ensuing months, he prevailed on American businessmen visiting Shanghai to appear at meetings as a show of support for Zhu and economic liberalism.

The hard-line politics in China troubled other American businesses there. Some firms pulled out, preferring a financial beating to unpredictable Chinese politics. Martin and Xerox stood their ground.

Even after the events of June 4th, Martin had faith in Zhu, who aspired to make Shanghai a regional entrepot by welcoming cutting-edge technological and infrastructure projects. Xerox was both a beneficiary and driving force in Zhu's plan. Despite top-level, government denunciations of capitalists, Martin—with Zhu's backing—forged ahead. He announced rather proudly that his joint venture had captured 44.5% of the Chinese market for desktop copiers, an increase of 31.8% in one year. In 1990, Xerox Shanghai opened two other plants within its compound. One made photoreceptors for installation in Shanghai product copiers and for field replacement. The other made toner, a lucrative addition to the product line.

How to account for such coolheadedness? Martin himself is enigmatic: "The mountains are high and heaven is far away," he says, smiling like an Irish Buddha. "China is a pragmatic government of personalities, not law. There's a wide range of economic and cultural activities in each region and city. A man has to know where he wants to participate."

For our third interview, Martin was at U.S. headquarters, studying the lay of the land before incorporating Latin America and Canada into his territory. Asked to think back to another beginning, his Far Eastern assignment, he summarizes his accomplishments.

He inherited an office in Hong Kong, 40 repairmen, a bare-bones plant in Shanghai assembling low-end parts imported from Fuji Xerox, and a goal of producing 30,000 copiers a year by 1992.

He put together a gung-ho team of managers, seven ex-pats and seven Chinese, rejecting any American who thought he was signing up for the colonial life. Because China was so challenging, Martin required that all managers had to have experience on another joint venture, preferably in India, Mexico, or Brazil. Everyone who needed it got training in the U.S.

A MONTH IN THE LIFE

Frequent Flier

Patrick Martin

President and General Manager
Xerox Americas Operation

September
13. Hong Kong. Xerox regional office
16. Shanghai. Xerox manufacturing complex
18. Beijing. Meetings
20. U.S. headquarters, Stamford, CT
22. Sao Paulo, Brazil
24. Buenos Aires, Argentina
27. Chile
29. Venezuela
October
1. U.S. headquarters
6. Brazil
Once a month: Visit Brazil, Mexico and Canada.
Every 3 or 4 months: Visit Far East.

He staffed the factory, a major headache because of constraints by Chinese civil service rules. Some of the "pre-hired" employees were fired based on experience with them during the four years of joint venture negotiation. Somehow, the team picked the 30 most promising workers.

Reflecting on the early part of his China stint, Martin says, "I realized China will take 50 to 60 years to industrialize. It's a long road to the Chinese people having competitive work skills. I think about Japan in 1958. We (Xerox Shanghai) are where they were then."

With the plant producing to Xerox standards, Martin faced the difficult task of selling. Recognizing that what made the best salesman in the U.S.—energy, cold calling, incentives, and the rest—didn't work in China, he tried the political approach.

With ties to Zhu locally and a solid relationship with Premier Li Peng in Beijing, Martin knew how to work around the government bureaucracy by forming powerful alliances. Martin was "politically correct" and his copiers sold, about 13,500 of them last year, most of those to Chinese government agencies, entrepreneurs, and office supply companies. The machines were so good that several thousand went to Rank Xerox Germany—a major accomplishment in pleasing the picky Germans.

Finally, Martin found a good product mix for products other than Xerox Shanghai's desktop copiers. Engineering copiers, photoreceptors, and toners seemed just about right. Martin's strategy has worked. Every year Xerox Shanghai produces and sells more copiers, parts, and supplies than the year before.

But the long-term success of Martin's strategic political alignments presents a risk. Backing the reformer, Zhu, and Li, the central-planning advocate, could be disastrous if either of them fall out of favor with the Chinese Community Party (CCP). This risk was highlighted in the September meeting of the CCP on industrial policy. The party spoke: "Large and medium-sized government plants must ceaselessly increase their vitality and efficiency in order to consolidate the preeminence of the public sector and raise confidence in socialism."

Such pronouncements make reformers nervous. A political and economic shift toward state-run enterprises could signal trouble for cities with flourishing enterprises. Martin can only watch and wait, hoping that the seeds of enterprise he planted will flourish rather than be crushed underfoot by the Old Guard.

If Xerox is a giant that has learned

to dance, what can it teach companies much smaller than itself? Martin explains: "I'm in a field office thousands of miles from Stamford. I have to run it as if it were my own business. I enjoy the obligations of making decisions. Xerox is very good at letting people do this. You have to have the intellect and the intuition to do this because there's not a lot of help from afar."

What to do about bumping up against foreign business practices that are Byzantine, corrupt, or just incomprehensible? Martin advises Americans to be careful, and not to knuckle under to pressure for bribes, gifts or other demands that are often expected to grease the wheels of foreign trade.

He points out, however, that countries—especially in the Pac Rim—are awash in cash and goodies from Japan. The Japanese are slated to spread $21 billion around the region during the next five years. Such largess will not go unnoticed and unrewarded.

So how do we compete? Martin says start with the assumption that things seem unbalanced and unfair. "Developing countries don't want to be exploited. If they see us coming in and selling our products to them, they see money being siphoned off from local goods, and they expect some compensation. They want us to honor trade obligations, to offer a guaranteed balance of trade." What happens to a Super Manager? He gets promoted, of course. Earlier this year Martin added Canada and Latin America to his turf. Fuji Xerox took over the rest of the Pacific countries, while the Middle East and Africa went to Rank Xerox (Europe). Martin ticks off the elements of his new strategy: The similarities between Canada and Australia are striking. They're both large and sparsely populated, with abundant natural resources. He's profiled their GDPs and major business problems and knows his jumping-off point.

'We set the pace for everyone. I gear my reward systems for people who know how to work hard.'

Mexico's on a roll. It's got fast growth in its gross national product and seems analogous to the Four Tigers (Taiwan, Hong Kong, South Korea, and Singapore). Like the Tigers, its economy is developing quickly, but its infrastructure is straining under rapid growth.

Both Martin's Mexican and Brazilian development teams remind him of the Shanghai setup. The plants' general managers are highly motivated; Martin finds them at their desks until 9 p.m. most evenings.

But Latin America presents headaches Martin didn't face in the Pacific. Inflation is rampant; some currencies are devalued 20% a month. How will he adjust his business strategy? "I'm studying the economic and political history of Brazil and I've got to talk to the finance minister. In 1988 they had a price freeze for 18 months . . . Hmm," Martin muses. In the welter of global changes and career moves, Xerox's Super Manager is eager for his new challenge.

Challenging Global MYTHS

An unprecedented look at Quality practices reveals gaping holes in the perception of most North American executives and delivers an explosive mandate.

Tracy E. Benson

It wasn't so many years ago that the notion of quality in manufacturing lifted eyebrows.

Why? Because producing quality products and services, it was believed, simply meant a more costly process. But years of grueling global competition and the ensuing exploration of the quality terrain have caused what was once a revelation to become common knowledge: The very pursuit of quality products, services, and processes results in lower cost, higher productivity, and greater market share.

Although these ideas are becoming increasingly accepted, they have until now been based largely on anecdotal evidence. Without a comprehensive database of quality-management practices to track and consult, business leaders around the world have had to rely on instinct, history, and experimentation.

The International Quality Study (IQS)[SM], a joint research effort launched by the American Quality Foundation (based in New York) and Ernst & Young, Cleveland, is the first known attempt to assess the level of quality practices across industries and across national borders. Participating businesses represent the automotive, banking, computer, and health-care industries and are based in Canada, Germany, Japan, and the U. S.

Designed to measure the extent of actual behavior, rather than attitudes, the IQS provides the framework for the first time to understand how quality practices impact market performance.

The most startling discoveries thus far indicate that almost across the board, companies in Japan behave far differently in the face of quality and related issues than was previously believed in the U. S.

The emphasis devoted to teams of employees with a specific quality focus, for instance, is far ***lower*** in Japan than was anticipated. And while change is typically slow and measured in Japan, trend data in the area of customer expectations indicate dramatic change will occur during the next three years.

Not surprisingly, companies in the U. S. consistently report they intend to dramatically step up efforts—on all fronts—in the quality arena. Though the intention in North America is noble regarding this trend, experts are concerned that in the face of global pressures, it may not be enough.

"Although this is our first look at the data," notes Joshua Hammond, president of the American Quality Foundation (AQF), "the performance level that Japan has achieved in numerous quality practices and the exponential plans Japan has for integrating the voice of the customer in strategic planning is greater than expected. National parity," he adds, "will come only if the existing rates of increase in management practices across the board in other countries are rapidly accelerated."

Initial top-line findings, issued by the AQF and Ernst & Young this month at the Quality Forum in New York, fall into five major areas: business performance, customer focus, competitors in the strategic process, process improvement, and employee involvement. In this first IQS report, Industry Week examines three major areas of quality practice from a country-by-country perspective: employee involvement, process improvement, and customer focus. During at least the next 12 months, IW will track further findings and interpret them in special quality reports.

Employee Involvement

Employee involvement in its early days was an outgrowth of the quality circles so widely in use in Japan during the 1950s and '60s. Today, charged with a dual mission of humanizing the workplace and creating more efficient workflow, em-

Reprinted with permission from *Industry Week*, October 7, 1991, pp. 12-25. Copyright © 1991 by Penton Publishing, Inc., Cleveland, Ohio.

ployee involvement often takes the shape of work teams. The increasing popularity of such teams (both cross-functional and departmental) around the world mandates taking a closer look.

IQS data show that the majority of Japanese businesses (64%) report an astonishingly *low* level of worker involvement on quality-related teams—one-quarter of the workforce or less.

Even more striking is the pronounced gap between the plans of Western companies and their Japanese counterparts in this area. As recently as three years ago, only 15% of surveyed companies in the U. S. and none in Canada involved three-quarters or more of their workers in quality-related teams. Three years from now, however, 34% of U. S. companies and 27% of those in Canada will achieve the three-quarters level. By contrast, the face of worker involvement in Japan will not have undergone any change at all in the same six-year period.

This insight into the behavior of Japanese companies vis-a-vis quality teams effectively shatters widespread notions on the subject. "I find this an explosive finding with major implications for U. S. industry," notes the AQF's Mr. Hammond. "The quality circle movement was founded in Japan, and it bombed in the U. S. in the '60s and '70s. But the persistent improvement in Japan led U. S. industry to refocus on teams during the '80s, without the structure of quality circles.

"At the same time," he continues, the Japanese "had either integrated quality so fully that it can no longer be distinguished, or they have taken care of quality issues so well that they've turned to other issues."

The discrepancy between formal quality-prompted employee involvement and the overall emphasis on quality in Japan does not surprise Joseph R. Bransky, director of corporate quality and reliability at General Motors Corp. In fact, he has seen firsthand a more deep-seated—and thus informal—manifestation of quality practices in the Japanese automotive industry.

"They are involved very much in improvement and quality-first kinds of ideas. But it is much more informal—mostly through their suggestion systems and programs. The number of suggestions submitted, as well as the number implemented, are a quantum leap in numbers compared with what you see in the U. S."

Though quality is not typically an explicit mission for work teams in Japan, Mr. Bransky argues that the quality-first philosophy is the foundation of those teams. "It probably represents what I would say is a greater maturity on the part of the Japanese with respect to the quality-improvement process."

Because of the limited potential of its domestic market, Japanese automakers were forced to think globally long before manufacturers in North America did so. "Having to push their products overseas caused them to realize that there's a tremendous diversity with respect to customer preferences and tastes all over the world," notes Mr. Bransky. "That really becomes an eye-opener.

"I think there's just a greater depth of understanding of the relationship quality has to all aspects of the business. It perhaps is more ingrained, if you will, in that culture than it is as we [in the U. S.] come down the learning curve."

Though not organized by teams on the subject of quality, Japanese workers indeed enjoy the highest rate of participation in regularly scheduled meetings concerning quality. Roughly 40% of Japanese companies report that three-quarters or more of their workers are involved in these get-togethers. In North America, only 15% of companies report that much participation, while in Germany, a mere 5% of companies do this.

Here, too, while Japan anticipates little movement in this area, companies around the world report big plans. In Canada, Germany, and the U. S., the number of companies planning to involve 75% or more of their workers in regular quality meetings will double three years from now. But even then, overwhelming participation in quality meetings will be routine in less than half of companies worldwide.

Conventional wisdom dictates that frequent and regular communications are critical to engender understanding and commitment. But the

THE AMERICAN QUALITY FOUNDATION

A nonprofit organization targets strategic issues of Total Quality Management.

For years American industry considered the issue of Total Quality Management (TQM) strictly from a technical perspective. In so doing, it raised the standards of its production processes significantly. The problem was, however, that as advanced as its tools and processes became, total quality had little relationship to either the marketplace or the overall corporate mission.

In 1987, the American Society for Quality Control spawned the American Quality Foundation (AQF), a nonprofit executive-led group whose mission is to support the long-term development and promotion of total quality improvement.

In its mission statement, called "New Horizons: A Declaration," the AQF challenges, "It is no longer enough to manage *for* quality; business must manage *by* quality." Through the International Quality Study (IQS)SM developed with Ernst & Young, the AQF hopes to develop universal reference points for accessing successful quality practices.

AQF President Joshua Hammond thinks the IQS will be a useful rallying point around which to create a national industrial policy. "We [in the U. S.] don't think in national strategic terms," he points out. "We think in competitive individual terms."

Through its campaigns on the global, national, and personal levels, the AQF has made great strides in its efforts to "make quality a national public and economic concern, to support the quality needs of executives, develop the next generation of quality-improvement strategies, and to promote the integration of the human side of the quality equation into existing and new quality practices."

Not only is its mission powerpacked. The group's board of directors includes such industry leaders as Robert C. Stempel (chairman and CEO, General Motors Corp.); Allen F. Jacobson (chairman and CEO, 3M Co.); Susan B. King (president, Steuben Glass); Ray J. Groves (chairman, Ernst & Young); and John E. Pepper (president, Procter & Gamble Co.).

AQF's Mr. Hammond suggests that meetings alone are not the answer. "American business has 'meetinged' itself to death. Yet we're lagging Japan and other countries in terms of regular meetings about quality.

"One of the tradeoffs here is, 'Do we add more meetings, but say these are special meetings, these are important meetings, these are critical meetings?' Or do we find another way to achieve the same thing that could be achieved as a result of meetings?"

Indeed, regular meetings may not be a panacea. But one way or another, companies must create opportunities for such dialog within the organization. Those that don't must ask themselves how they intend to build the culture and orientation that will foster quality awareness.

THE INTERNATIONAL QUALITY STUDY

It is the definitive examination of quality practices across four nations and four industries.

Since its initial successes in Japan under the tutelage of Dr. W. Edwards Deming, Total Quality Management has become a staple in U. S. corporate lexicon. Until now, though, its advocates have not had a fact-based body of knowledge on which to rely.

In an attempt to provide the first-ever empirical base of knowledge, the American Quality Foundation and Ernst & Young have developed and undertaken the International Quality Study (IQS)[SM].

This project is designed to shed some much-needed light on the correlation of quality practices with market performance. In so doing, it examines management practices across four countries—Canada, Germany, Japan, and the U. S.—and within four industries—automotive, banking, computers, and health care.

The need for such an examination was clear to Stephen L. Yearout, national director of operations and quality management for Ernst & Young's management-consulting group, Cleveland. "There is a lot of supposition about which quality-management practices work best. But there are very few factual data that prove that," he notes.

"So what you find is that companies will read something and try to apply it directly to their business, when, in fact, their business might be a much different business and may be strategically positioned much differently."

The IQS was designed to ask critical questions about quality management that have never been asked before. The idea was to puncture the veil of widely held assumptions about what constitutes quality management in an effort to get to real-life truths.

"As global markets emerge, the ability to benchmark quality-management practices against an international database will become critical," Mr. Yearout predicts. "This benchmarking will provide clues not only to the relative merits of particular practices, but, more importantly, it will also yield understanding of the speed with which competitors are adopting these practices. We believe this study and the ongoing analysis associated with it will provide the practical information needed by both manufacturing and service businesses."

Since most of business' quality efforts are often considered proprietary, it is noteworthy that more than 500 companies agreed to participate in the project. Because of the depth and breadth of the study, it took at least 16 hours per participant to complete.

The database, collected from March through August 1991, contains 1.5 million pieces of information. Though initial top-line findings were issued in a report based on a country-by-country perspective, further periodic reports will focus on other angles of the research. Future examinations will include how management practices impact business performance, cross-industry relationships, the impact of culture, and overall trends.

PROCESS IMPROVEMENT

Process improvement is perhaps the quintessential manifestation of the continuous-improvement concept. It is, in essence, a means of consistently improving the cumulative steps (the process) by which products and services are produced.

Only in Japan are process simplification and cycle-time analysis (two process-improvement tools) being aggressively pursued. One-half of businesses in that country report "always or almost always" using these tools.

Only one in five companies in North America, on the other hand, "always or almost always" use either tool, and a mere 6% of companies in Germany do so. Cycle-time reduction, perhaps a more familiar practice, is in somewhat more frequent use than process simplification in Canadian, German, and U. S. businesses.

Not surprisingly, the automotive and computer industries show dramatic leads over the banking and health-care sectors in the practice of both tools. Process simplification is consistently practiced by one in five automotive companies and almost one-quarter of computer businesses worldwide. Cycle-time reduction is "always or almost always" practiced by 32% of automotive companies and 23% of computer companies.

"The universal movement toward increased emphasis on process improvement comes as no surprise," asserts Stephen L. Yearout, national director of operations and quality management at Ernst & Young. "We've seen clients from all industries, the service and manufacturing sectors, experience dramatic improvements in quality, cost, and time performance by focusing on process imrpovement."

IBM Corp. and GM are two U. S. companies that put a premium on process improvement. "A few years ago, we said that we should look not only at manufacturing and development, but look really across all the areas of our business at the processes in effect," recalls Edward J. Fuhr, program manager for market-driven quality management systems at IBM.

"We started out from the point of view of the customer, looked back across IBM, and came up with 15-odd processes that produce something for the customer's benefit. This meant looking horizontally across the functional organizations where we have output to the customer."

After considerable time spent on defining these processes, IBM is currently involved in simplifying them.

The relationship between process simplification and cycle-time reduction is as important as either tool is alone. GM's Mr. Bransky says that by simplifying the process—and consequently reducing the time it takes for work in process to complete a cycle—errors and problems are forced to the surface where they can receive the attention they need.

"When you reduce in-process inventory between operations [a common result of process improvement], you really call out what your problem areas are very quickly because you don't have a big inventory bank to rely on until the problem is fixed or contained," Mr. Bransky says. Without that cushion to which industry had become so accustomed, "you're required to respond very quickly to get that problem stabilized and produce good product."

As technology continues to advance, many companies are discovering that product development is the next vast frontier—and tomorrow's competitive edge. "In the old world," Mr. Fuhr reflects, "we used to have to design something on paper, build a prototype, and test out the prototype.

"Today in the design world, engineers actually use computer terminals to design what they're doing. They can then test the product before it's ever built."

Increasingly, companies around the world are shedding their traditional vertical structures in favor of efficiency and agility. In such an environment, process-improvement tools can provide the critical competitive edge.

The challenge is clearly here to examine and then perfect the processes by which companies deliver their goods and services.

Customer Focus

Ask any quality expert what is the single greatest link in the pursuit of business success. The answer will be: meeting or exceeding customers' expectations. Despite worldwide consensus on this basic tenet, fewer than half of the IQS respondents have elevated customer satisfaction measurements to a "primary" status on the strategic-planning level.

Even so, customer satisfaction appears to be on nearly everyone's mind. Three-quarters or more of companies in all countries report that customer satisfaction is of "major" or "primary" importance in strategic planning. Not surprisingly, businesses in Japan are again ahead of the pack. Roughly one-quarter of companies in Canada, Germany, and the U. S. place secondary or less importance on customer satisfaction in strategic planning. By contrast, only 5% of Japanese respondents indicate the role it plays is minor.

"Despite general business claims by North America that customer satisfaction is of paramount importance," Ernst & Young's Mr. Yearout challenges, "our findings indicate that current planning practices do not fully mirror those claims. On the other hand, future plans to incorporate the voice of the customer in strategic planning is encouraging. The question is, given the aggressive plans, do businesses have the practices and infrastructure in place to make these goals reality?"

IBM is one U. S.-based company that has recognized the value of regular customer interface. In fact, that company has taken customer expectations so far that it involves not only current customers, but non-customers as well.

IBM's user groups are widely talked about in quality circles. "We actually have a software partner's laboratory where we get customers and business partners to come in and try out the software that's under development," Mr. Fuhr explains.

"There's a video I saw recently where one IBM customer said, 'I feel I'm part of the IBM design team, because every suggestion I made when I tested this product out—things that were not there before—are all in the product now when it's finally announced.'"

IBM is big believer in the notion that customer expectations play a significant role in a company's strategic planning efforts. An international group of customers was brought into an IBM strategic planning session as early as 1986. That, recalls Mr. Fuhr, was quite a learning experience.

"It turns out we didn't like what we heard. Customers complained about things such as product quality and the fact that IBM wasn't being attentive to their needs, that we were too slow in responding to what the customers wanted."

That brush with reality forced IBM's top execs to turn their attention back to basics. "Our chairman established unequivocally that the customer is the final arbiter in what we do. So let's determine what satisfies the customer and let's do that."

Technology appears to be the tool of choice—both currently and in the future—in the Japanese quest to meet customer expectations. The IQS study indicates that while nearly one-half of businesses in Japan place primary importance on technology for meeting customer expectations, only 22% of companies in the U. S. do so. Interestingly, businesses in both Canada and Germany place more importance on technology for these purposes than those in the U. S.

Although businesses in all four countries plan strong growth in this sphere during the next three years, companies in Japan will nevertheless continue to lead the way. U. S. companies plan to more than double efforts over the next three years, while Canadian and German firms likewise plan to nearly double their use of technology in meeting customer expectations. But study findings also indicate that although there has been little change during the last three years in Japan, companies there have targeted this area for significant expansion during the next three years. In fact, the growth planned in these efforts has been called "exponential" by some industry observers who are accustomed to seeing change in Japan take place in small, incremental stages.

Aggressive plans to expand the role of technology have effectively raised the stakes for business in all countries. The projected pace of technology application raises important questions for all businesses about the capability to implement these plans in short order.

Whatever tools businesses select for these purposes, the key, insists GM's Mr. Bransky, is linkage. "The customer-satisfaction focus has to have linkage with your vision, your strategies, your tasks, your activities, and your measurement and feedback systems. What I'm describing is really an integrated approach from the macro view at the corporate level."

The test, he challenges, is whether that overall corporate vision is reflected in every step of the chain. "They have to be related so that when you walk out onto the manufacturing floor or into the dealer's showroom or into the supplier's office, there's an alignment of understanding that says 'we understand what you're trying to do.' It's important for people to be able to personalize what those strategies mean to them."

IMPLICATIONS

At first glance, top-line IQS findings appear to support the notion that Japanese business executives typically take the time necessary to examine the issues and then carefully select elements that fit the overall mission. Once identified, those leverage points are then pursued with a vengeance. In Canada and the U. S., on the other hand, it appears that business leaders shoot for the moon in every area possible.

Have the great strides achieved by Japanese businesses more to do with cultural propensities, or, as GM's Mr. Bransky notes, has quality awareness simply reached maturation in Japan before it has in other nations? Whatever the answer, the AQF's Mr. Hammond sees a great deal of wisdom in deliberately selecting points of emphasis. "There is a fundamental tenet in any quality program, which is to pick your vital few. The Japanese have picked three of the 10 items we're reporting on," based on an initial analysis of the top-line findings. "It's exciting that Japan can do that."

Mr. Hammond urges business leaders in the U. S. to likewise craft an approach that maximizes our own unique cultural strengths. "It's O.K. to imitate *why* someone is doing something." But, he says, "we need to separate the *why* from the *how*. The *how* needs to be built on American strengths, on American peculiarities, and on American ideosyncracies. So if we are good at things that don't require a lot of planning, for instance, let's do those things."

Cycle-time reduction and process simplification are two areas in which U. S. businesses could excel, because, in Mr. Hammond's estimation, they play right into the American bias for action.

GM's Mr. Bransky agrees that U. S. businesses have a propensity for the touchdown, with little patience for the short-yardage plays to set it up. Even so, he urges, "there's got to be both innovation and incremental improvement. There needs to be a balance, a harmony. Incremental improvement is most likely to take place with the current product and current processes. It's the upstream activity in your product life cycle that can really contribute to the breakthrough or innovation improvement."

Selecting a path to excellence is no different for a corporation or a nation than it is for an individual. The key is to choose the strategies "that we can combine with our cultural strengths for the strategic business payoff," Mr. Hammond explains.

Top-line IQS findings indicate that Canadian and U. S. executives plan to unleash all the bulls into the quality ring at once. One would be hard pressed to find an executive or quality professional to say that we shouldn't try to do it all. Nevertheless, many use phrases like "let's get focused" when faced with the array of things it appears we'll be trying to accomplish during the next three years.

The key to harnessing the complexity of a company's quality efforts for the business payoff is in its ***integration***. Any orchestra can create a cacophony of sounds. But one that is well-trained and led by a seasoned conductor with a well-thought-out score can turn chaos into a beautifully executed symphony.

Business leaders around the globe must ask themselves: What are the threads of strength and continuity running through our businesses upon which these various tools can build? For Mr. Bransky, they are simply a focus on the customer and a fundamental set of values.

"The organization needs to have understandable, visible, and doable strategies based on a value system that is clearly articulated. The bottom line has to be around product and process improvement and innovation. And the customer is the one who votes," Mr. Bransky says.

It certainly isn't a secret that U. S. business leaders have not historically optimized strategic planning tools such as the business plan. Largely a formality until now, business plans have reflected only the financial dimension of a company's performance.

And maybe planning isn't the great American pastime. But in the face of growing global pressure, visionary leaders will dust these documents (or others like them) off and breathe new life into them. Tools such as these can provide the critical linkage between the disparate elements of an organization and its vision that is required to propel the ship efficiently toward its destination of total quality.

The Foreign Director: Boon or Babel in the Boardroom?

Santhanam C. Shekar

With many issues to consider, U.S. CEOs often find themselves sitting on the fence regarding who should be sitting on their boards. However, foreign representation—conspicuously absent in U.S. boardrooms—is increasingly vital to the success of all international companies.

Santhanam C. Shekar recently joined Heidrick & Struggles as a member of the firm's transnational search practice. Previously he was a Director with Arthur D. Little, Inc., and a Sales and Marketing Executive with Siemens. He is currently a member of three international advisory boards. *He gratefully acknowledges Robert K. Mueller, former Chairman of the Board of Arthur D. Little and the author of 13 books on statutory and advisory boards, for his contribution to this article.*

The role of the board of directors in the corporation has changed dramatically in recent years. U.S. companies are giving new constituencies, including women and minorities, enhanced representation on their boards. Yet conspicuously absent in most U.S. boardrooms are foreign accents—U.S. boards remain largely reserved for American nationals. However, as U.S. firms face the increased challenges of global competition in the 1990s and beyond, it is imperative that CEOs have a clear understanding of the role and value of a foreign national on their boards.

In the spring of 1989, the Conference Board surveyed 589 U.S. firms to determine the make-up of their boards. Of 268 manufacturing companies, only 24 percent had at least one non-U.S. citizen on the board. In the service sector, things looked even worse. Only 14 percent of 140 financial firms and 9 percent of 181 non-financial firms surveyed reported that they had foreign directors. Other surveys and studies paint the same picture.

Japanese companies have also traditionally had a poor track record regarding non-Japanese directors. In recent years, however, some top-ranked Japanese firms including Sony Corp., Nomura Securities Company, C. Itoh, and Yaohan Department Stores have all invited foreign nationals to join their boards of directors. Characteristic of Japanese companies, Sony's Michael Schulhof and Nomura's Ian Chapman are both inside directors from their respective U.S. operations. It should not be surprising that Sony, which also named a European to the board, leads the way in naming foreign directors. The company makes two-thirds of its sales outside Japan—27 percent in the United States alone.

Only 14 percent of 140 financial firms and 9 percent of 181 non-financial firms surveyed reported that they had foreign directors.

European companies seem to be the least parochial. Swiss and Dutch firms have gone the furthest in internationalizing their boards. Forbo, a Swiss manufacturer of wall and paper coverings has British, Dutch, and Swedish directors on its 12-man board. In 1988, Paul Volcker, the former chairman of the Federal Reserve, was asked to join the board of Nestle, the Swiss food

From *The Journal of European Business*, Vol. 3, No. 1, September/October 1991, pp. 25-31. Copyright © 1991 by Faulkner & Gray, Inc.

and beverage giant, which already includes two Frenchmen, a German, and a Spaniard. Mr. Volcker may not be a food and beverage specialist, but he brings invaluable expertise with regard to the world's biggest and most sophisticated capital market as Nestle continues its expansion in the United States through further acquisitions.

How can the corporate governance of a U.S. firm assess and advise on the firm's strategies and actions in unchartered foreign markets when its members have no experience abroad?

The board of ABB Asea Brown Boveri, the world's largest electrical engineering firm, consists of three Swedes, two Germans, two Swiss, and a citizen from Luxembourg. Philips, the most international of Dutch firms, already boasts six nationalities on its board—American, Belgian, British, Dutch, French, and German. Other European companies with multinational boards include Volvo, ICI, Unilever, and Fiat. Surprisingly, globally oriented firms Daimler-Benz, Siemens, and Electrolux still have only all-national board representation—in spite of the fact that in the former two companies more than 50 percent of the annual revenues accrue from overseas sales. An American member of the board at Siemens is long overdue, given that Siemens Inc. in the United States is the firm's largest foreign subsidiary.

All U.S. firms—multinationals, traditional exporters, new entrants into international markets, and purely domestically oriented firms—will face new opportunities and challenges as world markets are redefined and a new breed of foreign competition appears not only in other markets but also at home in the United States. One would assume that U.S. top management is preparing to meet these challenges and opportunities adequately. But the facts belie that assumption. Can a board without foreign participation have the mind-set and the know-how to do business in London, Frankfurt, Paris, Prague, Bombay, Tokyo, and Sao Paolo? How can the corporate governance of a U.S. firm assess and advise on the firm's strategies and actions in unchartered foreign markets when its members have no experience abroad?

Not only can foreign directors provide insight into new and/or foreign markets, but they can also provide valuable information on the company's competitors abroad, provide contacts with potential alliance and joint-venture candidates, and establish relations with foreign government, financial, and industrial authorities. Foreign directors can impress shareholders with a U.S. company's commitment to an international strategy, and, similarly, foreign directors can impress foreign customers, partners, and shareholders with a U.S. company's commitment to the foreign market. Furthermore, by sharing their experience of their countries' prevailing management techniques, organizational models, and information systems infrastructures, foreign directors can broaden and stimulate the thinking of U.S. directors and management.

Dispelling the Myths

U.S. companies are reluctant to invite foreign directors to sit on their boards for several reasons, many of which are spurious. Here are eight common issues U.S. companies raise to inviting foreign directors.

1. "Our own international managers can do the job." Some CEOs of U.S. companies may correctly argue they are bringing more foreigners with international experience into their management ranks who will provide the know-how and "feel" for spotting the changing needs in different national markets. However, those managers will need qualified boards that can match their vision and complement and support their strategies in order for them to be successful.

2. "Distance makes it difficult for foreigners to attend meetings." Jet aircraft have shortened distances dramatically. European board members can get to New York, Boston, or Washington via the Concorde faster than directors from Los Angeles, San Francisco, or Seattle. Further, as new broadband communication technologies such as videoconferencing become available, such barriers should lower even more. Foreign executives often have business connections in the United States and have the flexibility to coordinate their business trips with board meetings. The real issue for both U.S. and foreign board members is whether they can fit six to eight meetings a year into their heavy schedules as executives of other large firms.

3. "Language is a problem; they don't understand us." English is increasingly the international language of business. Excellent European and Asian boardroom candidates who speak English fluently and who understand the "American way of business" can be found without too much difficulty. Many top-notch European, Latin American, and Asian managers have spent years in the United States either studying or working for U.S. firms before going back to their native countries. Very often, this can be an attractive pool from which to recruit board members.

4. *"We don't need foreign directors because we have no business abroad."* Many U.S. firms that have no presence abroad, that have marginal exports, and that have concentrated on the home market, face a dual threat: a stagnant domestic market and rising entry barriers to new markets, such as the European Community.

It should not be surprising that Sony leads the way in naming foreign directors to its board. The company makes two-thirds of its sales outside Japan—27 percent in the United States alone.

Without international experience, U.S. companies will find it increasingly difficult to penetrate new markets abroad as they finish the job of structuring themselves. As foreign markets mature, entry barriers rise. By entering a new market early, companies can establish greater market shares and select from among more attractive merger, acquisition, and joint-venture candidates than those companies that wait. Further, new regulatory barriers may go up, as may be the case in the EC.

Also, domestically oriented firms will face new competitors from Asia, Europe, and Latin America *in the United States* in the near future as these regions restructure and their companies look for new markets. With 250-million affluent consumers the United States remains an attractive market for foreign companies that may have remained domestically oriented themselves.

Foreign directors can play an invaluable role in the board of domestically oriented firms by helping them review and define their international strategies and by providing early-warning signals with respect to foreign competitors invading the U.S. market.

5. *"The board will lose its cohesiveness and collegiality if its membership becomes too diverse."* By the same token, preserving like-mindedness can lead to "tunnel thinking" with regard to foreign markets, overseas opportunities, and new ideas from abroad.

The U.S. chief executive officer, who in most cases, is also the chairman of the board, is usually responsible for the choice of outside directors. The pressure to fill board positions with women and minorities often results in squeezing qualified foreign candidates off the lists. It should be borne in mind that the directors are not elected to represent any particular constituency—the primary responsibility of the director is to increase the value of the company for the benefit of the shareholders. Similarly, a European or Asian director should not be on a U.S. board to represent the interests of European and Asian suppliers and customers, but to enhance the firm's understanding of the dynamics of the region in question and how they will affect the firm's strategies and activities.

6. *"We have an International Advisory Board in place that meets with management once a year."* Many U.S. firms invite a panel of foreign luminaries and businesspeople to join international or regional boards to advise senior management on non-domestic issues. There are many problems attached to such advisory boards:

- They meet only once or twice a year or on an *ad hoc* basis.
- Due to the diversity of the international panelists, the agenda is frequently crowded and the panel cannot do justice to the issues at hand. Meaningful discussion, quite often, is difficult, given the egos of the various members, and the sessions take on a social character.
- The members have no accountability. Advice concerning foreign markets should have the same quality and integrity as that concerning domestic issues and hence must be tied to accountability.
- Management does not have to heed the advice of an advisory board as opposed to a statutory board, and this leads to frustration among advisory board members who may feel they are not taken seriously. (For appropriate uses of an International Advisory Board, see box, this article.)

7. *"Heads of U.S. subsidiaries of foreign firms make good board members."* This is a tricky issue. Many of these executives are excellent managers and know both the U.S. and the foreign side of business. Quite often, however, they are not free, indepen-

dent spirits. They are products of the values, norms, and cultures of their parent organizations and are not in a position to advise U.S. firms adequately. There is a clash between their employment and the SEC's requirement that boards of companies quoted on the New York Stock Exchange have members who are "independent, disinterested, and unaffiliated individuals."

8. "Retired executives of foreign companies make good board members." There are always exceptions to the rule, but given the dynamics of change in key foreign markets, it is extremely difficult for a retired executive to keep current on business and competitive issues. While he or she would have the time and flexibility to attend board meetings, the further away the individual moves from active business life, the more difficult it is to make a useful contribution.

Assessing the Drawbacks of Foreign Directors

While the above concerns should not prevent U.S. companies from inviting foreign directors to their boards, companies nevertheless must address a few very thorny issues connected with the selection of foreign board members.

• Foreign executives are unfamiliar with the written and unwritten laws governing U.S. business. U.S. companies, and the CEO in particular, must be prepared to spend the time it takes to indoctrinate the foreign board member to the workings of the U.S. board.

• Liability issues are a powerful deterrent to those being sought. It is not always a feather in the cap of a foreigner to be on a U.S. board, and the individual's firm or employer usually provides no real incentive. When inviting a foreigner to your board, one selling point may be that your company is in an industry that contributes to the foreign country's economy or its industrial development.

• The foreign board member often does not understand the difference between "accountability" and "responsibility."

• The "U.S. director's standard of conduct" often clashes with the culture and mind-set of the foreign national. The chairman of the board may have to mediate more often between the foreign member and the U.S. members on issues that seem natural and simple to the latter.

• The CEO must be more diligent than usual in explaining the trade-offs between long-term and short-term issues to the foreign board member as well as acquainting him or her with the organization, strategies, culture, power structure, and politics of the firm. These may also be highly countercultural to what the individual is used to in his or her own country.

• It is sometimes difficult to remove foreign board members from a statutory or advisory board. One multinational U.S. company that established a distinguished international advisory panel of prominent European corporate chairmen and CEOs had a problem with this issue. The company did not want to renew the contractual agreement for serving on an international advisory council when the member, a chairman of a major European bank, retired from his active role as bank chairman. However, in the member's native land to abruptly retire a distinguished executive from such an advisory role because he retired from his primary executive position would be unthinkable. The chairman of the U.S. company held firm on his policy of having only members in active business roles, and succeeded in replacing the retired banker with an equally prominent European, still actively responsible for a major European company.

The Role of the European Board Member

Regardless of the extent of a company's presence in Europe, any U.S. board that hopes to increase its company's presence there would do well to consider inviting qualified European executives to join a statutory or an advisory board.

Europe today represents a huge window of opportunity, but that window will certainly begin to close well before January 1, 1993. Current European trends will affect U.S. business in many ways. Among these trends are:

1. Corporate restructuring will sweep across Europe as companies seek internal efficiency gains. Formerly sheltered and conservative European companies are reexamining their operations to strengthen their competitive positions in both their expanded home markets and in world markets. Many observers have viewed European companies as high-cost goods producers in the past, primarily because of overengineering, inefficient production, high social cost, and a lack of economies of scale. Price levels of identical products in many sectors are 20 percent or higher in Europe than

Advisory Boards with Foreign Membership

Compared with a statutory board, members of an advisory board can avoid some unpopular powers and responsibilities, such as the legal right to depose management and legal responsibility to the public. American CEOs should consider the formation of an international or regional adivisory board:

• to fill the breach when the management or the statutory board of the company lacks the time or the expertise to handle the problem of managing a foreign market or organization;

• to support management and the statutory board by supplementing the expertise of the internal staff with regard to international issues;

• to complement the firm's information and intelligence-gathering capability in an international or strategic area of interest (*e.g.*, technology, markets/customers, economics);

• to identify and assess alternative courses of action management or the statutory board does not foresee; and

• to introduce the firm and its products or services to potential customers, suppliers, influencers, etc. in the relevant foreign markets; to develop business, government, and trade relations; and to keep abreast of political, social, and technical developments in the home regions in industry, government, and academic circles.

In establishing an advisory board, it is crucial that the company informs the board members that they are indeed an advisory group, and should not, *de facto*, make decisions or unduly influence the main board or the CEO and his management staff.

The issue of liability is unclear with regard to members of the advisory board. No regulations deal specifically with the legal liability of the advisory director, but it is likely that the liability would be the same as for any other management consultant or lawyer. Special care should be taken, though, that contracts for advisory board members are as strict and explicit concerning confidentiality and conflicts of interest as are those for statutory board directors.

The CEO must draw boundaries between the statutory and advisory boards very clearly or serious conflicts may arise, especially regarding accountability. The CEO must make the terms of the engagement explicit in the contract to avoid any implications of tenure. Contracts should include escape clauses for both parties.

The CEO is responsible for creating and maintaining the fellowship and social bonds among members of the advisory board. The social element is more important in advisory boards, which reward their members largely in psychological income, than it is in statutory boards. However, the CEO should remember one caveat: Watch out for status seekers.

An advisory board should never be considered an alternative or replacement for a statutory board. Advisory boards are useful as a precursor to a statutory board or as a stopgap when the statutory board or management cannot fulfill particular or temporary needs.

in the United States, but European companies aim to turn this around.

Operational changes and cost-reduction programs will almost surely make European companies more efficient and competitive. Corporate restructuring, seeking lower production cost facilities, reducing other overheads, and improving management and information systems will strongly reinforce this effort. U.S. firms involved in Europe, or those planning activities there, must realize that their current price advantage may be short-lived. The pressure on U.S. companies to be as lean and efficient as their European counterparts to compete effectively in the EC and world markets will only increase.

The role of the foreign director in the U.S. company, therefore, is to spot the trends in Europe and advise the company about how to take advantage of them. For example, a European director could advise a U.S. company that wants to structure its information systems to be compatible with those of its European partners and customers. Also, U.S. companies searching for new approaches to training and education would benefit from having a German director on its board who could share his or her knowledge of the highly regarded German apprenticeship system as well as German organizational models pertaining to management-union relations.

2. Merger, acquisition, and alliance activity is escalat-

ing. The number of mergers within the EC increased by 70 percent between 1985 and 1989, leading to fewer and larger European companies in such industries as electronics, defense, telecommunications, banking, food, and media services.

A European director should not be on a U.S. board to represent the interests of European suppliers and customers, but to enhance the firm's understanding of the dynamics of the region in question and how they will affect the firm's strategies and activities.

Daimler-Benz, over the past few years, has become Germany's largest defense and technology conglomerate by acquiring AEG, Motoren- und Turbinenunion, Dornier, and most recently, MBB. Mergers and alliances, however, have not been limited to the European continent. Daimler has formed a strategic alliance with Japan's Mitsubishi to share complementary technologies. And there is clear evidence that Europeans are moving toward the United States. Bertelsmann, a German media and publishing house has within a span of five years acquired Doubleday and RCA records, among others, to become a powerhouse in media services, probably second only to Sony.

U.S. multinationals and other large companies will soon face a new set of European competitors in world markets, ready to launch assaults on well-established U.S. positions. This new competition will possess broad-based technological and marketing capabilities and, more important, financial muscle. Extreme competitive pressure will force larger U.S. firms to run cost-efficient operations and to make long-term European investments in R&D, automation, and marketing. This comes at a time when many U.S. companies are strapped for cash and other resources.

Consider the benefits of putting a European banker on a U.S. board: A senior executive from Barclay's or Deutschebank, familiar with the financial terrain, could easily tackle issues of financing M&A activity and other projects in Europe. In addition, the foreign director with appropriate contacts could suggest and cultivate potential alliance and joint-venture partners in Europe.

3. The "pan-European niche company" will emerge. A new breed of European company is emerging in the EC. Take, for example, a medium- or small-size German company with a market share of 6 or 7 percent in its home market (Federal Republic of Germany). After 1992 the home market will be redefined, and the company's market share may drop to .4 or .5 percent. To survive in the new Europe, given its very small market share, the company will begin forming joint ventures and mergers with similar European companies to obtain a greater market share and more clout within the EC.

As smaller European suppliers develop a pan-European strategy, they will acquire more experience in selling, marketing, manufacturing, and distributing to what will then be the world's largest market. More important, the management of a pan-European niche company will acquire the international experience and the mind-set necessary to address successfully the needs of other markets outside the EC. How long will it then take these companies to exploit opportunities in what will then be the second largest market, the United States? Within the next five years, these pan-European niche players may become a sizable new threat to domestic U.S. players.

The foreign director can alert the U.S. company to these trends and to imminent competitive threats on the home turf as well as in Europe, and recommend some of these companies as acquisition candidates.

4. Venture capital will spur industrial growth in Europe. Traditionally risk-averse, European companies have lacked the venture capital available in, for example, Silicon Valley, where if a firm fails once it can often obtain the capital to try again. Unlike Silicon Valley, Europe has had no tolerance for failure. In addition, small home markets and the lack of capital have not fostered an entrepreneurial spirit in Europe.

Today, because capital tends to move toward regions of perceived high growth and sound return on investment, major changes in the flow of world capital into Europe are increasing the availability of venture capital and, in turn, improving the competitiveness of European business.

Venture capital is becoming increasingly available in Europe to entrepreneurs, especially in the high-tech arena. Technology parks and mini-Silicon Valleys are sprouting in Germany, France, Spain, England, Ireland, and Scotland. U.S. high-tech firms will face stiffer and better-financed competition than in the past from European entrepreneurs in certain sectors, and a revitalized Europe will attract worldwide capital. U.S. firms, meanwhile, may face reduced access to offshore investment funds.

The European director may be able to assist a U.S. company secure venture capital in Europe as well as lobby for the permission to participate in EC R&D projects.

A U.S. CEO must be more diligent than usual in explaining the trade-offs between long-term and short-term issues to the foreign board member as well as acquainting him or her with the organization, strategies, culture, power structure, and politics of the firm.

5. Many EC countries are revamping their corporate tax structure, as Britain did in 1987. A reduction and harmonization of the corporate tax rates within the EC could mean lower cost structures for those U.S. companies established in the EC as well as an enhanced competitive position for European companies that do business with U.S. exporters that have no presence in Europe.

Foreign directors can alert U.S. companies to such changes, advise them on how these changes will affect their companies, and may be powerful lobbyists in the Community, Member State, and local governments developing such regulations and legislation.

6. Eastern and Central European countries will rapidly push toward free markets and hard currencies. While Central European countries will not be profitable consumer markets for some time, they are attractive as manufacturing, assembly, and R&D bases. Czechoslovakia, for example, has a strong technological history in automobiles, electronics, and high-precision mechanical engineering.

The foreign director may be in a excellent position to recognize opportunities for a U.S. company in these countries and develop contacts.

Conclusion

In recent years, U.S. blue-chip firms such as Rubbermaid, Whirlpool, and the Sara Lee Corporation—traditionally non-multinational players in the domestic market—have made firm commitments to being global players. Many of them are enhancing the role of corporate governance to include foreign directors. Even professional service firms have recognized that they must address this need. Arthur D. Little recently appointed an influencial Japanese businessman and a prestigious German banker to its U.S. board.

The foreign director may be the linchpin in a U.S. company's European strategy and may provide a U.S. firm with a competitive edge over other non-EC firms competing for market share in Europe. By opening their boardroom doors to foreign directors, forward-thinking U.S. companies are opening the door to an exciting and profitable new Europe.

International Marketing

Most organizations get into international marketing on a gradual basis. They usually are small firms that get their first international contact as a result of an ad placed in an industry publication or, perhaps, at an industry trade show. This contact is not a result of a deliberate attempt to market their goods or services internationally, but as a by-product of their regular domestic efforts. It should be remembered by all businesspeople that U.S. industrial publications are read all over the world and that industry trade shows are attended, not only by locals in the industry, but by foreign buyers and sellers, all anxious to make contacts and profitable deals.

In today's world, communication is the key to successful marketing. The world has become so small that what is reported in the hardware business in the United States is known in Finland in a few weeks or even days. Information on the changes in technology and in the various markets of the world is readily available to business. The problem

Unit 4

is that managers frequently do not take advantage of the information that is already available. This is especially true of businesses with a monolingual background that makes finding out what is going on in Japan, Germany, or France rather difficult. However, many Japanese, German, and French managers already speak English and often look forward to receiving their English-language publications from the United States as a chance to practice their English.

While manufacturing and production have the ability to "go global," the case is somewhat different for marketing. The focus of marketing is not internal to the organization, but, rather, external to the customer. Indeed, the customer is the focal point of all marketing activities. The traditional "four P's" of marketing—product, place, promotion, and price—look to the customer as the final arbiter of success.

The one thing that all firms must remember is that the customer does not have to buy. There are alternatives. State-run economies, which characterized Eastern Europe until recently, have demonstrated the bankruptcy of trying to run an economy and a society without the necessary choice of products and services. All a state monopoly does is to create an alternative called a "black" (illegal) market. Choice is the essence of markets, and if the buyer does not like the products or services for which they are paying, then they can go somewhere else.

Marketing needs to be tailored for each market in which the product is being sold. The simple problems of language can create difficult situations. A classic example is that of the General Motors Corporation trying to market the Chevy Nova in Latin America. In Spanish, "Nova" translates to "no go"; not a particularly good name for a new car.

That is not to say that the French do not like the same kind of products as the Germans, or the Americans, or the Japanese. What it does say is that these products need to be marketed in the French way to Frenchmen, the German way to Germans, the American way to Americans, and the Japanese way to the Japanese. Each country and society has unique characteristics that the marketer can and must use to successfully market his or her product. Also, it is not correct to say that Americans cannot learn from the French or the Japanese from the British. Successful marketing techniques that have been traditionally applied in one market might be transferable to help create competitive advantages in another. There really is no end to the possibilities that alert international marketers can develop in the global marketplace.

While most of the marketing that occurs in the world is in developed countries, and the former Soviet bloc is now opening itself to the efforts of Western firms and goods, eagerly trying to learn marketing so that they will be able to compete in the global marketplace of the future, there is one country that has remained a very difficult market for corporations from developed countries: China.

China, along with Cuba, may be the last bastion of socialism/communism in the world. While Cuba's market and potential is relatively small, and remains a kind of anachronistic thorn in the side of the United States, China is another issue. Westerners have been fascinated with China and its potential, dating back to the days of Marco Polo. It is a vast sea of humanity, dating back thousands of years, with great potential for production and consumption. A distinct and ancient civilization, China, although not completely successfully, has resisted Western attempts to dominate it and change it. It has also successfully defended itself against Japan and the Soviet Union in this century. But China, today, is led by a gerontocracy that is trying to hold back the clock. The recent political repression is an example of this ruling group trying to hold back the evolution of Chinese society. The current rulers in China are caught in a quandary: they want and need the prosperity of the West and have experimented with it in Guangdong Province, which is next to Hong Kong. But to allow prosperity into all of China would mean the eventual loss of power for the ruling elite, and they dare not get off the tiger. Eventually, however, the rulers of China will have to change, if for no other reason than that the current ones will eventually die, and then, hopefully, China will start to experience real change in the form of markets both inside and outside of the country, for both Chinese and non-Chinese goods.

Looking Ahead: Challenge Questions

Unlike manufacturing, marketing does not lend itself particularly well to multinational applications. Why do you think this may be the case? What are some examples of the problems?

Most firms in the United States do not start out looking for business from international customers. Why do you think this is? How does it happen that they get this business?

China remains almost an elusive image for most Western business people. Why do you think this is so? When do you think that the markets of China will open?

Going global

As the international export market becomes more active with easing world tensions, the potential for untapped revenue sources grows geometrically

Ted J. Rakstis

If your business or professional practice is built upon an "America-only" foundation, you could be missing out on giant chunks of untapped revenues and profits.

Money is flowing in from the booming international export market in greater amounts than ever before. According to the United States Department of Commerce, export trade of merchandise, agricultural goods, and minerals produced in the US mushroomed from $227 billion in 1986 to $394 billion in 1990.

US exports of private-sector services exploded from $70 billion in 1986 to $120 billion in 1990. Both in products and services, those are astonishing four-year increases of nearly 75 percent.

As recently as 1983, Nation's Business magazine reports, only about 10 percent of all US companies exported their goods and services. But, in the late 1980s, two related phenomena changed that. American economic growth slowed at the same time the value of the US dollar declined.

With domestic trade weakening, many American businesses found eager buyers abroad. Yet the real potential scarcely has been touched.

A recent Dun & Bradstreet study shows that US companies with fewer than 100 employees represent 25.7 percent of all American organizations doing business on an international scale. That percentage may sound impressive, but it merely reflects the fact that most companies fall into the 100-and-under classification. Taken as a whole, only 8.5 percent of all US organizations in that bracket are in the export market.

By contrast, Dun & Bradstreet reports, 54.9 percent of all US firms with 10,000 or more workers are exporting. They comprise 31.6 percent of the export group and are the biggest money-makers.

Clearly, the trade possibilities for small businesses are enormous. Changing Times magazine observes: "Despite the obstacles, more American entrepreneurs are going global every day, and they're finding receptive markets.

"Selling overseas broadens your market, forces you to be more competitive, and reduces your per-unit cost of production. It can help hedge against a recession or a change in demand at home. It can even extend the life of a good product that is beginning to flag domestically, perhaps because a competitor has arrived on the scene. In short, it can boost your bottom line."

There are global opportunities in nearly every business sector. Here's how the US Department of Commerce breaks down 1990 merchandise trade: machinery, 30 percent; transportation equipment, 16 percent; chemicals, agricultural products, and crude materials, 10 percent each; and other manufacturers, 24 percent.

Travel and transportation accounted for nearly two-thirds of all service-business exports in 1990. But a hefty $32 billion in trade came from international banking, insurance, law, accounting, and other professional services.

The most lucrative export vistas today are Canada, Japan, Mexico, the United Kingdom, and Germany. Collectively, these countries brought in more than 50 percent of total 1990 US export revenues. Six other nations represented between $10 billion and $14 billion in annual purchases from US companies. The group consists of South Korea, France, the Netherlands, Taiwan, and Belgium/Luxembourg.

Kenichi Ohmae, author of *The Borderless World: Power and Strategy in the Interlinked Economy*, foresees a time when governments will shed their protectionist policies. They will, he believes, strive to obtain for their people the broadest choice of the cheapest goods and services on the market.

Ohmae envisions a "triad" of the US, Europe, and Japan as a dominating, one-billion-population, economic supermachine. The emergence of Eastern Europe next to the twelve-nation European Community already is creating that scenario.

There will be other trading kingpins. Gary S. Becker, a professor of economics and sociology at the University of Chicago, points out that Singapore's per capita income has grown by more than 7 percent each year since the early 1960s. And, he adds, a significant development is taking place in Latin America.

Says Becker: "By the end of 1994, Argentina, Brazil, Paraguay, and Uruguay will form a common market of 190 million people and account for more than half of the output of Latin America and the Caribbean."

At this writing, the trading power of the People's Republic of China was given a welcome boost with the renewal of its "most-favored-nation" status. The principal disputants were US President George Bush and certain members of the US Congress. Nevertheless, American business interest in China appears likely to accelerate.

Robert Mosbacher, US Secretary of Commerce, offers this appraisal: "US businesses, particularly mid-size and smaller companies, need to think of the entire world as a marketplace. If we're going to be more competitive in international sales, we can't rely on traditional single-market thinking.

"Regardless of what your business is,

Reprinted from *Kiwanis* magazine, October 1991, pp. 39-43. Copyright © 1991 by Kiwanis International.

there are tremendous opportunities. That's true whether you're selling doughnuts or high-tech products, or whether you're looking for capital or a place to get workers.

"There are great new markets in Eastern Europe and the Soviet Union," he continues. "Latin America, particularly Mexico, is burgeoning. Southeast Asia is still hot. Unfortunately, not enough people in the business world are able to see what's going on outside their own sphere."

If you're pondering an entry into the worldwide market, there are many steps to take. Together, they comprise a global marketing plan.

First, read. US government-produced works include *The World Is Your Market*, *A Basic Guide to Exporting*, and *Worker Training: Competing in the New International Economy*.

There also are many export-related books sold by commercial publishers. Among them are *Exportise*, *The Ernst & Young Guide to Expanding in the Global Market*, *Exporting from Start to Finance*, *Import/Export: How to Get Started in International Trade*, and *Inside Washington: The International Business Executive's Guide to Government Resources*.

Periodicals that cover the field are Business America, North American International Business, Export Today, and The Exporter. In addition, personal-computer software packages are available under such titles as *Export to Win*.

After you've done your basic homework, Nation's Business notes, you must ask yourself some tough questions. Is your product or service unique? Do you have the flexibility required to make changes according to world market demands? Are you personally committed? Can you bankroll a foreign start-up? Should you import your raw materials or build a factory abroad? Will you be able to sell at competitive prices?

If you pass this self-examination, the next move is to take advantage of US government services. Under the umbrella of the US Department of Commerce, the International Trade Administration (ITA) offers many programs through its US and Foreign Commercial Service (US&FCS).

US&FCS sponsors how-to seminars, free counseling, market-research aid, and assistance in finding buyers, agents, or distributors. ITA specialists track commercial developments by nation and industry. When this was written, there were sixty-eight US&FCS local offices throughout the US.

The US Small Business Administration (SBA) also provides free basic market research. It will help you pinpoint major importing and exporting nations in your product or service area. Further, the SBA's Export Legal Assistance Network furnishes free legal consultations.

International trade shows sponsored by the US Department of Commerce can turn up valuable information on potential distributors, customers, and competitors. A number of US states also have offices that supply advice on exporting and financing. Private export consultants can be helpful. And don't forget the local chamber of commerce.

As one example of grass-roots exporting aid, the Columbus Area Chamber of Commerce in Ohio operates an international trade office. Not long ago, the chamber sponsored a "fly-in" that brought twelve US Department of Commerce officers to Columbus for one-on-one consultations with executives of eighty-plus local companies.

A Columbus art-supply concern called Air Waves went into business in 1984 with four employees. By 1991, Air Waves had become America's largest designer and manufacturer of shirt transfers. At that time, the organization had 160 employees working on two shifts in a 70,000-square-foot facility.

In 1990, Brad Forward, an account representative at Air Waves, met with international consultants at the chamber of commerce. This year, the com-

Export expert imports advice

Like the traveling salesmen in the stage and film musical *The Music Man*, "you gotta know the territory" to sell in the international market.

Roger E. Axtell, author of *The Do's and Taboos of International Trade: A Small Business Primer*, makes that point. And, he adds, "If there's one cardinal rule that all experienced international managers agree upon, it's this: There's no substitute for getting out into the marketplace.

"For a potential exporter, the first trip abroad can be extremely significant. Lifelong relationships and steady, growing sales can result. But you could instead have a long string of headaches."

Axtell cites the ten most common mistakes of would-be exporters:

- A failure to consult export specialists and devise an international marketing plan. Without clear objectives and expert advice, your first costly move also could be your last one.
- An insufficient commitment by top management. If you're the head of your company, that means you. It will take time and financial resources to establish yourself in a foreign market.
- Poor judgment in choosing foreign distributors. Because of the complexity of overseas communications and transportation, you need a distributor who is well-known and respected in the market. Further, you must give him or her more independence than you're accustomed to granting in the United States.
- An absence of a plan for orderly growth. Don't become too ambitious too soon. Work with distributors in one or two geographical areas until you're certain that it's time to expand.
- A short-term attitude. As soon as business conditions improve at home, many companies neglect their export trade. The result: a foolish shutdown of a valuable source of plus profits.
- Unequal treatment of distributors. "Often," Axtell observes, "companies carry out special campaigns, discount and warranty offers, and credit plans in the US but fail to make similar aid available to their international distributors. This can destroy the vitality of your overseas marketing efforts."
- An unwillingness to modify products. When selling abroad, it's often necessary to make changes to satisfy local safety and security codes. You also must be aware of cultural differences. The US is not the entire world.
- Ignorance of the need to print service and warranty messages in local languages. Even if your overseas distributor speaks perfect English, it would be foolish to expect everyone on the sales and service staffs to be bilingual.
- A failure to look into the benefits offered by an export-management company. Unless you have your own export department, this is a virtual "must."
- Insufficient knowledge of licensing and joint-venture deals. "Any product that can compete on a national basis in the US," Axtell contends, "can be marketed successfully in most parts of the world."

pany is selling its shirt transfers in fifty nations. Foreign trade now accounts for 11 percent of Air Waves' sales.

"We were aggressive and followed up on every lead," Forward says. "Air Waves has become especially strong in Mexico, Central America, and South America. "We're also working on relationships with Eastern bloc countries by sending representatives to trade shows in Poland, Czechoslovakia, Hungary, and Russia."

Before you enter into any agreements, it's wise to attend commercial exhibits and make contacts in the nations where you intend to do business. The US Department of Commerce, SBA, and several state governments sponsor low-cost trade missions for entrepreneurs.

Barbara Esposito is one of the principals in Products Finishing, a family-owned maker of luggage carts located in Brooklyn, New York. She estimates that her company spent more than $50,000 for two months of travel in seventeen nations, as well as for mailings and shipments of samples. It paid off. Within two years, the company was selling in thirty lands.

Financing an overseas marketing venture can be tricky. Many banks have been unwilling to make direct loans for small businesses that are entering the global market. That's particularly true during tight economic times.

There are alternatives, however. Numerous US states are providing help. The Texas Department of Commerce, for instance, guarantees up to 85 percent of loans made by private lenders to small and mid-size organizations that need working capital and start-up equipment for exporting endeavors.

Nation's Business reports: "Most such programs are less than a decade old. (Their officials) work closely with the Export-Import Bank of the US (Eximbank), the chief source of export financing and guarantees at the federal level. In fact, Eximbank, which had its authority to make direct loans cut back sharply in recent years, has reformatted its programs to make them more compatible with those of states and cities."

Banks based outside the US may be the best sources for direct loans, the magazine points out. It singles out such financial institutions as Europe's National Westminster Bank, USA, and Japan's Daiwa Bank Ltd.

Lee A. Oster, tax manager at Miller, Cooper & Company, a large accounting and consulting firm in Northbrook, Illinois, says many novice exporters aren't even aware of available tax incentives.

"'Duty drawbacks' have been around for more than 200 years, but not many people know they exist," Oster comments. "If you're an exporter and you import and pay duty on components, you get that duty back when you export the products. Your costs are reduced. Also, it's cheaper to sell your products overseas."

Foreign Sales Corporations (FSC), Oster adds, represent another incentive.

How sweet it is—corn, that is

Ah, summer. Warm, sunny days filled with hometown parades, picnics on the lawn, and county fairs. The aroma of barbecued chicken grilled outside wafting through the crowds. Juicy, sticky watermelon being sold by the slice—accompanied by plenty of napkins. And always the smell of fresh, sweet corn on the cob—with plenty of butter—fills the air. The finer flavors of summer.

One of these finer flavors often is taken for granted. After all, corn is corn, right? It's grown in fields on tall stalks. Its yellow kernels taste great when served as corn fritters, corn muffins, and scallop corn. It comes fresh, frozen, canned, creamed, and popped. Once popped, it can be covered in caramel, cheese, garlic, butter, and a host of other flavors difficult to resist.

But if American Indians hadn't shown the pilgrims how to grow corn, the history of the United States might read differently today. And, if it weren't for Floyd S. Ingersoll, a senior member of the Kiwanis Club of Champaign-Urbana, Illinois, sweet corn would taste a lot different today as well.

"We introduced a new kind of sweet corn about thirty years ago, which is twice as sweet as normal sweet corn: It holds its sugar longer, and it has a longer shelf-life," says Floyd, the executive vice-president of Illinois Foundation Seed Company (IFSC) in Champaign-Urbana. "The only thing was, I was the only one who recognized it. Nobody would pay any attention to a geneticist who discovered it. So he came to us. In a matter of thirty years, we've become the second largest sweet corn seed company in the world.

"The market for sweet corn has surged because its quality has gone up," says Floyd. "We've done the best (marketing) in Japan. They are lovers of sweet corn. We've probably captured 75 percent of the total Japanese market in five or six years. And we also captured 90 percent of the total Taiwanese market. We've got lots of competition; that'll keep those young boys working.

"It's much more popular now than it was twenty years ago. Now all the other sweet corn seed companies are researching this type and marketing it."

Seed research is something in which the IFSC is expert, and although Floyd is knowledgeable about research, his expertise lies in marketing. Nicknamed "the Father of Modern Sweet Corn" by the US National Agri-Marketing Association, Floyd is described by the association as "a towering figure in the leadership of the American seed industry."

When he first became associated with IFSC in 1948 as the manager of three people, the company was nearly bankrupt. Today, the company has seventy-seven employees, and Floyd continues in his capacity as executive vice-president at eighty-two years of age.

A big part of Floyd's work in the sweet corn business is traveling—all over the world—with his wife, Marian, by his side.

"I've probably been to Japan at least a half-dozen times," he says. "One thing that really impressed us about Japan was the business people there always wanted her to come with me because the ladies, contrary to most businesses over there, got to go out to dinner and socialize. And they loved it. Marian's a good salesperson herself."

Aside from Japan, the Ingersoll's spent a year in Egypt in the '50s growing hybrid corn seed.

"That was the first it was ever grown in Egypt," Floyd says, "and now they have a pretty good size crop going."

In addition to introducing sweet corn to foreign cultures, Floyd served as president of the American Seed Trade Association in 1968 when it pushed for passage of the Plant Variety Protection Act of 1970.

This self-described "cornhusker from Nebraska" lives part of the year in Illinois and the other part in Scottsdale, Arizona. Floyd is the grandfather of fifteen grandchildren from his three daughters.

With his many years in the business he advises others: "There are a lot of people who spend a great deal of money and time on research without success. Now if you can hit something that is superior, then you can go export it successfully. This sweet corn was superior."

—Tamara P. Burley

An FSC is a separate foreign corporation designed to take advantage of federal tax incentives for exporters. By lowering the federal tax burden on foreign sales, an FSC decreases the cost of doing business. It also makes you more competitive.

"Once you set up an FSC," Oster explains, "you pay a commission to it for each foreign sale. The manufacturer deducts the commission, and the FSC records it as income. A portion of the commission income will be exempt from federal income tax. The remainder of the commission will be taxed currently. The benefit is that the deduction claimed for the commission expense will be greater than the taxable commission income. Thus, the overall income-tax liability is reduced by the tax-exempt commission.

"As an example of the savings, let's say you normally would make $1 on a sale. By using an FSC, you can make $1.05 or $1.10. You'll benefit from higher profit margins and lower costs of goods sold. And the savings are permanent."

An Interest Charge Domestic International Sales Corporation (IC-DISC) is similar to an FSC in that it's a separate "paper company," Oster elaborates.

But, through an IC-DISC, taxes are deferred on one-half of the earnings. By effectively borrowing an amount equal to the tax that would otherwise be payable on the deferred IC-DISC income, your working capital increases. Most states in the US also provide for a deferral.

"From the government at below-market rates," Oster says, "the IC-DISC is not subject to federal income taxes. Rather, the shareholders are taxed on the earnings of the corporation. One-half is taxed when earned by the IC-DISC. The other half is deferred until it's either distributed as divided or the IC-DISC fails to qualify as an IC-DISC."

Because FSC and IC-DISC structures are so complex, they're unknown to most people. In 1988, Miller, Cooper & Company surveyed a group of American exporters. More than 80 percent either didn't know about these incentives or weren't sufficiently knowledgeable to apply them to their own business situations.

"If you're getting into the overseas market," Oster stresses, "consult an accounting firm that knows exporting. Its specialists can help you to set up an FSC or IC-DISC."

When your market is targeted and your financing is in place, it's time to devise a plan to ship and sell on a worldwide scale.

An estimated 2,000 export-service firms are based in the US. Known as export-management companies (EMCs), these organizations usually specialize in a product category or an individual nation.

"Check their references and financial standings," Business Week magazine advises. "Get a list of the products that a company represents and verify it with the manufacturers. EMCs may take a commission of about 15 percent or work under a buy/sell agreement.

"Some also add a retainer. Such middlemen are convenient for companies new to exporting, but you will lose some control over how your product is marketed, priced, and serviced overseas."

Export-trading companies (ETCs) comprise another group of intermediaries. They differ from EMCs because they take title to your merchandise and pay you directly.

"ETCs tend to be less relationship-oriented than EMCs and are larger and more transaction-centered," says Richard Barovick, director of the (US) National Federation of Export Associations.

The alternative to a US-based middleman is a foreign agent or distributor. A bank with an international branch or a US Department of Commerce office can assist you in the search for a reputable representative abroad. But be cautious before you close a deal.

"In many countries, you're stuck with an agent or distributor once you appoint one," warns William Spitler, deputy director of the US Department of Commerce office in New York City. "You're either not allowed to get rid of them or the terms are exorbitant—for example, ten years' worth of commissions."

Another option is an alliance with a respected freight forwarder or customhouse broker. One such organization, Radix Group International in Los Angeles, has been working with US exporters for fifty years.

"The forwarder's role has shifted markedly during the past decade," says Matthew Sheppard, executive director of Radix. "Advanced technology and increased competition have caused many forwarders to become genuine partners with their customers.

"'Partner' conveys a number of meanings. To a small company undertaking initial exporting efforts, the forwarder often can become the organization's total traffic arm. It handles the many requirements needed to move goods properly and legally out of the US. A really valuable forwarder goes beyond even this assistance. With arrangements abroad through joint-venture operations or a network of seasoned independent agents, the forwarder can help the exporter to find customers."

The Lared Group, located in Century City, California, specializes in the implementation of another break-in method for small companies: "strategic partnering."

Lorraine D. Segil, Lared's managing partner, explains that the process entails the matching of a small organization with a bigger one. Her firm pairs companies through a chain of associates in Europe, the United Kingdom, and Australia.

Strategic partnering, Segil explains, is not the same as a joint venture. The partners may not be equal in terms of resources or profit division, but both have a stake in the same market.

Typically, Lared deals with a large and well-established company overseas that needs fresh products and ideas. They're most often supplied by a US entrepreneurial firm with innovative skills but limited capital. The probable result, Segil says, is a profitable match for both enterprises.

American franchisers constitute another growing segment of the export economy. The movement's leading spokesman is Arthur Karp, co-founder of the Great American Cookie Company. He served as the 1990 chairman of the International Franchise Association.

"Especially since the collapse of communism in Eastern Europe, the opportunities for exporting franchises are tremendous," Karp observes. "People in the new democracies are hungry for Western-style products, and their governments are eager to land US franchises."

As more American businesses enter the export market, highly specialized services are emerging to help them.

Small direct-mail marketers, for instance, usually can't afford to open their own offices overseas. TNT Mailfast, with headquarters in Garden City, New York, runs a private, full-service postal system in forty-one nations.

Through its International Reply Service, TNT provides local post-office boxes for direct-mail responses. Recently, it opened an office in Moscow and is focusing on other capital cities in Eastern Europe. TNT now handles more than 10 million pieces of international mail each week.

"Businesses can test the waters of new markets by establishing local mailing addresses for responses," says a TNT spokeswoman. A local address can help stimulate responses to virtually any type of US direct-mail campaign. As part of this service, TNT delivers the mail back to US-based businesses via air express. This allows many US companies—direct marketers, catalog houses, publishers, researchers, and manufacturers—to conduct market research and develop international sales campaigns."

No matter what marketing plan you settle upon, you must make periodic trips abroad to see what's happening. And, as anyone who has handled global business transactions knows, "cross-cultural shock" can be traumatic.

In 1977, Noel Kreicker and her then-husband, an attorney, went to Bogotá, Colombia, to open a branch office for his Chicago-based law firm. Because they had little knowledge of Latin American business or social customs, their effort was a disaster. The couple and their three children soon returned home.

Two years later, Kreicker founded International Orientation Resources (IOR), in Northbrook, Illinois. Her sole premise was this: Corporations never bring someone into the company without providing orientation and training, but few supply cross-cultural schooling when they send people abroad. IOR now has representatives in seventy cities scattered throughout thirty-six nations.

"What we do is lead people across boundaries," Kreicker explains. "With the expatriate and his or her family, we're a bridge between both the physical and psychological boundaries of a new country. Our clients learn to communicate effectively with their foreign counterparts, understand a different culture, and establish a home in a new land."

Since the end of World War II, global maps have been radically altered with the addition of scores of young and still-emerging nations. Yet, thanks to satellite telecommunications, the world actually is shrinking.

Unless yours is strictly a local enterprise, you should consider the challenges and rewards that lie abroad. It's no longer appropriate to think only in terms of Main Street, USA. We're now conducting business on International Boulevard, the planet Earth.

Finding the International Niche: A "How To" for American Small Business

Bonnie Heineman Wolfe

Bonnie Heineman Wolfe is president of New Venture Development Corporation, a consulting firm based in Washington, D.C.

More than 5.65 million companies in the U.S. were considered "small businesses" in 1987, generating sales revenues of $316 billion. These small businesses, defined by the government as companies with fewer than 500 employees, make up the vast majority of American concerns.

Most small businesses have never been in a position where they needed to look to the export market for increased market share. For 45 years the domestic market stretching from Maine to Alaska provided bountiful profits. American businesses grew accustomed to being contacted directly by companies overseas for new technology, quality products, and American "know-how."

Times are changing, however. Small companies are starting to review their marketing strategies. The small business owner sees quality competition from the East, price competition from lesser developed countries with cheaper labor, and looming competition from "Fortress Europe" coming in 1992. Small American businesses are quickly realizing that competition from overseas can affect their domestic market share.

An example of what is happening can be seen in Southern Gold Honey Company, a small honey producer in Vidor, Texas. Almost overnight in 1985 this 15-year-old company saw domestic sales drop off and its American market turn sour due to imports of less expensive honey. When the company realized they could no longer compete in the U.S. selling domestic honey, the owners looked overseas. Four years later sales have quadrupled—due solely to major exports to the Middle East.

The small business owner in Muncie, Indiana is starting to think, "If I am using a computer assembled in Taiwan, drinking from a Coca-Cola fountain manufactured in Germany, and writing at a desk designed in Scandinavia—why can't I export my auto parts to someone?" U.S. companies of all sizes are now thinking globally.

> *Small businesses may feel intimidated by the idea of overseas marketing, but plenty of assistance is available.*

An American Tomato in Finland

Although there may be a strong desire to enter the international market, the mechanics of exporting seem overwhelming for a small business owner trying to expand market share. A smaller company typically has limited resources, making it impossible to compete with the financial powers who can open up overseas subsidiaries overnight and take on the appearances of a domestic company.

There is only one hope for a small business in the international market—find a market niche. Finding the international market niche means targeting a few selected countries, finding the right local distributors, and gaining market share from a solid base.

Several obstacles appear immediately when the small business approaches foreign markets. The cost of marketing overseas is more expensive; unique country differences in politics, culture, language, and economics must be observed; and multinational companies often have a firm market share already in place. These factors mean the small business owner must use a nontraditional marketing strategy.

In carving out a niche, smaller companies need to look beyond traditional users of their product. For example, take the Finns and their tomato sauce. The Finns do not import large

Reprinted from *Business Horizons*, Vol. 34, No. 2, March/April 1991, pp. 13-17 Copyright © 1991 by the Foundation for the School of Business at Indiana University. Used with permission.

volumes of U.S. tomato products. In fact, Finland can't even be found among the statistics from the U.S. government—it falls into the category of "Other Countries."

Yet on the shelves of a gourmet grocery in Helsinki is "Paul Newman's Own Spaghetti Sauce." Finland doesn't show up as a big import market, but because the Finns like American products and because empty ships run regularly from the U.S. to Finland, a niche exists for an American tomato product.

RESEARCHING CONSUMER DEMAND

The small business first seeking a market niche can begin by turning to the U.S. government. Statistical information outlining what products are being exported to which countries is easily obtained from the Bureau of the Census, U.S. Department of Commerce. Looking at these numbers, a business owner can determine possible export markets. In addition, the Commerce Department's country desk officers and industry specialists can provide detailed information to assist marketing efforts regarding different products and countries. The Foreign Agriculture Service of the U.S. Department of Agriculture has background information and several programs to assist the exporter of agricultural products. The Foreign Commercial Service Specialists and the agricultural counselors in the American embassies can provide market information for various U.S. products. If the information readily available is not adequate, marketing studies can be performed for specific products in various countries for a nominal fee. American chambers of commerce overseas as well as foreign chambers of commerce located in the U.S. provide research information and marketing ideas. State offices and quasi-governmental organizations are also a good source of information about local markets, methods of distribution, and sales opportunities.

After collecting preliminary market information, the small business owner can begin to determine what countries to target and how best to market the firm's product. When starting out, targeted countries should be limited to between three and five. Although there may be other potential markets, it is better to focus on a few countries and establish a market presence there, because of the time that must be devoted to opening markets in each new country. Markets close to home such as Canada (the largest U.S. trading partner), Mexico, and the Caribbean are obvious targets due to lower transportation costs.

Differences in how consumers purchase items must be considered. For example, when exporting a food product, it is important to understand that most consumers overseas shop several times a week. In other countries grocery stores may not exist and shopping is done at markets. Each culture is unique and the small business must adapt to local customs and habits just as the multinational giants have.

Smaller U.S. exporters must also be aware that even though extensive market research may have been done, unique types of distribution channels are not always uncovered. For example, government regulations prohibit Venezuelan food producers from marketing certain products in Curacao. As a result, boats come into the coast of Curacao late at night selling those same prohibited food products at very low cost. Offering a quality American product and a stable supply may not always provide the competitive edge.

National Wealth

When targeting countries as potential markets, national wealth is an obvious consideration. The consumer must be able to afford the product. A quick look at per capita income, taxes, and disposable income are good indicators of national wealth.

Other intangible signals of wealth must also be observed. U.S. companies should be aware of whether the target country consumer is willing to give up quality for price on a certain product. Hidden markets such as tourism and foreign resident workers may create purchasing power where no obvious market exists.

Entry Costs

There are several cost barriers to entering a foreign market. Factors such as transportation, tariffs, and import regulations all add cost to the imported product.

Transportation is a real cost that must be added to the domestic price. A freight forwarder is one important resource that can be used when arranging shipments. A forwarder can provide all shipping services needed to get a product from point "A" to "B" for one fee. The freight forwarder can pull all the loose ends together, including a lot of paperwork that the small business owner may not be equipped to handle.

However, to become truly price competitive, the small business owner must be prepared to use several freight forwarders or contact shippers directly. For example, a Midwestern freight forwarder might charge a rate $1,000 more than the Saudi National Shipping Company of New York to ship an identical 20-foot container from Baltimore to Jeddah. The small business owner might be more comfortable dealing with a local freight forwarder rather than contacting shipping companies directly, but a high price is being paid for that comfort and convenience.

Tariffs, which are simply a form of taxation, are used to protect domestic industry and keep out certain imported products. Tariffs are a very effective form of protectionism. Canadian tariffs average 10 percent but range from zero to 27 percent. The European Community has tariffs ranging from zero to 30 percent and the Saudi tariffs average 12 percent. If the U.S. business owner finds no domestic production of a product within the targeted country, tariffs will probably be low.

Each country has its own import regulations which must be adhered to by the U.S. small business exporter. Regulations vary from country to country and change over time, so it is important that the U.S. business owner review the regulations frequently.

One type of import regulation involves labeling requirements for imported food products. It is not uncommon that labels be required in certain languages with specific measures. A product can be prohibited from entering a country due to incorrect labeling.

Labeling can also be an intangible trade barrier. In addition to national labeling requirements, some countries, such as Canada, may have local labeling requirements. It can be difficult for a small U.S. business to meet all the local labeling requirements. Since it is impossible to change the labeling requirements, this is a fact of global life the small business owner must understand and accept.

DISTRIBUTION CHANNELS

When researching a target country, it is vital to determine the best distribution method. For example, is it best to have a local distributor or should an office be opened in the target country?

For many small companies, the only affordable way to enter a market is through the use of a distributor. When this is the case, finding the right distributor can be the most important part of the marketing strategy. There are several ways to locate distributors (or agents). The Foreign Traders Index Service and The Agent/Distributor Service, both provided through the Commerce Department, can provide a list of potential distributors who have indicated an interest in marketing U.S. products. Contacts through the Commerce Department and Agriculture Department will also provide lists of distributors overseas. Attending international trade shows is possibly the best way to find and meet potential distributors.

It is important to learn of other U.S. companies represented by prospective distributors. The U.S. companies listed as references can easily be asked for additional information about the distributor.

Once the appropriate distributor is found, the U.S. company must treat that international distributor the same way as any domestic distributor. This means visiting the distributor, making joint sales calls, and bringing the distributor to visit the U.S. company's operation. Ignoring a good distributor overseas is throwing away an opportunity to do business in that country.

In talking to U.S. small business owners, it is not uncommon to find that many have been contacted in the past by foreign distributors. To the amazement of these business owners, the distributor just stopped calling one day. A U.S. company has to realize that any distributor working with them is working with companies in the same industry all over the world. If the U.S. company does not keep the distributor up to date on new products and prices, the distributor will naturally go to more interested sources.

In smaller countries, typically there are only a handful of key distributors that control the majority of the market share. Additionally, in smaller countries it is usually not common (nor appreciated) to have more than one distributor for a specific product. The distributors in specific industries all know each other and will avoid reducing their profit margins by competing against each other.

GOVERNMENT AND QUASI-GOVERNMENT ADVERTISING

Surprisingly, U.S. companies can directly market their products abroad through government and quasi-government organizations. The U.S. government provides several programs that allow companies to advertise their products overseas at no charge, or for a small fee. The Department of Agriculture's Buyer Alert program will advertise U.S. food products to more than 40 different countries free of charge.

The Commerce Department's Trade Opportunities Program publishes marketing leads in *The Journal of Commerce.* Requests for products from overseas are printed daily and provide easy introductions for U.S. companies.

U.S. chambers of commerce in other countries will advertise a U.S. product in their local newsletter if the U.S. company is looking for a local distributor. Advertising through local chambers of commerce lends credibility to the U.S. business.

THE BUDGET

Preparing a budget for international marketing is essential to control costs, but the small business owner will quickly learn that entry into the overseas market is not cheap.

Travel and communications are naturally more expensive than domestic marketing. Most communications are done by either fax or telex. Shipping samples will have a higher cost attached. A single booth at a major trade show will cost an average of $5,000. Perhaps the most difficult expense for the small business owner is the long lead time needed for payback.

Given the added costs of marketing overseas,

the U.S. business owner must use financial assistance programs, if available, and work wisely to reduce budget expenses.

Financial Assistance

The federal government is again a good place to seek various types of financial assistance. For example, the Department of Agriculture will sponsor pavilions at many international food shows, as well as provide ancillary services such as preliminary review of product labels and consolidation shipment. This can save time and effort on the part of the U.S. participant.

Quasi-governmental groups also sponsor trade shows and provide lower group rates. This was recently done by the Mid-America International Agri-Trade Council (MIATCO), which sponsored a food show in Curacao. MIATCO not only provided a group rate for the airline ticket (roughly half price) for U.S. participants; it paid for the entire flight for distributors on surrounding islands to attend the show and meet U.S. participants.

State governments also provide financial assistance to promote local exports. Indiana has a Trade Show Assistance Program for small to medium-sized Indiana businesses to help them enter and maintain sales in international markets. This program provides a reimbursement of 50 percent of expenses directly attributable to the cost of a trade show, up to a maximum of $5,000. The reimbursement includes translation of materials, cost of a translator, shipment of booth items, and the costs of renting the booth, furniture, and electricity.

Roughly a third of all U.S. states provide programs to assist in the short-term financing of exports. These states give loans that are intended to cover the company's actual shipment cost less its profit margin. The U.S. exporter becomes more competitive on a worldwide basis because products can be shipped giving the best terms possible for the importer.

Working Wisely

Working more wisely means contacting potential overseas distributors before leaving the U.S. to attend a trade show, using low-cost research sources such as associations and the government, meeting with trade missions in the U.S. when possible, and seeking out good, experienced distributors instead of opening offices overseas sooner than necessary.

In addition to the above, however, small business owners must be creative. For example, Indiana has offices in Korea and the Netherlands. These overseas offices can be treated as an extension of an Indiana business office.

Other low-cost product promotion options for the small U.S. business include the use of a U.S. Export Management Company (EMC) or Export Trading Company (ETC).

EMCs act as export departments for several manufacturers of unrelated products. The EMC will solicit and transact business in the name of the manufacturer represented. Payment is made through commission, salary, or retainer plus commission. ETCs purchase U.S. goods for resale in foreign markets. Many ETCs in the U.S. have offices in other countries, thus providing efficient sales and distribution.

Both the EMC and the ETC allow U.S. businesses to promote products abroad without forming an international department in-house and paying for increased staff assistance. The EMC and ETC also provide experience that can be expensive for the U.S. small business to obtain otherwise.

Small business owners must open their eyes to the global markets and take action. Otherwise, U.S. companies will not only miss revenue opportunities, but will run the risk of losing existing market share to overseas competition.

With instant communications available in the average office and electronic information at our fingertips, the world continues to shrink everyday. To survive, small U.S. businesses must look beyond their borders.

International marketing is not reserved for the multinationals or companies that can commit large sums of money for research. Cost-efficient ways for the small business owner to enter the market are available. The biggest stumbling block is under our American baseball caps. Once past that block, a world of opportunities exist.

An Exporter's Guide to Selecting Foreign Sales Agents and Distributors

Thomas F. Clasen

Poorly selected sales intermediaries not only cost the exporter sales, but they may be difficult and costly to terminate. While exporters can protect themselves by using carefully drafted agency and distribution agreements, the best step in minimizing problems is to use more care in selecting the intermediary.

Thomas F. Clasen is a member of the International Business Group of Foley & Lardner, a Milwaukee-based law firm. The author has adapted this article from his new book, International Agency and Distribution Agreements *(Butterworths, 1991), a multi-volume treatise on the appointment, use, and termination of foreign sales agents and distributors.*

Experts estimate that more than one half of all world trade is handled through agents and distributors. While the use of such sales intermediaries is commonplace, especially for small and medium-sized companies, it is also common for exporters to complain about their foreign agents and distributors. Unsatisfactory sales intermediaries not only cost the exporter sales, but as a result of protective laws in many foreign jurisdictions, they may be difficult and costly to terminate. New legislation in EC Member States under Directive 86-653, as well as the proposed extension of Article 85 of the Treaty of Rome to "non-integrated" agents, will present additional obstacles to the use of sales intermediaries in Europe.

While exporters can help themselves by using carefully drafted agency and distribution agreements, the best step in minimizing problems is to use more care in selecting the intermediary. It is not uncommon for manufacturing companies to appoint a local agent or distributor without any significant background check at all. This is particularly true where the intermediary appears to be bringing in a significant amount of business or where the market in the country appears marginal. Since costly disputes frequently arise even in these circumstances, however, it is wise to establish a procedure in selecting foreign agents and distributors and sticking to that policy in all cases.

An effective agent-distributor selection procedure normally involves a number of steps. While there are variations depending on the industry, the following core elements will generally be present:

1. Examine the legal and business considerations involved in appointing foreign intermediaries, and establish criteria that reflect the particular geographic market;
2. Assemble a list of potential candidates by using the various directories and consulting other sources of information;
3. Qualify such candidates by applying certain criteria and conducting a preliminary interview; and
4. Make a trip to visit the proposed intermediary to obtain additional information about its resources and facilities, to get a proper feel for the intermediary's compatibility with the organization, and to check the assumptions and objectives of the agent or distributor.

From *The Journal of European Business,* Vol. 3, No. 2, November/December 1991, pp. 28-32. Copyright © 1991 by Faulkner & Gray, Inc.

Setting the Criteria

Because the qualifications the intermediary should possess differ from country to country, the starting point for the development of criteria may be an analysis of the peculiar characteristics of the market. Is there sufficient demand for the product in the market to justify its own agent or distributor, or could the market be covered well by an intermediary in an adjacent country? Is the market too large to give exclusively to a single agent or distributor? Is it reasonable to expect an agent or distributor not to handle competing goods in the market? To what extent is the market already familiar with and receptive to the product? Will the establishment of a demand require a long-term strategy that can be pursued only by someone with significant financial resources? Is it desirable to go with a well-established intermediary that can immediately provide access to the market even though this may require more sharing of profits?

For customers that prefer to purchase "local" products, exporters may want to use a distributor that would sell the goods under its own label.

A related consideration is the nature of the customers. To the extent that the product will be sold exclusively to governmental agencies, it may be critical for the agent or distributor to have access to officials who influence procurement decisions. If the product is sold primarily as part of a larger construction or turnkey project, access to the project coordinators and the ability to work effectively with the project engineers may be key. Each of these would imply a long-term, focused sales effort for which an agent may be better suited than a distributor. In those instances involving sales to a broader base of ordinary consumers, on the other hand, a distributor with an existing network of sales outlets may be more appropriate. For customers that prefer to purchase "local" products, exporters may want to use a distributor that would sell the goods under its own label.

The nature of the product will obviously have a significant effect on the sales approach. For example, is the product of a highly complex, technical nature so that a sales representative will need to employ advanced engineering and technical personnel to sell it effectively? Is the product complimentary to another line of products making it desirable to "piggy back" on distributors of such other products? Is it essential for the intermediary to have sufficient resources to provide service and spare parts or can these be obtained elsewhere? Is the product susceptible to copying so that it is critical to saturate the market completely through a broad distribution network before knock offs begin to appear?

The special characteristics of the market, the customers, and the product determine many of the criteria the exporter should consider in selecting a foreign intermediary. There are, however, some additional characteristics of the relationship that may influence the choice. Many of these will dictate whether the intermediary will be an agent or a distributor. For example, when it is important to exercise a high level of control over the marketing and sales activities of the representative, an exporter may prefer to use an agent rather than a distributor. An exporter's preference to sell directly to the customer in order to build goodwill in the market may also make an agency arrangement more desirable. On the other hand, if the exporter is unwilling to assume the risk of nonpayment by the customer or is opposed to a commission-based compensation structure, a company may find a distributor to be more consistent with its objectives. As mentioned, distributors are also more likely to inventory product and parts and to provide repair and warranty service.

In addition to the basic criteria, there are a number of characteristics that the exporter should look for in the candidate. For example, what kind of track record has the proposed agent or distributor established in promoting comparable products? Is it clear that it was responsible for its past success? Are there adequate explanations for its past failures? What kind of reputation does the prospective intermediary have within the industry? Do potential customers uniformly regard the agent or distributor as a company with whom they wish to do business?

Another important area of consideration is the prospective candidate's financial condition and resources. Does the intermediary have a sufficient net worth or other sources of income to sustain a long-term promotional effort even if sales are not realized immediately? Has it shown a consistent pattern of paying its creditors and employees? Does the proposed distributor have sufficient credit to justify extending terms? Does it have sufficient funds to stock an inventory or meet its other needs? Does the *del credere* agent (one that guarantees the customers' payment to the exporter) have the financial resources to support its guarantee? Who are the owners and creditors of the prospective agent or distributor, and what is the extent of their commitment to the intermediary? Has the intermediary shown a practice of making necessary commitments of funds for advertising and promotional activities, personnel, and office and shop facilities?

Companies should also consider the level of interest and enthusiasm the candidate demonstrates in representing the product in the market. Did the candidate contact the exporter or vice versa? Has it prepared a business plan or otherwise outlined in detail its proposed strategy for market development? To what extent is it willing to put its own money into advertising and promotion? Is it willing to assume the risks associated with minimum sales or other performance criteria? What would be its expectation for an initial term of the agreement and in what circumstances should it be renewable? Are these consistent with the schedule the exporter believes to be appropriate for establishing a foothold in the market? These and other factors should be examined to confirm the level of the candidate's commitment to the promotion of the product.

While business considerations normally predominate in the choice of a foreign intermediary, legal factors can influence significantly the exporter's costs and risks in using agents and distributors abroad. Many legal considerations can be addressed in the contract regardless of the agent or distributor that is ultimately selected. Others are so fundamental, however, that they should be examined at the outset and included in the exporter's criteria for selecting the intermediary.

Perhaps the most important legal consideration relevant to the exporter's choice of a commercial intermediary is the effect of local law on the use of agents and distributors. Local laws limiting the use of certain types of commercial intermediaries, for example, or requiring the agent or distributor to meet certain conditions for qualification must obviously be considered in establishing the criteria for selection. In countries where local labor laws extend to protect individual agents, the exporter may require the agent to be a corporate entity. In countries whose protective legislation extends only to distributors, the exporter may decide only to consider agents. On the other hand, if the manner in which local tax law defines taxable "permanent establishments" makes it difficult to use agents without becoming subject to local taxation, the exporter may wish to limit possible candidates to distributors. The risk presented by the implied authority that agents are granted under local law may also favor the use of distributors rather than agents.

Identifying Candidates

Having developed the general criteria that will be used in selecting the foreign agent or distributor, the next step is to assemble a list of prospective candidates that appear to meet the criteria. For many manufacturers new to exporting, this may appear to be a somewhat daunting task. To be sure, the means of developing information on foreign firms that may be able and willing to promote a company's products abroad are not the same as those used to identify domestic representatives. There are, however, a number of specialized sources of information on possible candidates, including a number of directories (such as those identified in *Trade Directories of the World* and other publications of Croner, Dun & Bradstreet, and Thomas), assistance from the U.S. Department of Commerce (particularly under its Agent/Distributor Service and World Traders Data Report Service), and information available from trade associations, the commercial section of foreign embassies and consulates in the United States, commercial banks, international carriers, and other private firms.

Exporters should investigate who their competitors and other firms in related businesses are using abroad. The exporter should also consult with its existing and potential customers in the foreign territory about possible candidates. Customers are perhaps in the best position to provide accurate information about agents and distributors that know the industry and the product, can provide adequate service and support, provide prompt service, and in general enjoy a favorable reputation in the market.

Qualifying Candidates

Once the manufacturer or supplier has located

a number of candidates that appear to meet the its criteria, the next task is to qualify the prospective candidates. While the qualification process will clearly depend on the industry or product involved and will differ from country to country, it normally will consist of three steps: (1) investigating the background of the candidate based on outside sources, (2) contacting the candidate to determine its interest in serving as an agent or distributor, and (3) reviewing additional background information obtained from the candidate itself. The objective of the qualification process is to narrow the list of potential candidates to a small number of firms that are genuinely interested in the arrangement and that appear to meet the basic criteria the exporter establishes. This will eliminate the need to make a trip to a country to visit firms that are either unqualified for or uninterested in the relationship. It will also allow the exporter to concentrate its time on visiting serious candidates in a market where it identified numerous possible agents or distributors.

Conducting a background investigation on a potential candidate involves looking at many issues. What is the firm's reputation in its industry? How is it regarded by its customers? How extensive are its contacts and market position in the territory? How long has it been in this business? Who are its principals and what are their backgrounds? How strong are its sales and service personnel? Is it qualified to serve the entire market exclusively? Does it have sufficient facilities and personnel? Does it have adequate financial resources? Information on these and similar question can often be assembled from outside sources. These include trade and other publications, trade associations, foreign and U.S. government agencies and diplomatic posts, banks and consulting firms, and customers in the territory.

The next step is to contact the potential candidates to determine their interest in serving as agents or distributors. For smaller companies with limited resources, this first contact may be made by means of a letter. The letter should describe generally the exporter's plans for appointing an agent or distributor in the territory, provide some background on the exporter, and include complete information on the subject products, including applications and possible sales volume in the territory. The letter may also refer the candidate to existing users of the product in the territory, if any, to give the potential agent or distributor an opportunity to examine the product and discuss it with a customer. The letter should state clearly that it is intended only to determine whether the recipient would have an interest in selling the product, and that the actual appointment of an agent or distributor will be made only following a personal visit and pursuant to a written agreement. It is important to avoid any misunderstanding that the letter itself is an offer to appoint the recipient as the exporter's intermediary.

Before the exporter plans a trip to visit the candidates, it should obtain additional information on any candidates that respond favorably to the initial contact. Like the background investigation, this review is designed to ferret out firms that do not meet the criteria or that are not serious about representing the product line. In this case, the information is secured from the candidate itself. This may include additional information to confirm the accuracy of the information already gleaned from other sources. It should also include more subjective information such as details on how the candidate sees the new product line fitting into its existing business, general information on how the firm would promote the product, and what the firms requirements might be in terms of compensation. An exporter that has significant bargaining power due to the demand for the product may even require the candidate to prepare a detailed business plan on its proposed marketing and sales strategies.

Meeting with Candidates

Smaller manufacturers and suppliers that have limited financial resources frequently appoint foreign agents and distributors without visiting the intermediary first. They reason that the costs associated with making the trip outweigh the benefit in actually meeting the prospective agent or distributor. They may also feel that they have less to lose than larger companies if the appointment does not work out. In fact, it is probably more important for the exporter with limited resources than for the large multinational to actually meet with the proposed candidates before making a decision—a visit to the candidate's facilities and an opportunity to meet its principals and other personnel is perhaps the best way to confirm that it meets the exporter's criteria. Agents and distributors that meet this criteria are more likely to maximize the exporter's sales in the territory (thus maximizing the exporter's revenue) and less likely to require termination on unfriendly terms (thus minimizing the exporter's costs).

There are at least three separate objectives of meeting with the proposed appointee in person. The first, and most obvious, is to obtain additional information about the candidate's objectives and means of doing business in order to confirm that it is the proper choice. While the exporter should have secured extensive information before the visit, there is normally no substitute for the purely subjective evaluation a supplier can make by actually meeting with the candidate's personnel and spending a reasonable amount of time discussing each other's ideas on how to enter the market and maximize sales. It is not at all unusual for a supplier to conclude after such a meeting that while the candidate looked great on paper, the chemistry just was not right.

If the supplier finds the candidate acceptable, the meeting can help accomplish a second objective of providing the supplier with additional information useful in negotiating the agency or distribution agreement and improving ongoing communication throughout the term of the appointment. Once again, it is clearly possible to negotiate the agreement without actually sitting down together. Experienced negotiators know, however, that it is very difficult to assess the level of the other side's depth of feeling about a particular issue without sitting across the table from him or her. It is obviously possible simply to show the proposed appointee a printed form and tell it to take it or leave it. Even in these cases, however, it is helpful to spend time discussing the issues to determine the likelihood of the candidate's respect for the terms of the agreement after it is executed. An initial meeting also sets an important tone of mutual communication that can last throughout the term of the agreement. An agent or distributor is much more likely to call and discuss problems with an exporter whose salespeople it knows personally.

But if these were the only purposes for the meeting, then it could just as readily take place at the supplier's facilities or at an airport or trade show someplace in between. This is also undesirable. The third and equally important objective of the face-to-face encounter is to give the exporter an opportunity to personally examine the candidate's facilities and to meet more of its personnel to confirm that they are up to the task. The facilities may be more important in the case of a distributor that will be expected to maintain an inventory and provide service for the products. Both agents and distributors should, however, have acceptable means of communicating efficiently with the exporter and its customers (telex, facsimile, cable, etc.) and a sufficient number of trained personnel to handle the responsibilities of the appointment. This will give the exporter first-hand knowledge of the ability of the candidate to provide effective support for the product.

Finally, the visit to the territory should include calling upon potential customers and other sources of information both to develop additional background on the candidate and to obtain additional information on the market.

Maintaining the Relationship

After selecting an agent or distributor, the exporter should take the necessary steps to maintain the intermediary's goodwill. This involves (1) negotiating an agreement that is fair and mutually beneficial, (2) complying in good faith with the terms of the agreement, (3) continuing the communication between the parties, and (4) making occasional adjustments in the relationship in response to changing circumstances.

While there is no sure way to avoid the risks presented by the use of foreign agents and distributors, careful selection of the intermediary by the above steps is the best means of minimizing them.

IT'S in the MAIL!

Once limited to the United States, mail-order companies are entering the global marketplace — led by mid-sized firms like The Sharper Image and Patagonia.

Art Garcia

It's the first Wednesday of the month and a crowd of color and contrast gathers at the corporate headquarters of The Sharper Image in San Francisco's downtown financial district. This is Open House day, when Sharper Image's marketing staff will see any inventor, tinkerer or dreamer with an innovative and unusual product in hand, no appointment necessary. On this February day, there's a turnout of 115 hopefuls, carrying with them gadgets, proposals and dreams of striking it rich.

Some arrive in work clothes, some wear business suits and others are from the ranks of propeller heads. Only a small number will even make an impression. Fewer still will click with a product that eventually finds its way into the colorful Sharper Image catalog or a place on the shelves of its 74 retail stores in the U.S. and Sharper Image shops run by licensees in Japan, Switzerland, Mexico and Brazil.

Started as a mail-order operation in 1977, The Sharper Image typifies the opportunities and problems of big-scale catalog companies in the face of new economic realities. Also changing the catalog picture are competitors increasingly hungry for a piece of an expanding global mail-order market.

Long a leader in marketing new mail-order concepts, Sharper Image sells many of its products only through its award-winning, artsy and imaginative catalogs. Exclusively mail-order offerings reduce the costs of tracking and stocking every product through each of the stores in the Sharper Image system.

That reality helps boost the awareness of the potential for tightly-controlled mail orders on a global scale. L.L. Bean, Land's End, Tweeds and nine other U.S. mail-order companies, for example, have collaborated on a mega-merchandise catalog of made-in-America goods aimed at the Japanese market.

The group shipped 50,000 copies of their 28-page "American Showcase" catalog (produced in Chicago by R.R. Donnelley & Sons) to Japan last November. Another 500,000 followed in February. L.L. Bean itself just signed a deal with Matsushita Electric Industrial and Seiyua Ltd. to open five Japanese stores in five years. Why Japan as a first target? Consider this: Japan's mail-order market sales in 1990 were pegged at $11 billion—a slim 1.3% of that nation's total retail volume.

Mail order is still the driving force at Patagonia, Inc., international purveyors of

From *World Trade*, April 1992, p. 56-60, 62. *World Trade*, 500 Newport Center Drive, Suite 450, Newport Beach, CA 92660.
Reprinted by permission.

Different customer, different culture

Overseas customers buying American goods directly from U.S. mail-order firms often pay premium prices. In most cases, they must add costs of telephoning or faxing orders. On top of that, they're responsible for postage, duty and currency conversion. If there's a problem with what they ordered, they have to ship the product back to the U.S. and deal with customs to get their cash refund.

California-based Patagonia, Inc., began ironing out those wrinkles for its Japanese market four years ago by setting up a centralized mail-order operation in Tokyo.

What Patagonia has learned from its experience in Japan serves as a template for other companies interested in developing their overseas mail-order business. One of the first lessons: "The very different mental set to deal with there," says Libby Frishman.

Frishman, in charge of customer service at Patagonia's worldwide mail operations center in Bozman, Montana, also works closely with the company's Japanese market. "There's no real mail-order system set up in Japan, as there is in the U.S.," she says. "We have list brokerage services here—outfits that buy and sell names like crazy to get customer leads. In Japan, that's not the way it's done. The Japanese consider their customers' names highly proprietary. They wouldn't sell them to anybody else."

Patagonia advertises and promotes its seasonal mail-order catalogs in Japan. The catalogs are in English with an insert in Japanese giving instructions on how to order. The company has a retail store in Tokyo, with the direct-mail operation above it. Last fall, Patagonia established a wholesale distribution network of Japanese dealers who carry Patagonia products on a non-exclusive basis. The Tokyo outlet is its lone, U.S.-style Patagonia-only store in Japan.

Japanese mail-order customers go through the Tokyo office, which faxes orders weekly to Bozman. Products are shipped from Ventura, California in bulk. They're repacked in Tokyo and delivered. "Customers don't have to deal with duty hassles. It's all built into the price," explains Frishman. "If customers have a problem, they can talk to our mail-order personnel there about fit, sizing or help in placing an order."

Payment is made in yen to the Tokyo mail-order office. "We bill them," she says. "Customers don't have to convert yen into dollars or deal with exchange rates. Our office takes care of all that. With many mail-order companies there, that's not the case. Customers have to deal with the U.S. company directly."

Patagonia's Tokyo employees are English-speaking Japanese nationals. Catalogs are shipped to Tokyo by air for rapid distribution to customers, followed by additional bulk shipments by ocean carrier. Air shipments are correlated with advertising schedules in Japan. Total shipments: Between 15,000 and 20,000 catalogs for the company's "universal" fall/winter and spring/summer seasons. "We don't ship them all by air because that would cost a fortune," Frishman says.

Patagonia has no plans for similar mail-order activity in Europe. Besides an office in Paris, stores in Germany and France and a licensee in Italy, it has a fairly well-established dealer network in Europe. What customers can't obtain through those stores or dealers, they can get through U.S. mail order.

Now in its fifth year of shipping catalogs to Japan, Patagonia has learned a few key trade tricks. Credit cards, for example, aren't as popular with Japanese as with American buyers. "We get tons of Japanese orders just by cash," Frishman says. "They're just the opposite of Americans. In the U.S., we receive many more orders by credit card than by cash." The Japanese also use postal transfers. "Their whole economy is just set up differently," notes Frishman.

Companies considering entering the market "should really go over there and see what the market is, what the competition is and understand how people do business," she advises. "You can't make the same assumptions you can here. It is a different customer and a different culture."

She recommends "going over with the frame of mind that you're there to learn from them and that we don't have all the answers in the U.S. Be really receptive to different ways of doing things. Don't be arrogant—which Americans, as a culture, tend to be. The big goal," she says, "is just to get the customers the products they want."

---

rugged outdoor clothing and sportswear for adults and children. Patagonia's standards-setting garments and gear are designed and shipped from a 118,000-square-foot warehouse in the coastal community of Ventura, California, to dealers and individual customers around the world.

Patagonia also has won awards for its oversized catalog. Printed on recycled paper and colorfully illustrated with photographs shot by users of its products, the big book is assembled in Ventura by a full-time design staff of eight—larger than at some magazines. All mail and telephone orders, however, are booked at a dedicated central Patagonia operation in Bozman, Montana. (The off-the-beaten-path Bozman location reflects company founder and avid outdoorsman Yvon Chouinard's penchant for decentralization; it also mirrors his interest in rock climbing and fly-fishing in Wyoming and Montana, as well as in providing employment in that part of the country.)

A Patagonia affiliate, Great Pacific Iron Works, owns and operates domestic retail stores in San Francisco, Ventura, Santa Barbara, Seattle and Boston. Overseas stores are in Chamonix, France; Tokyo, Munich and Dublin. Patagonia products and catalogs are available abroad through company subsidiaries and independent distributors in the Netherlands, Canada, France, Germany, Italy, Japan, the United Kingdom, Sweden and Switzerland.

International orders are a "growing percentage" of Patagonia's overall sales of about $115 million, says Tom Lowe, export manager, but the private company won't reveal how fast the percentage is growing. Europe is the fastest-growing foreign market ("There are a lot more people there than in the U.S.," Lowe says). Overseas production of Patagonia wear is being stepped up, mostly in France and Portugal.

Sharper Image, which doesn't break out its foreign sales either, is busily expanding its overseas licensee program. "We've got two or three ready to sign on the dotted line, with several other prospects we're talking to," says Richard Thalheimer, president, CEO and founder of The Sharper Image. The company is "aggressively" pursuing the licensee route "because we view it as a way to have a little bit of our cake and eat it too," he says.

"From a marketing sense, we can exploit the overseas market without the investment in time and money," he adds. "We'd like to develop that market more because any time you're the franchisor or licensor and you have control, you tend to generate revenues with little expense. Somebody else is providing the money and the effort while we generate royalties or licensee income. It works for McDonald's, it works for us."

While muscling up abroad, Sharper Image has been slimming down at home. In fiscal 1990, the company posted the first loss in its 15 years in business, a reflection of Persian Gulf war worries, a sour economy, shifting consumer attitudes, shrinking margins and rising operating expenses. Final figures aren't out for the fiscal year ending January 31, but sales were around $175 million, the second off year in a row.

Publicly held Sharper Image's 1990 net loss of $2.3 million compared with the prior year's profit of $4.2 million. Sales in 1990 dropped to $181 million from fiscal 1989's record $209 million. Though disappointing, the red ink had a positive side, prompting a year of structural repositioning and reevaluation of merchandise and prices.

The company spent much of 1990 reviewing and overhauling nearly everything it does. Payroll was sliced and emphasis on brand-name products was dampened in favor of an invigorated mix of new and exclusive goods. As those changes took effect last year, the payoff was a doubling of fourth quarter earnings, despite one of the toughest Christmas seasons for retailers in 30 years.

The tightened operations and new lineup of products are restoring profit margins to sharply higher levels than Sharper Image has seen in years, says CEO Thalheimer. In the 1990 annual report, he promised shareholders that the company would eliminate the "frivolous and expensive products that became synonymous with the 1980s." Still, a key to Sharper Image's image remains ongoing promotion of "fun and functional" merchandise.

Some of those items blossom from the company's Open House affair, where acceptance of a product can be a ticket to global sales, if it makes the pages of Sharper Image's award-winning monthly catalog of items sold only through mail or 24-hour telephone order. Calls in the U.S. are to a free 800 number but overseas customers pay their own phone charges.

A core 32 pages of the catalog is designed and produced in the U.S. and shipped overseas. There, licensees add additional pages of products unique to their markets and described in the local language. While Sharper Image has put a $48 "subscription" price on its catalog for those requesting it overseas, the company is backing away from such solicitation. It still doesn't do vast overseas mailings but fulfills foreign requests for catalogs "one at a time," says Sydney Klevatt vice president of marketing.

Most overseas orders now are submitted by fax and similarly are handled on an individual basis. Sharper Image receives an "insignificant" number of phone calls from abroad. "Again, we've chosen to take the licensee route for exploitation of the international marketplace by having representatives in foreign countries solicit for themselves, but pay us royalties," Klevatt says. "We provide the catalog, they provide the language."

The heart of the catalog displays mainstream Sharper Image products. Additional local language pages feature merchandise procured by the licensees but approved by Sharper Image "because it bears our name," he explains. "If it's something that just doesn't strike us, we'll convince them they shouldn't include it." The company supplies the film for the core part of international versions of its catalogs but printing is done locally overseas. "It doesn't make much sense to ship finished catalogs around the world. That's pretty heavy stuff," notes Klevatt.

Sharper Image distributes about 25 million of its catalogs yearly and rings up 20 to 25% of its sales from mail orders,

SHARPENING THE IMAGE

A One-World Market of Big-Boy Toys

If it's in the catalog or on display at a Sharper Image store, it's for sale—from watches and airplanes to what the retail chain calls "getaway" chairs. Sit in one of these all-leather chairs with built-in radio, massager and heating element and "get away from it all."

So impressed was a sheik from a Gulf state in a visit to Sharper Image in New York City, he ordered 14 of the $2,000 chairs. Similar big-ticket sales are made to Japanese businessmen and other foreign buyers making runs at Sharper Image in Beverly Hills or any of the 73 other outlets they may cruise.

Whether an in-store sale or by mail, phone or fax, the company's glossy catalog has created a one-world market of big-boy tekkie toys and functional fashions. Among current items are a $100 "talking" two-channel pen that records reminders, the 50-flag windbreaker jacket popularized by President Bush, stereo karaoke systems and the bright-red, ultra-light, $20,000 plane hanging from the ceiling of the San Francisco downtown store.

"Everything's for sale," grins Sharper Image's senior vice president of marketing, Sydney Klevatt. "We're in the unusual gift business and something that's unusual to Americans tends to be pretty universally translated. After you allow for different electrical currencies for some products and different cultures and mores, the novelty grabs foreigners, too. Things that are best-sellers here tend to be best-sellers overseas."

Sharper Image has put new retail outlets on hold, giving it an opportunity to expand the catalog side of its business. U.S. customers have access to a 24-hour 800 number; those abroad pay the tab for phone and fax orders if they choose to deal directly with the San Francisco mail-order center, rather than a Sharper Image overseas shop.

International shipments are by DHL, Federal Express "or whatever method the customer wants," Klevatt says. Sharper Image makes no products itself, relying mostly on American manufacturers to turn out goods tailored to its specifications.

Most customers are male, 18 to 38, in the upper-middle to higher income ranges, less interested in high-tech and more price-conscious than five years ago. It's a shift in customer demographics Sharper Image is responding to by repositioning prices and product lines. "We don't have quite as many things for 500 bucks in the joint," Klevatt says. "Now we've got a lot of things under 100 bucks. We change with the needs of the customer."

volume that's expected to grow closer to 30% this year. So far, only about 10,000 copies are mailed to foreign customers. Many are international travelers who take a fancy to the exotica they've seen on display at Sharper Image stores in the U.S. and in other countries.

Patagonia's stores in Europe do very little mail-order business. "Now that people know our stores are there, they'll sometimes call those stores and place an order for something to be mailed," says export manager Lowe. "But we don't have a mail-order system there like we do in the U.S. Overseas, it's more of a service than an organized mail-order business. Here in the States, we maintain mail lists as a formal, organized way to sell product. We haven't reached that level in Europe."

Patagonia is giving thought to incorporating such a system in future planning for its foreign operations. "It might be a little more practical in a few more years when the European economies are a little more integrated," Lowe says. Patagonia has experimented with having its general catalog copied and printed in Europe and also printing an exclusively European version that includes only styles sold there.

In a more recent efficiency move, the company consolidated all its catalog efforts. It currently has a single universal catalog that's printed in the U.S. and shipped to Patagonia warehouses in Europe, Japan and Canada. In Europe and Canada, where Patagonia primarily has wholesale distribution systems, not mail-order service, catalogs are supplied to retail dealers by the warehouses. In Japan, the company has a wholesale operation and a mail-order business, plus a retail store in Tokyo, all working with their own customer lists.

Catalogs sent to Japan were the U.S. version until last fall, when Patagonia took its first stab at publishing an edition in Japanese. "We're still relatively new in Japan and fall/winter is the first season we've actually done a full-on translation," says Barbara Tebbel, international inventory manager and analyst at the Ventura corporate office.

In Europe, Patagonia catalogs are printed in French and German, as well as English. An Italian version is provided for the independent exclusive Patagonia distributor in Italy, while the counterpart in Sweden works with an English book. "We try to limit the number of versions of our catalogs that go out and the number of times we send them to the same customer," Tebbel says.

"Most companies believe you need to send a new catalog every month or two. We try to limit the number of catalogs we actually make and mail out so they don't become a form of junk mail," she continues. "We want our products to be important and unique. We don't want to throw them at the customer."

Have the economies of scale and the scale of the global market made the mail-order business a game strictly for big players or is there room still for entrepreneurial entries? With nearly five years at Patagonia under her belt, Tebbel believes the business remains open to innovators.

"That's how Patagonia began: As a small mail-order business," she points out. "We don't have strictly mail-order people working for us anymore, but then, we haven't done many things the way most mail-order companies do." In her global view, you can make book—or catalog—on creativity, imagination and fresh and better ideas.

GUESS WHO'S SELLING BARBIES IN JAPAN NOW?

It wasn't easy, but Toys 'R' Us finally cracked this tough market

Jumping out of his car in an empty parking lot 40 miles north of Tokyo, Larry R. Bouts stands back and admires the white, spanking-new building sprawling before him. "Can you believe this?" he exclaims. "Pretty amazing!"

White buildings and empty parking lots normally have little power to amaze. But Bouts is right to exult over this particular patch of real estate. Bouts, 42, is president of the international division of Toys 'R' Us Inc., and this is his first look at the company's inaugural store in Japan—and the very first large U. S.-owned discount store there.

SLOGGING. When Bouts's new Ibaraki Prefecture store opens on Dec. 20, it will culminate three years of heavy slogging through the swamps of Japanese bureaucracy, local vested interests, labyrinthine real estate practices, and heavy, often hostile, Japanese press coverage. And it will be the most visible payoff to date of the two-year-old, U. S.-inspired Structural Impediments Initiative aimed at prying open new markets for American companies in Japan. "We hope Toys 'R' Us will be the first in a long line of stores to locate in Japan," says Commerce Secretary Robert A. Mosbacher.

Small wonder Japanese toymakers and retailers are edgy. Toys 'R' Us Japan Ltd. hopes to be opening 10 stores per year from 1993 through the end of the decade. Each is expected to generate sales of at least $15 million its first year. That foretells minimum annual sales of $1.5 billion by the year 2000, roughly half of which would be from toys made outside Japan. Toys 'R' Us, with global revenue of $6.4 billion, can bring a lot of firepower to bear. The typical small Japanese toy store stocks between 1,000 and 2,000 different items, while Toys 'R' Us will start out with about 8,000 items, rising to 15,000 over time. If it can offer toys for 10% to 15% less than competitors, as it does elsewhere and as Bouts says is possible, Toys 'R' Us will have a huge impact on Japanese toy retailing. With more than $6 billion in annual sales, Japan is the world's No. 2 toy market after the U.S.

It was the size of that market that moved Toys 'R' Us to launch the effort in the first place. Anticipating the day when it would saturate its domestic market, America's largest toy retailer went international in 1984, first in Canada, then Europe, Hong Kong, and Singapore. Japan was always tempting, but the country's notorious Large-Store Law, aimed at protecting the country's politically powerful small shopkeepers, seemed an unbreachable barrier. Under the law, local communities and the Ministry of International Trade & Industry often managed to stall incursions by big retailers, such as Japanese supermarket operator Daiei Inc., for 10 years or more.

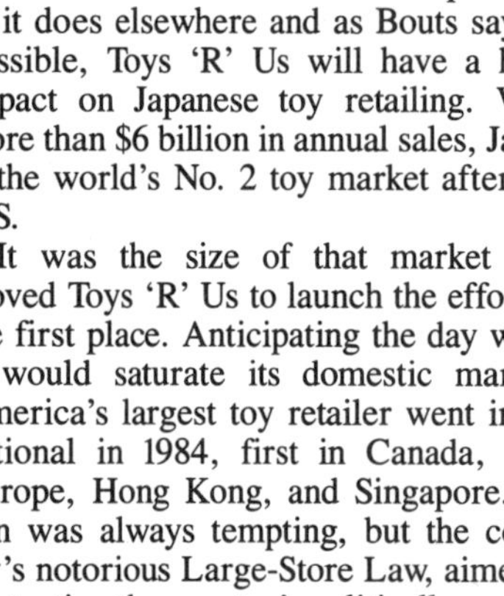

CHART BY ALBERTO MENA/BW

But by late 1988, recalls Toys 'R' Us Vice-Chairman Robert C. Nakasone, "there were rumblings MITI was thinking about a major change." Pressure was mounting from the U. S., big Japanese retailers, and consumers looking for the lower prices mass merchants could offer. Toys 'R' Us immediately began looking for a local partner to guide it through the ordeal it faced. In early 1989, Bouts's predecessor met Den Fujita, president of McDonald's Co. (Japan). "He was our kind of guy," says the U. S.-born Nakasone. "He was bicultural, and he had quickly grown a retail business in Japan. He really understood the impatience of a company like ours."

BIG MAC ABOARD. Fujita also liked what he saw. Since McDonald's serves a similar clientele—families with small kids—he figured it could profit from building restaurants on the same sites as Toys 'R' Us. And after 20 years of building McDonald's into Japan's largest fast-food operator, with $1.3 billion in sales, Fujita had acquired an encyclopedic knowledge of Japanese real estate. "If you name a city, I can see the post office, train station, everything," boasts Fujita, who estimates Japan has at least 100 sites suitable for a Toys 'R' Us. McDonald's Japan quickly agreed to take a 20% stake in Toys 'R' Us Japan.

In the spring of 1989, MITI unveiled its new retail industry "vision," which included eventual relaxation of the Large-Store Law. and the U.S. began proposing its Structural Impediments Initiative, aimed in part at cracking open Japanese markets. Nakasone, Bouts, and Fujita began lobbying their respective governments for help. Bouts and other Toys 'R' Us executives met directly with U.S. Trade Representative Carla A. Hills and

Reprinted from the December 9, 1991, issue of *Business Week*, pp. 72, 74, 76, by special permission. Copyright © 1991 by McGraw-Hill, Inc.

her deputy, Linn Williams. Bouts says Hills's backing was critical. Back in Tokyo, Fujita made the rounds of his government contacts, many of them former classmates and fellow alumni of the University of Tokyo's elite law department.

By April, 1990, MITI had agreed to shorten the big-store application process to no more than 18 months. "That was a major, major breakthrough," says Nakasone. He and Bouts already had handshake agreements with various landlords. Within weeks, the company had submitted building applications for several locations.

COOL RECEPTION. But the work had just started. Since then, Toys 'R' Us has been slowly negotiating the local barriers still in place after the Large-Store Law's amendment. Take the fairly typical case of Sagamihara, a Tokyo suburb of 520,000. In May, 1990, Toys 'R' Us started talks on opening a store there. The welcome was hardly a warm one. "The site Toys 'R' Us had chosen didn't fit our plans [for development]," says Goro Kakishima, senior managing director of Sagamihara's Chamber of Commerce & Industry. "But we couldn't legally prevent it." So in July, conforming to MITI-prescribed procedures, Toys 'R' Us submitted applications to the ministry, Kanagawa Prefecture, Sagamihara City, and the Chamber of Commerce.

> 'You won't see deep discounts,' says Bouts. 'Real estate and distribution costs are high here'

In August, Toys 'R' Us had to join in an "explanation meeting" at the local public hall. Next came presentations to Sagamihara's Commercial Activities Council, a MITI-inspired body of 18 consumers, merchants, professionals, and academics. After four meetings, the council gave the green light in June, 1991. Toys 'R' Us could open its store after Dec. 1. But like many other stores, it had to close every day by 8 p.m. and shutter itself 30 days a year. In addition, Toys 'R' Us had to consult with other bodies over possible traffic problems. By September, those consultations and construction delays forced a postponement of the Sagamihara opening until March, 1992. Determined to open one store this year, Toys 'R' Us turned to Ibaraki.

At Ibaraki, the store and 850-car parking lot are massive by Japanese standards. The colorful, English-language Toys 'R' Us signs jump out at passersby. Bouts says the store will get only minimal customization—some Japanese-language signs inside and perhaps a section for items especially popular with Japanese. Although he's aiming for discounts of up to 15%, he's not making any promises. "You won't see deep discounts," he says. "Real estate and distribution costs are high here."

The early stores will feature a mix of roughly two-thirds Japanese toys and one-third imports, including Huffy bikes, Mattel's Barbie dolls, and Tonka trucks. But Bouts says imports' share will gradually rise to as much as half. Meanwhile, local opposition seems to have subsided. "An integrated store for children is a good thing," says Katsuyuki Fujii, whose small Toy's House Joy sits just a half-mile down the road from the first Toys 'R' Us store. "My wife can't wait to go shopping there for our kids." Fujii says he'll survive by finding a profitable niche—which he won't specify.

HUE AND CRY. Nobody at Toys 'R' Us is predicting clear sailing, though. Last year, for example, frightened toy shop owners in the city of Niigata generated international headlines by clamoring against the application of Toys 'R' Us to build a store there. They succeeded in delaying the opening until 1993.

Toys 'R' Us still faces obstacles in Japan. It's having a hard time winning low-cost, direct-supply contracts from local toymakers, who don't want to upset powerful wholesalers and longtime customers. Such arrangements are key to the ability of Toys 'R' Us to discount. Only one major Japanese toymaker, Nintendo Co., has publicly stated it will sell directly to Toys 'R' Us Japan. And small retailers such as Fujii say they expect lower prices from wholesalers, and possibly financial support, if the heat from Toys 'R' Us gets to be too much.

Despite their anxiety over Toys 'R' Us, Japanese retailers probably don't have to worry about an onslaught of giant U. S. retailers. True, smaller specialty stores such as Computerland and Brooks Brothers Inc. are already in Japan. But their operations are a far cry from those of a "superstore" operator intent on commanding a market. As analyst Richard Baum of researcher Sanford C. Bernstein Inc. puts it: "Only a handful of big retailers have the kind of format, supplier relationships, and expertise that let them succeed globally." So, the intricate Japanese system of retailing may, by and large, remain undisturbed by U. S. companies. That larger issue isn't the giant toy retailer's problem, though. Toys 'R' Us is just intent on expanding its tenuous foothold in the world's toughest retail market.

By Robert Neff in Tokyo, with bureau reports

International Finance

Money is the grease that makes the wheels of international business turn. One of the challenges that faces the managers of multinational corporations is international finance. Currency exchange has always been a problem. When a customer in Germany buys French wine, he or she pays for it in marks, but, eventually, the French vintner will want francs to buy some German beer. Exchange rates fluctuate as the supply and demand for a particular currency changes. Relatively expensive currencies make for relatively expensive products and cheap currencies can make products a bargain. The currency trading markets are not for the faint of heart or the inexperienced. Many corporations and financial institutions have at one time or another suffered severe financial loss due to

Unit 5

changes in the currency exchange rate. When the Franklin National Bank failed, it was the largest bank failure in U.S. history up to that time. A big part of the reason it failed could be traced directly to bad currency transactions. Franklin was a very large financial institution dealing in a highly complex market, and it should be pointed out that Franklin's experience, while perhaps the most severe, was certainly not unique. Everyone who has ever engaged in currency transactions for any period of time has, at some point, lost money.

Over the past 20 years, dislocations in the marketplace have been reflected in the financial markets. When the first gasoline crisis arose in the early 1970s, the OPEC nations found themselves with a great amount of cash, mostly dollars, and they put the money in the banks. The banks, in turn, financed by petrodollars, went on a lending spree to Third World countries. Many of these loans have proven to be less than prudent over the years and, frankly, many banks are in financial difficulty today because they still have these loans on the books. They have had to put away reserves to cover the eventual, final, and expected default on these loans and that has meant higher prices and interest rates to the bank's good customers. It was not small banks with little or no international experience that fell into this trap, but the very large and experienced banks, such as Citicorp and Chase Manhattan, that have had to write off huge sums of money in bad loans to developing Third World countries.

One of the ways in which the international financial management process is conducted is through the mechanism of transfer pricing. Corporations are very careful to price their products in such a way as to maximize profit, and that means to minimize taxes. If a U.S. corporation sells a product to its Greek subsidiary, what price should it charge the subsidiary? The tax rate in Greece on corporate profits is very high, while the U.S. rate is relatively low when measured on a worldwide scale. If the U.S. parent sells the goods to the Greek subsidiary for slightly less than the Greek subsidiary has charged the final customer, then the profit will be taken in the United States with its lower tax rate and not in Greece, even though that is where the deal was made. The end result is that the corporation maximizes its profits, the U.S. government gets some tax revenue, and the Greek government gets virtually nothing because the Greek subsidiary does not show any profit. National governments are starting to look into this practice as they search for new sources of revenues.

For now, the banks will provide some of the more interesting developments in international finance during the next decade. The history of American banking since 1929 has been one of fairly close regulation. Banks are limited in the types of businesses they may enter and where they may do business. U.S. banks tend to be centered in one state, although there are multistate bank holding companies, but that is a fairly recent development. There are, in fact, two banking systems in the United States: one chartered by the national government (hence the word "National" in the title, or only the initials "N.A." [National Association] after the name) and state-chartered banks. American bankers are pressing the federal government for deregulation of their activities, back, perhaps, to pre-1929 levels of banking regulation. They are doing this so that they may better compete with foreign banks in international transactions. Many non–U.S. banks are able to offer services that U.S. banks cannot offer by law, and U.S. banks want to be able to compete directly with the foreign banks in this arena. Banks are in the service business. Like McDonald's, they are getting paid for a product, whether it is a "Big Mac" or a loan. The reason customers buy from them is because of the services they offer, and the more services they offer, the greater their ability to compete with non–U.S. banks that already offer many of these services that the U.S. banks wish to provide. Given the recent experience in the area of deregulation with the savings and loan associations, it will be interesting to see how far the banks will get in obtaining the deregulation they so ardently desire. As of now, the appropriate bills are pending in Congress, but many banks are not waiting and are seeking to merge under the theory that bigger means stronger and better able to compete in a rapidly changing international financial environment.

Looking Ahead: Challenge Questions

Transfer pricing has always been one of the more creative areas of international finance and accounting. How does it work? Why is it important?

Debt is a problem facing the Third World and the banking system. How did they get into this situation? How could they get out?

American banks want to be deregulated so that they can more effectively compete with their foreign counterparts. Do you think this is a good or a bad idea? Do you think there is any danger that this could turn into another savings and loan disaster? Defend your answers.

As Competition Rises In Global Banking, Europeans Have Edge

By Avoiding Excesses of '80s, They Take Fewer Big Hits, Rest on Solid Capital Bases

By Michael R. Sesit in New York, Craig Forman in London, Terence Roth in Frankfurt and Marcus W. Brauchli in Tokyo.

In the 1990s and beyond, the rough game of high-stakes international banking will probably get even rougher.

"We are in an era of aggressively intensified competition, rapidly shifting definitions of what financial products are, a general slowdown in world economic growth and much, much tougher risk-management demands," says Robert Dugger, chief economist for the American Bankers Association.

So rough is that looming competition, says George Vojta, chief of strategic planning at Bankers Trust New York Corp., that of 40 to 45 banks now aspiring to be global powerhouses, only six to 10 will make the grade by the end of the 1990s.

And some experts predict that most of the winners won't be America's big banks, which dominated world banking from the 1950s through the 1970s, or Japan's behemoths, which made a run for the top in the 1980s. Of a dozen banks picked as strong contenders by bankers, regulators and analysts, half are European (see box). One reason is a bit ironic.

"The European banking system is in the good shape it is in because it didn't have the same determination to dominate the world that the U.S. and Japanese did," says Alan Moore, director of corporate banking and treasury at Lloyds Bank PLC. European banks generally have been conservatively managed, treading more carefully in the risky, deregulated free-for-all of international finance. Now, some European giants have a lot going for them, including solid capital bases, strong balance sheets and dominant shares of home markets expected to grow quickly.

Difficult Problems

Yet all the big international banks face difficult problems. Global banking will change "from being a protected industry to a deregulated one. Everybody can invade your market; you can invade everybody else's markets," Mr. Vojta says. "Your survival will be based on your ability to take on all comers and succeed often enough to make sufficient profit to pay shareholders and build capital."

However, planning for survival is difficult. Nobody knows exactly what the future global bank will look like. But in general terms, global banks must be able to serve the financing needs of corporations, big and small, anywhere in the world. They also must be able to garner a commanding share of the increasing flow of capital across national borders and be flexible enough to shift resources to fast-growing areas and high-return businesses.

They must do all this while new technology and new financial products are shaking up the banking industry and while corporate clients and investors are becoming ever more global. Already, big banks are battling each other on many fronts: lending, underwriting, financial advice and new financing techniques for corporations, currency and securities trading, leasing, insurance, money management and consumer banking. The banks are also hurt by the industry's overcapacity—too many banks chasing too few customers—and many are struggling to meet international rules requiring them, by early 1993, to have capital equivalent to 8% of assets.

Cost of Failure

Moreover, the costs of trying to go global and failing will be high. "Mismanaging the process would be confusing to an organization, expensive for the shareholders and unsettling for clients," says Douglas A. Warner III, president of J.P. Morgan & Co. Banks losing out in the scramble could be taken over or become mostly domestic or niche institutions.

All the contenders enter the race with major handicaps and major advantages.

How They Stack Up

Many U.S. banks are plagued with weak capital bases and soured loans to less-developed countries, on real estate and for highly leveraged takeovers. They also keep losing business to nonbank rivals.

But after two decades of competing domestically against insurers, investment banks and money managers as well as internationally, U.S. banks have developed superior creative skills. "The Americans stand tall," says Lowell Bryan, chief banking consultant at McKinsey & Co. "European and Japanese banks are sitting on top of cartels that are going to have to change. The [global] winners are going to be the ones with the biggest skills; you don't get skills sitting in an oligopoly."

The Japanese giants, backed by a strong economy and powerful corporate

Reprinted by permission of *The Wall Street Journal*, March 25, 1991, pp. 1, A7. Copyright © 1991 by Dow Jones & Company, Inc. All rights reserved worldwide.

customers, are rich in assets. But the world's biggest banks are poor in capital and innovative flair and are learning that size doesn't guarantee performance. In the past year, Japan's banks have been ravaged by soaring interest rates, a plunging stock market and intensifying competition. Now, deregulation threatens many of them by narrowing spreads between borrowing costs and lending income.

"The era of Japanese banks' dominance, if it ever was dominance, is over," declares Daniel J. Kreps, a principal at SRI International, a consulting firm in Menlo Park, Calif. "They will play a role commensurate with the importance of the Japanese economy, which is considerable. But they won't run" world banking.

The well-capitalized European banks have mostly solved their Third World loan problems and are taking much smaller hits from bad real-estate and takeover credits than U.S. and Japanese banks are.

But they have little experience with head-butting competition. Europe's banking sanctuaries—local markets long protected from price-cutting competition by law or tradition—will be torn asunder by the planned 1992 integration of financial markets in the 12-nation European Community. The roughly 300 mergers and partial mergers among Europe's banks in the past two years foreshadow a further competitive shakeout; many analysts predict that today's roster of European banks will be halved to 800.

However, that attrition could leave the strongest European banks—Germany's Deutsche Bank AG, Union Bank of Switzerland, Credit Suisse, Swiss Bank Corp. and Britain's Barclays Bank PLC—mightier than ever. All but Barclays are rated triple-A; they are the world's only private-sector banks so designated by each of three major credit agencies. Barclays is rated triple-A by two and double-A by one.

Triple-A status lowers a bank's cost of funds and gives it a competitive edge in earning fees from municipalities and corporations that need back-up credit lines. It also attracts wealthy individuals, especially frightened ones. "In a crisis, people just throw money at us; it's almost an embarrassment," says Christopher Roberts, U.S. area head for Credit Suisse.

Each of the five banks, with a dominant position at home, has considerable leeway in setting domestic interest rates and can subsidize forays abroad. In Switzerland, according to Salomon Brothers Inc., four banks hold 53% of the assets; in Britain, 13 banks account for 57% of domestic sterling deposits. By contrast, each of the top 10 U.S. banks has an average of only 3% of industry revenues. And foreign banks hold 25% of U.S. banking assets, up from 14% in 1982 and 3.8% in 1973.

In home markets, Europe's banks have long been able to enter businesses, such as investment banking and insurance, mostly denied their U.S. and Japanese rivals. Continental institutions also hold large stakes in industrial companies, and many Japanese banks are in huge interlocking corporate groups, the *keiretsu*. In addition, banks in Europe and Japan can set up branches anywhere in their own countries. U.S. Treasury Department proposals to grant U.S. banks similar privileges face tough going in Congress.

Relying on the "universal" bank concept, Credit Suisse and UBS both pursue a three-pronged strategy: commercial banking, investment banking and money management. Unlike some British and Japanese banks, none of Switzerland's big three pursues consumer banking outside its home country.

Deutsche Bank and Barclays do. Preparing for 1992, the bank that awestruck competitors call "the Big D" has acquired subsidiaries—mostly retail branch operations—in Italy, Spain, Austria and the Netherlands. Last year, it shelled out the equivalent of $1.62 billion for Morgan Grenfell Group PLC, a premier British merchant bank. Barclays also has concentrated on Europe, acquiring banks in Germany and opening branches in Spain. It is purchasing Europeenne de Banque, once part of the Rothschild interests, to beef up its commercial banking in France.

But nobody matches Citicorp in its lust to be the world's consumer bank. The New York bank's two biggest profit centers are its New York branch system, with 1,200 automated teller machines, and its $30 billion credit-card business, with 27 million card holders. "It's going to be very unlikely we'll see many other global players in the consumer end of the business," says Richard S. Braddock, Citicorp's president.

In Japan, Citicorp is the only foreign bank competing in the consumer market with the Japanese giants. With designer-finished lobbies and top-of-the-line computer systems, it is targeting wealthy clients. In addition, Citicorp "is better positioned for 1992 on the retail side than many European banks," says Thomas H. Hanley, a Salomon Brothers managing director.

What the U.S. Air Force was to Operation Desert Storm, U.S. banks are to international finance. Their technological edge enhances their capabilities in trading and in designing and distributing myriad new services—capabilities widely expected to help them seize opportunities as European and Japanese markets are deregulated.

Some New Products

Last year, Bankers Trust sold securities permitting investors to bet on the direction of the Tokyo stock market. Meanwhile, J.P. Morgan and Citicorp arranged for banks around the world to reduce their loan exposure in Argentina by $4.6 billion by taking equity stakes in two newly privatized telephone companies.

"In corporate and investment banking, technology can make up for a lot; you don't have to have a physical presence within each country," Mr. Hanley says.

All three banks have invested heavily in servicing corporate clients and constructing sophisticated currency and securities trading systems. Bankers Trust, for example, spends about $350 million a year on its computer operations. "The cumulative technology is reaching the point where we've developed barriers to entry, where others don't even want to try to compete," the bank's Mr. Vojta says.

If the innovative American banks do get the right to operate without geographic and product constraints in the U.S., Mr. Bryan of McKinsey says, "we have potential winners in this country; we don't have to give them advantages" in competing with foreign rivals. "We just have to get out of their way."

That isn't true for most Japanese banks, despite their size. Just a few of them, analysts say, can challenge major U.S. or European banks. Only Industrial Bank of Japan Ltd., Sumitomo Bank Ltd. and Mitsubishi Bank Ltd. have "the experience, technological capability and capital strength necessary to succeed in providing a full range of commercial and investment bank services on an international scale," says Alicia Ogawa, a banking analyst at S.G. Warburg Securities Ltd.

Seeking Safety at Home

Paradoxically, many banks are retreating to the relative safety of their home markets just when their corporate clients and investors are becoming more global. One reason: Global expansion has caused a lot of disappointment.

In the past few years, Chase Manhattan Corp., BankAmerica Corp., Chemical Banking Corp. and other U.S. banks have sold or closed operations abroad to cut losses or meet the new capital standards. One big problem: Many banks venturing abroad never proceeded beyond their initial move. "Toeholds always look good because they're cheap, but it's sort of, 'Do you want to pay now or want to pay later?' " Citicorp President Braddock says. "The question is, if you buy the toehold, how do you build it into something substantial? That's a fundamental flaw in a lot of acquisition strategies."

Salomon's Mr. Hanley cites two examples in the U.S. "NatWest doesn't have real critical mass, and Barclays is still looking for market share," he says. NatWest's U.S. units had a 1990 loss of $352.4 million, and other big British banks—Lloyds, Midland Bank PLC and Standard Chartered Bank PLC—have sold U.S. banks to raise money. Japanese banks, hurt by soured buy-out loans and seeking to meet the capital rules, also are selling assets and slowing growth world-wide.

"The banking industry has lost multibillions of dollars in international markets," says Robin Monro-Davies, managing director of IBCA Ltd., a London bank credit-rating agency. "America has been a graveyard for foreign banks."

—Barbara Donnelly in New York contributed to this article.

Experts Select the 12 Big Banks They Expect to Be on Top by Close of 1990s

By a WALL STREET JOURNAL *Staff Reporter*

In interviews with bankers, regulators and analysts, 12 banks consistently turn up as most likely to be at the forefront of international banking at the end of the decade.

Some people say the global bank of the future doesn't exist yet—and won't until the U.S. and Japan implement proposed regulatory changes. In the U.S., one regulator conjures up a conglomerate consisting of a large money-center bank, a strong regional bank, an investment bank, a mutual-fund company and possibly also an insurer and industrial company—a sort of Citicorp, Banc One, Salomon Brothers, Fidelity, Equitable Life and General Motors all wrapped into one.

Nonbanking concerns appear on some people's lists. In terms of developing financial products and underwriting and trading securities on a world-wide scale, they see Goldman, Sachs & Co., Morgan Stanley & Co. and Japan's Nomura Securities Co. in the front rank of global powerhouses.

Nonetheless, here are capsule views of the 12, in alphabetical order:

Bankers Trust New York Corp. As a second-tier U.S. money-center bank in the 1970s, Bankers Trust faced a decision: change or wither. It changed, shedding its retail branches and other consumer businesses and investing heavily on the gamble that banks would get additional securities powers. Bankers Trust's core strategy is to manage the volatility associated with financial-market deregulation, whether in currencies, interest rates or oil prices. The bank also is emphasizing its merchant-banking operations. One bugaboo: Nonperforming assets soared 91.6% in the fourth quarter, to $2.75 billion, largely because of Mexican and Venezuelan debt.

Banque Nationale de Paris. One of the biggest French banks, 75%-government-owned BNP is a "universal" bank in France, with 2,000 branches and a complete range of retail, commercial and investment-banking operations. It also sells mutual funds and the insurance products of 10%-owned Union des Assurances de Paris. Outside France, BNP has operations in some 80 countries. Preparing for the European Community unification in 1992, the bank has been increasing its presence in Europe, most recently by acquiring a Belgian bank and opening branches in Spain. In the U.S., BNP has corporate banking and capital-market operations, plus an 85-branch retail bank in California.

Barclays Bank PLC. Britain's largest bank, with about 15% of the domestic banking market, Barclays operates in more than 70 countries and has about 52% of its assets outside the U.K. For 100 years, Barclays has been in America, where it is primarily a corporate and investment bank. Barclays also provides a rare example of a commercial bank successfully developing investment-banking expertise. It has built up its London-based Barclays de Zoete Wedd unit into one of the strongest players in the London securities markets. Barclays also has one of the strongest capital ratios of Britain's big banks, but its profits, like those of its rivals, have been squeezed recently by bad debts, rising costs and Britain's recession.

Citicorp. More than any other institution, America's biggest bank seeks to be all things to all people all over the world. To create a pan-European network with a single identity, Citi's 302-branch German consumer bank and 90-branch Belgium bank this year are adopting the Citibank name, which already adorns retail units in Italy, France, Greece and Britain. However, Citicorp is plagued by $10.44 billion of nonperforming assets, and, despite a $1.25 billion infusion from a Saudi prince and other investors, it is scouring the globe for capital. Insiders joke that the unspoken second half of the bank's slogan, "The Citi never sleeps," is "that's because of Brazil," which owes Citicorp $2.7 billion.

Credit Suisse. No other universal bank has pursued so ardently a course of being both a commercial and investment banker on three continents. That picture of success has been marred by problems at its CS First Boston investment-banking unit, which needed a $300 million capital infusion and has been wracked by high-level management changes. Nevertheless, Credit Suisse still is more of a heavyweight in more differing areas than any other European bank is. At home, its acquisition of Bank Leu AG last year consolidated its position as one of the top three domestic banks.

Deutsche Bank AG. The archetypical

universal bank, Deutsche Bank conducts commercial, investment and retail banking in addition to selling insurance. Germany's largest bank by far, Deutsche also holds influential stakes and many board seats in major German corporations. Within a year after the Berlin Wall crumbled in late 1989, it had 160 branches up and running in the former East Germany. In 1990, when many international banks were in retreat, Deutsche's assets grew about 16%. It also has been increasing its equity base to underwrite future expansion.

Industrial Bank of Japan Ltd. Respected for its lean operation—$328.5 billion in assets but only 5,500 employees—and a staff noted for talented Tokyo University graduates, IBJ wields more financial clout than virtually any other bank in Japan. With a client list that includes Hitachi Ltd., Nissan Motor Co. and Nippon Steel Corp., it has a guaranteed source of business anywhere in the world. Leading the push in Japan to package assets and resell them as securities—something not currently permitted—IBJ astonished Japanese rivals recently by setting up a special-purpose company in New York to securitize receivables from client companies and possibly its own assets. The bank also has developed sophisticated underwriting and trading operations in London.

Mitsubishi Bank Ltd. Among the most conservatively managed of Japan's banks, Mitsubishi is the only one listed on the New York Stock Exchange. Unlike its brethren, Mitsubishi has held down its real-estate lending—actually trimming direct loans to the industry last year—and has been quick to force corporate clients, even Mitsubishi group companies, to pay more for loans. Aggressive abroad, the bank owns a bank in California and is a big corporate lender in the U.S. Like archrival Sumitomo, Mitsubishi is building a swaps and capital-markets division and is trying to break into the securities business.

J.P. Morgan & Co. Regarded by many as a model client-driven corporate bank, Morgan probably has the most globally oriented management in banking. Roughly 40% of its approximately 350 most senior managers are either not U.S. citizens or were originally from outside the U.S. Morgan is beefing up its trading functions. Its customers? "There are some big ones, some little ones, some with sophisticated needs, some with simple ones. There are some American ones, some Mexican ones, some Greek ones, some Japanese ones," says President Douglas A. Warner III. "But the one defining element is quality."

Sumitomo Bank Ltd. Japan's most aggressive bank, at home or abroad, Sumitomo became its most profitable one in 1990. But disclosures last year that Sumitomo had lent money to a speculator accused of market manipulation and to a textile-trading company with nearly $10 billion in property-related debts forced Sumitomo's chairman to resign. To beef up its capital last year, it became the first Japanese bank to sell subordinated debt—with help from Goldman Sachs, in which it owns a 12.5% stake. Sumitomo's U.S. operations include a trust bank, securities unit, capital-markets unit and commercial bank. It also owns a California bank. Overseas, it has invested heavily in sophisticated technology to enhance its capabilities in international capital markets.

Swiss Bank Corp. The second-biggest Swiss bank, SBC is trying harder than top-ranked UBS to spruce up its commercial and investment banking operations. To consolidate at home, SBC acquired a major stake in Unigestion, a Geneva financial-services company, to gain effective control of Banca della Svizzera Italiana, one of the biggest banks in Italian-speaking Switzerland. SBC also is moving—albeit from a lower base than its Swiss rivals—into investment banking. In December, SBC formed a strategic alliance with a Chicago options firm, O'Connor Partners.

Union Bank of Switzerland. Switzerland's largest bank, UBS has a strong local base that alone would qualify it as a leading banking company in the 1990s. Few banks have the combination of such a strong capital base, powerful securities-distribution capacity and trading network. UBS has had difficulty swallowing Phillips & Drew, a big London broker acquired in 1984. Nevertheless, UBS is one of world's biggest fund managers, and recently those operations grew even bigger when UBS acquired Chase Manhattan Corp.'s $30 billion institutional money-management unit.

Competitiveness and the "Global Capital Shortage"

Alan Reynolds

To exercise influence over economic policy, it is first necessary to keep discovering alarming new "crises" that need to be fixed. This is why interest groups with completely opposite positions will nonetheless welcome and embrace such notions as a loss of U.S. "competitiveness" or a "global capital shortage." Ill-defined issues such as these can easily be cited as reasons for free trade agreements or protectionism, for tax incentives or tax increases, for tight money to keep inflation down or easy money to sink the dollar. These solutions remain the same; only the problems change.

There is no point in rehashing the many efforts to define "competitiveness." The word simply means different things to different people. The U.S. economy can certainly do better, regardless of how it stacks up against other countries. And there are surely some new and promising industries we would not want to lose.

Unfortunately, the political need to exaggerate problems in order to divert attention from numerous other issues and interests that compete for news and legislation has led to a grossly distorted perception of what has actually been going on in the U.S. and world economies. In particular, there is a common impression that most U.S. manufacturing industries have been in a state of chronic decay, facing "deindustrialization" and leaving only "hollow corporations" with offices here but factories abroad. It is likewise widely believed that most U.S. businesses can't compete on world markets, leaving this country importing more and more while exporting less and less.

Looking at the economy as a whole, rather than at separate industries, it is quite clear that U.S. manufacturing grew very rapidly in the past eight years, and that exports likewise boomed for the past five. The Index of U.S. Manufacturing Output primarily consists of physical measures, such as numbers of vehicles or tons of steel. It differs from the total index for industrial production because it excludes utilities and extractive industries (such as oil and coal, which have been hurt because of low prices and high costs). For comparisons with Japan, which has a much smaller mining sector, manufacturing output is more appropriate. From 1981 to 1989, manufacturing output rose by 5.2 percent per year, up from 2.8 percent in 1971-80. The 1981-89 gains were twice as large as in Germany (2.6 percent) and only slightly below Japan (6.7 percent) (see **Figure 1**).

> *The statistics do not support claims of U.S. competitive decline.*

Figure 2 shows U.S. exports, taken from the GNP statistics; it likewise speaks for itself. The

Figure 1
Index of Manufacturing Output

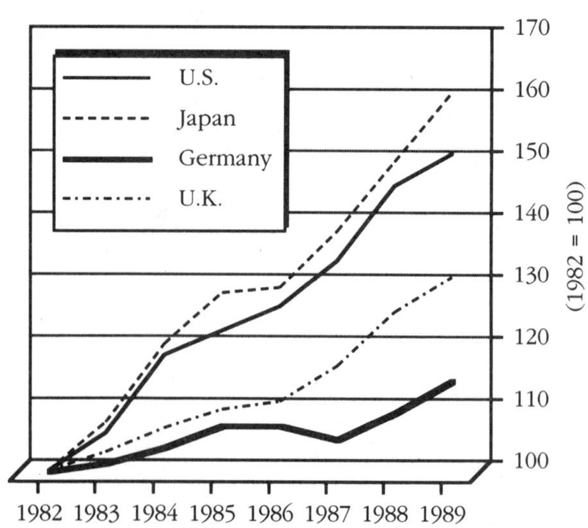

Reprinted from *Business Horizons*, Vol. 34, No. 6, November/December 1991, pp. 23-26. Copyright © 1991 by the Foundation for the School of Business at Indiana University. Used with permission.

Figure 2
Real U.S Exports

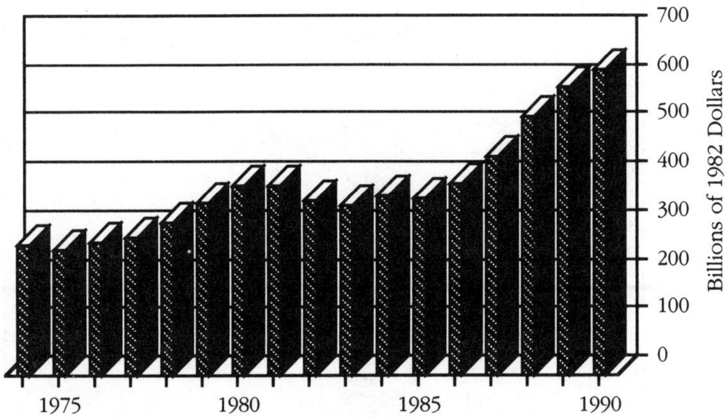

Figure 3
Growth Rates in Real GNP

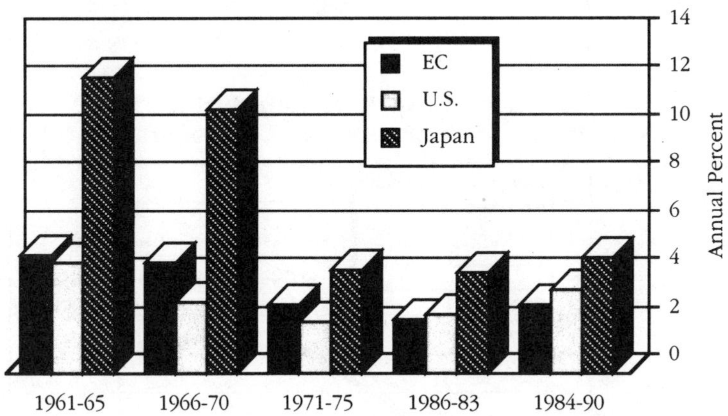

figures are adjusted for inflation, and they show the real volume of exports up more than 50 percent from any previous peak, and nearly doubling from the bottom of the 1982 recession. Exports continued to soar during the mini-recession of late 1990 and early 1991.

With manufacturing and exports way up, those who want to whip up some anxieties about "competitiveness" have had to keep redefining the problem that requires their pet solution. A favorite trick is to point to a long-term decline in the U.S. share of exports to the "world." Unfortunately, the United States is a very large part of the "world" import market, and the U.S. is the only country that cannot possibly export to the U.S.!

The U.S. economy grew faster than most other economies in 1983-87 (4.2 percent a year, even faster than Japan's 3.9 percent)—sucking in a lot of imports of capital equipment and industrial components and materials. U.S. industries were then busy supplying the needs of a rapidly expanding economy (such as aluminum and paper) and had no spare capacity for exporting. Yet such growing shipments from one domestic firm to another, rather than to foreign branches (as in the 1970s), were obviously not counted as exports. The U.S. share of exports to the *rest* of the world—aside from the U.S. itself—has held up quite well. From 1986 to 1989, for example, U.S. exports to non-OECD countries rose by 19.2 percent per year, compared with 11.3 percent for Japan and 9.3 percent for Germany.

Another source of confusion is that shares of world trade are measured in U.S. dollars, so the dollar's decline in 1990 appeared to give Germany a slightly larger share of world exports than the U.S. (Japan, surprisingly, is not even close). But the dollar's dramatic rebound in early 1991 likewise means Germany and Japan once again have a much smaller share of the *dollar* volume of world exports. Yet another problem with "shares of world exports" is that the U.S. share naturally declined after 1973, simply because OPEC oil claimed a much larger share.

A seemingly straightforward definition of competitiveness might be growth of real GNP. On this criterion, the common impression is that the economies of Japan and Europe have been speeding up, while the U.S. has slowed down. That was true of the past two or three years, but it is not true over any reasonable time frame, nor is it expected to be true in 1992. Looking at trends over a longer period give a quite different picture (see **Figure 3**).

Although the Japanese economy continues to grow more rapidly than more mature economies, particularly since cutting tax rates in 1987, growth rates in Japan have slowed to only a third of what they were in the 1960s. For all the fuss over "Europe 1992," the EC economies clearly grew far more slowly than that of the United States in the past decade. The EC average would look even worse were it not for a 4 percent growth rate in Britain following the Thatcher tax reforms of 1984-87. Economic growth in 1983-87 averaged only 2 percent in West Germany and was much slower than that in Belgium, Austria, and the Netherlands. All of these economies perked up after cutting marginal tax rates late in the decade, though Germany reversed that policy in early 1991. Compared with past performance, though, it is clearly Japan and Europe that have slowed down—not the United States.

An alternative criterion of "competitiveness" is living standards, which can be measured by the OECD index of real consumption *per capita*, adjusted by purchasing power parity (to avoid distortions from unstable exchange rates). On an index scale in which the OECD average equals 100, the U.S. rose from 138 in 1982 to 143 in 1989—43 percent above average. Japan rose from 89 to 91 in the same period, but that still left average living standards about 35 percent below the U.S. level. Britain rose from 88 to 95 percent of the OECD average. Germany dropped from 92

Figure 4
Current Account Balances as a Percent of GNP/GDP

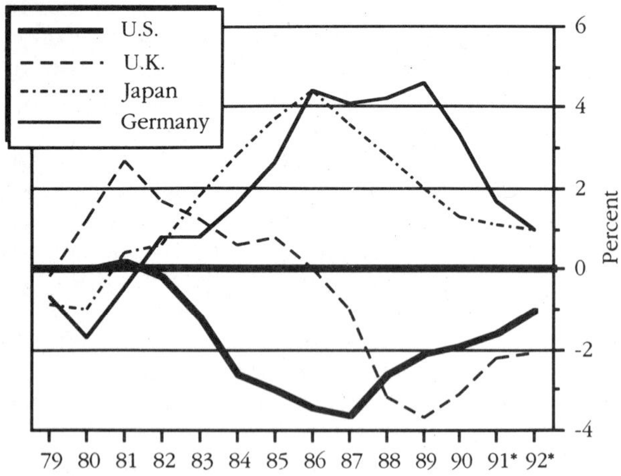

1991-92 are OECD estimates

Figure 5
Cumulative Changes in Employment

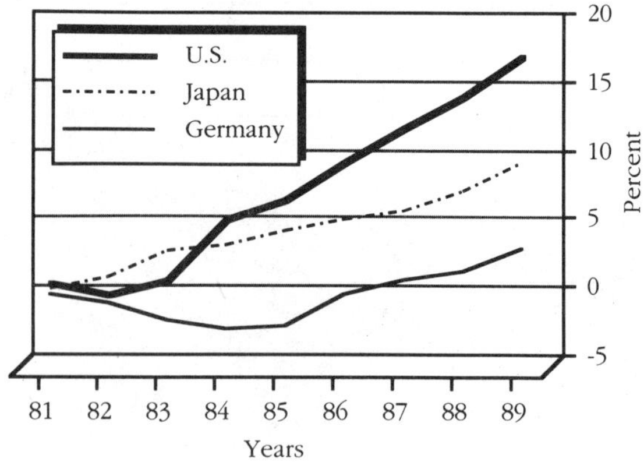

Figure 6
Rates of Return on Capital in the Business Sector

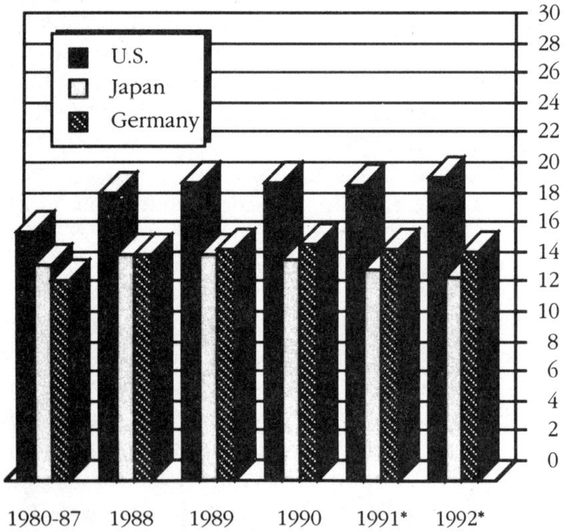

1991-92 are OECD estimates

Figure 7
Unit Labor Costs in Manufacturing: Trends Over Decades (in U.S. Dollars)

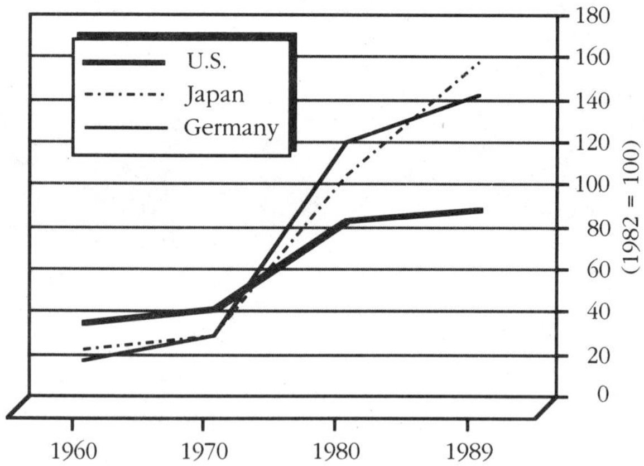

to 84. Clearly, on the basis of delivering the goods to consumers, the U.S. is far ahead, and (unlike during the 1970s) has been gaining on most other major economies in the past decade.

Much of the anxiety about trade, of course, refers to the large and rising U.S. current account deficit in 1984-87 and corresponding surpluses in Japan and Germany (see **Figure 4**). The U.S. economy was growing more rapidly than the other two at that time, so Japan and Germany were exporting capital equipment to the U.S. rather than investing their savings at home. In any case, the so-called "imbalances" in trade have been shrinking rapidly since 1987.

The claim that the U.S. has been slipping in competitiveness thus turns out to be difficult to pin on growth of manufacturing, GNP, exports, or living standards. Even trade deficits, which are a meaningless measure at best, are shrinking fast. Perhaps the inconvenience of all this evidence accounts for the excessive attention paid to labor productivity. From 1980 to 1989, cumulative increases in U.S. labor productivity in manufacturing were 42.9 percent, up from 26 percent from to 1970 to 1979. A 42.9 percent rise over nine years compares well with a 22.3 percent rise from 1980-89 in Germany, and even with a 59.3 percent rise in Japan. After all, employment increases were far more rapid in the U.S. than in any other major country (see **Figure 5**). If productivity were all that mattered, and jobs didn't, then we could raise average productivity by simply firing all new and inexperienced workers.

Moreover, the productivity of capital matters too, and OECD estimates show capital productivity *falling* by 1.7 percent a year in Japan from 1979 to 1988. Some of the apparent rise in Japanese labor productivity may actually reflect undercounting of the contribution of capital. Yet it is nonetheless plausible that new capital investment in Japan may not be yielding much "bang for the buck," considering high real estate and labor expenses. In view of the loose talk about a global "capital shortage" (which mainly means growing export markets for U.S. capital equipment), it is instructive that the OECD estimates that rates of return on capital in the U.S. will be more than competitive with those in Japan (see **Figure 6**).

Actually, what matters for "competitiveness" is the combination of productivity and pay, called "unit labor costs." On this score, the U.S. has few rivals (see **Figure 7**). Productivity gains have been brisk while compensation remained moderate, partly thanks to relatively low marginal taxation of pay increases.

Thus, the U.S. looks very competitive indeed in labor costs, return on capital, manufacturing growth and productivity, and real exports. This surely does represent a "competitiveness" problem—all those books about declining U.S. competitiveness may have to be recalled, due to shoddy workmanship.

References

OECD Economic Outlook, December 1990, p. 157.

OECD, *National Accounts,* Vol. 1 (Paris: 1990), p. 146.

U.S. Department of Labor, *Monthly Labor Review*, March 1991, p. 92.

Alan Reynolds is the Director of Economic Research at the Hudson Institute in Indianapolis, Indiana.

Big MacCurrencies

Some people read tea leaves to predict the future, others prefer hamburgers. What do they tell us about currencies?

The Economist's Big Mac Index was first launched in 1986 as a ready reckoner to whether currencies are at their "correct" exchange rate. It is time for our annual update.

The case for munching our way around the globe on Big Macs is based on the theory of purchasing-power parity. This argues that the exchange rate between two currencies is in equilibrium when it equalises the prices of an identical basket of goods and services in both countries. Advocates of PPP argue that in the long run currencies tend to move towards their PPP.

Our basket is simply a Big Mac, one of the few products that is produced locally in a great many countries. Many of our readers ask why we do not simply derive our PPPs from different cover prices of *The Economist.* But because the magazine is not printed in every country, local prices would be distorted by transport and distribution costs.

The Big Mac PPP is the exchange rate that leaves hamburgers costing the same in each country. Comparing the current exchange rate with its PPP gives a measure of whether a currency is under- or overvalued.

For example, the average price of a Big Mac in four American cities is $2.19. In Japan our Big Mac watcher had to fork out ¥ 380 ($2.86) for the same gastronomic delight. Dividing the yen price by the dollar price gives a Big Mac PPP of $1 = ¥ 174. On April 10th the actual dollar exchange rate was ¥ 133, which implies that on PPP grounds the dollar is 24% undervalued against the yen.

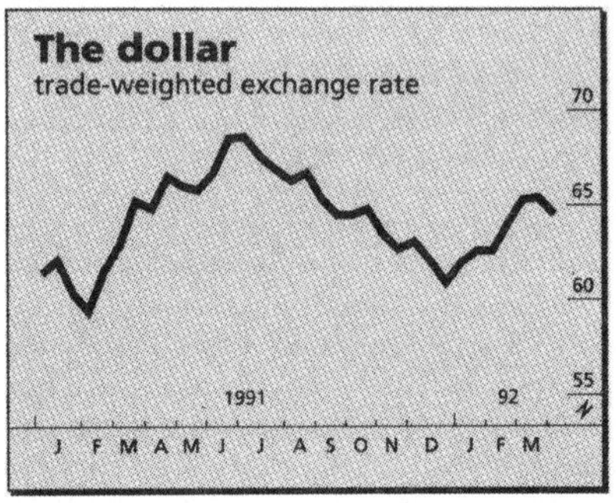

The hamburger standard

Big Mac prices Country	Prices* in local currency	Implied PPP** of the dollar	Actual exchange rate 10/4/92	% over(+) or under(-) valuation of dollar
Argentina	Peso3.30	1.51	0.99	–34
Australia	A$2.54	1.16	1.31	+13
Belgium	BFr108	49.32	33.55	–32
Brazil	Cr3,800	1,735	2,153	+24
Britain	£1.74	0.79	0.57	–28
Canada	C$2.76	1.26	1.19	–6
China	Yuan6.30	2.88	5.44	+89
Denmark	DKr27.25	12.44	6.32	–49
France	FFr18.10	8.26	5.55	–33
Germany	DM 4.50	2.05	1.64	–20
Holland	Fl 5.35	2.44	1.84	–24
Hong Kong	HK$8.90	4.06	7.73	+91
Hungary	Forint133	60.73	79.70	+31
Ireland	I£1.45	0.66	0.61	–8
Italy	Lire4,100	1872	1,233	–34
Japan	¥380	174	133	–24
Russia	Rouble58	26.48	98.95†	+273
Singapore	S$4.75	2.17	1.65	–24
S.Korea	Won2,300	1,050	778	–26
Spain	Ptas315	144	102	–29
Sweden	SKr25.50	11.64	5.93	–49
United States††	$2.19	—	—	—
Venezuela	Bs 170	77.63	60.63	–22

Source: McDonald's * prices may vary locally, ** Purchasing-power parity: local price divided by dollar price, † Market rate, †† New York, Chicago, San Francisco and Atlanta

On similar sums, the dollar is 20% undervalued against the D-mark, with an estimated PPP of DM2.05. The dollar has moved further away from its PPP over the past year: in April 1991 it was undervalued by only 13%. How can the dollar have become more undervalued when its actual exchange rate has barely budged? The answer lies in price movements. Big Mac prices have fallen by an average of 3% in America over the past 12 months; in Germany they have risen by 5%.

As the table shows, the dollar seems to be undervalued against most currencies. The exceptions are the currencies of countries where Big Macs cost less in dollars than in America: the Australian dollar, the Brazilian cruzeiro, the Chinese yuan, the Hong Kong dollar, the Hungarian forint and last, but by no means least, the rouble. Moscow is the best place for burger-bargain hunters: a Big Mac costs only 59 cents at the market exchange rate. In other words, the rouble is undervalued by 73% against the dollar.

An addition to our table this year are three Latin American currencies.

From *The Economist,* April 18, 1992, pp. 81-82. Copyright © 1992 by The Economist, Ltd. Distributed by The New York Times Special Features.

The Big Mac index signals, for example, that the Argentine peso is overvalued against the dollar (though much less so against other currencies). Brazil's cruzeiro, however, looks cheap.

Looking at cross rates within Europe suggests that most of the ERM currencies are overvalued against the D-mark on PPP grounds. For example, sterling's PPP is DM2.59, compared with its central rate of DM2.95. This supports those who argue that sterling joined the ERM at too high a rate. Other estimates, however, put sterling's PPP at up to DM3.10.

Some readers find the big Mac index hard to digest. To be sure, hamburgers are primitive predictors of exchange rates. Local price differences may be distorted by taxes, property costs or trade barriers. Nevertheless, the Big Mac can provide a rough and ready guide to how currencies might move over the long term. Experts who calculate PPPS by more sophisticated means come up with results that are not radically different. Indeed, many of them suggest that the dollar is even more undervalued than the hamburger standard indicates.

The message, therefore, is that the greenback should rise in the future. But when? Exchange rates can deviate significantly from PPPS for long periods.

Yet other economic fundamentals now seem to point in the same direction. Most currency-watchers expect interest rates to rise in America over the next 12 months as the economy picks up steam. Germany's interest rates may fall as its economy continues to stall. If so, interest-rate differentials will move in favour of the dollar and the greenback will rise. It has already gained almost 10% against the yen and the D-mark since January, and most forecasters are betting it will climb further this year.

The snag is that forecasters used the same arguments about relative interest rates a year ago, and that expectation helped to push the dollar up by 27% against the D-mark in the five months to July. As America's recovery faltered, the Fed cut interest rates again, and inflation fears caused Germany's Bundesbank to raise its rates further. The dollar slid, to end the year little higher than it began.

Forecasts of a firmer dollar are therefore only as firm as forecasts of economic recovery. Wise investors will not hold their breath—and will grab those cut-price Big Macs while they can.

Foreign Direct Investment: Gift Horse or Trojan Horse?

The last decade and a half witnessed a rapid increase in foreign direct investment (FDI) in the U.S. Some view this trend with concern, if not alarm. Foreign acquisitions of landmark U.S. corporate assets such as Columbia Pictures, Rockefeller Center, and MCA, are bemoaned as a wholesale sellout of America—worse yet, at bargain prices. To some, FDI seems tantamount to wheeling a Trojan horse inside the gates of the U.S. economy.

Others take a more benign view, ringing a variation on the equine theme: Don't look a gift horse in the mouth. Foreign investment, after all, is a vote of confidence in the U.S. economy, with ultimate benefits including new jobs and improved efficiency.

Which view makes more sense? This *Letter* reviews the recent trends in FDI in the U.S. and examines both the arguments and evidence pro and con. It concludes that FDI, like other forms of economic exchange, should be mutually beneficial to the parties involved. And indeed, the evidence suggests that any economic costs that may accompany FDI are amply outweighed by its benefits.

Background

While FDI conjures up an image of capital flowing across national borders to purchase new assets, it actually needs to involve neither capital flow nor investment in new capacity. What FDI measures is the extent to which foreign firms or individuals gain *control* over U.S. production. This element of control distinguishes direct investment from portfolio investment—for example when a foreign firm buys U.S. corporate bonds—which establishes a claim on domestic assets with the limited purpose of realizing a return.

To provide a concrete example of FDI, when Bridgestone, a Japanese tire manufacturer, took over the U.S. firm Firestone in 1988, financing was provided largely by U.S. domestic lenders. Although no new investment expenditure nor any substantial capital flow took place between Japan and the U.S., FDI occurred since the deal resulted in an international transfer in the control of corporate assets. Honda's opening of a new car factory in Maryville, Ohio is an example. This type of FDI is sometimes referred to as a "greenfield" investment to distinguish it from an acquisition or takeover that involves no new investment expenditure.

According to the Department of Commerce's definition, FDI occurs when a *single* foreign resident (usually a firm) acquires 10 percent or more of the equity in a U.S. firm. The idea is that a 10 percent stake is a large enough block of shares to provide the investor an effective say in the operation of the firm. It turns out that on average, foreign parent firms hold equity stakes of nearly 80 percent in U.S. affiliates; that is, FDI in the U.S. typically involves majority rather than fractional ownership by the foreign investor.

Figure 1 shows the growth in FDI stock in the U.S. from 1972 to 1990, computed from the balance of payments statistics. On average, FDI stock grew by 20.6 percent per year since 1972, reaching $404 billion in 1990. Two periods of accelerated growth are discernible: one from about 1977 to 1981 and another from 1987 to 1989. The FDI growth rate appears to have tapered off since then, but it is still too soon to predict future trends. Although not shown in the figure, a similar pattern is revealed in FDI stock as a percentage of the total net worth of all nonfinancial U.S. corporations. This ratio increased fivefold from 2.1 percent in 1977 to 10.5 percent in 1990.

FDI therefore is qualitatively more important in the U.S. economy today compared to fifteen

Figure 1:
Stock of Foreign Direct Investment in the U.S.
(Billions of Dollars in Book Value)

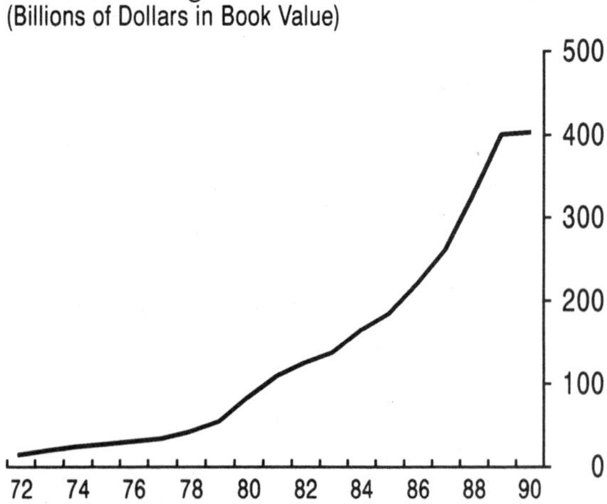

From *Weekly Letter,* Federal Reserve Bank of San Francisco, March 20, 1992, pp. 1-3. Reprinted by permission.

years ago. Graham and Krugman (1991) estimate that, depending on the measure used, foreign-owned firms attained control (that is, held 10 percent or more of equity) of between 10 and 17 percent of the manufacturing sector by the end of 1989, and some 14 to 21 percent of the U.S. banking industry by 1990. These numbers each represent about a 150 percent increase from their respective levels in the mid-1970s. It is worth emphasizing, however, that despite these rapid increases, the role of FDI in the U.S. is still relatively small by international standards. According to the latest available data, as of 1986 major European nations had twice the share of foreign-owned firms (in sales and assets) compared to the U.S.

Figure 2 shows that in book value terms, the United Kingdom has been by far the largest direct investor in the U.S., accounting for more than a quarter of the total. Japan's FDI increased considerably in recent years in relative terms, overtaking the Netherlands in 1987 as the second largest investor in the U.S. It is clear from the figure, however, that Japan has not singlehandedly caused the recent surge in FDI as is sometimes presumed. Japan is but one of the major direct investors, holding about one-fifth of the total stock of all FDI in the U.S.

Concerns

One concern about FDI is that foreign-controlled firms may have a greater tendency to procure production inputs from abroad than do domestic firms. The lower demand for inputs supplied by domestic firms therefore will result in reduced employment and a worsened trade balance in the U.S.

A second set of concerns stems from the so-called "headquarters effect." When a foreign firm acquires or displaces a U.S. firm in the U.S. market, it allegedly prefers to locate production involving higher skills and higher value-added, as well as research and development (R&D), near its headquarters. The reduction in R&D is seen as particularly problematic since these activities can generate significant spillovers from one firm to another—"positive externalities" in economists' jargon. The agglomeration of high tech firms in Silicon Valley is an example where innovative firms have mutually benefited from such positive externalities, and where the combined impact of such spillover effects has proved to be very substantial in contributing to economic growth.

Figure 2:
Major Foreign Direct Investors in the U.S.
(Billions of Dollars in Book Value)

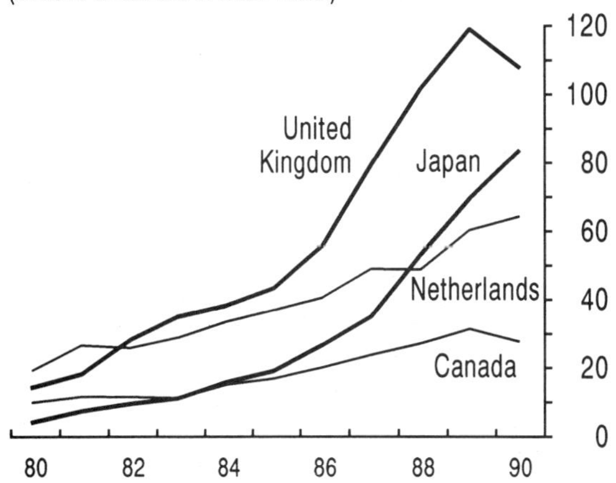

Benefits

The potential costs of FDI must be weighed against possible benefits, and these may be divided into two categories. The first set of benefits is closely related to the gains from international trade. Trade permits nations to specialize in producing goods and services where they have a comparative advantage, and thereby they achieve efficiency gains. A similar principle underlies FDI. A foreign firm acquires an existing U.S. firm or builds a new factory in the U.S. because, given its comparative advantage, it expects to generate higher returns than would a U.S.-owned firm. The foreign firm's comparative advantage may be knowledge or assets that translate into superior production and management skills compared to domestic firms. (The success of Japanese automobile and electronic manufacturers in the U.S. comes immediately to mind.) Alternatively, a foreign multinational may have technological knowledge generated from its R&D activities elsewhere that can be deployed to its advantage in the U.S. market through production by its subsidiary. In either case, FDI increases international integration and thereby fosters specialization according to comparative advantage, which should be to the mutual benefit of the source as well as the recipient country. The notable difference with international trade is that FDI achieves this efficiency gain through international transfer of corporate control rather than through movements in goods and services.

The second set of benefits amounts to turning an earlier argument on its head: FDI may generate beneficial technology spillovers in the domestic economy. Foreign-owned firms can bring foreign technology, know-how, and management methods that can be emulated by domestic firms. Foreign firms also train local workers who may subsequently transfer their skills elsewhere. FDI may therefore add to the U.S. economy's real output more than the foreign direct investor directly accrues.

Evidence

Whether the benefits of FDI outweigh its costs (or vice versa) is ultimately an empirical question.

Unfortunately, the benefits—gains from integration and spillovers—are inherently difficult to measure. What about the costs? Lipsey (1991), among others, finds evidence suggesting that, indeed, foreign-owned firms, and Japanese firms in particular, have on average a greater tendency to import production inputs compared to their domestic counterparts. Foreign-owned firms also tend to be less export-oriented with respect to their output, thus exacerbating the trade balance problem. But do these findings provide sufficient grounds to reject FDI?

There are at least two reasons to think that they do not. First, any cost engendered by foreign firms' greater tendency to import appears relatively small. Graham and Krugman (1991) estimate that as of 1988, this greater tendency to import worsened the U.S. current account balance by about $10 billion. Under reasonable assumptions, this implies a reduction in the equilibrium value of the dollar of about 2 percent. Stated differently, as a result of FDI, a given amount of U.S. exports purchased about 2 percent less of foreign imports. This deterioration in the terms of trade seems rather small a cost compared to the benefits conferred by FDI.

Second, the higher propensity of foreign firms to import may reflect the fact that a large proportion of FDI in the U.S. is relatively recent. Past history indicates that although FDI in manufacturing typically begins with assembly operation with low local content, local sourcing by foreign affiliates increases over time. This pattern holds for U.S. multinationals that were established in Europe during the 1950s and 1960s, and there is no reason to expect anything different from their foreign counterparts operating in the U.S. Indeed, data collected by the Department of Commerce indicate that the local content of products made by foreign multinationals has been rising. Any deleterious impact of FDI on trade balance and domestic employment should therefore decline further in the future.

What about the headquarters effects? Graham and Krugman find that when foreign-owned firms are compared to U.S. firms as a whole, both compensation and value added per worker are actually *higher* in foreign affiliates than in the average U.S. firm. When the comparison is restricted to manufacturing firms, no systematic difference could be detected in compensation or value-added between foreign and domestic firms. In other words, available evidence does not support the view that FDI depletes the U.S. of higher skill production or higher value-added production.

The authors reach a similar conclusion with respect to R&D. For industries, as well as for the subset of manufacturing, R&D expenditures per employee were again *higher* for foreign-owned firms than for U.S. firms. Thus, the possibility that foreign-owned firms favor undertaking R&D activities in their home countries is not supported by the data.

Conclusions

On economic grounds at least, FDI is not a Trojan horse as some fear. Rather, the increasing importance of FDI in the U.S. should be seen as a part of a larger trend toward globalization and increased international economic integration. To the extent that the process entails reorganization and reallocation of resources within the U.S. economy, some adjustment costs will be inevtable. If past experiences with increased international trade in goods and services are any indication, however, such costs should be amply offset by increased efficiency to the benefit of all countries concerned.

Sun Bae Kim
Economist

References

Graham, Edward M. and Paul R. Krugman. 1991. *Foreign Direct Investment in the United States.* Second edition. Washington, D.C.: Institute for International Economics.

Lipsey, Robert. 1991. "Foreign Direct Investment in the U.S. and U.S. Trade." *Annals of the American Academy of Political and Social Science* 516, pp. 76-90.

A Tenth Anniversary Report on the Debt Crisis

A number of middle-income developing countries have now put the debt crisis behind them, but for many others—especially the poorest—a great deal remains to be done

Masood Ahmed and Lawrence Summers

Masood Ahmed, Pakistani, is Chief of the Debt and International Finance Division in the Bank's International Economics Department. He taught at the London School of Economics.

Lawrence Summers, a US citizen, is Vice President, Development Economics, and Chief Economist of the Bank. He is on leave from his position as Professor of Political Economy at Harvard University, where he received his PhD.

Ten years have passed since Mexico's inability to service its debts triggered a rapid succession of similar moratoria by other debtor countries and led to what has come to be known as the "debt crisis." A tenth anniversary is a good opportunity to take stock of how far we have come since then. It is also an occasion to reflect upon the lessons learned, as a way of better understanding both the mistakes that led up to the crisis and the prolonged and still only partially complete process that was adopted to resolve it.

What have we learned?

One must extract lessons with a great deal of humility. If the debt crisis has taught anything, it is the fallibility of forecasts. It was not only Citibank President Walter Wriston, but a sizable part of the world's financial and economic community that believed in the late 1970s that sovereign countries did not go bankrupt. Even after the crisis broke, the pessimists did not predict the kind of stagnation suffered by the debtor countries during the 1980s, and many people dismissed the disruption in payments as simply a liquidity problem. As recently as five years ago, few could have predicted that much of Latin America would today be wrestling with the question of how to manage large-scale capital inflows. In that spirit of humility, listed below are ten key lessons.

(1) *Systemic thinking is crucial to avoiding bad lending decisions.* For much of the 1960s and 1970s, the growth of income in most countries significantly exceeded interest rates. In this environment, it was difficult for a country to appear insolvent. Even nations that borrowed to pay all of their interest bills could have improving debt indicators. Neither lender nor borrower questioned what would happen if the international economic environment changed dramatically, as it did with the sudden and sharp disinflation in the industrialized world in the early 1980s. As Chart 1 illustrates, growth collapsed just as real interest rates rose sharply.

One after another, countries to whom bankers had been eager to lend only months before ran into problems servicing their external obligations. Indeed, within two years of Mexico's default, 30 developing countries—representing half of developing country debt—were failing to service their debt as originally

Chart 1

Growth plummeted as real interest rates soared

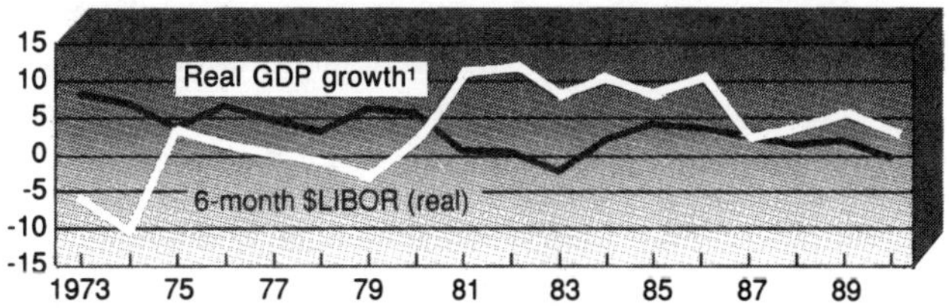

Sources: *World Tables* (World Bank); *International Financial Statistics* (IMF).

[1] Weighted rate in 34 severely indebted developing countries (Algeria, Argentina, Bolivia, Brazil, Burundi, the Congo, Costa Rica, Côte d'Ivoire, Ecuador, Egypt, Ethiopia, Ghana, Guinea-Bissau, Guyana, Honduras, Kenya, Madagascar, Malawi, Mauritania, Mexico, Morocco, Niger, Nigeria, Peru, the Philippines, São Tomé and Príncipe, Sierra Leone, Somalia, Syrian Arab Republic, Uganda, Uruguay, Venezuela, Zaïre, and Zambia).

From *Finance & Development*, September 1992, pp. 2-5. *Finance & Development,* published quarterly by the International Monetary Fund and the World Bank, Washington, DC.

Chart 2
Soon after Mexico's default, debt restructurings took off
(In millions of dollars)

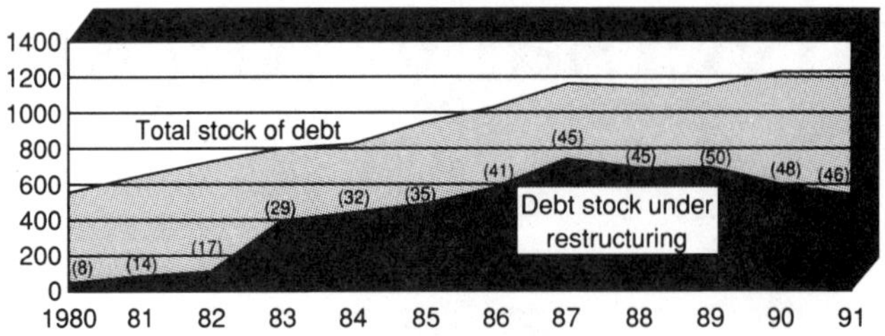

Source: Debtor Reporting System (World Bank).
Note: Numbers in parentheses refer to total number of countries that are subject to restructuring arrangements. New entrants are determined by the formal initiation of a restructuring agreement.

scheduled (see Chart 2). The pervasiveness of the debt problem is testimony to the dominant role played by a changed international economic environment. It also demonstrates the folly of assuming, as some prominent bankers did at the time, that simply spreading exposure across developing countries was an adequate way to diversify risk.

(2) *Heavy borrowing that is not accompanied by productive investment is a disaster for creditor and debtor alike.* If the money borrowed during the 1970s had been used wisely—that is, to finance high-return investments, or to underwrite necessary structural changes—debtor countries could have ridden out the disinflationary storm of the early 1980s. Indeed, some countries—such as Korea, whose external debt went up ninefold over the 1970s—followed precisely such a strategy and were able to stay their development course through the 1980s. Unfortunately, however, in too many other developing countries, the easy availability of international credit in the 1970s was used to postpone, rather than catalyze, necessary economic reforms.

Telltale signs that all was not well were rationalized by both borrowers and lenders in a willing suspension of disbelief. Neither side carefully examined what was happening to fiscal deficits and public enterprise losses; nor was the connection made between why residents were transferring funds abroad in ever increasing amounts, even as foreign creditors transferred resources in to shore up sagging public finances. The problem was exacerbated by the paucity of information and poor bookkeeping on how the borrowed funds were actually being used. The net result was to build up the "liabilities" side of the debtor country's "balance sheet," without a commensurate increase in the stock of productive "assets." Sorting out this disequilibrium would preoccupy national policymakers and international agencies for the subsequent decade.

(3) *Countries that "opted out" of the international financial system have generally done worse as a result.* During the last decade, a few countries tried at various times to resolve their debt problems unilaterally by opting out of the international financial system. They stopped servicing their external obligations and broke off relations with their creditors. Sometimes, this was preceded by a breakdown of negotiations on a stabilization and adjustment program with the international financial institutions. In the end, these actions have generally proved detrimental to the debtor country involved. One reason is that the financial costs associated with the building up of arrears has been added to the cost of delaying much needed adjustment—these costs include reduced trade and interbank credit lines, as well as higher prices (the "spreads") that have had to be paid for these lines. But even more important and damaging have been the adverse effects of isolationist action on domestic confidence. Trying to get the best deal within the mainstream, with the support of official development agencies, seems to be a more fruitful avenue for country action than trying to go it alone.

(4) *Good national policies are the key to capital market access.* The debt crisis was at least as much a symptom as a cause of bad economic performance. It is important to emphasize that private capital has continued to flow during the 1980s to a number of developing countries, notably the prudently managed economies of East Asia. For that region as a whole, net resource flows from private sources have been positive in every year of the 1980s, and foreign equity flows have gone up eightfold over the decade. A more recent phenomenon is the return to capital market access of a number of the debt-distressed Latin American countries, including Argentina, Brazil, Mexico, and Venezuela. It is not a coincidence that among these, Mexico, the country with the strongest track record in economic management in the region, is also by far the largest recipient of private portfolio flows to developing countries.

Underlying this widening access to international capital markets has been a revolution in economic policies across much of the developing world. Fiscal deficits and inflation are down, and exchange rates reflect market realities rather than national pride. Macroeconomic stabilization has been accompanied by deep-rooted structural change. The role of government is being greatly curtailed, trade barriers have come down, and the privatization of public enterprises is underway in virtually every World Bank borrower. One of the painfully learned lessons of the last several decades is that sustained growth depends on governments choosing an appropriate economic role—doing those things that governments need to do, such as providing infrastructure and basic human services, but leaving to the market that which the market can do best.

Trade deficits turn to surpluses, but economic growth turns down

	External debt $ billion	External debt (As percent of GNP)1982	Trade balance (As percent of GNP) 1979-82	Trade balance (As percent of GNP) 1983-86	Real GDP growth rate Avg. 1973-82	Real GDP growth rate Avg. 1982-90
Argentina	43.6	83.9	0.22	4.73	0.9	0.1
Bolivia	3.3	114.8	0.71	0.08	2.5	0.7
Brazil	92.9	34.4	(1.32)	4.06	5.1	3.5
Chile	17.3	76.7	(5.52)	2.19	3.6	5.3
Colombia	10.3	26.9	(1.60)	1.09	4.9	0.3
Côte d'Ivoire	7.9	111.4	(5.20)	8.28	4.5	4.2
Ecuador	7.7	66.9	(0.27)	4.45	5.9	2.1
Mexico	86.0	53.4	(0.75)	7.18	5.5	4.1
Morocco	12.5	84.8	(13.45)	(8.93)	6.3	1.0
Peru	12.3	49.7	(0.40)	2.09	3.0	-0.1
Philippines	24.6	62.5	(4.79)	(0.59)	5.4	1.2
Venezuela	32.2	41.4	2.59	7.24	2.0	1.7
All developing countries	883.3	33.81	(0.63)	(0.61)	4.2	3.5

Sources: *World Debt Tables 1991-92*; *World Tables 1992.*

(5) *Economic adjustment takes time and things often get worse before they get better, so attention to the political and economic sustainability of reform is in the interest of both the creditors and debtors.* It is now clear from the experience of Chile, Ghana, and Mexico, among others, that market friendly policies can help to improve the economic performance of economies previously hamstrung by a plethora of controls and distortions. But dismantling controls and opening up an economy takes time and involves substantial dislocations. This means that output at first declines, before gradually increasing—a process that creates enormous political pressures to reverse reform policies. The situation is greatly exacerbated when adjustment coincides with import cutbacks, which are caused by the need to use scarce foreign exchange to service foreign debts.

For policymakers, import compression during adjustment poses a cruel dilemma. Either they can seek to maintain consumption and reduce capital goods imports, thereby compromising the long-run economic viability of reforms, or they can seek to reduce consumption, even as economic dislocations increase, thereby risking political instability. Since creditors have a strong stake in the success of reform efforts, it may well be in their collective interest to avoid import compression. Yet no individual private creditor has an incentive to accept debt reduction or to put in new money; each would prefer to "free ride" on the activities of other creditors. This is where the presence of official lenders, with a longer-term stake in the debtor country, makes a vital contribution by limiting the need for initial cutbacks in consumption without distorting the short-term adjustment process to regain creditworthiness.

(6) *There is a compelling need for official action to overcome free rider problems that complicate debt reschedulings and reductions.* The problems of free-riding and holdouts among the banks have exacerbated coordination difficulties that would have resulted simply from the number and diversity of lenders. In purely domestic contexts, bankruptcy laws exist because of the recognized problem of dealing with conflicts among creditors, and between creditors and debtors. Without such laws regulating sovereign lending, there is a clear case for government action to overcome free-rider problems. This critical point was recognized when the crisis broke and the world financial system seemed to be at risk. But during the heyday of *laissez faire* enthusiasm during the mid-1980s, at least some officials lost sight of it.

The free rider issue is well recognized in the structure of the Brady Plan, which has provided the framework for commercial debt reduction agreements since 1989. The "menu" approach enables creditor banks with different preferences to choose the debt reduction option most suited to their needs, while the comprehensive nature of these deals minimizes the possibility of free riding by a small group of creditors at the expense of the other participants.

This comprehensive approach is based on the recognition that market buybacks (the repurchase for cash of debt) of only a small part of the outstanding debt stock, even at a discount to face value, generate few benefits for the debtor country, because they raise the probability that the country will repay its debt, and thus the market value of the country's remaining outstanding debt. Confronted with a steadily increasing price for their debt obligations, countries that are already financially strained will soon reach a point where further buybacks are economically unviable, rendering this mechanism unsuited for large-scale reductions in debt stock. In the same way, there is a real danger that partial debt-equity swaps may benefit creditors who hold on to their debt, without doing a great deal for debtor countries.

(7) *Treating the debt crisis purely as a liquidity problem delayed the search for a stable and real solution.* In the early years of the debt crisis, many observers felt that the indebted countries were suffering from a liquidity—rather than a solvency—problem, and thus the official work-out strategy relied on providing new funds to overcome the temporary shortage of finance. But in many instances, commercial lenders were unwilling to provide these new funds, essentially because they were uncertain about the prospects of recovering this money even in the medium term. It was only the debt reduction deals under the Brady Plan that finally helped to reduce this uncertainty by removing one part of the contingent claims on future public finances. More generally, this experience has demon-

strated the weakness of the basic liquidity-solvency distinction as applied to the debt crisis. This lesson is well learned now, but the cost of delay has been to put development on hold for a decade in many of these countries (see table). A lesson for the future is the importance of acknowledging reality sooner.

(8) *Debt reduction is sometimes necessary but only works well when accompanied by good economic policies.* The main benefit of a Brady-type debt reduction deal for a debtor country is that it eliminates the contingent liability represented by the unserviced part of the old debt. The debt reduction thus reduces uncertainty about the returns to any new investment and helps to create the climate of confidence for the private sector to undertake new investments. These benefits are best captured in countries where an established track record of sound policies and prudent economic management have already lifted the other impediments to renewed private sector confidence. Such an established record does not yet exist in some of the severely indebted middle-income developing countries that have not concluded a Brady-type deal with their commercial creditors. Waiting until it does will maximize the potential benefits of the deal to the country and ensure the productive use of the resources needed to finance the transaction.

(9) *Building risk-sharing contingencies into financial contracts is much less costly than renegotiating contracts when things go wrong.* The essence of the workout process during the 1980s was to agree on the terms for the ex-post rewriting of loan contracts to share the losses associated with an outcome that had turned out to be worse than either lender or borrower had envisaged. The process was made more difficult by the fact that virtually none of the original loan contracts had such "downside" contingency clauses, meaning that all the contracts had to be renegotiated ex-post and without a frame of reference that such a clause would have provided. Moreover, the predominance of syndicated lending to sovereign borrowers in the 1970s meant that the risk-sharing features of other forms of international finance, notably foreign direct investment and other equity flows, had been largely foregone.

The recent boom in portfolio flows to emerging stock markets in these countries shows that at least one set of international investors has learned from this experience. It is not clear, however, that many developing countries have fully realized either the potential for, or the implications of, using a more diversified set of financial instruments.

(10) *External finance for investment in low-income countries must come largely from official sources.* A key lesson of the debt crisis is that commercial banks are an inefficient instrument for channeling long-term investment finance to the poorest countries. During the next decade, their role in these countries is likely to focus on the provision of trade and short-term credit, and correspondent banking relationships to facilitate international trade arrangements, as well as limited-recourse project finance, where the repayments on the loan are linked to the success of the investment project financed by the money. Other commercial sources will also run up against internal, or externally imposed, regulatory or creditworthiness constraints.

Yet the financing needs of these countries continue to be pressing. During the past decade, per capita incomes in the severely indebted low-income countries have fallen by a fifth to well short of a dollar a day in 1991. Raising incomes from these pitiful levels will require both better economic management and an injection of foreign capital for investment in economic development. Because many of these countries are not likely to be creditworthy for a long time, the real need is to increase concessional financing. A doubling of all the net resource flows to developing countries last year would add a little over $16 billion to the aid bill of the industrialized world—just 1 percent of what the world spends on defense each year. It is also a small price to pay for reversing the decline in health, nutrition, and educational standards that has characterized so many of these countries during the 1980s.

Is the debt crisis over?

The preceding lessons are vital not only to avoid future debt crises but also to tackle the substantial unfinished agenda from the 1980s. Certainly, considerable progress has been made. National and international actions have helped avert any serious damage to the international financial system, which was a real concern in the early aftermath of the crisis. With the recently announced commercial debt reduction agreements for Argentina and Brazil, the normalization of external creditor relations is now well advanced for the middle-income developing countries. And sustained official financial support on concessional terms has complemented the very limited domestic savings of the poorest countries, ensuring that their basic import needs have continued to be met.

But the debt crisis is far from over for more than 40 developing countries, which continue to have difficulties in servicing their debt as originally contracted. In particular, much remains to be done for the poorest developing countries, 26 of which are classified as severely indebted. For these countries—mostly in Sub-Saharan Africa—official support has been strong through the 1980s, in terms of the provision of both new money and progressively more concessional debt relief. But external viability has remained elusive. On average, these countries have been allocating a quarter of their exports to debt servicing, although this still only enables them to pay half the scheduled amount.

Under any plausible future scenario, many of these countries will regain external viability only if some portion of their existing—largely official bilateral—debt is written down, reflecting the creditors' acceptance of a reduction in the stock of debt outstanding. Bringing scheduled debt-service payments to a level that can reasonably be expected to be paid would help reduce uncertainty and make new creditors feel more confident that their contractual arrangements were likely to be honored. Debt relief for these countries is thus a high-priority item. But the actual amounts required will have to be determined on a case-by-case basis and assessed within the context of the overall economic and structural adjustment program. It is clear, however, that in many countries, this relief will need to go beyond the 50 percent reduction in the present value of debt service that has characterized some of the most recent agreements reached with official bilateral creditors under the auspices of the Paris Club.

As for the remaining severely indebted middle-income countries, the objective remains to restore access to private international capital markets. The recent experience of a number of major Latin American countries, including Argentina, Brazil, Chile, and Mexico, has shown that private capital can flow back in substantial amounts under the right national and international conditions. Foremost among these is a sustained track record of economic and structural reform. Investor confidence has also been helped by the successful completion—or imminent conclusion—of Brady-type agreements for reducing part of the existing commercial bank debt. A similar sustained track record of sound national policies, complemented, in some cases, by an agreement on commercial debt reduction, should facilitate the return to market access for the dozen or so middle-income countries still classified as severely indebted. The same consideration also apply to some of the states of the former USSR, whose current debt-servicing problems have sharply curtailed access to private international capital markets.

In sum, the debt crisis may no longer be the principal preoccupation of the international commercial banks, but it is far from over for many of the countries involved, among them, some of the poorest. For a number of these countries, a combination of growth and cash flow relief through rescheduling should result in a resumption of normal creditor relations by the mid-1990s. For others, however, a return to external viability can only be achieved in conjunction with some reduction of their existing debt obligations. For all of them, the key to both improved economic performance and continued support from the international financial community will be sound economic policies. And the importance of these policies will increase in the 1990s, as international capital markets remain tight and the competition for concessional finance becomes stronger. Moreover, the tolerance for wrong policies will be sharply reduced in a world where capital account liberalization and financial market integration make large sudden outflows of capital a real constraint on government action.

Sound policies need to be nurtured by a supportive international economic environment. This means that the developing world's recovery and growth prospects would be helped by reducing protectionism in the OECD countries. Cutting current levels of industrial country protection in half would lead to a $50 billion increase in developing country exports—not including the sizable benefits to consumers in the developed world. It also means that developing countries, as price takers in the international capital markets, would benefit from industrial country policies that would bring down real interest rates from their current high levels. As long as real interest rates are above the growth rates for some developing countries, any net borrowing must necessarily worsen their debt indicators. Thus, actions by the industrial countries to raise their own level of saving, thereby reducing pressure on international markets, would do much to improve the creditworthiness and financing prospects of the developing countries in the decade ahead.

International Production

Perhaps the single most successful aspect of Japanese management, and the one that has possibly led to the success of the Japanese corporations in the world market, has been their success in production. The Japanese have been able to produce better goods with fewer resources than their U.S. or European counterparts. There is no doubt that Japanese production is efficient, and that this efficiency has led to lower costs and prices to the final consumer of their products.

Automobiles are the most obvious example of the Japanese success in production. Japanese labor in the automobile business is not cheap. In fact, the Japanese autoworker is now paid more than a U.S. counterpart, but Japanese production is more efficient. A typical Japanese auto plant can produce cars more efficiently and with less labor content than factories in other parts of the world. Part of the reason for this is that Japanese factories are more automated than factories elsewhere. The Japanese make extensive use of industrial robots (another example of an American invention that has been exploited more fully by the Japanese) that perform tasks normally associated with fairly low-skilled labor in the plants. Spot welding may be the best example of robotic efficiency in the plant. Every weld is identical when performed by industrial robots. There is little or no variation in time or material. Human welders, on the other hand, may use more or less material and time to perform their task, they need relief and benefits, and sometimes get sick, but robots do not. What robots do require is a large initial investment in plant and equipment, up front. They are a fixed asset and a

Unit 6

fixed expense, and if they are idle, they still have to be paid for. Workers can be laid off. The only problem for U.S. automakers is that this supposed "advantage" over more mechanized factories does not exist. Given the current contract arrangements between the automakers and the United Auto Workers, the cost is almost as much for a worker not to work in the plant as it is for the worker to perform a job. The cost saving for U.S. automakers when they lay off workers for anything but very extended periods of time is extremely marginal. The initial motive for the Japanese to go to robotics was very simple: they have a relatively restricted labor force and needed to find ways to free people up to do things other than simple repetitive tasks, the types of tasks that lend themselves to robotics.

Another aspect of the Japanese success in production has been their success with the "just-in-time" approach to inventory management, especially of parts needed for the assembly of products. In theory, just-in-time means exactly that: the part needed for the assembly of the product arrives at the designated work station just as the part is needed. This cuts costs significantly by reducing investment in the inventory of materials and making the production process run lean. It can only be accomplished, however, with the cooperation of suppliers and low reject rates for parts. Firms must work closely with their suppliers if they are to be successful with "just-in-time" approaches to production.

One of the problems in dealing with production for the international market is that the various national markets frequently require something slightly different in the product. There is more than the traditional tension between marketing and production, when marketing cannot seem to sell what the factory makes, and the factory never seems to make what marketing can sell. Elements of size, packaging, language, and technical specifications can change from market to market. A case in point is the continued use of the old English standard of weights and measures in many products in the United States, while the rest of the world has gone metric. Even the English do not use the English standard anymore, but the United States persists. This leads to inefficiencies in production and economies of scale as U.S. firms are sometimes faced with having to develop two products for the market, one metric and one English, while their competition needs only one.

The opening of the Iron Curtain represents another opportunity for organizations, but industries in the Commonwealth of Independent States (C.I.S.) seem hardly ready to enter into competition. After years of state control, it is going to be very difficult for C.I.S. managers to successfully deal with a competitive market. If the Americans, Europeans, and Japanese are going to successfully integrate the former Eastern Bloc countries into the world marketplace, several things need to be recognized and addressed. First, it is going to take longer than most people think. Second, much of former industry is obsolete and that which is not is frequently involved in the production of military goods. Third, the C.I.S. is going to have to learn how to compete and to significantly change the way it does business. The key to integrating the former Eastern Bloc into the Western economy is not just to sell them Western products, but through the trade of Western goods for Eastern goods that will allow them to build up their industries and to participate in international markets.

International production raises the question of what has been produced where and by whom? Governments have addressed this issue with domestic content legislation, requiring a certain minimum percentage of the product to be manufactured domestically or labeling it as an imported good. It is likely, however, that this type of legislation will become increasingly irrelevant as more and more firms look to the world market as their source of supply. Corporations, because of competitive pressure, seek to become as efficient as possible in the production of goods and will produce where it is most cost-effective and efficient. That could be the United States, Japan, China, or Europe; but wherever it may be, the choice will be dictated by the needs and requirements of the marketplace.

Looking Ahead: Challenge Questions

Robots were first developed in the United States, but have been put to greatest use in Japan. Why do you suppose that is? How have the Japanese benefited?

"Just-in-time" inventory approaches have worked well in Japan. What are some of their advantages? How could "just-in-time" work in a U.S. factory?

The United States uses the English standard of weights and measures while the rest of the world uses the metric system. How does this harm U.S. competitiveness? What can be done?

Domestic content legislation has been enacted by the federal government to help ensure continued U.S. manufacturing. Do you think this will work in the long run? Why or why not?

Manufacturing's New Economies of Scale

Manufacturing globally means rationalizing all the pieces of the production process.

Michael E. McGrath and Richard W. Hoole

Michael E. McGrath and Richard W. Hoole are directors in the Weston, Massachusetts office of Pittiglio Rabin Todd & McGrath, an international management consulting firm that specializes in global manufacturing.

In the 1990s, manufacturing companies face the challenge of globally integrating their operations. Just as companies were forced to rationalize operations within individual plants in the 1980s, they must now do the same for their entire system of manufacturing facilities around the world. Multinationals that can no longer rely on sheer size and geographic reach can still integrate far-flung plants into tightly connected, distributed production systems – and seize the opportunity for a new manufacturing scale advantage.

For years, the diverse operations of many multinationals made good business sense. At one extreme, companies manufactured products close to their customers, tailoring regional operations at scattered plants to meet local needs. Other companies chose to centralize manufacturing, offering a selection of standard, lower priced products to all of the markets they served. Yet given the current competition, which includes smaller, more focused companies as well as other multinationals, leading manufacturers must step beyond what has succeeded in the past. As our work with Xerox Corporation, Digital Equipment Corporation, Coulter Electronics, and other companies indicates, moving toward global integration is a long, involved process that begins at the top, filters down through the organization, and includes innovations across all functions.

Of course, there are no easy solutions to the need for change on such a large scale. All multinationals must grapple with their own unique problems; each must come up with its own innovations. Still, while the focus varies from company to company, many manufacturers have tried similar approaches. Some have created international teams for different functions: international design teams or commodity management teams, for example. Others have emphasized doing a critical activity only once, such as designing a core product or entering a customer order.

Regardless of the ways in which companies initiate change, one fact remains the same: multinationals *must* integrate their operations if they expect to compete in the volatile global arena. They cannot go backward to complete centralization of manufacturing, or they will lose access to essential markets. Nor can they remain a disconnected system of geographically scattered operations. With a tightly coordinated network of plants in high-cost end markets and low-cost manufacturing centers, multinationals can achieve new economies of scale and cut costs by eliminating redundant processes. But in becoming globally integrated, these same companies must balance the tension between a monolithic central authority and the need to integrate independent units. And they must focus specific changes in functions and at individual sites by articulating a vision shared by the entire organization.

First Steps: Globalizing Xerox

No multinational manufacturer can claim complete global integration, perfectly implemented,

Reprinted by permission of *Harvard Business Review.* "Manufacturing's New Economies of Scale," by Michael E. McGrath and Richard W. Hoole, May/June 1992, pp. 94-102. Copyright © 1992 by the President and Fellows of Harvard College. All rights reserved.

with no hitches or complaints, or provide an exact blueprint for others. However, Xerox Corporation, with its complex web of international operations, embarked on a general strategy of global integration – and affirmed it publicly – at the right time.

At the end of the 1970s, Xerox was a typical multinational. The parent company, Xerox Corporation, designed and produced products in the United States for the U.S. market; Rank Xerox, a 51%-owned Xerox company, developed products for the European market; Fuji Xerox, an equal partnership between Rank Xerox and Fuji, created products for the Japanese market; and a number of other Xerox operating companies manufactured and sold a variety of peripherals and subassemblies throughout the world.

Each Xerox company controlled its own suppliers, assembly plants, and distribution channels. Plants in Mexico, the United States, Canada, Asia, Europe, and Brazil produced according to independently set schedules, based on forecasts from each individual operating company. The managers of these scattered plants gave little thought to how each one fit into the overall production plans of Xerox Corporation and rarely communicated with each other. And since Xerox had a near monopoly on the worldwide copier market, no one, including top management at parent headquarters, felt pressured to do so.

In 1981, senior managers at Xerox began to rethink the company's structure.

Nevertheless, in 1981, senior managers at Xerox began to rethink the company's structure, focusing on ways to cut costs, reduce excessive inventory, and speed up product delivery. Global integration was far from a well-defined strategy at the time, and managers did not pursue it with any urgency. But they accumulated information on the benefits of moving from a collection of independent regional units to a more integrated company.

Then, as the 1980s progressed, the competitive landscape started to shift. Xerox competitors such as Canon and Ricoh penetrated the U.S. and European markets with low-cost copiers. In 1983, Xerox dominated the top ten copier companies in the world with a 57% share of revenue; just two short years later, Xerox's share had fallen to 52%. More tellingly, in 1985, Canon announced it was globalizing production of its copiers. Until that time, Canon had manufactured primarily in Japan and sold through a worldwide distribution network; it was, in effect, a typical centralized, export-oriented company. But with new design and manufacturing facilities planned for the United States and Europe, Canon transformed itself into a decentralized multinational.

As competitive pressures bore down, Xerox picked up its own pace, pursuing an explicit strategy of global integration. The graph, "Xerox Achieves a New Manufacturing Scale Advantage," illustrates changes in operating income and revenue that reflect the company's growth. During the critical period between 1982 and 1991, Xerox made rapid innovations in many functions, which are highlighted in the time line that follows.

1982: Senior managers at Xerox realized the potential for cutting costs if the company consolidated raw material sources. They created a central purchasing group that included representatives from over a dozen of Xerox's multinational operating companies. This group of commodity managers identified and cultivated suppliers that could provide Xerox with high-quality, low-cost components on a worldwide basis. In the process, Xerox trimmed its global supply base from about 5,000 suppliers to just over 400, which now accounts for more than 90% of raw material purchases. For instance, Xerox now buys many of the lamps for its copiers from a single supplier with plants in Asia, Europe, and the United States. Because the consolidation of raw materials simplified purchasing, overhead rates have fallen from 9% of total costs for materials in 1982 to about 3% today. The result: Xerox now saves over $100 million annually on raw materials.

1983: Xerox Corporation introduced its Leadership Through Quality program to improve product quality, streamline and standardize manufacturing processes, cut costs, and increase return on assets. Senior managers recognized the power of such a program to improve communication of new management principles throughout its entire system of multinational operating companies and within the ranks of each company. Leadership Through Quality provided a common language of quality and a standard set of management practices that all of Xerox's companies now share.

1985 to 1986: Xerox instituted a new product-delivery process designed to standardize procedures. Functionally and geographically integrated teams took responsibility for introducing a new product in all major markets. Each product team managed the design, component sources, manufacturing, distribution, and follow-up customer service on a worldwide basis. One team designed a new product with universal power supplies and dual-language displays – for example, in both English and French – to eliminate the cost of reengineering for new markets at a later date. In general, using integrated teams has cut as much as one year from the overall product development cycle and saved millions of dollars.

1988: Xerox created a multinational task force to gather more specific and focused data on global integration. This task force identified three levels of integration and used them as a basis for restructuring various operations at all facilities. Xerox plants were required to (1) adopt global standards for basic processes that apply to all operations (for example, databases for managing materials); (2) maintain common business processes but, where necessary, tailor them to local needs (for example, just-in-time programs); and (3) set site-specific processes for only those systems that must conform to local needs (for example, government reporting requirements).

Information from this task force allowed top managers at Xerox to compare product cost and inventory data at different plants so they could balance production levels and improve utilization of excess inventory. Over a two-year period, these activities saved Xerox $20 million. And when Xerox initiated a common just-in-time system, it also created a worldwide council that developed a set of metrics and goals for all plants to follow. At some plants, 90% of products are now delivered on a just-in-time basis, a quantum improvement, given that less than 50% were delivered in this way in 1988.

1989: Top managers at Xerox Corporation calculated that they could eliminate $1 billion in inventory and $200 million in inventory-related costs by linking customer orders more closely with production. They formed a multinational organization called Central Logistics and Asset Management (CLAM) and four multifunctional, product-focused teams to integrate the supply chain across geographic boundaries. The aim of CLAM is to base individual plant production levels on customer orders and to reduce excess inventory. One team developed a new process that took more than a month out of the production forecasting cycle. And Xerox has now reduced its worldwide inventories by $500 million.

> The global design process was fast – and saved Xerox $10 million.

1990: Xerox introduced its 5100 copier, the first product jointly designed for a worldwide market by Fuji Xerox and Xerox Corporation engineers. The 5100, manufactured in U.S. plants, was launched in

Xerox Achieves a New Manufacturing Scale Advantage*

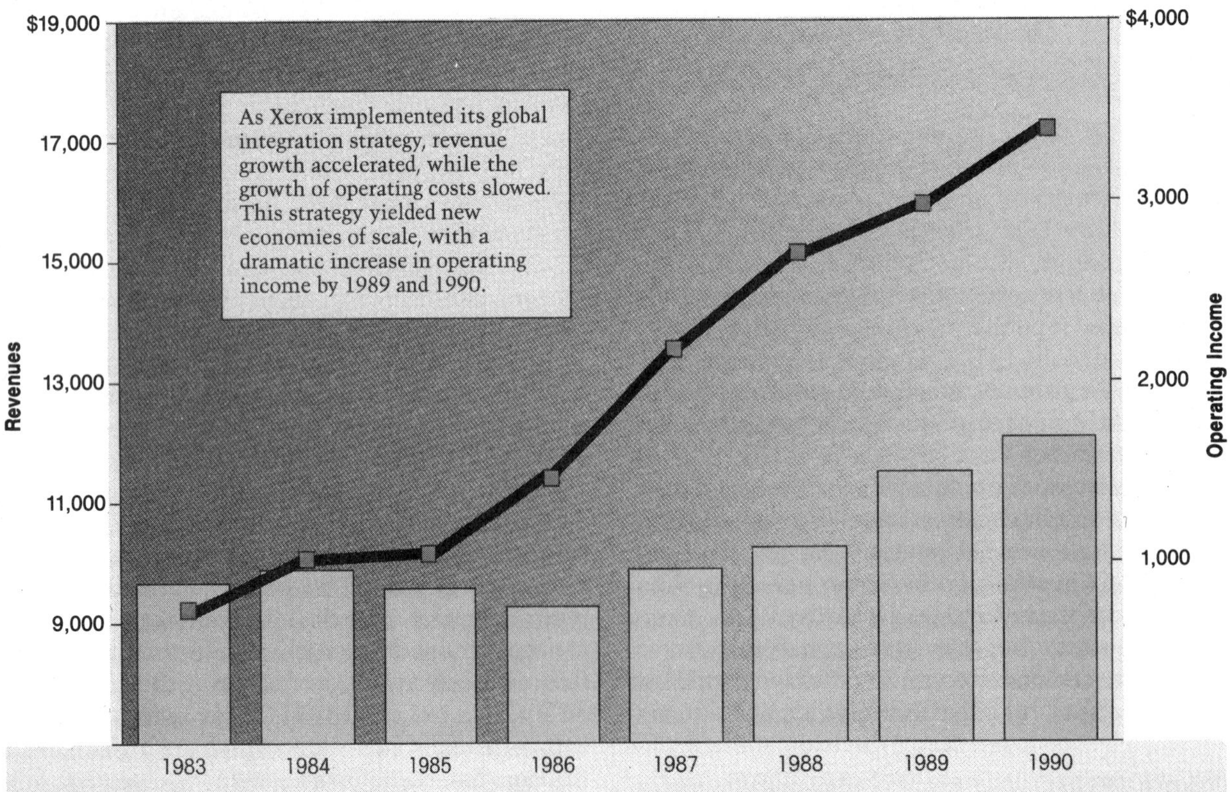

*Copyright 1992 by Pittiglio Rabin Todd & McGrath. Note that revenues and operating income are for Xerox's document processing and related businesses only. The figures have also been adjusted to include Fuji Xerox, which is generally not consolidated for financial reporting purposes.

Japan in November 1990 and in the United States the following February. Before that time, Xerox had never introduced a major product in two distinct markets so quickly.

In the past, the unique needs of the Japanese market, such as lighter weight paper, common use of blue pencils, and difficulties in copying *kanji* characters, meant separate product development programs for Western and Asian markets. That, in turn, meant products developed in this fashion required reengineering for other markets. However, Xerox assembled a team of Japanese and American engineers to design the 5100 copier from concept to finished drawings. The design team also received feedback from customer groups in the United States, Europe, and Japan. The 5100's global design process reduced overall time-to-market and saved the company more than $10 million in development costs.

1991: Xerox began integrating its product delivery activities. A CLAM team and several operating groups created a Western Hemisphere distribution center for spare parts, consolidating safety stocks previously held independently for the U.S., Canadian, and Latin American markets. Once again, such integration of operations saved Xerox several million dollars annually.

The Five Basics: Focusing Change

Xerox Corporation evolved its global-integration strategies over time and, to some extent, by trial and error. Realistically, changes at most multinationals do not happen neatly or in a fixed sequence. Similar small innovations may spark at the same time in several operating companies: automating certain parts of the manufacturing process, for example, or processing customer orders in a new way.

While there is no fixed starting point for globally integrating an organization, managers, both at the top and in individual operations, should begin with focused projects that address specific problems. It makes sense to focus first on a part of the organization where immediate and substantive improvement is possible. Xerox began its global-integration process in purchasing raw materials because management decided that was where it could make the most immediate and greatest gains.

The starting point might be in any of what we call the "five basics": product development, purchasing, production, demand management, or order fulfillment. The following sections provide suggestions for integrating each function and, while not definitive, show the range of possibilities.

Product Development. Designing products once and only once for the global market benefits companies in a number of important ways. Such a design process can eliminate costly, after-the-fact redesigns every time a company wants to enter a new market with a particular product. And combining this new process with international design teams can turn a multinational's scattered operations into a competitive advantage.

Each development project should revolve around the design of a core product, including the capacity for design variations and derivatives tailored to meet the needs of local markets. In some cases, companies have included derivative designs in software or a "country kit" that contains items such as preprogrammed memory chips, labels, documentation, and special power cords. In other cases, extra elements must be included in the core product so it can pass the regulatory requirements of specific countries. Often the cost of overdesigning a product to begin with is lower than that of redesigning the product later to meet idiosyncratic specifications in different countries. For example, one electronics company designs all of its products with additional shielding to prevent damage from liquid spills, even though only the United Kingdom and a few other European countries require such protection.

> Global contracts are so lucrative that suppliers can offer buyers better unit costs and schedules.

Creating international design teams is another crucial part of globalizing product development. If members of a product design team are located all over the world rather than clustered at a central site, each designer can monitor local tastes, technical standards, and changing government regulations. Designers in the field can also stay abreast of local technology developments and gain quicker access to competitors' products.

Of course, the global distribution of a design team introduces communication problems. But a good communications system, a necessary component of any world-class global enterprise, makes these problems manageable. For example, Digital Equipment Corporation, a pioneer in computer networking, created an electronic-mail network that links 100,000 employees worldwide. That means an engineer in Shrewsbury, Massachusetts can ask for help on a technical problem relating to disk-drive technology by typing a quick e-mail message. Within 24 hours, she may receive responses from fellow designers around the world that detail possible solutions. DEC estimates that the use of this application has contributed to a twofold reduction in product development time since 1988.

Purchasing. Economies of scale in purchasing come from consolidating raw material sources and paring down a company's supplier base. By purchasing on a global instead of a local basis, companies have the freedom to choose the best suppliers in the world, no matter where their operations are located. And because global contracts are often significantly larger than local ones, suppliers can offer buyers more favorable unit costs and delivery schedules. Some suppliers may even agree to set up local operations for a buyer if the contract is big enough.

To integrate purchasing, companies can create commodity management teams for all important materials. Commodity management teams select suppliers around the world and monitor their performance. Local plant-materials managers can execute the purchase orders and oversee daily supply flow. As for low-volume, low-cost commodities (particularly those with high transportation costs), individual plant staff can manage them based on local needs.

Each commodity management team is responsible for setting the cost, quality, and lead-time performance of the appropriate worldwide suppliers. Team members can be located anywhere in the world, although they must operate as a single group and make decisions for the company as a whole. Teams should include members from purchasing, engineering, finance, and quality assurance so that, as a group, they have the necessary expertise to identify world-class suppliers and ensure that the company gets the best performance for its money.

For example, Coulter Electronics, which produces medical electronics equipment, created commodity management teams that included representatives from all five of its plants. Early on, the semiconductor commodity team found that the company could consolidate half of all semiconductors it purchased into a few large contracts, saving more than $1 million a year. In another instance, the team discovered that the same three-way solenoid valve cost $20.87 in France, $17.50 in the United Kingdom, and $10.54 in the United States. By consolidating the purchasing of this valve, Coulter saved over $100,000 annually.

Production. To take advantage of their larger capacity and geographic diversity, multinational manufacturers must streamline the flow of inventory between plants. That means coordinating production of components in low-cost manufacturing centers with final assembly in high-cost locations close to customers. Mass producing component parts in Chinese or Malaysian plants, for example, can clearly cut production costs for a multinational. However, operating final assembly plants in places such as the United States or Germany is also essential for a number of reasons; for example, shipping the assembled product may be prohibitively expensive. In some instances, customers identify more closely with a company that has manufacturing facilities in their own country. In addition, many governments levy lower duties if final assembly is done locally; or they may require local assembly to sell products in that market, as in Brazil.

Of course, many companies are unable to coordinate existing production facilities after years of rapid and often haphazard expansion. While new ventures, acquisitions, or mergers may lead to new markets, they may also leave a manufacturer with too much uncoordinated worldwide capacity in locations that make little strategic sense. And because the age and type of capital equipment varies from plant to plant, the quality and cost of each plant's global production also varies.

Managers can begin restructuring production by analyzing how materials flow from plant to plant. Coordinating and simplifying materials flow requires two things: (1) balancing production *vertically* within the production pipeline, from component manufacturing to final assembly; and (2) balancing production *horizontally* between plants that manufacture the same or similar products.

Balancing production vertically requires tightening the connection between scattered final assembly, subassembly, and component plants. We have found that creating a global system analogous to single-plant, just-in-time inventory management ensures the tightest connection. To do this, companies should first take their end-product forecasts and communicate general requirements to all plants at all levels in the production process. Each plant can use these forecasts for capacity and materials planning. Then, operating in parallel, real customer

> When capital equipment varies from plant to plant, so will quality and cost.

orders become the "pull signals" for the upstream plant in the system to produce necessary components. But while a pull signal in a single plant is often a physical signal (an empty kanban bin, for instance), in a global system with multiple production facilities the signal probably would be an electronic message sent over a computer network.

Horizontal balancing, on the other hand, requires central coordination of plants that handle the same step in the manufacturing process, such as production of a particular component or final assembly. Because the same products are often manufactured by different plants in an organization, horizontal balancing involves assigning production based on cost, plant capacity, technical capabilities, availability of materials, and closeness to the customer.

For example, one company operates final assembly plants in two countries, each with dedicated metal-fabrication facilities that in the past manufactured many identical parts. One fabrication shop's outdated equipment produced complex turned parts very inefficiently. The other shop produced them quite efficiently, but because its skilled laborers received higher wages, its costs for manufacturing simple sheet-metal parts were far above the first shop's. By reallocating production – such as assigning more complex turned parts to the plant with highly paid, skilled workers – the company capitalized on the strengths of both shops and saved almost $1 million annually.

Demand Management. Managers use marketing and sales forecasts – the core of demand management – to set sales quotas, plan production schedules and inventory requirements, negotiate supplier contracts, and establish corporate revenue plans. If for no other reason than demand management, a sophisticated global forecasting system is necessary. Companies must gather information on the local level, integrate it into a central system, and then distribute the consolidated data back to all local operations.

However, before investing in a technical solution, management should first understand how the company uses current demand forecasts to set production. The biggest problem many multinationals face is that demand forecasting is a politically charged process. From central headquarters, which may be halfway around the world from the company's manufacturing facilities, senior managers set the annual forecast at the beginning of each fiscal year. This is then handed down to manufacturing operations to use for scheduling production. But because the forecast is also used by Wall Street analysts as a baseline for evaluating the company's performance, senior managers frown on any deviations from the plan. So if customer orders begin to fall, but production levels remain the same to meet corporate expectations, inventory accumulates and manufacturing managers are blamed. In fact, official adjustments to production forecasts often take months to make.

To address the problem, manufacturing managers should have the authority to adjust production levels to reflect actual orders. Over the last few years, Xerox has reengineered its global demand management process with this change in mind. Today teams of production planners and demand analysts at each operating company meet weekly to review production of each product family and adjust production and inventory levels. Each team uses an interactive modeling system that graphically displays historical and projected customer demand, production output, and inventory levels, including relevant data from other related Xerox companies.

These demand management teams have the experience to make informed decisions on production changes and the authority to implement them, which has shaved weeks and even months off production planning times. In one case, a quick change in a plant's production schedule of copiers saved $100,000 in inventory and freight costs.

Order Fulfillment. To gain a new scale advantage in order fulfillment, companies must focus on coordinating customer orders with distribution at the global level. The result is more efficient order management, a decrease in total finished goods inventories, and quicker, more direct delivery. Companies should strive to cut all unnecessary warehousing and transportation of finished products on their way to customers. Ideally, orders are linked to the most appropriate factory, which then ships the product directly to the customer.

Companies can move toward this goal by first creating a globally networked order management system that keeps track of where different products are made, how they can be configured, where the customer is located, and how products are priced in different markets. In addition, the system assigns product automatically to a plant close to the customer. And by electronically transmitting, validating, pricing, and scheduling an order, the company can cut significant time out of the entire fulfillment cycle.

Take, for example, the complex order fulfillment problems of Digital Equipment Corporation, which must bundle a unique set of components – computer platforms, displays, printers, storage units, and communications equipment – that are manufactured by a variety of plants around the world and then ship a single, complete package to the customer. Just a few years ago, DEC's unwieldy fulfillment system

> Manufacturing strategy should match business strategy; yet companies rarely connect the two.

involved endless negotiations between individual plants and distribution centers that added time and expense to each delivery.

Now DEC has simplified the process: the goal is to enter an order only once. Order processors use an expert system to configure each product, then coordinate production and shipment of each part to one of

DEC's new consolidation centers. Even before the component parts arrive, employees at the consolidation center prepare the shipping documents and schedule a carrier for final delivery. The new process reduces the number of transactions, streamlines the distribution flow, considerably improves delivery time, and increases the accuracy of orders – and customer satisfaction.

Setting the Stage for Global Integration

Specific functional changes each contribute to a new scale advantage: flexible products, reduced costs, simplified manufacturing processes, realistic planning based on demand, or better customer service. But once a multinational acknowledges the need for global integration, the ultimate goal should be to make changes in all five basics.

Obviously, this is not a simple task. Rationalizing every scattered facility and operation as part of a coherent whole and establishing new systems may take years to accomplish, especially for a large multinational. While Xerox, DEC, and other innovative companies have integrated some systems, even they are still in the early stages. We recognize that change often happens by fits and starts and doesn't always spring from an overarching vision. Still, companies can use three general guidelines to set the stage for global integration and drive the first changes in the right direction.

1. Affirm a global manufacturing mission.

The manufacturing strategy must support the company's global business strategy and be consistent across all facilities. However tautological this statement sounds, it rarely holds. At some companies, regional operations often set their own manufacturing priorities, and corporate management has little power to coordinate their strategies. At other companies, there is no formal manufacturing strategy at all, only a series of manufacturing decisions made at different times and under different conditions in the company's history. In both cases, the end result is a poor match between manufacturing strategy and business strategy.

To align the two strategies, top management should analyze existing plants, including their location, capacity, the range of products they produce, and the ability and willingness of their managers to communicate with each other. Studying the manufacturing infrastructure in the context of a worldwide business strategy can point up glaring weaknesses and provide a foundation for a meaningful manufacturing mission.

But creating the manufacturing mission is only the first step. Senior management must *publicly* declare its commitment to global integration, outlining to employees, customers, and suppliers the vision it holds for the company. In this way, everyone understands the context for any and all changes that follow.

In 1990, Gaynor Kelley, chairman of Perkin-Elmer Corporation, issued a call to become "one company, global yet compact, coordinated, efficient." His company plan, which was distributed to all employees, is an outline for shifting Perkin-Elmer's focus away from optimizing each plant's manufacturing assets toward the coordination of all plants.

Similarly, in early 1991, NEC Corporation's president Tadahiro Sekimoto publicly announced plans for globally integrating the company. "Until a few years ago," he said, "we expanded through linear globalization, with control flowing from Tokyo to overseas units. Now we are pursuing *mesh globalism,* which means decentralized but still connected." Companies such as NEC have not only recognized the need for "mesh globalism" but also the fact that integration cannot happen without the knowledge and support of everyone involved.

2. Develop a profile of capabilities.

Senior managers must first understand the strengths and weaknesses of the existing manufacturing structure. They must have a realistic idea of what capabilities the company still needs and where to focus attention first before they can draft a specific plan of action.

Any inventory of requisite capabilities should begin with an effective communications and information processing system. Teleconferencing equipment, electronic mail, electronic data interchange, distributed computing, and multivendor connectivity are all essential to tie facilities together. In fact, since achieving a new scale advantage depends on quick and accurate communication between far-flung plants, top managers should make compatibility of computer and communications equipment a corporate priority.

Of course, well-connected facilities are useless if employees don't understand each other. Creating a common management "language" – a universal set of management practices and measurement systems – is also crucial. At Xerox, for example, the Leadership Through Quality program set the stage for the company's global networking efforts.

As a company evolves its information network and improves its global communication skills, it should also evaluate how to rationalize operations, but on a global rather than single-plant basis. For instance, by benchmarking its capabilities against the competition, a company can identify performance gaps. Managers then use this information to set aggressive goals for improving capabilities.

More important, benchmarking not only provides

information on the product or plant level but also illuminates strengths and weaknesses at the corporate level. One international electronics company benchmarked its plants by function (purchasing, logistics, manufacturing) along a number of critical dimensions (customer satisfaction, product and process quality, cost) and uncovered several performance gaps. But in the process, management found that several plants had extremely efficient manufacturing processes. At the time, there was no mechanism for transferring such expertise to other plants. However, by identifying successes, the company could then focus on transforming the manufacturing process throughout the organization rather than just addressing specific performance gaps.

This company has now set up a database that includes information on all plants, organized by 250 separate performance measures. Top management actively encourages individual plant managers to use the database to compare their facility's performance with others in the organization and share knowledge of the most successful practices.

Well-integrated facilities are useless without a common set of management practices and measurement systems.

3. Identify options, pick a plan of action, and target specific results.

The most immediate, nuts-and-bolts issues senior managers will address are redeployment of plants and equipment and the reengineering of critical processes. Managers must decide which plants to close immediately and which ones to target for expansion. They must determine which manufacturing processes require reengineering and which ones can continue as they are.

One large capital equipment manufacturer, for example, considered the entire range of choices for restructuring its five plants, from total centralization to total decentralization. It developed a model for all options, which included the impact of each location on local sales volume and the company's cost structure over time. The company also included the effects of varying 11 critical functions in each scenario it studied. For instance, management looked at what product development process would work best in a system of four manufacturing plants as compared with a system of two, weighing the costs and the benefits of each scenario. While time consuming, this company's analysis produced a final plan that was widely supported across the organization.

Manufacturers that successfully coordinate global resources will become stronger, more responsive companies.

Of course, once a company has selected a plan of action, it must also get quick, highly visible results. Even though change is a long-term process, management needs to demonstrate progress in the short-term. Otherwise, its larger mission may fail, given the competitive marketplace. Coulter Electronics started coordinating its worldwide purchasing by setting up a simple, PC-driven database. The system was up and running within a few months at minimal expense and paved the way for other fundamental organizational improvements in purchasing.

In fact, a company can target specific results in any of the five basic functions to establish early victories, set the stage, and build momentum for the ultimate goal: a fully integrated global manufacturing system. Taken one step further, a multinational's new scale advantage will come from increased interaction *across* functions. When companies globalize the design process, for example, they may also create products that are easier to manufacture. And when companies globalize purchasing, manufacturing is no longer tied to a specific plant, and designers are not limited by local suppliers.

A multinational of the future, fully integrated yet still flexible, may supply its component plants with raw materials from a single source; standardize the manufacturing process in its British, German, and American final assembly plants; enter customer orders into a worldwide order fulfillment system so that products are assembled in and distributed from the most convenient site; and install a sophisticated electronic network that links product designers, demand analysts, and production planners at all facilities. Companies like this will rationalize operations from a global perspective, even if it means making hard and initially costly decisions, such as laying off workers at one plant in Tennessee to expand another in Brazil.

Those multinational manufacturers that successfully coordinate and balance their global resources will evolve into stronger, more responsive companies, better able to cut costs and serve their customers around the world. And multinationals of all sizes that integrate their operations–and achieve a new manufacturing scale advantage–will control the competition today and in the future.

The Search for a Truly Pan-European Manufacturing System

Nigel Dunham and Robin Morgan

Though pan-European manufacturing systems are new, the availability and market for them will certainly increase. The potential benefits are great to the company that very carefully selects and implements the systems.

Dr. Nigel Dunham is Head of KPMG's European FMCG Group, London, England, and Robin Morgan is a Senior Managing Consultant in KPMG's Manufacturing Systems Group.

The successful development of a pan-European manufacturing strategy relies on systems that can operate in a multi-plant, multi-base currency, multi-language, and multi-legal entity environment. Software that offers such features for pan-European manufacturing systems is now coming onto the market.

A pan-European system is a single package of programs that may be implemented in multiple European countries without the need for modification. The implementation can take the form of using the same basic package in a variety of related or unrelated businesses, which form part of the same overall organization (see Figure 1). If the businesses are related, the option exists to control these as though they were a single integrated entity, while meeting local statutory requirements, particularly as they relate to financial reporting, VAT, and market accountability. Country, business, or plant variations are implemented by means of parameters or "keys" set at installation. A pan-European manufacturing system includes both manufacturing and distribution—in other words, sales order processing, resource and material planning, inventory control, purchase order processing, and distribution requirements planning. Accounting and payroll are excluded.

The Needs of an Integrated Pan-European Manufacturer

Many companies, particularly those specializing in fast moving consumer goods, are examining the way they currently operate in order to determine whether it is still appropriate in the context of the EC's Single Market. Historically, companies located plants to serve the needs of only a particular country or region, but many now realize that the removal of trade barriers allows them to operate as integrated European businesses. Therefore, companies are changing their manufacturing strategy, which in turn is fueling the demand for pan-European software. This software allows companies to make supply, production, and distribution decisions without regard to natural boundaries, while at the same time satisfying the requirements of the different legal entities in the countries in which they operate. Typical system requirements that flow from this type of situation include:

1. Forecasting

• collation of forecasts from different markets/countries at product group and/or item level;

From *The Journal of European Business*, Vol. 3, No. 1, September/October 1991, pp. 43-47. Copyright © 1991 by Faulkner & Gray, Inc.

Figure 1. Pan-European Manufacturing Systems

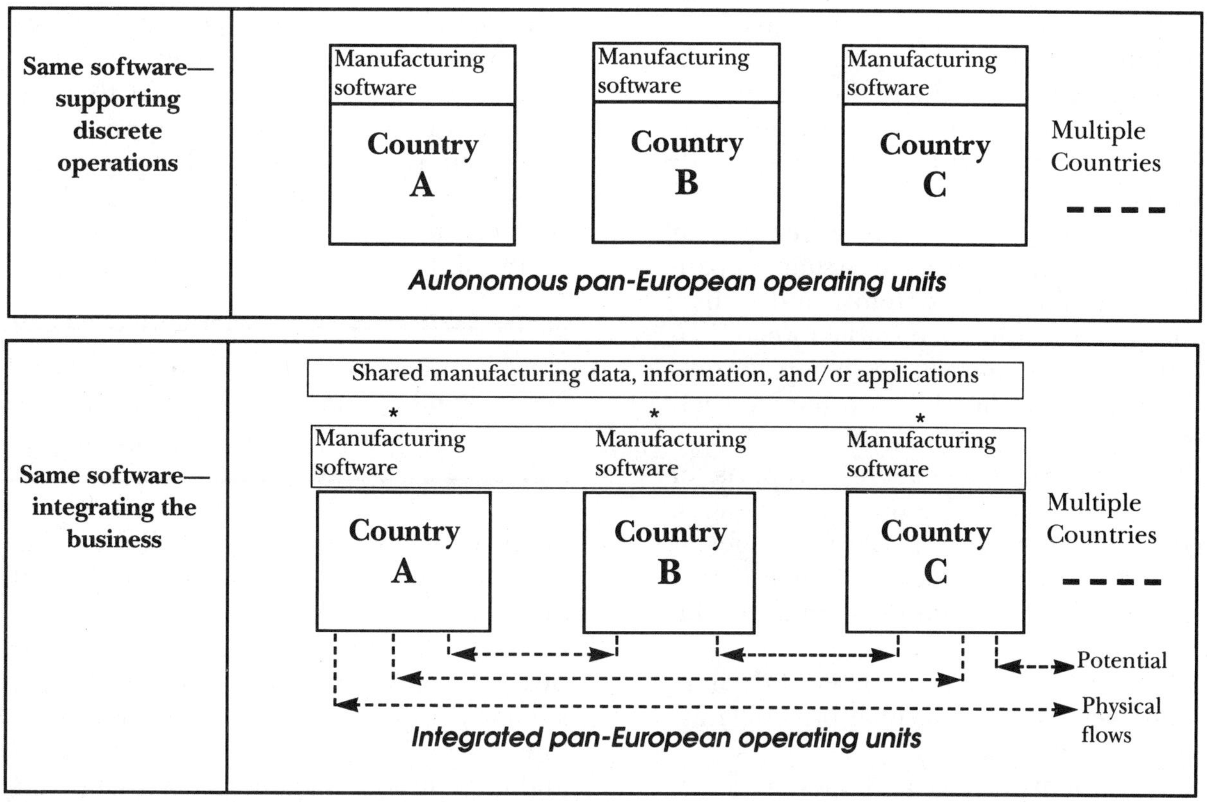

2. Logistics/inventory planning

• aggregating market/country stocks to derive European inventory;

• netting demand against inventory to determine market/country and European net requirements;

• flagging out-of-balance demand/inventory situations at both market/country and European levels;

• providing inventory deployment "what-if" capability that identifies and supports inter-company/country transfer opportunities;

• providing shipment schedules to individual site systems.

3. Product data

• central updating of bills of materials, formulations, process details, etc. that reside on remote systems.

4. Production planning

• aggregation of forecasts, sales orders, and finished goods levels across all remote sites;

• the ability to link demand by item or customer to the preferred site of production;

• rough cut capacity planning and "what-if" simulations across plants and key production resources;

• splitting and downloading of aggregate production plans to individual site systems.

5. Purchasing

• feeding of some or all purchase requisitions from remote sites to a central purchasing function;

• updating of purchasing orders placed by remote sites;

• feeding of some or all goods-received data at remote sites to central purchasing;

• invoicing either centrally or at remote sites.

6. Product costing

• analysis of manufacturing costs across all European production facilities.

7. Management information

• analysis of sales, stock turns, etc. across multiple systems.

Pan-European Issues

Businesses that want to select and implement a pan-European system need to address a number of key issues. For example, is there a need to have a standard pan-European system? Only if there are measurable benefits should a company install of a pan-European system. These expected benefits must be carefully quantified at the start of the process and compared to actual results at the end of the implementation. Obviously, there is no point in embarking on the project if the costs outweigh the benefits.

Another important issue to consider is: Can you find a suitable pan-European system? A pan-European manufacturing system is more than just a U.K. package translated into a foreign language. The generic requirements of a pan-European system include the ability to handle such situations as:

- multiple languages on-screen, in reports, in documentation, and in help and error messages. Some countries require multiple languages at the same site (*e.g.*, Belgium and Switzerland), the language used on-screen depending on the particular user.
- widely varying field sizes, number of decimal places, currency symbols, decimal place characters, and thousand separators.
- different systems of VAT and sales tax. Non-EC countries each have their own set of reports and methods of calculation.
- various reporting requirements, particularly with regard to analyzing data by legal entity, country, market, customer, plant, warehouse, and store.

The system must be flexible enough to meet all of these challenges. Such systems are now available in Europe, although not in large numbers, and even some of these are still unable to meet all the major requirements. Software houses seeking to compete in this growing market have created packages capable of operating in a number of European countries, both within and outside the EC. There are also a number of companies working on pan-European manufacturing systems, but it will be several years before there is a mature market with a reasonable choice available.

As with all changes there will be an issue of acceptance, particularly: Will users accept a new and "foreign" system where they have been used to a local manufacturing system that has probably been modified?

A steering group that contains an appropriate balance of user and systems representatives must drive the pan-European manufacturing system project. The desire to adopt a common Europe-wide system can often subject certain businesses or plants to undue pressure to accept a compromise. The elegance of a potential system's solution should not blind systems personnel to the business needs of a particular company. Experience shows that there are no packages that are uniformly good at meeting the system requirements of all types of businesses from make-to-order companies, such as shipbuilders, to continuous-flow operations such as oil refining.

A pan-European manufacturing system is more than just a U.K. package translated into a foreign language.

The complexities of the task will pose the question: Can one system cope with all the national and business differences? There is a very real danger with manufacturing systems that the sum of the systems requirements of many apparently similar companies can lead to the selection of one system that is functionally rich but expensive and difficult to implement. Increasing complexity also tends to slow implementation, thereby delaying the realization of business benefits. Companies must carefully consider the issue of balancing system complexity, the number of sites able to use the features provided by a very comprehensive system, and potential cost savings. Unless these issues are fully explored at the feasibility stage, there is the danger that subsequent resistance to implementing a complex system will reduce the anticipated number of users, thereby eroding multi-site software savings.

Finally, support is a key issue with any software product, and pan-European manufacturing systems are no exception. How will a pan-European system be supported? The detailed issues in this area will depend on whether support will be undertaken externally or internally. Most hardware suppliers have a good European network of offices and distributors, but the situation for software companies and dealers is much more patchy. Support is a key area software suppliers must address if they are to succeed in this market. Because the system will be the same throughout the organization, a pan-European system offers the possibility of a centralized, internal support function, which can be supplemented by local visits from local experts. This

Case Study

The company: a major international manufacturer in the "FMCG" (fast moving consumer goods) market with operations in nine countries and sales in more than 135 countries around the world.

The objective: to select an integrated software package encompassing distribution, manufacturing, and financial accounts, which could be implemented throughout Europe in support of the company's pan-European business strategy (see Figure 2).

The process: The company's European project team generated a statement of pan-European business requirements. This required significant commitment and an effective and efficient communication structure to ensure adequate input from the individual European sites.

Selected vendors were invited to demonstrate their systems' fit with the company's requirements. During the process it became apparent that while the vendors could offer multi-plant solutions, they were unable to truly support the company's pan-European vision of both manufacturing anywhere in Europe and distributing throughout Europe. Specific European requirements that a single version of the software should support included multi-base currency, multi-currency, multi-legal entity, pan-European inventory deployment, and distribution.

Initially the software vendors' development staffs did not appear to appreciate fully the requirements of trading in a pan-European environment across several legal entities. However, by working with the vendors, the company was able to establish the necessary functionality a true pan-European manufacturing software package should possess. This base functionality was then used to specify required software enhancements necessary to support the company in the short term. More important, the base functionality was used to check that the vendor's long-term development plans would deliver the required functionality as part of their standard package.

The selection process was judged a success not simply because a vendor/solution was selected that is capable of supporting the company's current and future European trading vision, but also because user ownership of the system has been readily accepted across all European sites, thereby providing firm foundations for a successful implementation.

Business benefits:

- reduced inventory holding throughout the entire distribution chain from centralized planning;
- improved customer service resulting from pan-European inventory deployment;
- reduced manufacturing costs by enabling the lowest-cost production site to be identified and exploited;
- enhanced purchasing leverage.

System benefits:

- the ability to utilize key systems personnel on a pan-European basis;
- shared expertise, experiences, and development;
- opportunity to benefit from corporate purchasing (*e.g.*, the company negotiated a reduction on the software purchase price of more than one-third).

The company is now in the process of implementing the chosen solution.

Figure 2. Supporting Systems for Pan-European Trading

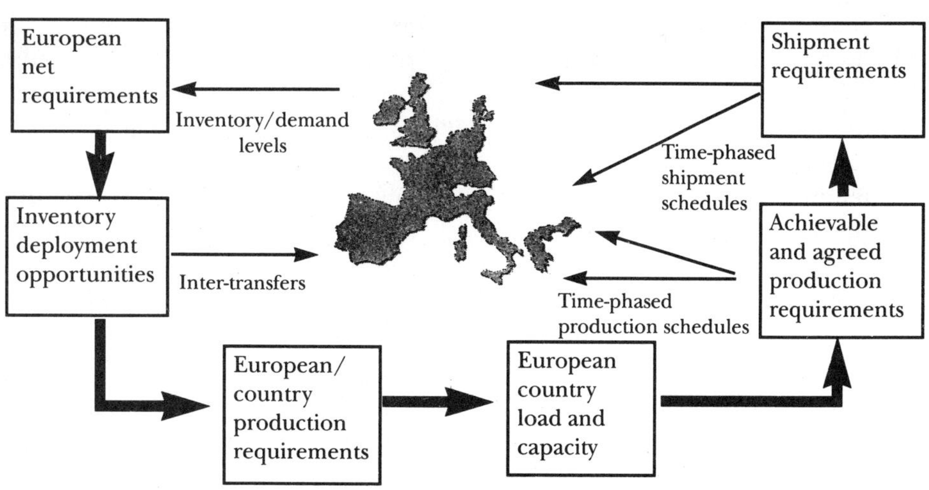

will require setting up the appropriate organizational structures and controls.

Benefits

A successful implementation of a pan-European manufacturing system should give rise to a number of benefits to the organization as a whole. These benefits should accrue from better management of the supply chain, enhanced management control, and reduced system costs. These benefits, however, depend on the particular nature and structure of the organization. Typically, benefits for an organization moving toward becoming an integrated pan-European manufacturer will result from improved purchasing power, optimal manufacturing capacity, reduced stock levels through the entire supply chain, and a streamlined product range.

Cost saving, through economies of scale, should also be a benefit. For example, companies (1) may obtain discounts for multiple software licenses, (2) do any needed development work only once, and (3) centralize training. In addition, if a company selects a pan-European accounting system in conjunction with a manufacturing system, it can usually reduce the number of accounting interfaces.

Companies should also be able to benefit from a centralized internal support function for pan-European systems. An international internal support function will understand the business better than an external function, be able to devote all its resources to the one organization, and provide company-specific training. The ability to transfer staff among countries, because the systems would be the same, may also be a great benefit to some organizations.

A further benefit should be improved efficiency, through a simplified management reporting and consolidation process. The adoption of common manufacturing systems is frequently the catalyst to harmonize different practices, procedures, data structures, etc. The resulting adoption of the best practices and increased uniformity should provide the data required to spot opportunities, undertake more meaningful performance comparisons, and collate information relating to other pan-European suppliers and customers.

Constraints

One should consider both the benefits and the constraints in order to determine the most appropriate way forward for any particular manufacturing business. The constraints a company will need to manage will include such things as: resistance to change; complex and disparate requirements; cost, both in time and outlays; different cultures' currencies and languages; availability and knowledge of suppliers and software; expertise and knowledge of the pan-European systems market; expertise in multinational selection; and implementation. In addition, the lack of standard terminology and definitions for many manufacturing-related terms can cause misunderstandings both within an organization and between the organization and potential software vendors.

Conclusion

Key requirements for success include:

- the use of proven methods in the definition of requirements and selection of the system;
- a comprehensive knowledge of the available pan-European manufacturing systems, together with their strengths and weaknesses;
- an understanding of the opportunities and risks associated with pan-European manufacturing systems;
- the use of proven methods in managing the implementation, which will be a major project;
- the effective management of change.

It is possible to find and implement pan-European manufacturing systems, and the availability and market for such systems will increase. The potential benefits are great to the company that very carefully selects and implements the systems. A number of software houses are now putting resources into this area, but not all of them appreciate the differences between the requirements of a local manufacturing business and the requirements of truly integrated pan-European manufacturing and distribution organizations. Developing true pan-European systems requires considerable commitment in time and resources, but this commitment will produce significant benefits to these developers and their customers.

GLOBAL INNOVATION: WHO'S IN THE LEAD?

BW's new ranking of nearly 200 top companies tracks technological strength based on U.S. patents

Francis Narin is no ordinary detective. So when a consulting firm called three years ago and asked him to investigate a division of a major chemical company, he didn't start following anyone or probing financial records. Instead, he fired up the vast data base at CHI Research Inc., the tiny research firm he runs in Haddon Heights, N.J., and began his line of inquiry: analyzing patent trends.

All Narin knew was that the chemical company's division had a reputation for innovation—and that the consultant's unnamed client was thinking of buying the unit. A search of CHI's data base of more than 1 million U.S. patent records turned up a surprising fact: Many of the division's key patents belonged to just two researchers. Then, a second survey showed telltale evidence that something was afoot: The pair had stopped filing patents under the divisional name and were inventing for the parent company instead. "In anticipation of divestiture," Narin surmises, "the company had moved their key people out." Narin calls this selling "the empty technological shell." Though he can't say for sure what role the CHI report played, the acquisition never took place.

The technique Narin drew on is bibliometrics, a form of statistical analysis used to scan patents and scientific papers to figure out which ones are most important. Increasingly, savvy companies are employing it to spot technological trends, unearth competitor's moves before

A TEST OF HIGH-TECH STRENGTH

The **number of patents** granted by the U.S. government is a traditional test of high-tech strength. But CHI Research Inc. has come up with more sophisticated measures, based on earlier patents cited as building blocks in new patents. The **current impact index** measures how often a company's patents are cited relative to those of all other companies. The 1.45 for Toshiba, for example, means its patents are cited 45% more than average. CHI multiplies the index by number of patents to get **technological strength**, the basis for this ranking. **Technology cycle time** is the median age in years of patents cited in a company's new patents. The shorter the cycle time, the faster the company is developing new technology

Company (headquarters country)	Number of U.S. patents 1991	Current impact index 1991	Technological strength	Technology cycle time 1991
TOSHIBA (Japan)	1156	1.45	1677	5.4
HITACHI (Japan)	1139	1.43	1633	5.7
CANON (Japan)	828	1.45	1201	6.0
MITSUBISHI ELECTRIC (Japan)	959	1.24	1190	5.1
EASTMAN KODAK (U.S.)	887	1.34	1186	7.8
IBM (U.S.)	680	1.71	1161	5.9
GENERAL MOTORS (U.S.)*	863	1.32	1139	7.9
GENERAL ELECTRIC (U.S.)	923	1.16	1069	8.8
FUJI PHOTO FILM (Japan)	742	1.42	1056	5.8
MOTOROLA (U.S.)	631	1.54	969	5.5
AT&T (U.S.)	487	1.84	895	5.3
PHILIPS (Netherlands)	768	1.02	781	6.0
NISSAN MOTOR (Japan)	385	1.91	736	4.7
TEXAS INSTRUMENTS (U.S.)	380	1.87	709	6.2
NEC (Japan)	482	1.46	706	5.0
MATSUSHITA ELECTRIC (Japan)	561	1.24	694	5.6
DU PONT (U.S.)	631	1.06	669	9.7
XEROX (U.S.)	353	1.75	619	6.8
FUJITSU (Japan)	382	1.56	596	5.3
SIEMENS (Germany)	610	0.97	589	6.6
3M (U.S.)	374	1.39	519	10.9
HOECHST (Germany)	575	0.88	507	8.6
MINOLTA CAMERA (Japan)	315	1.61	506	5.1
AMP (U.S.)	275	1.84	505	7.1
SHARP (Japan)	388	1.27	493	5.4

*Including EDS and GM Hughes Electronics DATA: CHI RESEARCH INC.

Reprinted from the August 3, 1992, issue of *Business Week*, pp. 68-69, by special permission. Copyright © 1992 by McGraw-Hill, Inc.

they're apparent in the marketplace—and even help plan acquisitions, partnerships, and overall strategic direction. "You can spot right away the leaders and the followers in different technology areas, and you can detect companies shifting technological emphasis—or even strategies," attests Donald Milstein, manager of planning, coordination, and evaluation for Mobil Research & Development Corp., the oil company's technology arm.

Based on this technique, BUSINESS WEEK has teamed up with CHI Research to create a new Patent Scoreboard that tracks corporate technological power. It separates 197 of the world's top companies into 14 industry groups and ranks them by technological strength—a measure derived from the number and quality of patents.

As with any analytical tool, the new tables don't tell the whole story. They cover only U.S. patents—and while most important foreign inventions are also patented in the U.S., this isn't always true. Then, too, in order to keep research secret, some technologically strong companies restrict the number of patents they file. In addition, Japanese companies are being pressured by their backlogged government to curtail filings for minor patents—a trend that could mean lower Scoreboard numbers if they follow suit in the U.S.

Despite these caveats, the new Scoreboard shows key technological trends. The raw power of Japanese companies stands out, challenging the stereotype that they are mere copycats. Japan holds down the first four slots, led by Toshiba Corp's technology strength rating of 1,677. The best U.S. performer is fifth-place Eastman Kodak Co., at 1,186, with IBM a step behind. The top European: Philips Electronics, No. 11 overall.

COMEBACK KIDS? Within industry sectors, the story is more ambiguous. Given the prowess of Japanese auto makers, it's no surprise that only General Motors Corp. cracks the top five in tech strength. But Detroit may be catching up. Over the past five years, GM has gained an average of 10% a year, and Ford is up 16% annually. And while Nissan's rating has risen, Toyota's and Honda's have declined. Japan's carmakers downplay the numbers. True, they're patenting less, as requested. "But that doesn't mean technological development has slowed down," says Toyota Executive Vice-President Shiro Sasaki. Still, Detroit has recently gained market share, and some experts say its technological comeback may be a factor. "The changes that the domestics have made have been primarily in the technology," says Thomas F. O'Grady, president of Integrated Automotive Resources Inc., a Wilmington (Del.) consultant.

Among individual companies, General Electric Co. shows a seemingly ominous decline. Over the past two decades, GE has been awarded more U.S. patents than any other company. But since 1987, output has slipped an average of 8% a year—and its technological strength rating has fallen an average of 11% annually. GE attributes the decline to its downsizing from 30-odd businesses to just 13—and says it remains the world leader in most of those fields. On a brighter note, U.S. technology-strength leader Kodak has won 30% more patents annually since 1987, pushing into emerging fields such as electronic imaging. Its tech strength has jumped 44% a year. In 1991, Ko-

THE COMPANIES WITH HIGH-IMPACT PATENTS...

Company (headquarters country)	1991 Current impact index
CORDIS (U.S.)	2.25
INTEL (U.S.)	2.16
PROCTER & GAMBLE (U.S.)	2.08
ALZA (U.S.)	1.96
NISSAN MOTOR (Japan)	1.91
TEXAS INSTRUMENTS (U.S.)	1.87
AT&T (U.S.)	1.84
NIPPON TELEPHONE (Japan)	1.84
AMP (U.S.)	1.84
FUJI HEAVY INDUSTRIES (Japan)	1.83
MAZDA MOTOR (Japan)	1.81
MITSUBISHI MOTORS (Japan)	1.78
XEROX (U.S.)	1.75
COLGATE-PALMOLIVE (U.S.)	1.72
IBM (U.S.)	1.71

...AND THOSE CLOSEST TO THE CUTTING EDGE

Company (headquarters country)	1991 Technology cycle time
FUJI HEAVY INDUSTRIES (Japan)	4.1
MAZDA MOTOR (Japan)	4.5
PIONEER ELECTRONIC (Japan)	4.5
MITSUBISHI MOTORS (Japan)	4.6
RICOH (Japan)	4.6
NISSAN MOTOR (Japan)	4.7
OLYMPUS OPTICAL (Japan)	4.8
NIKON (Japan)	4.8
INTEL (U.S.)	4.9
AISIN SEIKI (Japan)	5.0
NEC (Japan)	5.0
SONY (Japan)	5.0
MITSUBISHI ELECTRIC (Japan)	5.1
MINOLTA CAMERA (Japan)	5.1
TOYOTA MOTOR (Japan)	5.2

DATA: CHI RESEARCH INC.

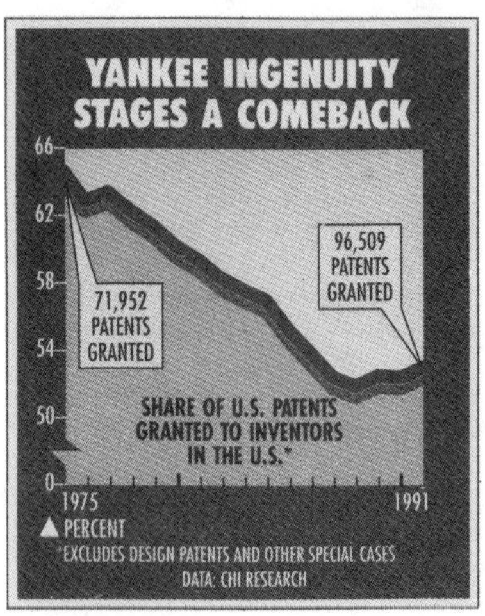

dak trailed Canon Inc. by just 15 points.

The new Scoreboard will mark the first time many companies have heard of bibliometrics. But others are well aware of it. Kodak forages through patent data to track particular inventors—to see what competitors are doing and whether they are moving star scientists to hot new areas. Philips has used patent analysis to track 30 rivals in 39 fields, from software to optical recording.

The uses of bibliometric data go far beyond intelligence gathering, however. Mobil Research & Development first used the technique in 1987, as part of an assessment of its technological competitiveness. As expected, the analysis showed Mobil leading the pack in the discovery of zeolites, synthetic catalysts used in oil refining and petrochemical production. But researchers were stunned to find that competitors were often better at patenting applications for the very materials Mobil had discovered. "Obviously, we were missing out on a potential opportunity," says Milstein. Over the next two years, Mobil R&D upped by a third the budget and personnel devoted to exploiting new zeolites. Without giving specifics, Milstein says the moves will pay off with a slew of new applications.

EARLY WORD. These same kinds of studies—charting output from individuals, universities, and corporate labs—can be done with scientific papers instead of patent data. The pioneer in this area, the Institute for Scientific Information in Philadelphia, assesses the importance of papers by determining how often they're cited in other reports. Moreover, several groups in Europe and the U.S. use ISI's raw data for their own studies. Leonard Simon, president of the Center for Research Planning in Philadelphia, says it's possible to pick up hot new fields or shifts in the direction of research before they're common knowledge.

Whether it tracks patents, papers, or both, bibliometrics can reveal vital information. And even if it spots nothing experts in a given area don't intuitively know, the technique can provide hard data that corporate executives need in order to act on the judgments of their technical staff.

What's more, advocates say, now and then they see something fundamental. "We can show companies that their research universe is in the midst of a whole revolutionary process—and that down the line, all their products will be obsolete because the science will change," Simon adds. Even enthusiasts warn against basing decisions solely on such analysis. But this technique gives companies another way to guard against being blindsided by technological change.

By Robert Buderi in Boston, with John Carey in Washington, and Neil Gross and Karen Lowry Miller in Tokyo

The Myth of 'Made in the U.S.A.'

ROBERT REICH

Mr. Reich teaches at Harvard's Kennedy School and is author of "The Work of Nations: Preparing Ourselves for 21st Century Capitalism" (Knopf, 1991). [In 1993 Mr. Reich was appointed Secretary of Labor in the Clinton administration. Ed.]

Last month the U.S. Customs Service charged Honda Motor Company with circumventing import duties by overstating the North American content of its Canadian-built cars. They weren't really Canadian, said the service.

In May, the Treasury Department disallowed certain expenses that CAMI Automotive Inc., of Ingersoll, Ontario—a joint venture of Suzuki Motors and General Motors—used to back its claim that its Geo Tracker truck had the 50% North American content required to be considered Canadian.

How to square these actions—and several others now pending—with the Bush administration's free-trade rhetoric? The White House is tightening up eligibility for duty-free access to the U.S., in light of the upcoming U.S.-Mexican trade talks. The administration wants to assure American producers that foreign companies won't be using Mexico, or Canada, as convenient entrepots into the huge North American free-trade zone.

Doomed Effort

The administration's effort is doomed to fail. In the emerging global economy, it's impossible to say what's a "North American" product. Once upon a time, products had distinct national identities. Regardless of how many international borders they crossed, their country of origin—the name of which was usually imprinted right on them—was never in doubt. Products were manufactured in one place because economies of scale necessitated a central location.

But in the emerging high-value economy, quantities can be produced efficiently in many different locations and combined in all sorts of ways to serve customer needs in many places. Precision ice hockey equipment is designed in Sweden, financed in Canada, and assembled in Cleveland and Denmark for distribution in North America and Europe, respectively, out of alloys whose molecular structure was researched and patented in Delaware and fabricated in Japan. An advertising campaign is conceived in Britain: Film footage for it is shot in Canada, dubbed in Britain, and edited in New York. A sports car is financed in Japan, designed in Italy, and assembled in Indiana, Mexico and France, using advanced electronic components invented in New Jersey and fabricated in Japan.

What's traded between nations is less often finished goods than specialized research, design, fabrication, management, marketing, advertising, consulting, financial and legal services, as well as components and materials.

When an American buys a Pontiac Le Mans from General Motors, for example, he engages unwittingly in an international transaction. Of the $10,000 paid to GM, about $3,000 goes to South Korea for routine labor and assembly operations, $1,850 to Japan for advanced components (engines, transaxles, and electronics) $700 to the former West Germany for styling and design engineering, $400 to Taiwan, Singapore, and Japan for small components, $250 to Britain for advertising and marketing services, and about $50 to Ireland and Barbados for data processing. The rest—less than $4,000—goes to strategists in Detroit, lawyers and bankers in New York, lobbyists in Washington, insurance and health care workers all over the country, and to General Motors shareholders all over the world.

The proud new owner of the Pontiac is not aware of having bought so much from overseas, of course. General Motors did the trading within its global network. This is typical. Most "trade" no longer occurs in arm's-length transactions between buyers in one nation and sellers in another, but between people within the same global network who are likely to deal repeatedly with each other across borders. They may be part of the same multinational corporation, collecting salaries from one source (more than half of America's exports and imports, by value, are transfers of components and services within the same global company), or they may be working in different companies that share in any profits from the joint venture, or they may simply contract with one another to perform specific services for a pre-established fee.

A sports car is financed in Japan, designed in Italy, and assembled in Indiana, Mexico and France, using advanced electronic components invented in New Jersey and fabricated in Japan.

Global networks like these cloak themselves in whatever national garb is most convenient. Because corporate accounting systems record transfers of intermediate goods and related services across borders, earnings and revenues can appear in all sorts of places around the world (often, not coincidentally, where taxes are lowest).

Global companies will characterize themselves as domestic when advantageous. In 1987 the Hyster Company, an American-owned manufacturer of forklift trucks, headquartered in Portland, Ore., accused several Japanese-owned firms of pricing their forklifts sold in America below what they charged in Japan, prompting the Commerce Department to impose special duties on the forklift imports. In response, the Japanese firms began to make forklifts in the United States. Hyster cried foul, arguing that the competing forklifts were still "Japanese," since many of their parts came from Japan. What Hyster carefully did not reveal, however, was that its own "American" forklifts contained even more foreign parts than those they were accusing of being "Japanese."

When there are greater advantages to being seen as "foreign," on the other hand, even the most native of goods and services are magically transformed into alien products. Consider Ford Motor Company's instant 1990 alteration. The Environmental

 From *The Wall Street Journal*, July 5, 1991, pp. A6. Copyright © 1991 Robert B. Reich. Reprinted by permission.

Protection Agency had required that every automaker's fleet of "American-made" cars achieve a certain minimum average fuel economy. Any foreign cars made or imported by the American firm would have to meet the same standard when these cars' fuel economy ratings were averaged together. By not allowing American automakers to average their small, fuel-efficient imports with their far more profitable American gas-guzzlers, the EPA had intended to encourage American automakers to retain small-car production in the U.S.

Ford, however, concocted a brilliant idea: by increasing the foreign-made parts in its American gas guzzlers just a tad, Ford could qualify the big clunkers as "foreign-made," thus permitting them to be averaged with all the high-mileage Ford imports. Presto! Overnight, Ford's "foreign-made" Mercury Marquis and LTD Crown Victorias could be sold in America without first having to be balanced by smaller (and far less profitable) high-mileage cars made in the U.S.

Official decisions about how much of a product must be produced within the nation in order for it to qualify as "domestic" rather than "foreign"—and how to measure such things—are consuming millions of hours of legal time, here and abroad. What percentage of its value must originate at home in order that it be deemed a domestic product? May the cost of advertising and marketing the product be included in the tally? What about interest payments to banks located within the nation? And so on.

Such decisions often require delicate diplomatic maneuvers. In the 1980s, French bureaucrats limited Japanese automobile imports to 3% of the French market, but then faced the awesome task of explaining to Margaret Thatcher why Nissan Bluebirds, assembled in Britain, 80% of whose parts came from Europe, would be subject to the quota. The bureaucrats failed. (France and Italy are now insisting that Toyotas and Hondas made in Britain be counted against the proposed 15% Community-wide quota for Japanese automobile sales.)

When in 1989 Taiwan tried to apply its ban on Japanese car imports to Toyotas assembled in the U.S., it was the Bush administration's turn to express outrage—and Taiwan backed down. In a remarkably facile, though somewhat less successful turnabout, the administration then attempted to beat back a European Community ruling that Ricoh copiers assembled in California were really "Japanese," and therefore subject to special import duties.

Vestigial Concerns

The notion that products have national origins is so deeply engrained that governments, and the publics they represent, are unable to adjust to the emerging reality. Preoccupied with vestigial concerns, they continue to focus on the wrong question: is it a "foreign" or a "domestic" product?

These contortions accomplish little more than distracting attention from a far more relevant issue: For any given product, which nation's workers are responsible for the high value-added activities—such as research, design, manufacturing engineering, complex fabrication and strategy? And which nation's workers do the lower value-added activities—unskilled assembly, warehousing and routine maintenance? A nation whose work force is largely in the former camp will achieve a high standard of living overall. One whose work force occupies the latter category will not.

International Issues of the Twenty-First Century

- **Ethics and Culture (Articles 32–34)**
- **Japan and Asia (Articles 35–37)**
- **Eastern Europe and Commonwealth of Independent States (Article 38)**
- **Western Europe (Articles 39–40)**
- **North America (Articles 41–43)**
- **Third World (Articles 44–46)**

The world is growing smaller. Cultures and the ethical systems that they include are coming into conflict with each other. What might be acceptable in one country might be unacceptable or even illegal in another. Dealing with these issues is going to be one of the more difficult tasks that will face industry in the future.

As the world economy enters the twenty-first century, it is faced with several issues that will have to be addressed. The first deals with the economic growth of Japan and its relations with the rest of the industrialized world. Japan now has a per capita gross national product higher than that of the United States. The Japanese have gone from zero and on the verge of starvation at the end of World War II, to being one of the three major economic powers in the world. The Japanese need not be ashamed of their accomplishments, because they have been nothing short of spectacular. They are, however, in a different position today than they were 45 years ago. The five largest commercial organizations in the world are Japanese. Over half of the ten largest banks in the world are Japanese. Japan is a mighty industrial power and the world's leading creditor nation. This means that Japan has to stop acting like the "poor little Japan" of the 1950s and start behaving like the "mighty industrial Japan" of the 1990s and beyond. Japan must open its markets to foreign goods on a broader scale than it already has. It must assume its rightful place in world leadership, perhaps, eventually, gaining a permanent seat on the Security Council of the United Nations (admittedly, not a very meaningful step in real terms, but one with great symbolic importance). Japanese organizations are going to be forced into becoming more multinational in scope as opposed to being focused on Japan. This is because they will be unable to ignore the talents of their non-Japanese employees if they want to be truly competitive in the world marketplace. It will take time for the Japanese to adjust to their new role and for the rest of the world to adjust to them, but with the recent events in Eastern Europe in mind, it may happen sooner and faster than anyone anticipates.

The new opportunities available in the former Eastern Bloc countries and the Commonwealth of Independent States are going to be at the forefront of events during the last decade of the twentieth century. This part of the world has been held back for the last 50 years (first with World War II and then the cold war), but now it may finally be opening. The only real problem in Eastern Europe will be one of patience. These people want what Western society has and they want it now. Unfortunately, the fact is that it is going to take time. It has taken the Japanese 45 years to get where they are today. The Poles and Hungarians are simply not going to be able to do it in a few years. Indeed, the story of economic development in the first half of the twenty-first century could easily be the rise of Europe and particularly Eastern Europe as an economic power. But it will not be a brief or simple story. These countries have a long way to go in their development. Capital investment in new plant and equipment, education, and a change in the culture of the population will be necessary for capitalism to take hold and be successful.

The big news in the coming decade will be the economic development of the European Economic Community (EC). This market represents a much larger market than that of the United States, but it is not without its problems. There is a great gulf between the standard of living in Portugal and Germany. Germany, the largest member of the EC, will be preoccupied with the assimilation of the former East Germany into its economic, social, and political life at least for the first several years of the decade. The next questions is, then what? If the EC does work economically, will it work politically? And even if it does work, will the member states be able to trust each other enough to go to a truly common currency, an issue that has been called into doubt in both France and Denmark in the past year? Political questions become very difficult. The English, the French, and the Germans have never really gotten along since the Middle Ages. Can they really undo 1500 years of history? The Germans with their robust economy and larger population must be careful not to dominate the union through the sheer force of their numbers and wealth. The British represent, perhaps, the greatest threat to bolt the community, as demonstrated by their recent withdrawal from the European currency agreement. British commitment to the EC remains tenuous, and it will be interesting to see what course they will take. The next ten years in the EC will be very interesting.

In North America, partially in response to Japan and the

Unit 7

EC, the United States, Canada, and Mexico are on the verge of forming a vast continental megamarket. While there will be many problems in integrating these three economies with each other, especially Mexico's, the trend is clear. Unite and be strong, or remain divided and be weak.

Finally, the developed countries are going to have to address questions concerning the lesser and least developed world, not just China, but Africa, Latin America, and India as well. These areas have the fastest population growth and the fewest resources. Many of these societies still contain the vestiges of tribal rivalry and conflict that need to be overcome before they can truly become a nation. The problems of the Third World continue to grow while the attention of the world is focused on the developments in Eastern Europe and the Common Market. And they will not go away. Any global agreements that ignore poor countries are doomed to failure. The Third World must be allowed and helped to participate in the economic growth of the planet or it will eventually pull down the rest of the world with the weight of its own poverty.

Looking Ahead: Challenge Questions

Ethical concepts and standards are different in many societies. How can a manager of a multinational corporation deal with these differences?

Japan has come a long way since 1945. What do you think the position of Japan will be in the twenty-first century? How do you think other countries will react?

Political and economic unification in the EC is not going as smoothly as many had thought. Why do you think this is?

Eastern Europe and the Commonwealth of Independent States have gone through a long winter of economic stagnation. How do you see them developing in the future?

The North American Free Trade Agreement will integrate the economies of Canada, Mexico, and the United States. Do you think this is a good idea? Why or why not?

The Third World seems to have been left behind in the new economic developments around the world. Do you think this is wise? Can they be ignored?

Adapting Ethical Decisions to a Global Marketplace

KENT HODGSON

A smaller planet has put nations and peoples face-to-face as never before. Only now are we coming to grips with how intertwined our customs and values really are. They are as different yet proximate as camels loping by Abram tanks in the desert; mud-and-thatch huts only minutes away from million-dollar suburban homes; or foreign nationals graduating from Harvard Business School and returning to villages in Yemen or Panama, while their American counterparts interview for Xerox and Citicorp in Manhattan.

In part of Africa, a "family" celebration at the conclusion of a business deal—a party for which you are asked to pay—may well be a sign of friendship and lasting business relationships, not a personal payoff. "Grease" payments to customs officials in some countries may be part of their earning a living wage—not blackmail. In a large number of countries, custom, law and religion support the fact that women are denied personal and professional rights of equality.

Each of these practices is part of some group's ethical standards and affects business dealings between you and the group's members.

Each of these practices also represents a problem of differences—a conflict of values and norms among stakeholders—but not necessarily of right versus wrong, truth against falsehood or knowledge encountering ignorance. It is certainly not a question of our "good ethics" versus their "bad ethics." Such a view begs the integrity question, but more important, it risks destroying any sense of cooperation based on mutual trust and goodwill.

The real challenge is to bridge differences and value gaps, and hurdle our own perceived obstacles (see related story in *MR* April 1992, page 42). In today's world, there is much to be accomplished and mutually gained through understanding and respect across cultural lines. The opportunities are there, but so is the clash of values and interests.

A basic step in finding practical solutions to cultural challenges in a global market is to answer two initial questions: First, do you accept the premise that most decisions involve both business and ethics? Second, are you an American businessperson or member of an organization that happens to do business overseas, or are you a global businessperson or member of an organization that happens to have headquarters in the United States?

Your answer to the first question embodies a key philosophical commitment. An affirmative answer means adoption of primary working values and principles—like the health and welfare of customers—from which action decisions will be made. Your answer to the second question determines a key responsibility commitment; it makes other countries and peoples either valued stakeholder partners or just potential profit centers and resource sites.

STAKEHOLDER VIEWPOINTS

Another step toward better global decision making is to be aware of, and acknowledge, the clash among different cultures, values and principles. This acknowledgement is really a process of learning about other cultures without making business or moral judgments based solely on American customs and mores. You should know the historical, ethnic, cultural, political, legal and religious facts about a country or region, as these facts influence the way the people think, interact and do business. Then you should

Excerpted from "A Rock and a Hard Place: Making Ethical Business Decisions When the Choices are Tough," by Kent Hodgson (AMACOM 1992), $19.95.

From *Management Review,* May 1992, pp. 53-57. Reprinted with permission of the publisher, from *A Rock and a Hard Place: Making Ethical Decisions When The Choices Are Tough.* Copyright © 1992 by Kent Hodgson. Published by AMACOM, a division of the American Management Association. All rights reserved.

allow those facts to affect your thinking and acting.

Acknowledgment of the differences between peoples should also include a tolerance of diversity. Our values, beliefs, customs and ethics are not the only acceptable ones. Many nations have value systems that did not evolve from Graeco-Roman and Anglo-Saxon roots, which emphasize the rule of law. Americans easily forget how relatively young and unique the U.S. Constitution and Bill of Rights are. Indeed, most other systems were practiced for centuries before the United States existed.

The values and customs of other nations are not necessarily primitive, degraded or wrong because they are different from ours. Hence, they don't call for our immediate suspicion, distrust or condemnation. Until proved otherwise, they are only different—having evolved under distinct geographies, conditions and heritages.

By example, let's look at the practical problems of bribery and payoffs. Most foreign governments, including many well known for corruption, have enforced statutes against most forms of private payoff. Yet in some countries of Africa, ancient traditions take precedence over law. Payoffs have become the norm and are rooted in a "communal heritage," in which a community leader's wealth was shared with the community; those who hoarded were scorned. The Nigerian practice of "dash"—private pay for private service—traces back to trade in the form of gifts exchanged for labor.

American organizations frequently deal through foreign nationals who have been educated in the United States, know American business ways, but are very much a part of their own culture. They may hold seemingly conflicting values: some instilled in the West, others a part of their local tradition and life. They may see no conflict in negotiating along Western lines and then reverting to communal traditions when discussing more private remuneration. These people need not be labeled completely corrupt; rather, they are drawn by both indigenous and Western values. They may have American ideals of personal business enrichment and want to adhere to communal obligations at the same time.

If you are involved in business with Third World countries, you need to understand three widespread traditions that affect business transactions and added remunerations: the inner circle, future favors and the gift exchange.

□ *Inner circle.* Communal societies divide people into two groups: Those with whom they have relationships, and those with whom they have none—the goal being group prosperity and protection. There are the "in" people and the "out" people. The "ins" are family; the "outs" are strangers. In East and West Africa, inner circles can be true relatives, comrades or persons of similar age or region. In China, they may be those who share the same dialect; in India, members of the same caste. These are not unlike the "old boy networks" in the United States. The effect in many of these countries is to restrict social and business dealings to those with whom the businessperson has safe, trusting relationships. Often that trust is forthcoming if Westerners willing to honor communal values become part of the inner circle.

□ *Future favors.* The system of future favors operates within the inner circles. In Japan it is known as "inner duty," in Kenya, "inner relationship," and in the Philip-

WORKING WITH YOUR PRINCIPLES—AND THEIRS

Awareness and acknowledgment of differences in values among regions should bring about changes in your thinking and initiatives.

Practices you view as questionable, illegal or simply exploitative may be revealed as local tradition, courtesy and even friendship. I'm not suggesting that you break or ignore your own country's laws or those of other nations. Nor am I condoning begging, blackmail or bribery. This would spell financial, legal and ethical trouble for you, your organization and possibly those of other countries. But you can take initiatives other than outright rejection of legitimate values different from yours on the one hand, or completely selling out your own values on the other.

You can capitalize on new and existing opportunities for business in the following general ways:

1. Become more sensitive to the customs, values and practices of other peoples, which they themselves view as moral, traditional, practical and effective.

2. Don't judge the business customs of others—when different from your own—as necessarily immoral, corrupt, primitive or unworkable. Assume they are legitimate and workable until proved otherwise.

3. Find legitimate ways to operate from their ethical and commercial points of view; do not demand that they operate only by your ground rules.

4. Avoid rationalizing borderline actions, which usually are justified by the following:

□ "This isn't *really* illegal or immoral."
□ "This is in the organization's and my best interest."
□ "We're safe; no one will find us out."
□ "The organization will condone this and protect me."

5. Refuse to do business when stakeholder options violate or seriously compromise laws or fundamental organizational values.

6. Conduct relationships and negotiations as openly and aboveboard as possible—including reports to stakeholders and public accountability.

7. Avoid purely legalistic but ethically questionable strategies, such as calling "agents" (who are accountable to employers) "distributors" (who are not).

—*K.H.*

pines, "inner debt." In these traditions, the person obligated to another is expected to repay the favor sometime in the future. Some form of favor or service will repay the earlier debt; this repayment then places the grantor of the original favor under future obligation. Lifelong shifting obligations create relationships of trust and are the basis for doing business.

□ *Gift exchange.* In many non-Western circles, the gift exchange tradition has evolved into a business tool: Gifts begin a process of future favors. They are an immediate sign of gratitude or hospitality, but upon acceptance, they generate an obligation that the recipient must someday repay.

Inner circles, future favors and gift exchanges exist in American society also, but they don't usually have the same sense of obligation—either in the present or in the future. Nor is there the same sense of "family" with ensuing trust or loyalty present. Rather, many Americans feel a sense of ethical wariness when the relationship seems to move beyond gratitude, courtesy or friendliness to even remotely suggest influence in decision making.

THE RESULTS SYSTEM

Looking closely at the consequences of foreign practices rather than the actions themselves can clarify difficult situations. Gift giving is a good example. Solicitation of gifts has no place in U.S. business circles when it smacks of exploitation. This may be true in other countries too, but foreign colleagues often are at a loss to know how to initiate honorable, lasting relationships that form around business ventures—especially when Americans have little time for social amenities, are ignorant of local traditions or are wary of the exchange of gifts that creates obligations and trust.

Foreigners often take on the role of initial giver or may suggest that gift giving is the traditional way of entering the local business system. This role is viewed as a courteous and acceptable means of furthering business. You should look at the true purpose and legitimate consequences of such gift giving, considered in a local context other than your own.

An American company that exclusively manufactured and distributed medical devices for human implantation was asked for payment outside the contract; if it did not comply, it would lose the right to sell in a certain foreign country. The company had to weigh payment to certain nongovernmental parties against its business interests as well as the life-and-death need of hundreds of citizens who could not obtain the device by any other means. Weighing the good consequences of an action against a questionably ethical "means to the end" makes for a tough call. Yet a decision for remuneration in some form could well be the right one, given the importance of the devices versus an unwanted but unavoidable payment.

THE RESPONSIBILITY SYSTEM

A promise to respond to important stakeholders in a spirit of cooperation also allows for new initiatives in doing business in foreign countries. Whereas directly granting requests for private monies exposes U.S. organizations to financial and legal threats, invoking the principle of responsibility to—but not for—other stakeholders makes alternate answers appropriate. Nonmonetary public service benefits could well replace payoffs and satisfy the needs of both sides, for instance.

I wonder if the specter of foreign payoffs and bribes doesn't sometimes blind American organizations to the fact that technical expertise, follow-up satisfaction and customer service also are powerful incentives to buy. Responsibility to the customer through quality, partnering and service is the name of the game today. It has top priority within the United States—why not overseas as well? While firmly rejecting direct private payoffs, you may counter with monies clearly directed at needed help to others not touched by the contracts themselves. Even if these funds make the foreign contacts richer, in the long run some portion of the wealth is often shared communally with many relatives and "mates."

In fact, Kenya and Indonesia have made such requests of U.S. companies. It is not uncommon for non-Western colleagues of American organizations to view requests for private monies as a way of helping themselves, but also as a means to aid larger groups and their nations.

Responsibility also may suggest that donations could be open contributions to build schools, hospitals, medical clinics or agricultural projects. Such donations could be directed to the provinces or villages of the foreign counterparts or colleagues. Donating services, tools or machine parts is another alternative to private payoffs. Tanzanian poaching patrols have been helped in this way by British companies, and Coca-Cola hired Egyptians to plant acres of orange trees. Both cases resulted in needed political favor, increased local employment and goodwill.

The object, of course, is self-interest on both sides. But cooperation and goodwill are the responsible means. Public service, donations, employment, social progress and the use of local customs and traditions are far superior to bribes, misunderstanding, or simply walking away from mutual business opportunity and benefit.

America's Foreign Corrupt Practices Act of 1977 (FCPA) prohibits payments to foreign officials, political parties or candidates for the purpose of influencing an act or decision intended to

In today's world, there is much to be accomplished and mutually gained through understanding and respect across cultural lines.

THE MAGNIFICENT SEVEN PRINCIPLES

1. Dignity of human life. The lives of people are to be respected. Human beings, by the fact of their existence, have value and dignity. We may not act in ways that directly intend to harm an innocent person. Human beings have a right to live; we have an obligation to respect that right to life. Human life is to be preserved and treated as sacred.

2. Autonomy. All persons are intrinsically valuable and have the right to self-determination. We should act in ways that demonstrate each person's worth, dignity, and right to free choice. We have a right to act in ways that assert our own worth and legitimate needs. We should not use others as mere "things," or only as means to an end. Each person has an equal right to basic human liberty, compatible with a similar liberty for others.

3. Honesty. The truth should be told to those who have a right to know it. Honesty is also known as integrity, truth-telling and honor. One should speak and act so as to reflect the reality of the situation. Speaking and acting should mirror the way things really are. There are times when others have the right to hear the truth from us; there are times when they do not.

4. Loyalty. Promises, contracts and commitments should be honored. Loyalty includes fidelity, promise keeping, maintaining the public trust, good citizenship, excellence in quality of work, reliability, commitment, and honoring just laws, rules and policies. One should honor and keep confidences, proprietary information and personal private information that is freely and willingly shared. People should fulfill written and verbal contracts and commitments. They should fulfill just rules, laws and policies.

5. Fairness. People should be treated justly. People have the right to be treated fairly, impartially and equitably. People also have the obligation to treat others fairly and justly. Everyone has the right to the necessities of life. Justice includes equal, unbiased treatment. Fairness tolerates diversity and accepts differences in people and their ideas. All employees have the right to fair treatment under work contracts, company policies and procedures, and the law.

6. Humaneness. This has two parts: Our actions ought to accomplish good; and we should avoid doing evil. We should do good to others and to ourselves. We should have concern for the well-being of others; usually, we show this concern in the form of compassion, kindness, serving and caring. We should act and speak in ways that benefit our valid self-interests and those of others. We must avoid actions that are evil.

7. The common good. Actions should accomplish the greatest good for the greatest number of people. One should act and speak in ways that benefit the welfare of the largest number of people, while trying to protect the rights of individuals.

—*K.H.*

obtain or retain business. Companies and their managers also are liable if they know, or had reason to know, that their agents used payments from a U.S. concern to pay foreign officials for a prohibited purpose.

Nowhere does the FCPA prohibit the use of funds to aid developing societies. You and your organization often can solve ethical/business dilemmas by turning potential private payoffs into public services. Such decisions then would be openly defensible and justifiable on ethical as well as legal grounds—a powerful argument.

THREE-STEP PROCESS

Ultimately, you will want to apply the following process to issues or dilemmas posed in the global marketplace:

1. Examine the situation. Acknowledgment of the histories, customs and values of the people involved gives added insight into the critical facts of the situation. You will be better able to identify the key stakeholders, who may be more numerous than in the United States. Communal traditions, inner circle relationships, and other non-Western colleagues lengthen the list.

2. Establish the dilemma. Identify the working principles and norms that drive each of the stakeholder options (i.e., why they want their options chosen). Since foreign values and principles are likely to differ from those you quickly assign to American clients, this will help you focus the issue or dilemma.

With a more balanced acknowledgment of why foreigners hold certain values and "stakes" when approaching business, you will better understand their intentions. Projecting the outcomes of the stakeholders' options should then be closer to reality and less colored by your own values and principles.

Then you can attempt to determine the actions that stakeholders will take to produce the outcome they want. At this point, ask whether those actions, as means to the end, violate your own or organizational principles. You may see significant clashes of your principles, your organization's principles, and your laws with theirs. But you also will find common values.

Awareness of their values and customs will help you judge more accurately and fairly whether the means they will use in fulfillment of their options are acceptable or unacceptable ground rules for you.

3. Evaluate the options. The key to value-based decision making is to choose an option for action that flows from business values and principles rooted responsibly in the Magnificent Seven General Principles (see box this page). Given your awareness of the similarities and differences in interpretation of these principles by other people, identify which principle is driving each stakeholder option, including your own.

Finally, compare the General Principles behind each option. Which is the most responsible principle in this situation? The answer to this question will come as a result of weighing the General Principles that drive all the options.

One step toward better global decision making is to be aware of the clash among different cultures, values and principles.

MOVING FORWARD

Awareness and acknowledgment of differences, respect for traditions other than your own, changes in thinking and in initiatives, principled and responsible decisions flowing from a practical decision-making process—all these will help open the door to waiting opportunities.

It would be naive to think that all the differences and contradictions between our business and ethical systems can be overcome to the mutual satisfaction of all. Some differences will never be reconciled.

No country or its businesspeople should have to sell out to another. But Americans have not been sensitive and open enough to business and ethical systems other than our own. While different from yours and mine in many ways, the cultures and customs of other countries are not beyond a working spirit of what we both would call, in our own ways, cooperation and shared moral responsibility. □

RJR NABISCO:

TRANSNATIONAL TOBACCO TRAFFICKER

Philip Mattera

Philip Mattera is the author of Inside U.S. Business *(Business One Irvin) and* World Class Business: A Guide to the 100 Most Powerful Global Corporations *(Henry Holt & Co., 1992), on which this article is based.*

THE DOMINANT U.S. CIGARETTE COMPANY until the early 1980s, R.J. Reynolds, — now RJR Nabisco — has been most widely known in recent years as the object of a dramatic takeover battle. That contest, which became a symbol of the financial excesses of the 1980s, resulted in the largest corporate transaction ever consummated: a $25 billion leveraged buyout. The resultant debt, critics charge, has put pressure on RJR to aggressively hawk cigarettes to vulnerable populations—African Americans, poor women and children in the United States, and people in the Third World and Eastern Europe.

From Camels to Fig Newtons

RJR's origins can be traced to the arrival of 25-year-old Richard Joshua Reynolds in the town of Winston, North Carolina in 1875. Winston was the production center of the new flue-cured leaf that made the best chewing tobacco. For several decades Reynolds built a prosperous chewing-tobacco business, selling the plugs under dozens of brand names.

During the 1890s, the company fell prey to the tobacco empire being assembled by James Duke, who controlled the rights to cigarette rolling machines. After the Supreme Court broke up the Tobacco Trust in 1911, R.J. Reynolds, independent once again, charged into the cigarette business. Like many "advances" in the tobacco industry, this initiative took the form of a marketing blitz. Using a massive advertising campaign announcing that "the Camels are coming," the company succeeded in creating the first national cigarette brand.

Camels became so popular during World War I — thanks in large part to the free samples given to the U.S. troops — that General Pershing himself contacted the company to be sure that the doughboys would not run out of smokes. After the war, the brand was etched onto the U.S. consciousness with the famous slogan "I'd walk a mile for a Camel." That line was most conspicuous on a billboard (which emitted real smoke rings) that stood in New York's Times Square for many years.

RJR, like its brethren in the tobacco industry, took great pains to resist the growing realization of the hazards of smoking — an awareness that began to be created on a large scale by a 1952 article in Reader's Digest. RJR advertised, for example: "More doctors smoke Camels than any other cigarette." While downplaying the significance of the evidence of smoking's hazards, RJR hedged its bets in 1954 by introducing a filtered cigarette brand called Winston, which went on to become one of the perennially best-selling brands in the United States.

When the pressure on the industry became more intense in the wake of the U.S. Surgeon General's 1964 report, Reynolds began to diversify its operations. Among its purchases were Chun King foods, Del Monte and Sea-Land shipping. In 1970, the company took the word "tobacco" out of its name and rechristened itself R.J. Reynolds Industries.

RJR accelerated its diversification strategy in the 1980s. In 1982 the target was Heublein, a distilled spirits producer founded in 1875. Heublein sold the first prepared cocktails and survived Prohibition by selling A-1 Steak Sauce. After World War II, the company transformed U.S. drinking habits by heavily promoting

From *Multinational Monitor,* January/February 1992, pp. 38-41. Reprinted with permission of *Multinational Monitor,* P.O. Box 19405, Washington, DC 20036, $25/yr.

vodka and introducing mixed drinks, such as the Bloody Mary, that used the Russian liquor. In 1971, Heublein acquired the Kentucky Fried Chicken fast-food chain.

Once it had swallowed Heublein, Reynolds turned its appetite to a $5 billion deal: Nabisco Brands. The target was the product of the 1981 merger of Nabisco and Standard Brands. Nabisco itself was born of the merger of two rival baking groups in 1898. Originally known as the National Biscuit Company, it developed the first brand name cracker (Uneeda) and went on to dominate the cookie and cracker market with brands such as Ritz, Oreo and Fig Newton. Standard Brands was built on Fleischmann yeast and gin, Royal baking powder and Chase & Sanborn coffee.

The transformation of Reynolds continued through the 1980s. In 1986, the Kentucky Fried Chicken operation was sold to PepsiCo and the following year most of the rest of Heublein was purchased by Britain's Grand Metropolitan for $1.2 billion. The Canada Dry and Sunkist soft drinks businesses, which had been acquired only a few years earlier, were sold to Cadbury Schweppes.

But the real drama came in 1988. A bold proposal by chief executive F. Ross Johnson to take the company private through a leveraged buyout prompted an intense bidding war, as well as a great deal of public criticism of the greed and ruthlessness of the parties maneuvering for control. In the end, the winner was Kohlberg Kravis Roberts & Co. (KKR), which acquired the firm for $25 billion, the largest takeover ever.

As part of the effort to service the company's gargantuan debt load, nearly $6 billion in assets have been sold off since the KKR takeover. These have included several European and Asian food businesses, Chun King and much of Del Monte Foods. In 1990 and 1991, the company also engaged in an extensive recapitalization, which involved the trade of debt for equity, including the reissuance of common and convertible preferred stock.

The company's 1990 annual report, the first in three years, tried very hard to dispel the idea that the leveraged buyout had stifled investment and promoted short-term thinking. "The impact has been just the opposite at RJR Nabisco," the report said. "We have a new sense of urgency and entrepreneurial energy." Yet the report put an inordinate emphasis on generating cash flow, vital to the company's struggle to meet its debt payments.

This quest has made the company obsessive about cutting costs, so today's RJR is a much less flamboyant operation than it was during the days of Ross Johnson, when millions were spent on a fleet of corporate jets. Even so, interest payments keep the company's bottom line solidly in the red.

A pushy pusher

Through all of its turbulence and diversification efforts, RJR has maintained its core commitment to selling cigarettes, with tobacco sales accounting for 58 percent of the company's 1990 net income. RJR and its subsidiaries and licensees manufacture cigarettes in the United States and 30 other countries. The company's tobacco products are marketed in approximately 160 nations.

The company's leading cigarette brands are Winston, Salem, Doral, Camel and Vantage. Nearly all of RJR's domestic tobacco-manufacturing facilities are located in and around Winston-Salem, North Carolina. Among these is the 2 million-square-foot Tobaccoville plant that went into full operation in 1987.

Having established itself as the U.S. market leader after World War I, RJR remained the top cigarette company until 1983, when it lost the position to Philip Morris. Savvy marketing of Marlboro and other brands enabled Philip Morris to pass RJR, which market analysts came to view as being a step slower. RJR's 1991 U.S. market share stood at 28 percent.

Entering the second half of the 1980s, RJR was losing market share to Philip Morris and cheaper, discount cigarettes on the one hand, and, on the other, facing the industry-wide problem of a shrinking market as customers quit smoking or die. The company's problems multiplied with the KKR takeover and resultant debt accrual. Desperate to boost sales, RJR has been "extremely aggressive" since the takeover, says Greg Connolly, director of the Massachusetts state office for Nonsmoking and Health. The company has pursued, with varying degrees of success, a number of controversial marketing strategies over the last five years.

- In 1987, RJR introduced the Premier brand, designed to be a "smokeless" cigarette. The company withdrew Premier from the market in 1989 due to unfavorable consumer response.
- In 1989, RJR ran a four-page pullout advertisement for its Camel brand which offered tips on "how to impress someone at the beach." The advertisement suggested, "Run into the water, grab someone and drag her back to shore, as if you've saved her from drowning. The more she kicks and screams, the better." In the wake of widespread protests from women's and health advocacy groups, RJR pulled the ad, with RJ Reynolds Tobacco chair James Johnston saying, "The ad should never have been run."
- In 1990, RJR planned to introduce a cigarette aimed at African Americans. A wave of protest led by Health and Human Services Secretary Louis Sullivan forced RJR to cancel the brand, known as Uptown, before it was test-marketed. Sullivan blasted the company for "pursuing profits at the expense of the health and well-being of our poor and minority citizens." RJR did not give up Uptown happily. A company official stated, "We regret that a small coalition of anti-smoking zealots apparently believes that black smokers are somehow different from others who choose to smoke."
- Shortly after the cancellation of Uptown, the Washington Post disclosed RJR plans to market a new brand called Dakota, to be aimed at young, poorly educated, white females. The Dakota revelations drew criticism from Sullivan and other anti-smoking advocates, who again denounced the company for targeting

vulnerable populations. The new brand also generated protests from many North and South Dakotans, who formed a group called Dakotans Against Dakota Cigarettes and collected 25,000 signatures on petitions opposing the cigarettes.

RJR denies that Dakota is aimed at women, claiming that it rejected the widely publicized marketing plans. RJR spokesperson Didi Witt says, "The cigarette was never meant to be targeted for any market other than adult male and female smokers, particularly Marlboro smokers." RJR did not withdraw the Dakota brand, and it is currently test-marketing Dakotas in Houston and Phoenix.

- In late 1990, the company began to mount an aggressive challenge to Philip Morris with the splashy introduction of super-low-tar Camel Ultra Lights. The company earned plaudits from market watchers for introducing the brand before Philip Morris began marketing its Marlboro Ultra Lights nationwide.
- One of RJR's most successful—and most criticized—strategies has been the use of the cartoon figure "Joe Camel" to promote its Camel brand. The cartoon figure, which appears in a leather jacket and is often surrounded by admiring women, was introduced in 1987 and is credited with bolstering Camel's market share. Joe Camel has generated intense protests from anti-smoking advocates, who claim that the character is designed to appeal to children and teens.

Like the rest of the tobacco industry, RJR is also turning to international markets to bolster its sales. Although Philip Morris's international presence is much stronger, RJR's Tobacco International has reasonably good brand presence in much of Europe and some other key foreign markets. In late 1990, RJR and Philip Morris were asked by the Soviet Union to supply 34 billion cigarettes to alleviate a dangerous shortage of tobacco products in the country. The company has also moved to take advantage of the transformation of Eastern Europe by acquiring the Club brand, one of the best-selling cigarettes in the former East Germany. In 1991, it was exploring additional investments in Poland, Hungary and Czechoslovakia. RJR is the only U.S. cigarette company with a manufacturing facility in China, the world's largest cigarette market.

Labor relations

R.J. Reynolds has a reputation as one of the most anti-union employers in the country. It has been on the AFL-CIO boycott list for nearly 40 years. Unions have organized the company, but they tend to get dislodged as a result of company resistance. This happened after both World War I and World War II. RJR beat back an organizing effort by the Bakery, Confectionary and Tobacco Workers (BCTW) in 1974, and a 1989 BCTW organizing drive did not lead to an election. Raymond Scannell, research director of the BCTW, says the company remains virulently anti-union, but that it has grown more sophisticated in its tactics. "It is still fair to say that RJR is one of the most anti-union employers in the country," he says. "They have become one of the premier practitioners of what is called 'union-free' management." Overseas, however, several of the company's tobacco operations are unionized.

The BCTW does represent workers at Nabisco, and the union continued to have a working relationship with the company even after it was taken over by RJR, with relations improving after the KKR takeover. Helped by federal mediators, the company and the union began cooperating on projects such as a $5 million jointly administered fund to help workers learn the higher-tech skills needed in modern bakeries. In recognition of the new labor-management harmony, the company and the BCTW were given an award for "excellence in industrial relations" by the Federal Mediation and Conciliation Service in 1991. Some rank and file workers, however, are not pleased with the results of this labor-management cooperation. In September 1991, BCTW members at a local union in Portland, Oregon, concerned that seniority and job security were being eroded, voted to abandon the team concept.

Deadly hypocrisy

Any company that markets a product which causes as much death and suffering as cigarettes will naturally draw widespread condemnation. Connolly, of the Massachusetts Office for Nonsmoking and Health, uses words like "despicable," "reckless" and "irresponsible" when he speaks of RJR.

Ultimately, however, Connolly argues, RJR is most morally culpable for profiting from products that people like Henry Kravis, the main engineer of the KKR takeover of RJR Nabisco, would never use. While the health-conscious Kravis and his peers in high society have rejected smoking, they are marketing cigarettes to, and inflicting severe health problems on, poor and disadvantaged people.

Companies Use Cross-Cultural Training To Help Their Employees Adjust Abroad

Joann S. Lublin

Staff Reporter of The Wall Street Journal

BOULDER, Colo.—Dale Pilger, **General Motors** Corp.'s new managing director for Kenya, wonders if he can keep his Kenyan employees from interrupting his paper work by raising his index finger.

"The finger itself will offend," warns Noah Midamba, a Kenyan. He urges that Mr. Pilger instead greet a worker with an effusive welcome, offer a chair and request that he wait. It can be even trickier to fire a Kenyan, Mr. Midamba says. The government asked one German auto executive to leave Kenya after he dismissed a man—whose brother was the East African country's vice president.

Mr. Pilger, his adventurous wife and their two teen-agers, miserable about moving, have come to this Rocky Mountain college town for three days of cross-cultural training. The Cortland, Ohio, family learns to cope with being strangers in a strange land as consultants Moran, Stahl & Boyer International give them a crash immersion in African political history, business practices, social customs and nonverbal gestures. The training enables managers to grasp cultural differences and handle culture-shock symptoms such as self-pity.

Cross-cultural training is on the rise everywhere because more global-minded corporations moving fast-track executives overseas want to curb the cost of failed expatriate stints. "Probably between $2 billion and $2.5 billion a year is lost from failed assignments," says J. Stewart Black, an associate professor of business administration at Dartmouth's Tuck School. Nearly half of major U.S. companies now give executives cross-cultural training before foreign transfers, compared with about 10% a decade ago, consultants estimate.

The number of cultural-training providers also is growing. **Berlitz International** Inc. will set up a cross-cultural division this year, officials say, because a recent survey of 200 corporate clients found they needed cultural orientation more than its foreign-language training.

American businesses "are dumb if they don't use cross-cultural training," says Richard B. Jackson, personnel vice president of **Reynolds Metals** Co.'s overseas arm. The big aluminum maker's high rate of expatriate burnout fell "to almost zero," Mr. Jackson notes, after the company began using cross-cultural training in the late 1970s. Other concerns train U.S.-based executives as well because their global duties often take them abroad.

But as cross-cultural training gains popularity, it attracts growing criticism. A lot of the training is garbage, argues Robert Bontempo, assistant professor of international business at Columbia University. Even customized family training offered by companies like **Prudential Insurance Co. of America**'s Moran Stahl—which typically costs $6,000 for three days—hasn't been scientifically tested. "They charge a huge amount of money, and there's no evidence that these firms do any good" in lowering foreign-transfer flops, Prof. Bontempo contends.

"You don't need research" to prove that cross-cultural training works because so much money has been wasted on failed overseas assignments, counters Gary Wederspahn, director of design and development at Moran Stahl.

General Motors agrees. Despite massive cost cutting lately, the auto giant still spends nearly $500,000 a year on cross-cultural training for about 150 Americans and their families headed abroad. "We think this substantially contributes to the low [premature return rate] of less than 1% among GM expatriates," says Richard Rachner, GM general director of international personnel. That compares with a 25% rate at concerns that don't properly select and coach expatriates, he adds.

The Pilgers' experience reveals the benefits and drawbacks of such training. Mr. Pilger, a 38-year-old engineer employed by GM for 20 years, sought an overseas post but never lived abroad before. He finds the sessions "worthwhile" in readying him to run a vehicle-assembly plant that is 51% owned by Kenya's government. But he finds the training "horribly empty . . . in helping us prepare for the personal side of the move."

Dale and Nancy Pilger have just

Reprinted by permission of *The Wall Street Journal,* August 24, 1992, pp. B1, B9. Copyright © 1992 by Dow Jones & Company, Inc. All rights reserved worldwide.

spent a week in Nairobi. But the executive's scant knowledge of Africa becomes clear when trainer Jackson Wolfe, a former Peace Corps official, mentions Nigeria. "Is that where Idi Amin was from?" Mr. Pilger asks. The dictator ruled Uganda. With a sheepish smile, Mr. Pilger admits: "We don't know a lot about the world."

The couple's instructors don't always know everything about preparing expatriates for Kenyan culture, either. Mr. Midamba, an adjunct international-relations professor at Kent State University and son of a Kenyan political leader, concedes that he neglected to caution Mr. Pilger's predecessor against holding business dinners at Nairobi restaurants.

As a result, the American manager "got his key people to the restaurant and expected their wives to be there," Mr. Midamba recalls. But "the wives didn't show up." Married women in Kenya view restaurants "as places where you find prostitutes and loose morals," notes Mungai Kimani, another Kenyan trainer.

The blunder partly explains why Mr. Midamba goes to great lengths to teach the Pilgers the art of entertaining at home. Among his tips: Don't be surprised if guests arrive an hour early, an hour late or announce their departure four times.

The Moral Stahl program also zeros in on the family's adjustment (though not to Mr. Pilger's satisfaction). A family's poor adjustment causes more foreign-transfer failures than a manager's work performance. That is the Pilgers' greatest fear because 14-year-old Christy and 16-year-old Eric bitterly oppose the move. The lanky, boyish-looking Mr. Pilger remembers Eric's tearful reaction as: " 'You'll have to arrest me if you think you're going to take me to Africa.' "

While distressed by his children's hostility, Mr. Pilger still believes living abroad will be a great growth experience for them. But he says he promised Eric that if "he's miserable" in Kenya, he can return to Ohio for his last year of high school next year.

To east their adjustment, Christy and Eric receive separate training from their parents. The teens' activities include sampling Indian food (popular in Kenya) as well as learning how to ride Nairobi public buses, speak a little Swahili and juggle, of all things.

By the training's last day, both youngsters grudgingly accept being uprooted from friends, her swim team and his brand-new car. Going to Kenya "no longer seems like a death sentence," Christy, says. Eric mumbles that he may volunteer at a wild-game reserve.

But their usually upbeat mother has become increasingly upset as she hears more about a country troubled by drought, poverty and political unrest—where foreigners live behind walled fortresses. Now, at an international parenting session, she clashes with youth trainer Amy Kaplan over whether her offspring can safely ride Nairobi's public buses, even with Mrs. Pilger initially accompanying them.

"All the advice we've gotten is that it's deadly" to ride buses there, Mrs. Pilger frets. Ms. Kaplan retorts: "It's going to be hard" to let teen-agers do their own thing in Kenya, but then they'll be less likely to rebel. The remark fails to quell Mrs. Pilger's fears that she can't handle life abroad. "I'm going to let a lot of people down if I blow this," she adds, her voice quavering with emotion.

The Pilgers' experience suggests that U.S. managers and their families may need extra training overseas. At **Procter & Gamble** Co., for instance, cultural familiarization doesn't even begin until expatriates reach a foreign country. "For deep-rooted, subtle concepts, it's more effective" to train people that way, says Dartmouth's Prof. Black. "But it's more effective to do it before" expatriates leave home "than not at all."

JAPAN'S PACIFIC OVERTURES

HOW JAPAN SEES ITSELF

AT HOME, IN ASIA, AND AROUND THE WORLD

Kenneth B. Pyle

Kenneth B. Pyle is a professor of East Asian studies at the University of Washington. He was the founding editor of the Journal of Japanese Studies, *serving from 1974 until 1986, and the director of the Henry M. Jackson School of International Studies at the University of Washington from 1978 to 1988. This article is based on a paper presented to the U.S. Institute of Peace and is the basis of his book* The Japanese Question: Power and Purpose in the New Era *(AEI Press, 1992).*

On the eve of President George Bush's visit to Japan, the editors asked one of our country's leading experts on Japan to tell our readers what we should expect from Japan today and why. Kenneth Pyle begins his essay by examining Japan's postwar strategy—its singular commitment to economic growth, its deliberate shyness abroad. He observes that while this strategy produced the economic success Japan now enjoys, it left unformed those institutions necessary for a well-developed foreign policy. Japan is now wrestling with its role abroad, and its early steps to define that role can be seen in its activities in Asia and its use of foreign aid. Pyle argues that in response, America needs to devise positive measures to link U.S. and Japanese economic and security concerns.

Japan made its way in the post-World War II era by pursuing its own carefully defined self-interest and by deliberately frustrating all attempts to engage it in collective security arrangements. This strategy and the foreign policy that underlay it were a brilliant success. Japan could rely on its alliance with the United States to guarantee its security and at the same time maintain the international free-trade order, while it was free to follow policies of economic nationalism.

From time to time, Americans complained about the absence of reciprocity in the alliance, but these complaints were always met with rejoinders from the Japanese about their country's pacifism, the constitutional constraints that had been placed on them after World War II, the fears of Japan's neighbors about potential expansion, and the specter of a revived Japanese militarism. These assertions of Japan's inability to play a broader role in the international community are now losing much of their persuasive power abroad and even in Japan as a result of recent changes in the international system. Japan's emergence as an economic power and the winding down of the Cold War have radically changed the context of the alliance. Furthermore, the grudging and limited Japanese contribution to the Persian Gulf coalition has raised questions abroad about Japan's future national purpose, its policies toward collective security arrangements, and its capacity to change from a country intent on its own economic aims to one that is capable of becoming an international leader.

Within Japan, these developments are causing an intense self-examination, an exercise that will be especially difficult given the unwillingness of postwar Japanese leaders to lay a foundation in public opinion for international responsibility. Japan's reflection on its postwar experience and its examination of its future role form the backdrop for President Bush's visit this month.

America has a unique opportunity to put itself at the head of long-range trends in Asia, and to do this we must redefine our relationship with Japan. To understand what President Bush can do to further these goals on his visit to Japan, it is important to understand how we and Japan have come to views each of us now holds about the relationship. The changes in the Soviet Union make this exercise particularly critical now.

TOGETHER WITH THIS PRIMARY COMMITMENT TO ECONOMIC NATIONALISM WAS A DETERMINATION TO AVOID ANY COLLECTIVE SECURITY COMMITMENTS AND ANY INVOLVEMENT WITH SECURITY AFFAIRS BEYOND THE HOME ISLANDS.

Two Versions of National Purpose

Largely because of their preoccupation with the Cold War, Americans were slow to understand Japan's fundamental national purpose

From *The American Enterprise,* November/December 1991, pp. 28-37. Copyright © 1991 by The American Enterprise. Distributed by The New York Times Special Features.

in the postwar period. Essentially, Japan has had two coexisting versions of its national purpose since the end of World War II. One, which Americans did understand, was a popular, public position that was based on the imposed constitutional order and its associated reforms and that had the support of most groups across the political spectrum. According to this version, Japan was rebuilding its national livelihood on the basis of a new democratic order and in line with the role that its constitution envisioned for Japan in the world. Their experience as the first victims of the atomic age convinced them that the sovereign prerogative to go to war must be renounced. Japan would lead the world into a new era in which states forswore the settlement of disputes by resort to arms. Japan, in short, had a unique mission and would be an exception to the pattern of all other nations.

JAPAN ALONE AMONG THE ADVANCED INDUSTRIAL NATIONS HAS BEEN SHIELDED FROM THE SOCIAL STRESSES OF AN ACTIVE FOREIGN POLICY. THE COST OF THIS LOW-PROFILE POLICY IS BECOMING INCREASINGLY CLEAR.

This was the face the Japanese showed to the outside world. It was the way, for example, that a Japanese foreign minister addressing the United Nations would explain his country's goals in the world community. There is no doubt that this version of the national purpose appealed to, and was fervently held by, a substantial segment of the Japanese people. But it is clear that this view was sometimes cynically used by the postwar conservative leadership and that it served as a pretext for what was their more fundamental and genuine purpose of concentrating exclusively on the goals of economic nationalism. As former vice minister of the Ministry of International Trade and Industry (MITI) Naohiro Amaya wrote in 1988: "Postwar Japan defined itself as a cultural state holding the principles of liberalism, democracy, and peace, but these were only superficial principles. The fundamental objective was the pouring of all our strength into economic growth."

Together with, and corollary to, this primary commitment to economic nationalism was a determination to avoid any collective security commitments and any involvement with security affairs beyond the home islands. It is scarcely remembered today that in 1950 John Foster Dulles, then the special emissary of the secretary of state, tried to establish a regional security organization like NATO in the Pacific. Dulles proposed to Japan and other countries a Pacific Pact, a regional defense alliance that would facilitate Japanese rearmament but keep it under international control. The pact would have initially included the United States, Japan, Australia, New Zealand, the Philippines, and perhaps Indonesia. Dulles believed that such an alliance would internationalize Japanese military forces and "ease reconciliation" with the Japanese constitution. He was prepared to offer guarantees and override the objections of other Asian countries in order to secure their acquiescence to Japanese remilitarization and entry into a regional security organization. Such an arrangement, which would have paralleled the approach taken at the time toward Germany, remains in some form an option today for drawing Japanese defense efforts into a multilateral context and thereby defusing the tensions in the bilateral security treaty. It would encourage a responsible Japanese security commitment and ease concerns that its neighbors would have of an eventual independent Japanese military.

Shigeru Yoshida, who served as prime minister for nearly the entire period from 1946-1954, steadfastly refused to participate in such a multilateral Pacific security system. Instead, he was determined to use the circumstances of the Cold War to Japan's maximum advantage and to pursue a narrowly defined sense of economic self-interest. Yoshida contrived to trade bases on Japanese soil for an American guarantee of Japanese security. It might seem "devious," he confided to an aide, but the constitution provided a perfect pretext for resisting American pressure.

Yoshida and his successors built an elaborate set of policies to prevent Japan's being drawn into any overseas commitments whatsoever. When the Japanese Self-Defense Forces were organized in 1954 because of American pressure, the Upper House of the Parliament passed a unanimous resolution opposing the dispatch of forces overseas. It became the fixed position of subsequent prime ministers that participation in any collective security agreement would be unconstitutional. Other policies limited defense spending to 1 percent of GNP, proscribed arms and military technology exports, and prohibited Japanese production or possession of nuclear weapons and the introduction of nuclear armaments on its soil. Without these policies and their seemingly incontestable constitutional sanction, the pressure on Japan to contribute to the Cold War effort would have been well-nigh irresistible. As Sunao Sonoda, who served as foreign minister in 1977–1978, recalled: "The Americans were always asking us to do this and to do that, to take over part of the burden of their Far Eastern policies. But all their efforts were sabotaged by one Japanese cabinet after another."

The Casualties of Japan's International Isolationism

The advantage of maintaining a low posture in international affairs since World War II has been the ability to concentrate exclusively on economic growth while avoiding the extreme internal political divisions that an active foreign policy would have engendered. For most of the postwar period, there has been a tacit agreement between the conservative mainstream of the Liberal Democratic Party, which has held power since its formation in 1955, and the left-wing progressive camp to avoid the divisive issues of rearmament and constitutional revision. Japan alone among the advanced industrial nations has been shielded from the social stresses of an active foreign policy.

On the other hand, the cost of this low-profile policy is becoming increasingly clear. The Yoshida strategy began as a means of handling the international politics of the Cold War and the domestic politics of pacifism. But as it continued over the years, its success lengthened, and many of the institutions and processes required for an active and independent foreign policy were left undeveloped. While the Ministry of Finance, MITI, the Economic Planning Agency, and (on some issues) big business dominated the formulation of foreign policy, the growth of institutions of autonomous policymaking in the security field was stunted. Institutions of intelligence gathering, strategic thinking, crisis management, policy implementation, and of course the armed forces went undeveloped.

But a more costly and basic result of the moratorium that Japan has enjoyed on international involvement is the state of internal Japanese opinion. As a result of the Yoshida strategy, the conservatives abnegated the responsibilities of leadership in a democracy to inform and educate its citizenry about international responsibilities. The internal debate over the role Japan would play in the Gulf War demonstrated the divisions, parochialism, and isolationism that sway Japanese views, even among the elite. The opposition to a more positive foreign policy, that is, toward acceptance of collective security commitments, is less ideological today than it was in the past. Instead, opposition to the government's wholly innocuous United Nations Peace Cooperation Bill in the autumn of 1990, which would have permitted dispatching personnel to the Gulf, came from a mix of complacency, anti-American nationalism, and residual distrust of a situation in which the postwar restraints on an expanded military would be removed. Decades of shunning collective security arrangements, of accommodating left-wing opinion, and of minimalist interpretations of their constitution have left Japanese opinion adrift and reactive in its attitudes toward post-Cold War foreign policy. The Gulf crisis demonstrated once again that Japan's capacity to change, to develop policies that transcend its own narrow self-interest, and to play a role of international leadership in a way that would satisfy world expectations is severely limited by the institutional legacies of the postwar experience.

Japan's Asian Ascent

There is, however, one emerging role of leadership that will follow almost naturally from the trajectory of the postwar Japanese state: to lead Asia's emergence as the world's most dynamic economic region. This role is developing almost ineluctably from the needs of the Japanese economy, from international political-economic trends, and from the predilections of Japan's bureaucratic and business leadership of the country's dominant postwar institutions. The implications of this development for the United States and the international system are substantial.

A remarkable convergence of circumstances in the mid-1980s provided the opportunity for Japan's emergence as the core economy of an increasingly cohesive and interdependent region. Since 1985, Japan has acquired an impressive array of economic tools that make it possible to establish economic leadership in the region. The developments that made this power possible include the agreement negotiated at the Plaza Hotel in New York in 1985 that led to the rise in the value of the yen, Japan's emergence as the world's largest creditor and donor of official development assistance, liberalization of the Japanese capital market, and foreign pressure to restructure the Japanese economy so as to reduce its trade surpluses and increase the importation of manufactured goods. As a consequence of these developments, Japan was prepared to offer other Asian countries a persuasive set of economic inducements to follow its leadership: foreign aid, commercial loans, technology transfers, direct investment, and preferential access to the Japanese market.

In the late 1980s, Japanese bureaucrats began to devote their attention to the disposition of these sources of economic influence within the region. The task of formulating a comprehensive and coordinated approach to Asia in terms of economic policies very much fit the postwar inclination of the Japanese state, with its strength in economic institutions, capacity for bureaucratic planning and coordination, and ability to fine-tune policies to enhance market forces. Given Japan's reservoir of private capital for investment, its commitment to provide massive official aid, and its stores of transferable technologies, the bureaucrats could use a mix of government and private resources to promote Japanese influence and power. Concern that rising protectionism and development of trading blocs would restrict that access to Europe and North America further focused Japan's attention on Asia.

Speaking in Bangkok in June 1991, Kiichi Miyazawa, a former finance minister and perennial candidate for prime minister, said that Japan should lead an Asian economic bloc that included ASEAN (the Association of Southeast Asian Nations, established in 1967 and composed of Brunei, Indonesia, Malaysia, the Philippines, Singapore, and Thailand) and South Korea: that is, that Japan should use its economic resources to build the region's economic infrastructure for the long term and to help this bloc "outdo" the North American and European blocs. "The Asian economic zone," he said, "will outdo the North American economic zone and European economic zone at the beginning of the twenty-first century and assume a very crucial role." Economic complementarities, geographic proximity, and cultural traditions all further enhance the attractiveness of the proposed Japanese role in Asia.

The Ministry of Finance, MITI, the Economic Planning Agency, and the Ministry of Foreign Affairs undertook in the late 1980s

A 1988 STUDY BY [JAPAN'S] ECONOMIC PLANNING AGENCY RECOMMENDED A COMPREHENSIVE INTEGRATION OF THE ECONOMIES OF ASIA, WITH THE JAPANESE BUREAUCRACY SERVING AS THE MASTERMIND "ASIAN BRAIN," DETERMINING THE REGION'S DEVELOPMENT.

THE FAVORITE METAPHOR FOR THIS PATTERN OF DEVELOPMENT IS THE "FLYING GEESE" FORMATION, A LEAD ECONOMY WITH OTHERS RANKED BEHIND IN THE ORDER OF THEIR ECONOMIC STRENGTH AND TECHNICAL SOPHISTICATION.

major examinations of Japan's relations within the region and the ways in which Japan might promote the region's economic integration. A 1988 study by the Economic Planning Agency recommended a comprehensive integration of the economies of Asia, with the Japanese bureaucracy serving as the mastermind "Asian brain," determining the region's development through investment and technology. In 1987, MITI announced its New Asian Industries Development Plan, or New AID Plan, designed to relocate Japanese industry into lower-cost Asian countries, something that was happening anyway owing to normal economic forces. What the New AID Plan did was give MITI a tool to guide the market forces and thereby assert its influence over the process of restructuring the economy, easing trade frictions, and promoting future commercial advantage. Private investment, trade, and official development assistance should be coordinated, the report said, so they serve as "three sides of the same body."

Given the long experience that Japanese bureaucrats have had in creating institutions and formulating policies to promote Japan's own economy, what is likely to emerge is a series of policies to direct the regional division of labor under distinctly Japanese leadership. The goal of these various policies is a Japanese-style economic leadership that will advance the cause of Japan's domestic restructuring and improve its trade imbalance with the United States at the same time that it lays the basis for a loose, regionwide integration of economies under Japanese leadership.

Bureaucratic thinking envisions a kind of "benign division of labor" coordinated and presided over by Japan. The favorite metaphor for this pattern of development is the "flying geese" formation, a lead economy with others ranked behind in the order of their economic strength and technical sophistication. This analogy suggests a vertical division of labor not wholly unlike what was envisioned in Japan's prewar Pan-Asian ideology. For example, the report of the Ministry of Finance's Committee on Asia-Pacific Economic Research envisions a three-tier division of labor in Asia composed of Japan, the Newly Industrializing Economies (that is, South Korea, Hong Kong, Taiwan, and Singapore), and the ASEAN countries plus China. While denying that this would be a fixed structure, the report seems to minimize the possibility of changing the order of countries when it describes future development in the region:

"While each area continues to develop, a new international division of labor will be formed in a far higher dimension than in the past.... For the development of each of the three tiers, it is necessary that what Japan used to do should be done by the Asian NIEs, what they used to do should be done by the ASEAN countries, and Japan should enter into a far higher division. For this, it is indispensable for Japan to encourage maturer industries to make inroads abroad positively."

This means that under Japanese leadership, the countries of Asia would move successively up the ladder of the production cycle.

Aid is a powerful instrument for Tokyo bureaucrats to wield in planning the coordination of Asian economies. The Ministry of Finance's new vice minister for international affairs, Tadao Chino, declared in August 1991 that he would bend all his efforts toward transforming Japanese official development aid into a magnet for private capital, using it as "seed money to attract Japanese manufacturers." American aid has also been used to create markets, but what is distinctive about the emerging Japanese development aid program is its more highly coordinated and guided nature and its more unmitigatedly commercial purpose.

U.S. Influence Now

In the past, the United States exercised unchallenged leadership in the Pacific Basin. Through its support of international institutions such as the World Bank and the GATT, it created a favorable environment in which the economies of this region could flourish. The American government provided aid, and American multinationals made direct investment in the region. Technology was transferred, and American universities trained large numbers of Asians in science and engineering.

Thailand is the most dramatic example of how leadership roles have changed. From 1970 to 1985, American investment in Thailand was slightly higher than Japanese investment, but in the years since, Japan's share has increased and now outstrips the American. The Japanese ambassador to Thailand estimated in 1991 that "a new Japanese factory will open in Thailand every three days for the next several years." It is estimated that Japanese economic aid to Thailand in 1991 will run about $500 million, while the United States will provide less than $20 million.

The new Japanese role in Asia will increase the problems of the Japanese-American alliance; it will especially challenge the willingness of the United States to continue providing security for the region while it cedes economic leadership to the Japanese. As Japanese economic power in Asia becomes more marked, Americans will confront in a stark way the need for a coherent policy of their own that integrates new strategic and economic realities. It appears that the U.S. security system will be keeping order for a thriving region dominated by Japan. Such an arrangement is of questionable stability. Despite the fact that American forces have been in Japan not only for the defense of Japan but also to serve American interests, it is unlikely that American opinion will continue to support the maintenance of over 40,000 military personnel in Japan, even though under an agreement signed in 1991 the Japanese government will assume by 1995 approximately half the cost of keeping American bases and forces in Japan. Americans are not likely to accept indefinitely a situation that thrusts them into a role akin to mercenaries.

Left to their own wishes in Asia, Japanese policymakers would have the Americans continue to carry the burdens of their security. As one Japanese political analyst observed recently, Japan "is concerned about the United States declining [at home and in the world] too early and too fast so that she will no longer be able to shoulder the burdens others have thrust on her." American decline is assumed, although its leadership is still needed. There is, of course, resentment over the continued deference to American political leadership that this dependence on the alliance implies, but Japan is willing to pay that price.

The remarks of the top Marine Corps general in Japan reported in the *Washington Post* on March 27, 1990, caused intense private anger among Japanese. He told a correspondent that U.S. troops must remain in Japan at least until the beginning of the twenty-first century because "no one wants a rearmed, resurgent Japan. So we are a cap in the bottle, if you will."

Another incident, in April 1990, also implied that a future purpose of the Treaty of Mutual Cooperation was containment of Japanese rearmament. A high-profile Pentagon report, "A Strategic Framework for the Asian Pacific Rim: Looking Toward the 21st Century," listed a key strategic American objective in Japan as "discouraging any destabilizing development of power projection capability." A senior Defense Department official explained that the United States did not want to see Japanese aircraft carriers deployed in the Indian Ocean. These incidents stirred understandable resentment within the Japanese diplomatic and defense establishment. What is significant, however, is that when Japanese policymakers discussed these incidents, they suppressed their anger in deference to Japan's interest of keeping the U.S. military in Asia and maintaining the stability of the region.

These incidents not only reveal the changing tone of the bilateral relationship, they raise the larger issue of Japanese-U.S. relations in Asia in the post-Cold War era. To assign the Mutual Security Treaty the purpose of containing Japanese power and influence in the Pacific will not square with the prevailing nationalist mood in Japan. The reaction of Shintaro Ishihara, former cabinet member and coauthor of the book *The Japan That Can Say No*, to such an arrangement when he was queried in 1989 was characteristically inflammatory while nonetheless pointing to the larger issue: "Japan's franchise is Asia. I think Japan should assume greater responsibility than the United States or Europe in the development of the Asian region. It is extremely unpleasant to watch the United States drive a wedge between Japan and other Asian countries by propagating the idea that the U.S. military presence is preventing Japan's invasion of the region. In combining the human capital of the Newly Industrialized Countries of Asia with Japan's high technology and knowledge-intensive industry, Asia could become a powerful economic bloc." The day is likely to arrive when Japan will reject the anomaly of financing foreign bases that are there in large part to "contain" Japan, particularly when this situation contributes to a politically deferential and dependent foreign policy.

What America Must Do

American initiative in establishing a new U.S.-Japanese equilibrium is necessary now, while Washington still maintains substantial leverage on these issues and while Japan is still divided, adrift, and reactive in its post-Cold War foreign policy. There is a growing constituency in Japan for cooperation with the United States in more international affairs. Cooperation in building a new multilateral security arrangement in the Pacific appeals to the new internationalism that is stirring among the Japanese elites, although this new, larger vision arises less from any fundamental liberalism than from a broadened conception of Japan's own national interest. In the mainstream of the Liberal Democratic Party, in major ministries, among leaders of big business, there is a dawning recognition that Japan's stake in the international political-economic order is so great that to be a Japanese nationalist now is to be, in a certain sense, an internationalist. The view that is beginning to take shape is that having caught up with the West after a century-long struggle, and having a confident vision of Japan's future economic and technological prowess, Japan's own interests are no longer best served by narrow mercantilist policies and a passive role in international organizations.

LEFT TO THEIR OWN WISHES IN ASIA, JAPANESE POLICYMAKERS WOULD HAVE THE AMERICANS CONTINUE TO CARRY THE BURDENS OF THEIR SECURITY.

The internationalist point of view is still in a formative stage, and as demonstrated most recently by the Gulf crisis, this view clearly is not yet a national consensus, nor is it likely to be so for some time. Except in response to outside pressure, there is not the political will, the necessary institutions, or the values and cultural resources that would readily impel Japan to abandon its heretofore highly successful but narrowly self-generated vision of its world role. Abandoning that narrow vision is in Japan's own long-term interest.

Nevertheless, because it is still only partially formed, this new internationalism is tractable and susceptible to intelligent American leadership. The Department of Defense has already set in motion a decrease in the size of American forces in Japan, but these decisions appear driven by budgetary exigencies rather than a new strategic vision. The new conditions in Asia suggest that the U.S. approach to Asia-Pacific security should be rethought, with greater emphasis on multilateral arrangements, mutuality, consensus, and local contribution. Thought should be given to increased cooperation and coordination with Japan and other countries of the region, common military doctrine, and coordinated training. In fact, some initial steps in this direction were taken in the 1980s: for example, Japan now has greater responsibility for defense of its sea-lanes, and there is an increased level and sophistication in joint military training with forces from the United States and other Pacific nations. In light of new circumstances in the U.S.-Japan relationship and lessened Soviet tensions, it is appropriate to move substantially beyond these steps. A reduced American presence might lead to new forms of security maintenance, internationalized defense of sea-lanes, joint use of bases, and other new arrangements.

More than is often realized, the countries of Southeast Asia (in contrast to China and South Korea) are prepared to accept an enhanced Japanese security role, provided that the United States remains centrally involved even at a reduced level. There is much recent evidence of this attitude. In April 1991 when Prime Minister Kaifu met Thai Prime Minister Anand Panyarachun, the latter said that Thailand hoped Japan would play a multifaceted role and not restrict itself solely to economic activities. A year earlier, the Thai prime minister had surprised Japanese officials by proposing joint Thai-Japanese naval exercises. Also in April 1991, the Philippine defense secretary proposed to members of Japan's Liberal Democratic Party that Asia establish a regional security system. The previous month, Indonesian President Suharto told Michio Watanabe, a senior LDP politician, that Indonesia would understand if Japan were to send its armed forces on overseas peacekeeping missions. Singapore's new prime minister said the same. At about the same time, Malaysia tried to persuade Japan to take the lead in forming a new East Asia Economic Group, demonstrating receptivity to a more active Japanese leadership in the region.

The United States, as the provider of security and the primary market for exports from the region, retains a good deal of leverage. While welcoming Japan's investment, aid, and technology, Asians remain wary of Japan's potential domination of the region. Recognizing these concerns, Japanese policy favors a continuation of the U.S. security role as essential to maintaining the stability of the region that is required for Japanese economic interests. Even in the United States, many policymakers favor an international division of labor: the United States will provide security for Asia, while Japan will provide aid. Such a solution, while necessary in the immediate future, is not workable or wise in the long run. Japanese aid, whether or not it is formally tied to purchases of Japanese goods, overwhelmingly serves Japan's commercial interests, and even if it were to be given through international organizations, this division of labor would leave Americans with the unpleasant and controversial role of policeman. The international, and especially the American, reaction to Japan's simply putting up money for the Gulf coalition rather than sharing in a balanced way the contributions of the international community illustrates the inadequacy of this approach.

It is not in America's interest to try to keep Japan as an abnormal country. While the Yoshida strategy has largely been responsible for the perpetuation of this state of affairs, it is also true that the United States has been ambivalent about requesting that Japan do a great deal more in the security area—there is residual distrust of the Japanese national character and memories of the militarist period. But a continuation of the "cap in the bottle" approach brings with it what amounts to a mercenary role for American forces in Japan and a policemans' role in Asia while Japan's economic domination of the increasingly prosperous and self-assured region increases. It assures continued conflict with Japanese pride and its nationalist mood. Across a wide spectrum in Japan, there is an increasing impatience with a deferential foreign policy and a growing will to exert leadership in the region, even while there is no agreement on quite how this should be done. In the short run, if the Japanese sense that the Americans would prefer Japan simply to put up more money for bases and foreign aid, then the Japanese system, given its inclination and inertia at this point, will fall into line. But such a policy of drift ignores the new realities and trends of the region and is not in accord with our long-term interests.

It would be more far-sighted to put ourselves at the head of the long-range trends in Asia. Rather than attempting an indefinite containment of Japanese pride and power through a continuation of the security treaty in its present outmoded form, greater realism would dictate American initiative to form an organization of Pacific nations, of which a revised U.S.-Japan alliance would serve as the core. Such an organization would link economic and security interests and responsibilities and be less exclusively dependent on American resources than has been the case in the Cold War era. By weaving a positive Japanese security role into an expanded multilateral context, the goal of preventing an independent Japanese "power projection capability" would be achieved through positive measures rather than by an effort to contain Japan through the present bilateral relationship that is of questionable stability.

DOES JAPAN PLAY FAIR?

While official protectionism is largely gone, Americans still battle cartels, old-boy networks, and outright corruption. The U.S. must keep the pressure on.

Edmund Faltermayer

DOES JAPAN tilt its economic playing field against the rest of the world? The question is crucial, for despite years of pressure to open the world's No. 2 economy to foreign goods and investment, Japan has amassed an unheard-of trade surplus now soaring above $100 billion a year. If Japan's policies and business culture really do deny foreign companies a fighting chance, what can be done to set the balance right? Unless it is corrected, governments around the world, including the U.S. President elected in November, are sure to feel rising protectionist demands.

This article examines specific markets and business practices that shed light on Japan's openness. Sizing up a country's business terrain is relative. Difficult or easy compared with what? In making the assessment, FORTUNE judged access to markets in Japan in relation to hardships Japanese companies face in the U.S.

Overall, is the playing field level? In a word, no. "The Japanese market is not as closed as Americans think," says Akio Morita, chairman of Sony, "but not as open as the Japanese think." The long answer is more complicated, however—and more encouraging. Japan has changed greatly since the mid-Eighties. In many markets today's tilt is less steep than it was, and an official, orchestrated policy of thwarting the *gaijin* (foreigner) is mostly gone. Americans with high-quality goods and services can make a dent in Japan. Because of remaining governmental roadblocks and a business culture that can be extraordinarily inhospitable to outsiders, however, U.S. companies still have to work harder than Japanese companies in the U.S. And sometimes the Americans need diplomatic pressure to help laissez faire along, particularly when they are trying to penetrate industries dominated by entrenched oligopolies.

For those willing to take lots of bruises and stay in the game, Japan has compensations. The customers the Yank wins are often more loyal than those back home. Makoto Kuroda, managing director of Mitsubishi Corp., tells an American visitor: "Your market is easy to enter, but it's also easy to be kicked out. In Japan, once in, your people may stay much longer." Depending on the industry, the Americans may also reap outsize profits. Says William Wheeler, who heads Asia-Pacific operations for FMC Corp.: "The margins here are some of the highest in the world."

Many Japanese insist that their country's barriers have fallen and that Americans have little to grouse about. "In terms of formal government policies," asserts Noboru Hatakeyama, vice minister for international affairs at the Ministry of International Trade and Industry (MITI), "Japan is much more open" than the U.S. Japan has cut average tariffs on manufactured goods below America's (2.1% vs. 5%). The country may also be one of the few in history to *subsidize* imports. For the past three years, Japanese companies that substantially boost imports of a wide array of manufactured goods can get a 5% tax credit on the increase.

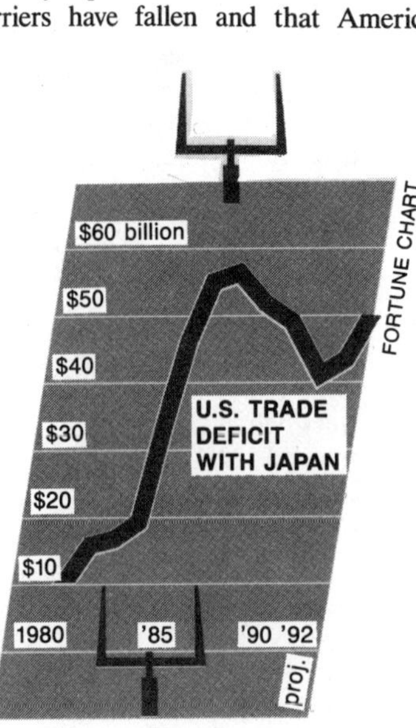

Japan has some gripes about the U.S. too. In semiconductors, for instance, Washington has resorted to managed trade with quotas, demanding that Japan buy 20% of the chips it uses from foreign companies. The U.S. has also leaned on Japan to curb exports of such items as cars and machine tools, forcing a shift of production to American transplants. Light pickup trucks from Japan face an unusually high tariff of 25%. And let's not ignore recent protectionist outbursts, as when opportunistic politicians in Los Angeles canceled a subway car contract with Sumitomo in favor of Morrison Knudsen.

For Japanese executives running businesses in the U.S., life is no Zen garden. They must often contend with a poorly educated, ill-trained labor force. The U.S. used to be ranked among the lowest-risk countries in which to do business, says Tachi Kiuchi, CEO of Mitsubishi Electronics America, a sales subsidiary of Mitsubishi Electric. But because of "all the lawsuits," he says, "the U.S. is no longer in the top five."

Still, for all America's blemishes, one giant fact stands out: Gaining entry is like falling out of bed compared with what a foreign company confronts in Japan. Though

REPORTER ASSOCIATES *Sally Solo, with Cindy Kano and Jessica Skelly von Brachel*

From *Fortune,* September 7, 1992, pp. 38-42, 46, 50, 52. Copyright © 1992 by The Time Inc. Magazine Company. Reprinted by permission.

formal barriers there *are* mostly gone, a forest of others remains. Many impede any newcomer to a particular market, Japanese or foreign, and in that sense foreigners are getting what trade negotiators call national treatment. But because Americans find conditions harder in Japan than vice versa, they are handicapped in redressing the trade imbalance.

Topping the list of adverse conditions, according to U.S. companies surveyed in 1991 by the A.T. Kearney consulting firm, is "the high cost of doing business." The rise in the yen against the dollar since the mid-Eighties has made a bad situation worse. Kearney itself pays $160 a square foot for its Tokyo office, nearly five times what equivalent space would command in New York City. Assuming that an American company lands orders, survival in the early years can resemble life in a piranha tank. Unless the product is unique and can't be readily duplicated, says Kearney vice president William Best, "you'll have competition faster than you can believe."

Americans who bend your ear about the perils aren't all crybabies, for the Japanese themselves acknowledge that their country is a rough go. Listen to Seiichi Takikawa, the jovial president of Canon Sales, a marketing and importing offshoot of the Japanese camera and copier company. He says that in the Seventies, when he built up Canon's operation in the U.S.—"where it's a much simpler task"—it took only six years to lift sales tenfold. Returning to Japan, Takikawa needed 15 years to achieve similar growth. Reason: a smaller market, fiercer competition, and a government that, he says, "has a habit of sticking its nose into everything it sees." And Takikawa was born into the culture. For an American, he says, success in Japan requires "two to three times as much as energy."

Daunting as this sounds, it was worse when Japan practiced flagrant protectionism. Edmund Reilly, president of Digital Equipment's Japanese subsidiary, recalls that when he first went to Japan for his company in 1970, the government was nurturing a home-grown computer industry and "the odds *really were* stacked against us." Overt discrimination against foreign products is now limited, though Japan still keeps out rice. The ban flies in the face of free-market principles: The home-grown variety costs seven times as much as imported rice would.

These days, when the Japanese government makes life difficult for foreigners, it's mainly through regulatory moves that rarely get headlines. Etak, a California company now part of Rupert Murdoch's News Corp., was the first to begin electronic mapping of Japanese cities in 1987, hoping to enable ambulance services and others to find addresses on computer screens. But a year later the government decided that Etak needed a license. By the time it came through, the company's head start was gone and a Japanese competitor had moved in.

This is but one example. Says Clyde Prestowitz Jr., president of the Economic Strategy Institute, a Washington research group: "The procedures that you go through are typically not transparent." He means they are neither open nor based on criteria known to all who are affected. In that atmosphere, American executives say, Japanese who have good entree with bureaucrats can delay the entry of competitors. The effects are sufficiently serious that Japan, in the latest round of talks with the U.S. under the so-called Structural Impediments Initiative, has agreed to reform its regulatory practices.

What really leaves many foreign companies out in the cold is the business culture. The word keiretsu suggests giant industrial groups linked by cross-ownership, such as Mitsubishi or Sumitomo. But the term can apply to longstanding business relationships without financial ties. When Sony developed its videocassette recorder in the early Seventies, Chairman Morita relates, it needed a new, high-quality recording tape. At the time, a major U.S. chemical company passed up Sony's invitation to supply the tape because it was reluctant to invest in new production equipment. Sony enlisted two Japanese companies that, Morita says, "invested money at their own risk." To this day Sony holds no equity stake in these suppliers, he adds, "but once they invest money and make a good product, that situation is a keiretsu, and we feel some kind of obligation."

Outsiders sometimes fail to understand why they can't instantly displace such suppliers by underselling them. As Morita explains: "An American company says, 'Our product is good, our price is good, why don't you buy?' But with an industrial product that needs continuous improvement, you need a long-term relationship." The U.S. company that originally declined Morita's invitation now has some of the business, but less than it might have had.

Productive relationships are the good side of keiretsu, which America has begun to emulate. But all too often, keiretsu exclude new players or give preferential treatment to members. Says Reilly of Digital Equipment, who is also president of the American Chamber of Commerce in Japan: "Keiretsu links, bidding cartels, and the old-boy network still present us with formidable obstacles that Japanese corporations do not face in the U.S. market."

Obstacles or no, more and more companies find they must be in Japan. Applied Materials, a Silicon Valley company with sales of $644 million a year, is one of the few flourishing American manufacturers of chipmaking equipment. One reason: It gets valuable customer feedback from Japan, which accounts for 35% of its revenues. Tetsuo Iwasaki, CEO of Applied Materials Japan, explains how the company benefits from working closely with Japan's semiconductor industry, the world's largest. Japan excels in manufacturing DRAM memory chips, he notes, which require finer circuitry than the microprocessors in which the U.S. has the leading position. Says Iwasaki: "In production, DRAMs are the technology driver."

The examination that follows concentrates on markets where Americans have a strong competitive edge or a chance to improve the trade numbers dramatically—if only the playing fields were level. One notable theme that emerges: It's relatively easy to sell to Japanese consumers as opposed to the purchasing agents of big companies. We also assess Japanese fairness in two important areas that cut across many businesses—direct investment and patent protection.

> *"American companies have an advantage in anything related to youth and lifestyle."*

■ CONSUMER ITEMS. The Apple computers jumping off Tokyo store shelves and BMWs tooling down the elevated expressways dispel the notion that Japanese citizens shun all foreign products. When it comes to marketing, says Tokyo consultant George Fields, "American companies have an advantage in anything related to youth and lifestyle." Fields, the son of an Australian father and a Japanese mother, spent time in each country in his youth. He notes that Japan's No. 1 soft drink is Coca-Cola, the No. 1 fast-food chain is McDonald's, the No. 1 theme park Disneyland, and the list goes on.

Many of the successful products are made in Japan rather than exported from the U.S., but the earnings help America's balance of payments. The main difficulty in marketing consumer goods is penetrating the convoluted distribution system. Kodak's entry in the mid-Eighties shows the unexpected routes a company might have to take: It used a mail-order company to sell film and a dry-cleaning chain as a collection point for developing.

Distribution is an impediment for the supreme consumer item: the automobile. When Japanese carmakers entered the U.S., they were able to sell through existing American dealers, who have long been allowed to offer more than one make. Japanese automakers own much of the sales network in Japan, and dual dealerships are rare. Bowing to pressure from Washington, Japanese carmakers are starting to offer a few American models. But the only real answer may be a direct stake in a distribution network. BMW carved out a respectable niche in Japan's market after it bought an ailing chain of showrooms in 1981 and expanded it. Ford, the most aggressive of Detroit's Big Three in Japan, has just raised its ownership in the Autorama sales chain from 34% to 36.5%, making it an equal partner with Mazda.

■ **SODA ASH.** The Japanese market for this mundane substance, used in glassmaking, is only \$360 million a year. But Japan's reluctance to import it illustrates a widespread pattern studied by economist Peter Petri of Brandeis University. Analyzing where Japanese imports go, he found that businesses and government agencies were far less inclined than consumers to buy foreign goods. The soda ash story is "entirely consistent" with this reluctance, Petri says. Patriotism on the part of senior executives may partly explain it. Says Douglas Shinsato of the Tohmatsu Touche Ross consulting firm in Tokyo: "Older managing directors, 50 and above, still think it's a sin to import."

Soda ash is cheaply mined in Wyoming by FMC, the leading importer into Japan, and the quality is as good or better than what's produced artificially in Japan's chemical plants. If pure economics ruled, imports might have half the market. In the early Eighties, following a complaint by the U.S. government, Japan's Fair Trade Commission found that a cartel of chemical and glass companies was setting price and volume limits on the imported stuff. Before long the import share leaped from 3% to

Noguchi dismisses the idea that Toyota's keiretsu exclude outside suppliers.

17%. The cartel must still have some power, because while imports have exerted steady downward pressure on the price, their share has been stuck around 22% since 1987.

■ **FLAT GLASS.** The same Japanese companies that overpay for soda ash manage to hold U.S. glass imports to less than 0.5% of the market. Three producers have divvied up the business in virtually unaltered proportions for decades. That's far different than the U.S., where Japanese companies have 10% of the market either directly or through stakes in American producers. Michigan's privately owned Guardian Industries wants to smash through Japan's glass wall. The company can typically deliver its American-made product direct to a Japanese customer for 20% less, claims Peter Young, Guardian's director of international business. But, he says, "Japanese construction companies tell us, 'We can work with you outside Japan but not inside.' They fear they won't be able to buy from domestic glassmakers when they need to."

Among many commitments made by the Japanese government during President Bush's January visit was an agreement to take steps to "substantially increase" foreign companies' access to the flat glass market. As part of this effort Japan's Fair Trade Commission, which in the past has issued cease-and-desist orders against the Japanese oligopoly, is conducting a new survey of competitive conditions in the industry. PPG, which has taken a lower-key approach in Japan than Guardian, welcomes the study. "It might do some good," says PPG executive John Reichenbach Jr. "But there's no need to get euphoric at this point."

■ **AUTO PARTS.** This Japanese door is opening wider, partly because salesman Bush has his foot in it. Auto parts got heavy attention during his Japan trip because of their huge sales potential. It may take years for Detroit's automakers to increase their minuscule 0.3% share of the Japanese market, but American parts makers assert that a lot of what they make could be put into Japanese cars right now, both in Japan and at U.S. transplants. Cars and parts made up 72% of last year's \$43.4 billion U.S. trade deficit with Japan.

It's been a tough sale. Many components must be designed into a new car long before it goes into production. Two years ago, a white paper by the American Chamber of Commerce in Japan charged that American parts makers couldn't get in on the ground floor: "Typically, participation in the design phase is only open to Japanese companies." The transplants have been boosting the U.S. content of their cars, but many of the parts come from Japanese parts makers that followed the carmakers to North America. In many cases they are members of keiretsu back home, and the carmakers own some of their stock. Says CEO John Reilly of Tenneco Automotive, which is stunningly successful at selling parts everywhere but

JAPAN'S GRIDIRONS RUN UPHILL

Individual playing fields studied by FORTUNE, shown here in ascending steepness, range from the nearly wide open financial services market to the small but difficult-to-penetrate market for flat glass. The tilt of each field represents the relative difficulty U.S. companies encounter in Japan when compared with the hindrances Japanese face in the U.S.

PLAYING FIELD	FINANCIAL SERVICES	CONSUMER ITEMS	PATENT PROTECTION
	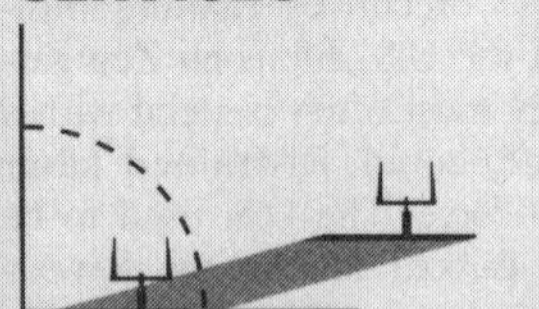		
SLOPE OF FIELD FOR U.S. BUSINESS	Practically level	Moderately steep	Moderately steep
MAJOR DIFFICULTIES FACING U.S. COMPANIES IN JAPAN	■ Regulation delays new products; keiretsu make it hard to sell property and casualty insurance to large companies.	■ Penetrating the convoluted retail distribution system.	■ Long delays in receiving patents during which Japanese companies can pore over patent applications to duplicate technological advances.
MAJOR DIFFICULTIES FACING THE JAPANESE IN THE U.S.	■ Very few.	■ None for electronics and other products. Auto imports are limited by voluntary agreements; light truck sales by 25% tariffs.	■ Litigious business culture in which suits for patent infringement are more common than in Japan.

FORTUNE TABLE

Japan: "You can't have it both ways—a keiretsu relationship with a supplier and a free and open market."

Oh, yes you can, asserts, Koichiro Noguchi, Toyota's urbane general manager of international purchasing at Toyota City, who dismisses the idea that his company's keiretsu with suppliers is exclusionary. On average, he says, Toyota orders the same part from four or five companies, of which only one is typically in the family. Each of Japan's parts manufacturers, he adds, ships to an average of five automakers. "In an industry as competitive as ours," declares Noguchi, "conducting business on a restrictive basis is only for those with a death wish."

Toyota is striving to buy from more American-owned parts makers, Noguchi notes, and to include them in new model development. But many need to learn to control costs better, he says, and Toyota still encounters 100 times as many defects from U.S. companies as from Japanese suppliers. The average reject rate from an American firm, Noguchi says, is 2,000 parts per million (ppm), vs. the 20 ppm average from Japanese companies. Noguchi reports that U.S. defects have fallen, "steadily but not dramatically," by 60% since 1988. "I don't want you to make it sound discouraging," he tells a visitor. "I believe in a rosy future."

American parts makers, loath to reveal their defect rates, stoutly maintain that they are competitive on price and quality. A study commissioned by the University of Michigan's Transportation Research Institute shows that on average U.S.-made parts are 19% cheaper than those produced in Japan. On quality, though, Richard McClain, TRW's Asia-Pacific vice president, concedes that some American suppliers may well fall short. Among makers of major components, he says, "there's a larger disparity between the best and worst in the U.S. than in Japan." But, he adds, "the best American suppliers are world-competitive."

One that surely qualifies is TRW, whose global business with Japan's carmakers has reached $500 million a year and is growing fast. "It takes a unique technology to sell to the Japanese in Japan," McClain says. TRW ships air bags and sensors from the U.S. and supplies steering gear from a 100%-owned plant in Nagoya. Another company to make it into Japanese auto factories is Timken, which began selling tapered roller bearings for wheel assemblies to Nissan and Mazda in 1987. When Nissan began planning three new luxury cars not sold in the U.S., it included Timken in the "design-in" phase. Timken bearings from Bucyrus, Ohio, now go into a made-in-Japan Toyota pickup truck.

During the Bush trip, Japan's automakers said they would try to double purchases of American-made parts in the U.S. and Japan to $19 billion by 1994. Toyota's president, Shoichiro Toyoda, says that "we know there's a trade imbalance we should be concerned about." Does he think his company can meet its own stepped-up goal for buying American-made parts? "We will make good-faith efforts," he responds. Altering close supplier relationships like Toyota's won't be easy, however, and the Americans are waging an uphill campaign.

> *"Older managing directors, 50 and above, still think it's a sin to import."*

■ CONSTRUCTION. Japanese companies do plenty of business in the U.S., where *Engineering News Record* estimates their new contracts at $1.5 billion last year in a $401-billion-a-year market. It's a different tale in Japan, where it has taken threats of retaliation from Washington to open up public works projects to American firms. Commerce Department officials put the value of total U.S. construction work in Japan at about $200 million a year.

That meager presence may be a loss for Japan. John Moore Jr., who runs the Far East business for Bechtel Group, the biggest U.S. operator in Japan, says construction costs there are two to four times higher than in the U.S. Bloated costs help explain why Japan's construction industry, running at $651 billion in 1991, is nominally bigger than America's. Back home and in other countries, Bechtel keeps a lid on expenses by arranging for just-in-time delivery of materials and components. But because it is only one member of a consortium putting up half of a terminal at Osaka's new Kansai airport, one of six Japanese projects it's involved in, Bechtel cannot impose its usual computerized cost and scheduling controls. At Kansai, Moore says, 200 subcontractors are at work, and "nobody knows where all the trucks are going."

Though its construction companies are aggressively competitive abroad, Japan tolerates inefficiency at home. The reason, Moore says, is that the construction industry "is designed to maintain full employ-

AUTOMOBILE PARTS

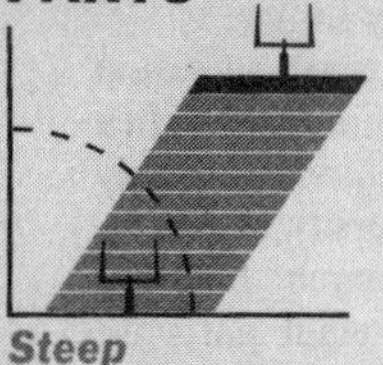

Steep

■ Reluctance of Japanese automakers to switch from traditional suppliers, many with keiretsu ties.

■ None.

DIRECT INVESTMENT

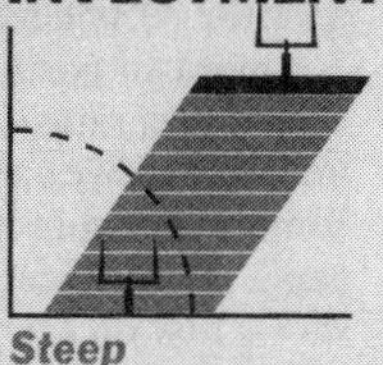

Steep

■ Cross-ownership of most shares by keiretsu members keeps outsiders from buying control of large companies.

■ None, except where law prohibits foreign control, as in defense industries.

CONSTRUCTION

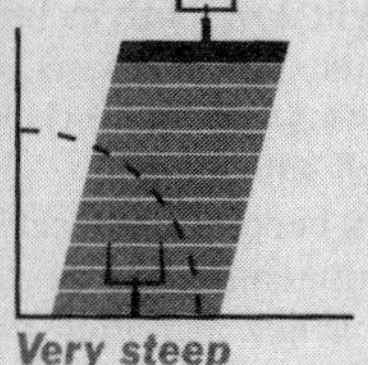

Very steep

■ Corruption, including collusion among Japanese bidders.

■ None.

SODA ASH

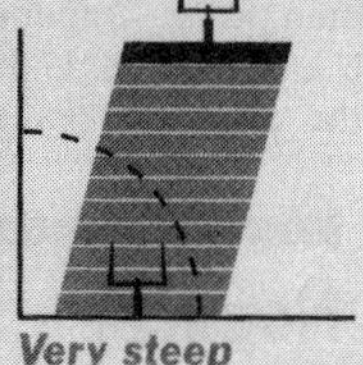

Very steep

■ Industrial customers are persuaded by domestic producers not to buy the cheaper American product.

■ None; Japanese companies do not export to U.S.

FLAT GLASS

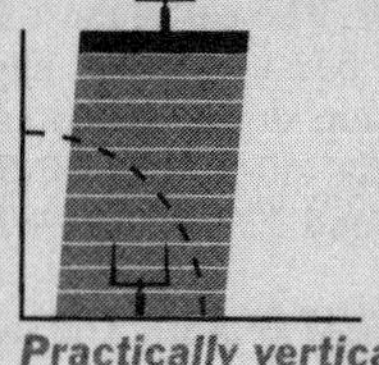

Practically vertical

■ Pressure by Japanese glassmaking cartel on construction industry and other users restricts U.S. imports to less than 0.5% of the market.

■ None; Japanese companies have built U.S. plants and now have 10% of the market.

Right now, says Stern, 38 high-tech Japanese companies are up for sale.

ment regardless of costs." Collusion is rife. Recently, Japan's Fair Trade Commission uncovered a bid-rigging scheme, known as a *dango*, not far from Tokyo but took relatively mild action against the companies. Japan's ruling Liberal Democratic Party, which gets major contributions from the construction industry, has been in no hurry to crack down. America's construction industry isn't always simon-pure, but Akira Goshi, who teaches at Nihon University's business school, flatly says that in his country, "construction is corrupt." Change, he says, will require "flak from outside Japan."

■ FINANCIAL SERVICES. America excels here, and the big surprise is that some foreign companies enjoy privileges in Japan that local competitors don't. Under exceptions to Japan's version of the Glass-Steagall Act separating commercial and investment banking, Citicorp owns a brokerage firm while Salomon Brothers has a bank. In that sense, the playing field runs *downhill.* But factor in heavy-handed regulation and keiretsu, neither of which hampers Japanese financial firms in the U.S., and the gradient runs moderately against the Yanks.

Citibank, the largest U.S. commercial bank in Japan, has few beefs. It is no sign of discrimination, says Masamoto Yashiro, Citi's executive vice president in Tokyo, that American institutions control only 1% of the assets in Japan's banking system while Japanese banks have a tenth of America's. Citi is free to buy a Japanese bank, Yashiro says, but with price/earnings multiples still high and Japan's stock market traumatized, "Who in their right mind would want to?" Citi's big push in Japan is in consumer banking, and one gripe is that the bank can't get access to as many automated teller networks as it would like.

At the opposite end of the satisfaction spectrum are U.S. investment advisory firms and banks eager to apply their sophisticated money management techniques to Japan's $225 billion in pension funds. So far, despite a push by the U.S. Treasury Department, regulations from Japan's Ministry of Finance (MOF) have held the foreigners back.

The cup is half full for brokerage firms. Salomon is one of 25 foreign securities houses on the Tokyo Stock Exchange, four times the number in 1986, and its $180 million in profits in Japan last year placed it second only to Nomura. That sounds like nirvana, except that new products Salomon wants to introduce—such as securitized credit card receivables—require MOF's approval, which takes time.

The keiretsu system hems in American International Group, the big insurer. Not that AIG is bleeding. Entering Japan just after World War II to serve American GIs, it has become the largest foreign seller of life and accident insurance to the Japanese and sends splendid profits back to headquarters in New York City. But while the company sells all kinds of personal accident insurance, it is effectively frozen out of mandatory automobile liability insurance, which auto dealers arrange when they sell new cars.

As for property and casualty insurance for business, AIG sells to small companies but not big ones. Keiretsu connections, including stock holdings, between big companies and insurers, plus regulation, AIG says, "create a web that small and foreign companies cannot penetrate." AIG claims that to land a big client it would have to join the keiretsu, in effect, by taking a 3% to 5% ownership stake in the prospect. Says Evan Greenberg, AIG's chief operating officer for Japan and Korea: "You're talking of an investment of hundreds of millions just to sell to one customer."

Ryozo Kanno, in the MOF section that regulates P&C, says he has trouble understanding such complaints. The answer, he contends, may simply be more "sales effort." He likes to point out that foreign insurance companies have 2.8% of the P&C business in Japan while his country's insurers have only 0.1% in the U.S. CEO Maurice Greenberg, Evan's father, argues that the Japanese insurers' small American market share is beside the point. Japanese insurers have "absolute carte blanche" in the U.S., he says. "I thought the rules had to do with market access, not market share."

■ DIRECT INVESTMENT. The flow of direct investment between the U.S. and Japan is even more lopsided than trade. According to figures compiled by MITI, foreign companies control less than 1% of corporate assets in Japan, while outsiders own 20% of U.S. assets. Though many American companies have shunned investing in Japan because of the high cost and the tough business climate, they didn't have much choice prior to the early Seventies. Government policy made it virtually impossible for outsiders to buy control of a Japanese company. Since then, cross-ownership by keiretsu—which economist Robert Lawrence of Harvard's Kennedy School calls "an explicit device to prevent foreigners from buying Japanese companies"—has kept a majority of each member's shares off the market.

By contrast, except mainly in defense-related industries, the U.S. welcome mat has always been out. States avidly court foreigners, as Kentucky did when it offered Toyota $140 million in incentives to build an assembly plant in Georgetown. Says Walter Shill III of McKinsey & Co.'s Tokyo office: "The U.S. is beyond open; it's promiscuous."

The unequal investment flows have far-reaching consequences. One is a largely one-way transfer of technology from start-up companies, which the U.S. hatches in disproportionate numbers. Since 1986, according to the American Electronics Association's office in Japan, Japanese companies have bought 50% or more of at least 65 U.S. electronics outfits, most of them startups. Over the entire Eighties, American companies acquired major stakes in a mere seven Japanese electronics companies.

Skewed investment also skews trade. That's a major point of a new book, *Rivals Beyond Trade*, by Dennis Encarnation of the Harvard business school. Intracompany transactions by multinational corporations now dominate the world's movement of goods, Encarnation says, as when a Japanese car transplant brings in engines from the parent company. To control intracompany trade, Encarnation says, corporations need majority control of their overseas affiliates. But he argues that "persistent asymmetries"—first in policy, then in business practices—have severely held down the number of majority-owned foreign subsidiaries in Japan.

The situation is not hopeless. American companies, Encarnation says, are "desperately trying to overcome the legacy of the past." Right now, says John Stern, who heads the American Electronics Association's Japan office, 38 high-tech Japanese companies are on the market, and not all are turkeys. Toshihiko Yamamoto, president of an investment banking boutique called Advisory International Inc., knows of companies available in chemicals, retailing, warehousing, and financial services.

■ PATENT PROTECTION. Both Japan and the U.S. find plenty to criticize in each other's practices. The Japanese are incensed that American companies, in many cases failing to do the hard work of turning their technology into winning products, are going to court and nailing Japanese companies that did. The Japanese are not being singled out in the new aggressiveness on patent enforcement, but it poses a special hazard for foreign companies in the U.S.

Outweighing it are deficiencies in Japan's protection of intellectual property. A Japanese company can get a patent in 18 months on average from the U.S. Patent and Trademark Office. In Japan the pro-

According to MITI, foreigners control less than 1% of Japan's corporate assets.

cess can easily take five years. Texas Instruments waited 29 years for a patent on its basic integrated circuit design. While the U.S. patent system rewards breakthroughs, the Japanese system is designed to *diffuse* technology. Eighteen months after an application is filed in Japan, competitors are free to pore over it. They are then in a position to design around the new technology.

The sheer delay in getting a patent can wipe out a company's Japanese sales effort. In 1982, Silicon Technologies, a small private outfit in New Jersey, applied for a Japanese patent on a system that helps prevent damage to wafers as they are sliced off silicon crystals by diamond-tipped saws. The patent still hasn't come through. CEO George Kachajian charges that a Japanese company that opposed its issuance has incorporated a copy of the system into its own machines. After Kachajian threatened to bring Washington trade negotiators into the picture, the Japanese company began discussing royalties. There is nothing to prevent the recurrence of similar cases. Under U.S. prodding, Japan has promised to speed the granting of patents.

If American business is to make further headway in Japan, two strategies are essential. Some companies clearly need the help of *gaiatsu*, or foreign pressure, in the form of crowbars applied by the U.S. government. "There's plenty of work to be done for further accelerating access to this market," says Michael Armacost, U.S. ambassador to Japan. That may sound like market meddling, but prying open Japan's doors is preferable to the protectionist alternative of closing America's. In return, Japan gets to exert its own *gaiatsu*, goading the U.S. to shape up its schools and boost a low savings rate.

THE OTHER strategy is for companies to try harder. Kodak's innovative distribution system is one example. Another who went the extra mile—or should we say the extra scooter ride—is Ernest Higa, a Hawaiian-born American who introduced Domino's pizza to Japan seven years ago. To make sure the pizzas arrive in the promised 30 minutes, Higa developed proprietary maps locating all the families in a store's delivery radius. David Baskerville, Asian vice president of Siecor International, a joint venture of Siemens and Corning, battled for six years to become one of the top five suppliers of fiber-optic cable. Says he: "Never give up, keep pushing."

And—surprise—the Japanese really are trying harder too. A new report by the Keidanren, Japan's prestigious organization of top industrial leaders, calls for *kyosei* (symbiosis) with the U.S. One way to achieve it, the report says, is "for keiretsu members to provide ample opportunities for newcomers, particularly those from foreign countries." Kazuo Nukazawa, the Keidanren's managing director, says he hopes for a future in which critics like Edith Cresson, France's former prime minister, will no longer describe his country as an anthill. "We'll catch up with you in humanizing capitalism," Nukazawa tells an American. "We'll cut working hours, first passing you and then Germany."

MITI, too, has mellowed. Minoru Masuda, chairman of the Japan External Trade Organization, its trade arm, drives around Toyko in a Cadillac with an "Import now!" sticker. Americans who distrust Japan might dismiss all this as public relations designed to keep export markets open. But Brandeis economist Petri believes the desire for something resembling economic detente "is serious on the Keidanren and MITI's part." The trouble, he says, is that access to Japan's markets "has much more to do with the fabric of the business system, and the Keidanren and MITI are not going to change that overnight." Japan will continue to open up, but foreigners can expect to keep looking uphill at the goal posts.

"The mountains are high, the emperor is far away"

The tired old autocrats still rule in Beijing, but down on China's southern coast a capitalist revolution has started. Without a shot being fired, it is spreading throughout the vast country.

Andrew Tanzer

THAT VENERABLE Chinese saying—"The mountains are high, the emperor is far away"—applies neatly to the situation today in Guangdong province, 82,000 square miles and 60 million people, 1,200 miles away from Beijing. While Beijing's octogenarian communist hard-liners remain stuck in a time warp, Guangdong province is firmly set on a road to capitalist prosperity.

A $1 billion six-lane toll-levying superhighway, scheduled for completion in mid-1994, will tie Guangdong closer to adjacent, free-enterprise Hong Kong and further integrate the two economies. When it is finished, Guangdong will be far closer ideologically as well as geographically to Hong Kong than to Beijing. The highway is being constructed by a Hong Kong civil engineering firm, Hopewell Holdings, in a joint venture between Hopewell and a Guangdong provincial corporation.

In Hong Kong's teeming Wanchai district, Gordon Wu, the irreverent managing director of Hopewell, traces on a map the road through the heart of the Pearl River Delta *(see map)*, already probably economically the fastest-growing region in the world. Wu says the 75-mile freeway was inspired by his traveling on the New Jersey Turnpike during his college days at Princeton in the 1950s. "What I see in Guangdong today is another Taiwan in the making," says Wu. "Guangdong will have a profound impact on China. It's an economic revolution."

This isn't the sort of revolution that Chairman Mao Zedong had in mind. Ignoring the repressive, stubbornly communist autocracy in Beijing, Guangdong's businessmen and politicians are moving rapidly from a planned to a market- and incentive-based economy. Says John Kamm, an American chemical company executive who has done business with the province for 19 years: "Old-style communism is dead in Guangdong."

As recently as 1984, Guangdong ranked fifth among provinces in China in exports, but that was before economic reforms and a massive migration of industry from Hong Kong transformed the economy. Now the province ranks first in exports ($10.5 billion in 1990, up from $3 billion in 1985), industrial production, foreign investment and retail sales.

As in Korea and Taiwan in the 1960s and 1970s, Guangdong's exports are fueling a blaze of growth. Visit the Pearl River Delta, a region with 20 million people that radiates 150 miles out from the capitalist enclaves of Hong Kong and Macao. Over the past decade, the province's economy has grown 12% a year and the Delta's over 20%—rates that exceed even those of newly industrializing economies such as Taiwan and South Korea during peak growth years. Economists put per capita output in the Delta at over $1,500, four times the national average.

Drive around the Delta and the signs of economic boom and prosperity are everywhere. Banana plantations and rice paddies worked with water buffalo are being bulldozed to make way for roads, apartment buildings and thousands of factories. (Guangdong is already one of the world's largest exporters of such things as toys, electric fans, down jackets, footwear and watch parts.)

Shenzhen, the special economic zone in Guangdong just across the border from Hong Kong, has the look

Reprinted by permission of *Forbes* magazine, August 5, 1991, pp. 70-75. Copyright © Forbes, Inc., 1991.

and feel of a cowboy boomtown. Prostitutes, mainly comely girls from Shanghai and farther north, lure Hong Kong businessmen in the city's sleek new hotels and Japanese-style karaoke bars. The girls don't come cheap: They typically charge $40 a trick, or almost two months' average wages in most of China. Shenzhen's young stock and property markets have become almost as volatile as Hong Kong's. Local businessmen flaunt their portable phones and pagers. Shenzhen's population has mushroomed from 50,000 in 1980 to 1.7 million as tens of thousands of shabbily clad migrants from the rest of China flock in looking for lucrative work. Shenzhen's industrial output has surged from $11 million to $3.8 billion, 80% of it exported, and the zone is still growing 40% a year.

Many of the city's hotel towers are topped with revolving restaurants. The first McDonald's outlet in China is here, packed with brightly dressed locals paying for their Big Macs with Hong Kong dollars, instead of with the local renminbi. So pervasive is the trading in Hong Kong currency that Hong Kong dollars fetch a mere 7% premium on the black market.

In Guangzhou (Canton), the provincial capital of Guangdong, across the street from the train station there are giant billboards. Maoist slogans? No, advertisements for Head & Shoulders shampoo, Levi's and 7UP. Take a stroll down Guangzhou's Liberation Avenue, a main thoroughfare clogged with buses, taxis and motorbikes, and you'll find shops stuffed with goods like Johnson roach killer, Remy Martin cognac, Rejoice shampoo, Parker pens, Sony CD players and Barbie dolls, purchasable in either local or hard currencies. In a development that must have Mao turning in his grave, late last year thousands of commission-earning Avon ladies began peddling cosmetics door-to-door in Guangzhou, the first direct selling in China since the communist revolution in 1949.

Every evening, speedboats laden with VCRs, stereo equipment and Marlboro cigarettes race from Hong Kong to the Guangdong coast. Legal? No, but nobody much cares or interferes. Each month hundreds of cars are stolen in Hong Kong and smuggled to Guangdong in six-engine jetfoils. Favorite makes: Mercedes-Benz, BMW, Toyota.

Ironically, this runaway capitalism was started by the communist panjandrums in Beijing themselves. In 1978, when Deng Xiaoping launched his open-door policy, they picked Guangdong as the main laboratory for testing economic reforms. Three of the four original special economic zones, which were intended to attract foreign investment and to allow the study of capitalistic practices, were situated in Guangdong.

An immediate result of the reforms was the disappearance of the political commissars from Guangdong factories. "In 1980-84 there was always the political hack who ruined deals," says Robert Theleen, an American venture capitalist with long experience in the Delta. "Suddenly, in 1985, the political cadres began to disappear from factories."

Foreign investors were given the freedom to hire, fire and train workers without political interference. Patrick Wang, for instance, managing director of Johnson Electric, a big Hong Kong micromotor maker, says he shuns workers from the grotesquely featherbedded state corporations. They grew up under "socialist laziness" and are used to working two-hour days. Instead, he prefers fresh high school graduates: "We brainwash the workers to do it right the first time."

Foreign investors were allowed to devise incentive systems for workers to boost productivity. Hong Kong investors typically pay workers bonuses and overtime in Hong Kong dollars. In a toy or garment factory, for instance, bonuses, which can easily double a worker's income, are paid according to piece rates. Female workers might be showered with gifts such as imported stockings, cosmetics and soap as part of their incentive payments.

While other parts of China still discourage foreign investment in low-tech, wholly owned consumer ventures, Guangdong welcomes any foreign investment that creates jobs and foreign exchange earnings. Thus does Heinz produce baby food, General Foods make Maxwell House coffee, American Standard manufacture toilets and Procter & Gamble turn out Head & Shoulders shampoo and Oil of Olay skin cream in Guangdong.

Once capitalism had its foot in the

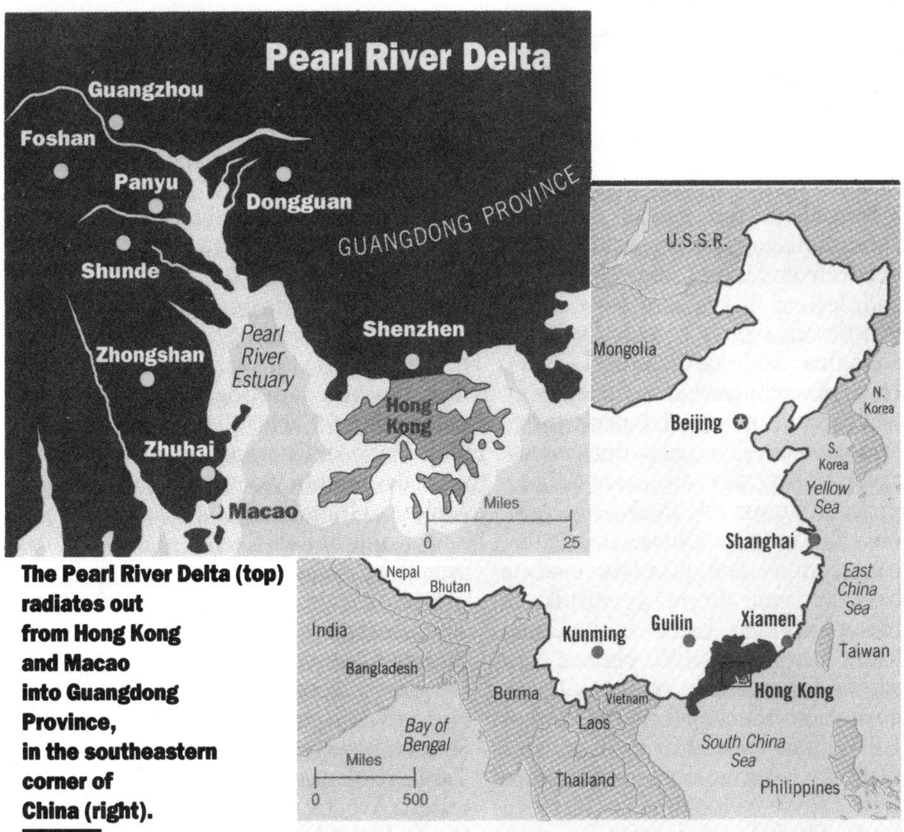

The Pearl River Delta (top) radiates out from Hong Kong and Macao into Guangdong Province, in the southeastern corner of China (right).

door, communism was doomed. Beijing overestimated its ability to control things. Cantonese society (the population of Guangdong) is deeply pragmatic, materialistic, entrepreneurial. Nearly four decades of communism did nothing to eradicate these deep impulses, which bubbled over once repression was lifted. "The central government realizes it's impossible to change Guangdong now," comments Simon To, managing director of Hutchison China Trade. "You can't turn the clock back."

The great catalyst for change in Guangdong has been the stunningly swift migration of manufacturing from Hong Kong across the border into the Delta since the mid-1980s. This marriage made in heaven combines the business acumen, technology and capital of Hong Kong industry with the bottomless pool of cheap Chinese labor. Essentially, Guangdong has become Hong Kong's factory, while the British colony is increasingly a service center.

An estimated 3 million factory workers in Guangdong toil in 30,000 plants owned by or subcontracting for Hong Kong manufacturers. This compares with just 715,000 factory workers in Hong Kong's rapidly shrinking industrial work force. At least 80% of Hong Kong producers, such as toy, watch, garment and electronics makers, have moved some production to Guangdong. Taiwanese industrialists have also moved production of labor-intensive products like umbrellas, footwear and handbags to Guangdong. In a typical subcontracting relationship, the Hong Kong side brings in capital equipment, components and raw materials and sends factory managers and supervisors to the satellite factories. An estimated 50,000 Hong Kong managers commute regularly by car, train or ferry across the border.

Hong Kong industrialists pay in foreign exchange for land, labor and utilities, hence that growing volume of convertible currency behind the rotting bamboo curtain. Here's how the deals work: If it's a subcontracting deal, the Hong Kong company typically pays the Chinese partner a processing fee based on a volume of production. After processing, most of the goods are brought back to Hong Kong and reexported to the world. Hong Kong's trade with China has jumped from $2 billion in 1978 to $50 billion in 1990.

Wages are far higher in Guangdong than in noncapitalist China, but far lower than in Hong Kong. An assembly worker in Guangdong will earn from $60 to $100 a month; the workweek is typically six eight-hour days. That is 10% to 15% of what an equivalent worker gets in Hong Kong, but at least three times average wages in China. Moreover, with the easy availability of hard currency in Guangdong, the wages will buy real goods. "They come from rural villages [to the factories of Guangdong] and after working two or three years they take home things they only dreamed about, like color TVs, refrigerators, radios and bicycles," says Johnson Electric's Patrick Wang. His company employs 4,000 workers in three factories in the Delta; every day it trucks in six containers of parts and takes out six containers of finished micromotors for export around the world.

Guangdong officials understand the high wages are not enough; there must be goods available to make the money worth having. The local government saw to it that there were goods in the stores to motivate workers. Park'N Shop, a retailing unit of Hutchison Whampoa, is setting up a chain of supermarkets in the Pearl River Delta; Robert Theleen plans to bring Domino's Pizza to the area.

In less than a decade the Delta's workers have graduated from bicycles and watches to color TVs and refrigerators. "Now they're on the threshold of motorcycles," says Hopewell's Wu. "Give them five years and there will be a great increase in car ownership and they'll be coming to Hong Kong in droves as tourists."

What is most remarkable is the seemingly spontaneous explosion of entrepreneurship. In Guangdong the private sector is growing rapidly but is mainly made up of small-scale businesses such as poultry and fish farms, restaurants, wholesalers and retailers.

Also on the increase are so-called collective enterprises. These can be set up by individuals, such as wealthy farmers, but are more often established by local village or township governments. They compete fiercely in Hong Kong for investment—many have set up offices there—and buy materials and sell merchandise on the market. Like the small private businesses, these respond to the market rather than to some state plan.

Does Beijing know what is happening in Guangdong? Yes, but, says Miron Mushkat, chief regional economist at Baring Securities (Hong Kong), the province is skilled at parrying Beijing. "It's defiant in a subtle way. It says yes to Beijing but does its own thing. It's the major challenge to Beijing; it's a state within a state."

Why have the ideologues in Beijing such as Premier Li Peng tolerated this wayward province? Wu explains: "They settle their differences in very practical ways: Guangdong pays more taxes for more autonomy. As long as the tax money keeps coming in, the central government will keep its hands off." If the Beijing hard-liners cracked down on Guangdong, they would deprive themselves of desperately needed tax revenues and foreign exchange. Last year China suffered a record budget deficit, largely the result of snowballing subsidies shoveled to moneylosing state corporations. As in any communist system, these overstaffed industrial dinosaurs have stockpiled a mountain of poor-quality, unwanted goods. Someone must finance all this. Guangdong, however repugnant to the socialist ideologues, is a big help.

Will the capitalist virus spread to other parts of China? It has already started to do so. Beijing will face an expansion of the labor force of frightening proportions in the 1990s—more than 10 million new job-seekers a year—thanks to a baby boom generation born during the disastrous Cultural Revolution. The jobs needed can be created only by market-oriented private and collective enterprises, not by state corporations. Hence a slow but more or less unimpeded spread of the capitalist virus to other parts of China.

Nicholas Lardy, a specialist on China's economy at the University of Washington, calculates that 50% of China's industrial output is now generated outside the state sector, compared with just 20% before economic reforms were launched in 1978.

Since the Tiananmen massacre in June 1989, the U.S. media have mostly reported that hard-line ideologues are in full control in Beijing and are rolling back economic reforms and recentralizing the economy. Not so. "Beijing talks about recentralization, but what they've actually done over the past two years is decentralize," says Anthony Chan, China economist at Business International Asia/Pacific.

Last fall, for instance, provincial governors led by Guangdong's feisty Ye Xuanping rejected Beijing's attempt to write tax increases and recentralization policies into its new five-year plan. "The old guard is horrified of Guangdong, but after Tiananmen they're too weak to resist," comments Theleen. "What they gained in political repression, they lost in economic control, because it's easier to extract political allegiance from the south in return for economic autonomy."

As 1997 approaches, the date when Britain returns Hong Kong to Chinese sovereignty, Beijing is growing fearful of Hong Kong-Guangdong economic integration. "A Hong Kong-Guangdong alliance could create a speed and momentum of economic reform that could jeopardize political stability, meaning the Communist Party in Beijing," says Robert Broadfoot, managing director of the Hong Kong-based Political & Economic Risk Consultancy.

Clearly worried, Beijing seems to be promoting Shanghai's newly created Pudong zone for foreign investment as a counterweight to Guangdong. China's traditional industrial center, Shanghai has seen its role usurped by Guangdong because the city has been milked by Beijing for tax revenues and has been a hotbed of radical politics since the revolution.

Growth of the Shanghai region may create a political counterpoise to Guangdong, but it will speed, not slow, China's creeping capitalism. "Every provincial governor and official wants to come to Guangdong to see how they're doing it," says David Li, the patrician chief executive of Hong Kong's Bank of East Asia. Li helped bring Avon to Guangzhou and IBM to Shenzhen for a software-writing venture. He expects Guangdong to shift lower-value-added processing to other provinces, just as Hong Kong has done to Guangdong, as the province integrates upstream to parts and materials.

One silk garment factory FORBES toured in Shenzhen was a joint venture between a Zhejiang province corporation and a Hong Kong partner. Three hundred blue-jeans-clad girls, all from Zhejiang, near Shanghai, stitch shirts and pants for overseas customers like Marks & Spencer and Daniel Hechter. These workers and managers, also from Zhejiang, will bring money, skills and ideas back to their home province.

Is there anything Americans can do to encourage the spread of China's capitalist revolution? Yes. We can persuade Congress that the best way to end repression in China is not through external pressure on the hard-headed autocrats of Beijing but through encouraging the resourceful capitalist counterrevolutionaries. In its misguided determination to reject President Bush's bid to continue extending most-favored-nation status to China, Congress is harming the coastal reformers and playing right into the hands of the reactionary, nationalistic rulers in Beijing.

"Ending most-favored-nation status would disproportionately injure the province in the forefront of economic reform [Guangdong], with the least human rights violations, that is developing most like the U.S. wants," argues John Kamm. William Simon, managing director of Hong Kong-based Odyssey International, a big down jacket producer, concurs: "Nothing can stop this move toward free markets, incentives and profits except for shutting them off from the world."

Cutting off most-favored-nation privileges would, for example, raise the tariff on imports of stuffed toys from China from 7% to 70%, sweaters from 6% to 35% and watch bands from 14% to 110%. The worst-hit economies would be those of Guangdong and Hong Kong. Kamm estimates that 18% of Guangdong's domestic product last year was accounted for by exports to the U.S.

Although the withering away of communism in China has none of the drama or swiftness that it had in Eastern Europe, its course is equally irresistible. "Guangdong is the model," says David Li. "The rest of China will gradually change. It has to change. Everybody wants a high standard of living." The U.S. can hasten the process. Or it can slow the process. But nothing can stop it.

DOING BUSINESS WITH THE SOVIET REPUBLICS

How republics make the grade

The Soviet Union is breaking up.[1] The Baltics have claimed their independence. The other republics are taking charge of their economies. If you're thinking of doing business in that vast land, which of the 15 Soviet republics would be most welcoming for U.S. companies?

USA TODAY asked Michael Claudon, president of the Geonomics Institute in Middlebury, Vt., to work with us to develop an investment report card for the 15 republics.

Claudon's criteria for grading:

► Living standards. "Higher incomes imply faster market growth once reforms take hold," Claudon says.

► Capacity for earning hard currency. Because Soviet rubles are worthless to U.S. companies, many businesses want to find or make products that can be exported from the Soviet Union to Western nations.

► Government posture toward market reforms.

► Conversion of defense plants to civilian use. The change will drain local economies. Conversions will take time and money and will mean plants must close, then reopen with fewer workers, leaving many former workers of the overstaffed factories unemployed.

► Mix of industry. Consumer goods and energy are potentially the fastest-growing.

► Amount of business contact with the West in the past.

The republics were graded on a curve, comparing them with one another, not to the outside world. Otherwise, the Baltics would rate on par with Mexico.

One thing to keep in mind: The Soviets have lied about their economic figures for so long, no one is sure of such things as gross national product. Consider the numbers as relative guides.

Geonomics is a not-for-profit group that has worked closely with Soviet leaders and U.S. businesspeople to help promote economic reform in the Soviet Union.

Report Card

Each republic's grade reflects its overall potential for business.

Republic	Grade	Republic	Grade
Estonia	A	Moldavia	C
Latvia	A	Armenia	C–
Lithuania	A–	Uzbekistan	D
Ukraine	A–	Azerbaijan	D
Russia	B+	Turkmenistan	D–
Georgia	B–	Kirghizia	D–
Kazakhstan	C+	Tadzhikistan	D–
Bvelorussia	C		

Source: Geonomics Institute

Business travel: Getting to Moscow isn't too tough. Getting to Ashkhabad, in Turkmenistan, or Irkutsk, in Siberia, can be another matter entirely. Some basics:

► The flight. A Pan Am-Aeroflot joint venture flies nonstop to Moscow from New York or Washington, D.C. The flight takes about nine hours. European carriers such as Lufthansa will get you from the USA to Moscow with one or two stops.

That's where the fun begins. Often, the only way to get to a remote Soviet city is to make a connection in Moscow. But when you land at Moscow's international airport, you have to go to a different airport to fly to a domestic destination. If you want to fly to a republic to the south or east, the airport is an hour's drive away. Some of the European carriers will fly from Western Europe directly into Soviet cities such as Kiev or Minsk, an option worth checking out.

► The visa. The Baltics have taken control of their visas. You can get a visa on arrival when you land at the airport. For the rest of the Soviet Union, visas still are being issued by the Soviet Embassy in Washington. You need an invitation from a Soviet to get a business visa, which can take up to two weeks. Tourist visas can take much longer.

► The money. It's confusing, but rubles are worth different amounts at different times. You can only change money at official locations in the Soviet Union, where you usually will get the tourist rate—1 ruble for about 3 U.S. cents. But restaurants, shops and hotels that take only hard currency list

Reprinted by permission of *USA TODAY newspaper,* September 30, 1991, pp. 6B and 7B. Copyright © 1991, USA TODAY.

prices in rubles, then convert at the commercial exchange rate of 1 ruble for $1.60. Keep U.S. currency—small bills—on hand. It can work magic on taxi drivers and just about anyone else in the Soviet Union.

► Fitful phones. Expect the worst when it comes to communications. All international calls must go through Moscow. There are just 91 circuits between Moscow and the USA. AT&T is asking to activate 42 more. AT&T plans to begin direct service to Armenia next month. When available, one of the best ways to communicate with Soviets is by facsimile machine. Faxes are abundant in Riga, Tallinn, Vilnius, Leningrad and Moscow but rare elsewhere.

► Talking business. If you want to impress your host, try these Russian business phrases:

Ocheen priyatna bilo s'vami rabochatz. (It's a pleasure to be able to do business with you.)

Bolshoi spaseebo. (Thank you very much.)

Skolyaka eta sto-eet? (How much is it?)

Mozhna priglaseetya vass na abyet? (May I invite you to lunch?)

Five ranked best among the lot

ESTONIA A

"An excellent transportation system and highly developed consumer-goods manufacturing sector are complemented by a highly educated populace having longstanding ties to Finland and a strong Western orientation. They welcome Western investment and are prepared to accommodate special needs."

GNP: $10 billion.

Population: 1.6 million.

Per capita GNP: $6,240.

Major city: Tallinn (capital, 478,000).

Ethnic groups: 65% Estonian, 28% Russian.

Languages: Estonian, Russian.

Climate: Moderate.

Infrastructure: Good internal roads, railroads; ports on the Baltic; connections to Leningrad, Helsinki, Moscow is 1 1/2 hours away by air; technology and phones are among the best in the Soviet Union, though international connections still must be made through Moscow.

Agriculture: A net food exporter; major products are dairy, cattle, pigs, grain, potatoes.

Industry: Electronics industry makes computers, electric motors and measuring instruments. It also is a major furniture-making center.

Registered joint ventures: 104.

Lodging: In Tallinn, the Viru, a large, basic foreign-tourist hotel; the Tallinn, older but less hectic.

History: Founded by Danes and ruled in turn by Germans, Swedes and Russians. It was independent from 1918 to 1940, when annexed by Stalin in pact with Hitler. Proclaimed independence after Aug. 19 coup failed.

Current situation: After recently claiming independence, it has been passing strong laws toward a market economy. New laws allow property ownership and give Soviet-seized property back to former owners or heirs. Some will get securities equal to the value of the property. Privatization of industry has begun, giving Estonians preference, though foreigners may buy firms using hard currency. Food prices were freed, and prices doubled.

Leader: President Arnold Ruutel.

Investment opportunities: Furniture, electronics (especially electric motors at Volta plant in Tallinn), consumer goods, garment industry.

LATVIA A

"Latvians are of average education and strong Western orientation who enjoy a high standard of living. They are well-versed in details of international commerce and have developed ties in Austria and Sweden."

GNP: $18.2 billion.

Population: 2.7 million.

Per capita GNP: $6,740.

Major city: Riga (capital, 1 million).

Ethnic groups: 54% Latvian, 33% Russian.

Languages: Latvian, Russian.

Climate: Moderate.

Infrastructure: Excellent road and rail transport; ice-free Riga port is second only to Leningrad's; Moscow is 1 1/2 hours away by air; technology and phones are excellent by Soviet standards.

Agriculture: A minor role in the economy. Main products: potatoes, grain, eggs, dairy.

Industry: Major electric-products industry, making telephone switches and electric buses and railway cars. Made half of Soviet motorcycles, 20% of radios. Also biotech, textiles, chemicals. Has few raw materials.

Registered joint ventures: 39.

Lodging: In Riga, the Latvia, busy, basic but only hotel set up for foreigners.

History: Long held by various European forces, it was part of Russia from 1800 to 1918, when it proclaimed independence. Annexed by Stalin in 1940 in pact with Hitler. Proclaimed independence after Aug. 19 Soviet coup failed.

Current situation: Having newly claimed independence, it is making moves toward privatization of land and business. Hasn't gone as far as other Baltics in freeing prices and allowing market forces. Still squabbling with Moscow over what factories and infrastructure left in Latvia belong to Soviets and what Latvia can claim.

Leader: President Anatoly Gorbunovs.

Investment opportunities: Railway-car, motorcycle plants; biotech; electronics and scientific equipment; food processing; synthetic-fiber manufacturing.

LITHUANIA A–

"Well-educated and pro-Western, their transition to a thriving market economy will be aided by the strong and financially successful Lithuanian population in the U.S., which is now eagerly investing in the country."

GNP: $21.8 billion.

Population: 3.7 million.

Per capita GNP: $5,880.

Major city: Vilnius (capital, 566,000).

Ethnic groups: 80% Lithuanian, 9% Russian, 7% Polish.

Languages: Lithuanian, Russian.

Climate: Moderate.

Infrastructure: Good internal roads, railroads; ports on the Baltic with connections to Leningrad, Helsinki; Moscow is 1 1/2 hours away by air; technology and phones are excellent by Soviet standards.

Agriculture: Grain, potatoes, beef cattle, pigs, poultry; relatively productive.

Industry: Well-developed electronics industry making computers, industrial robots, TVs and stereos; shipyards along the

Baltic coast; wood products such as furniture and building materials; amber. Big drawback: few indigenous raw materials.

Registered joint ventures: 18.

Lodging: In Vilnius, Lietuva, one of the soviet Union's best hotels; also the Astoriya.

History: The Grand Duchy of Lithuania united with Poland to create a large state in 1410, but it soon fell to Russia. Independent from 1918 to 1940, when it fell to Stalin as part of a secret pact with Hitler. From March 1990, it had been the most vociferous republic calling for independence from Moscow.

Current situation: Newly independent, the republic has been racing toward a market economy. Since early this year, it has been freeing prices, which has led to rampant inflation, readying businesses and property for privatization and squabbling with the Soviet government over what belongs to the Soviets and what belongs to Lithuania. Likely will introduce its own currency—perhaps the first republic to do so.

Leader: President Vytautas Landsbergis.

Investment opportunities: Precision machine tools, consumer electronics, amber.

UKRAINE A–

"The Ukraine combines a broad industrial base, substantial mineral deposits and a rich agricultural sector. It is outdistancing its rival republics in its efforts to convert defense plants to civilian industry. But Deutsche Bank gave the Ukrainians a failing grade on businessmindedness."

GNP: $243 billion.

Population: 51.7 million.

Per capita GNP: $4,700.

Major cities: Kiev (capital, 2.6 million), Kharkov (1.6 million).

Ethnic groups: 74% Ukrainian, 21% Russian.

Languages: Ukrainian, Russian.

Climate: Moderate, Mediterranean.

Infrastructure: Decent roads, railroads, links to Eastern Europe; Moscow is about one hour away by air; technology, phones are fair, worse in countryside.

Agriculture: Strongest in the Soviet Union. Contributes 46% of Soviet output; grows wheat, corn, tobacco, vegetables; 24% of Soviet beef cattle.

Industry: Made 12% of Soviet refrigerators, 32% of TVs, 23% of canned goods, 20% of chemicals. Biggest Soviet producer of computer processors and peripherals. Mines coal, oil, gas.

Registered joint ventures: 99.

Lodging: In Kiev, Dniepro, centrally located, best for business but small, often booked up. Others in Kiev: Lybid, Rus. In Kharkov, Intourist, Mir.

History: For centuries a part of the Russian empire. Peter the Great smashed an independence rebellion in 1709. In 1919, Lenin had to put down an independence movement. The 1986 Chernobyl nuclear accident left northern parts contaminated.

Current situation: Made limited breakaway moves before the coup—such as declaring that all state enterprises would come under Ukrainian control. But stayed communist until coup dissolved. Pressing for self-determination and a market economy but will keep economic ties to union.

Leader: President Leonid Kravchuk.

Investment opportunities: Farm equipment, computers, tourism, food processing.

RUSSIA B+

"The hub of the U.S.S.R., Russia is actively trying to attract Western investment by establishing free trade and special economic zones in Leningrad and on Sakhalin Island. But it was rated as unbusinessminded and is burdened by the conversion of 460 defense plants to civil enterprises."

GNP: $854 billion.

Population: 147.4 million.

Per capita GNP: $5,810.

Major cities: Moscow (capital, 9 million), Leningrad (5 million), Novosibirsk (1.4 million).

Ethnic groups: 83% Russian, 4% Tartar.

Language: Russian.

Climate: Ranges from moderate in the south to arctic. Moscow's is similar to that of Calgary, Alberta.

Infrastructure: Moscow has the nation's busiest and best international airport. Decent roads and rail links extend from Moscow to major cities. Land travel is nearly impossible in much of the countryside, especially Siberia. Technology, phones are decent in Moscow, fair to poor in most of the rest of the republic, worst in the far north and east.

Agriculture: The republic's 15 million people employed in agriculture produced half the nation's grain and potatoes and 43% of other vegetables.

Industry: Heavy industry and raw materials dominate. Russia made half of the Soviet Union's steel, most of its cars, 60% of its cement, 63% of its electricity, 84% of its paper. Siberia has a wealth of resources—half of the world's coal and natural gas, more oil reserves than Saudi Arabia, one-fifth of the world's gold.

Registered joint ventures: 1,072.

Lodging: In Moscow, the Savoy is best set up for Western businesspeople but hard to get into. Try the Radisson, National, Mezhdunorodnaya or Rossia. In Leningrad, the Astoria, newly restored. In Novosibirsk, Intourist.

History: The Kiev Rus, a Viking people, dominated much of what is now Russia by 1054. Borders and leaders shifted until the czars pushed to the Pacific and down through the Ural mountains by the 1700s. The heart of the 1917 revolution, Russia spread its control throughout the Soviet Union and Eastern Europe after World War II.

Current situation: Russia will be the powerhouse and catalyst behind any confederation of Soviet republics. Its leaders are pressing for a market economy, private property and strong legal framework for business, but those moves are only in beginning stages.

Leaders: Boris Yeltsin, president (popularly elected); Alexander Rutskoi, vice president; Anatoli Sobchak, Leningrad mayor.

Investment opportunities: Consulting, accounting and other business services; telecommunications; consumer products; tourism; medicine.

The other ten republics and their market niches

GEORGIA B–

"Though it has a relatively well-developed industrial structure, excellent agricultural sector and perhaps the most business-minded people of the Soviet Union, Georgia's low degree of self-sufficiency in industrial and consumer goods makes it particularly vulnerable to a breakdown of inter-republic trade."

GNP: $23.8 billion.

Population: 5.4 million.

Per capita GNP: $4,410.

Major city: Tbilisi (capital, 1.2 million).

Ethnic groups: 69% Georgian, 9% Armenian, 7% Russian.

Languages: Georgian, Russian.

Climate: Mild, Mediterranean on Black Sea coast.

Infrastructure: Good to fair roads and railways; Moscow is two hours away by air; technology and phones are fair to poor.

Agriculture: Hugely successful in grapes, citrus fruits, tea and spices. Georgian wine is popular throughout the Soviet Union.

Industry: Mostly food production—wineries, breweries, canneries. Mining, trucks and tractors. A tourism industry thrives on the Black Sea coast.

Registered joint ventures: 41.

Lodging: Tbilisi—the Iveria, modern, basic, swimming pool on roof; the Tbilisi, opened in 1914, city center, more elegant.

Current situation: Ethnic unrest and battles between political factions dominate Georgian life. Likely will stay in a confederation of Soviet states. Economic reform moving slowly. Some food rationing is in place despite the republic's agricultural output. Signed one of the first interrepublic economic agreements, trading Georgian food for Azerbaijani oil.

Leader: President Zviad Gamsakhurdia, under pressure to step down.

Investment opportunities: Tractor production, tourism (on Black Sea), wine, food products.

KAZAKHSTAN C+

"Blessed with potentially lucrative oil fields and huge deposits of rare minerals and led by charismatic, pro-Western leader, Kazakhstan is still unlikely to attract significant Western investment. Its population is relatively uneducated and divided into 100 nationalities that are unlikely to agree on common reform policies."

GNP: $60.3 billion.

Population: 16.2 million.

Per capita GNP: $3,720.

Major city: Alma-Ata (capital, 1.1 million).

Ethnic groups: 36% Kazakh, 41% Russian.

Languages: Russian, Kazakh.

Climate: Dry continental; half the republic is desert.

Infrastructure: Land travel nearly impossible—poor roads, difficult terrain and many off-limit areas (Soviet space launches and nuclear tests are done here). By air, Alma-Ata is five hours from Moscow. Technology and phones are poor.

Agriculture: Successful grain, tobacco, fruit, cotton growing; important meat exporter.

Industry: Abundant minerals, coal, oil and gas. Well-developed primary industry: iron, steel, chemicals, electricity.

Registered joint ventures: 10

Lodging: In Alma-Ata, the Otrar or the Zhetysu in city center. Both are basic and offer international calling.

Current situation: Government has moved swiftly to pass several economic measures—allowing private ownership of housing and setting foreign-trade priorities. But there's still a long way to go. Consumer-goods industry is underdeveloped. Strongly pushing for the confederation, Kazakhstan likely would be an economic force in the new nation.

Leaders: President Nursultan Nazarbayev, emerging as one of the strongest leaders in the Soviet Union.

Investment opportunities: Oil, gas and mineral mining.

BYELORUSSIA C

"While blessed with well-educated people, close proximity to Europe and relative self-sufficiency in industrial goods, the republic is burdened by low-quality textile, food, machinery and consumer-goods (radios, TVs, computers, watches) industries. It is poor in natural resources and has limited hard-currency earning capacity. Commercial ventures will likely service Byelorussia from neighboring Russia."

GNP: $60.8 billion.

Population: 10.2 million.

Per capita GNP: $5,960.

Major city: Minsk (capital, 1.5 million).

Ethnic groups: 79% Byelorussian, 12% Russian.

Languages: Byelorussian, Russian.

Climate: Moderate.

Infrastructure: Roads are moderate to poor, but there are good rail links to Berlin, Warsaw and Moscow. Kiev, Leningrad and Moscow each is a one-hour flight away; the Baltics are even closer. Technology and phones are fair to poor.

Agriculture: Grew 20% of Soviet potatoes, 30% of flax.

Industry: Heavy auto and agricultural-machinery industries (made 20% of Soviet motorcycles, 15% of tractors); refrigerators, machine tools (14% of Soviet total).

Registered joint ventures: 27.

Lodging: In Minsk, the Yubileynaya—comfortable, modern, city center; the Planeta—further out, more hectic.

Current situation: Will stay part of a confederation of republics. Continuing political battles have meant that economic reforms are scattered and ineffective. There are limited moves to free prices and make farms private. The 1986 Chernobyl nuclear accident has left parts of southern Byelorussia heavily contaminated.

Leader: Stanislav S. Shushkevich, first deputy chairman of the Byelorussian Parliament.

Investment opportunities: Food products; truck and tractor manufacturing.

MOLDAVIA C

"Moldavia is close to Western Europe, has an excellent infrastructure by Soviet standards and has highly productive fruit, vegetable, wine and tobacco industries—which have excellent hard-currency earning capacity. Manufacturing-investment opportunities are scarce. Industrial base is limited to small-scale manufacturing of appliances, TVs, farm machinery and electric transformers."

GNP: $16.5 billion.

Population: 4.3 million.

Per capita GNP: $3,830.

Major city: Kishinev (capital, 663,000).

Ethnic groups: 64% Moldavian, 14% Ukrainian, 13% Russian.

Languages: Moldavian, Russian.

Climate: Warm, equable.

Infrastructure: Better than elsewhere in the Soviet Union. Good road and rail links to Kiev, Romania and Odessa on the Black Sea. Technology and phones are fair to poor.

Agriculture: Favorable climate for vegetables, tobacco, grapes for wine.

Industry: Mostly food processing and some light industry.

Registered joint ventures: 14.

Lodging: Kishinev—the Intourist and Kishinev in city center; the Motel Strugurash a bit farther out.

Current situation: Likely will join the confederation but keep close links with neighboring Romania with an eye toward eventual reunification (Moldavia was part of Romania until the Soviet Union annexed it in 1940). Moving surprisingly fast on economic reform, freeing some prices this month and beginning an aggressive step-by-step program to privatize land and businesses.

Leader: Prime Minister Valeriu Muravsky.

Investment opportunities: Food, wine, tobacco production, possibly small-scale consumer products such as TVs, appliances.

ARMENIA C–

"Its strength is its population's free-enterprise orientation and a well-developed infrastructure. But its machine-building and chemical industries are unlikely to earn hard currency soon. Its people are poorly educated, and ethnic conflicts dim its attraction."

GNP: $15.5 billion.

Population: 3.3 million.

Per capita GNP: $4,710.

Major city: Yerevan (capital, 1.2 million).

Ethnic groups: 90% Armenian, 5% Azerbaijani.

Languages: Armenian, Russian, Azerbaijan.

Climate: Continental, hot.

Infrastructure: Better than elsewhere in the Soviet Union, though most mountainous regions are impassable by land. Links to neighboring Turkey. Three hours to Moscow by air. Technology, phones are poor.

Agriculture: The mountainous country isn't good for farming. Crops include grain, potatoes and grapes.

Industry: Machine tools, foundry equipment, plastics, footwear and textiles, notably woven carpets. Major deposits of copper, zinc, aluminum.

Registered joint ventures: 10.

Lodging: Yerevan—the Ani, central but bland; the Armenia, central but bland.

Current situation: Likely will stay in a confederation of republics. Armenia and Azerbaijan agreed recently to a cease fire in ethnic conflicts. Still, Armenia feels vulnerable to Azerbaijan to the east and ancient enemy Turkey to the west. Privatization has been erratic and laws continue to be revised, but the republic seems to be moving quickly to sell or give land and small businesses back to its people.

Leader: President Levon Ter-Petrosyan.

Investment opportunities: Metals, carpets, textiles.

UZBEKISTAN D

"Uzbekistan is the world's third-largest cotton producer, offering a relatively strong investment attraction for textile firms. But its environment has been devastated by irrigation and fertilization. The Aral Sea has shrunk 40%. Pervasive pesticide and chemical pollution of drinking water worries Westerners. The cost of cleanup of its water is estimated at 25 billion rubles."

GNP: $54.7 billion.

Population: 19.9 million.

Per capita GNP: $2,750.

Major city: Tashkent (capital, 2.1 million).

Ethnic groups: 69% Uzbek, 11% Russian.

Languages: Uzbek, Russian.

Climate: Continental, extreme temperatures.

Infrastructure: Fair to poor roads and railways. Tashkent is four hours by air from Moscow. Technology, phones are poor.

Agriculture: 9% arable land; cotton is chief crop.

Industry: Natural gas, chemicals.

Registered joint ventures: 11.

Lodging: In Tashkent, the Uzbekistan, relatively well-appointed but no business services. Other hotels are far inferior.

Current situation: Troubled by ethnic, social, political unrest. Too little food, raging inflation and one of the lowest-paid workforces in the Soviet Union. Limited moves toward a market economy. Likely will stay in confederation.

Leader: President Islam Karimov.

Investment opportunities: Cotton, textiles, natural gas.

AZERBAIJAN D

"The republic has poorly developed industry and infrastructure, and its people suffer from low education levels. But its raw materials' hard-currency earnings capacity is substantial."

GNP: $26.3 billion.

Population: 7 million.

Per capita GNP: $3,750.

Major city: Baku (capital, 1.7 million.)

Ethnic groups: 78% Azerbaijani, 8% Armenian, 8% Russian.

Languages: Azerbaijani, Russian, Armenian.

Climate: Continental, mild in Baku.

Infrastructure: Poor roads and railways; flights to Moscow take three hours; technology, phones are poor.

Agriculture: Weak and menaced by droughts; cotton, grain, sheep.

Industry: Most of the economy is oil-based. Azerbaijan has one of the richest oil fields in the world, still largely untapped. It refines oil and makes petrochemicals and has been the Soviet Union's major producer of oil-drilling equipment.

Registered joint ventures: 10.

Lodging: Baku—the Moskva, best in town for business, city center; Intourist, standard but near sea front.

Current situation: Probably will stay in the confederation, but popular movements call for uniting with neighboring Iran. Signed a cease fire with Armenia in ethnic conflicts. Stronger ties with United States than most republics because of its oil. A number of U.S. oil executives and government officials have visited, and several oil companies are seeking joint ventures—most notably Chevron. Few economic reforms.

Leader: President Ayaz Mutalibov.

Investment opportunities: Oil production, oil-field equipment.

TURKMENISTAN D–

"The republic is renowned for its fine carpets, Turkoman horses and Karakul sheep. The people have shown little appetite for economic reform."

GNP: $11.8 billion.

Population: 3.5 million.

Per capita GNP: $3,370.

Major city: Ashkhabad (capital, 398,000).

Ethnic groups: 68% Turkoman, 13% Russian.
Languages: Turkoman, Russian.
Climate: Extreme temperatures, 90% is desert.
Infrastructure: Poor roads; Ashkhabad is on the Transcaspian rail line linking the Caspian Sea to Uzbekistan; Moscow is 3 1/2 hours away by air; technology and phones are poor.
Agriculture: 2% arable land; main crop is cotton.
Industry: Oil and gas production, salt.
Registered joint ventures: One.
Lodging: In Ashkhabad, the Ashkhabad hotel—basic with no business services but two good restaurants.
Current situation: Mostly quiet since the Aug. 19 coup attempt. Little political or economic reform. President issued list of items that can't be privately owned—including weapons, drugs and printing equipment. Likely will join confederation.
Leader: President Saparmurad Niyazov.
Investment opportunities: Natural-gas production, carpets, cotton and textiles.

KIRGHIZIA D–

"Its poor transportation system and earthquake exposure make the republic an unlikely investment destination for Westerners. Its industry is relatively undeveloped and its population is less educated and business-minded than in other republics."
GNP: $13 billion.
Population: 4.3 million.
Per capita GNP: $3,030.
Major city: Frunze (capital, 630,000).
Ethnic groups: 48% Kirghiz, 26% Russian.
Languages: Kirghiz, Russian.
Climate: Continental, dry, half of mountainous republic 10,000 feet above sea level.
Infrastructure: Poor roads and railways; Moscow is three hours away by air; technology and phones are poor.
Agriculture: 7% arable land; potatoes, vegetables, cotton; beekeeping; mostly livestock breeding—sheep, goats, yaks.
Industry: Metallurgy, coal, oil and gas production, tourism (health spas).
Registered joint ventures: Two.
Lodging: In Frunze, the Ala Tau, three floors, no elevators, spartan.
Current situation: Ethnic tensions, land shortages and poverty are the rule. The government has passed market-reform laws and is seeking foreign investment, but that's made little difference to Kirghizia's sorry economy. Likely will stay in the confederation.
Leader: President Askar Akyayev.
Investment opportunities: Oil, coal and gas, tourism, wool.

TADZHIKISTAN D–

"Perhaps the republic's most notable characteristic is that it contains Communism Peak, at 24,590 feet the highest point in the Soviet Union. Interest in doing business is scarce."
GNP: $11.9 billion.
Population: 5.1 million.
Per capita GNP: $2,340.
Major city: Dushanbe (capital, 582,000).
Ethnic groups: 59% Tadzhik, 23% Uzbek, 10% Russian.
Languages: Tadzhikan, Russian, Uzbek.
Climate: From subtropical in regions to harsh in Pamir Mountains.
Infrastructure: Very poor roads and railways; Moscow is about four hours away by air; technology and phones are poor.
Agriculture: 6% arable land; grain, cotton, sheep, cattle, yaks.
Industry: Textiles, carpet weaving, metal mining and processing.
Registered joint ventures: One.
Lodging: In Dushanbe, the Tadzhikistan.
Current situation: The only republic where the Communist Party has reclaimed leadership. The republic is mired in unemployment and poverty and has made little economic reform. Likely will stay in the confederation but seek ties with nearby Iran.
Leader: Rakhman Nabiyev, president until Oct. 27 elections.
Investment opportunities: Carpets, wool, hydroelectric power.

Sources for this report

Information on the republics and business travel was prepared from the following sources:

- Geonomics Institute, Middlebury, Vt.
- Deutsche Bank reports available through Trans-Atlantic Futures, Washington, D.C.
- PlanEcon, Washington, D.C.
- *U.S.S.R.: The Economist Business Traveller's Guides* (Prentice Hall, $19.95).
- *Commersant,* a Soviet business weekly available through Refco Group, Chicago ($265 a year).
- *Berlitz Russian for Travellers* ($5.95).
- Intourist, the Soviet tourism enterprise, New York.
- *Doing Business in the Union of Soviet Socialist Republics,* Price Waterhouse, New York.
- *Meltdown: Inside the Soviet Economy,* Paul Craig Roberts and Karen LaFollette (Cato Institute, $9.95).
- *The Harper Collins Business Guide to Moscow* (Harper & Row, $9.95).

U.S. firms face legal hurdles in Soviet Union

After all the political hoopla in the Soviet Union, few changes have been made in the Soviet laws that are most critical to U.S. companies interested in doing business there.

Some of the key hurdles:

- Convertible currency. The Soviet ruble is worthless to U.S. companies, and laws governing it are confusing. Rubles can't be exchanged for other currencies. They can't be taken out of the Soviet Union. And they can't be used to buy anything on world markets.

That prevents foreign companies from taking profits out of the Soviet Union. The only way to make money is to use ruble profits to buy items on the Soviet market that can be shipped out of the country and sold in Western nations.

The Baltic states say they plan to introduce their own currencies as early as next year, and they'll try to quickly make the currencies convertible. The Baltics most likely will be the first Soviet republics to accomplish that. The republic of Russia may succeed in pushing the ruble to convertibility within the next two years but not without political fights and much more strain on its economy. The other republics likely will not have convertible currencies before Russia does.

► Private ownership. Owning private property is still illegal in most cases in any of the Soviet republics. That should change fastest in the Baltics. Lithuanian President Vytautas Landsbergis, for instance, says he wants to put almost all his nation's land and buildings into private hands by next year. Russia is beginning to experiment with handing over apartments and farms to private owners. Bureaucracy and inertia will keep most Russian property in state hands for years. Other republics will lag.

► Business laws. The Soviet Union had laws that prevented profiteering. Businesses had no legal guarantees that the state would not meddle or take them over at any time. Little has changed. Estonia is trying to push through business laws this year that are modeled on those in Western Europe. The other Baltics are close to doing the same.

Russia likely will pass more cautious business laws in the next few years. Most other republics may take much longer to reform.

---

[1]The Soviet Union was disbanded in December 1991 and replaced by the Commonwealth of Independent States. Ed.

LOCKING UP TOMORROW'S PROFITS

U.S. companies are searching for the key to business success in Europe, but commercial doors on the Continent may not open very wide

American business wants—and desperately needs—access to European markets. With the U.S. economy struggling to recover from a vicious recession, many companies in this country have become increasingly dependent on exports, one of the only sources of growth in the early 1990s. From a deficit of $25 billion in 1986, America chalked up a $19 billion trade surplus with Europe last year. Already the world's largest purchaser of cars, Europe is also one of the leading computer consumers. These facts have obviously made a big impression on companies like General Motors and IBM, which enjoy tremendous success on the Continent.

But garnering future profits in Europe may become difficult. Economic momentum in most continental countries has recently slowed, dampening demand for U.S. products. At the same time, competitive tensions between Europe and America have escalated over agricultural subsidies and threaten to undermine crucial trade talks. "Political tensions are going to rise," says economist Lester Thurow. "Everyone was scared of the Russian bear. Now that you don't have to cooperate economically to hold military alliances together, Europe will become assertive. They need us less."

A number of American companies have already found that out. Federal Express discovered that European companies don't change timeworn business practices overnight and is pulling out of the intra-European express-mail market. Though they are making inroads, American machine-tool makers are fighting entrenched German competitors. And U.S. warehouse clubs may receive a rude welcome if they try to cross the Atlantic and land in Great Britain.

The business climate in Europe could become even more tenuous if the Maastricht treaty, which provides for a common European currency by the end of the decade, falls apart. Despite the growing uncertainty, most U.S. companies have yet to scale back their designs on the European market. If they persist, they may find that cashing in on the Continent could take a lot longer than expected.

U.S. CAR MAKERS PREPARE FOR A COLLISION ON THE CONTINENT

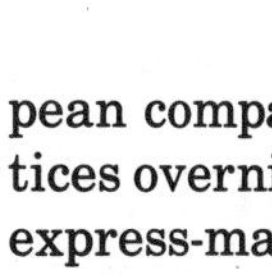

Ben Staartjes is the kind of customer that has executives at General Motors Europe grinning from ear to ear. For 20 years, the Dutch businessman proudly drove a succession of sleek, dark Jaguar sedans. But in late April, he forked over a cool $63,788 and change for a white Cadillac Seville STS instead.

From *U.S. News & World Report,* June 29, 1992, pp. 57-60. Copyright © 1992, U.S. News & World Report.

Staartjes's car conversion helps explain why GM has been such a success in Europe. With sales of 1.6 million autos expected this year, the company takes the checkered flag as one of the Continent's most dynamic car makers. But it was only after losing $2.3 billion between 1980 and 1986 that GM Europe managed a turnaround. Sales shot up 62 percent in five years and GM Europe made $1.8 billion on $25.4 billion in 1991, almost double the profits of Peugeot, the runner-up.

Lean management, efficient production, good labor relations despite job cuts in Germany, major savings in component sourcing and a complete model series are the main reasons GM has been able to pull itself out of the mud. But the American auto giant could easily get bogged down again in Europe because of intense Japanese competition. Nine Japanese car makers have 12.4 percent of the European market, despite quotas that limit them to 11 percent of the British market, 3 to 4 percent of France's and Spain's and a rock-bottom 2 percent of Italy's. These numbers may move higher, because the European Community and Japan have a shaky pact that will offer Japan free entry into the EC by 1999.

Europe is now the single-largest buyer of cars in the world

To combat Japan's onslaught, GM Europe is investing an estimated $1.4 billion over the next four years. Some of the money will be poured into a new car plant in eastern Germany and an engine factory in Hungary. But this new capital might not be enough to stop Japan's powerful drive through Europe.

AMERICAN COMPANIES COULD FEEL THE PAIN IN SPAIN

One deal in Spain seems to lead to another these days. With General Motors expanding its manufacturing operations in the country, Ingersoll-Rand recently paid about $15 million to snap up a majority interest in an auto parts business there. The purchase of the ball bearings company will beef up Ingersoll's business in Spain by some 20 percent. Faced with sluggish sales at home, PepsiCo has announced plans to invest $1 billion in Spain to build soft-drink plants and open fast-food restaurants. And Du Pont intends to invest $1 billion to develop several Spanish fiber-manufacturing plants over the next decade.

By providing Spain with a quarter of its foreign investment, American firms are betting that Europe's economic prodigy can live up to its promises. But some U.S. investors may have arrived too late. To fulfill Maastricht treaty requirements that govern entrance into Europe's monetary union, Spain has to meet tough targets on inflation, interest rates and budget deficits. During the late 1980s, Spain's gross domestic product grew 4.7 percent a year, outdistancing the average growth rate of 3.2 percent in the European Community. But Spain's GDP growth slowed to 3.8 percent in 1990 and to an estimated 3 percent in 1991. What's more, the Spanish inflation rate hit 5.7 percent last year, exceeding the EC's average inflation rate of 4.6 percent. At the same time, Madrid ran an $11 billion budget deficit.

America has a $19 billion trade surplus with Europe

Curbing those excesses could further constrain Spain's growth, dampen much-needed spending on the nation's transportation infrastructure and spark labor strife. Unfortunately, many American companies may have to pay the price as the country comes to grips with its incipient economic woes in the 1990s.

GERMAN TOOL PRODUCERS TRY TO GRIND DOWN U.S. RIVALS

After a decade of decline in the American machine-tool industry, an era that saw sales plummet and hundreds of companies fold, U.S. manufacturers have become savvy to the possibilities of global expansion and are targeting Germany and Central Europe as fertile ground for new sales. For the first time in years, American makers of milling and grinding machines, lathes and shapers have a unique opportunity to make headway in these markets, which have traditionally been dominated by the Germans. Cincinnati Milacron, the second-largest U.S. machine-tool maker, for example, sells its products in Europe and has selected a site for a new factory in Germany.

Tough export controls on German machine equipment have made foreign clients wary about placing orders with German companies. And high labor costs and the tendency of German manufacturers to rest on their laurels have added to the disenchantment. As a result, U.S. machine-tool makers increased their share of the German market last year by 50 percent, bringing their total share of imports into Germany to 6.6 percent. Encouraged by these numbers, the Association for Manufacturing Technology, an American trade association for machine-tool makers, has opened a Zurich office to promote U.S. machine tools in Central Europe.

But the continental market won't be easily won.

Most observers say the best way to stay in Europe is to manufacture within Europe. In western Germany, that means heavy taxes that can run as high as 50 percent on dividends and short working hours, which are disincentives to American companies. In eastern Germany and Central Europe, the hurdles have more to do with culture, language and geography. These obstacles are not insurmountable, yet American machine-tool makers are in for a very tough fight as they try to displace Germany from its pre-eminent position in Europe.

FLYING BLIND INTO EUROPE'S EXPRESS-MAIL MARKET

For nearly two decades Federal Express has flown high in the United States. Renowned for its service, the express-mail company has fended off an army of imitators and still commands nearly half the $10 billion American market for overnight delivery. But eight years after the Memphis-based company made its first flights into Europe, it has landed on the Continent with a thud. After losing as much as $200 million a year in Europe, FedEx has cut 6,600 employees and closed more than 100 European facilities. In its third fiscal quarter, the company had an operating loss of $250.6 million, which included a European restructuring charge of $254 million. This prompted Standard & Poor's to downgrade the debt rating on FedEx's commercial paper from A-2 to A-3.

What's behind the express-mail company's foreign fall from grace? "We made two fundamental assumptions that turned out to be incorrect," says Thomas Oliver, executive vice president for Federal Express's worldwide customer operations. First, FedEx assumed the European express-mail market would experience the explosive growth that made the company rich in America. FedEx spent millions to snap up trucking operations and establish a vast hub-and-spoke network based in Brussels. But despite the Continent's move toward unity, the majority of mail continued to travel within–not between–countries in Europe. "The average company in Columbus, Ohio, has more occasion to send packages to places like Phoenix than a Stuttgart company does to send packages to Milan or Paris," says Paul Schlesinger, an analyst with Donaldson, Lufkin & Jenrette.

FedEx's second error was its underestimation of costs. Packages coming into Great Britain from Germany, for example, had to first go through FedEx's hub in Brussels, then clear customs in England, adding to time, costs and paperwork. Including customs, FedEx's cost per package in Europe was four to five times what it was in the United States.

After selling its intra-European business to rivals, FedEx will concentrate on intercontinental deliveries instead. This will cut out $300 million a year in fixed costs and could help put the company back in the black. FedEx's big challenge now is to persuade European businesses to fly with someone who does less, better.

AMERICAN DISCOUNTERS MAY PAY THE PRICE IN BRITAIN

A battle is shaping up on the other side of the Atlantic, and the enemy hasn't even come ashore yet. Ever since rumors starting flying earlier this year that Costco, a $52 billion American warehouse club, was hunting around Great Britain for possible locations, British wholesalers and retailers have been on the lookout.

Costco has yet to sign a lease in Britain, but the company, which has seen its profits triple over the past three years to $85 million, admits it is searching for sites. And a Goldman Sachs study found there is room for 30 Costco-type warehouse in Britain. According to the analysis, these warehouses could generate sales of nearly $4 billion over the next five to 10 years.

European economic growth reached just 1.3 percent last year

Successfully transferring a U.S. retailing formula to the United Kingdom is easier said than done, however. The cost of doing business could turn out to be a stumbling block, for instance. Land in Britain is expensive, and a thicket of regulations and planning requirements govern the issuance of building permits. In addition, current laws in Britain prohibit wholesalers from opening their doors to shoppers. This could prove troublesome for Costco since two thirds of its customers are small businesses who buy at wholesale prices.

British merchants are also quick to argue that retailers won't patronize a wholesaler who competes with them for customers. "I think warehouse clubs will die here because of the tradition of the retailer despising the wholesaler who wishes to have his cake and eat it too," says Alan Toft, director-general of the Federation of Wholesaler Distributors.

But that may be wishful thinking. "To believe that even if they can obtain items more conveniently and at lower prices [that] small businesses will stay out of clubs out of a sense of moral outrage is naive," says Christopher Vroom of Alex. Brown & Sons. "It's the same attitude U.S. small wholesalers had before Costco eroded their business." Cultural differences aside, merchants in Britain may soon find out that a bargain is still a bargain no matter where it is found.

By Eva Pomice, John Marks in Berlin, Jonathan Kapstein in Brussels, Kathy Burton in Paris and Dana Hawkins

NOW THE NEW NEW EUROPE

The drive toward 1992 in Western Europe has converged with the growth of market economies in the old communist bloc. The result: big risks and big opportunities.

Shawn Tully

CALL IT the *new* New Europe. In a breathtaking rendezvous on the eve of 1992, the drive for a unified market has converged with the fall of communism to make Europe a far bigger and more competitive place to do business. In this special report, FORTUNE describes both the opportunities and the challenges facing Europe in the decade ahead.

The risks are real, the problems deep. For all its immense potential, the fissioning Soviet Union could explode into chaos, unleashing a flood of emigrants that would severely strain Western Europe's economy and poison its politics. Many of Europe's biggest companies—including most carmakers, airlines, and computer firms—are far less efficient than U.S. and Japanese rivals.

Europe's greatest asset is its new capacity to grow. The 12-member European Community, a sprawling bloc of 325 million free-spending consumers, may well expand to include at least 25 countries and 450 million people by the year 2000.

The EC is forging links with two big trading blocs: the European Free Trade Association, or EFTA, a long-standing confederation of Western European countries outside the Common Market; and Central Europe's three strongest economies, Hungary, Czechoslovakia, and Poland.

REPORTER ASSOCIATE *Thomas J. Martin*

The seven EFTA countries—Austria, Finland, Iceland, Liechtenstein, Norway, Sweden, Switzerland—are home to 32 million of the world's most affluent consumers. They have just concluded an agreement to start lifting all trade barriers with EC countries on January 1, 1993. Sweden and Austria have applied to become full members of the EC and should be admitted by 1995. Switzerland, Norway, and Finland are debating whether to join the club.

The EC is talking about admitting Poland, Czechoslovakia, and Hungary around the year 2000. In the meantime it is concluding sweeping agreements that will gradually establish free trade between the EC and the three countries, starting next year. In January the EC will begin negotiating similar pacts with Romania and Bulgaria.

The deals with Central Europe promise to be far more significant than those with EFTA. Major companies in the EC and EFTA already do a thriving business in each other's markets. Taking down the last of the barriers will simply make that trade easier. Central Europe is totally different. Since it now consumes minuscule amounts of Western goods, it amounts to rich terrain for new business. U.S. and Japanese companies will benefit too. Coca-Cola, General Motors, and Sony among many others consider Central Europe one of the world's most promising growth markets for the 1990s.

By meshing the economies of the EC, EFTA, and Central Europe, the new agreements greatly enhance the growth prospects for all three. The big dividends from Central Europe won't come right away because it is still trying to adjust to the collapse in trade with the Soviet Union. Scott Vicary, an analyst with the London investment firm of James Capel, thinks Central Europe will start growing slowly in 1993, then sprint ahead at up to an 8% annual rate toward the end of the decade. Says he: "That's roughly the same growth rate West Germany achieved after World War II."

Morgan Stanley projects that such rapid growth will lift the collective GDP of seven Central European countries—including Romania, Bulgaria, Yugoslavia, and Albania—by 170% in 15 years, to $1.6 trillion. Feeding that growth would in turn increase the combined output of the EC and EFTA by some 23%.

Western Europe can use the lift. After reaching 4% in 1988 and 3.3% in 1989, EC annual growth dropped to just over 1% in 1990. Now the outlook is brighter. Says J. Paul Horne, an economist with Smith Barney in Paris: "I had expected EC growth to coast along at 2.5% a year in the middle to late 1990s. Now, because of heavy demand from the East, annual growth could average 3.5%."

Even more bullish is Norbert Walter, chief economist for Germany's Deutsche Bank. "With 32 million wealthy consumers," says Walter, "EFTA will boost European growth starting next year." Central Europe's contribution will come later, he says, beginning in 1994 or 1995. A Europe-wide investment boom, not unlike

From *Fortune,* December 2, 1991, pp. 136-142. Copyright © 1991 by The Time Inc. Magazine Company. Reprinted by permission.

the one that has led up to 1992, should provide, Walter adds, "clear sailing from the mid-1990s onward."

The two things most likely to go wrong: a credit crunch, and chaos in the Soviet Union that sends millions of refugees west. Either event would play havoc with the one economy that Europe must depend on—Germany's.

Only Germany can lead Europe out of recession. And Germany is highly vulnerable to shocks from the East. To pay for unification, the German government raised taxes and shouldered a large budget deficit. At the same time, it reined in prices by tightening credit, which triggered higher interest rates across Europe, slowing growth in all EC countries.

Next year the threat of inflation should wane as eastern Germany begins to satisfy its tremendous appetite for goods and capital. That should allow Germany to cut interest rates sharply from the current 9%. With the tonic of lower rates, Europe should get back on a growth track.

A recession-producing credit crunch is either inevitable or unlikely, depending on what assumptions you make about who will pay to rebuild central Europe and what the final tab will be. On the scary side, the Centre for Economic Policy Research in London argues that *all* the money for capital investment—as much as $200 billion a year for ten years—must flow from *abroad* in the form of loans, aid, and direct investment. Most of the money, the Centre thinks, would come from Germany, Central Europe's neighbor and natural trading partner. The result would be a replay of unification. Central Europe's huge capital demands would raise interest rates and prolong the slump in Europe.

THERE IS a more hopeful view. It is more probable that Central Europe will pay for its own development. Fast-growing countries from Spain to Singapore have produced large tax surpluses, high domestic savings, and strong export growth that swells retained earnings. These countries have tapped those savings and profits to buy the bulk of their imported capital equipment. Says Barry Bosworth, an economist at the Brookings Institution: "Central Europe should follow the same pattern. The credit crunch is grossly exaggerated." According to Bosworth, Central Europe will absorb no more than $30 billion a year in foreign capital. Rapid growth, he reckons, could generate $150 billion a year in hard currency for computers, oil refineries, and machine tools.

The real peril is a huge migration. Germany is a magnet for refugees from Central Europe and the Soviet Union. If rising unrest forces Central Europe's governments to scrap free-market reforms, in the mid-1990s their economies will stall instead of taking off. Waves of impoverished refugees would flood into Germany. An economic cataclysm in the Soviet Union could unleash an even bigger influx.

Germany, which has by far the most liberal immigration laws in Europe, is already absorbing thousands of refugees. Since 1989 it has taken in more than 1.2 million immigrants, or 2% of its population of 61 million, chiefly from Poland, Yugoslavia, Romania, and the Soviet Union. Many are ethnic Germans, descendants of German settlers in Eastern Europe, whom Germany is obliged under its constitution to accept as citizens. Economic disaster could increase the flow: Another three million ethnic Germans are battling poverty in Poland and several former Soviet republics.

In the long term, a steady flow of immigrants will strengthen Germany: The number of native-born workers there will decline steeply in the 1990s, and immigrants will fill blue-collar jobs that the Germans increasingly shun. But the financial strain is already tremendous. Germany expects to spend more than $10 billion in 1991, equal to about 15% of its budget deficit, in order to provide housing, training, and welfare for immigrants. Massive immigration would multiply that figure—and magnify the traumas of unification. Instead of leading Europe's revival, Germany could be hobbled by swelling deficits, rising inflation, and high interest rates.

Fortunately, the new trade pacts should spread prosperity in Central Europe—and reduce threats of both migration and a shortage of credit. The EC's decision to embrace Central Europe is a stunning reversal accelerated by the aborted coup in the Soviet Union. Until the nations of Central Europe renounced their communist governments, they got the EC's least favorable treatment on trade, along with Vietnam and North Korea. In the late 1980s, Poland, Czechoslovakia, and Hungary supplied just 2% of the EC's imports, or about $9 billion a year, far less than the EC buys from Sweden.

In 1990 the EC greeted Central Europe's liberation with more generous terms of trade. The EC temporarily suspended all tariffs and quotas on manufactured goods as varied as cosmetics and electric motors, and lowered duties on politically "sensitive" items including shoes, TV sets, and chemicals. The catch: The EC kept tight restrictions on Central Europe's biggest export products—steel, textiles, and agricultural goods.

THIS YEAR negotiations for a new set of trade pacts, or association agreements as they are called, got off to a bad start. The EC offered few new concessions. But the attempted coup jolted the EC out of its protectionist stance. The looming breakup in the Soviet Union threatened to decimate already shrinking trade with its former satellites. Without an new outlet for its products, Central Europe faced an economic catastrophe.

That was a risk the EC couldn't take. Says Jan Truszczynski, deputy director in Poland's mission to the EC: "There's no question that the Soviet putsch convinced the members to open their markets to the East." In September, after France briefly blocked the proposal in a disagreement over meat imports, the EC presented Poland, Czechoslovakia, and Hungary with an improved formula for free trade. Slated to take effect in early 1992, the association agreements call for almost totally open borders between the EC and Central Europe within ten years.

That timetable is deceiving: Poland, Czechoslovakia, and Hungary have ten years to scrap their quotas and tariffs, which typically average between 15% and 20%, but the EC will dismantle its barriers far faster. The holiday on duties and quotas for consumer products, electric motors, and other manufactured goods will become permanent.

The key concessions by the EC came in steel, textiles, and agriculture. The 18-year-old limits on steel imports from Central Europe will cease in 1992, and the 5% tariff will stop in 1995. The EC plans to phase out restraints on textile imports by 1997, years before it lifts restrictions for its other trading partners under the worldwide Multi-Fibre Agreement. Exports of farm products, just 17% of Central Europe's sales to the EC in 1990, will get a substantial boost. The EC pledges to reduce tariffs on meat, fruit, and vegetables by 60% over the next three years and to increase quotas by 50% in five years.

The seed money for the big, rich market that Central Europe could become will come from Western European companies. Central Europe offers two major resources: a cheap, well-educated work force and vast, potentially low-cost agricultural production. Its workers earn Southeast Asian wages but boast a near Western European level of education. Though wages will hardly stay low forever, factory workers in Czechoslovakia right now earn $2,500 a year on average compared with $23,000 in western Germany.

Well-trained engineers, scarce in Western Europe, are plentiful east of the Elbe. Scientific education is especially strong in Hungary and Czechoslovakia. In 1988 a Swedish research institute tested high school students from 17 countries for achievement in science. Hungarian pupils finished first, far ahead of the Americans, Germans, and Japanese. Yet Hungarian engineers are a bargain. GE-Tungsram, a Hungarian light bulb manufacturer owned by General Electric of the U.S., pays its engineers $7,000 a year, including benefits, vs. more than $50,000 paid out by competitors like Siemens of Germany.

CENTRAL EUROPE is a sleeping giant in agriculture. Even today the three major countries and eastern Germany turn out half the milk, two-thirds the cattle, and three times the potatoes produced by France, the Netherlands, Britain, and western Germany. Despite primitive equipment—the Poles plow their wheat fields with antediluvian Soviet tractors belching black smoke—prices for many commodities are already lower than in Western Europe. Polish strawberries, for example, cost 18 cents a pound wholesale, vs. $1 in Britain.

In automobiles, Central Europe is a boon to producers seeking to escape Western Europe's high labor costs and tough union rules. Next year General Motors will start exporting 200,000 engines a year from a factory in Hungary to assembly plants in the EC. Volkswagen acquired Czech automaker Skoda, and plans to make it a major brand in Western Europe.

For the EC, the sting of competition will be soothed by the rise of the new market in Central Europe. The accords with EFTA are a fat bonus. The free-trade zone embracing the EC, EFTA, and Central Europe provides a sturdy foundation for Europe's future. It will reduce the threat of economic disaster in the East and help revitalize Europe as the glow fades from 1992. A true common market is coming into view, one so vast that even the Community's idealistic founders would have gazed in wonder.

MEGAMARKET

The North American Free Trade Agreement: a $6 trillion market gamble for 363 million consumers

BARBARA RUDOLPH

SUPPORTERS SEE IT AS THE BEST hope for escape from economic stagnation, a boost for trade and investment, a boon for employment, a lift for standards of living. Critics counter that it will strike a mortal blow at entire sectors of U.S., Canadian and Mexican industry, idling tens of thousands of workers whose jobs will move elsewhere, never to return. Europeans and Asians fret that it may accelerate a division of the world into giant protectionist trading blocs lurking behind new walls of tariffs and bureaucratic restrictions.

The subject of these conflicting visions is an edifice of daring scope and complexity, the North American Free Trade Agreement. Negotiators for the U.S., Canada and Mexico, at work virtually nonstop for the past 14 months, are in the final stages of preparing several hundred pages of regulation upon regulation, written in droning legalese. Yet once approved by the three governments, the trade pact will mark a dramatic turn in the history of the continent: at a stroke it will formalize a grand economic alliance, cement Mexico into a unity it has always occupied geographically, if not psychologically and culturally, and reshape the way North American business is done.

The agreement will bind together three major economies—two mature and wealthy, the third relatively poor but in the throes of rapid and profound modernization. Building upon a similar agreement between the U.S. and Canada that took effect in 1989, the expanded pact will create a $6.4 trillion megamarket of 363 million consumers. But it will also challenge the three governments with the prospect of far-reaching social dislocations. What worries politicians in all three nations is, Will the trade-off be worth it?

At its most basic level, the treaty will roll back as many as 20,000 separate tariffs over the next 10 to 15 years. Currently those barriers average nearly 11% in Mexico, around 5% in Canada and less than 4% in the U.S. (though duties on products like cocoa, for example, go as high as 20% in Mexico; in Canada tequila is slapped with a 183% duty). More important will be the steps that NAFTA takes to diminish nontariff barriers, such as dairy and cotton quotas in the U.S. and Canada, and various import licenses in Mexico. By rapidly widening the consumer market, the pact aims to spur capital investment across all three jurisdictions. This would be a striking change for Mexico, which has long banned outside ownership of strategic sectors like farm and border lands and oil.

While sweeping, the treaty will not cover everything: Mexico, in line with its constitution, has flatly ruled out foreign ownership in its energy industry, while Canada seeks to extend the blanket protection it won in its earlier agreement with the U.S. for "cultural industries" such as television and publishing. But in a major concession, Mexico has agreed to allow American companies to establish stakes in its banks and, under NAFTA, will include insurance and securities firms, institutions previously barred to foreign ownership.

Behind the numbing technicalities that define any trade agreement, the bot-

UNEQUAL PARTNERS

	U.S.	Canada	Mexico
GDP in billions of dollars (1991)	$5,673	$501	$283
Population in millions (1991)	253	27	83
Per capita income (1990)	$22,400	$21,980	$3,400
Hourly compensation in manufacturing	$14.77	$16.02	$1.80
Literacy rate	99%	99%	87%
Median age	33	33.5	19
Infant mortality per 1,000	10	7	29

Sources: Data Resources; U.S. Bureau of Census; U.S. Dept. of Commerce; CIA

From *Time*, August 10, 1992, pp. 43-44. Copyright © 1992 by The Time Inc. Magazine Company. Reprinted by permission.

tom line of NAFTA concerns growth and jobs. Proponents argue that the agreement will create both. Washington's conservative Heritage Foundation estimates that Mexico's growth rate, 3.6% last year, could rise to between 6% and 9% if the treaty is ratified.

The U.S. economy will not get anywhere near as big a jolt—it is eight times as large as the other two combined—but should enjoy an explosion in exports to Mexico. According to trade experts, those could increase substantially from a projected $40 billion this year, ultimately creating more and bigger American paychecks. Says U.S. Trade Representative Carla Hills: "For every billion dollars worth of exports, we gain 20,000 jobs." More important, she told a press conference last week, jobs in export industries pay on average 17% more than employment in the rest of the economy.

Labor leaders fear pain, rather than gain. They contend that tens of thousands of workers will be laid off as U.S. companies shift production south to take advantage of industrial wages in Mexico that are roughly one-sixth of those in the U.S. and Canada. The U.S. auto industry alone could lose thousands of positions. Mexican workers earning less than $20 a day are already building hundreds of thousands of Ford Mercury Tracers and Buick Centuries in Hermosillo and Ramos Arizpe and shipping them north. Under the pact, the Big Three's presence south of the border will surely grow in the next few years.

Yet many of those lost jobs would probably vanish anyway, either going under to foreign competition or moving to Asia. And there is an advantage to keeping even lost employment closer to home: manufacturers who move to Mexico are more likely to retain their proximate U.S. suppliers than are those who move to Asia. In fact, the trade pact may persuade many U.S. and other companies to shift production from low-cost Asian plants to low-cost Mexican plants, which could generate additional business for U.S. suppliers.

Zenith Electronics, for example, the leading U.S. producer of television sets, has already moved many of its operations from Taiwan to Mexico, and two months ago closed its Asian assembly plant altogether. Without a Mexican base, Zenith guesses, it would have lost about 4,000 U.S. jobs from its Chicago circuit-board plant and its Missouri molding and assembly factory. Another 2,000 to 5,000 supplier jobs would have vanished as well.

Despite the stakes, NAFTA has not made much of a splash in the U.S. presidential campaign . . . so far. The main reason is that Bill Clinton generally supports the idea of a free-trade treaty and believes it is in the best interest of American labor, at least over the long term. But he has criticized Bush Administration negotiators for not doing enough to protect American workers. "The President made clear representations on labor standards," Clinton said, "and there appears to be very little of that in the agreement."

What will be the pact's effect on the global economy? Most economists believe that the world is drifting toward three major regional trading blocs: North America, Europe and, more slowly, Asia. The question, says Michael Aho, a fellow at the Council on Foreign Relations in New York City, is whether these connections will turn out to be "benign or belligerent."

Some opponents of NAFTA argue that

How Trade Barriers Hurt U.S. Consumers

America's array of often contradictory trade restrictions are a major obstacle to raising its standard of living and strengthening its competitiveness, according to a study by economist James Bovard for the Dallas-based National Center for Policy Analysis. Tariffs and quotas cost each U.S. family an average of about $800 a year. Low-income households suffer more because they spend a greater share of their earnings on food and clothing, two of the most rigidly controlled imports. Despite efforts to eliminate quotas, more than 3,000 of them restrict foreign apparel and textiles, adding $40 billion to U.S. clothing prices. ■

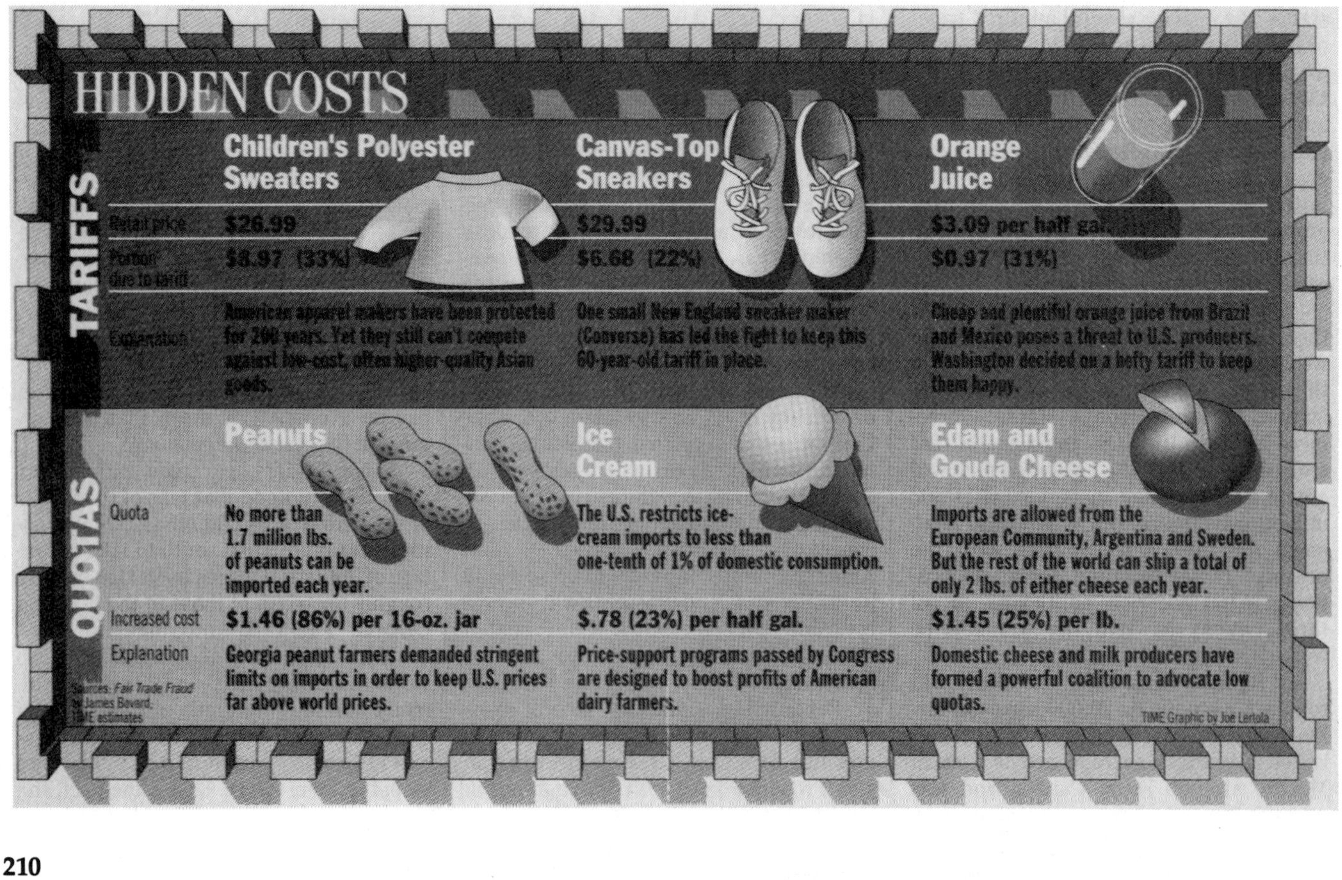

regional trade arrangements are inevitably destructive. "The NAFTA pact is managed trade," says economist and Nobel laureate Milton Friedman. "Worldwide reduction of tariff barriers is much to be preferred to regional trade agreements." That may be so, but the so-called Uruguay Round of global tariff reductions under the General Agreement on Tariffs and Trade is stalled. Proponents of the North American pact argue that nothing in the agreement will contravene the GATT accord, if it is ever reached.

And in any event, with or without NAFTA, the three North American economies are becoming ever more entwined. The U.S.-Canada trade relationship, for years the world's largest ($176 billion last year), grew at a substantially higher rate after the 1989 deal. Even without NAFTA, U.S.-Mexico trade has exploded to $43 billion, more than double the total five years ago.

The one certainty is that the trade agreement will not please everyone. Like all political accords, it will be packed with compromises, limitations and second-best solutions. The best basis for assessing the accord is not whether it causes dislocation for any given group of enterprises or people—international competition already does that—but whether it provides a better foundation for the economic security and future prosperity of 363 million people. The benefits derived so far from closer economic relationships between the three countries, and the benefits likely to ensue, make the proposed pact look like a gamble worth taking.

—With reporting by David Aikman/ Washington and Laura López/Mexico City, with other bureaus

QUEBEC: What Price Freedom?

Its drive for autonomy builds steam, but divorce may rend Canada

Deep in the recesses of a Quebec National Assembly annex sits a windowless room. It's much like any other conference room—except that on its walls are plans for a quiet revolution. In this "war room," staffers of a special commission on Quebec's sovereignty are making detailed plans on everything from a separate Quebec army to a national dairy farm policy. "We're preparing the real stuff, just in case," says one staffer. The commission expects to have a sovereignty blueprint before Quebec votes on its future in a late-October referendum. It's a vote that could unravel the nation of Canada.

French-speaking Quebec has been restive about its place in English-speaking Canada for decades, but now the tension is reaching a new high. Fed up by years of unmet demands, Quebec has given Ottawa a deadline: Either it presents Quebec with an acceptable plan for keeping the province within Canada, or Quebec will ask its voters to decide for themselves. If they vote *oui* for sovereignty in October, the province would break from Ottawa a year later.

As relations between English- and French-speaking Canadians deteriorate, it seems inconceivable that Canada will offer Quebec everything it wants. The central government on Feb. 28 made a proposal, but Quebec Premier Robert Bourassa quickly rejected it, calling it "domineering federalism." The proposal was even more bitterly condemned by Quebec's nationalists, who advocate immediate independence.

PLAYING CHICKEN. What makes the brinkmanship dangerous is that many Quebec leaders, executives, and citizens are confident they can go it alone. Quebec accounts for almost one-quarter of Canada's gross national product. Its corporate crown jewels include Hydro-Quebec, which with $34 billion assets is the world's No. 7 electric utility, and aircraft and transportation equipment builder Bombardier Inc., with nearly $3 billion sales. And its technocrats are pioneering an aggressive industrial policy—the most extensive in North America. Despite warnings from some that sovereignty would cripple the province, a poll of Quebec's business leaders last year showed 72% believed it would actually improve the economy over time.

Other Canadians are aghast at the prospect. The threat of Quebec's sov-

HOW QUEBEC WOULD STACK UP

STRENGTHS	WEAKNESSES
▶ World's 15th-largest economy, and 9th-largest trading partner of the U.S.	▶ Would have to assume its share of Canada's $340 billion debt, causing severe debt load
▶ Leading companies, including Hydro-Quebec, Bombardier, and SNC-Lavalin	▶ Creditors would force it to pay a stiff premium on international borrowings
▶ Strongly probusiness government, favoring free trade and pushing North America's most aggressive industrial strategy	▶ Would try to keep Canadian dollar. But this means ceding control over monetary policy
▶ Good labor relations with very few strikes	▶ Could face increasingly strained trade relations with both the U.S. and Canada
▶ Well-developed financial institutions in place, with over $110 billion in assets	▶ Unemployment, already 12%, would rise in the short run to higher levels

DATA: BW

Reprinted from the March 23, 1992, issue of *Business Week*, pp. 46-47, by special permission. Copyright © 1992 by McGraw-Hill, Inc.

ereignty "casts a dark shadow on everything we want to do," especially economic prospects, says Constitutional Affairs Minister Joe Clark. Leaders of the English-speaking business community also warn of a national apocalypse. But rhetoric aside, the rest-of-Canada, as Quebecers now refer to it, is not inclined to meet Quebec's demands for greater powers than other provinces enjoy. English-speakers argue that giving Quebec such leeway would undermine the nation as a whole. Many also warn that Quebec would be crushed economically by a breakup. It all shapes up as a national game of chicken that neither side can win. International nervousness over this showdown has helped drive the Canadian dollar under 84¢, from 89¢ last fall, forcing the Bank of Canada to raise interest rates.

Sovereignty for Quebec won't lead to civil war, as Yugoslavia's breakup has. Rather, Quebecers want political independence, a separate foreign policy, and full taxation and lawmaking powers. But they also want to continue using the Canadian dollar, maintain trade relations with the rest of Canada, and carry Canadian passports.

'BUILDING A NATION.' But even such minimal nationalism could have profound impact. For one thing, it would greatly complication relations with the U.S. just as Washington is trying to create a North American free-trade zone. Today, the U.S. and Canada are partners in $200 billion of two-way trade, and goods and services flow across the border under the rules of a four-year-old free-trade pact. But opposition to the free-trade agreement is mounting in English-speaking Canada, and if Quebec goes, the rest of Canada might try to renegotiate the pact.

Indeed, if Quebec secedes, the rest of Canada could come unglued. The depressed Maritime provinces would be cut off from others, while western provinces would reject Ontario's dominance. Eventually, predicts John Ciaccia, Quebec's Minister of International Affairs, some provinces, such as Alberta, might try to join the U.S.

No matter how the immediate crisis plays out, it is clear that Quebec's quiet revolution is moving ahead. *La Belle Province* is taking control of its affairs, including its economy, social programs and culture, step by step. "What they're doing is building a nation," says U.S. Consul General William C. McCahill Jr., in Quebec City. "They have cultural identity and purpose, they have pride in the institutions they've built up, and they want more of it."

Quebec's economic success has been a powerful boost to nationalist feeling. Alienated from English Canada, Quebec has developed its own model of close cooperation among business, labor, government, and banks, often called Quebec Inc. At the heart of this model is Hydro-Quebec, the province's powerhouse. Owned by the state, it's a world-class electric utility. Its cheap electricity has in turn fueled industrial development throughout the province, such as energy-intensive aluminum smelters. And Bombardier, originally a small snowmobile maker, is a transportation-equipment giant that builds subway cars for New York City and constructs planes in the U.S., Britain, and Canada. In January, it made a winning bid for the ailing Toronto-based de Havilland division of Boeing Co.

The Quebec government is actively orchestrating this economic drive. Quebec's Industry Minister, Gérald Tremblay, has a plan to create 550,000 jobs by the year 2000 and bring unemployment down to 7%, from 12% today. He has divided Quebec's economy into clusters. Some, such as aerospace, electrical power-generation equipment, and information technology, are already competitive. Others, including forest products and petrochemicals, need help. Tremblay gets key companies in these clusters to attack industry problems together and works to change inhibiting government policies.

ROUGH START. A thriving province is one thing; a sovereign nation something else again. Many economists figure that an independent Quebec would be in for rough times in the first few years. Already, Quebec has its weaknesses. With unemployment high, some of Quebec Inc.'s leaders are under pressure. Hydro-Quebec has postponed its $11 billion Great Whale hydroelectric project because of environmental opposition and New York State's desire to renegotiate its multibillion-dollar, 20-year contract on better terms. The forest-products and clothing industries have been pummeled.

Sovereignty could create more economic pain, especially in the short run. A sovereign Quebec would have to assume its share of Canada's $340 billion debt. That in turn could drive Quebec's debt load sky-high, and spooked foreign investors could then force Quebec to pay a premium on its international borrowings.

On the trade front, Quebec could see relations with the U.S. sour despite the province's free-trade stance, as Quebec Inc.'s policies of subsidization come under fire. The U.S. Commerce Dept. is already challenging the low rates Hydro-Quebec offers industrial customers. Trade with Canada would also be strained.

FALLOUT. The man trying to manage the growing crisis is Premier Bourassa, head of the ruling Liberal Party. A federalist who believes Quebec would be better off remaining as part of Canada, Bourassa is trying to quell separatist fervor by insisting that Ottawa cede substantial powers to Quebec. Specifically, his Liberal Party wants Quebec to have exclusive jurisdiction over 22 areas, among them culture, education, and regional development. The federal government would run only six, including defense and currency. Power would be shared in nine other areas. In this way, Quebec would operate with far more autonomy from Ottawa than other provinces—in effect, a nation within a nation.

While Bourassa tries to sell English Canada on this approach, the Parti Quebecois (PQ) is trumpeting sovereignty. PQ leader Jacques Parizeau argues that support for sovereignty is far stronger now than it was in 1980, when the first referendum on the issue was defeated. In November, polls found that 56% of Quebecers expect the province to be independent within a decade, while only 11% expect the status quo to remain. And 39% support sovereignty, while 32% lean toward federalism. The one-third in the middle sympathizes with Quebec's aspirations but worries about the economic fallout. So Parizeau has nimbly crafted a new definition of sovereignty. While Quebec would "leave" Canada, says Parizeau, it would then negotiate ties to minimize the disruption for itself, such as use of the Canadian dollar, free circulation of goods and services between Quebec and Canada, and the right of Quebecers to hold Canadian passports.

As the fall deadline draws nearer, optimists are betting that the Canadian genius for muddling through will eventually prevail. They may be right, since the costs of divorce are beginning to dawn on many Canadians on both sides. But Canada has never been this close to the brink. Even if the Canadians maintain a single nation, there are likely to be permanent shifts in relations between French- and English-speaking Canada. The consequences will resonate throughout the continent. Whether Bourassa or Parizeau prevails, Quebec's future direction is clear. It is only a question of how far, and how fast, it goes.

By William C. Symonds in Quebec City

Do we want free trade with Mexico?

Point ►►►►►►►►►►► | ◄◄◄◄◄◄◄◄ Counterpoint

Tommy G. Thompson

Tommy G. Thompson is governor of Wisconsin.

Today, as never before, states must take a strong interest in foreign trade. Governors are the foremost promoters of trade in the nation and building a state's economic base now includes traveling abroad.

My own state's economic prosperity depends on exports, and every state in the nation would benefit from greater economic opportunity abroad. In the 1980s, nearly 90 percent of U.S. economic growth came from exports. For this reason, states have a strong interest in promoting free trade with Mexico through the North American Free Trade Agreement.

A free trade agreement with Mexico can increase exports, create jobs and help alleviate certain U.S. environmental and social problems traceable to Mexican poverty.

By eliminating tariffs, the pact would benefit U.S. exporters more than Mexican exporters. Currently, Mexican tariffs average 10 percent on a trade-weighted basis, while the average for U.S. tariffs is only 3.4 percent. Because Mexican tariffs are higher, eliminating them will mean proportionately more U.S. exports to Mexico and thus more jobs for American exporters.

Since Mexico began lowering its tariff and non-tariff barriers in 1986, it has surpassed Germany to become our third largest trading partner, and U.S. exports to Mexico have grown by more than $28 billion.

An agreement would create additional jobs at home by allowing U.S. companies to combine low-cost Mexican labor with high-skilled American labor, making American products more competitive in the marketplace. Mexico's close proximity allows U.S. companies to employ unskilled Mexican labor for portions of their operations and higher-skilled American workers for more advanced production processes.

Since the 1960s, the "maquiladora" companies (which combine U.S. and Mexican operations) have produced 100,000 American jobs in export industries, and hundreds of thousands of jobs in export-support industries, such as transportation and storage.

John Peavey

Sen. John Peavey has served in the Idaho State Senate for eight terms and in leadership for the last five terms. He is a member of the Agriculture, Natural Resources and Conservation, and State Affairs committees.

The Mexican Free Trade Agreement may have dangerous consequences for U.S. agriculture and industries. Free trade has been sold to us by repeating the truism that we can compete against any nation on a level playing field. We are told the biggest impediments are the unfair barriers other countries raise against our products and the enormous subsidies they pay their producers. Japan and members of the European Common Market are among those cited as using unfair practices.

But, the threat from Mexico and many Third World nations is equally severe. In Mexico, a lower standard of living makes the cost of doing business minimal. Mexican producers and industrialists enter a free trade agreement with the United States with significant advantages, the first of which is labor costs.

In the United States, it is law that no one can be asked to work for less than $4.25 an hour (and that figure will soon reach $4.75) or for more than eight hours a day without overtime. Most Mexican workers may not earn our minimum wage in a 10-, 12- or 14-hour day. To maintain our standard of living, our direct labor costs are 10 to 12 times higher than in Mexico. This staggering cost differential is rarely addressed by those who are selling free trade with Mexico to a trusting public. But wages are only a beginning. We have compassionate child labor laws and encourage children to remain in school until 16. Any traveler to Mexico has seen young children illiterate, unkempt and begging, performing menial jobs and beginning a life from which there will be no advancement. We must avoid this at all costs for our children.

Indirect labor expenses also have an impact. U.S. workers have programs such as worker's compensation insurance. Long ago we decided that an employer had a social responsibility to pay a worker's medical bills and lost salary for on-the-job injuries. In Mexico and other Third World countries, there is no similar responsibility. Rather, it's a simple "adios amigo" if workers are unable to perform. We pay to have occupational safety and health, require safeguards against injury and keep

From *State Government News*, October 1991, pp. 16-17. Reprinted by permission.

Mexico's ability to prosper from a free trade pact will benefit the United States. First, greater Mexican purchasing power means more imports from the United States. Mexicans are eager to purchase U.S. products. Whereas 65 percent of Mexican imports come from the United States, less than 23 percent of Japan's imports are American, and for Germany the figure is only 7.5 percent.

In addition, by providing increased job opportunities and raising per capita income in Mexico, the free trade agreement will be far more effective in stemming illegal immigration than any amount of spending on border controls and will reduce the social service burdens in many U.S. cities and states caused by a flood of immigrants.

Similarly, the agreement could help solve the problem of airborne pollution. As we get control of land-based pollution sources, we are becoming more aware of airborne pollutants, which ignore national borders. Currently, 90 percent of the toxin PCB and mercury pollution entering Lake Superior is airborne. The pesticide DDT, which is still legal in Mexico, is entering the Great Lakes, years after being outlawed in the United States and Canada.

With increased prosperity, Mexico will have the will and the resources to clean up pollution. In addition, Mexican President Carlos Salinas de Gortari supports strong environmental protections in the agreement.

American states have a vital stake in the North American Free Trade Agreement. The jobs and increased prosperity from free trade are important to economic growth. Social problems that eat into state budgets, like illegal immigration and environmental pollution, are exacerbated by protectionist U.S. policies. A free trade agreement with Mexico is a vital interest we cannot ignore.

Free trade with Mexico will boost U.S. exports and jobs.

Free trade with Mexico will only lower our standard of living.

detailed records of job-related injuries or illnesses. No such requirements exist in Mexico.

As a nation, we are concerned with our environment and the health of our people. These issues are largely ignored in Mexico. Dangerous chemicals, long outlawed in this country, are available and used in Mexican agriculture. Often chemicals are applied while workers are still in the fields. In industry, highly toxic substances are routinely dumped into rivers and streams and recklessly released. Workers are subjected to chemical fumes in poorly ventilated factories.

In this country, taxes support public health, clean drinking water, waste disposal and sanitation systems. Mexico lags far behind in these areas. Our taxes support an educational system that allows our children to get a start at a better life. In Mexico, many children of age 10 or 12 are hard at work in fields and factories.

Politically, Mexico is dominated by a single party that has governed exclusively since the revolution of the 1930s. The government runs the labor unions. There is no force to lead the country on the reforms necessary to raise its living standard.

And who is pushing for a free trade agreement with Mexico? Proponents on our side of the border are food processors and large agribusiness entities, such as chemical and fertilizer companies. Banks and insurance companies — including the American Farm Bureau that is supposed to be an advocate for farmers — also are in the forefront on this selling job.

There is an outside chance that an expansive free trade policy may provide Mexico the incentive to raise its standard of living. However, with the United States facing a severe recession, there is a greater threat that our standard of living may be lowered as we, in a panic, attempt to compete with Mexico on its terms.

I am afraid the powerful forces at work on both sides of the border may dictate that the U.S. standard of living will be ratcheted down. Few of the trade agreement's promoters can be expected to lead the charge for Mexican minimum wage laws, workers' compensation, safety laws and environmental protection efforts when it would affect their profit-and-loss statements dramatically. Yet, without gigantic strides in these areas, total free trade and a level-playing field are impossible with Mexico. Instead, it seems a sure recipe for a vastly lowered U.S. standard of living and a continued exploitation of Mexican workers and farmers.

North-South Split

With Cold War Over, Poorer Nations Face Neglect by the Rich

Aid Programs Are Dwindling, And the Disappointment Could Blight Democracy

Playing the Ecology Card

Robert S. Greenberger

Staff Reporter of The Wall Street Journal

The New World Order is beginning to look like a bad place to be a poor nation.

The end of the Cold War spelled relief for Washington, Moscow, Berlin and other cities at ground zero. But the view is less pleasant from the economic hinterlands of Islamabad, Havana, Kingston and dozens of other Third World capitals.

For four decades after World War II, the two superpowers vied for the affections of poor nations. They showered the poor with military hardware, projects such as dams and steel mills and boatloads of subsidized food and other goods.

Now, as the dust settles on the East-West struggle, the world is dividing into the industrialized North and underdeveloped South–and the poor nations are being left to fend for themselves.

SOME MAJOR SHIFTS

Among the major shifts under way:

• Ideology is out, and economic interest are paramount. Third World nations watch warily as North America, Japan and Europe lead emerging trade blocs, each dominated by one major currency. After years of being urged to lift themselves by their bootstraps, the poor fear that they and their products will be locked out of the new global trading patterns.

• Slumping economies and the inward-turning moods sweeping the industrialized world are drying up overseas investment capital. The U.S. is trying to step up its economic growth and deal with domestic ills. Germany has all that it can handle absorbing the former East Germany, and Japan is deeply shaken by the plunge in its stock market. What's more, much of the limited aid and private capital that are available for overseas purposes is going to the North's own poor–the former Soviet republics and Eastern Europe.

• Looking for levers to pry money out of the North, the South has turned to the environment. At next month's global environmental summit in Rio de Janeiro–featuring more than 100 heads of state, a pop music concert, and even its own theme song–the poor will try to play on the guilt of the rich. But pre-summit negotiations at the United Nations suggest that this gambit won't produce much more for the Third World than get-lost money.

IMMIGRATION THREAT

Indeed, the main leverage that the poor now have over the rich is the threat that they may drop in–indefinitely. As disparities among nations grow, pressures to migrate are rising. According to the U.N., 75 million people are migrating illegally every year, shipping from country to country in search of work or food.

"Poor people can be stopped at borders, but poverty can't be stopped," warns Mahbubul Haq, Pakistan's

Reprinted by permission of *The Wall Street Journal,* May 14, 1992, pp. A1, A5. Copyright © 1992 by Dow Jones & Company, Inc. All rights reserved worldwide.

former finance minister and now an adviser to the United Nations Development Program. "Poverty travels in the form of drugs, terrorism, global warming and AIDS."

In Jamaica, a tiny island nation caught in the shifting tide from East-West to North-South contention, Peter Phillips, a cabinet minister without portfolio, waxes almost nostalgic about the good old days of superpower rivalry. Aid, trade and environmental assistance "were a lot easier to pry loose in the bipolar world," he says. "The peace dividend isn't being directed here."

OUT OF STRATEGIC FASHION

Once jealously projected by the U.S. from encroachment by Fidel Castro's Cuba, Jamaica is learning the hard way what it's like to fall out of strategic fashion. In the past, the military machines of the U.S. and the U.S.S.R. wanted Jamaican bauxite. The Pentagon paid dollars and stored the bauxite, the raw material for aluminum, in its strategic stockpile. The Soviet Union used the metal to build MiG fighters and paid with Ladas, the boxy little Soviet cars that weave through the streets of Kingston, Jamaica's capital. Now the Soviet Union is gone, and the U.S., to cut costs, may soon compete with Jamaica by selling its stockpiled bauxite.

At La Moda, an apparel factory near Kingston's waterfront, Dorothy Over senses disaster. Right now, business is brisk, she says above the din of 160 sewing machines stitching red fabric into blouses for Kmart shoppers in the U.S. But Ms. Over worries that the impending free-trade agreement between the U.S. and Mexico could silence her factory. The agreement would end a competitive advantage; U.S. law now permits La Moda and other Caribbean firms to finish U.S. goods and ship them back to the U.S. at preferential duties. And rumors that several big American textile companies will soon pull out and head for Mexico are racing like tropical squalls across Kingston. "If we aren't put on an equal footing with Mexico, we'll be wiped out," Ms. Over laments.

Ironically, this storm cloud is gathering just as Jamaica, like dozens of other Third World countries, has taken the harsh medicine prescribed by the West to build a free-market economy. Last September, the government loosened foreign-exchange laws so that its overpriced Jamaican dollar would find its market level and its exports would become more competitive. The currency plunged, and its drop raised the cost of imports, which account for nearly 70% of the country's consumer goods, including such basics as rice and flour. The result is 80% inflation, up from 9% four years ago.

The latest jolts don't affect the very poor; they already are on the bottom. Nor are they felt by the rich, who have assets abroad and live in affluent neighborhoods such as Arcada, in the hills above Kingston, in large houses surrounded by whitewashed walls splashed with red, purple and orange bougainvillea.

But they are jarring workers and the middle class—the people who form the core of a market economy and a liberal democracy. In a retail store called America Dream in Kingston's gritty downtown, a clerk, Angela Ellis, says she worries about stretching her shrinking wages far enough to feed her two children.

Many of America's other former Third World clients—stretching from Central American to South Asia—that once were well-paid pawns in the struggle against communism also feel short-changed. Just a few years ago, Pakistan was the pipeline for U.S. aid to the Afghan guerrillas, who battled—and bled—the invading Soviets. The U.S. gave billions of dollars in military assistance to Islamabad. Then the Cold War ended, and the Bush administration, citing a congressional prohibition on aid because of Pakistan's previously ignored nuclear program, cut off military aid.

ANGRY AMBASSADOR

Pakistan's ambassador to the U.S., Begum Syeda Abida Hussain, began seething soon after taking up her post last winter. Years of Pakistani friendship, she felt, were ending in cold shoulders and closed doors in Washington. She argued that the U.S. would need Pakistan again someday, perhaps as a bridge to the awakening nations of Islamic Central Asia. But U.S. officials aren't buying that line. "The Cold War is over, won by our friends the Americans," she says. "But we also recognize that now our American friends don't have a strategic need for us."

One of the few levers of power left to the poor nations is the environment. If global warming occurs, after all, it could damage everybody. But thus far, the South has found the environment an uncertain tool. "Firstly, those countries that induced climate change must accept that responsibility," argues C. Dasgupta, India's chief negotiator on global warming. "Secondly, we would hope for a substantial, if not massive, program of international cooperation."

That, in a nutshell, is still the South's hope for next month's Rio conference. As defined in a preliminary statement, environmentally responsible development includes everything from helping poor nations raise living standards to recognizing the vital role of women in environmental and population management.

But conservative thinking dominates many of the North's major governments, and the conservatives think they see a pig in a poke. "It's basically a redistributionist strategy," argues Jeane Kirkpatrick, who was the Reagan administration's first U.N. ambassador.

NO BIG SUMS IN SIGHT

No one expects the rich nations to come up with anywhere near the sums that many say will be needed to cure the world's environmental ills. Conference organizers estimate the global price tag for sustainable development to be $350 billion a year, with $70 billion a year coming from the rich countries. They are still hoping for a promise of a "down payment" of several billion dollars at Rio. In return, the poor nations would try to develop in ways that don't destroy irreplaceable resources such as the tropical rain forests.

Meanwhile, poor nations can make the rich feel some of their anger simply by not controlling emissions. Arguing that rich nations developed by polluting and now are refusing to act, India is wary of agreeing to limit emissions without more action from the rich. And if climate change and other global pollution prove as significant as the scientific evidence suggests, the rich must get the cooperation of the poor, whose coal and inefficient machinery eventually will produce most of the greenhouse emissions. "The North can't solve climate change without the South playing ball," says Scott Hajost, international counsel at the Environmental Defense Fund.

Another fault line is the new global economy, which is widening the gap not just between rich and poor but among the developing nations themselves. In Latin America, experts say, Mexico, Chile and Colombia will be economic winners; Peru and the Caribbean nations will be left behind. In South Asia, India is expected to emerge as a major exporter, but Bangladesh will slip further into the swamp. In Africa, Zambia's economy is strengthening, but the sub-Saharan region will fare even worse in the 1990s than in the 1980s.

DEMOCRACY AT RISK

As those nations fade from the radar screens of the affluent North, there is a growing risk that the widening divisions and bitter failures will bring profound disenchantment with democracy. All through the 1980s, developing nations heard the rich West tout democracy and free markets. The collapse of communism prodded them further. But if they are disappointed, authoritarianism and state-controlled economies could come back in vogue. Seen in this light, the attempted coup earlier this year in Venezuela and the suspension of democracy in Peru may be warning signs.

The success stories of the past decade, when the so-called Asian Tigers–South Korea, Taiwan, Singapore and Hong Kong–created miracles by spurring their economies with export growth, may not be repeated in the 1990s. During the past decade, as 60 developing nations were reducing trade restrictions, 20 of the top 24 industrialized nations were raising them. The new barriers will make it harder to find markets for the textiles, footwear and leather exports that typically help jump-start developing economies.

Meanwhile, prices of such Third World commodities as tea, coffee and cocoa have plunged to their lowest levels, on a relative basis, in 150 years.

In Africa, more than 30 countries have instituted International Monetary Fund reform programs. Ghana is considered a great success story. In 1983, it swallowed bitter economic pills, including a massive currency devaluation and a tightening of budgets and credit. Then the price of cocoa, its major export crop, collapsed. "They did everything right," says Gerry Helleiner, an economist at the University of Toronto, "and now even the World Bank says if they don't get more financing or stronger commodity prices, all these reforms won't get them the right results."

At least Ghana and Jamaica aren't former clients of the Soviet Union. Countries such as Angola and Mozambique have become the Flying Dutchmen of geopolitics. So has Cuba, just a few hundred miles north of Jamaica; it may be on the edge of breakdown. Cuba's economy is collapsing and its superpower patron, which until recently provided $5 billion annually in aid and subsidies, has died.

Now, ironically, Jamaica sees a new threat from Communist Cuba. "I'd really be concerned if Cuba were to become democratic and really open up its economy tomorrow," muses Morin Seymour, a Jamaican entrepreneur who is restoring Kingston's harbor area. "They have better beaches than we do."

–Staff reporter Rose Gutfeld contributed to this article.

Don't Forget Latin America

Jon I. Martinez • John A. Quelch • Joseph Ganitsky

THE INTRICACIES OF MARKETING PRODUCTS IN FOREIGN COUNTRIES ARE PERHAPS NOWHERE MORE APPARENT THAN IN LATIN AMERICA. FOR example, to manage in countries with hyperinflation, Procter & Gamble sometimes has had to raise its detergent prices as high as 30 percent every two weeks. But, as this article argues, the rewards can be great. The authors describe the changing economic and political conditions in Latin America that are making the region more attractive to foreign investors. They discuss how to decide which countries to enter and which products and services to offer, and they review the different approaches to participation, marketing, and organizational structure. Although Eastern Europe has garnered more attention, they argue, investors should not neglect Latin America.

Jon I. Martinez is Professor of International Business, Universidad Adolfo Ibanez, Santiago, Chile. John A. Quelch is Professor of Business Administration, Graduate School of Business Administration, Harvard University. Joseph Ganitsky is Professor of International Business at both Loyola University, New Orleans, Louisiana, and Instituto de Empresa, Madrid, Spain.

For most businesspeople the emerging world order includes a number of rising Asian players led by Japan, an integrated Western Europe, a newly opened Eastern Europe, and a less threatening and more attractive Soviet Union. Most leaders continue to forget the Southern hemisphere in general and Latin America in particular.

During the 1980s investors renounced Latin America because of its questionable political and economic situation. They tended to regard the region as an economic wasteland. It had an external debt of over $400 billion, a per capita income that had shown no growth since 1970, strong capital restrictions, and, in some countries, the stigmas of nationalization, government corruption, and four digit annual inflation. The prevailing conviction was that these countries were filled with drugs, debt, devaluations, or dictators. These negative perceptions contributed to the region's loss of almost a third of its world gross domestic product (GDP) share in the last decade, despite its abundant and diverse natural resources and large potential markets.

While in some cases this perspective was justified, now a growing number of firms operating in Latin America are profiting from recent political and economic developments. Investors are taking a second look at the region and finding it more attractive. In this article, we encourage investors to reconsider Latin America. We discuss recent changes in the region, the opportunities and challenges in selected countries, promising products and services, and various approaches to market penetration. We also include examples of marketing and organizational approaches used by several successful companies.

Taking a Second Look at Latin America

There are five reasons why investors should not ignore Latin America.

1. Most Countries in the Region Are Finally Undertaking True Reforms.

The severe problems of the 1980s shocked Latin American countries into abandoning policies they had clung to for decades. While the timing, sequence, and pace of change differs greatly among nations (ranging from Chile, which moved from a state interventionist economy eighteen years ago, to Peru, which is just beginning), all seem to be moving in the direction of liberal governments and open economies.

For decades Latin American countries achieved growth through a system of mutual political and economic favors exchanged between governments (and

From *Sloan Management Review,* Vol. 33, No. 2, Winter 1992, pp. 78-92. Copyright © 1992 by the Sloan Management Review Association.

their political organizations) and certain constituents. Corporations improved their performance through especially "close" relations with government rather than through efforts to develop genuine internal competitive advantages, such as enhanced technology, excellent training, or marketing expertise. Governments expanded their power with both internal and foreign constituents by limiting and controlling foreign investment and trade and by raising taxes. Unfortunately, in many instances the people's needs were ignored.

This symbiosis worked while governments could accumulate the resources to develop their nations and maintain loyalty, even if this meant inefficient state-protected monopolies or widespread corruption. However, in the early 1980s most governments, unable to pay their international financial obligations (whether interests or principal), could not attract more foreign capital nor raise additional taxes. This triggered a public confidence crisis, which increased private capital flight and significantly lowered hard currency reserves. The crisis also exposed the weaknesses of international banks and multilateral agencies and the rampant misallocation of resources. The ensuing inability of governments to lower their debt and expenditures at the same pace that resources declined led, in most nations, to endemic hyperinflation. This, in turn, lowered average living standards. The region's average growth during the 1980s declined to 1.1 percent as opposed to approximately 6.2 percent during the 1970s.[1] By 1989, terms of trade were 21 percent off their 1980 level and per capita income had dropped in nineteen of twenty-five Latin American countries. In summary, the region lost a full decade, as the following figures suggest:

	GDP Per Capita	Total Debt
	(1990 as a percentage of 1980)	
Argentina	36.4	206.7
Brazil	98.4	182.4
Peru	105.3	218.8
Venezuela	55.6	135.8

This dismal performance forced most countries to renegotiate the terms of their national debts. It broke off the symbiotic relationships and forced the power brokers to give up some of their influence. The new alliances increased the political leverage of previously underrepresented constituents and brought forward a new breed of government officials — many of them with advanced degrees and vast economic experience — who enacted reforms, including public expenditure reductions, economic deregulation, financial and trade liberalization, and increased fiscal responsibility.

The new leaders redefined the rules governing their relations with constituents. For example, Venezuela's development minister, Moisés Naim, encouraged businesspeople to search for sources of competitive advantage within their firms rather than begging for favors in lunches with government officials. Mexico's President Carlos Salinas, in an effort to eradicate corruption, sent to jail a leading stockbroker, the head of the petroleum workers' union, and a couple of public officials in his first 100 days in office. As a result, constituents acknowledged their diminished resources, power, and roles, and committed their efforts to create a new political and economic order. As public confidence returned, so did local capital, followed by foreign investment. Few experts believe that the road back from high inflation and instability will be quick or easy. Most likely, interest rates will remain high to encourage savings and investment, some labor unions will oppose privatization, and previously protected firms will resist efforts to make them more efficient.

Despite the difficulties, several countries are seeing positive results already. For example:

- Mexico moved from a budget deficit of 7 percent of GDP in 1988 to a 7 percent surplus, while inflation dropped from 160 percent in 1987 to 25 percent in 1990.
- Bolivia's inflation dropped dramatically from 8,171 percent in 1985 to only 18 percent in 1990. In 1990, the government decreed that it would privatize 100 out of 157 state-owned enterprises over the next five years.
- Chile and Colombia have successfully reentered the voluntary international private loan market.

In addition, the more successful nations have seen a significant decline in their debt's discount in secondary international markets, while it is still high for the others. Yet the debt crisis is not over, and bank lending to the region has not resumed.

2. Regional Integration Is Changing the Americas. Latin America's setbacks during the 1980s were also painful for the U.S. economy. Its financial system has not yet recuperated, and its manufacturing sector lost $130 billion in exports to the region from 1982 to 1988.[2] About one-third of the U.S. trade deficit resulted from the impact of the international raw material depression on Latin America, formerly one of U.S. manufacturers' best customers. To continue cutting its trade deficit (and indirectly ease its tensions with Japan), the United States had to recover Latin America as a customer for its manufactured goods or endure a very sharp recession.[3] In addition, Europe's integration is giving the United States and its Latin neighbors impetus to create a hemispheric bloc that can wield greater economic and political power.

Since mid-1990 President Bush has responded to these challenges by taking the following steps. He has:

- Proposed the Enterprise for the Americas Initiative

(EAI) to strengthen Latin and Caribbean economies through increased trade, investment, and reduction of official debt to the United States, backed by a $1.5 billion fund for improving conditions for private investment.

• Obtained "fast track" authority from Congress to negotiate a North American Free Trade Agreement (NAFTA) with Mexico and Canada.[4] This agreement would include 363 million inhabitants within a $6.2 trillion GDP market (1991 figures), which would be bigger than the European Community's 326 million inhabitants and $4.4 trillion market. A hemispheric common market would include twice as many inhabitants, but its total GDP would reach only $6.8 trillion.

• Signed fourteen bilateral and multilateral Framework Agreements on Trade and Investment with twenty-nine Latin American and Caribbean countries, each with the dual purpose of initially reducing trade and investment barriers and of later spreading open markets throughout the region.[5]

• Visited four Latin countries even during the Gulf War, thus giving an additional signal of his support to the region's reform-minded presidents.

• Sent teams of public and private leaders to the region to explore investment and trade options.

In addition, after decades of failure of regional trade entities — such as the Latin American Integration Association (LAIA), the Andean Common Market (ANCOM), and the Central American Common Market (CACM) — Latin nations have signed several bilateral and multilateral trade and investment agreements within the last year. In the March 1991 Treaty of Asuncion, the most ambitious of these treaties, the presidents of Argentina, Brazil, Paraguay, and Uruguay committed their nations to creation of a Southern Cone Free Trade Zone (Mercosur) that will eliminate all trade barriers by the end of 1994.

As these and similar initiatives transpire, exciting opportunities will emerge for foreign companies in Latin America.[6] Specifically, local markets will expand significantly, with benefits for industries sensitive to scale economies and the experience curve. For example, in the razor blade industry, where a plant's break-even point is about 100 million units per year, producers such as Gillette will concentrate production and rationalize operations of the seven plants that are currently located in five Latin American countries.

3. Geopolitical Forces Have Increased the Region's Attractiveness.

Decision makers are starting to realize that Latin America enjoys significant advantages over other formerly more attractive regions. Experts believe that it will be a great deal easier to turn Latin America's mixed economies into efficient and export-oriented countries than it will be to turn around the formerly closed and centralized economies of Eastern Europe. Latin American countries have an ample supply of well-trained engineers, entrepreneurs, accountants, economists, and lawyers, including many with advanced education in the United States and Europe who have been exposed to the processes and benefits of a free economy. Similarly, while much of Latin America's capital (up to two or three times its external debt) is currently out of the region in safer countries' banks, successful reforms may induce capital to return, as has already happened in some countries. Continuing high yields (such as a doubling of return on capital invested in the last four years) will also help bring monies to the region. In addition, Brazil alone has almost double the GDP of all of Eastern Europe, and U.S. trade with the region is already almost fourteen times greater than with Eastern Europe.[7] Eastern Europe lacks both experienced private and financial sectors and the people to manage them. It has an inefficient labor force and no legal system to sustain a market economy and protect investors. Eastern European countries are politically unstable, with their heterogeneous populations and ethnic conflict.

Finally, communism's collapse left Latin America's leftist movements ideologically orphaned and with diminished power. Thus, revolutionaries in El Salvador and Colombia, after lengthy negotiations, are integrating into their political systems; the Sandinistas play a very different role in Nicaragua; and the free market has become the region's guiding rule.

4. Global Competitors Develop Sustainable Advantages in Latin America.

The more intense competitive rivalry and limited growth and profit potential of the oversupplied developed markets have forced multinational corporations (MNCs) to turn their attention to less developed areas. These areas have sources of competitive advantage such as lower costs (from capturing larger global market shares or gaining access to globally competitive resources) and additional profit margins (from serving markets formerly protected or untapped). While in the past these sources seldom could be cultivated in Latin America, the recent changes have generated valuable opportunities.

In some countries, even before reforms are implemented, MNCs are establishing their beachheads. After all, the first mover advantages are immense. Developing relationships and contacts, cultivating goodwill, learning cultural and corporate nuances — these all take time. Companies that invest that time early, without expecting short-term profit, have a clear advantage when opportunities increase. They can solidify name and brand recognition before the influx of competing brands. They can develop a customer service network to back up sold or installed products.

These are some of the opportunities that have already been explored or tapped:

• Privatization of large state-owned firms, often through debt-equity swaps. According to a recent survey, more than one-fifth of the 500 largest companies in Latin America are state-owned, including seven out of the ten largest.[8] Argentina, Chile, Mexico, and Venezuela are pursuing aggressive privatization programs.

• Megaprojects to exploit the abundant natural resources.

• Investment in Latin America's profitable stock markets. Average annual compound stock returns in Mexico rose 41.5 percent between 1984 and 1990 and in Chile rose 30 percent between 1975 and 1990, well above those of Korea (26 percent) or the United States (11 percent). Performance differences have been even more acute during the first semester of 1991: Chile, 69.9 percent; Mexico, 68.8 percent; South Africa, 29.5 percent; the United States, 12.6 percent; Pacific Rim, 4.2 percent; Spain, 3.5 percent; Japan, 2.9 percent; France, -5.6 percent; and Germany, -7.0 percent. High performance can continue because the average price/earnings ratios of the region's stock markets have been fairly low.[9] During the last year a number of investment funds set up in the developed world and focusing on the region have extended these opportunities to smaller investors.[10]

5. Latin American Companies Are Good Partners for Strategic Alliances.

While Asia continues to be the region of choice for global production and sourcing, Latin American suppliers and partners have become more attractive. The following developments will likely increase their appeal to U.S. companies:

• Asian labor costs are increasing as industrialization and living standards advance.

• Concern is growing that Hong Kong, when it integrates with the People's Republic of China in 1997, will become less reliable.

• The value of speedy delivery, flexibility, and lower transportation costs is increasing as global competition shifts from cost and quality to speed and adaptation.

• U.S. resistance to Asian products may increase, especially if U.S. products continue facing substantial obstacles in Asian markets.

• Certain of Latin America's domestic markets are becoming more open and deregulated.

Some Latin American firms are already leveraging these advantages. For example, Brazil is the leading exporter of shoes and orange concentrate to the United States; Argentina and Chile export a high percentage of the jeans entering the U.S. market; the Dominican Republic is the sixth largest garment exporter to the U.S. market; and México's Vitro and the U.S.'s Corning, the housewares giant, formed a global marketing and manufacturing joint venture.

Interestingly, it is not only labor-intensive companies that are presenting sourcing opportunities, but capital-intensive ones as well. Fiat, the Italian automobile manufacturer, and Sevel, of Argentina, have established a strategic alliance whereby the latter is producing and exporting 2,000 engines per day. Fiat originally negotiated a licensing agreement but now owns 15 percent of Sevel.

Strategic alliances offer unique opportunities for partners to gain access to Latin American markets, the associated technology, and the other partner's expertise. For example, SONDA, a $60 million Chilean software firm, and the global giant Digital Equipment Corporation, second to IBM in the computer industry, have just signed a fifty-fifty joint venture to penetrate the entire Latin American market, except Brazil. Each partner is investing $30 million to establish fifteen subsidiaries in the region. Digital contributes its brand reputation and leading edge technology, while SONDA offers its expertise in software tailored to the unique, smaller institutions (such as special government offices) predominant in the developing world; its superior knowledge of Latin American markets; and its lower labor costs for computer programmers.

In summary, now is the critical time for investors to consider taking a competitive position in this complex but promising region. The situation is improving dramatically, and early arrivals will have the pick of partners, countries, and products. But before committing resources, executives must consider the following questions, which are addressed in the remaining sections: What purposes should be pursued? Which countries should be entered and in what order? What products or services should be offered? What form of participation should the company use? What marketing tactics should a company employ? How should a company organize to confront the region's unique issues?

Although the following discussion conveniently separates the analytic process into subcomponents, each component is related to the others. A comprehensive analysis requires an integrated set of answers.

What Purposes?

Multinational and local investors may differ in their strategic purposes. Multinationals have four basic options:

1. To serve open domestic markets with products and

technologies that they develop in the region or that have been developed elsewhere.

2. To gain a first mover advantage over global competitors in protected domestic markets or to reduce the early lead of competitors that are already there.

3. To secure reliable and competitive supply sources and to enhance the firm's global procurement and manufacturing base. This applies to traditional commodities (e.g., oil, copper, bananas), nontraditional goods (e.g., shrimps, macadamia nuts, lemon concentrate), and low-skilled manufacturing processes (e.g., assembly of electronic components, garments).

4. To enhance the firm's global competitive position by combining global synergistic benefits with competitive and comparative advantages from all locations.

Meanwhile, local investors have two basic options:

1. To enhance their competitiveness in their local markets and to defend themselves from upcoming foreign competitors.

2. To serve foreign market while gaining access to either export benefits (e.g., tax credits and subsidized credit), foreign hard currency, or foreign tax havens.

Local investors may also be able to invest abroad (e.g., Mexico's Cemex and Vitro, Venezuela's Petroven, and Chile's CMPC and Cochrane) to enhance their local and global competitive position, thus accomplishing the same goals as do multinationals.

Which Countries?

Foreign investors must understand not only the individual countries, but also how each country fits into the regional picture.

Regional Clustering

There is a common but erroneous tendency to view Latin America as a bloc of homogeneous countries. While countries can be grouped in various ways, differences are still evident on virtually every level (see Tables 1 and 2). These differences may make a country more or less attractive to investors. It is useful, though, to group companies by certain criteria, as we have below (see Figure 1 and Table 3).[11]

• **Development level.** There are three clusters using this criterion. The first comprises the three Southern Cone countries: Argentina, Chile, and Uruguay, which have somewhat higher living standards. Demographically, these countries also stand apart for having few Black or Indian residents, more European descendants, relatively low population growth ratios, and over 80 percent of the population concentrated in urban areas. In terms of health conditions and education, Costa Rica could be included in this cluster, although it is significantly different in geographical proximity and demographic composition.

The second cluster includes Brazil, Colombia, Mexico, Venezuela, and, considering only health and education levels, Paraguay. These five countries fall somewhat lower on the development scale, and all show similar patterns of population growth and urban concentration. However, they differ significantly in terms of language, size, and living standards.

The third cluster includes Bolivia, Ecuador, and Peru, which are relatively homogeneous in their geographic and demographic characteristics. Paraguay also falls in this category under the remaining criteria. This group uniformly exhibits the lowest development level in the region.

Note that this clustering approach provides much richer results than just using the per capita GDP, the most widely used classification (see second column, Table 2). A per capita GDP index would suggest six levels: (1) Argentina and Uruguay; (2) Brazil, Mexico, and Venezuela; (3) Chile and Costa Rica; (4) Colombia and Peru; (5) Paraguay and Ecuador; and (6) Bolivia.

• **Economic performance.** Countries can be classified into three economic clusters — good, medium, and bad performers. Good performers include Bolivia, Chile, Costa Rica, Colombia, Mexico, and Paraguay. Each of these exhibits moderate-to-strong growth, relatively low inflation, strong exports, and a foreign debt that is either declining or under control. Of these, Chile is the outstanding performer, with a GDP growth of 6.4 percent from 1988 to 1990, a rate that almost matches that of the newly industrialized countries (NICs) and far exceeds the Organization for Economic Cooperation and Development's 3.5 percent.

The medium performers include Ecuador, Uruguay, and Venezuela, countries that show mixed results but that generally have a mediocre outlook. Finally, Argentina, Brazil, and Peru are the bad performers, with Argentina showing signs of improvement in 1991, and Peru better characterized as chaotic.

These clusters bear little resemblance to those in the development category. Argentina, for instance, is among the highest in development terms, because of its superior past performance, but among the lowest in terms of recent economic performance. Additionally, these measures do not recognize ongoing changes that might rapidly change a country's outlook.

• **Political and economic liberalization.** Figure 2 shows four possible combinations of political and economic policies. Most developed nations are in square D; they are both politically and economically open. Since the

Table 1 Demography and Development in Selected Latin American Countries

	Population			Level of Development						
	Total 1990 (millions of inhabitants)	Average annual % increase 1988-1990	Urban % 1989	Life expectancy at birth, 1989 (years)	Infant mortality rate 1989 (per 1,000 live births)	Adult literacy rate 1985 (%)	Real GDP per head 1987*	Inhabitants per passenger car, 1989	Inhabitants per telephone, 1989	Inhabitants per TV set, 1990
Argentina	32.3	1.3	86	71	30	96	4,647	7.5	8.1	4.8
Bolivia	7.2	2.5	51	54	106	75	1,380	95.9	37.1	13.5
Brazil	150.3	2.1	74	66	59	78	4,307	15.5	10.5	5.4
Chile	13.2	1.7	85	72	19	98	4,862	19.4	15.0	4.1
Colombia	33.0	2.0	69	69	38	88	3,524	48.4	12.5	9.9
Costa Rica	3.0	2.6	47	75	17	93	3,760	36.2	7.2	4.9
Ecuador	10.6	2.6	55	66	61	83	2,687	152.0	15.2	12.8
Mexico	88.6	2.2	72	69	40	90	4,624	15.4	9.0	7.2
Paraguay	4.3	2.9	47	67	32	88	2,603	69.3	37.1	12.3
Peru	22.3	2.5	70	62	79	85	3,129	55.1	29.6	10.7
Uruguay	3.1	0.6	85	73	22	95	5,063	18.4	5.8	4.8
Venezuela	19.7	2.6	84	70	35	87	4,306	12.0	11.0	5.6

*Purchasing power per capita according to United Nations' Human Development Report 1990. Sources: United Nations, World Bank, BID, CEPAL.

Table 2 Economic Performance of Selected Latin American Countries

	Gross Domestic Product			Inflation	Investment		Foreign Trade		Foreign Debt		
	GDP total 1990 (billions US$)	GDP per capita, 1990 (US$)	Average annual % real growth rate, 1988-1990	Average annual % rate of inflation, 1988-1990	Average annual rate of gross inv. as % of GDP, 1988-1990	Average annual rate of foreign inv. as % of GDP, 1988-1990	Total exports, 1990 (billions US$)	Total imports, 1990 (billions US$)	Total foreign debt, 1990 (billions US$)	Average annual % change in foreign debt, 1988-1990	Price of foreign debt swaps %, June 1991
			-2.6								
Argentina	93.3	2,887	2.8	1,423.3	9.2	1.8	12.3	3.8	65.0	3.7	25.1
Bolivia	5.3	738	-0.6	18.7	13.3	n.a.	0.8	0.8	3.8	-3.2	n.a.
Brazil	383.4	2,550	6.4	1,443.5	16.4	0.4	31.4	20.6	122.2	0.3	32.9
Chile	27.2	2,066	3.9	20.3	16.6	4.9	8.3	7.0	18.6	-3.4	88.3
Colombia	44.4	1,345	4.1	28.9	15.4	0.8	7.1	5.1	16.7	2.2	72.8
Costa Rica	5.9	1,946	5.4	20.6	21.2	1.8	1.4	1.8	3.7	-5.5	46.4
Ecuador	11.5	1,087	2.8	62.4	14.4	0.8	2.7	1.7	11.2	3.0	22.3
Mexico	220.1	2,485	5.2	33.1	17.7	1.3	26.8	29.8	98.2	-1.4	55.1
Paraguay	4.5	1,043	-8.3	29.4	20.4	n.a.	1.2	1.5	1.8	-4.8	n.a.
Peru	34.1	1,526	0.4	3,336.1	17.2	0.0	3.3	2.9	17.3	4.1	6.6
Uruguay	8.9	2,890	1.1	94.2	10.8	0.3	1.7	1.3	7.4	7.8	n.a.
Venezuela	46.0	2,328		49.6	16.5	0.2	17.3	6.5	33.0	-1.8	60.2

Sources: CEPAL for columns 1, 7, 8, and 9. Own elaboration of data from CEPAL for columns 2, 3, 4, 5, and 10, and from Latin Finance for column 6. U.N. DIESA for column 11.

1950s, most Latin American governments followed protective political and economic policies (A), although some nations (e.g., Costa Rica) were politically open (B). Chile was the first, in the mid 1970s, to carry out open economic policies, albeit within protective political policies (C). Since the mid-1980s, most governments have shifted, first into more open political policies (from A to B), and then into more open economic policies (from B to D). In the late 1980s, Chile integrated its economic freedom with its new political openness (from C to D). No nation in the area has simultaneously moved toward more open political *and* economic systems (from A to D).

While open political systems have solidified throughout the region, economic liberalization proceeds unevenly. Not surprisingly, the countries with the best economic performance are also those with the most liberal and market-oriented economies. Bolivia, Chile, Costa Rica, Colombia, Mexico, and Paraguay are all relatively open economies with successful results to prove it. One of the biggest problems that investors encounter in setting up operations in most of these countries is government inexperience in managing the new openness.

Argentina, Peru, and Brazil, where until recently governments controlled the entire economy, have exhibited the poorest performance. Some progress is evident, though. Within the last few years they have introduced liberalization measures. However, the results are unclear. The remaining countries fall between these two broad groups.

Some companies have developed their own clustering approaches. For example, a Citibank executive in Chile told us:

> *At Citibank, we don't use the map to classify countries. Instead, we look at other criteria. For example, countries with debt problems in Latin America could be classified in two groups: "convergent" countries with effective solutions, as is the case in Chile, Uruguay, Colombia, and Mexico, and "nonperforming" countries like Peru, Argentina, and Brazil. Citibank, like others, tries to differentiate between past performance and future promise.*

Although the clustering criteria are generally useful, investors interested only in specific products or industries may find it better to compare individual countries. For example, investors interested in shrimp farming will recognize Ecuador's shrimping infrastructure, expertise, and experience as a source of global competitive advantage. Ecuador will then be more attractive than countries that rate better in the clusters.

In-Depth Country Assessment

Next, investors must understand each country's unique characteristics. Information is readily available from many sources, including executives doing business in the region, the U.S. and host governments (see the sidebar, "Where to Get Market Information and Trade Leads"), banks, research centers, multilateral agencies, and specialized publications (such as *Business Latin America, LDC Debt Report, and America Economia*).[12] This first analysis will prepare investors to visit those countries offering the most attractive opportunities (i.e., those consistent with the investor's expertise, resources, values, and goals). We cannot describe each country here, but the following discussions of Brazil

Figure 1 Summary of Clusters

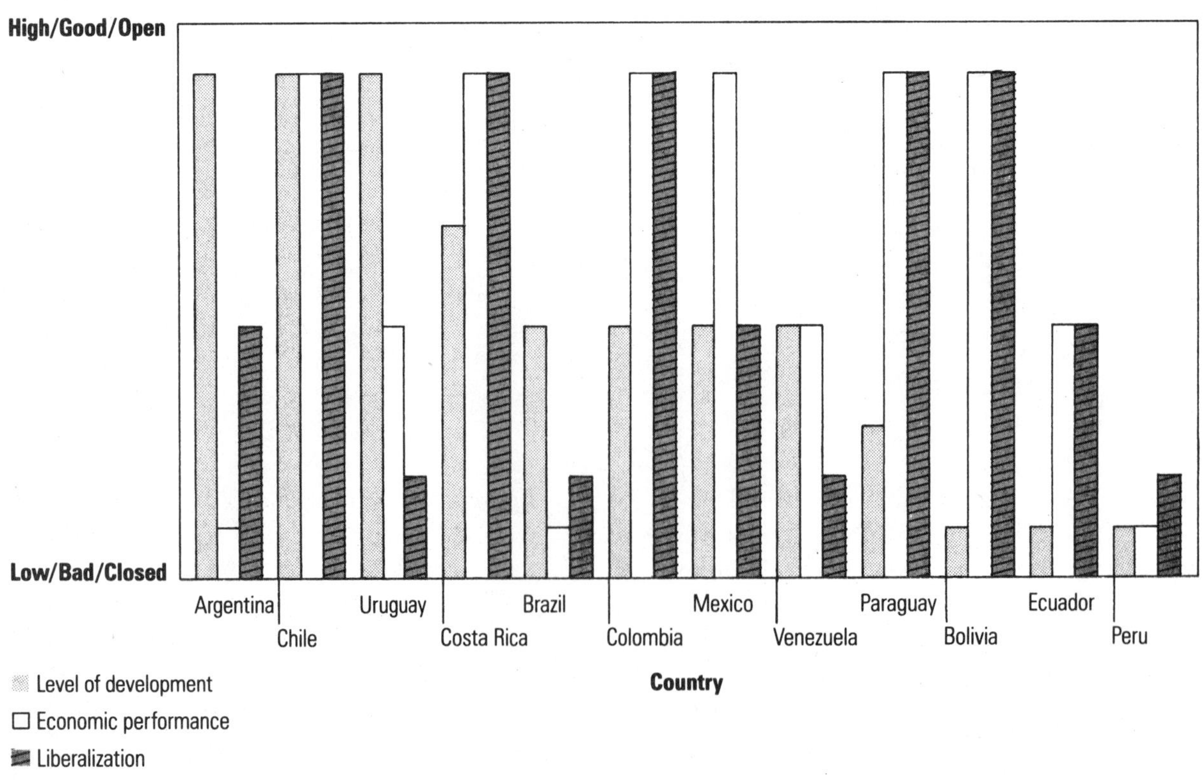

Table 3 Summary of Clusters

Country	Development Level	Economic Performance	Liberalization of Economy
Argentina	High	Bad	Starting to open
Bolivia	Low	Good	Open
Brazil	Medium	Bad	Attempting to open
Chile	High	Good	Open
Colombia	Medium	Good	Open
Costa Rica	High-medium	Good	Open
Ecuador	Low	Medium	Attempting to open
Mexico	Medium	Good	Newly open
Paraguay	Medium-low	Good	Open
Peru	Low	Bad	Recent attempt to open
Uruguay	High	Medium	Attempting to open
Venezuela	Medium	Medium	Attempting to open

Figure 2 Spectrum of Political and Economic Policies

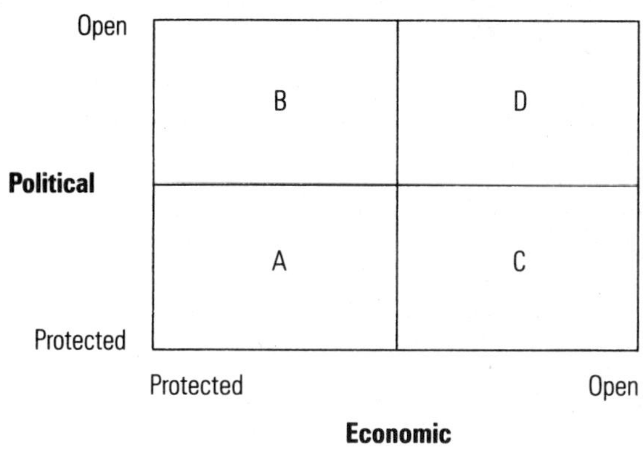

and Chile show how their unique situations affect foreign investors.

In Brazil, President Fernando Collor de Mello's 1990 anti-inflationary economic reform briefly cut the 84 percent monthly inflation to single digits but caused a massive recession and foreign exchange translation losses to foreign companies. By 1991 inflation returned and the failed program led to an economic crisis that is brewing a political crisis.[13] This caused many foreign multinationals either to downscale or to pull out to avoid rising losses. Black & Decker, for one, chose to remain, but it greatly reduced output and cut its Brazilian workforce in half to about 3,500 people last year. However, the country remains attractive to companies that can ride out the instability. Brazil makes up half of South America; it is actually bigger than the continental United States and ranks as the Western world's eighth largest economy. It has abundant natural resources and, with a population of 150 million, an ample labor supply. Companies such as AT&T are monitoring the situation carefully. Evidence in early 1991 suggests that the government is committed to continued liberalization. Average tariffs are expected to drop from 35 percent (reduced from 60 percent in 1988) to 20 percent in 1994 with maximum tariffs falling from 105 percent to 40 percent — 0 percent for many. The country's trade surplus of 12.6 billion was third largest in the world in 1989, and import restrictions on chemicals and computer equipment are being liberalized.[14] Furthermore, the government expects to privatize two large steel companies, Usiminas and Tubarao, in the coming months. The sale of Usiminas alone could bring $6.5 billion.[15] Benetton, the Italian clothing group, has responded to these indications of improvement by opening its first South American factory in Brazil.

In contrast, since 1985 Chile has reduced foreign debt by $6 billion, and its debt service ratio should be 20 percent to 30 percent sometime in the early 1990s. The Chilean economy has been growing at 6 percent per year with export growth predicted to be an even higher 10 percent to 15 percent for the next three years. Inflation remains the only drawback at 27 percent, but the government expects to reduce it to 18 percent in 1991. There is a single across-the-board tariff of 11 percent and no nontariff barriers or subsidies. The 1990 GDP was $27.2 billion, and a further $1.1 billion in foreign investment poured in. This 4 percent ratio of foreign investments over GDP is, by far, the highest in the region, and even higher than the 2.4 percent experienced by Asian countries. For example, Chiquita Brands recently purchased a fruit and vegetable exporter, and Kodak opened a plant to manufacture office furniture for export to the United States. The United States has recently upgraded Chile's credit rating to a "nonrestructuring" country, which means that U.S. banks no longer have to set aside provisions for loans made to Chile. In addition, Chile's sovereign bonds have been securing better terms than those issued by countries that are restructuring under the Brady plan. In September 1991, Chile signed a free trade agreement with Mexico, and a commercial agreement with the United States is imminent. Given these factors, Chilean companies may again be able to secure global financing.

Which Products?

Which product categories will have the most attractive business opportunities? Attractiveness depends, of course, on the investor's resources and goals. Agribusiness, whether oriented to domestic or foreign markets, has opportunities for developing, sustaining, and enhancing global advantage, as exports of cut flow-

Where to Get Market Information and Trade Leads

U.S. Department of Commerce/US&FCS Commercial Information Management System/National Trade Data Bank — Local Commerce District Office specialists can tailor information packages drawing from statistical trade and economic data, market research reports, and foreign traders indices. CIMS/NTDB house all relevant international trade publications published by ITA, including Foreign Economic Trends reports, Overseas Business Reports, and Industry Sector Analyses.
Contact: For your nearest Department of Commerce District Office, call (202) 377-4767, or see local telephone directory under U.S. Department of Commerce listing.

U.S. Department of Commerce/Comparison Shopping Service — A custom-tailored service provides firms with targeted information on marketing and foreign representation for specific products in specific countries. Fee varies.
Contact: For your nearest Department of Commerce District Office, call (202) 377-4767, or see local telephone directory under U.S. Department of Commerce listing.

U.S. Department of Commerce/Agent/Distributor Service — A customized search helps identify agents, distributors, and foreign representatives for U.S. firms based on the foreign companies' examination of U.S. product literature. A fee of $125 per country is charged.
Contact: For your nearest Department of Commerce District Office, call (202) 377-4767, or see local telephone directory under U.S. Department of Commerce listing.

U.S. Department of Commerce/Trade Opportunities Program — TOP provides companies with current sales leads from international firms seeking to buy or represent their products or services. TOP leads are printed daily in leading commercial newspapers and are also distributed electronically via the Economic Bulletin Board. The fee varies.
Contact: For your nearest Department of Commerce District Office, call (202) 377-4767, or see local telephone directory under U.S. Department of Commerce listing; For the Department of Commerce Economic Bulletin Board, call (202) 377-1986.

US. Department of Commerce/Minority Business Development Agency/Minority Export Development Consultants Program — This program helps develop marketing plans, identify potential overseas markets, and trade leads for minority business. It also provides assistance in documentation, short-term financing, and shipping.
Contact: Business Development Specialist, (202) 377-2414.

U.S. Department of Agriculture/Economic Research Service — The staff provides economic data, models, and research information about agricultural economics and policies of foreign countries and bilateral agricultural trade and development relationships.
Contact: Bob Robinson, (202) 219-0700.

U.S. Department of Agriculture/Trade and Marketing Information Centers — These centers, part of the National Agricultural Library, help locate relevant material form their large collection on trade and marketing and provide copies of research and data from the AGRICOLA database.
Contact: Mary Lassanyi, (301) 344-3704.

U.S. Department of Energy/Coal and Technology Export Program — This program promotes the export of U.S. clean coal products and services by acting as an information source on coal and coal technologies.
Contact: Peter Cover, (202) 586-7297.

U.S. Department of Energy/Fossil Energy-AID Database — The Office of Fossil Energy forwards prospective energy-related leads to AID for inclusion in its growing trade opportunities database in an effort to reach an extended audience seeking energy-related trade opportunities.
Contact: Denise Swink, (202) 586-9680.

Small Business Administration/Export Information System — Data reports provide specific product information on the top 25 world markets and market growth trends for the past five years.
Contact: Luis Saldarriaga, (404) 542-5760.

Agency for International Development/Trade and Investment Monitoring System — TIMS, a user-friendly computer-based system, provides a broad array of trade and investment information to potential U.S.investors and exporters on forty-two developing countries, e.g., general economic and business data: trade and investment policies and prospects; government regulation and incentives; sources of funding and corporate tax structures; production and labor forces; and business facilities and infrastructure.
Contact: Tracy L. Smith, (202) 647-3805.

Overseas Private Investment Corporation/Investor Information Service — This information clearinghouse provides "one-stop-shopping" for basic economic, business, and political information and data from a variety of sources on 118 developing countries and 16 geographic regions. This service is available for purchase in country- and region-specific kits.
Contact: Daven Oswalt, Manager, Public Affairs, (202) 457-7087.

Overseas Private Investment Corporation/Investor Services — A new OPIC initiative designed to assist smaller U.S. firms with their overseas investment planning and implementation needs. Fee-based services provide counseling to American firms on business plan development, project structuring, joint-venture partner identification, and location of project financing services.
Contact: Dan Riordan, Director, Investor Services, (202) 457-7091.

Overseas Private Investment Corporation/Opportunity Bank — This computer data system matches a U.S. investor's interest with specific overseas opportunities. A modest fee is charged.
Contact: Daven Oswalt, Manager, Public Affairs, (202) 457-7087.

Source: *Business America* (Washington, D.C.: U.S. Department of Commerce, 1991).

ers and counterseasonal fruits and vegetables already illustrate, or as wood, pulp, and paper products are about to demonstrate. Likewise, renewable and nonrenewable commodities offer great potential once the world economy pulls out of its current slowdown.

Nondurable and durable consumer goods of all kinds will offer significant investment possibilities once domestic markets open, if the economic reforms continue. In several Latin American countries, in Brazil in particular, the middle class is growing rapidly already. Many people can, for the first time, afford some of the capital goods they have been coveting. In Brazil only one-quarter of the homes with electricity have washing machines. In addition, the median age in many Latin American countries is low (18.4 in Mexico as opposed to 32.7 in the United States). As such, a large proportion of the population is just entering its years of highest consumption, a factor that is sure to affect demand for consumer goods.

Telecommunications has recently opened in Latin America. Many state-owned telecommunications companies have been privatized. Foreign companies see enormous potential: just 6 percent of the Latin American population is connected by telephone, compared to 71 percent in the United States, 45 percent in Europe, and 16 percent in Asia. France has more telephones than all of Latin America. Both AT&T and Motorola are already capitalizing; AT&T recently sold $130 million worth of fiber-optic equipment to Telmex (the Mexican telephone company), and Motorola just won the cellular license for a region covering northern Mexico. Similar opportunities exist as other public utilities are privatized.

Another thriving business in Latin America is tourism. The region has beautiful beaches, scuba diving, archaeological expeditions, and outstanding weather. The region's proximity to the United States and Canada virtually assures a constant supply of North American tourists. The Caribbean Islands alone received almost 17 million visitors in 1989. Mexico, where tourism employs one of every twelve Mexicans and where tourism revenues rank second behind those generated from oil, considers this industry to be its most promising source of economic growth. Investment opportunities are available in hotels, shopping centers, ski resorts, and airlines.

Some countries have already successfully attracted tourism investment. The Spanish group Sol-Melia is investing $1 billion in six hotels in Mexico; Marriott and Cementos Mexicanos have formed a joint venture to invest $500 million more in the same country; and the huge project to transform Buenos Aires's old port into hotels and shopping centers will attract some $500 million from foreign investors.

The pharmaceutical industry may open up soon. In Brazil, a government-appointed commission is developing a new intellectual property code, and other countries are expected to follow suit. The reforms protecting intellectual property could cause "substantial changes in investment and the formation of partnerships" in the pharmaceutical industry, says Eli Lilly vice president R.A. Cage.[16]

Other opportunities exist in the computer, auto, footwear, and apparel industries, although restrictions still apply in some countries. Yet their sheer size indicates their potential. For example, the region's computer hardware market already exceeds $6 billion a year, and the software market (despite lacking proper protection) is $1 billion, with annual growth above 10 percent.

How to Participate?

There are a variety of ways to enter the Latin American market, ranging from contractual arrangements to direct investments. We discuss some of the most promising below.

Exporting

Foreign companies can export either indirectly or directly. Indirect exporting means using a home-based export management company, an export trading company, or an export broker to market the investor's products. The middleman either can be paid a commission for services rendered or can take title, buying the goods at a discount and reselling them in Latin America. This strategy's short-term advantage is that it uses existing international marketing and distribution channels and avoids the expenditure of setting them up. However, if the company eventually wants to be directly involved in a Latin American market, this strategy may not be the most cost effective and sensible in the longer term.

The exporting company may also take direct responsibility for marketing its products in Latin America, either selling directly to the consumer or finding a national representative to sell its products locally. Choosing between the two methods often depends on financial capability, the level of import barriers, and the amount of risk or loss that the foreign company is willing to assume.

Strategic Alliances

For investors who know nothing about Latin America, alliances with local producers or distributors may be the best way to enter the market. An alliance allows an investor to share the risk and leverage its strengths with companies experienced in the region. The most common types of cooperative arrangements in the region have been joint ventures; licensing, franchise, and cross-distribution agreements; and subcontracting.

Governments generally support joint ventures (JVs) and will sometimes offer incentives for them. JVs bring in not only foreign capital, but foreign technology and expertise as well. Foreign companies generally benefit from cheap labor, abundant raw materials, access to both new and export markets, and access to local expertise. JV activity can be expected to increase in the near future for the following reasons: (1) as competition for Western investment and competition within global industries increase, foreign investment controls will progressively loosen; (2) as Western companies seek first mover advantages, a JV by one company can precipitate a scramble for similar deals by its global competitors; and (3) as JV regulations become more favorable, some companies currently exporting on a transaction-by-transaction or licensing basis may seek to upgrade their relations and form new JVs. Over time, some of these JVs can be expected to become wholly owned subsidiaries.

Successful JVs make strategic sense for both partners, as two examples illustrate:

• Chateau Lafitte-Rothschild from France has set up a fifty/fifty JV with Vina Los Vascos to export wines from Chile. For the French firm, the JV provided the opportunity to expand, at low cost, into a medium-priced market niche no longer available with its higher-priced domestic products. The Chilean winery obtained distribution access to huge markets in the developed world.

• Cadbury Schweppes signed a JV with Sanbra in preparation for its upcoming launch of Schweppes tonic water in Brazil. Sanbra will distribute the tonic water in Brazil's soft drink market, which is the world's third largest after the United States and Mexico. "Without the help of an experienced partner, we would have felt uncomfortable," says John Neilson, marketing vice president for Cadbury International. "But we feel confident that with Sanbra on our side, we can cope with Brazil's volatile economy."[17] Sanbra, for its part, will add higher margin products to its existing distribution system, improving its efficiency and enhancing its importance as a soft drink supplier.

Other firms prefer to sign long-term licensing agreements. These are a good alternative for small- and medium-sized companies that lack the experience, capital, and confidence to risk direct investment abroad. Licensing arrangements have their risk, however. The licensor's lack of control can cause severe problems if poor quality products undermine the brand name or product "leakage" into other countries at lower prices hurts relations with other channel partners.

Franchising in Latin America is still in the developmental stage. Perhaps Brazil is the most developed country in this field. Other countries are experiencing a boom. In less than three years, McDonald's, Kentucky Fried Chicken, Pizza Hut, and Benetton have established operations in Chile. Recent Mexican agreements have been concluded with Arby's, McDonald's, Baskin Robbins, Holiday Inn, Alpha Graphics, and The Athlete's Foot. Most are master franchise agreements that allow the franchisee to grant subfranchises and to open its own stores.

Other firms have signed crossdistribution agreements, by which they agree to distribute each other's complementary products in their own territories, as Digital Equipment Corporation (computer hardware) and Sonda (software) did until forming their recent joint venture, mentioned above.

Firms can also subcontract with existing companies that can provide activities and services for them. Even nonprofit organizations can use this strategy. For example, the United Nations Program for Development (UNPD) subcontracted with Fundacion Chile, a nonprofit organization with proven experience in transferring foreign technology into the exporting areas of its country's economy, to provide technical assistance to Argentina, Bolivia, Ecuador, El Salvador, and Guatemala.

In-Bond Assembly Plants

For years, American companies have operated border assembly plants, called maquiladoras.They have exported components into Mexico, then imported the finished product, paying only a modest duty, if any, on the added value. In many cases, a twin plant in the United States makes the components. Proximity permits close supervision by a company manager who may manage both plants. By February 1990, over 1,800 companies were operating maquiladoras, employing over 500,000 workers. This represented a 20 percent increase over 1989, a growth rate that appeared to have continued through early 1991. Japanese and Korean as well as American corporations are now operating in-bond assembly plants.

Formerly, there were few maquiladoras for agricultural uses. However, with recent changes in ownership rules and a newly relaxed attitude toward foreign investment, American capital and expertise have propelled the development of Mexico's promising food processing industry.[18] Agromaquilas now represent the fastest-growing segment of the $3 billion per year maquiladora industry, with the wholesale value of these agricultural goods totaling $100 million (they totaled less than $20 million in early 1989). One California-based firm grows onions in Mexico from imported seeds, then exports onion flakes and powder for distribution in the United States. Arrangements like this can benefit both sides. U.S. consumers get good products at reasonable cost, while Mexicans get jobs without having to cross the border. U.S. businesses use this method to compete against low-cost foreign competition.

Acquisitions

Acquiring an operating company is a relatively cost-effective way to enter a Latin American market. This method can be particularly attractive because heavy devaluations in most countries make local facilities excellent buys in home-currency terms. Experts believe that recent economic crises have created a buyer's market in Latin America. Procter & Gamble took advantage of these factors in the 1980s. Instead of starting subsidiaries on its own, it acquired Industrias Phebo in Brazil, Mammi in Venezuela, Inextra in Colombia, and Laboratorios Geka in Chile.[19]

Debt-equity swaps have made investments more attractive. Investors buy heavily discounted government debt paper in secondary markets. The investor then exchanges this paper for local currency (or state-owned assets) at much higher rates. The investor obtains an excellent price, and the government pays off some of its debts at favorable rates.[20] This method is particularly favored in privatization efforts.

Use of Debt-Equity Swaps in Privatizations ($ billions)

	1989	1990	1991 (est.)
Argentina	1.00	2.90	2.00
Brazil	0.88	1.50	1.80
Mexico	2.24	2.85	3.25

(Source: Institute of International Finance, *Fostering Foreign Direct Investment in Latin America,* Washington, D.C., 1990)

In the last two years, foreign MNCs have acquired, or are in the process of acquiring, the national telecommunications firms of Chile, Argentina, Uruguay, Mexico, and Brazil through debt-equity swaps. The U.S. Bell Atlantic and the Spanish Telefonica acquired 60 percent of the Argentine ENTEL, paying only $750 million for the equivalent of $5 billion of Argentina's external debt. The consortium of Scott Paper, Citibank, and the Chilean subsidiary of Royal Dutch Shell invested $350 million in Chile's pulp and paper industry. Campbell Soup's Argentine subsidiary, Swift, used debt-equity swaps to cut the cost of constructing a new meat packing plant by $41 million.

Green-Field Investments

Starting a company from inception is perhaps the riskiest and most difficult way to initiate Latin American operations. The bureaucracy and protectionism in many of these countries and the unique characteristics of these markets make it difficult to start a new business without a local network of contacts who can provide knowledge about local marketing practices, consumer behavior, and government relations. This method might be best for companies that are already familiar with or operating in Latin America.

Marketing Programs and Organization

Product Policy

To cope with volatile economic conditions, most multinationals manufacturing in Latin America try to ensure that they can export whatever they make and that production can be switched to lower-priced products during a downturn. Tariff barriers and local content rules have required multinationals to invest in manufacturing plants in most of the Latin American countries in which they wish to sell products. As these barriers and restrictions fall, multinationals will begin rationalizing their manufacturing as they are in Europe. Companies that have had to use low-quality, locally made parts and raw materials might be able to substitute higher-quality imported parts. Multiple product plants spread through Latin America might be replaceable by a few specialized plants with long production runs of products that meet the combined market needs of several countries.

Industrial products developed in the United States and Europe typically require little adaptation to be salable in Latin America. However, consumer packaged goods may require adaptation to local tastes and, when manufactured in Latin America, to local raw materials. Procter & Gamble found that its North American low-suds detergents, developed for North American washing machines, sold poorly to Mexicans who handwashed and believed that high sudsing indicated quality. In addition, consumer behavior differs widely across Latin American countries. For example, Chile's market for hair conditioner is almost eight times Peru's, while the Peruvian market for detergent soap is eighty times that of Chile. Multinationals are exploring panregional consumer products but most will continue to offer a mix of global and local brands in each market.

Foreign brands are widely known and highly regarded, even when local brands are of equivalent quality. This attitude may not last if freer trade spawns a wave of U.S. products and media that seem to threaten local cultural heritage. Meanwhile, many products retain English-language packaging, even when they are locally manufactured. Finally, the most popular package sizes are typically smaller than in the United States; Latin Americans have lower purchasing power.

Distribution

Trade concentration is increasing but varies widely by country. In Brazil, manufacturers are already contending with the power — and demands for lower prices — of three major supermarket chains. By contrast, small outlets still dominate consumer goods sales in Peru and Bolivia. Such outlets do not have the capital or space to stock much inventory and often carry only the most popular size of the leading brand in each category. In Peru, Procter & Gamble provides frequent deliveries of small orders to such stores along with fifteen to thirty day credit to encourage them to carry more inventory.

As tariff barriers decrease, more imported products will compete with domestic manufacturers for distributor representation. This will increase trade power and stimulate further trade concentration as only large, well-capitalized distributors will be able to offer broad selections of products.

Companies must look creatively for market development opportunities beyond the major metropolitan areas. BCE Ventures, for example, sells blocks of cellular phone airtime to rural storeowners, who resell it to villagers.

Communications

Advertising copy and budgets must be tailored for each country. First, advertising is highly regulated, and the rules differ from one country to another.

In Mexico, for example, all television advertising time is sold through a government agency, while Peru requires that all advertising be produced locally. Second, language cannot be assumed; in Paraguay and Bolivia, it's essential to translate radio ads into local dialects. Third, regional television is embryonic; only one program, Sabado Gigante, is broadcast simultaneously in eighteen countries. Fourth, the availability and reliability of media audience information varies widely, preventing easy cross-country comparisons.

The costs per thousand television advertising impressions, ostensibly low in most Latin American countries, are actually high when adjusted for much of the audience's minimal purchasing power. Mass advertising cannot be used efficiently for consumer durables, but automobile marketers in Mexico have found that television advertising on satellite-delivered channels does reach the target audience.

Many forms of consumer promotion cannot be used yet. Coupon redemption systems involving retailers are only gradually emerging. On-pack premiums are likely to be dismantled by store employees or consumers in the aisles. Mail refunds are unappealing to consumers in high-inflation environments, especially when postal services are unreliable. In-store sampling, however, is highly cost efficient owing to low labor rates.

Pricing

A common saying in Latin America is that it is cheaper to take a cab than a bus; in a bus, you pay when you get in, but in a cab, you pay when you reach your destination. Temporary price discounts are rare; instead, a marketer might raise a price in the afternoon rather than first thing in the morning.

Although many Latin American governments are attempting to curb inflation, most local businesspeople have learned how to live with it. Multinationals likewise have become proficient at minimizing inventories, managing their receivables tightly, and placing funds in interest-bearing overnight bank accounts. Kraft General Foods' Kibon subsidiary in Brazil astutely converted cash into milk just before President Collor's first economic reform plan froze all bank accounts. Molex, an electrical connector manufacturer, once had employees standing in lines all day at Sao Paulo banks depositing funds handed to them each hour by other employees. Colgate-Palmolive, like many other multinationals, uses an accounting system that adjusts all revenue and expense items daily in dollar terms in response to local currency devaluations; this minimizes the likelihood of a subsidiary discovering at year end that it has earned high profits in local currency but no profit in dollars.[21]

Marketers of widely sold consumer goods periodically find themselves subject to tightly enforced government price controls. It is therefore necessary to price ahead of inflation. Otherwise, it may become necessary to withdraw a product and relaunch it later under a different name; pharmaceuticals manufacturers have often used this tactic.

Industrial marketers of highly differentiated products who are not interested in aggressive market penetration or in doing business with government agencies may be able to demand prepayment in dollars, particularly in smaller countries. Most foreign companies, however, have to do business in the local currency and often negotiate complicated contracts with customers whereby different prices apply on the dates of order, shipment, and payment.

Organization

Multinationals use a variety of organizational structures, depending on their level of commitment and risk aversion. Some companies simply operate cash and carry warehouses in Miami. The Stanley Works pulled out of Venezuela and now fulfills dollar orders placed by its Latin American agents through its Miami distribution center; the company can achieve limited market penetration, but its return on investment exceeds 30 percent. Other companies without local manufacturing in Latin America commonly ship large quantities of their well-known brands to distributors in Panama, who then arrange for the goods to be forwarded into other Latin American countries.

Most multinationals with a strong commitment to Latin America have traditionally relied on a separate subsidiary headed by a country manager in each local market. Though expensive, this ensures good relations with top government officials whose support is often helpful in dealing with local regulations and bureaucratic impediments, and government agencies are often among the multinational's most important customers. In addition, unpredictable economic conditions and hyperinflation require decisive, on-the-spot management of the multinational's finances, especially when large investments in fixed assets and working capital have been made.

The ideal country manager has traditionally been a decisive, entrepreneurially minded, local national with financial acumen and the ability to cultivate high-level government contacts. Nowhere has the phenomenon of "country manager as king" been more evident than in Latin America.

The globalization of markets and the potential emergence of regional trading blocs within Latin America are causing multinationals to take a more panregional perspective. Increasingly country managers are not local nationals but Latin Americans from neighboring countries who have had assignments in multiple countries in the region plus a stint at corporate headquarters. This facilitates idea transfer, reduces myopia, and helps retain good executives. Latin American regional managers are becoming increasingly important in coordinating marketing and manufacturing strategies throughout the region. To prevent additional overhead and an extra layer of decision making, some companies appoint a senior country manager in a large market to regional manager. More typically, Latin American region managers are based either in Miami, for easy access, or at corporate headquarters, where they can advocate for the region's interests.

Conclusion

The climate of political and economic change sweeping through Latin America is as substantial as that affecting Eastern Europe, though less publicized. Trade agreements, tariff reductions, and privatization all promise a more competitive business environment and increasing opportunities for foreign multinationals. President Bush's Americas Initiative and the likely entry of Mexico and Chile into the North American Free Trade Area further reinforce the need for North American, Asian, and European multinationals — headquartered in and focused on the northern hemisphere — to look south and elevate Latin America in their strategic planning.

References

The authors thank Elisa Morton Palter, Aimee L. Stern, Pilar Santibanez, and Rainer Stehr for their research assistance on this project.

1. *D & B Reports,* January-February 1991, p. 21.

2. C. Hills, "U.S. Should Foster Stronger Trade in the Americas," *The Miami Herald,* International Edition, 8 July 1990, p. C-5.

3. P.F. Drucker, "Help Latin America and Help Ourselves," *Wall Street Journal,* 20 March 1990.

4. Nontariff barriers to export of U.S. goods to Mexico that would have to be eliminated include: import permits and licenses, "buy national" policies for selected sectors (such as telecommunications and construction), standards and testing procedures that unfairly impede the entry of foreign competitors, the absence of laws recognizing intellectual property rights, and direct foreign investment restrictions in key sectors.

5. "Enterprise for the Americas Fact Sheet," U.S. Department of Commerce, Office of Latin America, 30 August 1991, p. 10.

6. See "Rethinking Corporate Strategies for Latin America: A Blueprint for Success in the 1990s," a *Business International* research report.

7. J. Main, "How Latin America Is Opening Up," *Fortune,* 8 April 1991, pp. 84-89.

8. "The 500 Largest Companies in Latin America," *America Economia,* October 1990.

9. For example, in 1989 average price/earnings were: Brazil, 7.0; Colombia, 6.9; Chile, 4.7; Mexico, 9.7; and Venezuela, 5.7; as compared with United States, 16.2; United Kingdom, 13.4; West Germany, 15.6; and Japan, 53.8.

10. "Latin America Draws a Flood of New Capital," *Wall Street Journal,* 29 August 1991, p. A7.

11. Space limitations do not allow us to refer to Caribbean and Central American nations, except for Costa Rica.

12. For a checklist of country selection criteria, see:
J.A. Quelch, E. Joachimsthaler, and J.L. Nueno, "After the Wall: Marketing Guidelines for Eastern Europe," *Sloan Management Review,* Winter 1991, p. 85.

13. T. Kamm, "In the Political Trials of Brazil's Collor, Inflation and Economic Crisis Reign," *Wall Street Journal,* 13 September 1991, p. A-ll.

14. Main (1991).

15. "Privatization in Latin America Going, Going . . . ," *The Economist,* 23 March 1991.

16. "Turning the Hemisphere into a Free Trade Bloc," *Business Week,* 24 December 1990, p. 37.

17. "Schweppes Seeks a Tonic from Brazil," *Financial Times,* 21 March 1991, p. 12.

18. "There's Your Solution," *Forbes,* 7 January 1991, pp. 72 and 76.

19. "Southern Strategy: With Persistence, P&G Pursues Tough Market: The Latin Americans," *Wall Street Journal,* 18 June 1990, p. A1.

20. J. Ganitsky and G. Lema, "Foreign Investment through Debt-Equity Swaps," *Sloan Management Review,* Winter 1989, pp. 21-30.

21. "How Colgate-Palmolive Manages for Success in L.A.," *Business Latin America,* 12 February 1990.

BUT WHAT ABOUT AFRICA?

On the global economy's lost continent

Richard J. Barnet

Richard J. Barnet is a senior fellow at the Institute for Policy Studies in Washington. His most recent book is The Rockets' Red Glare: When America Goes to War, The Presidents & the People *(Simon & Schuster).*

Like the term *national security,* the word *development* artfully conceals an entire worldview. It is a word appropriated from nature and applied to man-made chaos. Flowers develop because they are genetically programmed to open and then to wither; babies develop by following biologically determined paths, the likes of which no one has yet discovered for any society, much less for the political economy of the earth. Healthy development in both flowers and babies requires a nurturing environment, and human beings have acquired considerable experience about how to achieve it. But we know much less about what societies and economies need in order to develop. While some of the ideological recipes—state socialism, social democracy, Japanese capitalism, capitalism under military rule, Reaganomics—obviously yield better results than others, no one has yet come up with a formula for assuring sustainable growth, a decent standard of living for all, and the promise of a more equitable distribution of wealth.

It has been forty-one years since Harry Truman set a national goal for the United States to "relieve the suffering" of people in the vast "underdeveloped areas" of the world through the spread of "industrial activity" and "greater production . . . the key to prosperity." Since the days of the Marshall Plan and Point Four (technical assistance for underdeveloped countries announced in Truman's inaugural address in 1949), brave talk of inevitable "takeoffs" into industrial prosperity has given way to the realization not only that the paths to development are different for different countries, depending upon their histories, cultures, and politics, but that for the poorest countries the paths are well hidden. Nowhere are the paths to development more obscured than in Africa.

The illusions proclaimed in early U.S. aid rhetoric—that the poorest countries could walk the same path to development that made the United States "preeminent among nations in the development of industrial and scientific techniques," and that with enough patience, hard work, and outside aid they could "catch up" or even "close the gap"—now seem hopelessly naive to anyone who visits the African continent, as I recently did. At the same time, most of the traditional hard-headed commercial and military reasons for pouring money into Africa's poor countries—keeping communism out of the Third World, making poor countries safe for economic penetration and resource exploitation—have begun to sound old-fashioned or off point. The Soviets are busy at home. Resources turn out to be well distributed around the globe, and, increasingly, synthetics can be substituted. Cheap labor is available almost anywhere. Poor people do not make good customers, and not very many of them get rich.

The World Bank began its quest for development in the late 1940s by setting a goal of "rapid industrialization." This meant financing huge projects—dams, roads, tourist meccas—that would generate capital. The benefits would eventually find their way to the poor. In the intervening years the doctors of development have tried many different remedies. When Robert McNamara was president of the World Bank in the early 1970s, he insisted upon paying special attention to the "basic needs" of the "poorest of the poor." But faced with the world recession of the early 1980s, in the wake of the "oil shocks," and the resulting trillion dollars of Third World debt, the World Bank switched course again. It shed its social-worker guise and became a stern economic taskmaster and cop.

The World Bank began tying its loans to the willingness of poor countries to make "structural adjustments" in their feeble economies. To qualify for a Structural Adjustment Loan, a government had to agree to devalue its currency, reduce government payrolls, encourage the export sector, let the market set food prices, and in many cases cut back health, education, and welfare programs. These austerity measures, applauded by bankers and businessmen as a long-

 Copyright © 1990 by Harper's Magazine, May 1990, pp. 43-51. All rights reserved. Reprinted by special permission.

overdue dose of realism, were denounced by some African governments as "neocolonial" schemes to take over their countries. The bitter pills, they declared, were nothing short of poison. The United Nations Children's Fund (UNICEF) lent some support for the charge that the World Bank and its sister agency, the International Monetary Fund (IMF), were trying to save economies at the expense of the people.

The decline in social spending has led to increasing malnutrition in countries in which the bottom 40 percent of the population, according to World Bank statistics, typically receives 10 percent or less of the national income. UNICEF has called for "adjustment with a human face." Having been greeted at its annual meetings by hundreds of demonstrators shouting "The World Bank kills babies" and subjected to devastating critiques by a variety of Third World economists, nongovernmental relief agencies, and the Economic Commission for Africa, the World Bank rededicated itself in 1987 to "dramatically revers[ing] the global trend of increasing impoverishment" by the year 2000. Bank documents were published that acknowledged mistakes of the past and addressed such critical and previously neglected issues as land reform and the exploitation of women—who do most of the work in many African and other Third World countries and get to spend little of the money. (This is more than a matter of injustice, since the women tend to spend money on their children while the men tend to spend it on themselves.) In November 1989 the World Bank published a study on Africa that showed much greater awareness of African sensibilities and more willingness to address the negative impact of austerity measures on poor people, which in Africa means most people. How much the World Bank's operations will change, however, is not yet clear.

A considerable portion of the money spent on foreign aid, in Africa as elsewhere, supports well-educated, well-paid officials and consultants from prosperous countries who have helped to design, finance, and construct big projects or to dispense money, food, shots, condoms, technology of all sorts—but mostly advice—to the governments of poor countries. Graham Hancock, a former correspondent for *The Economist*, has written a thundering denunciation of these "lords of poverty" and "aristocrats of mercy," as he calls them. The top-level administrators of largesse make easy targets: living like viceroys, with budgets for chauffeurs, gardeners, wine cellars, swimming pools, and tennis courts. Though they reside only a few miles away from the slums, these upscale modern missionaries behind their high walls and barred windows in the exclusive suburbs of Third World capitals could not be more separated, physically and psychologically, from the people they have come to help.

I have met conscientious aid administrators and dispensers in African nations who make heroic efforts

Most of the traditional hardheaded commercial and military reasons for pouring money into Africa's poor countries have begun to sound old-fashioned or off point.

to see their "patient" countries as more than a set of economic indicators and a blur of poor people. But for too many in the development business, their colonial life-style serves as a curtain. Under peer pressure not to "go native," they have no way of knowing how the money and advice they dispense actually affect the poor majority. Just doing their job—negotiating with ministers, fending off avaricious contractors, managing projects—encourages them to overlook the hidden strengths of people struggling out of poverty: the dignity and hope poor men and women exhibit, their ingenuity to survive in an increasingly hostile environment, their astounding entrepreneurial skills.

Do the ministrations of the doctors of development do more harm than good? I am not talking about famous mistakes—dams that dry up rivers, impoverishing the poor inhabitants on its banks and causing epidemics of onchocerciasis (river blindness). Nor am I referring to instances of well-intended development projects having accelerated the devastation of forests. (In East Africa, some 70 percent of the forests is already gone.) Nor do the seemingly endless stories of the human willingness to profit from the misery of other human beings—stories of swindling bureaucrats and thieving charities—decide the case one way or the other. What set of human institutions, especially one with $60 billion to spend—this representing the total expenditure on development last year by the World Bank, rich nations, and private aid groups—is free of corruption?

The real issue is whether the relationship between aid-giving countries and aid receivers is so fundamentally flawed that the doctors of develoopment would be better advised to take down their shingles. Faced with intractable and worsening poverty, a few despairing aid officials and consultants are beginning to sound like their radical critics. Feeling the burden of the Hippocratic oath—First, do no harm!—these disillusioned aid givers wonder whether it is not time to cut back, scale down, go home.

Africa is the continent most in need of intensive care. The continent has 650 million people, roughly 280 million of whom are poor by anybody's standards. The poorest of the poor live mostly in "sub-Saharan" Africa: black Africa minus South Africa and Namibia. With the fastest-growing population in the world and a total gross domestic product only about the size of Belgium's, sub-Saharan Africa is caught up in a process of development characterized by environmental destruction, political corruption, and dimming prospects for the poor majority. As the president of the World Bank, Barber B. Conable, put it a few months ago, "Overall, Africans are almost as poor today as they were thirty years ago." A senior official of the Agency for International Development pronounced all of sub-Saharan Africa—with a few enclaves excepted—to be a "basket case" and told me that pouring substantially more foreign money into the region would do no good whatever. Corruption, mismanagement, and the persistence of tribal politics all conspire to direct well-meant subsidies into the wrong pockets, much of the money ending up in numbered accounts in Zurich banks.

In the 1970s Africa caught the attention of the United States and other industrial countries because it appeared to be the next Cold War battleground. Soviet arms had poured onto the continent as military men espousing Marxist-Leninist rhetoric came to power in Ethiopia and Mozambique. U.S. interest in the continent heightened as the horn of Africa was incorporated into Zbigniew Brzezinski's "arc of crisis," and anxious admirals peddled panic to Congress. With U.S. encouragement, a number of African countries increased their military spending.

Today, however, the world's gaze is shifting away from Africa. The Soviet Union has lost interest in its African clients, and in Washington it is no longer fashionable to push for bases and "rapid deployment capabilities" in East African waters. Receding as a Cold War battlefield, too poor and unstable to attract much foreign investment, racked by regional and internal wars in Ethiopia, Sudan, Somalia, and elsewhere, sub-Saharan Africa participates at the fringes of international commerce. (The entire continent accounts for 3 percent of world trade.) I once heard the Nobel Prize-winning economist Gunnar Myrdal say that were the whole continent to disappear beneath the sea—South Africa aside—the world economy would hardly be disturbed. Africa today is threatened not so much by exploitation, as in the first half of the century, as by its marginalization in an increasingly integrated global economy.

Recently I went to Kenya, long considered a "middle income" African country by the World Bank ($330 per capita annual income), to try to understand better what development is, whether it is happening, and what role the dispensers of foreign aid are playing. Kenya seemed a good test case, perhaps the most hopeful country on a continent most of which seems to be sliding off the map. Kenya has enjoyed high growth rates and relatively low inflation since gaining independence. On a continent where the average ruler hangs on for seven months, Kenya has had just two presidents in the twenty-six years since the Union Jack came down. Unlike neighboring Ethiopia, Tanzania, Uganda, Sudan, and Somalia, Kenya has steered clear of wars. It is a tourist attraction, blessed with the best harbor in East Africa, the world's second-largest fresh-water lake, and a great stretch of the Great Rift Valley—the geological marvel in which the earliest known ancestors of *Homo sapiens* are thought to have appeared. It has a well-developed civil service. Although recent years have been rocky, it has grown almost enough food most years since independence to take care of its people. The World Bank's report *Sub-Saharan Africa* gave a moderately upbeat account of Kenya's success in navigating the disastrous 1980s, though income distribution is increasingly skewed to the rich. (The poorest 40 percent of the people in Nairobi received 17 percent of the income in 1969, 13 percent in 1985.)

With a total gross domestic product only about the size of Belgium's, sub-Saharan Africa is caught up in a process of development characterized by environmental destruction and political corruption.

Kenya is also the African country that has the longest experience with the World Bank's shock treatments for stalled economies. The nation received its first Structural Adjustment Loan in 1980. Officials of the World Bank exert pressure in three main areas: (1) They push for greater emphasis on exports to earn foreign exchange, which is needed to import foreign technology, drugs, machinery, and to service foreign debt. (2) They insist that the government stop setting artificially low prices on food and other basic necessities. (3) They encourage the government to get out of business and to "privatize" sectors of the economy that have been run by inefficient and corrupt publicly owned corporations ("parastatals").

There is compelling logic to the stern advice from the international lending agencies. Plainly, poor countries like those of sub-Saharan Africa cannot behave as if they were foundations or welfare agencies unless they can get some rich country to foot the bill. That prospect has evaporated. Eastern Europe, not Africa, is now seen as the patient most likely to recover. Where will the poor African countries get foreign exchange to import fuel, technology, drugs, and the "infrastructure" of development if they do not earn it? The catastrophic debt burden under which most of Africa staggers makes it clear that more borrowing in the international money market is not the answer. (Thirty-six cents of every dollar of foreign exchange Kenya earns goes to service its foreign debt.) Nor will billions in grants-in-aid from East or West fall like manna; the prospects are for reduced aid to these countries as the Cold War ebbs and aid-giving fashions change. Indeed, Africa is feeling the effects of a kind of Marshall Plan in reverse: In the 1980s more dollars were sucked from its poor countries—through interest payments and by flights of capital—than flowed into them.

Since equitable distribution of poverty is not a particularly inspiring goal, and certainly not a winning political slogan, most authoritarian African leaders have preferred to address their people's poverty by setting an example of opulent living. The record of African socialism, the ideology of most African states in the first flush of independence, is a story of dashed hopes and privation, equitably shared to some extent. Kenya never did more than nod in that direction. The prime goal was growth, not equity. More than most of its neighbors, Kenya let the market set food prices; and, though the state is still heavily involved in certain sectors of the economy, the government, appealing to the entrepreneurial spirit and tradition found among the dominant Kenyan tribes, always encouraged private enterprise.

It surely would have been unfair to do otherwise. The first two presidents of Kenya have been uncannily successful as investors, and while President Daniel arap Moi, now in the thirteenth year of his rule, has not matched the $5 billion President Sese Soko Mobuto of Zaire is supposed to have stashed away in banks and real estate around the world, it is widely assumed that his spare-time financial activities have done well enough to entitle him to inclusion on the *Forbes* list of the world's richest.*

No one can argue against structural changes in failing economies, but structural adjustment at the national level without a structural overhaul of the international economy is bound to fail. A country like Kenya cannot get out of its trap unless the ground rules of the world economy are reformed. There are hundreds of proposals for doing this, but the essential changes are two: If poor countries are expected to survive by exporting what they grow or make, the rich countries must open their markets, paying prices that do not further impoverish the exporters. If poor countries are expected to invest in future productivity, if they are ever to become good global customers, their crippling debt payments, or at least most of them, must be forgiven and forgotten.

Another problem with adjustment is that some of the medicine seems ill-advised, the dosages excessive—and, as a result, the side effects can be devastating. Take the great emphasis on pushing exports, for example. Kenya depends heavily on selling its tea and coffee on the world market. The country is also the world's fourth-largest exporter of flowers—mostly roses, orchids, and carnations. Arable land in Kenya is in short supply; more than 70 percent of the country is arid or semiarid. As more land is devoted to cash crops—coffee, tea, flowers—less land is available for subsistence agriculture. Some of the worst malnutrition in Kenya borders rich coastal lands used by Del Monte to grow pineapples for export.

Africa today is threatened not as much by exploitation as by its marginalization in an increasingly integrated global economy.

Further, the export market is notoriously volatile. There was a coffee boom in the mid-1970s; then prices plummeted more than 60 percent and are still depressed. The World Bank warns that consumers may soon have a choice between Kenya's justly famous AA coffee and "biocoffee" beans made in laboratories in the United States (and also warns that "laboratory-produced vanilla may soon put the livelihood of 70,000 vanilla-bean farmers in Madagascar in doubt"). The vicissitudes of the export market are infinite, almost totally unpredictable, and most likely to punish the world's poorest, frailest economies.

Kenya's greatest source of foreign exchange is tourism; the biggest attractions are the game parks. It is no longer lawful to shoot or sell rhinos, lions, hippos, and elephants, but they are rented every day to tourists who flock to the preserves for two-hour photo opportunities from the safety of a safari vehicle. Kenya's game parks are now under the direction of the famous naturalist Richard Leakey, and they are better managed than in some other African countries. But the tourist trade takes its toll on the environment. Safari vehicles racing over the bush to give the foreigners a rare glimpse of a leopard or a rhino have (along with stampeding elephants) reduced parts of the once lush Amboseli National Park to a dusty desert.

The hotel industry is also vulnerable. When I visited a coastal resort near Mombasa, the trade paper of the local tourist industry was full of the bad news from Sri Lanka: The political situation there had greatly improved, and tourists would be abandoning Kenya for the much cheaper beach hotels to the east. In the fiercely competitive export market that is barely growing, poor countries often make progress only at the expense of other poor countries.

The case for austerity is overwhelming; the issue is how the pain is to be shared. The determinant now is neither economics nor social justice, but raw political power. Thus the side effects of austerity fall on those with little power: the world's poor. As food prices rise and real wages fall, poor people, as one might expect, eat less. About 30 percent of the Kenyan population is

**It is claimed that a personal fortune is a requirement of office for a Kenyan president because of the peculiar institution known as* harambee, *a Swahili word meaning "let's pull together." If, say, a school is needed in a remote district, the president holds a rally in the community at which he pledges a large sum and calls upon the populace to come up with the rest, in effect a local taxation scheme triggered by presidential charity.*

malnourished, according to UNICEF studies, and severe malnutrition, I was told by doctors in Nairobi, is increasing.

Health care in Kenya is no longer free. Actually, in practice it never was. Patients learned to exercise their "right" to a bed or drugs by bribing the right person on the hospital staff or by bringing their own. Recently, the government has introduced a "cost-sharing" plan requiring patients to pay a small fee in order to be seen in government clinics and hospitals. As a consequence, hospital attendance is falling off. AIDS is rampant, but the extent of the epidemic is unknown because little testing is done.

There is public education in Kenya, but as the government is forced to cut back on its subsidies, the school dropout rate has increased. The future of the country depends on raising a new generation of aware, trained, self-sufficient citizens who can grasp the information and ideas that will enable them to escape poverty. Education is the key, but less government money will mean fewer Kenyans with even minimal schooling.

Neither the export boom nor the savings from the slashing of bloated bureaucracies touches the 60 percent of Nairobi's population who live in slums, typically with no electricity and but a single water source for as many as 200 families. Great, gaping, overpowering sewers crisscross these unimaginably squalid settlements, which no animal-rights group in the United States would tolerate as pigpens. The residents of Mathare Valley, reputed to be the largest slum in Africa, get scant attention from their government. There is a local office of the ruling party to get out the vote, a few devoted literacy teachers and health workers on government payrolls, and an occasional police patrol. A few private nongovernmental agencies are making valiant efforts with small resources to create jobs, teach people to read, and provide primary health care, but by and large the slum dwellers are part of the forgotten majority on the forgotten continent.

I was impressed with the intelligence, commitment, and absence of dogmatism of some officials from the World Bank, the United States Agency for International Development, and other donor agencies with whom I talked. A number of the agencies, including USAID, are funding local projects that seem extremely promising because they encourage and enable poor people to take some control over their lives. There is a growing understanding that "technology transfer" has much less to do with shipping machines abroad than with helping people to use and repair them. The more self-reliant they become, the less they are at the mercy of landowners, local bosses, and petty officials who keep them poor. One project sponsored by the Swedish International Development Authority for a community water supply and sanitation project was impressive because it combined specially designed technology—an easily operated and easily reparable hand pump—with the development of a local community to deal with health and sanitation problems.

If poor countries are expected to invest in future productivity, if they are ever to become global customers, their crippling debt payments, or at least most of them, must be forgiven and forgotten.

The World Bank has so much money to lend that most of its projects are huge. Little World Bank money is directly invested in poor people. It is a mammoth bureaucracy within which there are many contending ideas about what development is and what the role of lending agencies should be. The report *Sub-Saharan Africa* took months to be cleared, and some of its pages seem irreconcilable with adjoining pages. A number of aid bureaucrats and consultants I met kept alluding to the complex, codependent relationship between donor agencies and the host country. The aid bureaucracies in Nairobi need Kenya to justify their existence every bit as much as Kenya needs their money.

The charter of the World Bank imposes political blinders on the organization. It is supposed to be "above politics," dutifully servicing any government that meets its conditions, however repressive, however corrupt that government may be. In practice, the World Bank and other foreign-aid agencies exert major political influence through their choice of projects and by the conditions they impose. Nongovernmental agencies (NGOs) operate at the grass-roots level—building houses, running clinics, encouraging poor people to become their own leaders. But the government of Kenya is suspicious of NGO efforts to "empower" people by helping to organize and train them, for such people cannot then so easily be ignored or so cavalierly governed. Although it has become fashionable to ascribe an increasingly important role to NGOs and small projects, the government likes large projects because they are expensive and the usual 10 to 15 percent rake-off for the highest officials adds up to real money. But some Kenyans with whom I spoke worry that the NGOs are even less accountable for the money they receive and dispense than governments.

Virtually every Kenyan I talked to pointed out that the expatriate experts are at a distinct disadvantage because they do not, really cannot, comprehend the centrality of tribal politics, which affects almost every intervention into the economy. There are some forty-odd tribes in Kenya. The country's first president, Jomo Kenyatta, was a Kikuyu, and he favored his tribe in all sorts of ways, turning over the best government lands to its members, favoring them for admission to the university, and helping them to establish a dominant position in Kenyan financial and commercial institutions. For the last dozen years President Moi, a member of a small tribe, has been trying to cut the Kikuyus down to size, hounding them out of government and trying to reduce their influence in the economy. Almost every development decision is influenced by these bitter internal struggles, which often negate the intended beneficial effects. But they are not a matter for discussion between the donor agencies and the Kenyan government. The "white tribe" is kept at arm's length and can only guess what is happening behind the invective that cabinet ministers routinely hurl at one another in the daily papers. Diplomatic niceties make it mandatory to preserve the fiction that Kenya is well advanced on the road to "nation-building."

Kenya's economic growth is eclipsed by what is still the highest birthrate in the world and a declining death rate, one of the clear achievements of foreign aid. At the present rate of 4.1 percent a year, the population will double every eighteen years. The rapidly rising demand for food and fuel is producing an ecological crisis—overgrazing, deforestation, and soil erosion. According to Janet Brown of the World Resources Institute, per capita food production is down 38 percent in Kenya since 1952.

The case for austerity is overwhelming; the issue is how the pain is to be shared. The determinant now is neither economics nor social justice, but raw political power.

There is an obvious connection between the population explosion and ecological stress. The more people there are, the more forests are cut down, the more water and soil are depleted, and the more destructive carbon emissions are let loose on the planet. Despite the restrictions on funding abortion adopted by the Bush administration, USAID and other aid agencies are making birth control information and contraceptives more available. But relatively few Kenyans make use of either. Kenyans still favor large families—more hands to work in the fields, more children to support their parents when they become old. (For most, there is no other social security or retirement income.) In a country where in some areas just a short time ago half the babies were likely to die before the age of five, families still tend to produce eight or nine children as insurance. The death rate for children in Kenya has actually fallen dramatically over the last twenty years, but there is a long lag between this new reality and the perceptions of most Kenyans. A major problem is that

Although it has become fashionable to ascribe an increasingly important role to small projects, the African governments like large projects: The usual 10 to 15 percent rake-off for the highest officials adds up to real money.

women have few rights. The men want many children. Education levels for women have improved enough to increase fertility and infant survival—women now know more about how to take care of themselves and their babies—but not enough for women to gain the confidence that they have the right to decide how many children they should have.

So the cycle of poverty, ignorance, high birthrates, environmental and social stress leaves chaos—and invites coercive rule to provide a patina of order. There are links, less obvious but no less important, between poverty, the population explosion, and the absence of democracy. Governments unable or unwilling to educate poor people, or to provide schools and decent health facilities for the majority in the rural areas, or to create jobs for the dispossessed who flock to the cities, tend to act like an occupation force. Poor people who are landless, jobless, and vulnerable to disease and hunger, who are ever at the mercy of moneylenders and corrupt officials, do not respect the soil, water, and forests the way their ancestors did before the forced march to development began. (This is not to romanticize life in Africa before the white man came. Whether Africa is better or worse off than before it was "discovered" would make a good Oxford Union debate, but the deed is done.)

Greater equity and social justice is now a precondition for ecological balance. But neither can be achieved unless the great majority of the population, who are poor men and women, have much more control over their own lives and destiny. The building of democratic institutions, especially at the local level, in a form compatible with local culture and tradition, is the key to the struggle out of poverty. It may not be sufficient, but it is essential.

Kenya, however, appears to be in headlong retreat from democracy. At a moment when statues of monomaniacal leaders in Eastern Europe are being torn down, President Moi is bent on defacing Nairobi's principal park with a sixty-foot statue of himself. It is not that the population needs to be reminded of his erect carriage and unsmiling face. Pictures are mandatory in every public space, and the single-channel TV features little else but presidential appearances. Kenya is a one-party state, and it no longer has a secret ballot. Political prisoners have been detained without trial;

The building of democratic institutions, especially at the local level, in a form compatible with local culture and tradition, is the key to the struggle out of poverty.

and though this practice has ceased as a result of international pressure, the exile of government critics, the torture of dissidents, and the attacks on the independent judiciary and trade unions have had a chilling effect on debate. (So zealous are the police that an American judge was arrested while observing a Kenyan trial and held overnight.) No one with whom I talked in Kenya, whether a Kenyan or a foreigner, wanted to be quoted. A recent U.S. ambassador in Nairobi called the country "fascist."

Where, then, is there any hope? Some Kenyans are looking to the revolution in South Africa to sweep across the continent. The African National Congress and Fort Hare, the famous black university in South Africa, have had a profound influence on liberation movements all over Africa for almost eighty years, and the successful democratization of the only economic engine on the continent might prove contagious and serve to jumpstart other African economies. But perhaps the most promising source of change, in Kenya as elsewhere, is the "informal sector." In the face of absurd and contradictory government regulation, corruption, and harassment, poor people survive by their wits, energy, and entrepreneurial skill. By the side of the road or in the midst of a slum, they set up shop—as tailors, barbers, fixers of cars, makers of furniture. *Juicali*, it is called, meaning "under the sun." Hernando de Soto, the Peruvian author of *The Other Path*, which combines a wholesale attack on the state with a celebration of the informal sector in Latin America, recently visited Nairobi and aroused great interest among the aid givers there. Although he is a hero of the Right, many on the Left are also pinning their hopes on the informal sector, as the failures of anti-democratic government become more and more evident. Free of licensing and other restrictions that hamstring the production of goods and the rendering of services in the formal economy, this anarchic second economy is building an internal market in Kenya. The government had been hostile at first, but under pressure of lending agencies its attitude has become more positive. Some of the most impressive aid projects have involved the support of the informal sector—for example, a roof-tile factory employing 300 women in the Mathare Valley.

But the *juicali* economy is far from a panacea. It is small-scale. Incomes are low. Because it is unregulated, women and children are exploited, often outrageously. It can also be dangerous. *Matatus*, minibuses owned by small entrepreneurs, are often the sole means of transportation. The drivers are paid by the trip and number of passengers, and the result, of course, is that they are unbelievably overcrowded and they always speed. I saw four *matatus* overturned on roads during my stay.

The hope is that the informal sector could be expanded without reproducing the problems of the formal economy. People can become politicized by active participation in thriving small economies and mutual-support networks, which they themselves control. As the national government becomes more repressive and self-serving, democratic energy wells up at the local level to resist it—as happened in Eastern Europe. Thus, in response to the president's plans for a huge building to accompany his statue on practically the only piece of greenery the poor of Nairobi can claim as their own, a local greenbelt movement mobilized, and this helped to stall the project. Whether the park can be saved is not yet decided, but it is one of many examples of how the survival strategies of powerless people can force a change in repressive state structures.

The hope is that the informal economic sector can be expanded. People can become politicized by active participation in thriving small economies and mutual-support networks, which they themselves control.

The support that government, churches, foundations, and a variety of dedicated individuals are giving to small businesses, nongovernmental schools, clinics, children's homes, and credit unions is not only saving and changing lives but is laying the foundation for political transformation. However, these democratic possibilities can be nurtured only by making structural changes in the world economy to reverse the processes of impoverishment. Africa needs more support from the rich countries, not less, but how, where, and why money is to be spent on development—and what development is—are perhaps the most fateful political questions of the 1990s. The doctors of development will be under intense pressure to practice triage, shifting scarce resources away from the desperate countries of Africa to shore up the economies of Eastern Europe. But the world economy will not work as long as developed countries base their hopes on growth while the prospects for billions of people in Africa—in Asia and Latin America, too—continue to shrink. If people are denied the chance to be producers and consumers, they do not disappear. They make their presence felt—as participants in civil wars, as carriers of disease, as refugees, as despoilers of the environment, as a continuing reproach.

Index

Credits/ Acknowledgments

Cover design by Charles Vitelli

1. Overview of International Business
Facing overview—New York Stock Exchange.

2. The Multinational Corporation
Facing overview—New United Motor.

3. International Management
Facing overview—Saab-Scania.

4. International Marketing
Facing overview—Liaison Agency.

5. International Finance
Facing overview—New York Stock Exchange.

6. International Production
Facing overview—United Nations photo. 163-164—Chart by Alberto Mena/BW; Illustrations by Rob Doyle/BW.

7. International Issues of the Twenty-First Century
Facing overview—United Nations photo by J. Frank.

PHOTOCOPY THIS PAGE!!!*

ANNUAL EDITIONS ARTICLE REVIEW FORM

■ NAME: ______________________ DATE: ______________________

■ TITLE AND NUMBER OF ARTICLE: ______________________

■ BRIEFLY STATE THE MAIN IDEA OF THIS ARTICLE: ______________________

■ LIST THREE IMPORTANT FACTS THAT THE AUTHOR USES TO SUPPORT THE MAIN IDEA:

■ WHAT INFORMATION OR IDEAS DISCUSSED IN THIS ARTICLE ARE ALSO DISCUSSED IN YOUR TEXTBOOK OR OTHER READING YOU HAVE DONE? LIST THE TEXTBOOK CHAPTERS AND PAGE NUMBERS:

■ LIST ANY EXAMPLES OF BIAS OR FAULTY REASONING THAT YOU FOUND IN THE ARTICLE:

■ LIST ANY NEW TERMS/CONCEPTS THAT WERE DISCUSSED IN THE ARTICLE AND WRITE A SHORT DEFINITION:

*Your instructor may require you to use this Annual Editions Article Review Form in any number of ways: for articles that are assigned, for extra credit, as a tool to assist in developing assigned papers, or simply for your own reference. Even if it is not required, we encourage you to photocopy and use this page; you'll find that reflecting on the articles will greatly enhance the information from your text.

We Want Your Advice

Annual Editions revisions depend on two major opinion sources: one is our Advisory Board, listed in the front of this volume, which works with us in scanning the thousands of articles published in the public press each year; the other is you—the person actually using the book. Please help us and the users of the next edition by completing the prepaid article rating form on this page and returning it to us. Thank you.

ANNUAL EDITIONS: INTERNATIONAL BUSINESS 93/94

Article Rating Form

Here is an opportunity for you to have direct input into the next revision of this volume. We would like you to rate each of the 46 articles listed below, using the following scale:

1. **Excellent: should definitely be retained**
2. **Above average: should probably be retained**
3. **Below average: should probably be deleted**
4. **Poor: should definitely be deleted**

Your ratings will play a vital part in the next revision. So please mail this prepaid form to us just as soon as you complete it.
Thanks for your help!

Rating	Article	Rating	Article
	1. Are We Building New Berlin Walls?		23. As Competition Rises in Global Banking, Europeans Have Edge
	2. Global Frontiers of Business		24. Competitiveness and the "Global Capital Shortage"
	3. The Global Economy: Who Gets Hurt		25. Big MacCurrencies
	4. International Communication: An Executive Primer		26. Foreign Direct Investment: Gift Horse or Trojan Horse?
	5. The World's Trade Topography: How Level Is It?		27. A Tenth Anniversary Report on the Debt Crisis
	6. Global Corporate Competition II: Is the Large American Firm an Endangered Species?		28. Manufacturing's New Economies of Scale
	7. U.S. Companies Come Back Home		29. The Search for a Truly Pan-European Manufacturing System
	8. Globetrotter		30. Global Innovation: Who's in the Lead?
	9. Corporate Globalization: A New Trend		31. The Myth of 'Made in the U.S.A.'
	10. Stepping Up to Global Competition: Interview With Harold A. Poling, Chairman, CEO, Ford Motor Company		32. Adapting Ethical Decisions to a Global Marketplace
	11. Who Is Them?		33. RJR Nabisco: Transnational Tobacco Trafficker
	12. Sources of Information (and Misinformation)		34. Companies Use Cross-Cultural Training to Help Their Employees Adjust Abroad
	13. What Executives Should Know About Political Risk		35. How Japan Sees Itself
	14. Companies in Europe Seeking Executives Who Can Cross Borders in a Single Bound		36. Does Japan Play Fair?
	15. Super Manager		37. "The Mountains Are High, the Emperor Is Far Away"
	16. Challenging Global Myths		38. Doing Business With the Soviet Republics
	17. The Foreign Director: Boon or Babel in the Boardroom?		39. Locking Up Tomorrow's Profits
	18. Going Global		40. Now the New New Europe
	19. Finding the International Niche: A "How To" for American Small Business		41. Megamarket
	20. An Exporter's Guide to Selecting Foreign Sales Agents and Distributors		42. Quebec: What Price Freedom?
	21. It's in the Mail!		43. Do We Want Free Trade With Mexico?
	22. Guess Who's Selling Barbies in Japan Now?		44. North-South Split: With Cold War Over, Poorer Nations Face Neglect by the Rich
			45. Don't Forget Latin America
			46. But What About Africa?

(Continued on next page)

ABOUT YOU

Name____________________ Date________
Are you a teacher? ☐ Or student? ☐
Your School Name ____________________
Department ____________________
Address ____________________
City ____________ State ______ Zip ______
School Telephone # ____________________

YOUR COMMENTS ARE IMPORTANT TO US!

Please fill in the following information:

For which course did you use this book? ____________________
Did you use a text with this Annual Edition? ☐ yes ☐ no
The title of the text? ____________________
What are your general reactions to the Annual Editions concept?

Have you read any particular articles recently that you think should be included in the next edition?

Are there any articles you feel should be replaced in the next edition? Why?

Are there other areas that you feel would utilize an Annual Edition?

May we contact you for editorial input?

May we quote you from above?

No Postage Necessary if Mailed in the United States

ANNUAL EDITIONS: INTERNATIONAL BUSINESS 93/94

BUSINESS REPLY MAIL

First Class Permit No. 84 Guilford, CT

Postage will be paid by addressee

DPG **The Dushkin Publishing Group, Inc.**
Sluice Dock
Guilford, Connecticut 06437